An Economic and Social History of Britain 1760-1990

Second edition

Trevor May

LONGMAN

Preface to the second edition

When this book was first published in 1987, it was already apparent that its terminal date of 1970 was an arbitrary one although typographically a neat one. The opportunity to bring out a new edition has meant that a new but equally neat terminal date has become possible, but one which may prove a little less arbitrary than its predecessor. The year 1990 marked the departure from office of Margaret Thatcher, although not necessarily the end of Thatcherism. Because the economic and social problems which she sought to solve were not new, but had concerned her immediate predecessors, the opportunity has been taken to alter the division of those chapters which cover the period since the Second World War, and to re-examine the origins of the Welfare State.

Changes at the end of the book have been balanced by alterations at the very beginning, where the reader is introduced to the evolving interpretation of the industrial revolution over the past century, while space has also been found to incorporate material on proto-industrialisation, a concept that has been widely discussed in the past decade. What of the middle? Those readers familiar with the first edition will recognise the layout of the main body of the book, which has not been altered for the mere sake of change. However, attention has been paid to the cut and thrust of historical scholarship in the last 10 years and new interpretations have been incorporated where appropriate. Much of the contemporary material which is quoted remains the same, although where a more telling example has been found this has been included.

The pictorial sections are now spread throughout the book. As before, however, the reader is encouraged to engage with the visual evidence in an active manner and to consider some of the issues of interpretation.

Trevor May
June 1995

Contents

List of illustrations

Chapter one

Britain and the industrial revolution

Industrial heritage

The 1980s was a decade that witnessed profound changes to the structure of the British economy. Great swathes were cut through manufacturing industry, while the service sector rapidly expanded. Much of the latter growth was in financial services of various kinds and in retailing, where vast 'out-of-town' shopping developments seemed to spring up like mushrooms. Shopping, which at one time had been a more or less irksome chore, now became increasingly part of the leisure industry. A yet more remarkable area of growth was that of museums, a phenomenon not just for the fact that many were run as commercial enterprises (history as part of the holiday industry) but in its scale. The number of museums more than doubled from the late 1960s, from around 800 to more than 2,000. At the end of the 1980s it was estimated that one new museum opened every fortnight, not as fast as supermarkets but more surprising as objects of entrepreneurial activity. Some feared that Britain was condemned to a future as an island theme park, moored off the continent of Europe, to which it would be conveniently connected by the Channel Tunnel.

Many of the new museums rejected that title and set up, instead, as 'heritage centres', presenting a picture of a shared past which, though vanished, attested to the qualities of the British people. A significant part of that past was identified as industrial heritage, and by the middle of the 1980s no fewer than 464 museums – nearly a quarter of the whole – boasted industrial material. As fewer and fewer people found employment in manufacturing industry, so more and more found work in the heritage industry. The 'living museum' became the new orthodoxy, giving rise to the situation where ex-miners demonstrated how coal had once been cut; and ex-weavers, how cloth had once been woven. Such experiences can be poignant ones, both for those who have lost their jobs, and for children who face an uncertain future. As more and more industries declined, the new heritage centres presented the odd prospect of the working, non-working industry.

One of the most successful of the new museums is Ironbridge, in Shropshire, founded as a museum trust in 1968 with the task of preserving and presenting to the public what was hailed as 'the birthplace of the industrial revolution'. Writing of the museum in 1976, Barrie Trinder observed: 'In 1950 few would have thought a gas holder or a bottle oven beautiful, and the ruins of a blast furnace, a working cornmill or a row of weavers' cottages would not have been regarded as appropriate venues for family outings.'[1] The 1950s, however, was a time of growing economic optimism. The future looked bright, and most people chose to surround themselves with items of contemporary design rather than the nostalgic motifs that became so popular in later decades.

Nostalgia (from the Greek *nosos* – return to native land – and *algos* – suffering or grief) was once considered a physical as well as a mental condition. Nostalgia was seen as homesickness – a pathological longing to return home, or to return to one's roots. Such a longing is greater in times of uncertainty. Few would deny that the 1970s and 1980s were decades of greater uncertainty than the 1950s and 1960s, at least as far as economic and environmental issues were concerned. A concern for Britain's heritage is one aspect of that malaise; the Thatcherite concern to return to 'Victorian values' is another. Places like Ironbridge, or the North of England Open Air Museum at Beamish, or Quarry Bank Mill at Styal, point back to a time when Britain was the 'workshop of the world', and most people had jobs *making* things (if they were not *growing* them). Britain had been the first nation to pass through an industrial revolution and in that (and much 'else') its world leadership was undoubted.

In 1987 Robert Hewison in his controversial book, *The Heritage Industry: Britain in a Climate of Decline*, described Consett, in County Durham:

> Ten miles from Beamish is the town of Consett. Like Ironbridge, Consett has a long industrial history, and from the 1840s was dominated by its steel works. In 1980 the British Steel Corporation closed the works down, with the loss of 3,500 jobs, and many more jobs went with the removal of the town's economic *raison d'être*. Adult unemployment is around 25 per cent, and youth unemployment 80 per cent. New firms have been enticed to the area, but Consett's largest new employer is Derwent Valley Foods, where 110 people are engaged in the production of snacks packaged under the pseudo-nineteenth century patronage of Phileas Fogg. The site of the steelworks has been razed, in spite of the appeal from Beamish that one furnace should be preserved: as a tourist attraction. In Consett, such a relic would have a different meaning, as a monument not to industrial enterprise, but as a reminder of the near death of a town from de-industrialisation.[2]

Heritage museums, with their living history displays and their attempts to relive the past, have been the subject of scorn from many academics. The past which they attempt to convey is condemned as partial, or sanitised, or carefully packaged. It may even be condemned because it is popular, and has a huge following (far greater than the following of most academic historians). In fact, how historians view the past may not be so very different. They, too, are highly selective in what they investigate; they also package the past (even if that package is represented by the finite bounds of a book); and they, too, tie up loose ends which historical truth might leave untied. The historian is also concerned with 'living' history, if only because historical interpretation is never static but is forever changing. Nowhere is this more evident than in the interpretation of the industrial revolution. It has been the subject of serious academic study for little more than a century, yet in that time it has been interpreted in markedly different ways. Some historians have argued that the industrial revolution is itself a myth, at least to the extent that the changes which occurred between the mid-eighteenth and mid-nineteenth centuries do not justify such a dramatic term. It is important, therefore, to consider how our understanding has changed, and to consider how far such reinterpretations have been *endogenous* (arising from changes within the study of history itself) or *exogenous* (arising from external changes, in the sense of trends within the world in which the historian lives). In considering exogenous reasons for reinterpreting the industrial revolution, the most obvious starting point is the observation of the Italian historian and philosopher, Benedetto Croce (1866–1952) that 'all history is contemporary history', by which he meant that historians do not work in a vacuum and are inevitably influenced by the ideas, concerns and problems of their day. The most stimulating discussion of this idea in relation to the industrial revolution is that of David Cannadine, which he put forward in an article in 1984.[3] The historian's world undoubtedly provides part of the context of historical research, but so, too, do changes in the techniques and methodology of historical study itself. Among these endogenous sources of revision, the most interesting is the growth of the New Economic History or 'Cliometrics' (measurement in the service of Clio, the historical muse) which has brought rigorous quantification and the application of economic theory to the study of past economies. We shall consider exogenous and endogenous reasons for historical revisionism in the following two sections.

Historians and the industrial revolution, 1880–1990

It is not uncommon for foreign observers, more detached from events than are a country's nationals, to perceive fundamental changes taking place in a society. We should not be surprised, therefore, that the earliest recorded uses of the term 'industrial revolution', are to be found, not in the writings of British authors (although Britain was the first nation to experience the phenomenon), but in the comments of foreigners. Although the earliest use of the term has been traced to a French writer in the 1790s, the French economist, Jerome-Adolphe Blanqui, is generally credited with the first application of the term to Britain in 1837, when he claimed that economic and social change had affected Britain in the late eighteenth century in as fundamental way as political change had rocked France since the Revolution of 1789. Two years after Blanqui, the Belgian writer, Natalis Briavoinne, expanded on the idea, as did Friedrich Engels, a German cotton merchant resident in England, in his *Condition of the Working Class in England*, which was published in Leipzig in 1845. It was not, however, until the 1880s that the term came into general use in Britain, particularly following the publication in 1884 of Arnold Toynbee's *Lectures on the Industrial Revolution*, a book which soon sold out and went through five editions by 1908.

Toynbee took up the themes explored by Engels 40 years before, and painted a picture of an industrial revolution that had had catastrophic consequences for the mass of the people. This period, he wrote, had been 'as disastrous and as terrible as any through which a nation had passed'. That Toynbee's account should have been so pessimistic, and that it should have appeared when it did should not surprise us. As we shall see in Chapter 11, the 1880s was a decade in which poverty was 'rediscovered' (not for the last time) and there was considerable concern that, after half a century or more of economic growth which had brought the nation untold wealth, the lives of so many people were lived in poverty, squalor and ill-health. Something had gone wrong; a view that was reinforced by the growth of foreign competition and the increasing challenge to Britain's economic supremacy. Toynbee was followed by other historians such as J. L. and Barbara Hammond, and Sydney and Beatrice Webb. For such writers the industrial revolution had had consequences that were nasty, mean and brutish. And to complete that quartet of Hobbesian qualities, it had also been short. 'Revolution' was regarded as the appropriate term to describe changes that had come about suddenly, so suddenly that the American historian Charles Beard could write in 1901 that the industrial revolution had come 'suddenly, like a thunderbolt from a clear sky'.

This first phase of academic interest in the industrial revolution had two important legacies. Much of the emphasis was on the *social consequences* of industrialisation, giving rise to a debate on the standard of living which has yet to be concluded, and is considered further in Chapter 2. Second, it raised questions of timing; in particular,

I   Images of the factory

I   Arkwright's cotton works, Cromford, 1786

The watercolour of Cromford Mill (1) was painted in 1786, 15 years after Richard Arkwright had constructed it. The steel engraving of cotton factories in Manchester (2) was originally published as a book illustration almost 50 years after the Cromford watercolour. In what ways do the two pictures give a different impression of cotton mills? Why does one picture appear oppressive and the other not? Does the different atmosphere created by the two pictures reflect artistic intention, or the media by which they were produced? Or does the difference signify a change in attitude across half a century? Writing of engravings such as that of the Union Street mills, the art historian F. D. Klingender said: 'By now the cotton mills themselves have lost their pleasant country-house appearance . . . Immense and forbidding, contemporary engravers depict them as fortress prisons, fitted equally for defence against armed assault from without as for the tight maintenance of a rigid discipline within.' Does this seem a fair comment, or does it simply reflect Klingender's own Marxist views?

2   Cotton factories in Union Street, Manchester, 1829

3   Carding, drawing and roving cotton; from Edward Baines's *History of Cotton Manufacture in Great Britain*, 1835

Pictures 3 and 4 are often reproduced in history books; but is there reason to suppose that the one is any more accurate than the other? Is machinery shown as a way of easing labour, or as a form of enslavement? Edward Baines, from whose book Picture 3 is taken, wrote: 'On visiting mills I have generally remarked on the coolness and equanimity of the work-people, even of the children, whose manner seldom, as far as my observation goes, indicates anxious care, and is more frequently sportive than gloomy. The noise and whirl of the machinery, which are unpleasant and confusing to a spectator unaccustomed to the scene, produce not the slightest effect on the operatives habituated to it.'

Picture 4 comes from a novel by Frances Trollope which was antipathetic to factories. Both books would have been read by middle-class readers, unable to check their accuracy for themselves. How might they have reacted to each of these illustrations?

4   'Love conquered fear.' An illustration from *The Life and Adventures of Michael Armstrong* by Frances Trollope, 1840

5   Manchester mill operatives; *Illustrated London News*, November 1862

6   'The Dinner Hour' at Wigan, painted by Eyre Crowe, 1874

Picture 5 appeared in the *Illustrated London News* during the cotton famine caused by the American Civil War, and was intended to feature 'types' such as the mule-spinner in his top hat, and the 'knocker-up' with his long pole for waking workers in the early hours, by tapping on their windows. Does this source have implications for any ideas we may have about the 'cotton worker'?

Eyre Crowe (6) specialised in *genre* painting, or scenes from everyday life. Such paintings found a ready market among middle-class purchasers. What features might have made this picture appealing, and are they distortions of the truth?

the question whether 'revolution' is an appropriate term, or whether 'evolution' is a more apt description. This debate also continues.

Cannadine identifies a second phase in the historiography of the industrial revolution running from the mid-1920s to the early 1950s. In 1926 Sir John Clapham published the first volume of his *Economic History of Modern Britain*, in which he challenged a number of the accepted views of the earlier school of historians. He took a more evolutionary line, tending to draw out the process of industrialisation, and pointing out what had not changed by 1851, a date by which many had assumed the first phase of the industrial revolution to have been concluded. For many people the industrial revolution was associated with the rise of a factory system, but Clapham correctly pointed out that the factory worker had not become the 'typical' worker by the middle of the nineteenth century. He also demurred from the pessimistic view of the standard of living, producing evidence which he claimed justified more optimistic conclusions.

If the world in which the early historians of the industrial revolution lived affected their interpretation of past events, the same could be said of the period from the 1920s to the early 1950s. During those decades the world was rocked by two wars; the world economy was shaken by violent cyclical fluctuations, especially with the Great Crash of 1929, and unemployment at an unprecedentedly high level was a feature of the interwar years. These concerns could be projected backwards. Between 1688 and 1815 Britain fought eight wars against France and its allies. What effect had they had on economic growth? Were resources diverted from productive to destructive purposes, or did war exert a stimulus to growth, through technological spin-off, for example. While these questions taxed some historians, others were more concerned with the causes of fluctuations within an economy, whether in the short-term trade cycle, or in longer-term swings of activity. The economist Joseph Schumpeter stressed the importance of long waves, and the way they seemed to cluster around innovations, making the role of technology a vital issue. In *Economic Fluctuations in England, 1700–1800* (1959) T. S. Ashton paid particular attention to harvests, highlighting the role played by agriculture in economic growth. Each of these issues – the impact of war, the role of technology and the effect of agricultural improvement – is considered in more detail in later sections of this chapter.

Ashton's most popular book, *The Industrial Revolution, 1760–1830*, was published in 1948. In it he hailed the long-term advantages that industrialisation brought with it. His concluding paragraph confirmed the industrial revolution as the gateway though which nations passed from poverty to plenty:

> There are today on the plains of India and China men and women, plague-ridden and hungry, living lives little better, to outward appearance, than those of the cattle that toil with them by day and share their places of sleep by night. Such Asiatic standards, and such unmechanised horrors, are the lot of those who increase their numbers without passing through an Industrial Revolution.[4]

Writing about 20 years later, Peter Mathias described Ashton's words as 'one of the most influential paragraphs in the writing of economic history in the present generation'. But by that time, the historiography of the industrial revolution had passed into Cannadine's third stage, running from the mid-1950s to the early 1970s. In this period the countries of western Europe experienced economic growth which was the more remarkable in that it was sustained and promised to be continuous. For those countries which, led by Britain, had passed through an industrial revolution, the future looked bright. But this was an experience shared by only a minority of the world's population. What of the undeveloped economies of the world? The urgency of the question was spelled out in *North–South: A Programme for Survival*, the report (issued in 1980) of an international commission chaired by Willy Brandt, former Chancellor of the Federal Republic of Germany, and 1971 Nobel Peace Prize winner. The title, *North–South*, was a simple way of expressing how the world divides into rich and poor countries. Countries in the rich North included those of Europe and North America, the USSR, since broken up into much poorer independent republics, Japan, Australia and New Zealand. Those in the poorer South, sometimes referred to as the Third World, include most of Asia, Africa and Latin America.

The Brandt Report made clear the great disparities between the two regions. The North contains only one-quarter of the world's people, yet enjoys four-fifths of the world's income. Most of its people have enough to eat, and a person can expect to live on average more than 70 years. The North possesses over 90 per cent of the world's manufacturing industry, accounts for 96 per cent of the world's spending on research and development and owns nearly all the world's registered patents. By way of contrast, the poorer nations of the South have three-quarters of the world's population and only one-fifth of the world's income. People can expect to live to about 50 years, and one-fifth or more of the people suffer from hunger and malnutrition. According to the Brandt Report, about 800 million people (40 per cent of the South) are barely surviving. Although, with the break up of the Soviet Union and the development of the newly industrialised economies (such as Singapore, Hong Kong, Taiwan and South Korea), the distinction between North and South is diminishing, the gulf between rich and poor nations threatens to grow even wider. By 1990 Switzerland, at one extreme, enjoyed an income per head that was 300–400 times larger than that of Mozambique, the poorest of poor nations.

In grappling with the problems of economic growth in our own day, it was not surprising that economists, in company with economic historians, should seek a solution by examining in greater depth the mechanism of growth in the world's first industrial revolution, and to attempt to draw from the British experience a blueprint for growth that might be adapted to the needs of underdeveloped economies in today's world.

The thrust of many historical studies of the late 1950s and 1960s was therefore on economic growth and the causes of Britain's industrial revolution, with less emphasis than before on the social consequences. Foremost among the revisionists was the American historian, W. W. Rostow. His *Stages of Economic Growth* was published in 1960, with the provocative sub-title of *A Non-Communist Manifesto*, as if to challenge that strand of historical interpretation of the industrial revolution that stretched back to Friedrich Engels and his collaborator, Karl Marx.

In his book Rostow introduced a highly controversial theory which was to dominate the debate in subsequent decades, even though it failed to gain the support of all historians. He coined a phrase which has become part of everyday currency, namely, 'the take-off'. The analogy is with an aircraft taking off from the ground. Rostow implied that a certain rate of economic growth would sustain itself in the same way that an aircraft, having gained sufficient speed to leave the ground, can, so long as that speed is maintained, keep climbing. Rostow claimed that there were five stages for economic growth: the traditional society; the satisfaction of preconditions for take-off; the take-off itself; the drive to maturity; and finally, the age of high mass consumption. Rostow's work aroused enormous interest as well as a great deal of criticism, the latter focusing both on his general theory and his interpretation of the actual British experience. He argued originally that the take-off required certain preconditions, one being a rise in the rate of productive investment from, say, 5 per cent or less of the national income to over 10 per cent. He also stressed the need for one or more 'leading sectors' in the economy, that is to say substantial industries which forge ahead of the others and act as pacemakers. Each of these propositions has come under attack, and are considered more fully below.

The search for a blueprint for change proved abortive. Economic historians have so far failed to agree on the causes of the British industrial revolution, while some have argued that, in any case, Britain was the last place to look for the 'secret' of growth, if only because its industrial revolution was unique – there can be only one 'first in the field'. All others could follow its example (or try to avoid making its mistakes). Britain had more or less gone it alone. The failure of economic historians to agree was matched by an equal failure on the part of developmental economists to put forward a convincing explanation of growth.

In any case, by the early 1970s, the question of economic growth was starting to be reconsidered. The key moment was the world energy crisis of 1973–4, after which not only has the certainty of economic growth receded, but also its appropriateness has been called into question, as the environmental and ecological implications of industrialisation have become matters for concern.

It is possible to trace these new concerns in the historiography of the industrial revolution, with the appearance, for example, of studies in 'green history'. At the same time, the worldwide development of feminism has led to a more serious concern to investigate the part played by women both in the process of industrialisation and in the new industrial society. At a time when Britain appeared to be on the brink of deindustrialising, studies of the industrial revolution tended increasingly to stress the partial nature of Britain's transformation, while emphasising also the gradual build-up to change. For some, the very title 'industrial revolution' had ceased to have much meaning – Jonathon Clark claimed in 1986 that 'historians have been chasing a shadow'. The term, however, is likely to linger, if only because it has meaning for so many people, including the millions who visit industrial heritage museums. Inevitably, when academic expressions work their way into the language of ordinary people, they lose some of their precision. The implication for historians is that they should be aware of such limitations, rather than throw out terminology which makes *some* sense to so many people.

An awareness of the contemporary context in which historians have conducted their researches is enlightening, but too much should not be made of Cannadine's schematic framework. The issues which fascinated the historians of the 1880s are still debated, and though certain controversies take hold of the academic community at particular times, there has inevitably been (and will continue to be) a going back over old ground. Not only that, but some would claim that the historiography of the industrial revolution and its aftermath has been governed not just by evolving questions of contemporary concern, but by developments within the academic community itself. To these we now turn.

The New Economic History and the industrial revolution

Like the New World, from which it came, the New Economic History is getting on in years. The term is used to describe a school of history whose members, sometimes referred to as econometricians (or even cliometricians), construct 'models', and apply economic theory and statistical measurement to historical questions. The New Economic History thus represents an example of the interplay between the disciplines of social science and of history in the study of the past. The immediate origins of this particular approach to historical research are to be found in the economics departments of United States universities in the 1960s, where economists grappled with new methods for measuring national income (a question of vital importance to governments), and used historical data to test out hypotheses about the nature of economic growth. In some important respects, the paternity of the New Economic History can be traced even earlier. During the Second World War, economists were drawn upon to provide insights into the effectiveness of such military policies as strategic bombing. What would be the effect on the Germany economy, for example, of the knocking out of the Third Reich's entire railway system? The answer, it seems, was 'very little'. The question, however, pointed towards one of the most controversial techniques of the New Economic History, namely, the 'counterfactual'. Put simply, counterfactual technique is the attempt to measure the impact of variables within an economy by looking at how an economy would have fared at a predetermined moment in time if that particular element were removed. This technique has been used, for example, to attempt to measure the impact of railways on the economy, and is considered further in Chapter 6. The motto of the New Economic Historians might well be taken as: postulate a model; identify the variables; measure with vigour and rigour.

Of course, there is nothing new about the use of statistical evidence, and historians have always been quantifiers of sorts, if only implicitly. The cliometricians place quantification as the very bedrock of their research and are obliged to make their assumptions explicit (a point from which *all* historians can learn). However, some of the assumptions that have to be made are vast. In order to quantify, one must have access to the historical data. Very often they do not exist. The cliometricians therefore have to use surrogate measures. We may be interested in long-term changes in the price of shoes, for example. Lacking the precise data, we might have to make do with statistics relating to the price of leather, assuming that the price of the finished product will shadow the price of the principal raw material used. But it *is* only an assumption; and when one assumption is linked to another, we may easily stray from the path of historical reality. We have to be on our guard, therefore, because the apparent concreteness of statistics is very beguiling. David Landes has warned that 'numbers have power to lull the sceptical and intimidate the uncomprehending mind. They seem somehow more authoritative, and what's more, today's numbers are by definition better than yesterday's'.[5]

The New Economic Historians are generally concerned less with issues at the micro level – changes to the structure of the firm, or the family, or the life experiences of individuals – than they are with macroeconomic issues, where the emphasis is on aggregates, such as the growth of national income, the rate of capital formation, or the growth and composition of the labour force. It is at the macroeconomic level that the New Economic History has had important contributions to make to our understanding.

It was observed in the previous section that since the 1970s, historians have tended to place less stress on the changes brought about by the industrial revolution than they have upon the continuities between the pre- and post-industrial worlds. In 1971 R. M. Hartwell described the industrial revolution as one of the 'Great Discontinuities' of history, although it has proved impossible to pin down in time. When the French or Russian Revolutions happened does not present too great a difficulty, but as Joel Mokyr has observed, 'on the whole, economic changes, even economic revolutions, do not have their Bastille Days or their Lenins'. With tongue firmly in cheek, however, T. S. Ashton did once claim that those who like real precision might date the industrial revolution in Scotland from 1 January 1760, for on that day the Carron Ironworks lit its first furnace! In fact, Ashton identified the turning-point in the 1780s. On the other hand, Phyllis Deane and W. H. Cole pushed it back to the 1740s, while other historians have suggested different dates. It has been argued that if historians can differ by as much as 40 years, the turning-point may not only be difficult to locate but must even have a doubtful existence. The industrial revolution, of course, was not an 'event' that 'happened' in the conventional sense. It was a series of events that happened at different times, in some places faster than others, and affecting particular industries and activities differently. We may think of industrialisation as a syncopated process, with the rhythms of different aspects of economic and social change weaving around each other. To quote Mokyr: 'There is no "test" [of continuity and discontinuity] that we can apply: National income and aggregate consumption grew gradually; patents and cotton output grew much faster. Which one "measures" the industrial revolution?'[6]

These points are worth making, for the recent work of the New Economic Historians, measuring the eighteenth-century growth of the national income, for example, would tend to play down the discontinuities that have traditionally been associated with the industrial revolution. However, statistical aggregations have a natural tendency towards the smoothing out of discontinuities and to smother areas of great change and innovation. Mokyr vividly shows this ironing-out effect in the case of a two-sector model where there is a large 'traditional' sector and a smaller, innovative or modern one − as was the case with Britain in the eighteenth century. Assume, he suggests, that the modern sector in such a hypothetical model is growing at the rate of 4 per cent per annum, and that this sector originally produces 10 per cent of the total output. Assume, also, that the traditional sector (originally producing 90 per cent of total output) is growing at the rate of 1 per cent. Then the aggregate growth is at first 1.3 per cent (i.e. $0.9 \times 1 + 0.1 \times 4$). After 30 years, the share of the modern sector will have increased to 21 per cent, and after 50 years to one-third. It will take 74 years for the two sectors to be of equal size, at which point aggregate growth will be 2.5 per cent a year. After a full century, the traditional sector will have shrunk to about 31 per cent of the total economy. Like all models (and much more than most of those constructed by econometricians) this model is a simplification. For example, it neglects the way in which change is diffused because, in reality, 'traditional' sectors of the economy are not likely to remain unaffected by the improved means of production. Nevertheless, the example illustrates the point that aggregated quantifications of macroeconomic phenomena may fail to give due emphasis to major changes that are taking place in an economy, while the particular figures which it uses may not be so far from the actual British experience. One of the best available summaries of the data is that provided by N. F. R. Crafts in 1985.

Table 1.1   *Estimates of economic growth rates*

Years	National product	National product per head
1700–60	0.69	0.31
1760–80	0.70	0.01
1780–1801	1.32	0.35
1801–31	1.97	0.52

Source: N. F. R. Crafts, *British Eonomic Growth During the Industrial Revolution*, Oxford University Press, 1985, p. 45.

The second column shows annual average growth rates of total output, and the third shows annual average rates of output per person, the difference between the two columns representing the rate of growth of the population. Crafts's figures were noticeably lower than those of Phyllis Deane and W. A. Cole, which had set the tone of debate since the 1960s, and have been used as ammunition by those who have sought to minimise the extent of change.

The New Economic History, with its emphasis on theory and upon quantification, has given us fresh insights of enormous value, but, as with any approach to historical understanding, it is important to appreciate the limitations as well as the strengths of its methods. Economists usually add *ceteris paribus* (other things being equal) to their hypotheses. In reality, other things never are equal, and it is right for historians to stress the uniqueness of historical events and to avoid the temptation to squeeze facts to fit the form of some model or general explanatory law. It is also worth remembering that not all historical 'facts' are quantifiable, and that the work of cliometricians tells us little or nothing about the motives or responses of those who participate in economic change or are affected by it. David Landes refers particularly to technological change, but his forceful rhetoric has wider implications:

> What needs stressing . . . is the rapidity with which technological change impinged on the livelihood and consciousness of workers and translated into protest, much of it violent. Changes may have been making their way in some regions more than others, in some industrial branches more than others, and slower than some enthusiastic scholars may have thought. But do not tell that to the people affected: the pauper apprentices; the women who were sent to work in the mills where their husbands or fathers would not go; the displaced craftsmen; the residents of once-green valleys, now renamed the Black Country; the Irish immigrants who did the dirty work. Or, for that matter, to the winners of the new, industrializing world: the managers, merchants and shopkeepers, the newly skilled and the 'labour aristocracy', the consumers of the new commodities and of older ones now within reach, the multiplying professionals in growing towns and cities. The machine breakers did not need to wait 75 years for the new technology to work through its potential to know they were hurting. The doctors who had to deal with new health problems in mining villages and urban slums and wynds in the 1790s quickly understood that industry was growing and changing and injuring people . . . [P]ersonal experience was a good proxy measure of revolution; and for us, with our subtle number play and 20/20 hindsight, it is a fair reminder that there is more to life, work, and death than macrostatistics can tell.[7]

The causes of the industrial revolution in Britain

Recent trends in historical scholarship have tended to extend the industrial revolution and have placed greater stress on continuity than upon change. All revolutions, of course, have their evolutionary context. None start from an absolutely static position. The dynamics of change, therefore, still represent a legitimate area of study. Basic questions are still asked. Why Britain? Why then (whenever 'then' was)? Seeking answers to such questions has proved to be something like the search for the Holy Grail, perhaps because the existence of a single, prime cause is itself a myth.

In their attempt to explain these great changes, historians have sometimes drawn upon analogies taken from other disciplines. Joel Mokyr makes reference to the debate on Darwin's theory of evolution, and the view of some biologists that sudden leaps may occur in the slow evolutionary change. He has also referred to genetic theory, and the impact of random mutations; and to 'chaos theory' where comparatively minor events can set off a chain of events of greater moment.

A great many factors are tied up with industrialisation, and this is as true today as it was for Britain in the eighteenth century. Historians have at times stressed the role of population growth and of revolutions in agriculture, trade and transport. The impact of technological change has been emphasised, as has the willingness of capitalists to invest in the new technology. Willingness is, of course, a psychological and social phenomenon, and a willingness to take risks is determined by a range of complex factors. Social influences may determine the intensity of the desire of entrepreneurs for wealth and 'success'. Society will determine which goals are acceptable, while the actual riskiness of a venture will be influenced by socially determined institutional factors, such as the law, for the degree to which it protects property or guards the rights of groups such as investors will greatly affect business decisions. The willingness to accept change is another key factor. A static economy and society produce attitudes and institutions which favour continued stability, and to overcome them may require the strongest persuasion or coercion. The truth of this is apparent to those who, in the modern world, have seen economic projects in developing countries face the opposition of local people for wide-ranging cultural reasons. As an aside, it is salutary to point out that an unwillingness to undertake change is also a characteristic of economies that have passed their peak.

Some factors tending towards industrialisation were unique to Britain in the eighteenth century, but others were shared with its European neighbours. Intellectual, scientific and cultural advances proceeded on a broad front which transcended national frontiers. French foreign trade was comparable to that of Britain, and Holland enjoyed commercial and financial institutions as sophisticated as those of London. In many areas the Dutch excelled. It was there that many of the features which characterised progressive farming were pioneered, while in shipbuilding and shipping, as well as in foreign trade, Holland was the tutor rather than the taught.

Other features of the British experience were distinct. Even though it lagged behind France in many areas of pure science, Britain led in the broad field of technology. There was also a more widely based market than existed in France, which suffered from both social and geographical fragmentation. Geography was peculiarly beneficent to Britain. It was endowed with raw materials in a particularly favourable way. Coal was abundant. In 1814 a Swiss industrialist, touring Britain's industrial towns, observed: 'England owes its prosperity very largely to its coal deposits. Without its coal England would not have one-thousandth of the factories that she now possesses.' There were also good supplies of low-grade iron ore and of non-ferrous metals. Britain had hundreds of miles of navigable or potentially navigable rivers, while its deeply indented coastline, coupled with its comparatively compact land mass, greatly facilitated coastal shipping. As an Atlantic economy developed, Britain – on the north-western edge of Europe – was particularly advantageously placed.

While it is easy to draw up a balance sheet of features in which Britain excelled, producing one for where it lagged behind or where it shared in the common European experience is a futile exercise. It is the unique combination of features which accounts for its early lead. David Landes used the idea of 'critical mass' from nuclear physics, suggesting that it is the piling up of a large number of different factors which leads to an explosive chain reaction. The analogy is a good one, and warns us of the danger of accepting a narrow interpretation of the industrial revolution or of searching for one mainspring of economic growth.

Britain before the industrial revolution, and the concept of proto-industrialisation

It has been suggested that the term 'pre-industrial' to describe Britain in the middle of the eighteenth century is a 'grotesque misnomer' (Eric J. Evans). In so far as the economy was already well advanced, there is some truth in the assertion. Nevertheless, it is instructive to compare Britain before it experienced the industrial revolution with underdeveloped economies in the world today. In 1967 R. M. Hartwell wrote:

> The characteristics of poor and underdeveloped economies have been listed frequently by the economist, but rarely by the historian, even though England of the eighteenth century has often been described as underdeveloped. To the economist, underdevelopment means the following: a very high proportion of the population (more than two-thirds) in agriculture; incomes so low that most income is spent on food and necessities, savings are small, and there is little capital per head; an economically backward population (backward in education, skills, and attitudes) with a tendency to grow faster than output; poorly developed markets with a low volume of per capita trade, the result of poor communications and inadequate credit facilities; a low level of agrarian techniques and low yields per acre, and crude technology in industry. With both incomes and savings low, the economy is caught in a vicious circle in which insufficient demand and investment are incapable of stimulating growth.[8]

Many, but not all, of these features were to be found in pre-industrial Britain. *First* was the wide extent of poverty, accompanied by endemic hunger and disease. The Litany, drawn up by Archbishop Cranmer and contained in the Book of Common Prayer of 1549, contains the supplication that God will deliver his people 'From lightning and tempest; from plague, pestilence, and famine; from battle and murder, and from sudden death'. Unless he joined the army, the Englishman was not likely to die in battle and even if he did join up, a glorious death was likely to remain elusive. In the Revolutionary and Napoleonic Wars, soldiers had over 17 times as much chance of dying from disease or accident as they did of being killed by the enemy. The chances of being struck by lightning must be minimal, but the other potential disasters were real enough. If the plague died out in the seventeenth century, other forms of pestilence were ever present. Certain diseases were almost always in evidence including scurvy, pellagra and rickets. One medical authority argues that most of the poorer population of Tudor England suffered from sub-clinical scurvy after their winter diet of salt bacon, bread and peas. Pellagra, one of the scourges of the Third World today, was possibly widespread, being mistaken for leprosy to which it bears a superficial resemblance.

Rickets, arising from dietary deficiency contributed to the high infantile death rate. 'The only real defences against disease,' writes L. A. Clarkson, 'were wealth, luck, and common sense. The poor were more vulnerable than the rich: they lived in worse conditions, they were worse fed, worse dressed, and dirtier.'[9] Actual famine was perhaps rare, although hunger was known with monotonous frequency, and many slept with an empty or half-filled stomach. Yet, if we are to believe one or two contemporary estimates, by the standards of today's underdeveloped countries, the mass of the population was not poor. For example, at the end of the seventeenth century the statistician Gregory King calculated the national income of England and Wales in 1688. His figures suggest an average income of £8–£9 per head of population. In the 1750s it was probably £12–£13 a head, and at the end of the century averaged about £22. It is difficult to estimate what this sum would be worth in the early 1990s, but a rough estimate would suggest a figure above £100 per annum. Small though this sum may appear to a modern western European, it greatly exceeds the annual income of millions of people in the Third World. In terms of wealth, such people resemble not the Europeans of the seventeenth and eighteenth centuries, but rather those of the tenth and eleventh centuries. By comparison with the pre-industrial nations of today and the rest of the world of that day, western Europe was already rich before the industrial revolution, that wealth being the product of centuries of accumulation. Britain, says N. C. R. Crafts, was 'among the richest countries in Europe, but rich – as the rest were – by a traditional definition: productive if unscientific agriculture, busy if unmechanised industry, and vigorous if narrow commerce. The 80 years before 1780 are years of traditional success introducing two centuries of breaking and rebreaking of tradition.'[10]

This comparative richness may make our *second* distinction between a pre-industrial society and an industrial one appear paradoxical, namely that a pre-industrial society has a level of productivity and a standard of living which are relatively stagnant. By stagnant we do not mean static, for there may well be economic change and even economic growth in a pre-industrial economy, but it is painfully slow and all too easily reversed. To take up the Rostow analogy, the speed of change is not sufficient for the economy to take off. There are fluctuations both upwards and downwards, and though gains are sometimes made, they can easily be eliminated by a bad harvest, an epidemic or a war. The economy is much more dependent on the weather, which dominates the harvest (and thus agricultural incomes) and which indirectly affects a whole range of industries which are dependent on raw materials derived from agriculture.

This dependence upon agriculture is a *third* feature of pre-industrial economies, and it is very evident when we consider underdeveloped economies of our own day. The Brandt Report records that agriculture provides 83 per cent of the employment of the poorest countries of the world. How high the percentage was in Britain cannot be told with certainty before 1841, when the first occupational census was taken. Working from the figures of Gregory King, Phyllis Deane and W. A. Cole estimated that in 1688, 60–80 per cent of the labour force was engaged in agriculture, a figure that has more recently been reduced to around 55 per cent by P. H. Lindert. Gregory Clark suggests a figure of about 48 per cent of the British population thus employed in 1770, which may be compared with 66 per cent of the Indian labour force engaged in agriculture in 1981. Taking this measure, therefore, Britain was more developed than was once believed.

Peter Mathias has described agriculture as 'the great prime mover' of the pre-nineteenth-century economy, for many people were directly or indirectly tied to the agricultural sector. These included all those craftsmen such as blacksmiths and wheelwrights who were to be found throughout rural England, as well as all those whose industry depended upon some agricultural raw material, such as brewers, soap boilers, tallow makers, leather workers and wool workers. Indeed, it is hard to draw the line between agriculture and industry, for the products of many industries, such as the metal-working ones, went to satisfy the needs of farmers. In 1700 agriculture alone accounted for about 45 per cent of the nation's output, a figure which, by 1800, had fallen to 33 per cent.

If the economy was mainly agricultural, although not overwhelmingly so, the population was also predominantly rural. Gregory King estimated that a quarter of the population of England and Wales lived in cities and market towns, although most of the latter were little more than villages. Outside London (with about half a million inhabitants in 1700) only Norwich and Bristol had more than 20,000 inhabitants. Towns of 5,000 or more comprised only 13 per cent of Britain's population, and although, between 1700 and 1801, the number of people living in towns grew from under a fifth of the total population to almost a third, it was not until 1851 that the census showed Britain to have a predominantly urban population.

Fourth, the horizons of people living in a pre-industrial society are limited. Most

Englishmen before the nineteenth century, unless they succumbed to the blandish-ments of the army recruiting sergeant or the more violent tactics of the naval press-gang, never went further than the nearest market town. Several factors account for this parochialism. Communications were poor, and even walking cost money (meals and lodging along the way had to be purchased), while lost time meant lost work and lost wages. The word 'foreigner' had a much more localised meaning than we now give it. When Harrow School was founded in 1571, the distinction between local boys who were to be educated freely and 'foreigners' who were to pay was not an early attempt to milk overseas students, but a distinction between boys born within and outside the *parish*. You cannot get more parochial than that!

With the majority of the population tied to a subsistence economy, local markets coped with most needs. As late as 1841, more than 40 per cent of industrial craftsmen in England were supplying exclusively local markets, and the proportion must have been a good deal higher in the previous century. Poor communications were again a major constraint, hence it is more reasonable to think in terms of regional economies rather than a national one. To the producer in Kent or Essex, for example, customers in Cumberland or Cornwall were more remote than those in France or Flanders, while none were as accessible as those in nearby towns and villages.

Fifth, we may distinguish a lack of occupational specialisation. The industrial worker rarely produces a complete article, and is much more likely to perform a particular, limited task in a lengthy production process. On the other hand, the pre-industrial worker is more likely to be involved in the complete process, and even to be engaged in a variety of occupations. With a predominantly rural population many occupations were followed as an adjunct to agriculture, with the family as the unit of production.

The stereotype of an industrial revolution resulting in England's green and pleasant land being desecrated by dark, satanic mills is an all-to-familiar one, and is the very stuff and substance of the less reputable parts of the contemporary heritage industry, but historical truth is not that simple. It is not difficult to romanticise the domestic system or cottage industry, for the vision of the independent countryman, alternately tending his land and working at his loom, is easy to conjure up. In fact, there was no inherent reason why the two occupations should neatly dovetail, for busy periods in one might coincide with busy ones in the other, as might slack times. It doubtless brought some extra income to the family, but the supposed independence it is sometimes alleged to have created was frequently an illusion, for the outworker in domestic industry was often tied by debt to the middleman who supplied him with his raw materials or who purchased his products. The equipment used in domestic industry was generally simple and inexpensive, and had to be of such a size and nature as to fit easily into the worker's cottage or room. Thus, power-driven machinery could not be accommodated.

The widespread introduction of power-driven machinery marks one of the many changes brought about by an industrial revolution, for a *sixth* distinction between a pre-industrial and an industrial economy relates to its requirements of power, and the sources of that power. Although people in pre-industrial societies have performed tasks calling for prodigious amounts of power – think of the erection of Stonehenge or the building of the pyramids – the only sources known to them were muscle power (either human or animal), or the power of wind or water. Each had its limitations. Both wind and water are erratic and depend on the vagaries of the weather. The breakthrough came with the development of mineral energy sources, particularly coal and, much later, oil. The increased output of power which these give is enormous. In 1870 the capacity of Britain's steam-engines was about 4 million horsepower, equivalent (when one considers the working day of an engine, a horse, or a person) to the output of perhaps 12 million horses or 80 million people. One only has to note that the population of England and Wales in 1871 was less than 23 million to appreciate the scale of the transformation.

Two points are worth considering. The first is that neither handicraft industry nor domestic production ceased with the coming of the industrial revolution. As we shall see in Chapter 11, 'sweated labour' carried on in the homes of the workers was perceived as a major social problem at the end of the nineteenth century, while, in our own day, the spread of the computer has resulted in more and more people working from their own homes. Second, new lines of historical enquiry since the 1970s have led many to believe that in the eighteenth century there was a far greater measure of continuity between domestic industry and the factory system. Historians and social scientists have attempted to show how the one led to the other, and one of the results of their scholarly endeavour has been the development of the concept of proto-industrialisation.

Rather than the urban workshop, it is to the country cottage that many historians look for the transition from pre-industrial to an industrial organisation of production. It is there, between the seventeenth and the nineteenth centuries, that some of the key changes are thought to have taken place. The argument, as summarised by Maxine Berg, is that the world market for mass-produced goods grew at such a rate that traditional urban manufacturers could not keep pace, hampered as they were by guild regulations and high labour costs. At the same time that these markets were opening up, changes in agriculture were leading to an increasing differentiation between arable and pastoral regions. In pastoral regions it is claimed that the under-employed peasantry took up industrial occupations in their own homes, using material that were 'put-out' to them by a merchant. The possibility of complementary industrial employment broke down the traditional limitation on population growth set by the size of landholdings. The workers took less than the customary urban wage for their industrial labour, working more intensively, and subsisting partly from their agricultural activities. Because they were dispersed over a wide area, it was difficult for them to resist when merchants made reductions in the payments for their finished work; and because they had access to a cheaper labour force, those merchants involved in putting-out received a profit that was above the usual urban rates. In its turn, this provided a major source of capital accumulation. This proto-industrialisation, as it is called, gave rise to the labour and capital supplies, as well as the entrepreneurial skills that led to major increases in productivity before the factory.

While many of these phenomena have been well known to historians for generations, proto-industrialisation sets out to place them within the framework of a hypothetical model. It is this aspect of the research that has led to controversy, for some historians have claimed that proto-industrialisation is no more than, in the words of D. C. Coleman, 'the familiar findings of various scholars dressed up in long words and sociological finery'. At the same time, there is the objection that the model has been so tightly constructed that the empirical facts fit it in very few cases.

The model, as constructed originally by the American historian, Franklin Mendels, is distinguished by five main features. *First*, the unit of reference is the region (Mendels's original research was based on the region of Flanders). The emphasis is an important one, for whatever the problems may be of actually defining a 'region' (the Weald is an identifiable geographical region, but the West Country is not), we are reminded of the partial nature of the industrialisation process. The emphasis is thus somewhat different from that of most New Economic Historians whose concern tends to be at the national level, with investigations of *national* income and *national* rates of economic growth. Such investigations have their own validity, for much of the data upon which they work were produced by national agencies, while nationalism was one of the driving forces of history at the time that Britain's industrial revolution took place. But we need to remember that in Britain, as elsewhere, while the modern economy made progress in some areas, the traditional economy maintained its stronghold in many others. Concerns about the way in which nations industrialise may tempt us to forget these regional disparities.

The *second* feature of the model is that rural industry in the region involved peasant manufacturers who produced for the market. Their industry, such as weaving or stocking knitting, fluctuated with the seasons; and it slotted more satisfactorily into pasture farming, which was less labour intensive than arable agriculture. It provided a necessary income supplement for the household, but could ultimately develop into a full-time family occupation.

Third, the market for proto-industrial goods was outside the region. Indeed, it was frequently outside the nation, and entered into international trade. Such production was thus very different from the kind of small-scale manufacture that had long existed to meet purely local needs.

Fourth, there was a crucial linkage between proto-industry and commercial agriculture. Proto-industrial workers did not produce enough food for their own needs, either because their land was originally too small or too barren, or because manufacturing came to take up so much of their time.

The *fifth* feature of the Mendels model relates to the role of towns, which are regarded less as manufacturing centres than as the centres for mercantile activity (being the place where the 'putting-out' merchants lived); for marketing; and for finishing processes, such as the dyeing of cloth.

To what extent does proto-industrialisation further our historical understanding; or is it, as D. C. Coleman once suggested, 'a concept too many?'. One of the principle criticisms that has been levelled against the concept is that it is very restricted in the range of industries which it explains. Most of the empirical examples that have been offered relate to the manufacture of wool, linen and cotton, but the industrial revolution embraced more than the textile industries, and the concept has little to offer by way of explaining the development of more capital-intensive industries such as mining or iron smelting. The contribution of towns to manufacturing is also given insufficient weight; and little account is taken of the fact that many industries were located in rural areas *and* in towns, the distinction being in the quality of the final product. For example, woollen and worsted stockings were knitted in the country; jersey stockings were manufactured in such towns as Norwich and London; silk stockings were made in the capital alone. Similarly, coarse pottery was made in the country, but high-quality Delftware and creamware were produced in urban workshops. If you wanted the best knives, you looked to Sheffield; cheaper and inferior ones were made in the surrounding villages.

The difference between high-value goods manufactured in towns and goods of lower quality manufactured in the countryside is partly explained by differentials of skill. The more highly skilled (and more highly paid) workers were located in the towns, where closer supervision was possible. Cottage industry involved the making (usually by hand or by the most simple tools and machines) of plain, inexpensive goods. Little skill was involved, but much drudgery was entailed, the drudges including women and children as well as men.

Empirical studies have shown that capital for the establishment of factories often did come from domestic industry. A study of 150 Arkwright-type cotton mills operating in England in 1787 demonstrated the 'essential continuity of investment' between the putting-out system and factory production, while the majority of new mill owners had experience of the textile industry, either as manufacturers or merchants. However, the same study by K. Honeyman showed that a quarter of the mill owners in the cotton industry in that year lacked such experience, and were bankers, brewers, landowners and suchlike.

Not in every case did regions of proto-industrialisation progress to full-blown, factory production. East Anglia and the West Country, for example, both failed to live up to their early promise as cloth-manufacturing regions, and 'de-industrialised'. This may be to say no more than that their comparative advantage lay in agriculture, and that they came to specialise in what they were most efficient at, although there were other reasons, such as a greater worker resistance to machinery.

On balance, the concept of proto-industrialisation is probably much like many of those theoretical constructs which draw heavily on the social sciences. Their value to the historian lies less in the explanations that they offer than in the stimulus they provide to ask fresh questions.

Population change and economic growth

In 1990 the world's population stood at around 5.3 billion, having risen from around 1 billion at the beginning of the nineteenth century. By 2025 its estimated size ranges from 7.6 to 9.4 billion. Population growth is thus one of the key issues as we approach the twenty-first century. That there is a linkage between population growth and economic expansion has long been accepted, but the linkage is a complex one. That they do not go hand in hand is evident from the experience of, say, Ireland in the nineteenth century and Latin America and India today. It is therefore worthwhile to explore some of the ways in which a rapid expansion of population in Britain was linked to its industrial revolution.

The broad trends of Britain's population growth are not a matter of great controversy, and those of England and Wales are shown in Table 1.2. In the time between Gregory King's estimate for 1695 and the Registrar-General's for 1939 the population of England and Wales increased eightfold. Evidence for Scotland is scantier, but suggests that the population grew slightly more slowly, from around 1 million to 1.5 million between 1701 and 1801. By 1901 the population had reached 4.5 million, which again represents a slower rate of growth.

Table 1.2 shows that within the long trends there were considerable short-term fluctuations. Prior to the 1740s the population grew very slowly. The pace accelerated from the 1740s to the 1770s, but really took off in the next decade, the rate being twice as high in the 1780s and 1790s as it had been in the 1770s. At its peak – 1811–21 – the decennial increase was around 18 per cent. Though large, this has to be compared with the Third World in the twentieth century, where the rate has been much more dramatic. So different are these rates, in fact, that some historians have suggested that the problem is not to explain why Britain's population grew, but rather why it did not grow even faster.

It is possible that natural forces, beyond human control, were at work. For example, there is evidence that the virulence of certain diseases can undergo spontaneous change, and they can become more or less deadly for no apparent reason. Some diseases may have responded to the known improvement in climatic conditions which began in the later eighteenth century. Some natural forces, hitherto beyond people's control, came increasingly to respond to human intervention. Improved agriculture and new sources of overseas food supply eliminated the danger of severe food shortages and broke the vicious circle between malnutrition and disease. At the

Table 1.2   The population of England and Wales, 1695–1939

Date	Population (millions)	Rate of growth (% per annum)	
1695	5.2	1695–1701	1.2
1701	5.8	1701–11	0.3
1711	6.0	1711–21	0.1
1721	6.0	1721–31	0.1
1731	6.1	1731–41	0.2
1741	6.2	1741–51	0.4
1751	6.5	1751–61	0.4
1761	6.7	1761–71	0.6
1771	7.2	1771–81	0.5
1781	7.5	1781–91	1.0
1791	8.3	1791–1801	1.1
1801	9.2	1801–11	1.1
1811	10.2	1811–21	1.8
1821	12.0	1821–31	1.6
1831	13.9	1831–41	1.4
1841	15.9	1841–51	1.3
1851	17.9	1851–61	1.2
1861	20.1	1861–71	1.3
1871	22.7	1871–81	1.4
1881	26.0	1881–91	1.2
1891	29.0	1891–1901	1.2
1901	32.5	1901–11	1.1
1911	36.1	1911–21	0.5
1921	37.9	1921–31	0.6
1931	40.0	1931–39	0.4
1939	41.5		

Source: Neil Tranter, *Population Since the Industrial Revolution*, Croom Helm, 1973, pp. 41–2.

same time better medical and public health facilities allowed an attack to be mounted on the conditions which traditionally kept death rates high. There is much debate on these issues, which also raise the question of the relationship between death rates and birth rates. D. E. C. Eversley has suggested that the take-off after 1780 was in fact simply the result of the demographic experience of preceding generations. In pre-industrial societies, periods of demographic crisis – when population stagnates or declines – are invariably followed by high rates of population increase. The post-crisis population is small in relation to the number of economic opportunities, making it easier for people to marry earlier and to have larger families. The surviving population has demonstrated its robustness and relative healthiness, and is therefore less prone to fatal illness. And perhaps, also, disease itself has spent much of its previous force. Thus, a 'bulge generation' comes into being. Few would disagree with this thesis, but it is impossible to quantify the effect and, in any case, it could not have accounted for more than a small part of the upturn in the rate of increase. The explanation must lie elsewhere.

The problem is not only perplexing to historians; it also taxed contemporaries. Throughout the eighteenth century it was an accepted theory that the population was actually decreasing, but the quickening pace of economic activity towards the end of the century caused the opposite view to be put forward, and a lively debate ensued between 1770 and 1780. Arthur Young, in his capacity of Secretary to the Board of Agriculture, visited many parts of the country, and he trusted to the evidence of his own eyes:

> View the navigation, the roads, the harbours, and all other public works. Take notice of the spirit with which manufactures are carried on . . . . Move your eye on which side you will, you behold nothing but great riches and yet greater resources . . . It is vain to talk of tables of births and lists of houses and windows, as proofs of our loss of people: the flourishing state of our agriculture, our manufactures, and commerce, with our great wealth, prove the contrary.[11]

Arthur Young believed that the population was expanding, and was optimistic. Thomas Malthus also believed it was expanding – and was profoundly pessimistic. In 1798 he published his book, *An Essay on the Principle of Population*, of which he is reported to have said that few books had been more spoken of yet less read. Be this as it may, the ideas of Malthus (or what were believed to be his ideas) were of great influence. His great fear was overpopulation, with the country doomed to pauperism. Population, he believed, always tended to outrun the means of subsistence unless kept in check. Some checks were natural, such as war and famine. Others were within the power of human beings, chiefly 'moral restraint' from marriage. There was much that seemed to point to the validity of Malthus's views. The country was passing through an acute crisis, with a succession of bad harvests, accompanied by war at sea, pushing up prices to famine level in 1795–6. At the same time destitution was increasing, as reflected by the poor rate, which cost around £2 million in 1785 but had risen to £4 million in 1801. It was therefore inevitable that people would listen to Malthus, even if not everyone agreed with him. Robert Owen, for example, was one of those who foresaw that Malthus underestimated human beings' capacity to increase food supplies. In *A New View of Society* (1813), he wrote:

> Mr Malthus is . . . correct, when he says that the population of the world is ever adapting itself to the quantity of food raised for its support; but he has not told us how much food an intelligent and industrious people will create from the same soil, than will be produced by one ignorant and ill-governed. It is however as one, to infinity.
>
> For man knows not the limit to his power of creating food. How much has this power been latterly increased in these islands! And in them such knowledge is in its infancy. Yet compare even this power of raising food with the efforts of the Bosgemens [bushmen or hottentots] or other savages, and it will be found perhaps as one, to a thousand.
>
> Food for man may be also considered as a compound of the original elements; of the qualities, combinations, and control of which, chemistry is daily adding to our knowledge; nor is it yet for man to say to what this knowledge may lead, or where it may end.[12]

Malthus stressed the significance of a rising birth rate. This, together with the death rate and the rate of external migration, constitute the only factors which can affect the size of a country's population. External migration – immigration to and emigration from the country – can safely be ignored for this period. Numbers were comparatively small, and the net effect of migration is likely to have been on the quality of the population rather than the quantity.

The key will be found either in changes in the birth rate or the death rate, or a combination of both. The two are, of course, closely interlinked in a number of ways. There is, for example, the linkage through infant mortality. A child born one day and dead the next is a birth statistic and a death statistic. Infant mortality was high in eighteenth-century Britain, as it tends to be in pre-industrial societies of our own day. Parents were resigned to the possible death of their children. The Revd Sydney Smith (who knew from bitter experience) remarked that 'children are horribly insecure: the life of a parent is the life of a gambler'. Dr Johnson consoled Boswell on the loss of a child by reminding him that 'to keep three out of four is more than your share', and went on to observe that Mrs Thrale, a mutual friend, 'has but four out of eleven'. A child's life saved was of greater significance for growth than an old life prolonged, for every child surviving to marriageable age had the potential of producing more children.

The debate on the significance of rising birth rates and falling death rates has passed through many phases. For a generation between 1926 and the early 1950s the view that a falling death rate was paramount remained virtually unchallenged. This view had been put forward by G. T. Griffith, who argued that the significant change had been an improvement in medical knowledge and health care in the eighteenth century. However, this interpretation came under attack in 1955 when two medical historians, T. McKeown and R. G. Brown, argued that the medical improvements of the eighteenth century were more apparent than real. While they accepted that there had been a sevenfold increase in the number of hospitals in England between 1700 and 1800, they thought it improbable that this had had an appreciable effect on the death rate. They pointed out that the importance of segregating patients with infectious diseases was not appreciated, and that persons infected with cholera were admitted to the general wards of St Bartholomew's Hospital as late as 1854. Hospitals, they argued, might even have done actual harm. For example, a considerable number of lying-in (maternity) hospitals were established in the latter part of the eighteenth century but, because of the vulnerability of new-born babies to infectious disease, mortality rates in hospital were actually higher than in the case of home confinements. Despite the fame of such great eighteenth-century surgeons as John Hunter, McKeown and Brown argued that surgery had an unquantifiable effect on vital statistics until the advent – in the mid-nineteenth century – of anaesthesia and antiseptics. Even then, a surgeon could claim in 1874 that mortality following all forms of amputation was 35–50 per cent.

Despite this swingeing indictment of the medical case, McKeown and Brown still supported the idea of a falling death rate, which they attributed to environmental factors such as higher standards of housing, clothing and diet. Such conclusions were of profound importance, for clearly such factors are, in many instances, the consequence of economic growth.

Like Griffith's theory, the McKeown and Brown case became the accepted wisdom, but although it still retains wide support, it too has come under attack. On the one hand, it has been argued that the condemnation of eighteenth-century hospitals was too harsh: McKeown and Brown had demonstrated the inadequacies of hospitals in the mid-nineteenth century and had argued that there was a strong case for assuming that they must have been worse in the eighteenth century. But evidence has been produced that this was not the case, and that standards were surprisingly high in the eighteenth and early nineteenth centuries, declining thereafter under the pressures of a rising demand for treatment and inadequate resources to provide it. The evidence is not easy to interpret. As hospitals were voluntary institutions, relying on charitable bequests and donations for their support, they had to appear to be successful. When considering their 'cured and relieved' statistics, therefore, it is as well to remember that they pursued a cautious admissions policy and tended to discharge those patients whom they expected to die. On the other hand, P. E. Razzell has claimed that inoculation against smallpox (introduced in 1721) could theoretically explain the whole of the increase in population. Inoculation involved the injection of the small-pox virus itself into the patient. Vaccination, developed later in the century by Edward Jenner, consisted of injecting the less virulent cowpox virus. In support of his case, Razzell pointed to a study of life expectancy at birth of aristocratic women, which showed it to have risen from 36.3 years in the period 1700–24 to 51.7 years in the period 1800–24. Razzell held that any argument in the form of increased food supply or other environmental factor was irrelevant to such a prosperous group, but that inoculation – which was fashionable – could provide the answer. Smallpox had certainly been a great killer, but how far it declined because of inoculation (and, after 1798, through vaccination) or because the disease declined in virulence cannot be known. Its decline meant fewer deaths and, as recent research in India has shown, more births, for smallpox is a major cause of male infertility.

What of the birth rate, which Malthus had believed to be of such importance? The pre-industrial birth rate was high, partly as a counter to the high infantile death rate. As Leslie Clarkson comments: 'In the marriage bed at least, pre-industrial Englishmen and their wives outstripped the productivity of their twentieth-century counterparts.' Yet fertility in the eighteenth century, despite the absence of contra-ception, was less than half the biological maximum. By far the majority of children were born to married parents (although extra-marital births may have trebled in the eighteenth century), and therefore the age at which a woman married governed the number of children she might bear. The age at which most women married was between 24 and 27 years, reducing child-bearing years by a third. However, there is evidence that the age fell during the century, which would have had an important effect on the number of births. Much stress is placed by some historians, therefore, on those factors which, by removing restraints, led to earlier marriage and more child-bearing years for the wife. There were certainly some changes which pointed in this direction. For example, the practice of agricultural labourers 'living-in' with the farmer was in decline leading to more households being set up. Furthermore, the breakdown of apprenticeship in new trades meant that men did not have to wait so long before they reached maximum earnings, and were therefore less encouraged to postpone marriage. The demand for labour may have had some effect, especially that for child labour. The cost of child-rearing had to be offset against the possible earn-ings. Many people may have felt that they would be better off with more children. It was clear by the mid-nineteenth century that material rewards were greater for those with smaller families. What is noticeable is that the birth rate was higher in the late eighteenth century in the manufacturing areas than in the agricultural areas, and thus natural increase was a major factor in the changing regional balance of the population as between the north and south of England.

Did the subsidising of wages by the overseers of the poor (the Speenhamland system) encourage the birth of more children? The debate goes back to Malthus, who argued that it constituted a bounty on population. But did the allowance system perhaps have a greater impact on the death rate (by cushioning rural workers from the worst effects of rising food costs and unemployment) than on the birth rate? And is it not also possible that the allowance system was a consequence of higher birth rates and lower death rates rather than the cause?

The controversy over population growth is bound to continue, for while the evidence is fragmentary, the techniques to handle it are improving all the time, including the techniques of 'family reconstruction' pioneered by the Cambridge Group for the History of Population and Social Structure. Like the New Economic

Historians, the New Demographers, as they might be called, rely upon sophisticated statistical techniques, as well as on the power of computers to crunch numerical data as never before. Their approach involves a detailed investigation of the parish registers of the Church of England, for it should be remembered that civil registration of births and deaths did not begin until 1837. These registers, however, record not births and deaths but baptisms and burials, and a 'correction ratio' has to be formulated in order to adjust the figures. Can we be sure that registers were kept with the same degree of accuracy at all times and in all places? The answer seems to be that we cannot. For example, J. T. Krause has claimed that clerical zeal in keeping registers waned between 1781 and 1820 when clergymen increasingly held more than one living – non-residence was often a reason for not keeping registers properly. As the number of Nonconformists grew, the registers became less representative of the population as a whole, although the situation is complicated by other factors. It cost three times more to be buried in an Anglican churchyard than a Nonconformist one, so some members of the Church of England seem to have been prepared to be buried (or their economy-minded relatives preferred to have them buried) in a Nonconformist burial ground.

As this debate continues, so too does that on the relationship between population growth and economic growth. The links could be of a number of kinds, some more direct than others. The augmentation of the labour supply and more especially the extension of demand for industrial products are two of the most important. Contemporaries certainly had great faith in the power of numbers. Daniel Defoe, an important writer on economic and social matters, as well as being the author of *Robinson Crusoe*, wrote in 1728:

> As the Numbers of People increase, the consumption of Provisions increase, more Lands are cultivated; waste Grounds are inclosed, Woods are grubb'd up, forests and common Lands are till'd, and improv'd; by this more farmers are brought together, more farm-houses and Cottages are built, and more Trades are called upon to supply the necessary demands of Husbandry . . . As Trade prospers, Manufactures increase; as the Demand is greater or smaller, so also is the Quantity made . . . Trade has increased the People, and People have increased Trade; for Multitudes of People, if they can be put in a condition to maintain themselves, must increase Trade; they must have Food, that employs Land; they must have Clothes, that employs the Manufacture; they must have Houses, that employs Handicrafts; they must have Household staff, that employs a long Variety of Trades.[13]

Defoe's contemporary, Charles Davenant, observed that 'the bodies of men are . . . the most valuable treasure of a country, their increase or decrease must be carefully observed by any government that designs to thrive'. But it is clear that population growth does not automatically lead to industrial growth. If that were the case, most of the problems of developing countries in the Third World today would evaporate. If the rate of population growth is such as to outrun the economy's ability to supply the basic needs, demand for less essential products may well decline. For example, Eric Evans writes of eighteenth-century Ireland and Sweden, which 'could not channel [their population growth] into . . . productive enterprise either because they lacked the commercial superstructure or because their social structure was remorselessly battened down to the stolid conservatism of peasant proprietorship and subsistence farming'.[14]

The eighteenth century witnessed an extension of the market for industrial goods in Britain, although historians do not all agree on the precise manner by which this came about. It is not disputed, however, that during the period 1720–50, while population remained relatively stagnant, agricultural output rose substantially, and there was an immediate effect on consumer demand. As the cost of basic food grains fell, the average level of real wages rose. As a smaller percentage of income was spent on essential foodstuffs, more was available to be spent on less essential foods such as meat and dairy produce, and on cheap manufactured products. A common saying in nineteenth-century Bradford explained that 'when the poor live cheaply, they clothe well'. But in the second half of the eighteenth century, when the pressures of population growth and rising grain prices bore down on real wages, why did not the demand for manufactured goods among the labouring population decline? First, agricultural improvements meant that the supply of foodstuffs was more or less able to keep pace with population growth, so that the increase in food prices was minimised. Second, it has been argued that in order not to sacrifice newly experienced standards of consumption, labourers were willing to work harder and longer. For material ends, therefore, workers were willing to submit to the routine and hard regime of the factory. This materialism is itself one of the characteristics of an industrial (or industrialising) society. In traditional communities, where wants are simple, there may be a greater 'leisure preference', with individuals prepared to work only so hard as is necessary to satisfy basic needs.

The desire to increase their standard of living, even if this meant buckling down to industrial work, was very likely a factor persuading workers to migrate to the towns. A mobile population is advantageous to an industrialising nation, for migrant labour flows to the pressure points of the economy where the demand for workers is greatest. There were distinct differences in regional rates of population growth in late eighteenth-century Britain. Industrial counties, such as Lancashire, the West Riding of Yorkshire, Warwickshire and Staffordshire grew appreciably, while the agricultural counties of the South remained relatively stagnant. For example, between 1781 and 1801 the agricultural and commercial counties increased by a mere 10–12 per cent. Migration was one of the factors responsible, although economic conditions in the North were inducive of greater fertility.

Agricultural improvement

It is hard to see how the population of Britain could have expanded without a great rise in agricultural output, especially as it was accompanied by urbanisation and an increase in the number of those not producing their own food. It is clear that agricultural output expanded in the eighteenth century between 40 and 50 per cent. In 1700 one person engaged in agriculture could feed 1.7 persons, but by 1800 one agricultural worker could feed 2.5 persons, an increase of 47 per cent. This increase was due to two factors; higher yields per hectare and, more importantly, an increase in the number of hectares sown. Both of these features characterise what has been called the agricultural revolution. Traditionally this has been associated with a decline in open-field farming and a movement towards enclosure, together with a great improvement in agricultural practice, characterised by the introduction of new crops, better selective breeding of livestock and treatment of soil fertility, and the use of new machinery.

New crops included turnips and other root vegetables, and legumes such as clover, sainfoin, trefoil and lucerne. These improved fodder crops enabled more stock to be kept, whose dung increased the fertility of the soil. In addition, the legumes had nitrogen-fixing qualities which farmers appreciated pragmatically long before agricultural scientists were able to demonstrate the process involved. The impact of the increased use of legumes was great, and may have accounted for a third of the growth in agricultural output in northern Europe between 1750 and 1850. Further improvements to the soil were achieved by manuring and dressing with clay marl or with sand or chalk, depending on the natural deficiencies. Clay marl added to a sandy soil enabled it to retain water and manure, while chalk and sand added to heavy clay soil improved the tilth and assisted drainage. A wide range of fertilisers was employed, with a preference for materials of local origin because of the high costs of bulk transport. Near the coast, seaweed was used – either composted, burned, or ploughed in raw – and near the textile centres, waste rags. Around Sheffield bone and horn waste (left over from the manufacture of knife handles) was employed, and in the region close to all large towns the sweepings of streets and stables and the contents of privies were spread on the land. As early as the 1680s, the fertilisers spread on the grasslands of the Verney estates in North Buckinghamshire included dung, urban night soil, river mud, marl, lime and potash.

Innovation was biological rather than technical, for the development of farm machinery was remarkably slow when compared with the mechanisation of industry, and steam was not widely in use until the middle of the nineteenth century. However, improvements were made to the plough, and the use of the horse-hoe and horse-drawn seed drill gradually spread.

In the past many of the changes were assumed to have a 'heroic' quality, in the sense that much of the improvement was ascribed to the pioneering efforts of a small group of individuals. These included Jethro Tull (1674–1741), Charles Townshend (1674–1738), Robert Bakewell (1725–95) and Thomas Coke (1752–1842). Tull is best remembered for his advocacy of the seed drill which, by planting seed in rows rather than scattering it broadcast, enabled the soil to be more effectively hoed. He explained his ideas in *Horse-Hoeing Husbandry*, published in 1733. Jethro Tull's agricultural reputation is now much diminished. He did not actually invent the horse-hoe, and he held the quite erroneous view that air was the best fertiliser! Townshend – 'Turnip Townshend' as he came to be known – was noted for the introduction of marl to improve the sandy wastes of his Norfolk estates, and for the advocacy of the turnip for fodder and as an addition to the traditional rotation of crops. Robert Bakewell is best known for his work on selective breeding. Horse-breeding had long been a hobby of the gentry, and Bakewell's activities followed in this line. He was particularly successful with sheep, crossing Lincolns with Ryelands to produce the New Leicesters which fattened quickly, thus obtaining fat mutton for a growing market. The meat produced was not considered fit 'for genteel tables', but was rather seen as 'coal-heavers' mutton. Coke's improvements were many, most notably the granting of long leases to his tenants (the increased security of tenure encouraged improvement) and the dissemination of information. He was the pioneer of the agricultural show, holding an annual sheep shearing on his estate at Holkham in Norfolk attended by over 7,000 visitors .

It is this aspect of their work – publicity – which is now seen as the real achievement of the erstwhile pioneers. Most of the improvements with which their names are associated can be traced to an earlier period, but they helped to popularise existing sound practice. There were other agents of publicity. As literacy among farmers increased, so more books on agriculture were read. Among the most prolific writers was Arthur Young, who edited the *Annals of Agriculture* from 1784. He became Secretary of the Board of Agriculture which was formed in 1793, and wrote many of its County Reports. Another writer, of a somewhat earlier vintage, was William Ellis. Both Young and Ellis are examples of that not unknown phenomenon – the unsuccessful practitioner who goes on to become a best-selling author. In 1748

Ellis's village of Little Gaddesden in Hertfordshire was visited by a Swedish botanist, Peter Kalm, en route to study the flora of North America. Kalm noted in his journal that some of the arable fields of the village 'lay almost like beds in a kitchen garden', while others were carelessly managed. Kalm discussed this state of affairs with a local farmer:

> 'Who is the owner of this field, which to a great extent stands under water, and is so ill cultivated?'
>
> 'A Mr Ellis as he is called.'
>
> 'Mr Ellis,' I asked, 'you must have forgotten yourself, or is there more than one Mr Ellis?'
>
> 'No,' replied the man. 'There is not more than one Mr Ellis here, and to him the field belongs.'
>
> 'Who works on the enclosure away there where the moss has so excessively got the upper hand?'
>
> 'The same Mr Ellis.'
>
> I asked 'if it is the same Mr Ellis who is so celebrated for the many beautiful works he has published on Rural Economy'.
>
> The man answered that it was the very same, and that as for Mr Ellis's beautiful works on Rural Economy, he let them be for what they were worth; but this he said he was sure of, that if Mr Ellis did not make more profit out of sitting and scribbling books, and selling the Manuscripts to Publishers, than he did from his farming, he would soon have to go and beg – for 'Mr Ellis mostly sits at home in his room and writes books, and sometimes goes a whole week without getting out into his ploughed fields and meadows to look after the work, but trusts mostly to his servant, and young son, who is still a boy.'[15]

Ideas spread slowly, and a century after Tull's advocacy of the seed drill, Arthur Young could only find a dozen farmers using it in Hertfordshire. The impact of 'improving' agricultural literature can easily be exaggerated. The *Annals of Agriculture* only ran to 400 copies at the peak of its printing, and most farmers probably never read any such kind of book in their lives.

Other features of the agricultural revolution have been reinterpreted in recent years, including the alleged distinction between 'progressive' eastern counties and 'backward' western ones; the relationship between open fields, enclosure and agricultural improvement; and the impact of enclosure on the rural population. As for chronology, the agricultural revolution has proved even more elastic than the industrial revolution. As it is now commonly stretched to cover most of the period 1560–1880, the same controversies exist as to the appropriateness of the terminology.

Many of the improved techniques and new crops had their origin in Holland and, it was once strongly argued, took root in Norfolk and the eastern counties while the more distant western counties remained ignorant of them. It is now realised, however, that variations in agricultural practice were much more complex than was once supposed, and that as well as differences between counties, there were important differences within them. Many factors affected farming practice, including relief, soil and communications with the market. A more meaningful division than that between east and west is the division between scarp and vale topography, i.e. between light sandy soils on the uplands and heavy wet clays in lowland areas. There was not a uniform scope for innovation across these two divisions. There were variations from crop to crop, but the potential value of improvements remained greater on the light soils. These had previously been too infertile for permanent tillage, but were dry enough for stock (sheep especially) to be kept on the land during winter to feed off fodder crops, thus returning manure to the soil. This, in turn, allowed a following cereal crop. Once such thin soils could be kept fertile, cereals could be grown more cheaply on them than on the wet clays. There heavier ploughs had to be used (raising traction costs), the working season was shorter, root crops did less well and livestock could not be turned out to feed on them in the fields in winter as the land was too wet. During the eighteenth century, therefore, there was a marked extension of cultivation on to the former barren uplands, while many of the claylands went over to grass and farmers there specialised in fattening stock and dairying.

A large part of the increase of cultivable land is associated with enclosure, but whereas this was once seen as the basis of agricultural improvement, it is now thought to be the culmination. Open-field farming was not so backward as has sometimes been alleged. R. H. Tawney once described the open fields as 'a perverse miracle of squalid putrefaction', and their farmers as 'the slaves of organised torpor'. But, more recently, it is believed that if farmers inclined towards traditional practices it had a rational justification, while Gregory Clark has suggested that there are political overtones to the debate. 'In part,' he says, 'the weight given to the open fields as a retarding force in agriculture seems to have stemmed from a general ideological commitment on the part of many historians to pure private property as representing the improved state of society and communal property as representing the darkest forces of the tradition-bound past.'[16] It was not impossible to accommodate open-field farming to the new crops and techniques. Livestock breeding, for example, was facilitated by the widespread use of 'closes' (enclosed fields) in what were otherwise open-field villages. In order to appreciate the significance of enclosure, therefore, we must examine the nature of open-field farming and the changes which had occurred within it before the great period of parliamentary enclosure in the latter half of the eighteenth century.

Open-field agriculture was designed for a stable (or at most a slowly rising) population, and it fitted well the needs of subsistence. An expanding, urbanising population, such as that from the late eighteenth century, pushed agriculture more and more towards the market economy. In such conditions the farmer has to ask, 'What crops can I sell?' rather than 'What crops do I need in order to subsist?' The open-field system suggested an answer to the latter question, and allocated the ground according to the tripartite division of arable, meadow and pasture. The farmer needed arable to produce wheat and rye for his bread, and barley for his bread and his beer, and for his livestock. He needed pasture for his stock in the summer months, and he needed meadow so that in the summer he could lay up a stock of hay to feed his cattle during the winter. Otherwise they would have to be slaughtered at Martinmas (11 November).

There were complications, however. Instead of the host of crops grown by a modern arable farmer, there was little cultivation save of wheat and rye as bread corns with barley as beer corn, and pulses such as beans and peas. The farmer was therefore confronted with the problem of soil exhaustion, especially before the development of techniques of manuring. The usual method of allowing the soil to regain its fertility was by periodically letting it lie fallow, and to facilitate this there was a rotation of cultivation. In some areas the rotation was wheat or barley followed by fallow, and this was called a two-course rotation. A three-course rotation consisted of wheat followed by barley, followed by fallow. We associate the three-course rotation with the 'three-field system' but, in fact, the large open field was not the unit of rotation, which was the 'furlong' – a group of strips within the large open field. Thus it was actually possible to operate a four-course rotation with three open fields.

Meadowland, the second of the traditional farmer's basic requirements, was at a premium before the introduction of phosphatic manures in the nineteenth century, and the only mowing was in the natural water-meadows by the side of rivers or streams. Pasture consisted of the arable fields when they were in fallow, the meadowland after the hay harvest, odd scraps here and there, and the uncultivated waste land of the village.

The classic three-field system exists only in the pages of textbooks, for every village was in some way unique. Only half the area of England remained unenclosed in 1700, and the open-field system was not to be found everywhere. It had disappeared from Devon and Cornwall. It was rarely found in Wales, and had almost gone from the whole of the West Country from Monmouth and Somerset to Shropshire. It was hardly to be seen in Cumberland, Westmorland and Lancashire. It was unknown in Kent, and had early declined in Middlesex, Essex and large parts of Suffolk under the influence of the London market. Its stronghold was the great triangle stretching from Hampshire and Dorset through the Midlands to Yorkshire, although even here there were many scattered areas of enclosure.

Farmers cultivated scattered strips spread across all the open fields of the village, but when we speak of 'common field agriculture' it is essential to remember that what we are talking of is not common ownership but common practice. The manorial court, which was of medieval origin, fixed a communal timetable for sowing and harvesting, determined the rotation, and through the enforcement of 'customs of the manor' ensured a minimum standard of cultivation. The historian, Michael Turner, quotes an early nineteenth-century agriculturalist as saying that severalty (the separate and individual ownership of land) made a good farmer better but a bad farmer worse. However, the scattered nature of holdings in the open fields could make innovation both difficult and expensive. To overcome these difficulties many farmers consolidated their holdings by exchanging strips, and there was considerable enclosure by agreement. The problem for historians is that such enclosure is much more difficult to document than the parliamentary variety, the significance of which in the late eighteenth century has consequently been exaggerated, for it was merely the climax of a gradual transformation which had been taking place over a long period.

The emphasis on parliamentary enclosure has been heightened by the fact that it was heavily concentrated in certain periods. In the 1760s and 1770s some 900 Enclosure Acts were passed, while in the period of the Napoleonic Wars, 1793–1815, a further 2,000 acts were passed. Altogether, over 4,000 acts were passed between 1750 and 1850, of which nearly three-quarters were concentrated in these two periods of heavy enclosure.

The timing of parliamentary enclosure was determined principally by one factor – profit. In so far as gains were likely to be greater for the larger landowners, it was they who generally took the initiative, sometimes against the opposition of small landowners whose costs were proportionately higher. The expectation was that enclosure would result in higher rents, and it would appear that, on average, they did perhaps double.

The procedures were set in motion by securing agreement to petition Parliament for leave to bring in a bill, but it was weight of property rather than numbers which influenced Parliament. Large, powerful landowners therefore were able to override the interests of smaller ones. The bill would be prepared by the promoters' solicitor, and would be presented to Parliament by some interested Member. Once the bill was passed, the actual process of enclosure could begin. The act would call for the appointment of named commissioners who would, in their turn, appoint a surveyor. The commissioners would receive claims from landowners for an allotment of land, while the surveyor would measure each holding in the open fields as a preliminary to making an award. When all claims had been received, the commissioners would make their award, taking into account the size of the original holdings and, where waste and common pasture were enclosed, compensating (by an allotment of land) the commoners, who lost their common rights. At the same time old roads might be stopped up and new ones laid out.

The costs of enclosure were of two kinds, 'public' and 'personal'. The former included all the legal costs, commissioners' and surveyor's fees, and certain physical costs such as those for making new roads and for fencing the lands allotted to the tithe owners. The commissioners either raised a rate to cover the costs of enclosure or, as was increasingly the case in the nineteenth century, sold land. This eased the purely financial burden but meant that the land available for allotment was often severely curtailed, reducing that of some owners to an uneconomic unit. The principal personal costs were those involved with fencing, for each landowner was required (usually within three to six months) to fence his property from his neighbour's, and would, in addition, want to subdivide his allotment into manageable fields. Total costs might therefore be more than double the public costs. At the beginning of the nineteenth century £5 per acre (1 acre is equal to 0.4 hectare) was not exceptional, and if the owner took the opportunity to make capital improvements in order to get the full benefit of enclosure, this might reach £12.

How far did enclosure lead to a decline in the number of small landowners and cottagers, and to individuals being pressured to leave the land and enter the factories? Karl Marx certainly regarded enclosure as the key factor in the robbery of communal lands by landlords eager to create large, capitalist farms, and, by throwing large numbers off the land, to set free a proletarian workforce for manufacturing industry. By 1887 only about 12 per cent of the occupiers of land were the actual owners of it, and such was the concern for this alleged loss of a peasantry that around the turn of the twentieth century there were many historical studies aimed at explaining the phenomenon. Among the most eloquent writers were the Hammonds, whose classic study, *The Village Labourer*, appeared in 1911. Typical of their violent denunciation of enclosure is the following:

> The enclosures created a new organisation of classes. The peasant with rights and a status, with a share in the fortunes and government of his village, standing in rags, but standing on his feet, makes way for the labourer with no corporate rights to defend, no corporate power to invoke, no property to cherish, no ambition to pursue, bent beneath the fear of his masters, and the weight of a future without hope.

The Hammonds' interpretation is no longer tenable. As E. L. Jones says: 'The conspiracy theory of parliamentary enclosure may linger in the doctrinaire wings of economic history, but it is no longer a serious proposition that the enclosure commissioners were a kind of capitalist press-gang.' Indeed, J. D. Chambers and G. Mingay have observed that 'parliamentary enclosure represented a major advance in the recognition of the rights of the small man'.

It is true that cottagers and squatters lost their access to the common pasture and the waste, which may have provided the keep for a cow or some pigs or geese, as well as a supply of fuel. Yet, to some extent, compensation may have been afforded by the increase in both the volume and regularity of employment which followed enclosure. An increased demand for labour was created by the extension of the cultivated area, and there was much work involved in the erection and maintenance of fences and hedges, the laying out of new roads and the construction of new farms and buildings. There was surprisingly little introduction of machinery which, in any case (with the possible exception of the threshing machine), was not labour-saving. As late as 1831 wheat was still dibbled in Norfolk, while the scythe and the sickle reaped the harvest for a much longer period yet.

The numbers engaged in agriculture continued to climb, from around 1.7 million in 1801 to 2.1 million in 1851, but they did not match the increase in agricultural output. In other words, labour productivity was rising, which released workers from the land. This, together with the natural increase of population, created a labour supply which agriculture, for all its fresh demands, was unable to absorb.

The decline of small landowners can be traced back over a much longer period than that covered by parliamentary enclosure. G. Mingay argues, for example, that many of the causes of the decline date back to the seventeenth century. The argument of the Hammonds was that the expense of enclosure had forced out the small land-owners. Yet, apart from citing some instances (where the costs were unusually high), they produced little evidence that the burden was crushing. Small owners, like their larger counterparts, benefited from the rise in land values which enclosure usually brought about. While their costs may have been higher, for an expenditure of £50–£100 the small landowner might increase the value of his land from £450 to £900. To meet his expences he might raise a mortgage, or he might sell off one or two hectares. Alternatively, he might sell all his land at its improved value and set himself up instead as a substantial tenant farmer. There was a long-term trend towards larger farms, for they enjoyed economies of scale and in most cases were more efficient and flexible. What subjected the small farmers to greater pressure was not so much enclosure as the lower prices which prevailed after the Napoleonic Wars. Small tenant farmers were also in a weaker position than their larger brethren. They were easier to replace, and were in consequence less likely to receive abatements of rent in hard times, when a lenient attitude had to be shown towards the large tenants.

Finally, if enclosure did not eject labour into the factories, what were the links between agricultural expansion and economic growth? It should at once be said that agriculture itself did not provide the direct trigger for economic growth. As Leslie Clarkson has pointed out: 'Even modern experiences of economic growth offer few examples of countries developing rapidly on the basis of advances in primary production, not even in nineteenth-century Australia, where economic development came about more through urbanisation and industrialisation than the growth of agriculture.'[17] The elasticity of demand for the products of agriculture is limited by the elasticity of the human stomach! The demand for meat and dairy produce is more elastic than that for bread grains, as is also the demand for agricultural raw materials, although the major home-produced raw material – wool – supplied an industry that was growing only sluggishly. Thus, improved methods of agriculture did not open up the prospect of rapidly expanding sales, although the holding down of living costs is likely to have freed income which could be spent on manufactured products. Agriculture itself did not set up a great demand for the manufactures of other industries. It provided its own raw materials (such as seed corn and breeding stock) and there was little input from industry in the form of machinery, for example, or artificial fertilisers – both of which were important in the nineteenth century.

We therefore have to look to less direct links, in particular to the investment of agricultural income in industry and transport. Landowners played a noteworthy role in fostering industry by exploiting mineral deposits beneath their lands, and by developing their urban estates (see Chapter 3). Landed society remained less aloof from manufacturing industry than its European counterpart, and industrialists were freely admitted into its ranks. Indeed, it could be argued that the attraction of rural life could prove counter-productive. Richard Arkwright, for example, spent almost £250,000 on the purchase of an estate in Herefordshire, a sum equal to 60 per cent of the annual investment of fixed capital in the entire textile industry. There had always been this leak of fortunes made in industry into landownership, and it may not be without significance, therefore, that in the late eighteenth century the land market rather dried up, which may have kept more industrial and commercial money in the capital market.

There was some channelling by the country banks of agricultural profits into industry, but of greater importance than the volume was the direction in which such funds flowed. Landowners and farmers invested heavily in the communications network. Indeed, the canal boom in the south of England took place in response to the buoyant food prices during the French Revolutionary and Napoleonic Wars. The Kennet and Avon Canal, built by Rennie between 1794 and 1810, was one such project. Like other 'rural' canals, its aim was to cheapen the bulk carriage of agricultural inputs such as manure and chalk, and coal for the burning of lime and the manufacture of bricks for farm buildings; and to reduce the cost of transporting grain – the agricultural output. However, such canals had an obvious effect in permitting the wider diffusion of industrial goods. For example, the connection of the Kennet and Avon Canal with the Thames, into which flowed the Oxford Canal connecting with the Midlands, meant that Reading was soon able to import cheap coal, hardware and iron from Birmingham, pottery from Staffordshire, stone from Bath, and groceries from London or – via the port of Bristol – from Ireland and the Americas.

The progress of technology

A writer of 1752 spoke of 'the infinite numbers daily inventing machines for shortening business'. Two years later, another declared that 'at Birmingham, Wolverhampton, Sheffield and other manufacturing places, almost every manufacturer hath a new invention of his own, and is daily improving on those of others'. Dr Johnson observed: 'The age is running mad after innovation; all the business of the world is to be done in a new way.' And in 1814, Patrick Colquhoun was optimistic that the demand for British manufactures would rapidly increase, for goods were 'now capable of being augmented almost to any extent in consequence of the great improvements and incalculable mechanical powers of machinery'.

Conscious attempts were made to encourage inventiveness. For example, the Society for the Encouragement of Arts, Manufactures and Commerce (now the Royal Society of Arts) was established in 1754, with the aim of stimulating invention by way of competitions and the granting of awards and medals. More significant was the patent system, by means of which inventors were encouraged to reveal their secrets; in return they were promised the monopoly of exploiting them for a certain number of years (originally 14). The number of patents granted annually affords a very crude index of the pace of invention. The big break in the series comes in the 1760s when, for the first time, more than 200 were granted.

The patent figures do not tell anything like the whole story, however. In the first place, not all inventions were patented, partly because of the fee charged (£100 for England, or £350 for protection throughout the whole of Great Britain); or because the inventor might consider secrecy to be economically advantageous, provided it could be kept (not always easy: Richard Roberts, one of the foremost engineers of the time, bemoaned the fact that 'no trade secret can be kept very long; a quart of ale will do wonders in that way'). Second, the figures represent the quantity of inventions, but do not indicate the quality. Some inventions can clearly be shown to have been of enormous consequence; others were trivial; some were lunatic. Third, inventions have a practical effect only when they are widely adopted, which may be a long time after the initial patent is taken out. Fourth, it could be argued that, on balance, the patent system actually impeded technical progress, for it could enable an inventor to place a dead hand on further development of his ideas. For example, James Watt's original patent of 1769 was extended by Parliament for a further 25 years in 1775, thus giving great power to a man whose ideas were soon to become rigid. He refused application for licences to make engines under his patent; he discouraged experiments on locomotive models by his assistant, William Murdock; he was hostile to the use of steam at high pressure, and as T. S. Ashton has said, 'the authority he wielded was such as to clog engineering enterprise for more than a generation'. That steam power spread as fast as it did was partly because other manufacturers were prepared to pirate the Boulton and Watt engine, and because the older and more primitive Newcomen engines continued to be made. There was not the same restraint in the case of Arkwright and of Henry Cort. Arkwright's wide patents were annulled between 1781 and 1785; and in 1789 Henry Cort failed to protect his patent for iron puddling and rolling, which then went on to be more rapidly adopted than many other successful eighteenth-century inventions.

Table 1.3   Number of English patents sealed in each decade

1700–9	22
1710–19	38
1720–29	89
1730–39	56
1740–49	82
1750–59	92
1760–69	205
1770–79	294
1780–89	477
1790–99	647
1800–9	924
1810–19	1,124
1820–29	1,453
1830–39	2,453
1840–49	4,581

Source: B. R. Mitchell, *Abstract of British Historical Statistics*, Cambridge University Press, 1963, p. 268.

There was nothing new in mechanical ingenuity itself, as a visit to many museums will show. Since the Renaissance, and even earlier, many people had shown a remarkable degree of mechanical skill in the construction of elaborate timepieces, scientific instruments and other automata. In 1596, for example, Queen Elizabeth made a present to the Sultan of Turkey of an automatic organ built by the Lancashire clockmaker, Thomas Dallam. Like some jewelled juke-box, it played a sequence of four-part madrigals, while bells rang and birds flapped their wings, trumpets sounded and little figures gyrated and performed. So, what could an Arkwright or a Watt do that a Dallam could not? The significance of the new technology lies principally in three areas: the scale of the new machines, the materials used in their construction and the power with which they were driven. Earlier machines represented precision engineering in miniature. Many of the new machines were on a hitherto unprecedented scale, which changed the very nature of the operation and not just the degree of difficulty. New materials were employed, such as iron and steel, and new tools for boring, planing, cutting and turning had to be developed to work them. There had been some large machines before – windmills and water-mills, for example – but they had been constructed largely of wood, a material that was then worked mainly by hand.

Wind- and water-powered machines were only partially under the control of their operators, and their potential was limited. The average windmill or water-wheel could produce 5–10 horsepower, and the largest and most elaborate could produce only 30 horsepower. Wind and water power (and human and animal power) therefore came to be supplemented and eventually replaced by new energy sources, especially that of steam. However, the change did not come overnight. As late as 1839, while there were 3,051 steam-engines in the textile factories of the United Kingdom, there were still 2,230 water-wheels. All the engines built by Boulton and Watt up to 1800 totalled only 7,500 horsepower. Today, a single turbo-generator produces twenty times as much. Total steam power had risen to 500,000 horsepower by 1850, but the great expansion took place after that – to more than 9.6 million horsepower in 1907, for example. Water power had not entirely disappeared even then. Indeed, the famous New Lanark cotton mills in Scotland still had three water turbines (capable of raising 1,000 horsepower) when they closed in 1968.

Much of the steam power in manufacturing industry was concentrated in textiles, and it is the technical innovations of that industry which have received most attention. Donald McCloskey has estimated that between 1780 and 1860 productivity grew at a rate of 2.6 per cent per annum, and the worsted industry by 1.8 per cent. But even excluding the 'modernised' areas of textiles, iron and transportation, he finds other areas of the economy (such as chemicals, pottery, glass, gasworks, tanning and furniture) growing at a rate of 0.65 per cent per annum, on average. Had agriculture grown at 0.45 per cent per annum as he estimates, and had all other sectors of the economy, even textiles and iron, grown at the lower rate of 0.65 per cent, the national income per head would still have doubled between 1780 and 1860 (rising from £11 to £22 a head, rather than from £11 to £28). In other words, it was technical progress – much of it unspectacular – across a broad front which contributed to the industrial revolution. David Landes speaks of 'anonymous technical change', i.e. small refinements made to existing techniques, often by unrecorded inventors, which nevertheless led to a cumulative technical improvement; and Peter Mathias talks of an almost Darwinian evolution of technology, sustained over a long period of time. For example, James Watt managed to increase the efficiency of his steam-engine by two and a half times, but mining engineers in Cornwall, making a minor change here and a slight improvement there, increased the efficiency of steam-engines fourfold in the first half of the nineteenth century. It is easy to concentrate excessively on those 'heroic' inventors whose 'macroinventions' fill the pages of the history books. The economic impact of some was initially very slight. An extreme example would be hot-air ballooning (invented in France in 1783). This was a landmark event in the history of technology, yet the economic impact (and immediate military use, for that matter) was slight. On the other hand, many microinventions, consisting of improvements and adjustments to other people's great ideas could have an enormous impact on productivity levels.

At the time of the industrial revolution, there was an underlying awareness of the potential of technical progress, and there were linkages which helped to transmit advances in one industry to others. The intellectual stimulation to invention is important because of the questions it raises. Why do inventions occur when they do? What contributions did science make to technology? Many attempts have been made to produce a theory of invention, but none has been generally accepted. The matter is of some moment if we are to understand the relationship between technology and economic growth. We need to determine how far economic growth is due to technological change, or whether inventions are simply a response to prior economic pressures. The two possibilities are not, of course, mutually exclusive, but we still need to have some idea of the forces involved. So far, it has not proved possible to provide a hypothetical model for invention that can successfully explain questions of timing. On the other hand, the timing of innovation – the taking up of inventions and putting them to practical use – is more susceptible of economic explanation. Invention and innovation are, of course, complementary, and Joel Mokyr has remarked that 'asking whether technological change proceeds more by one or the other is like asking whether a pianist makes music with the left or the right hand'.

There was some transfer of knowledge from pure science to technology, although this can too easily be exaggerated. That the transfer was not automatic is revealed by the experience of France, for that country had a formidable scientific record that was not turned to practical application. There may be some truth in the idea that French science was rather abstract and formal, while in Britain it was more practical and applied. Many inventions were imported from across the Channel, including the Jacquard loom, chlorine bleaching, and the Leblanc soda-making process. Here again, it was improvement rather than originality that was crucial; and a Swiss calico printer observed in 1766 that for a thing to be perfect it had to be invented in France but developed in England.

There could be (and were) enormous time-lags between advances in scientific knowledge and technical innovation based upon it. For example, not one of the scientific ideas used by Bessemer, Siemens or Thomas, the great steel makers of the latter part of the nineteenth century, dated from later than 1790. In the same way, there could be dramatic time-lags between the empirical discovery that something worked and the scientific explanation of the process. Again, examples are to be found in metallurgy. Benjamin Huntsman began a long series of experiments in about 1743 which, after initial failure, led to the successful production of crucible steel in 1746. Five years later he began the manufacture of crucible steel on a commercial scale, an event of enormous economic significance, for this hard cutting-steel helped to emancipate the machine-tool makers. Yet Huntsman had no clear idea why his steel was so superior, for it was not until 1820, over 40 years after his death, that it was established that the difference between pig iron, wrought iron and steel depended upon the amount of carbon present; and not until 1831 that the German chemist, Justus von Liebig, perfected an exact method of determining the amount of carbon in steel.

More important than scientific knowledge may have been scientific method – experiment, observation and exact measurement. This is much more diffuse and difficult for the historian to evaluate, yet it may have been the decisive influence. This is the conclusion of Peter Mathias:

> . . . together both science and technology give evidence of a society increasingly curious, increasingly questing, increasingly on the move, on the make, having a go, increasingly seeking to experiment, wanting to improve. This may be the

prime significance of the new popularizers of science and technology . . . So much of the significance, that is to say, impinges at a more diffused level, affecting motivations, values, assumptions, the mode of approach to problem-solving, the intellectual milieu, rather than a direct transference of knowledge.[18]

Transfers of technology from one industry to another were affected in a variety of ways. Sometimes the techniques of one industry were capable of direct imitation in another, such as the use of rollers to attenuate material, be it bar-iron, textile, glass or paper. Techniques developed by John Wilkinson to bore iron-cannon castings were directly applicable to the boring of steam-engine cylinders. Incidentally, James Watt was thrilled with the result: 'Mr Wilkinson has improved the art of boring cylinders so that I promise upon a 72-inch cylinder being not further from absolute truth than the thickness of a thin sixpence in the worst part.' Sometimes an advance in one field was a condition of progress in another, as when the development of coke ovens made possible the extraction of tars; or an invention might break an equilibrium in a sequence of processes, as when the flying shuttle created a tremendous demand for yarn. Often the development of two industries went hand in hand. Abraham Darby's coke-smelting process required coal, yet coal production was hampered by the problem of pumping water from the mines. This was solved by the use of the Newcomen engine which, in turn, required large and intricate castings impossible to make without the iron made by Darby's process. And without Newcomen's engine, Darby could scarcely have obtained the blast he needed to produce iron on the scale required.

The impact of technological advance on industry was enormous, and facilitated the replacement of scarce by less scarce resources. The simple expedient of laying rails at collieries, for example, economised the high labour cost of loaders and wagoners. Resources could be economised. The eighteenth-century economy was heavily dependent on water, in the use of which spectacular economies were achieved by improvements to the waterwheel and the use of steam pumps to throw water back up to the mill ponds. To labour- and resource-saving economies must be added capital-saving ones. As T. S. Ashton says: 'When iron took the place of copper and brass in engine parts, of stone or bricks in bridges, and of timber for the beams and pillars in factories, there was a considerable capital saving.'

A final word of caution. The new technology did not sweep all before it. We should think in terms of 'coexisting technologies'. This might mean the continued use of older machines, or the continuance of hand technology. Improvements here could have great effect as when, in the early and middle years of the nineteenth century, the scythe came to replace the sickle in harvesting. Water power proved very resilient; for wheels were cheap, they lasted a long time, and they enjoyed low running costs. Such 'old' technology was capable of vast improvement, and wind power and water power, using vastly more sophisticated technology than might have been dreamed of in the eighteenth century, has enjoyed a revival in our own day.

The capital requirements of industry and the role of the entrepreneur

The role of capital in the industrial revolution has been subjected to much critical reassessment by historians in recent decades. Economists since the time of Adam Smith had stressed the role of capital and had agreed that a shortage of savings, and hence of capital for investment, was a critical constraint upon the growth of an economy. Karl Marx believed that the start of the process of industrialisation depended on the prior accumulation of capital, and that this was found at the expense of consumption. It was the masses, he argued, who would pay the price, either through taxes or inflation, or by a fall in their standard of living.

The emphasis on capital formation was heightened by economists grappling with today's problems of world economic growth. In 1955 W. A. Lewis argued that in order to increase the rate of growth of an economy from below 1 per cent per annum to above 2 per cent required a more than doubling of the rate of capital investment from 5 per cent or less of gross national product (GNP) to above 10 per cent. This idea was speedily taken up by W. W. Rostow as one of the preconditions of 'take-off'.

In 1961 Phyllis Deane claimed that the Lewis and Rostow figures did not fit the British experience, for she held that the rate of capital investment took a century to rise from 5 per cent to 10 per cent of GNP, and reached that figure only with the massive demands for capital made by railway building in the 1840s. More recently, however, Charles Feinstein has demonstrated that, in this respect at least, the Rostow hypothesis is valid. Figures never seem to last for long in the New Economic History, and N. F. R. Crafts has adjusted Feinstein's figures downwards, but the broad impression remains the same. His figures show a doubling of the ratio of total gross investment as a proportion of the gross domestic product from 5.7 per cent in 1760 to 11.7 per cent in 1830.

Comparison of Britain's pre-industrial economy with the underdeveloped economics of our own day may be particularly misleading when it comes to capital formation. Twentieth-century industry depends on sophisticated and expensive technology; today's developing countries demand enormous social investment in public utilities and health and education programmes; and governments press for high rates of growth in order to get back into the race.

Current research stresses the low capital requirements of industry in the eighteenth century, and draws a sharper distinction between fixed and circulating capital. It is important to understand these terms. *Fixed capital* consists of those assets, such as buildings and machinery, which continue in production for a length of time. *Circulating capital* includes those items which are used up in a short period (such as stocks of raw materials) and also goods in the process of manufacture or unsold finished goods. The sources of fixed and circulating capital are usually very different. As goods in the pipeline will eventually be sold, circulating capital can be supplied by short-term loans. Fixed capital − locked up in bricks and mortar or in machinery − presents a very different picture, for a much longer period of time will elapse before the asset realises its value. Hence there is a problem of long-term financing which usually presents greater difficulties.

Britain was fortunate in the timing of its industrial revolution, for capital costs were lower, and a greater proportion was tied up in circulating than in fixed capital. On the whole, the early technology was not expensive. In 1792 a new 40-spindle spinning jenny cost £6, and second-hand ones were frequently advertised at a lower price. Since the wages of hand-spinners were 2–3 shillings a week, it is evident that a 40-spindle jenny cost something like two weeks' wages of the 40 women it replaced. Insurance records have shown that, for example, in Stockport in 1795 a well-established jenny-spinner might have as little fixed capital as £150. It was possible to set oneself up in the iron industry with an equally small amount of capital. The Walker brothers established themselves in a foundry near Sheffield in 1741 with perhaps as little as £10. By 1754, and largely through their own self-denial, they had built it up to £62,500.

The really costly items were buildings and power. A large multi-storey spinning-mill of the type pioneered by Arkwright at Cromford cost perhaps £5,000 in the

1790s. At about this time a Boulton and Watt steam-engine would have cost around £850. It was, of course, possible to economise on expensive fixed capital. It was not usual for a person to set up in business in a purpose-built mill full of new machinery. Existing buildings, especially water-mills, might be purchased and adapted to a new use, and often they were either rented or leased. Power and machinery could be acquired in the same manner, or a cheaper but less efficient source of power than the Watt engine might be purchased.

A far greater proportion of total capital costs was represented by circulating capital. One of the largest manufacturing plants in the country in 1760 was the Truman, Hanbury and Buxton brewery at Spitalfields in London; yet, out of total assets of £130,000, fixed assets made up £30,000, or less than a quarter. The picture was not significantly different in other industries. While the cost of fixed capital was kept down by the relative simplicity of machinery, the cost of circulating capital was kept up by poor transport and defective market mechanisms which obliged manufacturers to hold large stocks of raw materials and finished products. In the course of time, as machinery became more complex and expensive, and as transport and distribution systems improved, the balance between the two forms of capital shifted.

It would be wrong to assume that raising capital presented no problems to the early industrialists. For a start, they had to face competing demands for finance. Building the infrastructure of the economy – roads, canals and river improvements, for example – absorbed large amounts of capital, as did agricultural improvements. The enclosure of 3 million acres (over 1.2 million hectares) of land between 1761 and 1801 may have involved investment of about £7 million. The government also competed for funds, principally to wage war, and in the half century between the outbreak of the Seven Years War and the Peace of Amiens in 1802, borrowed about £10 million a year which might otherwise have been available for economic growth.

The actual sources of capital varied. Modern industry obtains much of its capital from the ploughing back of profits, and there is no doubt that the same was true during the industrial revolution. T. S. Ashton observed: 'Whatever may be said against the early employers, the charge of self-indulgence can hardly be laid at their door. The records of firm after firm tell the same story as that of the Walkers: the proprietors agreed to pay themselves small salaries, restrict their household expenses, and put their profits to reserves.' However, some capital had to exist in the first place in order that a business could be established, and it could happen that entrepreneurs might want to invest capital for expansion at a faster rate than profits were accumulating. It was also the case that the key sectors of growth during the industrial revolution – cotton manufacture, iron making by the new techniques of coke-smelting, and engineering, for example – were, because of their very newness, the ones least likely to have access to ploughed-back profits, at any rate in their initial phase. Profits might be transferred from other activities such as agriculture or overseas trade. The Coalbrookdale ironworks of Abraham Darby was financed by his Bristol merchant partners, and the New Lanark cotton mill was founded by David Dale from his profits as an importer of linen yarn.

The role of the banks is an interesting one, for they were evolving at the same time as industry was expanding. There were about a dozen country banks in 1750, rising to around 700 by 1815. Successful banking, like any other business, involves risk taking; and bankers need information and experience in order to make sound decisions. Much of the work of the country banks had been in servicing agriculture, and the risk involved in lending money to meet the expenses of enclosure, say, or to build or expand a flour mill, could be assessed with reasonable ease. It was much harder to assess the creditworthiness of new industrial firms wishing to use innovative technology. Furthermore, it is sometimes argued that the contribution of banks to Britain's industrial revolution was minimal because they tended to lend for short terms rather than for long periods. This conclusion is unsatisfactory for two reasons. First, if they helped to provide circulating capital (which, we have seen, constituted the bulk of the industrialists' needs) they freed manufacturers to use their own funds, or funds from other sources, for fixed assets. Second, it is simplistic to say that they did not lend for long terms. What started out as a short-term loan sometimes ran for a long time on a 'rolling plan', rather like an overdraft. There was also a large measure of interlinking between banking and industrial personnel. Peter Mathias describes the relationship thus:

> Banks, and the partnerships of banks, throughout the country showed a very intimate connection with wealth made in trade and industry. Rich industrialists not uncommonly became partners in banks . . . Where a merchant or an industrialist or a mine-owner was a partner in a bank he felt he had special claims for accommodation . . . Where bankers became wealthy men on the profits of banking they were highly desirable candidates for partnerships, or as creditors of businessmen – and in so far as they supplied capital from their private resources, and not from the funds of the bank, this lending (which in aggregate economic terms would be designated from the banking sector) would not be identifiable in the account books of the bank.[19]

We may be guilty of laying too much stress on banks and other financial institutions simply because of their importance in our own economy. The eighteenth-century economy worked on a much more personal level, and it was often to his family or his friends that the industrialist first turned. Mrs Thrale was a friend of Dr Johnson and the wife of Henry Thrale, a London brewer. She described how the brewery came through the depression of 1772:

> First we made free with our mother's money, about three thousand pounds, 'twas all she had; and big as I was with child, I drove down to Brighton to beg of Mr Scrase . . . six thousand pounds more: dear Mr Scrase was an old gouty solicitor, friend and contemporary of my husband's father. Lady Lade [Henry Thrale's sister] lent us five thousand pounds more.[20]

It was to a politician friend that Richard Arkwright turned for his first loan; James Watt borrowed from his friend and mentor, Dr Joseph Black.

The taking of a partner was another possibility. The law of partnership was very strict in England, and each partner became personally liable for the debts of any firm from which he received a share of the profits. In fact, elaborate partnership agreements were frequently drawn up whereby the strict letter of the law was tempered, and there are many examples of young men with little capital taking on wealthy partners who took little active part in the business, but who contributed capital and received their share of the profits. Thus, long before joint-stock companies became the regular form of business organisation, the distinction between those merely contributing capital and those making management decisions had begun to emerge.

There is something exciting about inventions and technological change; so much so that the inventors and technologists of the industrial revolution may have gained more of the limelight than they deserve. However brilliant a new machine or technical process may be, it can have no impact upon economic growth until it is adopted and put to work. The decision to do this is taken not by the inventor but by the entrepreneur – the person who is willing to undertake the risks inherent in production, and who is prepared to organise the productive process. Most entrepreneurs in the late eighteenth century were not themselves inventors, and few possessed great technical skill. They needed to know enough to foresee the commercial possibilities of the new technology, and enough to control their managers and workers. Their inventiveness lay not in the techniques but in the organisation of production, from the purchase of raw materials right through to the marketing of the finished product. Their skill lay in sensing a market opportunity and in exploiting it.

Entrepreneurs have therefore been described as 'the shock troops of economic change' (Mathias). Harold Perkin describes the entrepreneur as the 'key figure' and the 'linchpin of society'. According to what Perkin describes as 'the entrepreneurial ideal', the entrepreneur was 'the impresario, the creative force, the initiator of the economic cycle'.

It is remarkable that, at a time of increasing division of labour, the entrepreneur should have fulfilled so many functions, yet this is the case. He was capitalist, financier, works manager, merchant, salesman – and in many cases, community builder. Labour had to be recruited, a task made more difficult by the popular repugnance to factories which, both in their architecture and in the discipline of the work they offered, bore marked similarities to the workhouse. Yet it seems that factory labour was attracted, rather than repelled from elsewhere (by changes in agriculture, for example), as was once supposed. The principal attraction was higher wages, for the sake of which (and the material advance which they promised) irksome conditions were endured. In many cases the relationship between the entrepreneur and his workforce did not cease when the workers left the factory gates. Factories often grew on isolated sites, tied to water power or cheap coal. The entrepreneur therefore had to provide houses, as well as shops and other services. Several spinners built churches and chapels and a number opened Sunday schools. It was more rare for the factory owner to open an inn within the community, although Arkwright did just this at Cromford in 1779. The company shop has received a bad press, because of its associations with payment in kind ('truck') and the 'tommy shop' system of credit sales. No doubt workers were often exploited by being charged high prices for goods of poor quality, although in isolated areas (where costs were high anyway) the company shop could provide a genuine service. Paying workers was no simple task, and the use of truck was partly a response to the great shortage of low-denomination coinage, especially in the provinces.

If the tasks which entrepreneurs were called upon to perform were so complex, what were the motivating forces which drove them on? Clearly, the main drives were the profit motive and aspirations towards social advancement. Both profit and position had to be fought for in competition with others, but as Perkin points out, competition during the industrial revolution had particular features: 'Competition was not the bloodless competition between material products and between abstract corporations of the modern "free enterprise" economy; it was individual competition, the competition between flesh-and-blood men for wealth, power and social status.'

The origin of eighteenth-century entrepreneurs is a matter of some importance, for clearly this is relevant to the question of why Britain was the first nation to experience an industrial revolution. At first glance it seems impossible to make any generalisations, for they came from diverse backgrounds. Some, like the Duke of Bridgewater, who helped to create a new transport system, were aristocrats. Many others had their origin on the land, such as Richard Crawshay, 'the iron king', whose father was a small farmer; or the Peels, in cotton, who had been prosperous farmers. Richard Arkwright, who died (a knight and a millionaire) in 1792, started life as a barber. Peter Stubs, an eminent file manufacturer and tool dealer, had been an innkeeper. Edmund Cartwright left the pulpit for the power loom, and Samuel Walker (a former teacher) left the classroom to become a leading figure in the north of England iron industry. Entrepreneurs were sometimes joined by the bonds of marriage. Ironmasters married ironmasters' daughters; and potters the daughters of potters. 'Hence', wrote T. S. Ashton, 'arose dynasties (such as those of the Barclays and the Wedgwoods) as powerful in industry as royal houses in international politics.'

If entrepreneurs did not arise from a particular social class, there is one link common to many of them which has aroused the interest of historians. This is the bond of religion or, more precisely, of Protestant Nonconformity. It is difficult to obtain precise figures, but one fairly random sample of prominent entrepreneurs and inventors of the industrial revolution suggests that 49 per cent were Noncon-formists. The alleged connections between religion and capitalism were developed in the late nineteenth century by a German scholar, Max Weber. He argued that the 'spirit of capitalism', which he defined as 'the pursuit of profit, and forever renewed profit by means of rational capitalistic enterprise' was stimulated by Protestantism in a way that it was not by Catholic teaching. At the heart of the Protestant ethic was the doctrine of the 'calling' which regarded everyday work, however menial, as divinely ordained. It therefore had to be accomplished successfully in order to glorify God, and as a way to salvation. The Weber thesis has been extensively criticised. The alleged differences between Catholic and Protestant economic thought are felt to be exaggerated, and the historical record does not reveal that economic develop-ment was always more rapid in Protestant than in Catholic countries. Calvinist Scotland, for example, lagged behind Catholic Flanders. Nor does the thesis explain why the transformation of economic life was so long delayed after the Reformation. The influence of religion cannot be simply dismissed, however. The hold on industrial enterprise of some Nonconformist groups, especially the Quakers, was quite out of proportion with their numerical presence in the population as a whole. Some have argued that their minority status and their exclusion from the mainstream of society is the clue to the relationship. Nonconformists who were strict to their faith were excluded from civil and military office, and were barred from the universities of Oxford and Cambridge. They therefore established their own educational institutions – the dissenting academies – which, through their broad and practical curriculum, provided the best commercial and scientific education available in England at that time.

Nonconformists may also have had particular psychological drives. Denied access to the universities and hence to the learned professions, and suffering from a sense of social alienation, they may have striven with increased vigour to rise in those careers which remained open, mainly business and industry. Such drives may have been implanted in infancy, for recent work by historians of childhood (many of them with a background in psychology) have laid new stress on attitudes to child-rearing.

Transport

It is instructive to observe the hazards from which people pray to be protected. Those churchgoers who used the words of Cranmer's Litany to invoke protection from plague, pestilence and famine went on a few sentences later to pray for the protection of 'all that travel by land or by water', coupling with that endangered species pregnant women, sick persons and young children, and all prisoners and captives. Indeed, Dean Swift, the author of *Gulliver's Travels*, confessed that he preferred to start his journeys on a Sunday, for he felt supported by the volume of intercession ascending heavenwards on that day. The dangers were real enough, and travel in pre-industrial England was a luxury, costly in both money and time, to a degree that we would find hard to comprehend. Parochialism was a feature of pre-industrial Britain as it is in underdeveloped countries of our own day. Horizons were widened by the industrial revolution, which was both the producer and the product of far-reaching changes in transportation.

At the beginning of the eighteenth century, the basis of the English road system was the network of Roman roads designed, more than a thousand years before, for the rapid movement of troops between strategic points. Two features provided the basis of this remarkable system: highly skilled engineering and an efficient, national administration. When the Romans departed, these skills departed with them – although the bare bones of their system lingered on, the skeleton of their network being discernible even on today's road maps. Stagnation was not complete, but attention in the Middle Ages was concentrated on key points such as bridges, while roads were dealt with haphazardly.

The crucial factor in the deterioration of the roads was the passage of their administration from central authority to local hands. The common law assigned the responsibility to local people for the maintenance of their roads. In practice, this meant that the manorial courts exercised authority. As the manorial system gradually broke down, new administrative arrangements became necessary, and in 1555 the Highways Act was passed, the first piece of English legislation applying to roads in general. The act remained the basis of local control until 1835. It provided for the annual election in each parish of a Surveyor who was to supervise the stint of four (later six) days' unpaid labour, which each householder, labourer or cottager had to perform on the roads each year. There were obvious weaknesses in the system. The grand title, 'Surveyor', hides the fact that no technical qualification was required. Indeed, the very persons with leisure and education which might have fitted them for the task were exempted by the law, including the clergy, landed proprietors above a certain small value, and lawyers. In practice, the Surveyor was usually a small farmer, tradesman or innkeeper knowing little about road-making, and lacking real authority to direct the work of his neighbours. In addition, the reaction of statute labourers, conscripted to do a job that was not of their choosing, was to turn the occasion into a holiday. While local people were the main beneficiaries, there was some sense in making parishioners maintain their own roads, but when roads became regional or national thoroughfares, linking distant centres of trade and population, it became unrealistic to expect farmers and labourers to bear burdens which were mainly to the benefit of strangers.

There were (and contemporary experience with juggernaut container lorries shows that there remain) two ways of dealing with road transport problems. The traffic can be made to fit the roads, or the roads can be made to fit the traffic. Both approaches were tried. Much legislation addressed itself to the design of vehicles, imposing minimum wheel widths, for example, in an attempt to reduce damage to the roads. Other legislation attempted to fix maximum weights which could be carried. These acts tended to work in opposition to each other – a broader tyre enables you to carry a heavier load – and there was much evasion of the law. Economic progress demanded that the roads should be fitted to the new demands made upon them, demands which had implications for highway administration and for engineering.

Administration was tackled first. In 1663 a stretch of the Great North Road passing through Hertfordshire, Cambridgeshire and Huntingdonshire was placed by statute under the management of the Justices of the Peace, who were given the power to erect gates and to charge a toll. This was the first Turnpike Act to be passed, and within ten years the practice developed of investing trustees, rather than Justices, with the power to maintain roads. In the early acts turnpike trustees were given powers for a limited number of years (usually 21), a renewal at the end of that time being a partial explanation for the great increase in the number of acts after 1751. Over the next 20 years some 870 acts were passed, and as the trusts became self-perpetuating, more and more roads came under their control. By the 1830s there were around 1,100 separate turnpike trusts, deriving their powers from 4,000 individual acts, and controlling about 22,000 miles of road. It has to be remembered that turnpike roads at no time accounted for more than about one-fifth of the total road mileage of England and Wales. On the other hand, it is now felt that there was rather more of a national 'system' than was once believed, even though the formation of the trusts was left almost entirely to local initiative. For example, by 1730, 57 per cent of the 1,560 miles of the 13 main roads into London had been turnpiked, and another 31 per cent had been added by 1750, by which date only 182 miles remained to be improved. Even so, the setting up of turnpike trusts merely made possible an improvement of road conditions; they established the conditions under which improvement might take place, but this by no means followed automatically.

The accounts of foreign travellers in Britain suggest that they found a road system which they greatly envied. The accounts of British travellers often tell another story. Both sets of views probably tell us more about the writers than about their subject. A correspondent to the *Gentleman's Magazine* in 1752 remarked on the main London to Falmouth road: 'You have such roads as the lazy Italians have fruits, namely what God left them after the flood!' Whether the turnpike trusts would effect an improvement to the roads depended on their administration and upon their success or failure in attracting sound road engineers. It is difficult to generalise about the trusts. Some were notorious for the inept and sometimes fraudulent manner in which they carried out their appointed tasks. Others made a conscious effort to maintain and improve their roads as economically as possible. There can be no doubt that more money was spent per mile on turnpike roads than on parish ones, even after allowances are made for administrative costs. In 1838 the expenditure of the trusts was equivalent to £51 per mile of road whereas only £11 3 s was spent on each mile of parish highway.

It was due to the turnpike trusts that a new breed of civil engineers was able to exercise their skills. Britain produced a number of excellent road-builders, of whom the two most noteworthy were John Loudon McAdam (1756–1836) and Thomas Telford (1757–1834). McAdam repaired more roads than he built, and was as important for his administrative ability as for his engineering skill. His methods were remarkably simple, but were capable of standardised application. To him, a thick (and costly) road-bed was not of great importance, for he pinned his faith on good drainage and an impervious and indestructible surface. His methods rapidly gained recognition. Three sons followed in his footsteps, and together they supervised the work of 107 trusts with 2,000 miles of road by 1823. Telford (nicknamed 'the Colossus of Roads' by the poet Robert Southey) was a stonemason by training, and emphasised a solid foundation of large stones, topped off with a compacted mass of smaller stones. His roads were more expensive to build, but there were stretches of the Holyhead Road (A5) north of Shrewsbury which, in the late 1960s, remained largely as he had engineered them a century and a half before. This particular road assumed a great importance after the Act of Union of 1801 which gave rise to a need for speedier communication with Ireland. Thirty turnpike trusts maintained the road, but parliamentary intervention after 1803 turned it, in effect, into the nearest thing to a 'national' highway. The seven trusts across the Welsh border were amalgamated, while the 23 in England were placed under the aegis of a commission appointed to superintend work on the road. Some £250,000 was spent on the road which, when completed under Telford's direction in the early 1830s, represented the only substantial national investment in road-building until the arterial motor roads of the twentieth century.

Improvements to the roads enabled goods to be carried in greater volume and with more speed. Packhorses had been widely used, but the maximum weight they could carry was about 2 hundredweight (1 hundredweight is equal to approximately 50 kilograms), whereas the same horse could draw 10–12 hundredweight on wheels, given a good road surface. Charges nevertheless remained high, so that water carriage enjoyed a cost advantage. Charges rarely fell below 10d a ton-mile, although there was a great variation between different classes of goods. As late as 1830, for example, Pickfords used a tariff in which the maximum rates for plate glass and gunpowder were five or six times greater than those for sacks of grain or barrels of ale. Pickfords was a large firm in an industry dominated by small businesses. A directory of 1835 lists more than 800 public carriers operating in London alone, and there were some 14,000 regular wagon services each week in all parts of the country. A Leeds directory of 1822 lists 163 carriers, of whom 131 were small family businesses operating in the immediate vicinity, while 32 operated on a larger scale.

It was in the business of passenger transport that large firms were to be found. Of the 342 principal coach services operating from London in 1836, 275 were provided by the three largest proprietors: W. J. Chaplin (106), B. W. Horne (92) and E. Sherman (77). Chaplin's business employed over 2,000 persons and 1,800 horses in 1838, in which year he joined forces with Benjamin Horne to negotiate with the London and Birmingham Railway – the first main line into London.

The development of coaches greatly enhanced the opportunities for travel, and helped to turn it into an item of personal consumption, to be undertaken for pleasure as well as business. In 1740 there was one coach a week between London and Birmingham; by 1783 there were 30, and by 1829 there were 34 each day. Taking 10 of the leading urban centres of Britain – Birmingham, Bristol, Edinburgh, Exeter, Glasgow, Leeds, Liverpool, Manchester, Newcastle and Sheffield – the number of coach services increased eightfold between 1790 and 1836. The increase in passenger transport was greater than these figures suggest, for coaches in 1836 had a much larger capacity, so that it would not be excessive to claim that 15 times as many people were travelling by coach in the mid-1830s as were doing so 40 years before. Journey times were also faster. In 1836 it took just over 45 hours to travel from London to Edinburgh, whereas in the 1750s it had taken 10 days in summer and 12 in winter. At that time it took two days to reach Oxford from London; in 1828 it took six hours. The impact on the conduct of business was dramatic. In the mid-eighteenth century it would take more than a week for a London businessman to receive confirmation of an order sent to Birmingham, whereas after 1785 – when Royal Mail coaches began to operate in the Midlands – a reply could be expected in two days.

As we shall see in Chapter 6, long-distance coach services soon fell victim to the cheaper and more rapid railways, although horse-traffic in general did not decline, due to the enormous local traffic which the new competitor fostered. The swing of the pendulum back to local traffic gave the local administration of roads a new lease of life. The 1835 Highways Act gave 15,000 parishes the power to levy a rate for road maintenance, and enabled them to combine for greater efficiency. Few in fact did so and, although compulsion became possible in the 1860s, as late as 1882 over 6,000 parishes still acted as highway authorities. Turnpike trusts were hit hard by the railways. Between 1837 and 1850 their receipts dropped by one-third and many became barely solvent. Nevertheless, the system was so entrenched that the trusts were slow to disappear in England, although the Welsh trusts were abolished after the Rebecca Riots of the early 1840s. There were still over 800 trusts in 1874, when Parliament began to take a tougher line. Thereafter the number fell, and within 12 years it had dropped to 113. By 1890 only two trusts were left, and on 15 October 1895 the last toll was levied on the last piece of turnpike road in the country.

However much roads might be improved, they remained unsuitable for the bulk transport of goods, for the mechanical efficiency of the horse could not be fully utilised. On soft roads a team of strong horses pulling a heavy wagon might shift a ton of goods, or double that amount on a good macadamised road. But a single horse might draw 30 tons of goods on a river barge or, on the more placid waters of a canal or artificial cut, up to 50 tons. That attention should have been paid to inland navigation was therefore inevitable.

Britain enjoyed peculiar advantages when it came to inland navigation, for it enjoyed more sea coast per square mile of land than any other European country. Its coastal waters had always borne a considerable traffic, especially as many of the ports were on navigable rivers which gave access to and from their interiors. Some ports, like London, Bristol, Gloucester, Hull and King's Lynn thus tapped very large areas. King's Lynn, for example, collected vast quantities of corn via the Great Ouse and its tributaries, shipping half of it abroad and the other half up and down the coast. Gloucester and Bristol performed similar functions for the West Country shipping out agricultural produce and distributing goods to the hinterland via the Severn and the Avon.

In the course of the seventeenth and eighteenth centuries there was much interest in river improvement but it was neither easy nor straightforward. Vested interests held back developments which might remove a local monopoly or give advantages to a rival market, and there were the added problems that rivers served other needs than those of transportation. Watermills and weirs presented serious impediments to navigation, and agreement therefore had to be reached between the various users of rivers, as well as the owners of property through which they passed. Added to these problems was the fact that much new industrial activity was based in the Midlands, perched high on the central Pennines in areas accessible only by road transport. For these reasons and because of the fluctuating water levels in rivers, attention was turned to the construction of artificial waterways. It should not be thought, however, that river improvement chronologically preceded canal construction, for the two developments were interlinked – in some cases directly. This can clearly be seen around the Mersey, where the canal age had its birth. Between 1720 and 1760, Liverpool's trade grew more than threefold, but continued expansion depended very much upon improving communications with its hinterland. By an act of 1694, the Mersey was made navigable as far as Warrington, but an expanding trade in salt necessitated improvements to its two tributaries. These were the Sankey Brook (serving the South Lancashire coalfield, whence came the fuel for refining), and the Weaver (which served the salt-fields around Northwich). The main improvements to the Weaver were completed by 1733, but the vastly different technical problems of improving the Sankey Brook led to the cutting of a canal, the Sankey Navigation (opened in 1757), which was separated from the Brook by a lock, and used the river only as a reservoir.

It was in the same region that the first canal was built entirely independent of an existing river. In the year that the Sankey Navigation was opened, the Duke of Bridgewater took possession of his valuable estate at Worsley, which contained extensive coalfields. He immediately set about reducing the cost of transporting his coal to the expanding markets of Manchester and Liverpool. He secured powers from Parliament in 1759 and 1760, and his drive – combined with the skills of James Gilbert (his agent and mining engineer) and of James Brindley (a barely literate ex-farm labourer turned millwright) – resulted in the opening of the first 10-mile stretch from Worsley to Stretford, a Manchester suburb, in July 1761. People marvelled at Brindley's aqueduct, which carried the canal over the River Irwell at Barton. The *Manchester Mercury* reported on 21 July 1761:

> On Friday last His Grace the Duke of Bridgewater with the Earl of Stamford and several other gentlemen, came to Barton to see the water turned into the Canal over the River Irwell, which drew together a large number of spectators and it is with pleasure that we can inform the Public that the experience answered the most sanguine Expectations of everyone present. As soon as the water had risen to the level of the Canal a large boat carrying upwards of 50 tons was towed along the new part of the Canal over arches across the River Irwell which were so firm, secure and compact that not a single drop of water could be perceived to ouze thro' any of them, although the surface of the Canal is 38 feet above the navigable river under it. This canal will be carried to Manchester with all expedition and we are creditably informed will be completed before Lady-Day next, every seeming difficulty being now removed, and that in the meantime the subterraneous Navigation to the Collieries will be perfected so that we may expect to have a supply of coals as will reduce considerably the price of coal to the consumer and this work will be of great use as well as ornament to the town of Manchester.

The 'subterraneous Navigation' was a second wonder, and consisted of the cutting of underground canals into the actual coal workings, which eventually totalled 46 miles. The Worsley Canal brought down the price of coal in Manchester from 7d to $3\frac{1}{2}$d a hundredweight (approximately 50 kilograms), thus dramatically demonstrating the economic potential of canals.

The construction of the main trunk routes quickly followed. The Staffordshire and Worcester Canal linked the Mersey with the Severn at Stourport in 1772. Hull was linked with Liverpool by the completion of the Trent and Mersey Canal (Grand Trunk) five years later. In 1789 the Thames and Severn Canal linked the Thames estuary with the Bristol Channel, and the Coventry and Oxford Canals in the following year connected the Trent and Mersey networks to the Thames. By 1792 the market price of Grand Trunk shares was more than three times their nominal value, and the growing success of the early ventures sparked off a canal mania. Between 1791 and 1796, 51 new canal companies were authorised, with a capital of over £7.5 million, of which the most important was the Grand Junction (opened in 1805), providing a more efficient link between London and the industrial Midlands.

Most of the initiative and much of the capital for canal building came from local landowners and entrepreneurs. For example, Josiah Wedgwood was treasurer of the Trent and Mersey Canal and could see the potential of canals both in bringing in the raw materials he needed and carrying away his finished pottery with a greatly reduced risk of breakage. Nevertheless, speculative investment appealed not just to local people but to investors further afield. The canals thus differed from the turnpikes, which were managed by supposedly disinterested trustees, and resembled much more closely the railway companies which were to follow them. Their aim was to produce a profit, and having secured control of a trade route (often by breaking the monopoly of road and river interests) companies frequently acted as monopolies themselves. The full benefit of improvements was not passed on to the public, nor were the long-term interests of the companies themselves served. Avarice for short-term gain was short-sighted, for reinvestment in improving their service would have placed canals in a better position to face the railways. Here lay one of the disadvantages of local initiative and control, for canals were built in all shapes and sizes, and there was no national network until the waterways were taken over by the state in the twentieth century.

The economic effect of the canals was none the less great. They had the initial effect of lowering the costs of overland carriage by at least a half, and on the most efficient canals by three-quarters. When the Grand Trunk was opened, freight rates between Manchester and Lichfield were reduced from £4 to £1 a ton, and on canals generally tolls and carriers' charges amounted to around $2\frac{1}{2}$d a ton-mile. The reduction of freight rates helped to overcome a fuel crisis by facilitating the transport of abundant supplies of cheap coal. The Duke of Bridgewater declared that 'a good canal should have coals at the heels of it', while a writer of 1803 claimed that 90 of the 165 canal acts obtained since 1758 served collieries.

In addition, the actual building of canals provided a great stimulus through the massive employment of 'navvies', and the creation of spending power at a time when a number of industries were looking to mass markets. In this way also the canals anticipated the railways, while the construction of 3,000 miles or more of canal and improved river navigation between 1760 and 1830 was the main influence on the creation of a civil engineering profession so necessary to the railway age. Railways came late on the stage of the industrial revolution, and their development is traced in Chapter 6. In the early stages of economic growth it was to other forms of transport that the industralists had to turn, and the greatest of these was the canal.

Foreign trade, government policy and war

Just as internal trade grew in the eighteenth century so, too, did overseas trade. Although expansion was not entirely smooth, imports expanded by 523 per cent between 1700 and 1800, exports grew by 568 per cent, and re-exports by 906 per cent. Not all industries were equally dependent on export markets. In 1700 only 7.5 per cent of industrial output other than woollen cloth was exported, and even in 1831 only 7.7 per cent of output was exported in trades other than iron and textiles – by which time, cotton had pushed well to the fore. By 1815 Britain was exporting four yards (3.7 metres) of cotton cloth for every three (2.7 metres) that were produced for the domestic market. However, whether trade was the child of industry or industry that of trade is debatable.

There was a great growth in the size of the merchant fleet, the tonnage of which went up by over 326 per cent between 1702 and 1788, and this was paralleled by the rise of the Royal Navy which doubled in size between 1714 and 1763. What is quite clear is that Britain successfully used its naval power to secure a major share of new and expanding markets and sources of raw materials. At the beginning of the eighteenth century English foreign trade was heavily concentrated on the European continent, but by the end only 29 per cent of its imports were European in origin and only 21 per cent of its exports went there (although the majority of re-exports continued to do so). This relative decline was due to the expansion of colonial trade, especially across the Atlantic. Combined exports and re-exports to the North American colonies and the West Indies grew by a staggering 2,300 per cent during the eighteenth century. Imports from that source increased sixfold during the same period, and represented 32 per cent of total imports at the end of the century. Britain was geographically well placed within Europe to benefit from the growth of the Atlantic economy, and the reorientation of its trade is reflected in the rise of the west coast ports such as Liverpool and Bristol.

Britain's dominant position in North America, as well as in India, was the outcome of four wars fought between 1739 and 1783, wars which had a political and dynastic significance to the continental powers involved but which, in Britain's case, primarily served commercial ends. Through them it acquired its first empire, administered so that it might gain commercial advantage. Whether the system was as effective as was once believed is now doubted. Using sophisticated statistical techniques, some historians have argued that the gains of empire were slight and that, in the case of the West Indies for example, the costs outweighed the benefits. Why then were they maintained? Because what may have been a public loss was undoubtedly a private gain to the farmers and planters who were so powerful at Westminster. Their vested interest guaranteed the continuation of government policies which may, in fact, have impeded the development of the economy.

That government schemes to expand economic growth could be counterproductive is quite clear from European experience, where the wrong entrepreneurs, in the wrong industries, sited in the wrong places, were sometimes given state aid. By conscious acts of policy governments on the continent could attempt to follow an economic master plan, taking Britain as their model. But Britain had no model to follow, so an integrated plan for boosting the economy was out of the question. The government could, and did, intervene however, and had done so for centuries. Elaborate provisions for the training of skilled labour and the regulation of wages were contained in the Statute of Artificers of 1563, which still remained in force. That act restricted the mobility of labour, which was further hampered by the Law of Settlement. The Bubble Act of 1720 put severe limitations on the creation of joint-stock companies, while the Usury Laws set a limit of 5 per cent on the rate of interest which could be charged for loans. The export of a number of goods was prohibited, and duties were imposed on the importation of a great many others.

The removal of these restrictions might be seen as a great liberating force for the economy. Hence the significance attached to *laissez-faire* – the belief that governments should stand aside so that the wealth of the nation might be maximised through the collective efforts of individuals each pursuing their own best interests. This was the view of Adam Smith, whose great work, *The Wealth of Nations*, was published in 1776. However, there is often a time-lag between the formulation of new ideas and their actual practice, and this was true of *laissez-faire*. There was some rationalisation of import duties in the 1780s, and some modification of the navigation system and the regulation of colonial trade after the loss of the American colonies, but there was no clear abandonment of the so–called 'mercantilist' policies of state interference until the second decade of the nineteenth century. Even then the change was a gradual one. Chronology, therefore, would indicate that the adoption of *laissez-faire* ideas can hardly be used to explain the origins of the British industrial revolution.

If, however, we look at all the government regulations which remained in force throughout the eighteenth century, it is clear that some were more apparent than real. This is the case with those mentioned above. The Statute of Artificers was a dead letter, while the hindrance to migration constituted by the Law of Settlement was minimal. The ban on joint-stock enterprise presented little hardship for, as we have seen, most industrial undertakings had low fixed capital requirements; and the heavy consumers of capital – turnpike trusts and, more particularly, canal companies – could obtain the powers they needed by act of Parliament. There were various ways of getting round the Usury Laws, and it was not too difficult to evade restrictions on overseas trade. The smuggler, bringing in 'Brandy for the Parson, baccy for the Clerk', was a respected member of the community. Adam Smith described him as 'a person who, though no doubt highly blameable for violating the laws of his country, is frequently incapable of violating those of natural justice'. To the extent, therefore, that existing regulations were not, or could not be, enforced, a more congenial environment for growth may have been provided than is at first apparent.

It was not only by allowing restrictive legislation to remain unenforced that the government showed its sympathies for industrialisation; for new law, favourable to industrialists, was passed. It banned trade unionism in particular trades and, through the Combination Acts of 1799 and 1800, made that ban general. As putting-out manufacture spread in the eighteenth century, laws were passed which criminalised the appropriation of waste materials by outworkers although this had often been regarded as a 'perk' – a traditional perquisite of the trade. The export of machinery was banned in the interests of domestic manufacturers, and the emigration of artisans (who might take skills and trade secrets abroad) was also made illegal.

In the late seventeenth century the economic writer Sir Dudley North observed that 'no People ever yet grew rich by Policies, but it is Peace, Industry and Freedom that brings Trade and Wealth, and nothing else'. Was peace a causal factor, or did war – which engaged the country for 75 years between 1689 and 1802 – provide a greater stimulus to the economy? The arguments over defence expenditure are hotly debated in our own day, when there is much talk of 'peace dividends' on the one hand, and 'spin-off' on the other. 'Spin-off' normally relates to technological advance, where innovations in the military sphere are seen to have civilian applications. Questions of expense and of practical difficulty are not allowed to inhibit development in wartime, and L. T. C. Rolt has pointedly observed: 'Though we have not yet acquired the wisdom to convert the one into the other, by producing better swords we certainly learn how to make better ploughshares.'[21]

Many examples can be found which bear out this point. The army and navy were great consumers of iron, and Henry Cort, who revolutionised its manufacture, was a navy agent in the 1760s anxious to improve the quality of the product. Likewise a number of ironworks depended on government contracts for cannon. The Carron Ironworks developed the famous carronade (another product of the year 1776), and Wilkinson's boring machine – without which steam-engine cylinders of high quality could not be produced – was designed initially for boring cannon. The output of pig iron increased spectacularly during the French Wars. In 1788 the estimated production was 68,000 tons; eight years later it was 125,000 tons; and by 1802 the figure had risen to 170,000 tons. Technical developments in the use of coal for smelting purposes were encouraged by the wartime demand for metals, while supplies of timber for charcoal (the fuel previously used) were diminished by the voracious demands of naval shipbuilding.

The navy stimulated technical developments in a number of other fields. A 74-gun ship required 922 pulley blocks, and it was estimated that the annual consumption by the Royal Navy at the beginning of the nineteenth century was 100,000. To expedite their manufacture and to reduce cost, Sir Marc Isambard Brunel designed 44 machines (built by Henry Maudslay) which were set up in a fully mechanised production line at Portsmouth Dockyard. Elm logs started at one end, and finished blocks emerged at the other, with 10 men able to produce 160,000 blocks a year. Previously, 110 men were employed at a cost to the Admiralty three times as great.

Some of these machines remained in use into the second half of the twentieth century, yet the immediate 'spin-off' into the rest of the economy does not appear to have been great.

Naval purchasing increased the number of beasts coming to Smithfield market in wartime, and in the War of 1812 the first English canning factory was established at Bermondsey in order to supply preserved meats and soups for men-of-war. Certain branches of the textile industry, such as those producing canvas and cheap cloth for shirts and uniforms, benefited from government contracts. Since such contracts had to be met on time and the goods had to be of acceptable quality, it was worth a businessman's while to introduce new techniques if they would help him win an order and then fulfil it.

The effect of eighteenth-century wars on the export trade varied, but after 1793 the French Wars probably did more good than harm to Britain's industrialisation. Exports to Europe grew faster than those to other markets, while the Royal Navy's command of the high seas enabled Britain to deny markets to French and French-occupied competitors. Being cut off from trans-Atlantic trade, France found its momentum for growth crippled, and a gap opened between its economy and that of Britain, which forged ahead. British exports between 1793 and 1815 expanded at the rate of 3.8 per cent per annum, faster than before or subsequently.

Not everything was gain, for war brought disruption and losses which may appear less obvious, yet were perhaps of equal or greater substance. Peacetime economic activities were dislocated. In order to pay for the war, the government was obliged to borrow massive amounts of money. To what extent did this 'crowd out' other investment? In other words, had there been no war, what proportion of those investable funds would have been used to build up productive (rather than destructive) assets, that might have contributed more to economic growth? HMS *Victory*, launched in 1765, cost £63,174 to build. That was five times the fixed capital value of Ambrose Crawley's iron works, one of the industrial wonders of its age. The capital value of the whole fleet was perhaps five times greater than the total value of the West Yorkshire woollen manufacture. Would not the money have been better invested there? The problem with this line of argument is that the investable funds might not have been there at all (or in anything like the same amount) had the government not called them forth. Wealthy landowners and others lent their money to defend their property rights and privileges (with, perhaps, a dash of patriotism). There is no guarantee that they would have invested anything like the same amount in peacetime industry. Not only that, but the successful conclusion of the wars, and the security which this brought from foreign aggression, was itself very likely to have been an encouragement to investors in later years.

It is impossible to balance all the gains against the losses. In 1955 T. S. Ashton wrote that 'the case for war as a stimulus to economic expansion is, to say the least, unproven'. Although our knowledge has increased in the 40 years since then his conclusions would still gain widespread acceptance today.

Notes

1   Barrie Trinder, 'Industrial conservation and industrial history: reflections on Ironbridge Gorge Museum', *History Workshop*, Autumn 1976, p. 173.
2   Robert Hewison, *The Heritage Industry: Britain in a Climate of Decline*, 1987, p. 95.
3   David Cannadine, 'The present and the past in the English industrial revolution 1880–1980', *Past and Present*, 1984.

4   T. S. Ashton, *The Industrial Revolution, 1760–1830*, Oxford University Press, 1948, p. 161.

5   David Landes, 'The fable of the dead horse; or, the industrial revolution revisited' in Joel Mokyr (ed.), *The British Industrial Revolution: An Economic Perspective*, Westview Press, 1993, p. 168.

6   Joel Mokyr (ed.), op. cit., p. 2.

7   David Landes, op. cit., p. 161.

8   R. M. Hartwell, *The Causes of the Industrial Revolution in England*, Methuen, 1967, pp. 22–3.

9   L. A. Clarkson, *Death, Disease and Famine in Pre-Industrial England*, Gill and Macmillan, 1975, p. 112.

10 N. C. R. Crafts, 'The eighteenth century: a survey' in Roderic Floud and Donald McCloskey (eds), *The Economic History of Britain since 1700*, Cambridge University Press, 1981, vol. 1, p. 1.

11 Quoted in Paul Mantoux, *The Industrial Revolution in the Eighteenth Century*, 1928 (Cape, 1961), pp. 344–5.

12 Robert Owen, *A New View of Society*, 1813–14 (Penguin, 1970), p. 192.

13 Quoted in Neil Tranter, *Population since the Industrial Revolution*, Croom Helm, 1973, p. 139.

14 Eric J. Evans, *The Forging of the Modern State, 1783–1870*, Longman, 1983, p. 104.

15 Vicars Bell, *To Meet Mr Ellis*, Faber, 1956, pp. 148–9.

16 Gregory Clark, 'Agriculture' in Joel Mokyr, op cit., p. 250.

17 L. A. Clarkson, *The Pre-Industrial Economy in England 1500–1750*, Batsford, 1971, p. 72.

18 Peter Mathias, *The Transformation of England*, Methuen, 1979, p. 66.

19 Ibid., p. 106.

20 Peter Mathias, *The First Industrial Nation*, Methuen, 2nd edition, 1983, p. 150.

21 L. T. C. Rolt, *Tools for the Job*, Batsford, 1965, p. 41.

Chapter two

The social impact of industrialisation before 1850

The birth of class

'Words are witnesses which often speak louder than documents,' wrote Eric Hobsbawm in the introduction to his book, *The Age of Revolution*, and he listed a number of words, each representing a new concept, which gained their modern usage in the 60 years between the French Revolution and the mid-nineteenth century. These include 'industry'; 'industrialist'; 'factory'; 'capitalism'; 'socialism'; 'liberal' and 'conservative' as political terms; 'statistics'; 'sociology'; 'proletariat'; (economic) 'crisis'; 'strike'; 'pauperism'; 'railway' and 'engineer'. The list also includes 'middle class' and 'working class', concepts which indicate the profoundest of all the changes brought about by the industrial revolution, for they represent a fundamental change in the very framework of society. As though to mark the revolutionary nature of these social changes, the first recorded use in English of the term, 'working class', was in the fateful year of 1789.

Social class is a concept which we now take for granted, and most people have some idea of the class to which they belong. In 1988 G. Marshall and others interviewed nearly 2,000 people of working age in England, Scotland and Wales, well over 90 per cent of whom felt able to place themselves in a particular class category; while almost three-quarters of the respondents felt class to be an inevitable feature of modern society. The concept is a difficult one, however, and sociologists interpret the term in different ways, nevertheless accepting that classes are not sharply definable groups whose precise numbers in any society can be determined simply by gathering enough information about each individual. E. P. Thompson, whose seminal book *The Making of the English Working Class* (1963) was a major contribution to the study of the origins of a class society, declared that 'the finest-meshed sociological net cannot give us a pure specimen of class, any more than it can give us one of deference or of love'.

The historian, Arthur Marwick, arrives at a definition of what a class society is by first considering what it is not:

A class society is not the same as a caste society, nor is it the same as a pre-industrial society of estates and orders (though some of the elements of modern class were already apparent in such societies). It is not the same as a status society (if such a society has ever actually existed) in which there is a continuous gradation of strata rather than a relatively small number of fairly discrete social classes. It is obviously not the same as a classless society, in which either there are no inequalities at all, or in which any inequalities are totally based on variations in natural talent, or in assessable variations in contributions made to the well-being of the community. In modern societies, there are manifest inequalities based on sex, race, and age; but class is different in kind from these sources of inequality since they are biologically determined, which class is not. In certain societies the inhabitants of particular regions, or the members of particular religious faiths, have been at a disadvantage; these are not class distinctions. By looking closely at what classes are not, we come closer to seeing what classes are: classes are groupings across society, broadly recognised by members of that society, involving inequalities, or, certainly, differences, in such areas as power, authority, wealth, income, prestige, working conditions, lifestyles and culture; people of any one class, it is assumed, associate much more with one another than they do with members of other classes.[1]

At one level, then, social class is simply a means of classifying or placing people into recognisable groups. This is how James Nelson used the term in 1753, when he wrote that 'every Nation has its Custom of dividing the People into Classes'. Such classification involves all sorts of factors including: occupation, income, education, where people live, their religious convictions, how they spend their income, how they dress and so on. The last factor might seem a trivial one, yet before the days of cheap fashionable clothing how a person dressed could be a very visible sign of his or her social position. The novelist George Gissing wrote that the great social divide was between those men who wore a collar and those who did not (a distinction we still make when we talk of 'white-collar jobs'); while in Glasgow, at least, headwear so clearly defined social position before the First World War that there were separate clubs for 'hat girls' and 'shawl girls'.

In the final analysis objective social stratification may be unattainable, for in large part a person's class is what he or she believes it to be and, more important, what others accept it to be. Robert Roberts, who lived in Salford at the beginning of the twentieth century, gives a vivid account of the intricacies of social classification:

> One 'papist' family, I remember, set the district a pretty problem in social assessment, the mother had been a teacher and a headmistress to boot. This should have placed her way above anyone else. Unfortunately she had been head of a Catholic school. Moreover, her husband, once a drunkard, was now a permanent invalid. They lived in considerable poverty. All this called for realistic evaluation. The woman spoke in an educated way (good) but with a brogue (bad). She kept her house clean and her two daughters from any contact with the other girls in the neighbourhood (very good), but they could not prevent the younger son from consorting with all the rapscallions of the village (very bad). In due time the girls became shorthand typists and went to 'business' in hat, coat and shoes (excellent, since their contemporaries were mill girls in clogs and shawls) and out of all assessment when one became the wife of a solicitor (Catholic, true, but still a solicitor). Balance was restored, however, after the son married into a labouring family, Irish Catholic from a 'low' street. The old lady herself, ignorant of all the social anomalies her family had caused, or indifferent anyway, went on treating everyone with the same simple courtesy and goodwill. The whole affair puzzled our class fixers, who never succeeded in slotting Mrs O'T. and her family into any agreed social niche.[2]

When sociologists consider social stratification, they often use the categories first outlined by the late-nineteenth-century German sociologist Max Weber who identified three dimensions: class, status and party. These concepts can be useful to the historian, for they refer to three different types of social group with which men and women can identify. With Weber, as with Marx, class is an economic grouping dependent upon the value of a person's labour and his or her share of property. Those who share similar work or are in a similar position in the labour market draw together in classes. Status arises from the basic tendency for people to attach positive and negative values to human attributes and to accord respect or contempt accordingly. A wide range of factors will determine a person's status, and when Robert Roberts spoke of 'class fixers' in Salford, he should, perhaps, have talked of 'status fixers'. Members of the same social class may well be accorded a different status by society. Not all barristers, for example, are accorded the same respect, and a black, woman barrister may well feel at a double disadvantage in an occupation that is dominated by white men. Party represents the organisations through which people with shared social objectives join together in order to obtain and to wield power. Political parties are obvious examples but so too are pressure groups and other kinds of association. In effect, in Weber's model the economic structure of society is defined by classes, the social by status groups and the political (in a broad sense) by parties.

Historians need to exercise care when confronted with the theoretical models of social scientists. Such models may help us to make sense of the past, but the temptation to squeeze the known facts in order to make them fit some hypothesis or general law should be resisted. Nevertheless, Weber's distinctions are useful, for what we may think of as class struggle in the past may well prove to have been status struggle; while status groups may include some which were of great significance in earlier periods but which have less meaning in our own. The nineteenth century did indeed have two such status divisions, namely the 'gentleman' and the 'respectable'. They were groupings of enormous significance, but they cut right across class lines. The gentleman, exhibiting noble qualities and patterns of behaviour, might be a member of the aristocracy, but could equally be a member of one of the middle-class professions. Likewise, although respectability was a quality particularly associated with the middle class, the ranks of 'the respectable' included many peers and peeresses (but not all), and many (but not all) working men and women.

We also have to be careful not to assume that our contemporary threefold division of classes (upper, middle and working classes) can be meaningfully transposed to earlier societies. Marxists stress a division into two groups since the industrial revolution – the bourgeoisie and the proletariat. Although Marx made such a two-fold division central to his theories, he was not the first person to see society in such dichotomous terms. They were very common in pre-industrial society, where classifications such as gentry/common people, rich/poor, or high/low were frequently used. Others have argued that more than three classes are required to explain nineteenth-century social stratification, while some stress the significance of divisions within the working class between the unskilled and the skilled 'aristocracy of labour'. Weber distinguished between four classes in late nineteenth-century Europe: (i) the manual working class; (ii) the petty bourgeoisie; (iii) propertyless white-collar workers; and (iv) those privileged through property and superior education. More recently, the historian R. S. Neale offered a five-class model, although this has been criticised because of his blurring of class and status. Nevertheless, what Neale and others have to say about the complexities of the relationship between different social groups does remind us of the dangers of projecting on to the past groupings with a purely twentieth-century significance.

Social stratification is a many-faceted phenomenon but, ever since Karl Marx drafted *The Communist Manifesto* in 1847, class has had further connotations in terms of class consciousness and class struggle. In Marxist ideology class is not merely *a* social reality, but *the* great social reality which transcends all others and constitutes the great moving force in history. Class membership, according to Marx, is determined by the relationship of the individual to the economic structure, that is to say, to the control and use of the means of production. Marxists argue that under capitalism one set of persons owns and controls the means of production and gives orders to another set of persons who labour under their direction and in accordance with what the ruling class conceives to be its interests. These two classes they call respectively the bourgeoisie and the proletariat, and they regard the struggle between them as the fundamental factor in directing the course of modern history. Non-Marxists have strong reservations about this theory, questioning, for example, how far the existence of classes must inevitably lead to class struggle, and how far the facts of history support Marx's views about the dominance of two classes in nineteenth-century Britain. Social relationships proved to be much more complicated than Marx anticipated. Far from dividing conveniently into a bourgeoisie and a proletariat, important social groupings either survived from earlier periods (such as the aristocracy); evolved from earlier groupings (such as the labour aristocracy out of the old artisan craft élites); or developed as marginal groups (like the growing number of professional men, and the lower middle-class shopkeepers, clerks and schoolteachers). Struggle there was, and friction aplenty, but that conflict was much more likely to be seen by its participants as one of status than one of class, however the intellectuals might have theorised

Class consciousness did not arise overnight. 'No one will ever find a point in history,' writes R. J. Morris, 'at which the whole of the working class got out of bed one morning with a total awareness of their own identity.' Nevertheless, he claims: 'There is a tendency in the literature to look for the birth of class as a sharp change. Increasing knowledge of the eighteenth century is likely to emphasise that class formation was a slow process.'[3] Nor did all groups in society achieve class-consciousness at the same time; and there are good grounds for suggesting that the middle class anticipated the working class in this respect.

What then was the social structure of traditional England, and how was this affected by the industrial revolution? Eighteenth-century English society was hierarchical, and was often conceived as a pyramid, stretching down from a tiny minority of the rich and powerful at the top, through layers of lesser wealth and power, to the great mass of the people – poor and powerless – at the bottom. In 1709 Daniel Defoe suggested a sevenfold division of society, based on wealth and consumption:

1 the great, who live profusely
2 the rich, who live plentifully
3 the middle sort, who live well
4 the working trades, who labour hard, but feel no want
5 the country people, farmers, etc. who fare indifferently
6 the poor, who fare hard
7 the miserable, who really pinch and suffer want.

One's position on the slopes of the pyramid was determined by the amount and kind of property one owned, the most important type being the freehold possession of land. Status derived from property, as did dignity and title. From the seventeenth century onwards knighthoods, baronetcies and Irish peerages could be freely purchased by those with sufficient cash and land, as could (with a little more difficulty) an English peerage. By the eighteenth century few English peers could claim continuity in the male line from a medieval grant; all the rest owed their title and their status to their property. Despite the privileges which the ownership of land gave, there were no legal obligations attached to it other than the payment of property tax. Yet there were strong moral obligations owed to those lower down the pyramid, in return for deference received. Cobbett spoke of 'the great chain of connection' between the rich and the poor, an apt description of this pervasive system of social obligation. The system of patronage which it implied was far wider than the mere filling of jobs or providing of pensions, and it stretched from the Court at its apex right down to the poor at the base – for the 'respectable' and 'deserving' poor, for whom squire or person would vouch, were likely to have the first claim on charity. Everyone knew his or her place in the hierarchy, and obligations were reinforced by the catechism of the Church of England:

> My duty towards my Neighbour, is to love him as myself, and to do to all men, as I would they should do unto me: To love, honour, and succour my father and mother: To honour and obey the King, and all that are put in authority under him: To submit myself to all my governors, teachers, spiritual pastors and masters: To order myself lowly and reverently to all my betters . . . Not to covet nor desire other men's goods; but to learn and labour truly to get mine own living, and to do my duty in that state of life, unto which it shall please God to call me.

The tense employed in the last line should be noted – 'unto which it shall please God', not 'unto which it has pleased God'. Social mobility was provided for. By honest striving (and with divine assistance) a person might rise to a higher state. No rank in the system was closed, and people (especially those in the 'middling ranks') were ever attempting, often with success, to rise in the hierarchy. So long as the system could absorb them it remained comparatively stable.

Industrialisation affected this pattern of society in a number of ways. The greatly increased opportunities for the creation of private wealth led to an expansion in the number of middling people which the system could not absorb. There therefore emerged a 'middle class' increasingly aware of its identity, and with its own character and ideals. Of these, free competition and individual effort were the most significant. Industrialisation also brought about a self-conscious working class. The link was through the industrial town rather than through the factory. Class feeling was largely absent in the rural mills of the water-power phase of the industrial revolution. In the little communities built round these mills, master and worker retained a face-to-face relationship in much the same manner as before. The isolation of the mills obliged the masters to take care of the material needs of their workers, in return for which they expected the usual deference, and exercised a discipline over their private as well as their working lives. The paternalism of Robert Owen (somewhat ironically regarded as 'the father of socialism') at his New Lanark mill was an extreme case of the establishment of a microcosm of the old society, albeit much reformed.

When steam power transferred the centres of industry to the towns, workers were thrown on their own devices, and there was little contact between them and their employers outside the workplace. Friedrich Engels remarked on this geographical separation as it affected Manchester in the 1840s:

> The town itself is peculiarly built, so that a person may live in it for years, and go in and out daily without coming into contact with a working-people's quarter or even with workers, that is, so long as he confines himself to his business or to pleasure walks. This arises chiefly from the fact, that by unconscious tacit agreement, as well as with outspoken conscious determination, the

working-people's quarters are sharply separated from the sections of the city reserved for the middle class . . . [4]

The chain of connection was broken, but it was a two-sided process. On the one side the lower ranks sought to break the links of dependence on and obedience to the higher ranks. On the other, the higher ranks rejected not the whole relationship (for they were quite happy for those beneath them to remain deferential), but their own paternal protection and responsibility which, in the old society, had justified deference to their position.

While industrialisation provided centrifugal forces tending to the break-up of the old society, for a while the Napoleonic Wars gave a counterbalancing centripetal force, binding the nation together in the face of a common foe. The economic and social distress which followed the advent of peace, however, marked the time when the modern class society had its birth. The exact nature of the process by which class consciousness developed remains a matter of some controversy as does the length of time the process took. E. P. Thompson was among the foremost of those historians who advocate what has been described as 'the conspiratorial theory of the birth of class', stressing the influence on working-class consciousness of Tom Paine and the Radicals of the 1790s. However, it is debatable how far the Painites were in any sense 'proletarian', while the extent to which the workers as a whole (as distinct from tradesmen and artisans) supported them is even more conjectural. Many historians would argue that working-class consciousness did not develop fully until very late in the nineteenth century, a point that is taken up in Chapter 8.

Society under strain

For many people the period of the industrial revolution was one of great distress. With hindsight we can see that the miseries of the time were, in fact, labour pains accompanying the birth of industrial capitalism and the new industrial society. But to contemporaries there was nothing inevitable about the process, and their sufferings could be just as easily interpreted as the death throes of a social order which would soon pass away and be replaced by a society quite different from that which actually came about. As Hobsbawm puts it:

We, who see the period from the 1780s to the 1840s in the light of later developments, see it simply as the initial phase of industrial capitalism. But might it not also be its final phase? The question seems absurd, because it so obviously was not. This is to underestimate the instability and tension of this initial phase – particularly of the three decades after Waterloo – and the malaise of both the economy and those who thought seriously about its prospects. Early industrial Britain passed through a crisis which reached its stage of greatest acuteness in the 1830s and early 1840s. That it was not in any sense a 'final' crisis, but merely one of growth, should not lead us to underestimate its seriousness, as economic (but not social) historians have persistently inclined to do.[5]

The French Wars for a while exercised a cohesive influence upon society. Coleridge, writing in 1817, for example, felt that it had 'brought about a national unanimity unexampled in our history since the reign of Elizabeth'. Even so, domestic troubles in 1812 tied down 12,000 troops, while of the 155 barracks constructed between 1792 and 1815 many were deliberately sited in the 'disaffected' districts of the Midlands and the north. The coming of peace abroad in 1815 ushered in a period of unprecedented domestic unrest, the like of which has never been seen since. One disturbance seemed to follow another: Luddism between 1811 and 1818, the East Anglian and the Spa Fields riots in 1816, the March of the Blanketeers and the Pentrich rising in 1817, Peterloo in 1819, the Swing riots in the early 1830s, Reform Bill riots in 1831, Rebecca riots in 1838–9 and again in 1843, and the Chartist riots of 1839 and 1842. In the latter year Sir James Graham, the Home Secretary, was prompted to suppose that treason was stalking the land in the shape of a 'mad insurrection of the working classes'.

Whether or not Britain came close to a political revolution on the continental model is a matter of debate between historians. In 1924 the French historian, Élie Halévy, put forward his famous thesis that religion had acted as a great social stabiliser, and that Methodism, in particular, probably saved Britain from the revolutionary fate which overtook France. E. P. Thompson saw the connection in reverse, however, and argued that the failed revolution was not the consequence of Methodism, but rather that Methodism became popular because the revolution never came. As the millennium was not to be enjoyed here, disappointed working men turned to revivalist religion. So, too, did working women, who formed the major element in the new factory proletariat. Yet, as F. M. L. Thompson has suggested:

> It could be that they contributed a decisively non-violent and non-revolutionary tone to the nascent proletariat at the one moment, in the late 1830s and 1840s, when for a variety of reasons social tensions were so acute that a determined move from the mills might have tipped the scales towards disintegration of the social order.[6]

All this assumes that there was an actual revolutionary situation. Many people, of very different political persuasions, talked of revolution, but the situation was very unclear. The government relied for its information on spies. The dividing line between spy and agent provocateur was a thin one, and there was a vested interest in sending back lurid reports. Richard Brinsley Sheridan, who was a Member of Parliament as well as a playwright, told the House of Commons in 1795 that 'the present alarm had been created solely by ministers, for the corrupt purpose of libelling the country'. This they had done through their spies and informers, who invented the worst atrocities for gain; and he told of a man who was given a retainer of one guinea (21 shillings) a week for information, but two guineas for really alarming pieces of news. Thereafter he ensured that all his news was of the more lucrative kind. It must not be supposed, however, that the government lacked all sense of quality control, and there is ample evidence that it did wish to learn the truth (although it might be happy to have a supply of untruths for public consumption). The reaction of the government to the disorders appears to have been one of panic, for while many people wished for a changed society, the leaders with the largest following wished to reform the constitution, not overthrow it. Robert Owen, whose influence was wide (albeit diffuse), wrote in 1857 in his *Life*:

> Society did not destroy the old gravel roads before it commenced and completed the railways which were to supersede them. And when the railways were made ready to receive travellers, even then the gravel roads were allowed to remain for the use of timid persons. In like manner, without destroying or injuring the old system of society, the new will be made ready to receive willing passengers from the old. And thus will conflict be prevented.

Owen was one of many contemporary reformers who considered that society was on the wrong track, and he formulated a different social order. He looked forward to a new era of cooperation and community and, as an alternative to the evils of industrial capitalism, as he saw them, he advocated multi-functional communities in which men and women would realise their true potential. In his 'Report to the County of Lanark', published in 1821, he wrote.

The new wealth which one individual, by comparatively light and always healthy employment, may create under the arrangements now proposed, is indeed incalculable. They would give him giant powers compared with those which the working class or any other now possesses. There would at once be an end of all mere animal machines who could only follow a plough, or turn a sod, or make some insignificant part of some insignificant manufacture or frivolous articles which society could better spare than possess. Instead of the unhealthy pointer of a pin, – header of a nail, – piecer of a thread, or clodhopper, senselessly gazing at the soil or around him, without understanding or rational reflection, there would spring up a working class full of activity and useful knowledge, with habits, information, manners, and dispositions, that would place the lowest in the scale many degrees above the best of any class which has yet been formed by the circumstances of past or present society.

Owen's ideas did not seem as hare-brained to many of his contemporaries as they may do to us. In E. P. Thompson's view:

It was not Owen who was 'mad', but, from the standpoint of the toilers, a social system in which steam and new machinery evidently displaced and degraded labourers, and in which the markets could be 'glutted' while the unshod weaver sat at his loom and the shoemaker sat in his workshop with no coat to his back.[7]

Owen's cotton mill at New Lanark in Scotland was one of the most widely publicised social experiments of the nineteenth century, and it was visited by nearly 20,000 people between 1815 and 1825. It was a repudiation of much that accompanied the factory system, and it provided the prototype of the villages of cooperation of his new moral world.

Many workers shared Owen's view that capitalism was not the only possible economic structure, but in order to organise production in a more equitable fashion, with the basic needs of all being met, and labour receiving its due reward, capital still had somehow to be raised. Hence the great interest in cooperative trading as a means of raising capital to establish socialist communities. The coming together of the Rochdale Pioneers in 1844 is often considered to be the starting point of cooperation, but many hundreds of societies existed before them. Sidney Pollard has shown that the Rochdale Pioneers mark the start of a second phase of cooperation. Originally no dividends were paid, but profits were saved in order to provide the capital for community building. The Secretary of the British Association for the Promotion of Cooperative Knowledge put it thus in 1830:

The grand aim of cooperative societies is not to combine to raise the wages of its members by buying at wholesale prices and selling the same for ready money . . . but, on the contrary, to raise a capital sufficient to purchase and cultivate land and establish manufactories of such goods as the members can produce for themselves, and to exchange for the production of others; likewise to form a community thereby giving equal rights and privileges to all.[8]

The decision of the Rochdale Pioneers to pay dividends represents the abandonment of the idea that workers could opt out of capitalist society. The infant capitalism, which had appeared so sickly that it might soon pass away (or be strangled by its opponents) proved to be a healthier child than had been anticipated. The new phase of cooperation took on the characteristics of Victorian self-help, whereby workers could raise themselves up within the system. A commentator of 1861 wrote of the Rochdale Pioneers:

> The chief ambition . . . appears to me to be to raise themselves by raising the class to which they belong, without desiring to leave it, and without the slightest wish to depress or injure any other class. Their object and ambition appears to be that the working class should be well fed, well clothed, well housed, well washed, well educated – in a word that they should be respectable and respected. If any taint of the socialist and communist theories in which the society originated still cleaves to them, it is being rapidly worked off, and will, I am persuaded, shortly disappear.[9]

That this change should have come about in the 1840s is significant, for by then the worst of the unrest was over, and the fruits of industrialisation, which for so long had largely been withheld from the mass of the workers, now fell increasingly into their hands, and their standard of living clearly began to rise for the first time.

The standard-of-living controversy

The degree of social unrest in the first four decades of the nineteenth century might be taken as strong evidence that industrialisation caused the standard of living of the mass of workers to fall, but this need not have been so. At the turn of the twentieth century A. L. Bowley, who did important work on wages and income, made the point that progress is largely psychological, and is certainly relative. People, he said, 'are apt to measure their progress not from a forgotten position in the past, but towards an idea which, like an horizon, continually recedes. The present generation is not interested in the earlier needs and successes of its progenitors but in its own distresses and frustration considered in the light of the presumed possibility of universal comfort and of riches'. Sociologists talk of 'the revolution of rising expectations' – of people becoming more discontented when their condition improves at a rate slower than they might wish, or less than it seems to have for others. Certainly, there is no reason why people who are materially better off, should not be unhappier than before because the means of earning their livelihood becomes harder or less congenial.

Strong evidence that the standard of living of the mass of workers rose in the first half of the nineteenth century might be thought to follow from the fact that the national income per head of population at constant prices almost doubled between 1800 and 1851. This too would be misleading. Whether or not this represents an actual rise in living standards would depend on the proportion of the national income diverted from consumption to investment. It would depend, too, on the way that proportion of the national income devoted to consumption was distributed between the rents and profits going to the property owners, and the wages and salaries going to the workers.

The standard-of-living debate has been described by Peter Mathias as 'the most sustained single controversy in Britain's economic history', and he suggests two reasons why, apart from its intrinsic historical importance, it should have enjoyed such a vigorous life. In the first place he argues that 'there seems no possibility of an unchallengeable answer to such a diffuse, many-sided question'. Partly this is due to the nature of the evidence, for as Arthur J. Taylor has pointed out, 'where evidence is fragmentary and disputable, argument can be readily sustained but agreed conclusions rarely reached'. Mathias's second point is that 'the debate has always been suffused with current political values. Essentially it has been a judgment on capitalism, about the social consequences of the operation of the free-market economy'. David Landes made a similar point in 1993 when he reiterated his earlier view that 'what keeps the controversy going . . . is that the two adversary opinions are also seen as shibboleths, as clues to and tests of political stance'. The argument has been fierce; so fierce, indeed, that one historian has observed that it has generated heat rather than light.

Like many issues of historical interpretation, the question was one which was hotly debated by contemporaries. The 'Condition of England Question' attracted many participants between 1825 and 1850, ranging on the 'optimistic' side from Edwin Chadwick, G. R. Porter and Andrew Ure (who likened factory children to 'lively elves at play') to Friedrich Engels, Benjamin Disraeli and John Stuart Mill on the 'pessimistic' side. Mill wrote in 1848:

> Hitherto it is questionable if all the mechanical inventions yet made have lightened the day's toil of any human being. They have enabled a greater proportion to live the same life of drudgery and imprisonment and an increased number of manufacturers and others to make fortunes. They have increased the comforts of the middle classes. But they have not yet begun to effect those great changes in human destiny, which it is in their nature and in their futurity to accomplish.[10]

That opening 'hitherto' and the date are significant, for just as social unrest seemed to die down in the late 1840s so, too, did the Condition of England Question. Like Chartism it was killed, it has been suggested, by free trade, railways and prosperity. The question was opened up again at the end of the century when the investigations of Booth and Rowntree demonstrated that, despite half a century of undisputed progress, nearly a third of the population of London and York still lived in poverty. Now it was socialist intellectuals, like the Webbs and the Hammonds, who raised the old issues again. Of the Hammonds' *The Town Labourer* (1917), Malcolm Thomis has written that it is

> a passionate and committed book, the classic presentation of what has come to be known as the pessimist case on the Industrial Revolution, the grand denunciation featuring all the villains unequivocally denounced, the capitalist owners of factories and mines, the politicians such as Pitt and Wilberforce who collaborated with them. It is the popular view of the Industrial Revolution with all the eloquence and all the embellishments, not necessarily the view of the majority of academic historians but the Industrial Revolution of popular tradition, which has supplied sustenance to a wealth of ideologies and philosophies of life. It is what people know of the Industrial Revolution even if they have never read a history book.[11]

The response to the moral indignation of the Hammonds took the form of a number of empirical studies, firmly based (so the authors believed) on fact. Thus, Sir John Clapham and T. S. Ashton argued that while economic change left some workers displaced and distressed, the majority benefited from falling prices, more regular employment and a wider range of employment opportunities.

In the 1950s and 1960s the debate developed into a confrontation between the 'pessimist' (and Marxist) E. J. Hobsbawm and the 'optimist' R. M. Hartwell, with contributions from many others. In this scholarly war of attrition, the participants became increasingly moderate in their claims and sought to occupy ground not far from a central position, far removed from that occupied by the Hammonds. Hobsbawm himself admitted in 1975 that 'an agnostic position is probably the most reliable', and although he remains pessimistic, even he is prepared to acknowledge a very modest rise in average living standards, while Hartwell is not inclined to push much beyond that. E. P. Thompson's assessment in 1963 remains an apt one, even after more than 30 years:

> All in all, it is an unremarkable record. In fifty years of the Industrial Revolution the working-class share of the national product had almost certainly fallen relative to the share of the property-owning and professional classes. The 'average' working man remained very close to subsistence level at a time when he was surrounded by the evidence of an increase of national wealth, much of it transparently the product of his own labour, and passing, by equally transparent means, into the hands of his employers. In psychological terms, this felt very much like a decline in standards. His own share in the 'benefits of economic progress' consisted of more potatoes, a few articles of cotton clothing for his family, soap and candles, some tea and sugar, and a great many articles in the *Economic History Review*.[12]

Just because the debate has proved inconclusive is no reason for not paying it close attention, for it throws up important questions of historical method. Imprecise definition is one factor which has tended to exaggerate the differences of interpretation. We have to ask precisely what we mean by 'standard of living' and then decide whose standard of living we are talking about, where and during what period. Only then are we ready to tackle the technical question of the direction in which the standard of living was moving.

The standard of living is a matter of material existence and, as such, is an economic phenomenon. It is measured by a person's real income which, in turn, is governed by his or her money earnings and the price of the goods he or she needs to buy. But the boundary lines of this material well-being are difficult to draw, even if accepted in principle. E. P. Thompson put the point as clearly and vividly as anyone:

> From food we are led to homes, from homes to health, from health to family life, and thence to leisure, work-discipline, education and play, intensity of labour, and so on. From standard-of-life we pass to way-of-life. But the two are not the same. The first as a measurement of quantities: the second a description (and sometimes an evaluation) of qualities. Where statistical evidence is appropriate to the first, we must rely largely upon 'literary evidence' as to the second. A major source of confusion arises from the drawing of conclusions as to one from evidence appropriate only to the other. It is at times as if statisticians have been arguing: 'the indices reveal an increased per capita consumption of tea, sugar, meat, and soap, therefore the working class was happier', while social historians have replied: 'the literary sources show that people were unhappy, therefore their standard of living must have deteriorated'.[13]

This distinction between 'standard of living' and 'way of life' is an essential one, for the industrial revolution was no mere economic expansion, but a profound social change. It was these social changes, as much as anything, that contemporaries argued about. The loss of status and of independence by the worker, the disruption of traditional family patterns, the monotony of factory work, and the breakdown of traditional cultural values were all keenly felt, and caused at least as much unrest as straightforward 'bread-and-butter' questions.

Second, we need to be clear precisely what period we are talking about. The later the period considered, the more the evidence supports an 'optimistic' conclusion, while the earlier the period, the more 'pessimistic' the result. For example, the real-wage index of artisans in London, produced by R. S. Tucker, showed a decline in real wages of 11 per cent between 1780 and 1840, but an increase of 25 per cent between 1790 and 1850. As the two sides in the controversy have moved towards the middle ground, the period for which there remains the greatest difference of opinion can be narrowed down to that between the 1820s and the early 1840s.

Third, we must be clear just whose standard of living is under consideration. It is tempting to see 'labour' as more homogeneous than in reality it was. This applies to agriculture as well as industry, for in farming the yearly men, with some special skill or responsibility, fared much better than the day-labourers. There was likewise a great range of skills in industry, each rewarded differently. For example, mule-spinners were (apart from overlookers) the highest paid artisans in the cotton industry, enjoying a semi-independent status within the mills, and recognised in the wider community by having the best rooms in some public houses reserved for 'mule-spinners only'. S. D. Chapman has shown that in one typical small spinning-mill of the mid-1830s, which employed 40 people, half of the weekly wage bill of £24 was paid to four mule-spinners and their piecers. And, to remind us that there was no such thing even as the average cotton worker, we might note that the 1841 census enumerated 1,225 subdivisions of heads of employment in cotton manufacture alone. Nor was the factory hand the typical worker of the period, for the artisan and the hand-worker continued to dominate the employment picture and, as late as 1851, only around 27 per cent of the British labour force worked in industries which had been directly affected by the industrial revolution.

Finally, we should note that a number of local studies have revealed a regional variation in the standard of living. T. C. Gourvish, for example, has shown that only the better-paid Glasgow workers improved their lot between 1810 and 1831, while R. S. Neale calculates that labourers in Bath did not raise their real wages between the 1780s and the start of local railway construction after 1839. The case of rising living standards is strongest when attention is confined to the industrial north of England and the Midlands, rather than the agricultural south; and weakest when the Irish experience is added to that of Great Britain.

The ideal method of determining changes in the standard of living would be to construct an authentic money-wage and price index. The latter, divided by the former, would give us an index of real wages – a measure of what money will buy. This quantitative approach is very attractive, but there are enormous difficulties with the construction of such indices. The data present numerous problems. Most price indices are based on long runs of institutional accounts but these, being wholesale prices paid by institutions (mainly in the south of England) possibly bear little relationship to the retail prices paid by individual workers in, say, the industrial districts. And very often the prices of raw materials have to be used, rather than the prices of the actual manufactured goods or processed foods purchased by the individual. For example, one major cost-of-living index deduces changes in the price of clothing from such sources as the Admiralty ledgers for leather and the prices paid by Westminster School for broadcloth. It has suggested that more use might be made of the provisions accounts of parish workhouses, for overseers made regular purchases of a wide range of groceries and provisions which were of a similar kind and quality as those featuring in the household diets of the locality. It is also suggested that such accounts, being kept with local suppliers, can afford a closer insight into the relationship between contract prices and retail prices.

There are also problems associated with drawing up the 'basket of goods' (the list of representative goods purchased by the consumer) used in a cost-of-living index to represent the pattern of spending. If statisticians are to make comparisons over time, the goods in the 'basket' must remain the same, but as patterns of consumption change, the index will become less and less representative of what the consumer actually purchases. They must also decide what weight to give to any item in the index. This is done on the basis of assessing what proportion of a person's income might be spent on a particular item. Something like 70 per cent of the worker's income in the early nineteenth century went on food, for example. This meant that expenditure on other goods was normally extremely responsive to changes in the price of foodstuffs.

Similar problems arise when one attempts to measure changes in money wages. First, the available indices may not be representative of workers as a whole. Second, money wages by themselves give no real indication of the amount of money which the worker has to spend at any particular time, for they take no account of unemployment or of supplementary earnings. We know too little of the actual earnings of workers employed on piece-rates, whose wages depended on the amount of work available as well as on their individual inclinations and aptitudes. Our ignorance of unemployment is also great. E. J. Hobsbawm has given us figures for Leeds in 1838 which indicate the degree to which weekly wages have to be adjusted in order to take account of unemployment. He lists trades which worked 12, 11, 10 and only nine months. Thus, a tailor earning 16s a week, for example, but working only 11 months, has a corrected wage of 14s 8d. Two months' unemployment brought the 13s a week wage of a weaver down to an average of 10s 10d, while a dyer, employed for only nine months, received an average weekly wage of only 16s 6d although his nominal wage (when employed) was 22s. Third, we have again to remember regional variations, for there existed high- as well as low-wage areas. These applied to skilled as well as unskilled workers. Compositors in the printing trade, for example, might in the early years of the nineteenth century expect to earn 12–19s in Scotland; 18–22s in northern England; 18–24s in the south-east; and as much as 25s in London. Finally, we must also think in terms of family income, which obviously showed considerable variation. Generally speaking, however, the earnings of a wife, a son and a daughter working in the textile industry might double the wages of the husband, a fact of deep psychological and sociological impact as well as of economic significance.

So great have appeared the technical difficulties of constructing a realistic index of real wages that historians have turned increasingly to changing patterns of consumption. They have been encouraged in this by an awareness that during the process of industrialisation consumption may, for theoretical reasons, come under pressure as more resources are diverted to investment. Historians take different sides on this point. Hartwell's optimism is supported by his contention that the cost of investment was low during Britain's industrial revolution. On the other hand, Hobsbawm's pessimism gains strength from his view that the investment mechanism was so inefficient that a large proportion of accumulated savings were not directly invested in industry at all, leaving the rest of the community to bear a greater burden than might have been necessary in other circumstances.

In so far as an industrial revolution is largely about producing more and more goods at less and less cost, one might suppose that a greater quantity and variety of goods were available to the masses, but it is hard to make firm statements. Consider clothing, for example. It has been estimated that the price of cotton cloth fell by about one-third between 1830 and 1850, as mechanical weaving took over from the hand loom. This must have had some effect on the clothing of the workers (which, Engels noted in Manchester in the 1840s, was largely made of this material). However, few people bought new clothes, and it is likely that, as with so many of the other products of industry, other classes benefited more. Fuel was certainly increasing in availability and falling in price, as improvements in transport assisted in the exploitation of the inland coalfields. In 1815 the price of best coal in Newcastle and Sunderland was 13s a ton, while it cost 39s a ton in London; by 1845 the price had fallen to 8s and 13s a ton respectively.

We know less than we would like to about house rents although, in relation to wages, they probably rose relative to other consumer items throughout the industrial revolution. This was the conclusion reached by Peter Lindert and Jeffrey Williamson in 1983, although their data reveal just how fragile may be the foundations upon which New Economic Historians build. Their rent series was based upon a few dozen cottages in Trentham, just outside Stoke-on-Trent in Staffordshire. In reality, there were considerable regional differences in rent. Between 1830 and 1914 London was the most expensive place to live. In the early 1840s a double cellar could be rented in Liverpool for 1s a week. In parts of central London similar accommodation cost 1s 6d–2s. There an unfurnished room cost on average 4s 3d in 1839, while the same could be had in Bristol for 1s 3¾d. Jerry-building was the response of the private builder to filling the gap between supply and a rapidly rising demand. Contrary to many people's belief, jerry-builders were not vast profiteers for, compared with the quick profits to be made in industry or trade, house-building was not a particularly attractive field of investment. A back-to-back house at mid-century might cost £150 to £200, and was expected to repay its capital cost after about 20 years, at a rent of around 4s a week. After food, rent represented the largest item of expenditure of most working people, and the failure of many model housing schemes indicates the inability of most workers to pay for more than the barest minimum.

Much attention has been focused on changes in the consumption of various items of foodstuffs, but there is disagreement between historians not only on the quantities involved, but also on the significance of changes. It is possible to regard foodstuff simply from a nutritional standpoint, and to forget that particular items also have status in the mind of the consumer, and that some items of low nutritional value may enjoy a high social status. Thus the substitution of an item of low nutritional value by one of higher value cannot be taken as evidence of a rising standard of living if it represents, to the consumer, the substitution of a low-status food for a high one; and the reverse is also true.

One item of unequivocal social as well as nutritional value is meat, a decline in the consumption of which can be taken as a prima-facie case for a deterioration of living standards. One of the major sources for information consists of the 'Returns of Smithfield Market', from which Hobsbawm has argued that consumption declined after 1800. However, the figures are difficult to use, for they indicate only the number of beasts brought to market, and not their weight. At one time it was held that the agricultural revolution led to a doubling in the weight of animals brought to market in the eighteenth century. G. E. Fussell disproved this, but it would be foolhardy to carry over his conclusions into the nineteenth century. Again, the figures do not include all classes of meat, the major omission being the pig, often kept in the worker's back yard, or raised with the aid of a pig club, and providing a substantial alternative to butchers' meat. The Smithfield figures also apply only to London and, it has been argued, do not even represent accurately the meat consumption of the capital, for there were other markets such as Newgate and Leadenhall. All in all, John Burnett, who has done much work on the history of diet, argues that there appears to be no evidence of a general rise in the consumption trends of meat over the period 1815–50. Fish, in our times a major source of protein, was less favoured in the eighteenth and early nineteenth centuries, possibly because of religious (i.e. anti-Catholic) prejudice, but also because of its high price. This, however, fell with transport improvements. The kipper came on the market in 1843, but it was not until the 1880s that the first fish-and-chip shop, using new supplies of cheap cod and vegetable oils, was opened. This was one of Britain's contributions to world cuisine; it was also a contribution to the development of working-class culture. Milk consumption was low, and even as late as 1902 Britain was the lowest milk-drinking nation of Europe.

Bread was a staple part of the diet in the eighteenth and early nineteenth centuries, but there is some debate about the significance of its partial replacement by potatoes. It seems evident that in the south of England the potato had a low reputation, and its increased use is properly regarded as a mark of a lower standard of living. In the north, however, it was appreciated as a useful variant to the diet, whether as an ingredient of an Irish stew or a Lancashire hotpot.

The trend in sugar and beer consumption was downwards until about 1845, while tea remained stationary throughout the period. Burnett suggests that sugar and beer are better indicators of working-class standards than tea, which was regarded as a near-necessity, and which consequently had an inelastic demand. Burnett's conclusion is that the evidence from food consumption points to a fall rather than a rise in standards of living, although there are strong indications of an upswing in food trends after 1845.

In recent years, historians have turned to a biological indicator of living standards. It is generally accepted that height is a function of net nutritional status; in other words, the amount of food taken in by children and adolescents net of demands made upon their bodies by either labour or disease. Other things being equal (always the qualifier in such calculations) children born in a family that enjoyed a higher standard of living would grow up to be taller. In 1990 Floud, Wachter and Gregory published findings that showed that net nutritional status, as measured by stature, increased between 1760 and 1820, and then went into decline for half a century. The year-groups born between 1850 and 1854 were shorter than any other year-group born in the nineteenth century. They conclude that if there were significant gains in real income for the working class between the 1820s and the 1850s, they were bought at a very high price. If there were such gains, they argue that they did not lead to physical improvements in the lives of English men and women at that time. In 1993 Stephen Nicholas and Deborah Oxley published the results of an investigation which drew similar conclusions regarding the standard of living of English women between 1795 and 1820. Using the records of convicts transported to New South Wales, Australia, they demonstrated that average heights declined over the period; and if literacy can be taken as an indicator of the quality of life, that also fell.

Work-discipline

Such improvements as there may have been in the standard of living of the workers in the first half of the nineteenth century were slight. The benefits of industrialisation trickled down to them only slowly, and standards of material comfort remained abysmally low. But material standards were not the only, nor it seems the main, source of unrest among the working population. Some of the bitterest conflicts arose not from money matters but from onslaughts on traditional practices: for example, the notion of the family and the family economy, the distinction between work and leisure, and the ability to make individual decisions or realise individual potential under conditions of harsh factory discipline. Industrialisation resulted in a profound cultural change which, for the worker, involved a loss of independence and individuality. We can say this without falling into the trap of regarding traditional patterns as idyllic. Farm workers laboured from dawn to dusk, but such work – especially in the harvest months – could seem natural. Nature demanded that the grain be harvested before bad weather set in, just as cows naturally have to be milked, whatever the inclination of the worker. Such 'task-orientation' of time is more humanly comprehensible than a working day dictated by the machine or the assembly line. With task-orientation, what constitutes 'work' and what constitutes real 'life' are less clearly demarcated. With industrialisation many workers came to take an 'instrumental' view of work – something to be suffered because of the things it secured, whether material goods, a measure of 'leisure' or, often, plain survival.

Friedrich Engels, writing in the mid-1840s, vividly described the deadening impact of factory work:

> The supervision of machinery, the joining of broken threads, is no activity which claims the operative's thinking powers, yet it is of a sort which prevents him from occupying his mind with other things. We have seen . . . that this work affords the muscles no opportunity for physical activity. Thus it is, properly speaking, not work, but tedium, the most deadening, wearing process conceivable. The operative is condemned to let his physical and mental powers decay in this utter monotony, it is his mission to be bored every day and all day long from his eighth year. Moreover, he must not take a moment's rest; the engine moves unceasingly; the wheels, the straps, the spindles hum and rattle in his ears without a pause, and if he tried to snatch one instant, there is the over-looker at his back with the book of fines. This condemnation to be buried alive in the mill, to give constant attention to the tireless machine is felt as the keenest torture by the operatives, and its action upon mind and body is in the long run stunting in the highest degree. There is no better means of inducing stupe-faction than a period of factory work.[14]

Time assumed a new significance during the industrial revolution. For the upper classes, time frequently seemed the enemy, and was something to be 'killed'. Not so with middle-class entrepreneurs. 'Time is money' became a fitting slogan for a situation in which it became a currency to be 'spent' rather than something to be 'passed', and where workers came to see a greater distinction between their employer's time and their 'own' time. The start of the employer's time was signalled by the factory bell, which Wordsworth saw as:

> Of harsher import than the curfew-knell
> That spoke the Norman Conqueror's stern behest –
> A local summons to unceasing toil!

Josiah Wedgwood, who boasted of 'making such machines of men as cannot err', is credited with implementing the first system of clocking-in, and he backed this up with stiff fines of 2s if any worker were late. Time for the factory masters was capital, and their profits were partly determined by the velocity of circulating capital, that is, the speed with which they could turn over the stock of goods tied up in the production process and marketing.

Toil dominated by machinery could seem unceasing. Workers could not leave their machinery for a drink of water (and there was no 'water-boy' as there was on American convict chain gangs), and even natural functions were a problem. In many factories workers could not go to the privy without permission from the overlooker, and in at least one a tub was brought round for the male operatives to use three times a day. The closer supervision of workers was, indeed, one of the reasons why many factories were established, for technological change was not the sole motivating force.

Old habits died hard. Few trades had not celebrated 'Saint Monday' by taking the day off and doubling efforts later in the week in order to catch up. The song, 'The Jovial Cutlers', captures well the irregularity of artisan labour.

> Brother workmen cease your labour,
> Lay your files and hammers by,
> Listen while a brother neighbour
> Sings a cutler's destiny;
> How upon a good Saint Monday,
> Sitting by the smithy fire
> Telling what's been done o't Sunday
> And in cheerful mirth conspire.

John Rule, who quotes this song, notes that in a subsequent verse, 'The cutler's wife enters and indicates, by reference to her ragged attire, that she at least would welcome a little less leisure preference and a little more consumer response to monetary incentive'.[15] This attitude to work was the despair of the new factory masters. Absenteeism was rife. As late as the 1840s it was estimated in south Wales that the workers lost one week in five, while in the fortnight after the monthly pay-day, only two-thirds of the time was worked. Regularity had to be enforced by punitive fines, ranging from 6d to 2s 6d for ordinary offences, or the equivalent of between two hours and a day's wages. No assessment of workers' wages is complete which ignores this fact. Nor were workers outside the factories unaffected by the new work discipline, for their work also tended to become harder and more monotonous, often because work practices in the handicraft industries were altered so that they might better compete with factory production.

Industrialisation and the family

The 1980s presented contradictory images of the family. On the one hand, advertisements in the media presented the 'ideal' nuclear family, where father went off to win the family bread, mother stayed at home and worried about stained laundry or the state of the kitchen floor, while two bouncy children fought over breakfast cereal. On the other hand, the press was full of reports of marriage breakdown, juvenile delinquency and child abuse, while the government railed against the breakdown of 'family values'. There is of course nothing new in the perception that the actual functioning of institutions is falling below some accepted, often traditional ideal; and at the time of the industrial revolution the 'breakdown of the family' was as keenly debated as it is today. That the industrial revolution did, indeed, mark a watershed in the evolution of the modern family came to be a generally accepted proposition, but this has been seriously questioned in recent decades. Michael Anderson, for example, has suggested that many of the features of the 'modern family', far from being products of the industrial revolution, date only from the twentieth century, or even from the period after 1945.

Historians have questioned older ideas in other ways, asking not only how industrialisation affected the family, but how the family affected industrialisation – at the stage of proto-industrialisation, for example. This changes the emphasis from the family as a 'passive' agent, buffeted by the waves of economic and social change, and assigns it a more active role.

There can be little doubt that the industrial revolution placed great strains upon the family, yet despite considerable advances in the fields of demography and family reconstruction, surprisingly little is known about the precise nature of the impact. Few records of the day-to-day life and feelings of the family were ever kept, especially of working-class families, which were almost certainly the most affected. We have, therefore, to rely on incidental remarks in the autobiographies of working men (the gender-specific language is here intentional – when David Vincent undertook his study of the 142 working-class autobiographies between 1790 and 1850 which he had succeeded in locating, only six had been written by women). Failing that, we are forced back upon the observations of middle-class investigators and novelists, which may present no more than a projection of their ideals, assumptions and prejudices. The concern which middle-class commentators expressed over the working-class family was not purely altruistic, for they looked to such families for their domestic servants.

Victorian comments on changes within the working-class family were usually adverse. Peter Gaskell, from whom Engels derived most of his notions on the development of the family, wrote in 1836:

> A household thus constituted, in which all the decencies and moral observances of domestic life are constantly violated, reduces the inmates to a condition little elevated above that of the savage. Recklessness, improvidence, and unnecessary poverty, starvation, drunkenness, parental cruelty and carelessness, filial disobedience, neglect of conjugal rights, absence of maternal love, destruction of brotherly and sisterly affection, are too often its constituents, and the results of such a combination are moral degradation, ruin of domestic enjoyments, and social misery.[16]

Much of the debate on industrialisation and the family, both among contemporaries and by historians, has been related to the factory system, and on textile mills in particular. The factory system was alleged to have broken the traditional worker's family in a variety of ways. First, it led to a physical separation of the members of the family for much of the day; second, the efficiency of the married woman, both as wife and mother, was greatly reduced; third, the system is alleged to have had an adverse effect on sexual morality; and fourth, the position of the father within the family was weakened.

Under the domestic system, the members of the family had been together at work and at leisure, all the day and every day. Now, with some or all of the members going to the mill in the morning and not returning until night, the family might be split up for 12–14 hours a day, spending only a few hours sleeping and eating together, or at recreation on Sunday or on occasional holidays. Separation of the members of the family made child labour all the more irksome as kinship discipline came to be replaced by the impersonal discipline of the overseer. The breaking up of the family as a productive unit did not come about all at once, but was governed by certain technological developments. In spinning, the introduction of the smaller, hand-operated 'cottage' jenny increased the gains of the females in a family, and of the family in general, and kept the family together. The subsequent introduction of the water-frame took some women and children into the mills, but in the early days these were country mills, and with domestic weavers enjoying high earnings, these new workers were often the wives and children of labourers and the like (who usually worked away from home, anyway), so the changes were not regarded as revolutionary. When the factory jenny and the mule took men into the mill, it was usual for these highly skilled spinners to hire their own assistants for piecing and scavenging, and this was done from among their own relatives. The spinner paid his assistants from his own wages, and normally the master did not deal with them at all. Thus the family stayed together as a unit – but within the factory. However, the longer mules and the self-acting mules of the 1820s required more piecers and scavengers than could normally be recruited from the spinner's own family, and this led to the employment of children without their parents, often directly by the factory owner and under his overseer's control. In weaving, the story was somewhat different, for power-weaving demanded young persons and women, but very few adult males. From the very beginning, therefore, recruitment fell into the hands of the masters. The crisis in the factory worker's family coincided with the factory reform agitation of the 1830s and 1840s and contributed, in Harold Perkin's words, 'much of the emotional pressure and some of the more paradoxical of its tactical twists and changes'.

The second area of change was in the domestic efficiency of the wife. The working wife and mother did not have time to do housework, sewing or cooking, except in the evenings, when she was tired, or on Sundays, when she needed recreation after the week's toil. Children received less attention and had to be weaned earlier so that the mother could return to work. This imposed additional strains, as breast-feeding was an accepted means of birth control. While less time might be available to manage the household, totally new skills were demanded. Principal among these was that of budgeting, for with the spread of the cash economy only the wage packet stood between the family and distress. Few cottages in the expanding towns had a plot of land for growing vegetables, and more and more commodities had to be purchased from the shop (and often a corrupt, company 'tommy shop' at that). Budgeting usually seems to have fallen to the woman, on whose skill the welfare of the family depended. The irregularity of earnings made it difficult to take a long-term view of the future, and in consequence the worker often adjusted his domestic expenditure to his lowest rather than his average earnings, and 'squandered' any surplus that might have accrued. Drink no doubt made the poor poorer, but it is hard to condemn the working man (or woman) for seeking some consolation from the dismal life which had, perforce, to be endured. Middle-class observers frequently failed to appreciate this, just as they had misguided ideas about the practicality (and, from the point of view of the workers, the desirability) of 'frugal cookery'. The labouring poor may have lacked food, but there was no shortage of books offering them advice on how they might make do with less palatable and cheaper food. One example will suffice. Esther Copley's *Cottage Comforts* and *Cottage Cookery* circulated widely in the 1820s and 1830s, the latter containing economical recipes for such delights as stewed ox cheek and scrap pie. Another delicacy offered was mutton chitterlings – or small intestines. The chitterlings were to be obtained immediately the animal had been killed, scoured many times with salt and water, and put into soak for 24 hours, all of which would make them quite white and free from smell. Such recipes as this completely neglected the fact that working women had neither the time nor the inclination to cope with any food which required such extensive preparation. The kind of food which the workers wanted was not necessarily that which commended itself to the economists or the dieticians. They wanted their food tasty, hot – and quick.

Third, it was argued that unmarried girls in the factory not only lacked the time and opportunity to learn skills of housewifery, but were encouraged by mill life into sexual immorality. A witness before the Factory Commission in 1833 claimed that 'it would be no strain on his conscience to say that three-quarters of the girls between 14 and 20 years of age were unchaste', while another argued that 'some of the married women were as bad as the girls'. There are great problems, of course, over evidence for this kind of assertion. James Kay-Shuttleworth, the Manchester doctor and social reformer, wrote in 1832 that while crime could be 'statistically classed', the 'moral leprosy of vice cannot be exhibited with mathematical precision', for he concluded that 'sensuality has no record'. Illegitimacy figures might be regarded as sufficient evidence. Modern demographic research has revealed that the illegitimacy ratio (illegitimate to all births) rose from 1.5 per cent in the 1670s and 1680s to 3 per cent in the middle of the eighteenth century. By 1810 it was up to 6 per cent, and by 1850 to almost 7 per cent. Peter Gaskell, writing in 1836, argued that contemporary statistics on illegitimacy were 'worse than useless' because they showed a higher rate in agricultural than in manufacturing districts. Because this fitted middle-class preconceptions so badly, he argued that the reason was that mill girls had greater skill in 'destroying, prematurely, the fruit and the evidence of their guilt'. In other words, the proof of 'sin' lay in the lack of evidence of it! There are alternative interpretations. One is that the distinction between the 'industrial' and the 'agricultural' family was exaggerated. There were complaints about the immorality of those employed in farming, such as those of Alfred Austin, an Assistant Poor Law Commissioner, in his evidence of 1843 in the 'Reports on the Employment of Women and Children in Agriculture':

> There is no doubt that the mixed employment of men and women in hay-making, and perhaps in the corn-harvests, tends to immorality. Hay-making is a season of comparative license; hard work is expected by the master; but if it is performed he overlooks conduct on the part of the work-people which he might not suffer to pass unnoticed at other times . . . But one-half of the women and girls employed in the hay-field are never engaged in any other kind of farm-work, and the licentiousness of that season, as far as the women are concerned, would appear to proceed from those occasionally employed. Women who work the whole or the greater part of the year are too much accustomed to work in the company of men, and moreover are too much inclined to look upon their work in the serious light of an important part of their means of subsistence, to conduct themselves in a reckless manner at any particular season; and generally the testimony in favour of such women's good conduct is abundant.[17]

As F. M. L. Thompson puts it:

> The teenage promiscuity in the mill towns, widely reported in the parliamentary enquiries of the 1830s and 1840s and almost as widely denied, was . . . not a new industrial or urban phenomenon but was to be found in highly traditional rural and agricultural communities, and was less a prelude to lifelong casual sex than an anticipation of marriage. The great majority of the youths who appeared to exhibit 'a want of delicacy or decency' no doubt grew up to be responsible adult parents.[18]

Finally, it was held that the factories undermined the position of the father in the family. There was a lack of balance between adult and child labour in the early factories. At Arkwright's Cromford mills in 1789 there were 150 men in a total labour force of 1,150, or 13 per cent of the total. In the early 1830s between one-third and one-half of the labour force in cotton mills was under 21, and considerably more than half of the adults were women. Men were often employed in some sort of day work, or as a carter or porter, so that the labour of their wives and children might be secured. The man's wage of 10s or 13s a week might be less than half what his wife or children might earn as power-loom weavers or worsted spinners. The father's status as breadwinner was thus undermined, which must have had a demoralising effect. Richard Oastler, one of the central characters in the factory reform movement, once observed that he had witnessed 'full-grown athletic men, whose only labour was to carry their little ones to the mill long before the sun was risen, and bring them home at night long after he had set'.

It is hard to cut through the contemporary propaganda and to reach a balanced assessment of the impact of industrialisation on the family, but J. F. C. Harrison sums the situation up thus:

> Probably the children were better off when the mother could interrupt her spinning or weaving to suckle them and when, as they grew bigger, they were subject to their father's training and correction. The married woman factory worker may have gained a new sense of independence in being away from the home and contributing to the family income; the unmarried girls certainly did. On the other hand the traditional measure of a woman's status was her skill in all the arts of home-craft, and by this conventional wisdom the factory girl, married or unmarried, was made to feel wanting. The removal of industry from the home to the factory was from the housewifely point of view a blessing. A home that was also a workshop could become very squalid. . . Emancipation from the noise and dirt and smell of domestic industry must have been very welcome to those housewives who remained at home – and these, after all, were more numerous than those who went out to work.
>
> The trouble with this somewhat mechanical assessment of the situation is that the gains and losses were often intangible: feelings and emotions that were hard to measure, personal relationships that were not always easy to recognise.[19]

Child labour and factory reform

Within the family, children might themselves act as agents of change. It was often they who introduced literacy to their elders or, because child labour was so important, introduced new work habits and new technologies. Child labour was one of the most hotly debated of subjects, where exaggerated statements were made both by the reformers and their opponents. In 1830 Oastler likened the child workers of the Bradford worsted industry to negro slaves:

> Let truth speak out . . . Thousands of our fellow-creatures and fellow-subjects both male and female . . . are this very moment existing in a state of slavery, more horrid than are the victims of that hellish system 'colonial slavery'. These innocent creatures drawl out, unpitied, their short but miserable existence, in a place famed for its profession of religious zeal. . . The very streets which receive the droppings of an 'Anti-Slavery Society' are every morning wet by the tears of innocent victims at the accursed shrine of avarice, who are compelled (not by the cart-whip of the negro slave-driver) but by the dread of the equally appalling thong or strap of the overlooker, to hasten, half-dressed, but not half-fed, to those magazines of British infantile slavery – the worsted mills in the town and neighbourhood of Bradford!!! . . .[20]

2   Publicising the impact of child labour

If 'a picture is worth a thousand words', then its power to shock is also likely to be much greater. This proved to be the case with the engravings that appeared in the *First Report of the Children's Employment Commissioners: Mines and Collieries*, which was presented to Parliament in April 1842. We have become so hardened to pictures of degradation, in the press and on television, that it is difficult for us to imagine how shocked Victorians were when these illustrations were printed in an official report and reprinted in literary and political journals.

The engravings included one of Ann Ambler, aged about 15, sitting astride 14-year-old William Dyson as they were raised up the shaft of a coal mine, both children being shown naked from the waist up (1).

1   Ann Ambler and William Dyson being winched out of a coal mine; from the *First Report of the Children's Employment Commissioners: Mines and Collieries*, 1842

In the House of Lords, the Marquess of Londonderry, a prominent colliery owner complained that 'the manner in which the report had been accompanied by a picture of an extravagant and disgusting, and in some cases of a scandalous and obscene character, was not such as should have been adopted in a grave publication, and was calculated to excite the judgment'.

Punch made a contrast between scenes of luxury above ground, and of misery below (2). Victorians would have recognised the woman with the anchor as an allegorical representation of Hope – firmly locked out.

CAPITAL AND LABOUR.

2   A cartoon from *Punch*, 1843

Stories of physical atrocities in the mills abounded, and there were allegations of accidents from unfenced machinery, excessive heat and lack of ventilation in spinning rooms, which were thick with cotton dust, and general physical over-exertion. Propaganda campaigns against these abuses were sustained and varied, and included verse (such as Sadler's 'The Factory Girl's Last Day'); novels, like Mrs Frances Trollope's *Life and Adventures of Michael Armstrong, The Factory Boy* (based on *A Memoir of Robert Blincoe, An Orphan Boy*, one of many alleged autobiographies of child labourers); and medical reports, such as C. T. Thackrah's 'The Effects of the Principal Arts, Trades and Professions. . . On Health and Longevity'. Parliamentary papers added to the stream of propaganda. Sadler's Committee of 1832 was certainly rigged. No evidence was given under oath; and Sadler arranged that the supporters of reform should give their evidence first. When parliamentary time ran out he published their evidence without comment, and without the counterbalancing views of the masters. There appear to have been 'professional' witnesses who kept appearing, year after year, before one enquiry or another, such as a Bolton weaver, Richard Needham, who appeared before no fewer than four committees between 1803 and 1834. The reformers were not immune to the loaded question. One witness was asked, 'Is it your impression that your growth has been very much stunted, your health injured, and your constitution thus early destroyed by excessive labour?' Not surprisingly, the answer was, 'Yes it is'. We should therefore be guarded in our judgements, for conditions varied between large and small mills, country and town mills, and mills of an earlier and of a later period. But we ought not to overcompensate, for the weight of evidence would suggest that life in the 'dark satanic mills' could be very black indeed. Nor should we be complacent for, in 1993, the Low Pay Unit estimated that nearly 2 million of Britain's 4 million secondary school children were currently at work, around 74 per cent of them illegally.

In the early nineteenth century, observers were quick to point out that children worked in domestic industry and in agriculture, where conditions were held to be equally if not more gruelling. However, when discipline was imposed by the parents, as it was in domestic industry and in the early factories, child labour aroused little concern. Not surprisingly, therefore, the early legislation such as Peel's Health and Morals of Apprentices Act of 1802 applied to children outside the kinship system. Parish apprenticeship, while admirable as far as some trades were concerned, was a complete misnomer as far as it related to textile mills, for there was no great skill to be imparted, and no possibility of the 'apprentice' ever becoming a master. Nor did it guarantee a job in adulthood. S. D. Chapman noted that in one mill that he had investigated, more that a third of the apprentices died, absconded or had to be returned, while only two of the 780 apprentices taken on were subsequently employed as adult workers. Rather, the system provided a convenient method whereby parish overseers could dispose of their child paupers, and country mills (often in isolated areas) could obtain cheap juvenile labour. The act of 1802 stuck to the pretence that there was a real master/apprentice relationship, and marks the end rather than the beginning of a legislative era. It attempted to enforce good behaviour on the masters by restricting apprentice hours to 12 a day, and gradually eliminating night work. It required minimal sanitation, adequate ventilation of the mill, the provision of clothes and a certain amount of educational and religious instruction. But as inspection was to be undertaken by local Justices of the Peace, rather than by salaried inspectors appointed by the government, the act was largely ineffective. In any case, parish apprenticeship experienced a decline by the 1820s as steam-powered mills developed in urban areas, and these tended to recruit 'free' children.

The act of 1819, therefore, was an attempt (campaigned for by humanitarian mill-owners, like Robert Owen and Sir Robert Peel) to extend protection to free labour. Several years of parliamentary campaigning were required before a bill was passed, and in the process many of its teeth were drawn. Cotton-mill children generally were limited to 12 hours' labour daily, but as a proposal for salaried factory inspectors was again dropped, the act was of limited impact.

The agitation for factory reform was mounted by a number of interested groups who may be collectively considered 'philanthropists', and by groups of working men. The philanthropists included doctors, clergy and Tory protectionists. A number of pioneers of social medicine drew attention to the pernicious effects of factory labour on health, while many clergy (mainly Anglican) raised Christian objections to the system. Oastler, though not a clergyman, raised similar objections. He claimed that 'the Factory-question was indeed . . . a Soul-question – it was Souls against pounds, shillings and pence!' Tories such as Lord Shaftesbury were as much influenced by hostility to *nouveau riche* mill-owners as they were by feelings of pity for the mill workers. However, it has been argued that the view, popular with some historians, that the factory movement was simply an aristocratic and squirearchic counterattack on presumptuous capitalists who had assailed the sacred concepts of political deference and were eventually to repeal the Corn Laws, is a gross oversimplification, for the 'agricultural' and 'industrial' interests were far from monolithic. Working men were also involved, for they saw that child labour cheapened adult labour, and believed that if child labour were regulated, they could hope that the demand for adult labour would rise – as would its price. There was little hope that the hours and conditions of adult males would be regulated so long as politicians held it to be wrong for Parliament to interfere in the arrangements made between masters and men who were held to be 'free agents'. Children, however (and in some degree women), could not be held to be 'free agents', and many working men thought that there might be an incidental improvement in their own conditions once those of children were regulated.

In 1832 Michael Sadler secured a controversial Select Committee to investigate factory conditions, but he lost his parliamentary seat in that year when Aldborough in Yorkshire, the constituency which he represented, was disfranchised by the Reform Act. Leadership then passed to Lord Ashley (later seventh Earl of Shaftesbury) who agreed to reintroduce Sadler's Bill in 1833. As a delaying tactic, opponents of the bill proposed another enquiry, by Royal Commission, to counteract Sadler's notorious committee of the previous year. It was instructed to examine magistrates, masters, adult operatives and children, and to re-examine – this time under oath – those who had appeared before Sadler's Committee. The commissioners reported against legislation to limit the hours of all workers to 10, as this would interfere with adult 'free agents', but they were prepared to justify government interference in the interests of children.

The ensuing Factory Act of 1833 provided that children aged 9–14 should be restricted (by stages) to eight hours' actual labour in most textile mills, with two hours at 'school' (often spent, it seems, in a factory corner with some illiterate employee). Young persons under 18 were limited to 12 hours. Most important of all, perhaps, for this was to become an agency for central control in a number of areas of social reform, four factory inspectors were to be appointed to enforce the act. One of the problems was to determine the age of children, at a time when there was no civil registration of births. Attempts were made to tell their age (like that of horses) by their teeth, but a criterion of height (by no means accurate) was preferred. A child of less than 3 feet 10 inches (1.17 metres) was presumed not yet to be 9, while 4 feet 3½ inches (1.3 metres) was adopted as a minimum height for children claiming to be 13.

The act marked a crucial step in the emergence of the new, more specialised family, for kinship links at work were shattered by the different shifts worked by children and adults, and by the formal provisions for schooling which helped to take education outside the family. The men were bitterly disappointed by the act, for children could be worked in relays with the consequence that adult hours would not indirectly be limited. Violations of the act were frequent, and were committed not only by the masters, but by operatives eager to restore those family controls which the act weakened. After 1833 there was a swing to the demand for a general Ten Hours Act, which was gained (legally for women and children, but indirectly for men) in 1847.

In 1843 Sir James Graham introduced a bill designed to reduce working hours of children aged 9–16 to six and a half hours each day, to be worked either in the morning or the afternoon. For three hours each day education would be made compulsory. There was bitter denominational opposition to the education clauses, which were dropped when the act was passed in 1844, although the half-time system was introduced, and inspectors were given powers to inspect factory schools and to remove incompetent teachers. Dangerous machinery was also to be fenced.

All the above legislation was restricted to textile mills. In mining, amelioration of conditions was not enough, and in 1842 the Mines Act prohibited entirely the employment underground of women and of boys under 10. Thousands of children continued to work in unprotected trades such as agriculture, brick-making and scores of other occupations, many of them noxious. Gradually control was exerted over them, but the only real cure was the adequate provision, by the state if necessary, of sufficient schools. This, together with compulsory education, did not come about until much later in the century, as we shall see in Chapter 5.

Resistance to change: Luddites and hand-loom weavers

Economic necessity forced many workers to accept the new way of life which the factory system imposed. But what if the appeal of traditional ways were stronger, and the workers resisted? Large numbers, in fact, did so usually with disastrous results to themselves.

Until quite recently the Luddites had received a very poor press, largely because of the drastic short-term measures which they took to long-term problems. E. P. Thompson talked of Luddism lingering on in the popular imagination as 'an uncouth, spontaneous affair of illiterate hand workers blindly resisting machinery'; while Hobsbawm notes the view, held by some, 'that the early labour movement did not know what it was doing, but merely reacted, blindly and gropingly, to the pressures of misery, as animals in the laboratory react to electric currents'. They even proved something of an embarrassment to the Hammonds, who made a pioneering study of the movement. The Fabianism of these historians made it difficult to fit the violent Luddites into their framework of a labour movement gradually moving forwards to the Trades Union Congress (TUC) and the Labour Party.

The question also remains whether Luddism was a purely industrial affair ('collective bargaining by riot') or was a revolutionary movement aiming for the violent overthrow of society, as many believed at the time. The sources present a problem, for we are forced to rely very heavily on Home Office files, which are made up largely from the reports of the government's own spies. The Luddites themselves were remarkably secretive. On 12 April 1812, for example, 150 masked and disguised men attacked Cartwright's Mill, halfway between Leeds and Huddersfield. Having been warned of the impending attack, the factory owner had heavily fortified the mill – the defences included carboys of acid. Forty Luddites were wounded in the fray, two fatally. One of these, John Booth, was questioned by Cartwright as he lay dying. Booth eventually whispered, 'Can you keep a secret?' 'I can,' came the hopeful reply from Cartwright. 'So can I,' gasped Booth. And he died, revealing nothing. Although vast rewards were offered, it took a long time to get information from others, although eventually a trial was held at York Assizes in January 1813, at which eight were sentenced to death, including five for the attack on Cartwright's Mill. One who was acquitted was John Hirst, who never talked about Luddism until, in the 1870s, some of his reminiscences and songs were taken down by Frank Peel (a Yorkshire local historian) who used them as the basis of a published account on Luddism. Reminiscence and song are, of course, valid sources of historical evidence, but they need just as much care in their interpretation as do the reports of government secret agents.

While numerous instances of resistance to machinery can be found throughout the nineteenth century, Luddism proper was confined almost entirely to three geographical areas and to three occupations, and was an active force for only a short period. In the West Riding, croppers in the woollen trade were active; in South Lancashire it was the cotton weavers; and in Nottinghamshire, Leicestershire and Derbyshire the movement sprang up among the framework knitters. The unrest began in 1811 and was largely over by 1818. The three strands of Luddism should be carefully distinguished, for the characteristics of the workers involved varied, and only in one instance was machine-breaking a direct response to the introduction of machinery.

The croppers of Yorkshire were skilled and privileged workmen whose craft was associated with the finishing of woollen cloth, which had to be cleaned, stretched (or 'tentered' by drawing out on 'tenter-hooks') and pressed. The key process was raising the nap of the cloth which then had to be cropped, or sheared. The nap was raised by teazels, and the shearing done by heavy hand shears, sometimes 40 pounds in weight and four feet in length. The use of such equipment led to deformity of the right wrist; and 'croppers' hoof' became a ready identification of the members of this élite craft. So important was the process, and so great the skill of the croppers, that it was claimed that their work could, for good or ill, make a difference of 20 per cent to the value of the cloth. The croppers' skill, however, was directly threatened by two machines, the gig-mill and the shearing-frame. The former was a device which raised the nap by cylinders set with teazels (for which no adequate substitute has ever been found). It was not a new invention and had, in fact, been banned by a Statute of Edward VI. The shearing-frame was simply a device which mounted two or more shears in a frame and dispensed with the need for skilled craftsmanship. The threat to the croppers was great, and they complained that 'now gigs and shearing frames are like to become general, if they are allowed to go on many hundreds of us will be out of bread'. However obsolete the Statute of Edward VI might appear to have been to some, to the croppers it gave what they considered a constitutional right. However, petitions to Parliament in 1802–3 and again in 1806 failed to secure an enforcement of this and other protective legislation. The tide of economic thought was running the other way, toward the removal of restrictions on trade. Thus it was that Parliament, far from enforcing the law as the croppers wished, in 1809 repealed all the protective legislation in the woollen industry, which covered gig-mills as well as apprenticeship and the number of looms. This was sound, 'progressive' *laissez-faire* – but to the croppers it was not freedom which was gained, but the reverse. Threats were therefore made. A Gloucester clothier was the recipient of a note made more rather than less alarming by its idiosyncrasies of spelling and punctuation:

> Wee Hear in Formed that you got Shear in mee sheens and if you Dont Pull the Down in a Forght Nights Time Wee will pull them Down for you Wee will you Dammd infernold Dog. And Bee four Almighty God we will pull down all the Mills that heave Heany Shering me Shens in We will cut out Hall your Damd Hearts as Do Keep themand We will meock the rest Heat them or else We will Searve them the Seam.[21]

While the croppers' objections were to machinery, per se, the conditions of the framework-knitters and cotton weavers were somewhat different. They were outworkers, faced with a devastating loss of status, to whom machine-breaking represented a method of putting pressure on their employers – what Hobsbawm has aptly described as 'collective bargaining by riot'. The hosiery trade was highly localised, with nearly 90 per cent of all British frames (and over 60 per cent of the estimated number of frames in the world) situated in the Midlands in 1812. There was some specialisation between counties. Leicester's trade was mainly in wool, cotton was concentrated in Nottinghamshire, and silk was divided between that county and Derbyshire. The industry was largely rural – 82 per cent of the frames were scattered among 253 villages – and this isolation made the work of the machine-breakers that much easier.

The grievances of the framework-knitters were complex, and relate to the pressures of industrial change on skilled craftsmen. Few knitters owned their own looms or frames, and the majority rented them either from a hosier or from an independent capitalist. The hosiers could thus reduce the knitters' wages in two ways – by lowering the piece-rates or by raising the frame rents. The knitters claimed that they were frequently defrauded. Hosiers arbitrarily determined the quality of work produced, upon which the piece-rate depended; numerous deductions from earnings were made; and in some villages payment in wages was almost entirely displaced by 'truck'. There were also complaints about the practices of 'cut-ups' and 'colting', which affected the craft status of the knitters. Cut-up stockings, for example, were manufactured from large pieces of knitted material which were cut out and sewn to the shape of the leg, instead of being knitted in one piece. Although, at first, cut-ups might be difficult to distinguish from the legitimate article, they soon lost shape and had a tendency to split. Not only did this hurt the craftman's pride, but the new cheap techniques of production encouraged an influx into the trade of cheap, unskilled labour. This was exacerbated by the hosiers taking on too many apprentices ('colting'), and both practices threatened to undermine the skilled knitter.

Machine-breaking began in Nottinghamshire and spread throughout the Midlands. The spark was the restriction of foreign markets by Napoleon's Continental System and the collapse of the American market in 1811, which caused demand to fall, stocks to pile up and acute distress to be experienced by the workers. 'Ned Lud' was the name taken by the leaders of the machine-breakers, but the destructive force was supplied by 'Enoch', the giant sledge-hammer used to smash doors and machinery. Ironically, many of the hammers were made by the same man who made the frames – Enoch Taylor of Marsden. 'Enoch made them; Enoch shall break them!' cried the Luddites, one of whose songs ran:

> Great Enoch still shall lead the van,
> Stop him who dare, stop him who can:

Press forward every gallant man,
With hatchet, pike and gun!

Between March 1811 and February 1812 about 1,000 frames were destroyed, valued at between £6,000 and £10,000. Remarkable organisation and discrimination was shown by the Luddites, who generally spared frames not used for cut-ups. In Lancashire and Yorkshire the machines were chiefly to be found in mills, which were easier to defend, and whose masters were less easy to intimidate. It was here, therefore, that the legendary pitched battles – like the attack on Cartwright's and Rawfolds Mills – took place. In February 1812 Parliament made frame-breaking a capital offence, despite a passionate address in the House of Lords by Lord Byron:

> By the adoption of one species of Frame in particular, one man performed the work of many, and the superfluous labourers were thrown out of employment. Yet it is to be observed that the work thus executed was inferior in quality; not marketable at home, and merely hurried over with a view to exportation. It was called, in the cant of the trade, by the name of 'Spider work'. The rejected workmen, in the blindness of their ignorance, instead of rejoicing at these improvements in arts so beneficial to mankind, conceived themselves to be sacrificed to improvements in mechanism. In the foolishness of their hearts they imagined that the maintenance and well doing of the industrious poor were objects of greater consequence than the enrichment of a few individuals by any improvement, in the implements of trade, which threw the workmen out of employment and rendered the labourer unworthy of his hire.[22]

How effective Luddism was as a workers' movement is hard to assess, although Hobsbawm argues that it was at least as effective a means of bringing pressure to bear as others which might have been employed, for men with little scarcity value could gain nothing from strike action. Luddism was also an effective means of enforcing group solidarity (operating in the same way as any gang), while the destruction of property – or the threat of its destruction – might prove an effective means of intimidating smaller employers. Except in Lancashire and Cheshire, at least a temporary redress of grievances was granted. Yorkshire woollen masters withdrew their shearing-frames and, in the Midlands, negotiations between the men and their employers quickly followed.

There are many misconceptions about the cotton hand-loom weavers, who were the third group to be numbered among the Luddites. They are sometimes imagined to have been domestic workers, lingering on from the traditional economic system, and finally destroyed by the factories. Yet in fact they were in a sense both created and destroyed by the industrial revolution, the three generations which witnessed the industrial take-off seeing also the rise and the fall of hand-loom cotton weaving. Once the new fabric could be made, its cheapness and variety commended itself to home and foreign markets, and it was to satisfy this demand that an army of cotton hand-loom weavers was called into being. Spinning, as we have seen, was mechanised early, but the power-loom, though invented in the 1780s, was not quickly introduced for a variety of technical and economic reasons. In the early nineteenth century it was the hand-loom which was improved, and the eventual triumph of the power-loom was not accepted until the 1820s. Even as late as 1830 it was estimated that there were no more than 60,000 power-looms in England and Scotland, although there were four times as many hand-looms. By the 1830s and 1840s there were, with their families, over 800,000 persons engaged in hand-loom weaving, forming the largest occupational group in the country, after agricultural workers and domestic servants.

Contrary to popular belief, hand-loom weaving was not a skilled trade; and entry into it was easy. Three weeks was reckoned sufficient time to learn plain weaving, while a lad of 16 was considered capable of learning muslin weaving in six. Many weavers from the older fustian trade moved into cotton weaving, as did many domestic spinners, displaced by the new machinery. Little capital was necessary, and a loom and lodgings could be hired at Burnley and Colne for as little as a shilling a week. There were no apprenticeship regulations, and much of the work could be done by women and children.

At first the wages proved attractive, but the ease of entry led to distress. Hand-loom weaving came to be seen as a last refuge, and as more and more people entered the trade, so piece-rates fell. From a peak of 23s a week in 1805, earnings had dropped to 6s by 1831. It was this demoralising competition among the weavers, rather than the competition of the power-loom, which led to distress, for their misery was great even before the power-loom came to be widely adopted in the 1820s. The popular ballad, 'John O'Grinfield', captured well the desperation of the hand-loom weavers in the years immediately after the Napoleonic Wars:

> I'm a poor cotton weaver as many a one knows,
> I've nowt t'eat i' th' house and I've worn out my clothes;
> You'd hardly give sixpence for all I've got on,
> My clogs they are bursten and stocking I've none.
> You'd think it wur hard to be sent to the world
> For to clam [starve] and do best that you can . . .

The response to falling piece-rates was to produce more - which only lowered the rates yet further. It is a plausible estimate that in the 1820s output per weaver increased by 20–30 per cent. The manufacturers found a combination of power-looms and hand-looms attractive, for they could base their steady trade on the former, and put on or lay off hand-loom weavers as demand fluctuated.

Classical economic theory would have led one to believe that hand-loom weavers would have quit such an overstocked trade, but there were many reasons why they might find it difficult to secure alternative employment in the factories, even if they could overcome their deep antipathy towards them. In the first place, there were geographical difficulties which are sometimes overlooked, for the earliest power-looms were located outside the old weaving districts which tended to be in rural areas. Second, the demand in the mills was mainly for the labour of women and children. Even well-disposed masters might find difficulty in employing men. John Fielden, for example, recalled in 1835: 'I was applied to weekly by scores of hand-loom weavers, who were so pressed down in their conditions as to be obliged to seek such work, and it gave me and my partners no small pain . . . to be compelled to refuse work to men who applied for it.' Third, there was the suspicion and hostility of workers in other sections of the industry who feared for their own jobs, and who were anxious lest employers use hand-loom weavers as blacklegs. Finally, there were the social factors, which might exert a stronger pull than economic ones. There was nothing idyllic about the life of the hand-loom weaver in his cottage, but it had its compensations. The weaver felt a measure of independence, just as he felt that he had a certain status as a real maker of cloth which no mere factory 'hand' ever had. Again, it is folk-song which captures the resentment:

> So come all you cotton-weavers, you must rise up very soon,
> For you must work in factories from morning until noon:
> You mustn't walk in your garden for two or three hours a-day,
> For you must stand at their command, and keep your shuttles in play.

To 'stand at their command' was, as E. P. Thompson suggested, the most deeply resented indignity. There is no doubt that hand-loom weavers suffered, and differences between historians can only be about the degree of that suffering.

Notes

1   Arthur Marwick, *Class: Image and Reality*, Fontana, 1981, pp. 18–19.
2   Robert Roberts, *The Classic Slum*, Penguin, 1973, p. 171.
3   R. J. Morris, *Class and Class Consciousness in the Industrial Revolution 1780–1850*, Macmillan, 1980, p. 20.
4   Quoted in Kate Flint (ed.), *The Victorian Novelist: Social Problems and Social Change*, Croom Helm, 1987, pp. 26–7.
5   E. J. Hobsbawm, *Industry and Empire*, Penguin, 1969, pp. 72–3.
6   F. M. L. Thompson, *The Rise of Respectable Society 1830–1900*, Fontana, 1988, p. 26.
7   E. P. Thompson, *The Making of the English Working Class*, Gollancz, 1963, p. 804.
8   Quoted in Patricia Hollis, *Class and Conflict in Nineteenth-Century England, 1815–1850*, Routledge and Kegan Paul, 1973, p. 158.
9   Quoted in Eric Evans, *Social Policy, 1830–1914*, Routledge and Kegan Paul, 1978, p. 108.
10 Quoted in Arthur J. Taylor, *The Standard of Living in Britain in the Industrial Revolution*, Methuen, 1975, p. 37.
11 Malcolm Thomis, *The Town Labourer and the Industrial Revolution*, Batsford, 1974, pp. 2–3.
12 E. P. Thompson, op.cit., p. 318.
13 Ibid., p. 211.
14 Quoted in Alasdair Clayre, *Nature and Industrialisation*, Oxford University Press, 1977, p. 244.
15 John Rule, *The Vital Century*, Longman, 1992, p. 192.
16 Quoted in Harold Perkin, *The Origins of Modern English Society*, Routledge and Kegan Paul, 1969, pp. 149–50.
17 Quoted in Kate Flint, op cit., 1987, p. 250.
18 F. M. L. Thompson, op. cit., 1988, p. 114.
19 J. F. C. Harrison, *The Early Victorians*, Fontana, 1979, pp. 103–4.
20 Quoted in Patricia Hollis, op. cit., 1973, p. 194.
21 Quoted in E. P. Thompson, op. cit., p. 526.
22 Quoted in Roy Palmer, *The Sound of History*, Oxford University Press, 1988, p. 103.

Chapter three

Landed society in the nineteenth century

The landed interest

It would be a mistake to think that at some determinable moment in time Britain became 'industrialised' and that the old pattern of social and economic relationships ceased to exist. The transformation came about gradually, and affected particular sectors of the economy and social communities at different times. In a sense, traditional Britain shrank, while the new industrial society grew alongside it. Change came about most quickly in the towns, while the old order persisted longer in the countryside.

Although much of the history of Britain since the Industrial Revolution can only be understood in terms of social class, people in the nineteenth century spoke of 'the landed interest', including in that phrase all those who derived an interest from land, whether as landowners, farmers or labourers. These three groups related to the land in different ways, and although they shared some common concerns, what was in the interest of one group was not necessarily in the interest of the others. Even within these broad groups interests could vary. For example, what was good for the arable farmer was not always good for the stock-breeder or dairyman, and what would benefit one landowner might injure another.

Although it is helpful to divide the landed interest into these three tiers, it does not give us the whole picture. Many rural artisans and small traders, as well as professional men such as surveyors and country attorneys, might well claim to be included. Furthermore, there were parts of Britain where these divisions made less sense, such as Wales, the Highlands of Scotland and parts of the north of England (as well, of course, as Ireland) where a simple division between landlords and peasants, with a few small farmers, is more representative.

In addition to the minority of landowners who themselves farmed their land, there were those who looked to the land for sport, for income in the form of rent, or for political and social influence. 'You see,' said Archdeacon Grantley in Anthony Trollope's novel, *The Last Chronicle of Barset*, 'land gives you so much more than rent. It gives you position and influence and political power – to say nothing of the game.' Land, more than any other kind of property, provided social influence, for it was the most visible form of wealth. As late as 1870 a writer in *The Economist* could claim that so great was the effect of such conspicuous wealth upon social status, that it would pay a millionaire to sink half his fortune in buying 10,000 acres of land to return only one shilling per cent, and live upon the remainder, rather than live upon the whole without land. He would be a greater man in the eyes of more people.

Between 1835 and 1899 some 500 country houses were either built or substantially remodelled, roughly half the activity being on behalf of new families who were either first or second generation on their estate. However, while many of those who amassed wealth in the industrial revolution aspired to set up as landed gentry, the desire was not universal; and it has been shown that in the early 1880s no more than 10 per cent of the total number of landowners consisted of members of new families who had purchased their estate in the course of the previous hundred years.

The distribution of landownership

The exact extent and distribution of landownership was a matter of conjecture to contemporaries, and remains so to the historian. The occupation tables of the decennial census (described by F. M. L. Thompson, a leading historian of nineteenth-century landed society, as 'shifting sands' in a 'sea of conjecture') were the main source of evidence, and gave rise to the popular view, in the middle decades of the century, that landownership was concentrated in the hands of a mere 30,000 individuals. To confound this potentially explosive idea an official return of the landowners of the United Kingdom was procured by the Conservative peer, Lord Derby, in 1872. *The Return of Owners of Land*, published in the following year, and commonly called the *New Domesday Survey*, seriously misfired as a political weapon. It certainly proved over a million people to be owners of land (though frequently their 'estate' was no larger than a cabbage patch) but the mythical 30,000 were reduced to a group of fewer than 7,000 who were shown to possess four-fifths of the United Kingdom. Such a contentious document was immediately subjected to a great deal of scrutiny, and many errors and inaccuracies were discovered. One of the most extensive examinations and revisions was made by John Bateman, a Tory landowner from Essex, whose book, *The Great Landowners of Great Britain and Ireland* (originally entitled *The Acreocracy of England*) ran through four editions between 1876 and 1883. Table 3.1, which appeared as an appendix to the fourth edition, gives a clear and reasonably accurate picture of landownership at that time, and is broadly indicative of the previous decades as well.

Table 3.1   *Summary table of landowners in England and Wales, 1883*

No. of owners	Class	Extent in acres*
400	Peers and peeresses	5,728,979
1,288	Great landowners	8,497,699
2,529	Squires	4,319,271
9,585	Greater yeomen	4,782,627
24,412	Lesser yeomen	4,144,272
217,049	Small proprietors	3,931,806
703,289	Cottagers	151,148
	Public bodies: the crown, barracks, convict prisons, lighthouses, etc.	165,427
14,459	Religious, educational, philanthropic, etc., commercial and miscellaneous	947,655 / 330,466
	Waste	1,524,624
973,011	Total	34,523,974

* 1 acre = 0.4 hectare
Source: John Bateman, *The Great Landowners of Great Britain and Ireland*, 1883 (1971).

Bateman's class of great landowners includes all estates owned by commoners of at least 3,000 acres (1 acre is equal to 0.4 hectare), provided that the rent reached £3,000 (thus realistically excluding the owners of vast tracts of bog or unusable moorland). Squires include estates of 1,000–3,000 acres, and such larger estates as would have been included in the former group had their rental been above the minimum £3,000. The estates of greater yeomen were classed as 300–1,000 acres, lesser yeomen as 100–300 acres, while small proprietors possessed 1–100 acres. Cottagers (who made up the majority) held less than an acre. When it is remembered that the population of England and Wales in 1881 was nearly 26 million, the significance of the figures becomes immediately apparent.

At the top of the tree was the aristocracy – the peers and peeresses of the realm. Some could trace their noble lines to medieval times, but for the majority nobility was of more recent creation. Around 1830 Sir Robert Peel wrote of titles, 'The voracity for these things quite surprises me. I wonder people don't begin to feel the distinction of an unadorned name.' Peers continued to be created, and the situation by the late 1960s was that only one-fifth of the 1,100 or so peers of that time could trace their title to before 1800, while one-half dated from 1906 or later.

The possession of land was virtually essential for the aristocracy. In 1873 only 60 of the existing 585 peers and peeresses held no land. So strong was the mystique of landownership that, in 1847–48, Disraeli had to be set up by his political friends with 750 acres at Hughenden, in order to make him respectable to the Tory Party. As the nineteenth century progressed, the new wealth of the industrial revolution came increasingly to be represented in the peerage, although the traditional connection with land remained strong. Some 200 individuals were ennobled between 1886 and 1914, of whom more than a third came from industry and another third from the professions; yet a great many of both groups were the sons of men who already had a landed status. The entry of new classes into the House of Lords was popularly typified by the brewers (although there were only five of them in the House by 1911) who lent themselves to the opprobrious epithet, 'the beerage'. Whatever their origins, wealth remained a prerequisite for holders of noble rank. As late as 1919 Field Marshall Haig informed the Prime Minister that 'unless an adequate grant was made to enable a suitable position to be maintained', he must decline a peerage. He eventually accepted an earldom and a grant of £100,000.

A writer of 1882 claimed that 'a man who only wanted all the conveniences and comforts that London and the country could give, could have them for £10,000 a year. To spend more than this, he must go into horse-racing or illegitimate pleasures'. However, the income range of 300 or so families who made up the aristocracy was wide. Some, like the Earl of Clarendon, could hold their head high on an income from land as low as £3,000. Others, such as the great Dukes of Bedford, Devonshire or Northumberland, could already boast of incomes of over £50,000 at the very beginning of the century. Bateman estimated that the estates of the last-named peer totalled 186,397 acres (74,559 hectares) – an area greater than the combined acreage of all the cottagers of England and Wales shown in Table 3.1.

Foreign commentators were often amazed at the wealth of the British aristocracy. Hippolyte Taine recorded the invitation which Lord Hertford gave to one of his French friends: 'I have a castle in Wales. I have never seen it, but I am told it is very beautiful. Every day twelve places are laid for dinner and the carriage is ready at the front door in case I might arrive. Do go and stay there – it won't cost me a penny.' In 1856 the American poet and essayist, Ralph Waldo Emerson, visited Britain and recorded how the Marquis of Breadalbane could ride 100 miles in a straight line across his own property, while the Duke of Sutherland owned the whole of the county of that name, from sea to shining sea.

Increasingly, landowners turned to sources of wealth other than agricultural rents. For example, mineral resources were exploited by many. A French visitor to Tyneside at the end of the Napoleonic Wars described landowners eagerly searching for coal on their estates, in their anxiety to establish 'farms underground'. Lord Londonderry referred to his collieries as his 'black diamond trade', and more than one country seat was literally founded upon coal. The Earl of Durham (or 'His Carbonic Majesty' as he was once called) had to spend £20,000 on filling the workings beneath Lambton Castle; while mining beneath the Yorkshire estate of the Lowther baronets brought about the subsidence of Swillington House.

At first landowners frequently worked their own pits, but as time passed the practice declined, and they came to rely on mineral leases instead. In 1829, for instance, John Buddle, the leading colliery engineer of the day, calculated that only five of the 41 owners on Tyneside actually worked their own mines. Income from mining leases could be considerable. The mineral income of the Dukes of Northumberland rose from £3,000 in 1800 to around £25,000 in the 1860s and 1870s, while in 1889 coal, iron, and other metal royalties for the country as a whole were estimated at £4,665,043, with a further £216,000 for wayleaves (the charge for carrying minerals across or beneath another's land).

A further source of income was provided by the rise in urban land values. Many landowners appreciated the jingle in a contemporary handbook:

> The richest crop of any field
> Is a crop of bricks for it to yield.
> The richest crop that it can grow
> Is a crop of houses in a row.

It has been estimated that urban land values rose from £3 million in 1845 to £8.6 million in 1857, and to £30.1 million in 1882. The Duke of Portland estimated his London rents at £50,000 a year in 1844, while the rental of the Duke of Bedford's London estate grossed £70,000–£80,000 per annum from 1830 to 1870. The lucky possession of land in prime urban areas could make a family. The Grosvenors, for example, had started as modest Cheshire squires, but the acquisition (through marriage) of land in what was to become London's West End led to great wealth and to the title of Dukes of Westminster. By 1914 the Duke had an income of £1,000 a day. Nor were the profits from estate development confined to the metropolis. Nine-tenths of the £120,000 income of Lord Calthorpe came from his estates at Edgbaston, a prosperous suburb of Birmingham; and the student in many a provincial town should find little difficulty in tracing the urban enterprises of local landowning families.

Railway development proved an asset to other landowners, and in 1856 Robert Stephenson worked out that, out of £286 million invested by the railway companies for line construction in 25 years, one-quarter of the sum had been spent on purchasing land. The fruit of these various sources of income was, of course, unevenly scattered, and most landowners continued to rely on their agricultural rents for the bulk of their income.

Below the aristocracy and other great landowners in Bateman's table came the more fluid group of the gentry or squirearchy, whose income for most of the nineteenth century ranged from a lower limit of £1,000 a year to an upper limit of £10,000. Their influence was more local than that of the aristocracy (whose estates often crossed county boundaries) yet the power of the local squire was none the less tremendous, as George Brodrick illustrated in his *English Land and English Landlords* of 1880:

> To an Englishman born and bred in the country, it appears the natural order of things, if not the fixed ordinance of providence, that in each parish there should

be a dominant resident landowner, called a squire, unless he should chance to be a peer, invested with an authority over its inhabitants, which neither the Saxon chief, nor the Norman lord, in the fulness of his power, ever had the right of exercising. This potentate, who, luckily for his dependents, is usually a kind-hearted and tolerably educated gentleman, concentrates in himself a variety of rights and prerogatives which, in the aggregate, amount to little short of patriarchal sovereignty. The clergyman, who is by far the greatest man in the parish next to himself, is usually his nominee, and often his kinsman. The farmers, who are almost the only employers of labour besides himself, are his tenants-at-will, and, possibly, his debtors. The petty tradespeople of the village community rent under him, and, if they do not, might be crushed by his displeasure at any moment. The labourers, of course, live in his cottages . . . but this is by no means his only hold upon them. They are absolutely at his mercy for the privilege of hiring allotments, generally at an 'accommodation' rent; they sometimes work on the home farm, and are glad to get jobs from his bailiff, especially in the winter; they look to him for advice in worldly matters as they would consult the parson in spiritual matters; they believe that his good word could procure them any favour or advancement for their children on which they may set their hearts, and they know that his frown may bring ruin upon them and theirs. Nothing passes in the parish without being reported to him. If a girl should go wrong, or a young man should consort with poachers, or a stranger of doubtful repute should be admitted as a lodger, the squire is sure to hear of it, and his decree, so far as his labourers and cottage-tenants are concerned, is as good as law. He is, in fact, the local representative of the law itself, and, as a magistrate, has often the means of legally enforcing the policy which, as landlord, he may have adopted. Add to all this the influence which he may and ought to acquire as the leading supporter and manager of the parish school, as the most liberal subscriber to parochial charities, as the patron of village games and the dispenser of village treats, not to speak of the motherly services which may be rendered by his wife, or the boyish fellowship which may grow up between the youth of the village and the young gentlemen at the Hall; and it is difficult to imagine a position of greater real power and responsibility.

As Brodrick indicates, it was his seat on the Justice's Bench which gave the squire so much of his power. Many country houses possessed a 'justice room', where (until it was specifically forbidden in 1848) it was possible to deal with cases in private. Many game offences were dealt with in this manner, and it was said that 'the sporting squire bagged his birds in the morning, and his poachers in the afternoon'. Apart from the magistrate and the accused, only two persons were required, one to 'lay the information' and the other to act as witness, although in the early nineteenth century these could be one and the same person – usually the magistrate's own gamekeeper, or that of his neighbour. Although serious charges were referred to the Quarter Sessions, the single Justice, sitting in Petty Sessions, could deal with many offences including certain statutory offences created in the nineteenth century and relating to railways and factories, for example. Before 1888 the Justices executed much county business. They supervised gaols, visited lunatic asylums, and were ex-officio members of the poor-law Boards of Guardians. None of the work was paid, but it added greatly to the prestige of the office-holder.

The paternalism described by Brodrick was almost unique to the countryside, for although Disraeli and the supporters of the Young England movement hoped to transplant it into the towns, the soil was not ripe there for it to take root. Later attempts by people like Octavia Hill to use the 'urban gentry' to oversee and supervise the poor proved equally disappointing, although considerable effort, much of it female, went into visiting.

It was the gentry who represented the main agency of mobility into landed society, for direct entry into the aristocracy required resources beyond all but the greatest industrialists or financiers. The process of assimilation had advantages both for the middle-class aspirants towards landed status, and for the gentry who received them, while the relative ease with which the transition could be made acted as a major social and political safety-valve.

There were numerous ways in which contacts between the two classes were maintained. Experience of the worlds of industry and commerce was gained not only through the exploitation of mineral and other resources but also through other business activities like those recorded by the Duke of Devonshire in his diary for 1869:

> I attended the monthly meeting of the Royal Agricultural Society which lasted nearly three hours though there was no business of much importance. I then went to Currey's (his lawyers) where we had meetings of the Furness Gas and Water Co, and of the Furness Railway Directors and the Barrow Steel Directors. At the Furness meeting we had a good deal of discussion about the Belfast steamer and the question of improving the present paddle wheel boats or substituting screw steamers . . . At the Steel meeting we sanctioned outlay of various kinds which including a new furnace will amount to £37,000, the furnace alone costing £10,000 . . . I afterwards saw Mr Purdon with reference to the Fernway and Lismore line.[1]

In addition, the law of primogeniture, which ensured that an estate passed wholly to the eldest son, obliged the younger sons to look elsewhere for a living, and thus many entered business and the professions. Middle-class entry into landed society was effected by marriage (the traditional method) or by the purchase of an estate. The mere acquisition of land, however, did not automatically or immediately confer the new status; although, if not upon the purchaser himself, it would usually be conferred on his children or grandchildren, educated alongside the children of the landed classes.

It could be argued that by the end of the nineteenth century landownership proved somewhat less attractive as demands for land reform gathered strength. Between 1881 and 1884, *Progress and Poverty*, written by the American economist Henry George, went through 10 London editions. George's ideas were based on the observation of David Ricardo, the classical economist, that good land produced at a cost well below the market price, which was set by much poorer land, and that landlords took this 'unearned increment' in the form of rent. George argued that the state should impose a tax on this unearned increment which, he believed, would produce sufficient revenue to allow for the abolition of all other taxes. There was much talk of land nationalisation, and in 1894 for the first time death duties were imposed on agricultural property. When the Liberals were returned in 1906 they had far-reaching plans for land reform, which partly explains the great increase in land sales which took place around that time. In 1910 the value of land sold was £1.5 million, and in 1911, £2 million. As the Secretary of the Farmers' Club put it in that year: 'Wealth in the immovable form of land is easily taxed or confiscated. Wealth in the form of sovereigns is more moveable, and therefore more secure.'

Aristocratic power in the nineteenth century

In a letter which he wrote to his free-trade colleague, John Bright, in 1849, Richard Cobden bewailed the power which remained in the hands of the aristocracy 'and their allies, the snobs of the towns':

We are a servile, aristocracy-loving, lord-ridden people, who regard land with as much reverence as we still do the peerage and baronetage. Not only have not nineteen-twentieths of us any share in the soil, but we have not presumed to think that we are worthy to possess a few acres of mother earth. The politicians who would propose to break up the estates of this country into smaller properties, will be looked upon as revolutionary democrats aiming at nothing less than the establishment of a Republic upon the ruin of Queen and Lords . . .[2]

In 1857 Cobden was forced to say: 'During my experience the higher classes never stood so high in relative social and political rank, as compared with the other classes, as at present.' The landed class retained a clear majority in the House of Commons until 1885, and in the Cabinet until 1893, if not 1905. The number of hereditary peers in the House of Lords rose from around 350 in 1832 to over 570 by 1914, and the powers of that House were not drastically reduced until the Parliament Act of 1911. The landed class controlled recruitment to the civil service until at least 1870, to the army until 1871 and to the Church for even longer. Local government was dominated by it until at least 1888. If one excepts Disraeli, the first Prime Minister not to belong to a landed family was Herbert Asquith, who took office in 1908.

How, then, is the marriage to be effected between the often held view that the middle class 'came to power' in 1832, and the idea that the landed class remained in control until much later in the century, if not even into the next? In the first place, the power base of the landed classes was strengthened by the 1832 Reform Act which, while giving the vote to the urban middle class, also increased the number of county members from 188 to 253. A second solution to the paradox was offered by Walter Bagehot in *The English Constitution* (1867). Bagehot made a distinction between the 'dignified' and the 'efficient' parts of the constitution, and he developed the concepts of 'deference' and a 'deferential society'. The 'dignified' parts of the constitution, he claimed, were represented by the monarchy and the House of Lords, institutions of great antiquity and augustness, but little real power, while the 'efficient' part (the House of Commons, and especially the Cabinet) exercised real power by a kind of remote control. The 'dignified' part was necessary to bring government within the limited powers of understanding of the masses and to make it acceptable to them, for 'the fancy of the mass of men is incredibly weak; it can see nothing without a visible symbol'. 'A Royal Family,' wrote Bagehot, 'sweetens politics by the seasonable addition of nice and pretty events. It introduces irrelevant facts into the business of government, but they are facts which speak to "men's bosoms" and employ their thoughts. To state the matter shortly, royalty is a government in which the attention of the nation is concentrated on one person doing interesting actions.'

Likewise, the imagination and reverence of the masses was captured by the aristocracy, who gave the appearance of having been born to lead:

In reverencing wealth, we reverence not man, but an appendix to a man; in reverencing inherited nobility, we reverence the probable possession of a great faculty – the faculty of bringing out what is in one. The unconscious grace of life may be in the middle classes: finely-mannered persons are born every-where: but it ought to be in the aristocracy: and a man must be born with a hitch in his nerves if he has not some of it. It is a physiological possession of the race, though it is sometimes wanting in the individual.

Britain was the very model of a deferential society. A German commentator of 1851 wrote: 'A principal trait of an Englishman's character, and the basis not merely of the conventions but also of the political structure of his nation, is his willingness to subordinate himself to anyone in society who is superior to him.' The concepts of 'deference' and of a 'dignified' part of the constitution were, of course, linked – in a way in which Bagehot portrayed:

In fact, the mass of the English people yield a deference rather to something else than to their rulers. They defer to what we may call the theatrical show of society. A certain state passes before them; a certain pomp of great men; a certain spectacle of beautiful women; a wonderful scene of wealth and enjoyment is displayed, and they are coerced by it. Their imagination is bowed down; they feel they are not equal to the life which is revealed to them. Courts and aristocracies have the great quality which rules the multitude, though philosophers can see nothing in it – visibility . . . Philosophers may deride this superstition, but its results are inestimable. By the spectacle of this august society, countless ignorant men and women are induced to obey the few nominal electors – the £10 borough renters, and the £50 county renters – who have nothing imposing about them, nothing which would attract the eye or fascinate the fancy. What impresses men is not mind, but the result of mind. And the greatest of these results is this wonderful spectacle of society, which is ever new, and yet ever the same . . . The apparent rulers of the English nation are like the most imposing personages of a splendid procession; it is by them the mob are influenced; it is they whom the spectators cheer. The real rulers are secreted in second-rate carriages; no one cares for them or asks about them, but they are obeyed implicitly and unconsciously by reason of the splendour of those who eclipsed and preceded them.

Nevertheless, to put it in terms which the middle class would have understood, the aristocracy was expected to give value for money, as, of course, it did. For a start, those whose wealth was unearned had the leisure which a life in politics required, and they often entered the political arena at a younger age. The *Westminster Review* said in 1833:

The landed interest must always exercise great sway in public affairs; for that class alone have much leisure to meddle in them. The intelligence of the other classes is absorbed, if not exclusively, yet in a great degree, in the business of money-making . . . The men who have the leisure for intrigue, from whose coteries the ministries are formed, and whose leisure finds no other occupation than to tattle on the politics of the day, to clog the steps of officials, and flutter from club to club – are of the landed interest.[3]

The parliamentary burden on MPs grew heavily from the 1830s onwards, and Eric Evans has pointed out that the amount of time a Member might spend in the House (if he was so inclined) is indicated by the fact that 25 volumes of *Hansard* suffice to report the debates of the decade 1820–30, but 63 are needed for the 1840s. Politics was time-consuming, and land provided both the time and the income for many men to pursue a political career.

Finally, it has to be admitted that the aristocracy showed a remarkable capacity for self-preservation, and proved extremely flexible in facing the buffetings of the new industrial society. English society may have contained inequalities, but they were *removable inequalities*. The leaders of rising groups within society had for long past been absorbed into the élite, while their major demands had been, wherever possible, accommodated. The aristocracy was prepared to make a tactical retreat from the most untenable positions of inherited privilege and thereby ward off their total annihilation. During the debates on the Reform Bill, Lord Althorp had predicted that MPs 'would continue to be selected from the same classes . . . but with this beneficial change, that they would then be acting under the influence of their constituents'. His forecast was a shrewd one, for if, after the 1832 Reform Act, the aristocracy still retained the main positions of power, their possession had to be bargained for, and was no longer an automatic right. Harold Perkin makes the point that 'the radical change produced by the Reform Act was from aristocratic rule by prescription to aristocratic rule by consent', and the fear of creating an antiaristocratic block vote (rather than the actual existence of one) thereafter acted as a brake.

The education of a gentleman

Squire Brown, in Thomas Hughes' novel *Tom Brown's Schooldays*, had very definite views about his son's education and, before Tom's departure for Rugby School, had the following thoughts:

> To condense the Squire's meditation, it was somewhat as follows: 'I won't tell him to read his Bible, and love and serve God; if he don't do that for his mother's sake and teaching, he won't for mine. Shall I go into the sort of temptations he'll meet with? No, I can't do that. Never do for an old fellow to go into such things with a boy. He won't understand me. Do him more harm than good, ten to one. Shall I tell him to mind his work, and say he's sent to school to make himself a good scholar? Well, but he isn't sent to school for that – at any rate, not for that mainly. I don't care a straw for Greek particles, or the digamma; no more does his mother. What is he sent to school for? Well, partly because he wanted so to go. If he'll only turn out a brave, helpful truth-telling Englishman, and a gentleman, and a Christian, that's all I want', thought the Squire; and upon this view of the case he framed his last words of advice to Tom, which were well enough suited to his purpose.

Unlike Squire Brown, Dr Arnold did give a straw for Greek particles (and demanded a high level of active scholarship from his staff) but he would have approved of the advice in other respects. Before he took up his headmastership in 1828, he wrote to a friend:

> With regard to reforms at Rugby, give me credit, I must beg of you, for a most sincere desire to make it a place of Christian education. At the same time my object will be, if possible, to form Christian men, for Christian boys I can scarcely hope to make; I mean that, from the natural imperfect state of boyhood, they are not susceptible of Christian principles in their full development upon their practice, and I suspect that a low standard of morals in many respects must be tolerated amongst them, as it was on a larger scale in what I consider the boyhood of the human race. But I believe that a great deal may be done, and I should be most unwilling to undertake the business, if I did not trust that much might be done.[4]

Elsewhere he wrote: 'My love for any place or person, or institution, is exactly the measure of my desire to reform them.' And reform Rugby he did. Dr Arnold was a remarkable man. His 14 years at Rugby (1828–42) spanned three reigns, and

3   The fourth-form room at Harrow School

I   Harrow School, 1816

2   Harrow School, c. 1880

Picture 1 shows the main teaching room at Harrow School, taken from a print by
A. C. Pugin, published by Rudolph Ackermann in 1816 in a history of the nine great public
schools. Picture 2 is of the same room as it appeared in the 1880s. Do they give a similar
impression? Does Pugin's view support the description of the room that appears in the
text of the book? There it is described as having 'a gloomy appearance', and having 'little
claim to attention, but the uses to which it is consecrated'. The photograph gives a
different impression; but have we any right to suppose that it is more accurate?

although he survived for only four years of Victoria's reign, he earned a place in Lytton Strachey's influential but iconoclastic book, *Eminent Victorians*. His inclusion was not without justification, for Arnold's influence on the Victorian public school was very great. Some historians talk of the 'myth' of Thomas Arnold, and it is certainly true that his reputation was spread in part by a work of fiction. *Tom Brown's Schooldays* was first published in April 1857, and had gone into a fifth edition by November of the same year. Before 1892 52 editions were brought out by Macmillan, the original publishers, and the book has never been out of print. It is one of those books which illustrates the interesting proposition that, while literature usually reflects life, life may come to follow art; and most historians are prepared to accept that the book helped to create the Victorian public school as much as describe it. There is less agreement as to the accuracy with which the book actually portrays the Rugby of Arnold's day. Patrick Scott has pointed to some of the dangers which confront the historian who attempts to use literature as evidence. A novel must be set against other contemporary evidence if its accuracy is to be determined, for the tests of 'realism' applied by the literary critic may prove inadequate. Scott has shown that those parts of *Tom Brown's Schooldays* which, to the modern reader, seem less 'realistic' are, perhaps, historically the most accurate:

> The contemporary evidence . . . goes to show that the piety and high-mindedness of Part Two of Tom Brown's Schooldays was a true presentation of Arnold's Rugby as Hughes would have experienced it, while the gentlemanly philistinism of the first part, authentic enough in its outline, is much closer to previous literary simplification of life at Rugby School. The historian will find safer evidence of Arnold's Rugby in Part Two than in Part One, splendid though it is. Once more, as is also the case with Dean Farrar's school novels, the literary-critical test of 'realism' proves a poor aid for the historian attempting to discern the real.[5]

The most important of Dean Farrar's novels, mentioned by Scott, was *Eric, or Little by Little* (1858). Farrar, a master at Harrow School, and later headmaster of Marlborough, wrote much more critically of the public schools than did Hughes, and his criticisms coincided with a more direct attack on the schools in both the *Cornhill Magazine* and the *Westminster Review*. The spotlight of public attention was turned on the schools, culminating in the establishment of the Clarendon Commission in 1861.

The Clarendon Commission is important as a mid-century 'stocktaking' of the public schools. None of the members of the Commission were hostile critics, and although criticisms of the curriculum were made – there was not enough teaching of mathematics, science or modern languages – the classics were vindicated, and the system itself was praised. The schools had already achieved a great measure of internal reform, for which much of the credit must be given to Arnold. The Clarendon Commission investigated the nine 'great' public schools (Eton, Harrow, Rugby, Westminster, Winchester, Charterhouse, St Paul's, Merchant Taylors' and Shrewsbury). The criteria for selection were narrow, and they excluded many schools which would have been accepted as 'public schools' at that date. Such schools are difficult to define, and although it is now customary to accept as public schools those whose headmasters are members of the Headmasters' Conference (dating from 1869) some other criterion has to be selected for the nineteenth century. Perhaps the best is acceptance by the charmed circle of undoubted public schools themselves. J. R. de S. Honey has developed this concept of 'interaction', which could take various forms. Schools might compete with each other for university scholarships, for example, or they might meet at corps camps or field days. In particular, they met at sport. Who was willing to play with whom gives a firm indication of the relative status of schools. For example, Mill Hill School was founded in 1807 yet, more than 60 years later, a challenge to Harrow (founded 1572) brought the withering response, 'Eton we know, and Rugby we know, but who are ye?' Of course, just as Harrow refused to interact with Mill Hill at this time, so would the latter have considered itself superior to many other schools. The various levels of interaction, therefore, cover a spectrum, with the nine great public schools at one end and minor public schools at the other.

At the beginning of the nineteenth century the public schools were at a very low ebb, and those members of the landed society who could afford to educated their sons privately. There was a deeply rooted tradition in the schools that boys should be left to govern themselves, with the consequence that mob rule prevailed and boys and masters were in a state of almost constant warfare. Rebellions were frequent. At Harrow there were uprisings in 1805 and 1808, and on the latter occasion a train of gunpowder was laid in the headmaster's house, but – thanks to the efforts of the young Lord Byron – was not ignited. Troops with fixed bayonets were called in to quell a riot at Winchester in 1818, and at Eton in the same year the desk of Keate, the headmaster, was smashed with a sledge-hammer. Keate was a notorious flogger, and took such savage reprisals that he could soon claim that 'the boys are as quiet as lambs'.

Arnold was not the first headmaster to try to end this warfare between masters and boys, but when he went to Rugby in 1828 he made an intense effort and applied certain novel remedies. He assumed autocratic control, while at the same time raising the status of his assistant masters by paying them higher salaries and associating them with him in the government of the school. He also encouraged them to take boarders, with the intention that they should take greater pastoral care of the boys while, at the same time, the school would be welded into more of a corporate unit. Boys who were considered to be deriving no benefit from the school, or who were doing positive harm, were weeded out and Arnold wrote: 'Till a man learns that the first, second, and third duty of a schoolmaster is to get rid of unpromising subjects, a great public school will never be what it might be, and what it ought to be.' Floggings were thus reduced, as was repression generally, but there was a consequent tendency to concentrate on an élite, a situation which Edward Thring, another great Victorian headmaster, found decidedly improper. In his view each boy had his merits which it was the duty of the school to seek out and foster.

Perhaps the two most notable innovations were the use which Arnold made of prefects and of the school chapel. Prefects were not his invention, but are an example of his taking an existing institution and using it to his own ends. 'You should feel,' he charged them, 'like officers in the army or navy where want of moral courage would, indeed, be thought cowardice.' When instructing them in their duties Arnold declared: 'What we must look for here is, 1st, religious and moral principles; 2ndly gentlemanly conduct; 3rdly intellectual ability.' It was this thinking which underlay the stress which he placed on the school chapel, where his sermons, simple in language and direct in message, achieved a large measure of success. It is important, however, not to exaggerate the changes which he effected there. As Kathryn Chidwick puts it: 'Before Arnold, public schools were bearpits. After Arnold, they were still bearpits, but with the bears required to put in compulsory attendance at Chapel.'[6]

Arnold had many disciples among his assistant masters and old boys, and the work of reform that he began at Rugby which continued until his death in 1842 was carried on in other schools, such as Harrow under Charles Vaughan and Marlborough under George Cotton. After Arnold's death, a great surge of new schools were founded in the public school mould, including Marlborough in 1843, Rossall in 1844, Radley in 1847, Lancing in 1848, Hurstpierpoint in 1849, Wellington in 1856 and Clifton, Haileybury and Malvern in 1862. Arnold's influence was clearly one of the factors in the renaissance of the public school, but there were others. The development of the railway greatly facilitated the transport of large numbers of boys around the country, while of greater significance still was the growing demand for this type of schooling. At first this may seem a little surprising. One might not expect that the world's leading industrial nation would demand a system of secondary education which largely spurned science and had a limited curriculum in mathematics and modern languages. But this is to ignore the order in which Arnold outlined his requirements to his new prefects; moral education came before intellectual teaching. Country gentlemen continued to require a classical education for their sons, for their vocational requirements were limited and easily satisfied. Training for the professions tended to be given 'on the job', and the classics fitted well the amateur ideal which was part of the gentlemanly mystique. In the same way, 'urban gentlemen' from the middle class wanted their sons to be made socially acceptable, and this the public schools could do. 'County gentlemen and urban "gentlemen" need not after all assimilate to one another,' writes Geoffrey Best, 'or even undergo the embarrassment of meeting.'

> Their sons could do it for them. The urban 'gentleman' would retain un-disturbed ascendancy in his own social sphere and would seek no more of the reality of county life than the make-believe landownership of the suburban villa; his sons, however, would mix with the sons of the county on the common ground of a 'public school', and come out stamped as gentlemen together. Thus did the so-called public schools (the name is a classic instance of protective coloration!) begin during our period to perform the socio-political function they have performed ever since: preserving the quasi-hereditary social elite and satisfying the status ambitions of variously talented or wealthy professional and 'business' families, by endowing their children with a sense of shared superiority to everyone else. By the eighties, the uncertainty which had hung over the use of the word gentleman . . . had given way to this certainty at least, that anyone was a gentleman who had been to a public school or who successfully concealed that he hadn't.[7]

Nor was it just the middle class who were changed, their sons acquiring a veneer of gentlemanly qualities. The aristocracy imbibed some of the middle-class earnestness and high regard for hard work, together with some of their competitive spirit, as displayed in the classroom, the examination hall and the games field. In *The Great Schools of England* (1865) Howard Staunton observed that the public schools were 'less to be considered as educational agencies, in the intellectual sense, than as social agencies'. In terms of mere mental or intellectual development, he added, they might in many respects be defective, but 'they are the theatres of athletic manners, and the training places of a gallant, generous spirit for the English gentleman'. The training which they gave was in *leadership*, and their products went on to form the country's political, military and administrative élite. Some anthropologists have seen in the public schools' accent on isolation from mother and home, together with their stern, at times spartan, regimen, many attributes of tribal initiation. Once initiated, the public schoolboy was supported by the 'old boy network', an extension into the modern era of the tradition of patronage; and to be a 'public school man' was to possess a ticket of general social acceptability at a time of rapid social change.

The intellectual and social achievements of the public schools were acknowledged by the Clarendon Commission:

> Among the services which they have rendered is undoubtedly to be reckoned the maintenance of classical literature as the staple of English education, a service which far outweighs the error of having clung to these studies too exclusively. A second, and a greater still, is the creation of a system of government and discipline for boys, the excellence of which has been universally recognised, and which is admitted to have been most important in its effects on national character and social life. It is not easy to estimate the degree to which the English people are indebted to these schools for the qualities on which they pique themselves most – for their capacity to govern others and control themselves, their aptitude for combining freedom with order, their public spirit, their vigour and manliness of character, their strong but not slavish respect for public opinion, their love of healthy sports and exercise. These schools have been the chief nurseries of our statesmen; in them, and in schools modelled after them, men of all the various classes that make up English society, destined for every profession and career, have been brought up on a footing of social equality, and have contracted the most enduring friendships, and some of the ruling habits, of their lives; and they have had perhaps the largest share in moulding the character of an English gentleman. The system, like other systems, has had its blots and imperfections; there have been times when it was at once too lax and too severe – severe in its punishments, but lax in superintendence and prevention; it has permitted, if not encouraged, some roughness, tyranny, and license; but these defects have not seriously marred its wholesome operation, and it appears to have gradually purged itself from them in a remarkable degree.

Any purging which remained to be done was largely left to the schools themselves. The Public Schools Act of 1868 was largely concerned with improving the governing bodies of the schools, although, as a corollary to making the schools a fit place for the assimilation of the middle class into the landed gentry, provisions were made to extinguish the remaining rights of local tradesmen, farmers and others to a free education for their sons at Harrow, Rugby and Shrewsbury.

As in the case of Arnold at Rugby, reforms continued to be made by influential headmasters, including Edward Thring, headmaster of Uppingham, 1853–87; H. M. Butler at Harrow, 1859–85; and F. W. Sanderson at Oundle, 1892–1922. Sanderson, both personally and educationally, stands outside the Arnoldian tradition. He was a great believer in the educational value of science, at a time when it was still held that the classics were pre-eminent in 'training the mind', and he added laboratories and workshops to his school with great success. Some of these reforms came to other schools as a result of outside pressure, especially as amateurism in the army and the civil service came under attack. Previously, amateurism had been regarded as gentlemanly, and high technical skill as rather degrading:

> The qualities valued in an officer were the qualities valued by the country gentry: courage, physical toughness, a determination to stand up for one's rights, a touchy sense of honour. Almost the only acquired skill highly regarded was horsemanship, and that was taken for granted. The notion that an officer should be a professional soldier, qualified by technical knowledge as well as the traditional virtues of a gentleman was derided and looked down upon, except in the engineers and artillery, two corps which were only rather doubtfully fit for gentlemen to serve in.[8]

As entry to the professions became competitive, however (open competition was laid down for nearly all departments of the home civil service in 1870, and the purchase of commissions in the army was abolished a year later), the schools came under pressure to revise their curricula. Harrow provided a 'modern side' in 1869, Manchester Grammar School started a Civil Service Form in the same year, and many other schools followed suit.

The 'public school spirit' influenced more than just the landed gentry and the more prosperous middle class. The ethos of the public school had a great impact on the twentieth-century state grammar school, while still humbler boys imbibed a moral and social education of sorts from the many published school stories, especially the novels of Frank Richards (centred on the imaginary Greyfriars School) and such comics as *The Magnet* and *The Gem*. Robert Roberts recalled his boyhood in Salford, a working-class area of Manchester, before the First World War:

> The standards of conduct observed by Harry Wharton and his friends at Greyfriars set social norms to which schoolboys and some young teenagers strove spasmodically to conform. Fights – ideally, at least – took place according to Greyfriars rules: no striking an opponent when he was down, no kicking, in fact no weapon but the manly fist. Through the Old School we learned to admire guts, integrity, tradition; we derided the glutton, the American and the French. We looked with contempt upon the sneak and the thief. Greyfriars gave us one moral code, life another, and a fine muddle we made of it all. I knew boys so avid for current numbers of the *Magnet* and *Gem* that they would trek on a weekday to the city railway station to catch the bulk arrival from London and buy first copies from the bookstall. One lad among us adopted a permanent jerky gait, this in his attempt to imitate Bob Cherry's 'springy, athletic stride'. Self-consciously we incorporated weird slang into our own oath-sprinkled banter – 'Yarooh!' 'My sainted aunt!' 'Leggo!' and a dozen others. The Famous Five stood for us as young knights, *sans peur et sans reproche*. Any idea that Harry Wharton could possibly have been guilty of 'certain practices' would have filled us with shame. He, like the rest, remained completely asexual, unsullied by those earthy cares of adolescence that troubled us. And that was how we wanted it.
>
> With nothing in our own school that called for love or allegiance, Greyfriars became for some of us our true Alma Mater, to whom we felt bound by a dreamlike loyalty. The 'mouldering pile', one came to believe, had real existence: of that boys assured one another. We placed it vaguely in the southern counties – somewhere between Winchester and Harrow. It came as a curious shock to one who revered the Old School when it dawned upon him that he himself was a typical sample of the 'low cads' so despised by all at Greyfriars. Class consciousness had broken through at last. Over the years these simple tales conditioned the thought of a whole generation of boys. The public school ethos, distorted into myth and sold among us weekly in penny numbers, for good or ill, set ideals and standards. This our own tutors, religious and secular, had signally failed to do. In the final estimate it may well be found that Frank Richards during the first quarter of the twentieth century had more influence on the mind and outlook of young working-class England than any other single person, not excluding Baden-Powell.[9]

The ancient universities of Oxford and Cambridge performed a similar socialising function to that of the public schools, from which the majority of the under-graduates came. At the time of the Clarendon Commission's Report in 1864, about one-third of the Oxford undergraduates came from the nine great schools, as did just over a fifth at Cambridge. The seeker after mere intellectual improvement might have done better to go to one of the Scottish universities (and many Englishmen did); for John Stuart Mill wrote in 1867: 'Youths come to the Scottish universities ignorant, and are there taught. The majority of those who come to the English universities come still more ignorant, and ignorant they go away.' But they went away with something different, and more valuable, perhaps, than knowledge – they went away with a further endorsement of their status as gentlemen; for throughout most of the nineteenth century the universities of Oxford and Cambridge acted as finishing schools for young landed gentlemen.

The exclusiveness of the ancient universities was maintained by their expense. 'On the whole,' commented the Royal Commission on Oxford University, in its report of 1852, 'we believe that a parent, who, after supplying his son with clothes and supporting him at home during the vacations, has paid for him during the University course not more than £600, and is not called upon to discharge debts at its close, has reason to congratulate himself.' Taine observed that many young men had £500 a year or more to spend and, moreover, got credit from tradesmen. The educative influence of the hunting field was as much sought after by some as that of the lecture room. The Commissioners reported:

> Driving, riding, and hunting are also causes of great expense. The University regulation, which imposes a heavy fine on those who are found driving, unless they have obtained permission from an officer of their College and one of the Proctors, is more or less enforced, and restrains the practice to some extent. Undergraduates are forbidden by Statute to keep horses without the sanction of the Head of their college; a rule which, however, is only partially enforced, and may be easily evaded by the use of hired horses. Of these amusements the most expensive is hunting. It seldom costs less than four guineas a day. Some of those who indulge in it are accustomed to it at home, and can afford it; and on this ground, as well as on the supposition that it often takes the place of worse pursuits, it is in several Colleges overlooked or permitted.[10]

To the social exclusiveness was added a religious one. The colleges were originally religious foundations, and the proportion of future clergy among the undergraduates high. Twelve of the oarsmen who rowed in the first Oxford and Cambridge boat race in 1829 became Anglican clergymen, two of them rising to be bishops, and two deans. Dissenters were effectively excluded by religious tests, which were especially severe at Oxford. There, every undergraduate had to subscribe to the Thirty-nine Articles before he matriculated (a point to which Wesleyans did not object), whereas at Cambridge a man might enter as an undergraduate, but must declare himself a member of the established Church before he took his degree. In 1834 the House of Commons passed a bill enabling dissenters to graduate, but it was thrown out by the Lords, and the religious tests were not finally abolished until 1871. However, dissenters came to be served by the University of London, which received its charter in 1836. Its curriculum was much wider than that of the ancient universities (and of Durham University, which was modelled on them and received its charter in the same year) and included a new principle – training for a specific career, such as medicine, law and engineering.

Like the public schools, the ancient universities reformed themselves from within, the process proceeding faster at Cambridge than at Oxford, which for 10 years was torn by religious agitation. Royal Commissions of 1850–52 and acts of Parliament of 1854 and 1856 accelerated the process, but in essence they remained as they had been before – places providing a liberal but not a professional education for gentlemen.

Some commentators argue that the enormous prestige of the public schools and ancient universities, with their stress on aristocratic values and their contempt for commerce and industry, played a significant role in Britain's eventual industrial decline. This is the view of Martin J. Wiener:

> Revivified public schools and ancient universities furnished the re-formed and cohesive English elite with a way of life and an outlook that gave little attention or status to industrial pursuits. This development set England apart from its emerging rivals, for in neither the United States nor Germany did the educational system encourage a comparable retreat from business and industry. In education, as in the composition and character of its elite, later-Victorian England marked out its own path, foreshadowing its twentieth-century achievements and difficulties.[11]

Wiener's interpretation has been challenged, however. W. D. Rubinstein, for example, has calculated that more than one-quarter of boys who entered Rugby School in 1870 went into manufacturing or trade (rising to a third if those who pursued business careers abroad are included). A similar proportion of Old Harrovians went into business. Even heavy industry acquired managers from the landed classes. Charlotte Erickson calculated that one in four of British steel manufacturers active between 1865 and 1953 were the sons of landowners and professionals. The cultural background to Britain's late nineteenth-century economic retardation is still a matter of controversy, and is taken up again in Chapter 11.

Farmers

Although a great many landowners farmed some of their land – some enthusiasts possessing 'model farms' employing the latest techniques – most of Britain's agricultural land was farmed by tenants. These, together with small owner-occupiers, made up the second tier of the landed interest.

In the nineteenth century only a little over one-tenth of the land was farmed by owner-occupiers; and even if he owned some land the farmer often rented a further amount, for it rarely paid him to put money into this resource when he could use it more profitably to buy new equipment or to extend the scale of his operations. Farms varied in size. In 1851 the average for England and Wales was 115 acres (1 acre is equal to 0.4 hectare), and over two-thirds of the 215,000 farms at that date had fewer than 100 acres. There were, however, a substantial number of much larger farms, including 16,840 of 300 acres or more, and around 800 of more than 1,000 acres, most of which were in areas of sheep or corn husbandry. Many of the smaller farms were in dairying, and in capital-intensive sectors of agriculture such as market gardens, orchards and hop gardens, which secured a good income to their occupiers. The pattern of land-holding hardly changed over the second half of the nineteenth century, for while there was some amalgamation of small farms in the grain-growing and stock-breeding regions, the development of small market gardens was a trend in the opposite direction. There was, however, an increase in owner-occupiers from the beginning of the twentieth century, when land sales increased (as has been mentioned). From a low point in the late-nineteenth century, when owner-occupiers possessed about one-seventh of the total acreage, the proportion rose to a third by the 1920s, an unprecedented level.

The most common form of tenure was the annual agreement, or a tenancy at will on six months' notice. Leases were generally confined to the larger farms, for both landlords and tenants had a distrust of long-term agreements which took no account of fluctuations in markets and prices. Despite this, little insecurity resulted. Large tenants were hard to replace, while landlords felt responsible to smaller tenants so long as they cultivated the land reasonably well, and were not disrespectful.

In some respects tenant farmers filled an uneasy position in the rural social system. They often shared in the pleasures of the hunting field with the landed proprietors, but they took little part in running local affairs. They might, it is true, serve as churchwardens or guardians of the poor, but a position on the Justices' Bench was socially (and in some cases educationally) beyond them. Nor did they have the same political voice as landowners. It was rare for a farmer to have a seat in Parliament, and it was not until 1908 that their independent pressure group, the National Farmers' Union, was formed.

In the nineteenth century, pressure might be brought to bear on tenants to make them conform to their landlord's political views. For example, the Duke of Newcastle evicted 200 residents of Newark who in 1829 failed to vote for his parliamentary candidate. 'Have I not a right to do what I like with my own?' he asked, invoking *Matthew 20:15*. The 1832 Reform Act gave the vote to tenant farmers paying more than £50 a year in rent, but it was a brave man − before the introduction of the secret ballot in 1872 − who would vote against his landlord's declared wishes. Intimidation became a burning issue later in the century, particularly in Wales, as men became more politically aware; and even after the introduction of the secret ballot, tenants dared not openly support a candidate of a different political hue from that of their landlord. In 1873, for example, George Hope, a notable farmer who (like his father and grandfather before him) farmed Fenton Barnes in East Lothian, found his lease was not renewed because eight years previously he had stood as a Liberal candidate against Lord Elcho, a friend of his landlord.

The relationship between landlord and tenant was a strong, personal one, bearing many of the features, both good and bad, of a feudal society. In Trollope's novel, *The Vicar of Bullhampton*, written in 1869–70, appears the Marquess of Trowbridge, whose relations with his tenants are thus described:

> The Marquis's people were all expected to vote for his candidates, and would soon have ceased to be the Marquis's people had they failed to do so. They were constrained, also, in many respects, by the terms of their very short leases. They could not kill a head of game on their farms. They could not sell their own hay off the land, nor, indeed, any produce other than their corn or cattle. They were compelled to crop their land in certain rotation; and could take no other lands than those held under the Marquis without his leave. In return for all this, they became the Marquis's people. Each tenant shook hands with the Marquis perhaps once in three years; and twice a year was allowed to get drunk at the Marquis's expense − if such was his taste − provided that he had paid his rent. If the duties were heavy, the privileges were great. So the Marquis himself felt; and he knew that a mantle of security, of a certain thickness, was spread upon the shoulders of each of his people by reason of the tenure which bound them together.

This 'feudal relationship' was not without its advantages to the tenant, as W. Bence Jones pointed out in an article in *The Nineteenth Century* in 1882, during the agricultural depression. Many landlords remitted rent during these hard times, reflecting a kindness and goodwill not often duly recognised (although, of course, it would have been hard to find alternative tenants). But if farming were to be simply a business, as many tenant farmers wished, such consideration would be neither expected nor forthcoming. 'Tenants,' declared Bence Jones, 'cannot have the advantages arising from the right of free contract, and the advantages arising from feudalism too. It must be either one thing or the other.'

The agricultural labourer

The town-dweller, now as in the past, may be apt to suppose that all agricultural workers are the same, and he or she often has in mind a crude caricature of the country-dweller. Just how crude this stereotype could be was pointed out by Thomas Hardy in an article on the Dorsetshire labourer, written in 1883:

> When we arrive at the farm-labouring community we find it to be seriously personified by the pitiable picture known as Hodge; not only so, but the community is assumed to be a uniform collection of concrete Hodges.
>   This supposed real but highly conventional Hodge is a degraded being of uncouth manner and aspect, stolid understanding, and snail-like movement. His speech is such a chaotic corruption of regular language that few persons of progressive aims consider it worth while to enquire what views, if any, of life, of nature, or of society are conveyed in these utterances. Hodge hangs his head or looks sheepish when spoken to, and thinks Lunnon a place paved with gold. Misery and fever lurk in his cottage, while, to paraphrase the words of a recent writer on the labouring classes, in his future there are only the workhouse and the grave. He hardly dares to think at all . . .

But, says Hardy, if the well-off city-dweller could live with a farm labourer for six months, he would discover no 'typical Hodge', but would find a collection of distinct individuals:

> Six months pass, and our gentleman leaves the cottage, bidding his friends good-bye with genuine regret. The great change in his perception is that Hodge, the dull, unvarying, joyless one, has ceased to exist for him. He has become disintegrated into a number of dissimilar fellow-creatures, men of many minds, infinite in difference . . . Dick the carter, Bob the shepherd, and Sam the ploughman, are, it is true, alike in the narrowness of their means and their general open-air life; but they cannot be rolled together into such a Hodge as he dreamt of, by any possible enchantment.[12]

The condition of the agricultural labourer also showed marked regional differences, and was generally worst in those areas where farming was the sole occupation, with little or no industry to compete for labour and thereby raise wages. In 1850 James Caird demonstrated this with a comparison throughout the country (Table 3.2).

'The influence of manufacturing enterprise,' wrote Caird, 'is thus seen to add 37 per cent to the wages of the agricultural labourers of the Northern counties, as compared with those of the South.' The line was distinctly drawn at that point where coal ceased to be found, to the south of which only one county – Sussex – showed wages reaching 10s a week; this exception being due, claimed Caird, to the additional demand for labour afforded by Brighton and other watering places along the coast.

The standard of living of farm labourers was higher in the north. Cheap coal was more readily available, which enabled labourers to keep their cottages warmer and

Table 3.2   The rate of agricultural wages, 1850–51

Midland and western counties	Weekly wages		East and south coast counties	Weekly wages	
Northern counties					
	s	d		s	d
Cumberland	13	0	Northumberland	11	0
Lancashire	13	6	Durham	11	0
West Riding	14	0	North Riding	11	0
Cheshire	12	0	East Riding	12	0
Derby	11	0	Lincoln	10	0
Nottingham	10	0			
Stafford	9	6			
Southern counties					
Warwick	8	6	Norfolk	8	6
Northampton	9	0	Suffolk	7	0
Bucks	8	6	Huntingdon	8	6
Oxford	9	0	Cambridge	7	6
Gloucester	7	0	Bedford	9	0
North Wilts	7	6	Hertford	9	0
Devon	8	6	Essex	8	0
			Berks	7	6
			Surrey	9	6
			Sussex	10	6
			Hants	9	0
			South Wilts	7	0
			Dorset	7	6
Average of west	10	0	Average of east	9	1
Average of all northern counties				11	6
Average of all southern counties				8	5
Average over the whole				9	6

Source: James Caird, *English Agriculture in 1850–51*, 1852 (Cass, 1967) p. 512.

allowed them to prepare more hot, cooked food. Diet tended to be better, and more milk was drunk. Improved diet made greater productivity possible, and it may be that part of the regional difference in wage rates arose from this. It was said that 'a Lancashire workman at half-a-crown a day is not dearer than most Welsh labourers at a shilling', and at the turn of the twentieth century it was claimed that the men of the north of England constituted 'a finer race, physically and intellectually, than the Southerner . . . because good feeding for generations has done much for them in body and in brain'.

There were further important differences between the north and the south; northern farmers tended to hire their labourers on an annual basis, rather than from week to week. Thus the Northumberland labourer, for example, was assured a guaranteed wage, and was normally paid even when he was sick or unable to work because of bad weather. It was quite usual for the entire family to be hired in this way, thus raising family income considerably, and making the lot of the northern labourer more comfortable than that of his southern counterpart. It is significant that the Swing riots of the early 1830s were largely confined to the south of England,

and when agricultural trade unionism developed during the 1870s, it made little headway in the north.

The prosperity which farmers enjoyed during the Napoleonic Wars was not, by and large, extended to the labourers, and while the former class strove to acquire the trappings of the gentry, the latter sank to new depths of misery. Hitherto many farm servants had lived in the farmer's household, but the widening social gap led to a decline of 'living-in', especially in the south. While the practice lingered in the north of England and in Scotland, social differentiation led to farm servants being moved out into bothies (small, roughly built outhouses), where they slept and ate by themselves. Farmers' wives were relieved from a certain amount of inconvenience, while their husbands found it cheaper to oblige labourers to fend for themselves from their wages.

As the war ended 400,000 servicemen were demobilised, thus adding to the rural surplus of labour, and the explosiveness of the situation was shown by the riots in East Anglia in 1816. Bands of labourers, sometimes several hundred strong, took to firing farmhouses, barns and ricks. Armed with weighted staves, and under a banner inscribed 'Bread or Blood', they terrorised the countryside, demanding cheaper bread and meat and extorting money. The hanging of five starving rioters and the imprisonment or transportation of many more discouraged similar outbreaks – but only for a time.

It is often alleged that the impoverishment of the farm labourer was exacerbated by the working of the Old Poor Law; in particular, by the Speenhamland system of allowances, and by the settlement system. It was in 1795 that the Berkshire Justices of the Peace, meeting at Speenhamland, near Newbury, attempted to deal humanely with the rising tide of pauperism and the threat of famine. They rejected the expedient of a minimum wage, and decided instead to subsidise low wages out of the poor rates in cases where the labourer's income fell below subsistence level, either because he had too many children to support, or because the price of bread was too high. A sliding scale of allowances was introduced which, although never given the force of law, was soon widely adopted throughout the country, with the exception of the extreme north and west. The outcome was unanticipated, for farmers found that by lowering wages they could throw some of the burden of their wage bill on to the parish. Likewise, the labourer had little incentive to exert himself, for his income was pegged to a subsistence level; there were also allegations that the system placed a bounty on children, legitimate or otherwise.

Poor rates certainly rose at an incredible pace. One Buckinghamshire village reported in 1822 that its expenditure on poor relief was eight times the sum it had been in 1795. In the Weald of Sussex, rent and poor rate exactly changed places between 1792 and 1833; rent at the earlier date was 8s an acre and poor rate 4s, while at the latter date rent was 4s an acre and poor rate 8s. However, more recent interpretations tend to see the heavy Poor Law expenditure as a consequence of low wages and unemployment rather than the cause, and attention is focused on the large stagnant pool of surplus labour and the high level of structural and seasonal unemployment.

Caird's table of wage rates indicates the importance of alternative forms of employment in fixing agricultural wages. The local economy of the south was almost entirely dependent on farming, and underemployment was constant except, perhaps, at the height of the harvest. There were wide seasonal variations in the demand for labour. Threshing accounted for perhaps a quarter of the entire annual labour requirement of a farm, and the task went on throughout November, December and January, if not longer. These winter months, when the need for fuel, food and clothing was greatest, were the time of greatest burden to the men. The introduction of threshing machines – slowly at first, as hand labour with the flail was so cheap – enabled farmers to stand off more men at their time of greatest need. It is not difficult to see why the machines were so hated by the labourers.

It is harder, perhaps, to understand why more labourers should not have migrated from those areas of the south where there was a labour surplus, to the north of England where there was an industrial demand for labour. For this, the Law of Settlement has traditionally been blamed, whereby a labourer could only receive poor relief in the parish in which he was 'settled', and to which he was required to be returned if he should become destitute. There were certainly many contemporary voices declaring the law to be a hindrance to migration. Once again, however, opinions have changed, and it is now believed that the laws were never applied as severely as they might have been. The parochialism of the average farm labourer no doubt proved a stronger obstacle to mobility than any legal impediment.

The opportunities for self-defence or protest open to the labourer were few, but there were some. The very existence of a surplus of labour made mere protests against wage cuts, or demands for higher wages, futile – unless accompanied by a mass movement. The labourer could fall back on the Poor Law, which was fast sinking into chaos; or he could turn to crime, either as a means of social protest or as a means of obtaining food. As Harry Hopkins has put it: 'The labourer, knocking over a hare for the pot, was not certainly making a declaration of the rights of man, and yet might feel more of a man for having done so.'[13] Cobbett once enquired of a young Surrey labourer how he managed to survive on the half-crown dole which he received from the parish for breaking stones. 'I poach,' was the reply. 'It is better to be hanged than starved to death.' Many countrymen saw no sin in poaching, and in some years nearly two-thirds of all convictions before the courts were under the game laws. Poaching represented a blow against the farmer and the landowner; if such blows failed to achieve their end, then outright terrorism might. Hence the labourer was led to arson and machine-breaking.

It is not altogether clear why the Swing revolt should have come in that particular year. The worsening economic conditions of the previous two years no doubt had something to do with it, as may have the revolution in France and the political tension at home. Whatever the cause, the revolt began in Kent in the summer of 1830, and exploded like a train of gunpowder throughout the southern and eastern counties in the following months. The pattern of events varied from district to district. In some areas the stress was on wages and allowances; in others labourers resorted to the torch and sledge-hammer. A total of 387 threshing and 26 other agricultural machines were destroyed in 22 counties between August 1830 and September 1832. The total damage is difficult to assess, but a figure of £100,000 has been suggested for damage caused by arson, and £20,000 for agricultural and other machinery destroyed.

The revolt was a remarkably disciplined affair, and many Swing bands appointed officers such as treasurers and 'captains', no doubt drawing on friendly society experience. Contemporaries were surprised at the number of 'respectable' men involved. More than half of those convicted were married, and many were in their middle and late twenties. The rioters were not headstrong youths on the rampage. There is little evidence that outside agitators played a crucial part, and there was no revolutionary threat to the social order. Like the Luddites, the farm labourers sought the restitution of lost rights, customary wages and poor relief, and the removal of threatening mechanical innovations.

The rising was not without results. Wages were temporarily raised in the southern counties, although the state of the labour market made permanent improvement impossible. More significantly, the spread of threshing machines was held up; and as late as 1843 it was claimed that in many farming districts of the south the threshing machine could not be used, 'owing to the destructive vengeance with which the labourers resisted its introduction'.

By that date, however, 19 labourers had swung from the gallows and nearly 500 more had been wrenched from their families and transported 12,000 miles away to Australia, with virtually no hope of ever returning. In subsequent years others were to follow, the more enterprising as emigrants, the more desperate as fellow-transportees. For those who remained on the land there was continuing bitterness and hatred. 'What was once the most stable working-class group has now been drawn into the revolutionary movement,' wrote Engels in 1844. 'What do my readers think of this state of affairs in the peaceful, idyllic English countryside? Is this social war or is it not?' Many historians would agree that it was. A.J. Peacock writes:

> Until the appearance of efficient police forces halfway through the century, the labourer had, as the town dweller did not have, ample means of squaring his scores with his employer. The labourer was adept at slacking in the most effective and undetectable ways. More serious, he could steal his employer's fruit, corn or game almost with impunity. Stacks could be fired, farm buildings lit, animals maimed, fences destroyed, banks breached. This went on continuously in rural England, a check on the farmers without a doubt, a psychological release for the labourer for certain. Usually vengeance of this kind would be wreaked, as far as one can tell, by individuals or small groups. Only when conditions became really overpowering, as in 1816 or the early 1830s, did the labourers unite on a grand scale; then they appear in the pages of the history books. But they appeared all the time on the pages of the local press. The usually immovable, completely cowed, soporific Hodge is a figment of imagination – at least in East Anglia. He protested all the time, and most of the time very effectively indeed.
>
> Very rarely, again except where conditions were so bad that villages and villagers united, were the rural 'criminals' caught, and so Home Office, Treasury Solicitors and Assize papers reveal little about what went on in the 'peaceful', normal years of the nineteenth century.[14]

The labourer had much to protest about, over and above the low level of wages. Hours of work were long, and he was out in all weathers. In the 1840s a 15-year-old ploughboy was interviewed by Alexander Somerville, one of the writers working for the Anti-Corn Law League. The lad slept in a loft where the sheets were changed once a year, and he never had a fire. Somerville asked him if he did not find his bed disagreeable, to which the ploughboy replied:

> Do I! I bees too sleepy. I never knows nought of it, only that I has to get up afore I be awake, and never get into it afore I be a'most asleep. I be up at four, and ben't done work afore eight at night.

Although he toiled for such long hours producing food, the agricultural labourer's own diet was monotonous and in many respects inadequate. Improved railway communication meant that farmers often found it more convenient and profitable to transport produce, especially dairy products, in bulk to the towns, rather than letting their men have it in small quantities. With the exception of bacon, meat was very seldom eaten, unless it was from diseased animals which the farmer killed and sold cheaply to his labourers. Some farmers forbade pig-keeping for fear that their men would steal grain for food, but vast numbers of labourers kept pigs, subscribing to what F. G. Heath described as a 'live savings bank'.

Much rural housing, seemingly so picturesque, was in reality as bad as anything to be found in the towns; and even in these foul dwellings the labourer frequently had no security of tenure, for many cottages were 'tied'. If a man lost his job, he might be evicted. The problem of eviction became acute during the agitation of the 1870s. Joseph Arch, the farm-workers' leader, gave an example drawn from a district only seven miles from his own house in Warwickshire; a new junction railway was being built through the district and the company offered young, strong men from 3s 6d to 3s 10d a day for work on the line. Many men who were at work on the land for 11s a week left their jobs, but were warned that if they refused to return to work for 12s, they would be evicted from their cottages.

From the 1850s the lot of the farm worker improved, though less in the form of direct spending power than in fringe benefits such as allotment gardens, better cottages on the larger estates, and amenities such as the provision of village schools and reading-rooms. The gains were real, if meagre. The labourer's appetite for improvement was whetted, and the 'Revolt of the Field', as the movement of the 1870s was called, may be another example of the 'revolution of rising expectations', that concept to which reference was made in the last chapter. The Revolt of the Field was the first large-scale and overt outburst of agrarian discontent since the riots of 1830. Although there were some similarities between the two movements, in the main they were very different. The movement of the 1870s was part of a general trade union movement of the time, and in fact drew much help from urban unions. The leaders were known men, no longer using sinister pseudonyms such as 'Captain Swing', and discontent was expressed in strikes rather than by the destruction of property. The Revolt of the Field was more widespread than the Swing riots, and there was better communication between the areas of discontent. Cheap newspapers helped. One Dorset MP remarked in 1872: 'You can't suppose those newspapers are not read; and the people see full well that the wages of mechanics and artisans in different towns have been raised considerably.' Joseph Arch's National Agricultural Labourers' Union (NALU) soon produced its own weekly journal, the *Labourers' Union Chronicle*, which claimed a circulation of 35,000 by 1873. In addition to the press, however, the railway and the penny post (both post-'Swing') helped the leaders to keep tighter control.

The NALU was formed in 1872, and taking non-affiliated unions into account, it had a membership of around 150,000 at its peak. The labourers enjoyed some initial successes; there was a general rise in wages and a widespread reduction in working hours, but the farmers soon rallied. The power of the union was broken by a lock-out in 1874. The labourers had counted on being indispensable, at least during the harvest. However, by a greater use of machinery and by relying on loyal non-unionists and unskilled female, child and town workers, the farmers coped. A special payment – 'harvest money' – was customarily paid to labourers for this essential work, and the lump sum was traditionally used for the purchase of boots and clothing. This loss proved disastrous, and eviction from their tied cottages threatened many.

Union numbers declined after the lock-out and with the onset of the agricultural depression, when many farmers economised by abandoning labour-intensive methods. There was rivalry between the unions, and they did not always pursue intelligent policies; the Kentish union, for example, broke up when its leader foolishly brought the men out on strike in the autumn, when the demand for agricultural labour was at its lowest. A number of small unions disappeared altogether, and by 1881 the NALU had shrunk to 15,000 members. Only in Norfolk did it retain any vitality, and in that county the newly enfranchised labourers returned Arch to Parliament in 1885.

Many men left the land. The census of 1901 recorded rather more than 1 million men and boys employed in agriculture in England and Wales and 165,000 in Scotland, as against 1.5 million and 232,000, 50 years earlier. The proportion of occupied males employed in agriculture fell from about a quarter in 1851 to about 17 per cent in 1881 and barely 12 per cent in 1901.

The decline was due both to demand and supply factors. The introduction of machines reduced the demand for labour, mechanisation of threshing alone accounting for the loss of winter work for as many as 200,000 workers. Laying down to grass also economised labour, one contemporary estimate being that 2 million acres (800,000 hectares) of arable lost between 1881 and 1901 threw out of work 60,000–80,000 labourers. On the other hand, many farm workers experienced a growing desire to leave the land, which seemed to offer little hope for an improved standard of living. Many of the best men migrated to the towns, or emigrated to the colonies, where their energies could find wider scope.

The Church in the countryside

One place in which landowners, farmers and labourers might meet together was the parish church, although social distinctions were to be found even there. If the squire was one pillar of the rural community, the parson was the other. In *Lark Rise to Candleford*, Flora Thompson described the vicar of a parish in the north-east corner of Oxfordshire in the 1880s:

> Mr Coulsdon preached to his poorer parishioners contentment with their divinely appointed lot in life and submission to the established order of earthly things. To the rich, the responsibilities of their position and their obligations in the way of charity. Being rich and highly placed in the little community and genuinely loving a country life, he himself naturally saw nothing wrong in the social order, and, being of a generous nature, the duty of helping the poor and afflicted was also a pleasure to him.[15]

Poverty was no bar to the acceptance of the Anglican (but not the Noncon-formist) clergy into the upper ranks of rural society. When, in Trollope's novel, *The Last Chronicle of Barset* (1867), Archdeacon Grantly greeted the battered perpetual curate of Hogglestock in his library, he was able to say, despite his visitor's worn clothes and boots: 'We stand on the only perfect level on which such men can meet each other. We are both gentlemen.' Admittedly, the poor curate was a graduate of Oxford University, and his degree represented the hallmark of a gentleman; indeed, such a degree was deemed sufficient qualification for ordination. Theological training was rudimentary; not until 1838–9 was a small seminary attached to the cathedral at Wells, while Cuddesdon, the first theological college with a corporate life, was not opened till 1854.

There were institutional links between landownership and the Church, through the power of patronage, which grew out of a world in which the squire owned the parish, perhaps built the church, and needed a clergyman of whom he approved; he thus retained the right (known as an advowson) to appoint to the vacant benefice. In 1831, 7,268 out of a total of 11,342 livings in England and Wales were in the hands of private patrons. Church patronage could be used to secure a living for a younger son, debarred by the land laws from inheriting a portion of the estate, or it could be used to reward friends. The advowson could also be sold, which gave it a certain investment value. Until 1898, when Parliament passed the Benefices Act, advowsons were offered at auction through the columns of the *Ecclesiastical Gazette*, and numerous other associated malpractices continued. That act did not abolish church patronage, however (although it was abolished in the Church of Scotland in 1874), and the right still exists. In the late 1960s approximately 2,300 out of a total of 12,000 livings remained in private hands, and although about 800 were held by peers and their children, and at least 70 per cent of the remainder by members of the landed gentry, the noble patrons now had some strange associates. Smiths Potato Estates, the crisp manufacturers, appointed to one living, while Cornish Manures Ltd shared the right with a bishop.

Had private patronage been totally discreditable it would no doubt have been abolished in the nineteenth century. There were, however, more serious abuses in the Church of England, including pluralism and non-residence. Of 10,533 benefices returned in 1827, the incumbents of only 4,413 were resident; and although this excludes many clergymen who lived near their church but outside the legal bounds of the parish, it reflects a system which had many unhealthy characteristics. The remuneration of curates, paid to perform the duties of absentee incumbents, was often pitifully low. They might expect £100 a year, but many were offered less; a respectable butler or coachman, by comparison, would hardly accept less than £70 a year unless board and lodging were added. A curate might also have to wait a considerable time before acquiring an incumbency of his own. In the diocese of Exeter in 1866, 68 clergymen remained curates on an income of £100, though all had served at least 15 years, and some up to 50 years.

Much attention was focused on these abuses in the early 1830s. A short poem appeared in *The Times* in 1832, in which St Jerome returned to earth and made a tour of inspection of the Church of England. He tried in vain to find Dr Hodgson – Dean of Carlisle, rector of St George's, Hanover Square, and holder of two other livings – for wherever the saint looked, the reverend gentleman was always at *another* of his residences. He went to see Bishop van Mildert of Durham:

> He found that pious soul van Mildert
> Much with his money-bags bewildered.

Others, too, were bewildered at the finances of Durham, considered the most scandalous of all the cathedrals. Each of the 12 canons received about £3,000 a year, while The Revd Francis Egerton, eighth Earl of Bridgewater, held a prebend for 49 years while living in Paris. It was a hurried attempt to put the cathedral endowments to good use before they were confiscated which led to the chapter resolving to establish a university, which they did in the same year, 1832.

Many of the worst abuses of the Church were remedied later in the decade. Peel established an Ecclesiastical Duties and Revenues Commission in 1835, which produced its report in the following year, when it was reconstituted as the Ecclesiastical Commission, a permanent body charged with reform of the structure of the Church. Among these reforms were the equalising of bishops' revenues (1836); placing severe restrictions on pluralism (1838); and suppressing excess revenues of cathedrals for redistribution to those of greater need (1840). These were not the only changes which were made. The Tithe Commutation Act of 1836 abolished tithes in kind, substituting a money payment based on the average price of grain over the preceding seven years. The Registration Act of the same year tackled a grievance of dissenters by putting the work of registering births, marriages and deaths in the hands of a civil official instead of the incumbent; and the Dissenters' Marriage Act of 1838 ended the obligation of Nonconformists to marry in the parish church.

As the abuses of the Church of England were gradually tackled, so the quality of the clergy improved. In the 1830s and earlier, many gentlemen looked on holy orders as the most attractive of the professions. It afforded leisure, social standing, a life of reasonable comfort and the chance of preferment. By the 1860s a different attitude prevailed, and parochial responsibilities were taken more seriously. The number of clergy sitting alongside the squire on the bench fell. In 1816, 36.8 per cent of the magistrates for Oxfordshire were clergymen; in 1827, 27 per cent; and in 1851, 21 per cent. However, because the position of magistrate was a life office, the number of clerical Justices fell only slowly in response to critical pressure from the 1830s onwards. The rapid decline in clerical magistrates did not set in until after 1873 when two local rectors, sitting on the bench at Chipping Norton, sent 16 women to prison for intimidating blackleg labourers during the farm-workers' strike. By 1906 there were only about 32 clerical magistrates left.

It was not easy for a country clergyman to defy the local landowners, and dissension between parson and squire could tear a village apart. A gamekeeper in Charles Kingsley's novel, *Yeast*, could appreciate how carefully the parson had to treat the squire: 'How else are they to get a farthing for schools, or coal-subscriptions, or lying-in societies, or lending libraries, or penny clubs? If they spoke their minds to the great ones, sir, how could they keep the parish together?' Kingsley himself showed great zeal in the 1840s when he was incumbent of Eversley in Hampshire. He founded coal and shoe clubs, a loan fund and a maternal society, and started adult classes and a lending library.

Another radical clergyman was Canon Edward Girdlestone who, in 1862, moved from a parish in Lancashire to become Vicar of Halberton, a small village in North Devon. He was filled with horror at the contrast between the comparatively well-paid labourers in the north and those he found in his new parish, subsisting on 7–8s a week. He tried remonstrating with the farmers, but to little effect, and during the cattle plague of 1866 preached on the text, 'Behold the hand of the Lord is upon thy cattle', declaring that the plague was a judgement on the farmers for the mistreatment of their men. Bitter fury was provoked, and many of the farmers left the parish church for the nearest Nonconformist chapel. Girdlestone decided that only by draining of the surplus labour could wages be made to rise, and he wrote to *The Times*, describing the men's condition and asking for offers of work elsewhere. The response was considerable, and he set to work organising a regular system of migration from Devon to farms in the north of England. Between 1866 and 1872, when he left Halberton, Girdlestone assisted between 400 and 500 men, many with their families, to move from this and the neighbouring villages. Once the movement started it continued under its own momentum, even after he left. During those years his own lot was one of subjection to every kind of vilification and abuse, not only from the farmers, but from local squires and fellow clergy. His greatest service, perhaps, was in gaining publicity for the plight of the farm workers so that when, in the early 1870s, they began to help themselves, there was no lack of informed support from other sections of the community.

In spite of the efforts of men like Kingsley and Girdlestone, many labourers remained aloof towards the Church, even though the view that church-going was more regular in the countryside than the towns appears to be substantially true. It is not easy to make generalisations, because figures are hard to come by. Only once, in 1851, was an attempt made to secure national statistics of church-going. The religious census, which was taken on Sunday, 30 March, revealed that about 60 per cent of possible worshippers had attended church or chapel on that day. Such an attendance figure may seem impressive to us, but at the time it caused great concern and dismay.

The Church of England was shocked to discover that it commanded only about one-half of the practising Christians of England and Wales, its strength being in the rural south-east where its hold had been secure since early times. In Wales, which had a high level of church- and chapel-going, the Anglicans could claim fewer than one-fifth of attendances. Some supporters of the Church of England cried foul, declaring for example, that a number of chapels had billed special, popular sermons in order to boost the returns. Some even claimed that bad weather had disrupted Anglican attendance, conveniently ignoring the fact that it rained on Nonconformists too. The trend of church-going after this mid-century stock-taking is somewhat conjectural. Owen Chadwick claims: 'The country churches were not empty on a Sunday. But they were less full. The clergy, at least, believed that they were less full, and we have small reason to doubt.' Nevertheless, there was much variety from village to village, and a fine pastor could still draw in the congregation.

There was also regional variation in the strength of Nonconformity which, though largely an urban religion, was strong in places like Cornwall, Lincolnshire and the northern counties. Its fastness, however, was Wales, where the chapel catered more than the church for Welsh cultural identity and language. The pattern of land-ownership accounts for some local variation. The Established Church tended to be strongest where there was a single large landowner, while Nonconformity thrived where there were many small freeholders, and where people lived in scattered and isolated communities less subject to landlord dominance. On the whole it does not appear that the chapel gained where the church lost. Some, like Joseph Arch, did come to reject the social order apparent in the parish church, and found the chapel both socially and spiritually less remote. He wrote in his autobiography:

> I can remember when the squire and the other local magnates used to sit in state in the centre of the aisle. They did not, if you please, like the look of the agricultural labourers. Hodge sat too near them, and even in his Sunday best he was an offence to their eyes. They also objected to Hodge looking at them, so they had curtains put up to hide them from the vulgar gaze. And yet, while all this was going on, while the poor had to bear with such high-handed dealings, people wondered why the Church had lost its hold, and continued to lose its hold, on the labourers in the country districts . . . First, up walked the squire to the communion rails; the farmers went up next; then up went the tradesmen, the shopkeepers, the wheelwright, and the blacksmith; and then, the very last of all, went the poor agricultural labourers in their smock frocks. They walked up by themselves; nobody else knelt with them; it was as if they were unclean . . . I ran home and told my mother what I had seen, and I wanted to know why my father was not as good in the eyes of God as the squire, and why the poor should be forced to come up last of all to the table of the Lord.

The social stratification which Arch observed in the order of taking communion was also evident in the distribution of pews. Indeed, Richard Gough's classic local study, *The History of Myddle* (a village in north Shropshire) written between 1700 and 1706, was structured around the arrangement of pews in the church, where the gentry were placed at the front, the yeomen farmers in the middle and the cottagers at the rear. The renting of pews provided a source of church income until late in the nineteenth century, and while the practice proved highly controversial among churchmen, it proved very resistant to change.

While many labourers no doubt felt themselves unwelcome in the church, many more probably found that Sunday simply gave them a chance to rest from their arduous labour, gossip with friends, or work on their gardens or allotments. Richard

Jefferies captured this mood in his essay, 'A modern country curate', published in his book, *Hodge and his Masters* (1880):

> Some few young cottage people who had good voices, and liked to use them, naturally now went to church. So did the old women and men, who had an eye to charity. But the strong, sturdy men, the carters and shepherds stood aloof; the bulk and backbone of the agricultural labouring population were not in the least affected . . . They cleaned their boots on a Sunday morning while the bells were ringing, and walked down to their allotments, and came home and ate their cabbage, and were as oblivious of the vicar as the wind that blew. They had no present quarrel with the Church; no complaint whatever; nor apparently any old memory or grudge; yet there was something, a blank space as it were, between them and the Church.

Notes

1 J. T. Ward and R. G. Wilson, *Land and Industry: The Landed Estate and the Industrial Revolution*, David and Charles, 1971, p. 47.
2 Norman Gash, *The Age of Peel*, Edward Arnold, 1968, p. 179.
3 Harold Perkin, *The Origins of Modern English Society, 1760–1880*, Routledge and Kegan Paul, 1969, p. 314.
4 Arthur Penrhyn Stanley, *The Life and Correspondence of Thomas Arnold*, 1844, vol. 1, p. 85.
5 Patrick Scott, in Brian Simon and Ian Bradley (eds), *The Victorian Public School*, Gill and Macmillan, 1975, p. 48.
6 Kathryn Chidwick, *Empire and the English Character*, I. B. Tauris, 1990, p. 216.
7 Geoffrey Best, *Mid-Victorian Britain, 1851–70*, Fontana, 1979, p. 276.
8 W. J. Reader, *Professional Men*, Weidenfeld and Nicholson, 1966, p. 74.
9 Robert Roberts, *The Classic Slum*, Penguin, 1973, p. 160–61.
10 G. M. Young and W. D. Handcock (eds), *English Historical Documents*, vol. XII (1), Eyre and Spottiswood, 1956, p. 879.
11 Martin J. Wiener, *English Culture and the Decline of the Industrial Spirit, 1850–1980*, Cambridge University Press, 1981, p. 24.
12 Thomas Hardy, 'The Dorsetshire labourer', reprinted in Harold Orel (ed.), *Thomas Hardy's Personal Writings*, Macmillan, 1967, pp. 168–71.
13 Harry Hopkins, *The Long Affray: The Poaching Wars in Britain*, Macmillan, 1985, p. 26.
14 A. J. Peacock, 'Village radicalism in East Anglia, 1800–50' in J. P. D. Dunbabin, *Rural Discontent in Nineteenth-Century Britain*, Faber and Faber, 1974, p. 27.
15 Flora Thompson, *Lark Rise to Candleford*, Penguin, 1984, p. 404.

Chapter four

The course of agriculture to 1914

Farming under the Corn Laws

Rapid industrialisation without an expansion of the capacity to produce food for the population of the growing towns is hard to conceive. Yet agriculture owed little to industry in the form of increased mechanisation. With the possible exception of the threshing machine, little machinery was used in farming before the middle of the nineteenth century; and even thereafter many operations continued to be carried out by hand. Some increase in productivity did come about through progress in what we should today call 'intermediate technology'. There were improvements in traditional implements such as the plough; and a perfection of the scythe, which gradually came to replace the sickle in harvesting.

It was in other ways that agriculture expanded its output. The best traditional practices were applied more widely, while more and more land, previously waste and rough pasture, was brought under cultivation. At no time did this proceed faster than during the French Wars. In 1795 the Board of Agriculture had claimed that 8 million acres (approximately 3.25 million hectares) of waste land existed, but by 1815 most of the waste and moorland which survived was uncultivable. To this day traces of abandoned ploughland dating from the French Wars can be found far up on the chalk downs and in places like Dartmoor and the New Forest. Landowners and farmers were encouraged to increase agricultural output by a marked upswing in farm prices, especially in the case of wheat which is generally subject to the greatest fluctuations. In the early 1790s the price hovered around 48–50s a quarter, but shot up to 90s in 1795, and to 126s 6d in 1812. In only six of the 23 years from 1793 to 1815 did the average price fall below 65s, and in only 10 years did it fall below 75s. At the same time, barley and oats as well as meat experienced significant price rises.

A large part of these price increases must be attributed to the peculiar conditions of war, although other factors were at work, including monetary inflation and the weather. The initial upswing in 1795 resulted from one of the three worst seasons of the eighteenth century, resulting in a yield which was between a fifth and a quarter less than usual. The whole period 1795–1800 was remarkable for poor seasons, and there was a further run of bad seasons between 1808 and 1812. The summers of 1808 and 1809 were wet, and serious outbreaks of sheep rot added to the disaster of spoilt harvests. The long run of bad seasons meant that there was an absence of reserve supplies of grain which sent prices up to famine level. The run of wet seasons also hid the fact that the potential supply of grain had been greatly overexpanded by the vast extension of cultivation, a problem revealed by the bumper harvest of 1813, when prices slumped.

The lifestyle of many farmers changed during the war years, much to the disgust of some commentators such as Cobbett, who, in *Rural Rides* (1830), described a

4   The Anti-Corn Law League: a pioneer of pressure-group politics

1   A commemorative poster dedicated to Richard Cobden, leader of the Anti-Corn Law League

The Anti-Corn Law League mounted a propaganda campaign on an unprecedented scale. By the end of 1841, over 1.25 million handbills and similar items had been distributed. By October 1842 it was contemplating spending £1,000 a week on propaganda, and was able to announce that 5 million tracts had been printed and circulated. The League's publicity material extended to transfer-printed tea and breakfast sets, together with that modern device, the 'sticker'. These were provided in sheets containing 35 mottos, 'grave and gay, serious and witty', for attaching to letters and envelopes.

The commemorative print (1) was issued shortly after the Corn Laws had been repealed, its design being very similar to those of the slightly later trade union membership certificates. The two membership certificates each contain a biblical quotation: from the Lord's Prayer in picture 2, and from the Book of Samuel in picture 3.

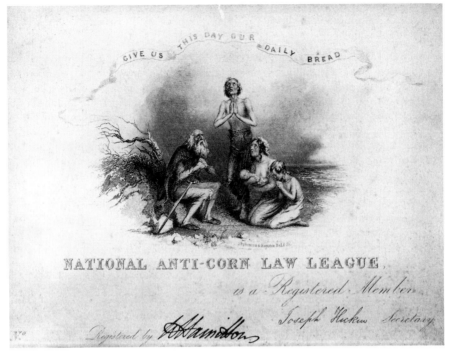

2   A League membership card

3   A League membership card

farmhouse which he visited near Reigate. Although written after the wars had come to an end, it illustrates well the rise in the position of many farmers – which they wished to maintain:

> When the old farm-houses are down (and down they must come in time) what a miserable thing the country will be! Those that are now erected are mere painted shells, with a Mistress within, who is stuck up in a place she calls a *parlour*, with, if she have children, the 'young ladies and gentlemen' about her: some showy chairs and a sofa (a *sofa* by all means): half a dozen prints in gilt frames hanging up: some swinging book-shelves with novels and tracts upon them: a dinner brought in by a girl that is perhaps better 'educated' than she: two or three nick-nacks to eat instead of a piece of bacon and a pudding: the house too neat for a dirty-shoed carter to be allowed to come into; and everything proclaiming to every sensible beholder, that there is here a constant anxiety to make a show not warranted by the reality. The children (which is the worst part of it) are all too clever to *work*: they are all to be gentlefolks. Go to plough! Good God! What, 'young gentlemen' go to plough! They become *clerks*, or some skimmy-dish thing or other. They flee from the dirty *work* as cunning horses do from the bridle. What misery is all this!

As the war neared its end, and the prospect of peace presented the threat of imports from the Continent (a threat which, in fact, was greatly exaggerated) farmers became fearful of the future. The wars had lasted, on and off, for 20 years. Pre-war days and pre-war prices seemed too remote to contemplate, and the abnormal prices of the war years came to be accepted as the norm rather than the exception.

Parliament, responsive to the farmers' cries of distress, in 1815–16 repealed income tax and a wartime malt duty, and passed a new Corn Law aimed at keeping out foreign grain. Further relief followed in what were two of the five lowest years for wheat prices in the first half of the century: in 1834 a new Poor Law lowered poor rates, and in 1836 the Tithe Commutation Act rationalised these irksome payments.

The Corn Law of 1815 allowed imported wheat to be sold only when the home price reached 80s a quarter, and barley and oats when they reached 40s and 27s respectively. It would be misleading to interpret the Corn Laws as simply a piece of class legislation, even though the landed interest did dominate the legislature. Broader arguments were brought forward. The strategic importance of agriculture was emphasised. Malthus, one of the more disinterested advocates of protection, stressed the importance of keeping farming profitable since it contributed more than a third of the national income, and gave employment to roughly the same proportion of the working population, the maintenance of whose purchasing power was vital in terms of the domestic market.

The Corn Laws were largely ineffective, for it was overcapacity in domestic agriculture that kept prices low, rather than the much-feared foreign competition. Not that prices *were* low by comparison with those which had prevailed *before* the war. The post-war talk of depression was largely due to the habit of making comparisons with the abnormal war years.

Much twentieth-century historical writing on agriculture has been derived from Lord Ernle's book, *English Farming Past and Present* (1912), in which the author paints a dismal portrait of agriculture after the Napoleonic Wars: 'Between 1813 and the accession of Queen Victoria falls one of the blackest periods of English farming . . . Farms were thrown up; notices to quit poured in; numbers of tenants absconded. Large tracts of land were untenanted and often uncultivated.' But, as E. L. Jones has pointed out, Ernle was guilty of 'the all-embracing generalisation'.

'He described,' says Jones, 'the experience of agriculturalists all over England, whatever their system of farming, from evidence . . . taken from the worst-hit districts in the very worst spells of distress.' Ernle based his interpretation largely on testimony before public enquiries – by the Board of Agriculture in 1816, and by Parliamentary Commissioners in 1821, 1833 and 1836. At all these enquiries the loudest representations were made by arable farmers and landowners of southern and eastern England cultivating large areas, eager to secure relief from rates and taxes (which tended not to fall commensurately with the fall in grain prices), and to increase their protection against imported cereals. But the arable farmers of heavy claylands were classic victims of agricultural depression, as they were to be again in the 1870s, and after 1921. They were not, however, representative of the whole of British agriculture, which has always been far from monolithic. Many farmers were involved in livestock raising, only indirectly affected by the level of wheat prices; and in mixed farming which depended on receipts from livestock fattening as well as from grain growing.

When Ernle argued that 'prosperity no longer stimulated progress' after the Napoleonic Wars, he failed to acknowledge the degree to which progress can be stimulated by adversity, a point which is not lost, however, to J. D. Chambers and G. Mingay:

> It is not often appreciated how much agricultural development stemmed from the stimulus of low prices, bad seasons and the threat of bankruptcy . . . The difference between improvements in periods of low prices and those in periods of prosperity was really one of emphasis. Both low and high prices resulted in a search for greater efficiency; but in the first the emphasis was on greater economy through reduction of costs; in the second it was more concerned with expansion of the cultivated acreage and higher output.
>
> When it was appreciated that at the post-war levels only efficient farming could be made to pay, there was renewed interest in techniques and improvements and a willingness to invest in them.[1]

Thus many farmers – less vocal perhaps than the protectionists (although many, especially from Scotland, gave evidence before the Select Committee on Agriculture of 1836) – turned to economic rather than political solutions. In consequence there are portents, during this period of 'depression', of that 'high farming' which is usually associated with the quarter century *after* the repeal of the Corn Laws. Pioneering work on land drainage and in the use of fertilisers was carried out; and as a forum for these new ideas the Royal Agricultural Society of England was formed in 1838, with the motto, 'Practice with science'.

It is hard to separate political and economic attitudes in the case of nineteenth-century agriculture, for subtle questions of relationships were at stake between different groups, both within the landed interest and between it and other sections of the population. It did not always follow that what made economic sense also made social or political sense, and there could be tension between different motivating forces. For example, the main social function of English land law was to pass estates intact from one generation to another, but this same law put many impediments in the way of raising capital to improve the land.

We can detect the play of economic and political forces in the repeal of the Corn Laws. Many writers consider repeal in simple terms, as a case of political surrender by the landed interest to pressures from the urban middle class. The notion that repeal represented a landmark in the rise of middle-class power contains some truth, and Asa Briggs has described the Anti-Corn Law League as 'a uniquely powerful

instrument in the forging of middle-class consciousness'. In many ways the movement for the repeal of the Corn Laws must be seen as a continuation of the radical
movement which had led to the passage of the Reform Act.

By the late 1830s the Radicals, disappointed that the Reform Act had not
brought about the promised millennium, sought out other targets of attack. Cobden,
however, saw the importance of rallying support behind a campaign for a single,
generally acceptable reform, and the target seemed clear. The Corn Laws had great
significance as a *symbol* of aristocratic misrule, and an attack mounted here would
force the opponents of reform to fight on poor ground. Although the agricultural
party was a powerful vested interest, such interests were less and less regarded if they
conflicted with economic theory, which was against protection. The monopoly of
the East India Company in the China trade was abolished in 1834, for example; and
as protection to interests other than agriculture was gradually whittled away, the
Corn Laws increasingly seemed in conflict with the spirit of the times. Here, then,
was a target that could unite a wide body of radical opinion.

The attack was organised by the Anti-Corn Law League, founded in Manchester
in 1839. The country was bombarded with propaganda material, sent out with
military precision from the Manchester office. It was estimated that 60–70 bales of
pamphlets, 'from three to three and a half tons of arguments', were sent off each
week. Words were not minced. To Cobden, the Corn Laws were 'the Bread Tax',
and landlords were variously described as 'monsters of impiety', 'relentless demons',
'heartless brutes', 'rapacious harpies', 'merciless footpads', 'inhuman fiends', 'swindlers',
'plunderers of the people' and 'murderers'. Tracts were not the only propaganda
material. The League produced a whole miscellany of promotional objects, ranging
from adhesive wafers for envelopes to anti-Corn Law tea and breakfast sets. Even
the League's membership cards carried the message; one showed a starving family
surrounded by the legend 'Give us this day our daily bread', with a view of
Bethlehem printed on the back!

The league employed lecturers who toured the country preaching the gospel of
free trade in corn — and were frequently attacked for their pains. At Cambridge a
lecturer 'was assailed . . . by a gang of unfledged ruffians in caps and gowns, who,
after exhausting their obscene and blasphemous vocabulary, exhibited themselves in
the character of prize-fighters with the rest of the audience'. In one place in Suffolk
a speaker had the parish fire engine turned on him, and at Saxmundham was thrown
over the banisters of his inn before being escorted out of town (for his own
protection) by the police. However, the word was relentlessly put across from the
platform and the pulpit, and in pamphlet and press (including *The Economist*,
founded by the League in 1843).

Sir Robert Peel, Prime Minister, 1841–6, had a liberal attitude towards fiscal
policy, in the tradition of Pitt and Huskisson. He had been a prominent member of
the government in 1828 when the absolute prohibition of the import of corn when
the home price was below 80s a quarter was replaced by a sliding scale, a principle
which he retained in his 1842 budget, when he halved the previous scale of protection. This move enabled the League to have the best of both worlds. Any improvement they could attribute to Peel's partial implementation of their theories, while
any continuing depression they could blame on the remaining vestiges of protection.

However, it was the failure of the potato rather than the success of propaganda
which was the immediate cause of repeal. A large part of the rural Irish population
had become dependent on the potato, and the appearance of blight in the autumn of
1845 proved a disaster of catastrophic proportions; the disease was virtually unknown
to British and European scientists who, for another generation, were unable to

diagnose a specific remedy. From famine and disease the population of Ireland fell by 1.5 million between 1845 and 1851.

To avert famine and revolution, Peel repealed the Corn Laws in 1846. He prevented the latter, though not the former – and he split the Conservative Party for 20 years. The traditional – that is to say, 'political' – interpretation of repeal goes no further, but D. C. Moore argued that the move was part of a deliberate attempt to stimulate cost-reducing improvements in British agriculture. In the same speech in which Peel outlined his plans for repeal, he outlined a scheme for a drainage loan and a number of other measures designed to encourage farmers to refocus their hopes on high productivity rather than high prices. Most historians regard these measures as mere 'sops', but Moore disagrees. Peel, he stressed, was a charter member of the Royal Agricultural Society, and was eager to encourage efficient farming techniques among those who still resisted the application of more scientific methods, or who claimed that they could not afford them. In Moore's view, 'Peel used both the carrot and the stick. Yet because the stick was the same shape as the bludgeon with which the Leaguers hoped to beat their rural opponents, the existence of the carrots has been almost totally ignored and the purpose of the stick seriously distorted.' By no means all historians would agree with him, and critics point to the small size of the original drainage loan (a mere £2 million) which, however, he argues was only meant to prime the pump.

Whether Peel intended to jerk the farmer into improved husbandry or not, repeal of the Corn Laws undoubtedly ushered in a generation of 'high farming', sometimes described as the 'Golden Age' of British agriculture.

High farming

'Chemistry and mechanism have beaten politics and protection,' wrote Philip Pusey, a great reforming agriculturalist, in 1852. In the same year, appeared James Caird's *English Agriculture in 1850–51*, a collection of reports previously published in *The Times*. Caird described the best as well as the worst contemporary practice; and what he had to say about agriculture in Leicestershire reveals much of the philosophy of high farming:

> The best landlords in the county are said to be capitalists from the towns, who, having purchased estates, manage them with the same attention to principles and details as gained them success in business. They drain their land thoroughly, remove useless and injurious timber, erect suitable farm buildings, and then let to good tenants on equitable terms. Nominally these rents are high; but farms provided with every facility for good cultivation can far better afford to pay a good rent, than can a dilapidated estate any rent, however apparently moderate.

Of those 'capitalists from the towns', a representative in fiction is Mr Jorrocks the cockney grocer turned farmer. In R. S. Surtees' novel, *Hillingdon Hall, or the Cockney Squire*, published in 1845 (with an ironical dedication to the Royal Agricultural Society), Mr Jorrocks, as he sat at breakfast one morning, waxed eloquent on the joys of high farming:

> 'Ah! by the way, you're a great farmer,' observed his Grace . . . 'delightful occupation, farming – monstrous nice occupation – wish I'd been born a farmer.'
>
> 'Wish I'd been born a duke,' grunted Mr Jorrocks, as he stuffed a large piece of tongue into his mouth.

'Tell me now,' continued his Grace, without noticing Mr Jorrocks's observation, 'have you an agricultural association about you? Society for promoting science, agricultural chemistry, improved farming? Best cow, best bull, best two-year-old horse?'

'No, but I intend to, your Grace,' replied Mr Jorrocks, 'shall teach them a thing or two – farmers are a long way behind the intelligence o' the age, Your Greece.'

'That's just what I say, Mr Jorrocks,' replied his Grace, 'that's just what I say!' repeated he. 'Too much of "what my father did I do" style about them – want brushing up: you take yours in hand, Mr Jorrocks – make them drain.'

'Drainin's a great diskivery, your Greece. It's the foundation of all agricultural improvement. . . .'

'Guano! nitrate o'sober gipsey manure!' continued Mr Jorrocks . . . 'We'll have sich a Hagricultural 'Sociation. President, John Jorrocks, Esq., Dine in a tent – dance in a barn – cuss it, there goes the hegg all over my chin . . .'

The farming press witnessed an extraordinary explosion well before the repeal of the Corn Laws. J. C. Loudon's *Cyclopaedia of Agriculture* appeared in 1825 and three years later the *Quarterly Journal of Agriculture* began publication, to be followed in the 1830s by the *Mark Lane Express* and *Farmers' Magazine*, and in the 1840s by the *Agricultural Gazette*. Justus von Liebig's seminal work on fertilisers, *Organic Chemistry in its Applications to Agriculture and Physiology*, appeared in 1840, and a flood of textbooks followed including William Youatt's *The Complete Grazier* which had run to eight editions by 1846, and David Low's *Elements of Practical Agriculture* which had reached its fourth by 1843. There was a similar spawning of farmers' clubs, agricultural associations, and scientific and educational institutions. In 1843 Sir John Lawes established an agricultural research station at Rothamsted in Hertfordshire, and three years later the Royal Agricultural College was opened at Cirencester. The intention was that it should provide a sound education in scientific agriculture for the sons of tenant farmers, but this class rarely availed themselves of the opportunities afforded. When Caird visited the college in 1850 he remarked that all of the 60 students then enrolled were the sons of solicitors, clergymen, officers or landed proprietors.

In most cases drainage was an essential preliminary to high farming, and government drainage loans, it will be remembered, formed part of Peel's 'package' of 1846. Properly executed drainage, explained Caird, 'renders the land so much warmer and wholesome for plants and animals, everything upon it becomes so much more thrifty, and all operations so much more easy and certain in their results, that it is sure to pay'. Great strides were made in the manufacture of cheap drainpipes and tiles, such that the cost of drainage was brought down to £3–4 an acre (1 acre is equal to 0.4 hectare) by 1851.

To the well-drained field the high farmer added new fertilisers, guano being one of the most popular. This substance consists of the excrement of seabirds, deposited in strata several metres thick on the coast of Peru. It was first imported into the country in the early 1840s, and cost the farmer around £10 a ton. Higher yields made the outlay worthwhile; Henry Stephens, for example, claimed: 'When tried on turnips against farm-yard dung, at the rate of only 3 cwt per acre, it produced 20 cwt 6 stones, on a similar piece of ground, that 18 cubic yards of dung per acre produced 19 cwt.'

There were many impediments to the introduction of new ideas. Farms were frequently too small to benefit from high-farming methods. Large, regular fields were required, and it was said that at least 300 acres (about 120 hectares) were needed for many of the new techniques to pay. Yet in the 1850s such farms numbered fewer than 17,000 and occupied only a third of the cultivated acreage. Insecurity of tenure may have acted as a further brake to progress. Improvements which the farmer made to his land might lead to his rent being raised, while the loss of his farm could result in the loss of the capital which he had invested in it, for a statutory right to compensation for improvements was not given until 1875. However, some historians claim that while many farmers (particularly in the south of England) complained bitterly about insecurity, their customary rights were stronger than might be imagined.

There were both physical and financial hindrances in the way of mechanisation. Either the fields had to be made to fit the machines, or the machines developed to suit the fields. The latter was easier. Between 1851 and 1870 almost 300 reaper patents were taken out in Britain alone, in a quest to perfect machines which could cope with the small fields and uneven terrain typical of so many farms. Even so, many machines could not be used all the year round, but lay idle for months until each came into its own season. The industrialist in his factory did not face the same problems. The spread of agricultural machinery was therefore slow, and in 1874, at a time when around 80 per cent of the American cereal harvest was carried out by machine, in Britain the figure was only 47 per cent.

It should not be imagined, therefore, that the whole of British agriculture was transformed by high farming. The 'Report of the Select Committee of the House of Lords on the Improvement of Lands' (1873) showed the limits of what had been achieved. A leading authority on drainage, Bailey Denton, estimated that only 3 million of the 20 million acres of land requiring drainage in England and Wales had as yet been drained, while Caird calculated that, taking all kinds of improvement into consideration, only one-fifth of what was required had been accomplished. Five years later Caird glanced back over the quarter century or so since he had surveyed British agriculture in 1850–51:

> The most striking feature of agricultural progress within the last twenty years has been the general introduction of reaping machines . . . Next to it is the steam plough . . . But it is as yet a costly implement, beyond the reach of all small farmers except when hired as an auxiliary, and not capable of doing its work with economy within small enclosures . . . Next to the economy of labour may be ranked the increase of produce by the expedient of taking two corn crops in succession where the land is clean and in high condition, and can bear the application of special manure, and where the agriculturalist is free to follow a rational system of farming . . . The old plan of relying on the resources of the farm by depending on the manure made upon it . . . will not answer now . . . One cwt of nitrate of soda will give a more certain return of corn than fifty times its weight in farmyard manure, and can be carried to and spread upon the ground at one-fiftieth of the labour. The proof of this, in Mr Lawes' experiments, has been before the country for more than thirty years, and yet it is only beginning to be generally recognised . . .
>
> But, with the exception of the reaping machine and steam-plough, and other implements and machines, there is really little that is new in the practice of the last quarter of a century. The present system of drainage was previously well understood. Bones, guano, and nitrate of soda were fully appreciated by those who then used them. Covered buildings and autumn cultivation had been introduced . . . In running my eye over the account which I wrote of English agriculture in 1850, I find descriptions of good farming in nearly every part of the country, the details of which differ very little from the practice of the present day . . .

The change has been not in any considerable progress beyond what was then the best, but in a general upheaval of the middling and worst towards the higher platform then occupied by the few.

Towards this end, but beyond all efforts of the agriculturalists themselves, or of the engineers and chemists who have done so much to aid them in developing the capabilities of the land, has been the influence of the general prosperity and growing trade and wealth of the country.[2]

Did high farming in fact pay? During the mid-Victorian period the investment of landlords in agriculture was considerable, yet research based on surviving estate records suggests that a return of no more than 3.5 per cent can generally have been made. This was far below the return on investments in banking, commerce and industry, and only a little above the yield of risk-free Consols. The Duke of Northumberland invested £992,000 on his estates between 1847 and 1878, which gave him a meagre 2.5 per cent between 1876 and 1879. Questions of prestige and *noblesse oblige* were involved in many of these improvements, but the real beneficiaries were the good tenant farmers. Their rents rose, but not in proportion to the rise in farm prices, and out of all proportion to their landlords' investment. The land was in fact over-capitalised, and all hope of a satisfactory return was lost when cold winds blew across British agriculture in the last quarter of the century.

The great depression of British agriculture

A sharp fall in agricultural prices was predicted once the Corn Laws had been repealed. During the 30 years after repeal, however, the price of wheat remained fairly stable and, at an average of 53s a quarter (1 quarter is equal to approximately 12.5 kilograms), was only 5s a quarter less than the average price of the last 26 years of protection. Farmers' profits rose, and the landlords' rents increased by a quarter between 1851–3 and 1878–9.

The reasons for this are not too difficult to see. Population increase supplied 5 million more mouths to feed between 1851 and 1871, while rising living standards increased per capita consumption of foodstuffs. However, in the course of time rising prosperity led to dietary changes which worked to the detriment of the wheat grower. As one commentator put it in 1899: 'The sort of man who had bread and cheese for his dinner forty years ago now demands a chop.'

Table 4.1   Net imports of wheat and flour into the UK

Annual average	Millions of cwt*
1820–9	1.6
1830–9	3.7
1840–9	10.7
1850–9	19.3
1860–9	33.7
1870–9	50.4
1880–9	70.3
1890–9	85.9
1900–9	102.6

*1 cwt = approx. 50 kg
Source: François Crouzet, *The Victorian Economy*, Methuen, 1982, p. 160.

Imports of foodstuffs certainly increased – by the mid-1870s nearly half the wheat consumed in Britain was imported – but supplies did not increase fast enough to swamp demand and depress prices. Foreign supplies were not in any position to undercut the domestic price. In 1850 four-fifths of Britain's corn imports came from Europe (France, Russia and the Baltic) while the remaining fifth came from the USA. Any grain which was surplus to the needs of their own expanding populations had to bear the cost of insurance and freight to Britain which raised its price. International dislocation further favoured the British farmer. The Crimean War disrupted Russian exports and gave home producers their most agreeable years, while the American Civil War struck at another potential source of supply. Not until the years after 1865 did the American railroad and the British steamship combine to bring the products of the prairies within easy reach of the British market.

Several decades passed, therefore, before the effects of the repeal of the Corn Laws came to be felt, although the shock had been bound to come, sooner or later, as G. W. P. A. Bentinck, MP, observed to the Royal Commission on Agriculture in 1881:

> I have been preparing for the results of free trade from the year 1846 up to the present time, having been always thoroughly convinced that it would entail great distress upon the country generally, and more especially upon the agricultural interest.
>
> Can you explain to the Commission how it is that the fulfilment of those prophecies has been delayed for so long a time, because we have passed through a period of great prosperity since that? – I think I have already stated that the discovery of gold and a series of great wars averted for a number of years the effects of free trade, and it was only when those great wars ceased, and when things were left to find their own level, that the effects of free trade made themselves fully felt in the country.
>
> Then, in fact, it is only within the last few years, probably since the present severe depression began, that we have begun for the first time to feel the real effect of the passage of those laws which you deprecated so much? – I think that is decidedly the case.

However, the traditional picture of the whole of British agriculture being battered by 'the great depression' can no longer be accepted. The variety of forms which British agriculture takes is now more fully appreciated, and it is clear that the years 1870–1914 mark a restructuring of farming, with resources being transferred from sectors of agriculture which no longer paid to others which did. For some farmers the period was indeed one of severe hardship, for others it was one of quiet prosperity, but for all it was one of inevitable change.

If there has been a new understanding of the problem, it stems partly from a reinterpretation of the evidence upon which the old generalisations were made. This applies to both the quantitative and the qualitative sources. As to the statistical evidence, too much can be made of the index of wheat prices, for the historian has to consider how representative such prices were of agricultural prices as a whole, while he or she must also ask whether wheat contributed the same proportion of agricultural output and earnings throughout the period.

As to the literary evidence – the writings of contemporary observers, and the oft-quoted proceedings of the two Royal Commissions of 1879–82 and 1894–7 – the historian should reflect on the general character trait which makes the voice of the discontented speak loudest. The late T. W. Fletcher drew attention to the biased representation of the two Royal Commissions. The Richmond Commission of

1879–82 was firmly led by the landowning aristocracy and gentry, all with properties in the Midlands and the south of England. The witnesses were equally unrepresentative. Thirty-five farmers, nearly all of them tenants, were called. Their holdings were nearly all larger than average; the average size of an English farm being then less than 100 acres (1 acre is equal to 0.4 hectare), a farm size which applied to only one of the witnesses. By contrast, 31 farmed more than 300 acres, 25 more than 500 acres and 10 more than 1,000. Their geographical origin was similarly unbalanced. Twenty-six came from the 'corn' counties of the east and south, while only nine came from the 'grazing' counties of the north and west. Likewise, the 10 leading wheat-growing counties between them produced 14 witnesses, as against five contributed by the 10 leading dairy counties. It is tempting to see this preponderance of large, arable farmers as an attempt to distort the facts, but such a sinister assumption is unnecessary. It is natural that such men, with foremen to manage their farms, should be willing to travel to London to give evidence to the Royal Commission. The working dairy farmer was tied to his farm, where the cows needed milking twice a day every day of the year.

Both the members of the second Royal Commission, and the witnesses called, were more generally representative. Twenty-two of the farmers giving evidence still came from the east and south, but 18 now came from the west and north, while the dairy counties provided 12 witnesses as against 13 from the corn counties. Even so, the final report devoted a mere three pages out of nearly 200 to dairy farming, and the subject received nothing like the attention given to the plight of the arable farmers in some districts.

One of the immediate causes of distress, and one which received frequent attention, was the inclement weather. The wet autumn of 1875 was followed by abnormally heavy rainfall in the winter of 1876–7, while the spring of 1878 ushered in a two-and-a-half-year period of exceptional cold and wet. The abnormal rainfall was worst in the south and east (Bury St Edmunds had 50 per cent more rain than usual in 1879) but it diminished progressively to the north and west, Cumberland and South Wales, for example, receiving rather less than the local average. The run of wet weather had a cumulative effect, exacerbating the problem of weeds, while it also brought an epidemic of liver rot in sheep and foot and mouth disease in cattle which raged from 1881–3.

Increased imports made the situation worse. A little over 40 million hundredweight (2 million tons) of wheat and flour were imported in the early 1870s, rising to an average of nearly 70 million hundredweight (3.5 million tons) in the late 1890s. By 1894, when wheat reached its lowest price of 22s 10d a quarter (12.7 kilograms), the corn grower could look back over 25 years of almost continuously falling prices.

At first many farmers explained away the rising imports by pointing to the good harvests which were being enjoyed in North America during the wet years in Britain, but it soon became clear that the change was a permanent one. The cost of carrying a quarter of wheat from Chicago to Liverpool averaged 11s between 1868 and 1879, 4s 4d by 1892 and only 2s 10$\frac{1}{2}$d in 1902. As F. R. Leyland, the owner of a major shipping line, put it in 1881: 'Every line of railway that is projected in America brings an additional corn growing area into competition with the farmer here; and you see what the cost of conveyance is, it is so trifling. For all practical purposes, Chicago is no further distant from this country than Aberdeen is from London.'

The livestock farmer did not fare as badly as the corn grower at first. One of his main *inputs* was corn for feed, so imports could do him nothing but good, especially as cheaper bread gave the consumers more money to spend on his products. It was not for at least another decade that he began to feel the effects of foreign competition, for imports of meat had to await the introduction of the refrigerated ship. Thereafter, imports rose rapidly; by 1895, 500,000 tons of meat, roughly a third of the estimated consumption, came from abroad. In 1896 it was calculated that a lamb could be killed in New Zealand, frozen, shipped to London, and there be delivered to a retailer for as little as $2\frac{1}{2}$d a pound. Between 1870 and 1900 per capita meat consumption rose by almost 50 per cent. However, it was at the cheaper end of the market that competition was most keenly felt, for the discerning buyer still preferred home-produced meat.

With returns to arable farming falling relative to those in other branches of agriculture, there were two courses of action which the farmer could adopt. One of the most obvious remedies, though not necessarily the most effective in the long run, was to economise on cash outlay, including (where remissions could be obtained) outlay on rent. 'Only what is absolutely necessary is done', was a Lincolnshire comment. Repairs were postponed, hedges and ditches neglected, less fertiliser was used, weeding was skimped and outlying fields allowed to fall into rough pasture. There was little satisfaction in this kind of farming although it no doubt enabled some farmers to survive.

Farmers could also diversify, and the period saw the development of fruit farming and market gardening, as well as the first tentative experiments in the growing of sugar beet. Much of the increased fruit production went into the manufacture of jam. As one commentator put it in 1883: 'As our dairies cannot furnish butter for those who are unable to give them 1s 5d to 1s 8d per pound for this luxury, they use jam for themselves and their children.' The Chivers family began a jam factory outside Cambridge in 1873, while a similar industry developed around Tiptree in Essex and Blairgowrie in Perthshire.

Farmers who turned to dairying could profit from the growth of the trade in liquid milk, a commodity so perishable as to be practically invulnerable to foreign competition. Of all farm prices, that of fresh milk, especially of winter milk, fell least during the depression; and milk could be produced on new grasslands or within a variety of arable systems. The railways conveyed it fresh to the towns. The Great Western Railway – 'the milky way' – doubled its milk traffic between 1892 and 1910, by which time it was conveying milk to London from distances up to 130 miles away. Dairy farmers began to be assisted by new machinery such as cream separators and milking machines. The *Preston Guardian* in 1896 forecast the demise of the milkmaid; the second verse of a poem appearing in that paper runs:

> For grim Invention – sentiment's
> Most pertinacious snubber –
> Has shaped a thing of wire and string,
> And tape and indiarubber;
> Has, out of brass, and zinc, and glass,
> And webbing soft as silk, made
> An apparatus meant henceforth
> To play the part of milkmaid.

In fact, milking by hand predominated until the First World War, and it remained one of the most burdensome tasks of milk production.

The changing structure of British agriculture is revealed by the acreage devoted to different types of husbandry. Between 1873 and 1904 the orchard acreage increased from almost 150,000 to about 250,000 acres (60,000–100,000 hectares), and the small fruit acreage, estimated at 37,000 in 1881, was recorded as 70,000 when first calculated in 1897. The most dramatic change was in the balance between arable land and pasture. The wheat acreage fell from 3.4 million in 1871 to 1.7 million in 1901, while during the same period the area under permanent grass rose from 11.4 to 15.4 million acres. The adjustment was a formidable one, involving in some cases the conversion of entire arable farms to pasture.

Some historians have criticised the slowness with which British agriculture was transformed, but change was not easy, as a writer in the *Journal of the Royal Agricultural Society* observed in 1896: 'The farmer's position is different from that of the tradesman, who, when he finds one line of goods is not wanted, merely has to order no more of the same kind, but to re-stock with something which will sell.'

Table 4.2   Crop acreage in Great Britain

	Millions of acres★			Percentage of the total		
	1872	*1895*	*1913*	*1872*	*1895*	*1913*
Wheat	3.6	1.4	1.8	12.0	4.0	5.5
Other corn	6.0	6.0	5.2	19.0	18.0	16.0
Cereals (total)	9.6	7.4	7.0	31.0	22.0	21.5
Green and root crops	3.6	3.2	3.0	12.0	10.0	9.0
Market gardening	0.2	0.3	0.4	0.8	1.0	1.0
Surface cultivated	13.4	10.9	10.4	44.0	33.0	31.0
Fallow grass, pasture	17.3	21.8	21.9	56.0	67.0	69.0

★1 acre = 0.4 hectare
Source: François Crouzet, *The Victorian Economy*, Methuen, 1982, p. 170.

The wet years at the start of the depression misled farmers as to the necessity for permanent change, and diminished their capital resources. This was a vital consideration since conversion to pasture required weed-free fields, a long period of careful management, ample supplies of manure and fertiliser, and then the livestock which formed the whole object of the exercise. There was, however, a measure of conservatism. Many farmers did not look upon horticulture as 'real' farming, however profitable it might be, while dairying was considered to be a decided step down the social scale, tying farmers to their farms day in, day out. The eminent agriculturalist A. D. Hall noted in 1913 that the resorts along the west coast of Wales were apt to run short of milk, butter, cream, eggs, fruit and vegetables in the holiday season, while farmers within 10 miles were still scratching a living producing wool and store stock, oats and hay.

Notes

1 J. D. Chambers and G. Mingay, *The Agricultural Revolution, 1750–1880*, Batsford, 1966, pp. 130–31.
2 James Caird, *The Landed Interest and the Supply of Food*, 1878, pp. 16–29.

Chapter five

Social problems in the age of *laissez-faire*

The nature of nineteenth-century social problems

The nineteenth century experienced many harrowing social problems, but we would be mistaken were we to see them as some do, solely as an urban pheno-menon. Many of the problems with which contemporaries grappled were evident in the countryside as well as in the towns and cities. Pauperism, for example, was a major issue in the agricultural counties, and Lord Macaulay was one of many who saw pauperism as a basic *rural* problem:

> (The) poor-rate is very decidedly lower in the manufacturing than in the agricultural districts . . . the amount of parish relief required by the labourers in the different counties of England, is almost exactly in inverse proportion to the degree in which the manufacturing system has been introduced into those counties. The returns for the years ending in March 1825, and in March 1828, are now before us. In the former year, we find the poor-rate highest in Sussex – about 20s to every inhabitant. Then come Buckinghamshire, Essex, Suffolk, Bedfordshire, Huntingdonshire, Kent and Norfolk. In all these the rate is above 15s a head . . . But in the West Riding of Yorkshire, it is as low as 5s; and when we come to Lancashire, we find it at 4s, – one-fifth of what it is in Sussex . . . These facts seem to indicate that the manufacturer is both in a more comfortable and in a less dependent situation than the agricultural labourer.[1]

Housing, too, was a problem which was evident in rural as well as in urban England, as F. G. Heath pointed out in 1883, in *Peasant Life in the West of England*, where he described a cottage near Minehead in Devon:

> Never had we witnessed so sad a sight as we saw in that miserable garret of a miserable hut. There was one bedstead, besides two other – we cannot say articles of furniture – things purporting to represent a table and a chair, on the bare floor. On the bedstead, in the darkest corner of the room, which might have been twelve or thirteen feet long, by some eight or nine feet wide, and perhaps seven feet high, lay the poor old bedridden grandmother, her poor wrinkled face looking the picture of patient and uncomplaining misery. Nothing on the floor besides the wretched bedstead and the table and chair; no pictures, even of the rudest kind, on the walls. One tiny window, cut through the thick wall of the cottage, admitted a little light into this chamber, and there, with her head in the darkest corner, had lain for years this poor old creature, the helpless mother of an English peasant.
> It is terrible to witness want and misery in the foul slums of a great city; but it is assuredly much more terrible to find it in rose-bound cottages –

emblazoned in the most charming of rural nooks, where the very richness of nature seems to rebuke the meanness of man.

Had the countryside been free of social and economic problems, the stream of rural migrants to the towns would hardly have been as it was.

We should also avoid the temptation to see urban problems exclusively in relation to the new towns, to be shocked, that is, only by cities like Manchester, the 'shock city' of the 1830s and 1840s. Many of the most unsanitary districts in the country were to be found in the old parts of old towns such as Exeter, which was ravaged by cholera in 1832, when nearly one citizen in 20 was struck down by the disease. The Health of Towns Association recognised the extent of the problem for, after its formation in 1844, it was at pains to stress in its propaganda that the battle for public health had to be fought as fiercely in small towns and cities, unsullied by industrial smoke and grime, as in the soot-stained industrial giants. Half a century later the nation was shocked to discover from Rowntree's investigations that the proportion of primary poverty in York, an ancient city revitalised by the railway in Victorian times, was the same as in London, a city of some 6 million people. Likewise, much pollution came not from new industries, but from the multiplication of traditional 'dirty trades'. Leicester, for example, had 87 town slaughterhouses in 1859, and pigs were fed on the offal.

All of this is not to say that there were no new social problems during this period, or that such problems as existed were unrelated to the growth of towns. Among the new features were a vast increase in the scale of problems with a long history, and a breakdown of social relationships in the cities which greatly exacerbated the situation. The industrial revolution created new problems of insecurity caused by fluctuations of employment among large concentrations of workers with no natural protectors to turn to in distress, as had existed in traditional rural England.

Increasingly, the social classes came to be physically separated from each other in the towns, each living and working in their distinct localities. The classes became foreign to each other, so that it could be said of Manchester in the 1840s that 'Ardwick knows less about Ancoats than it does about China, and feels more interested in the condition of New Zealand than of Little Ireland'. Likewise a commentator on the East and West Ends of London in 1856 observed that on the rare occasions when the inhabitants of the two areas came into contact they 'surveyed each other with much the same curiosity and astonishment as would nowadays be exhibited by a native of this town at the appearance of an Esquimaux in Hyde-Park or Regent Street'.

Not only were the *classes* separated from each other, but *individuals* increasingly experienced isolation and alienation – what sociologists call *anomie*, a feeling of powerlessness, meaninglessness and self-estrangement. Dickens noticed this in his first book, *Sketches by Boz*, written at the age of 23: 'It is strange with how little notice, good, bad, or indifferent, a man may live and die in London. He awakens no sympathy in the breast of any single person; his existence is a matter of interest to no one save himself; he cannot be said to be forgotten when he dies, for no one remembered him when he was alive.'

As the century progressed, however, there was not only a growing awareness of the problems but also a serious concern to provide solutions. Numerous influences were at work to bring the issues before the public eye. There was an explosion of social investigation, with many of the enquirers enthusiastically brandishing the newly forged sword of statistics. The Board of Trade set up a Statistical Office in 1832; the British Association established a statistical section in 1833; and the

Statistical Society of London was founded in 1834 in order to procure, arrange and publish 'Facts calculated to illustrate the Condition and Prospects of Society'. But statistics spoke more to the head than to the heart, as Elizabeth Barrett Browning observed in her verse-novel, *Aurora Leigh*, of 1857:

> A red-haired child
> Sick in a fever, if you touch him once,
> Though but as little as with a finger-tip
> Will set you weeping; but a million sick . . .
> You could as soon weep for the rule of three
> Or compound fractions.

Dickens was one of those who appreciated that statistical abstractions may have the effect of distancing the reader from the human experience, and he satirised those who:

> see figures and averages, and nothing else – the representatives of the wickedest and most enormous vice of this time – the men who, through long years to come, will do more to damage the real useful truths of political economy than I could do (if I tried) in my whole life; the addled heads who . . . would comfort the labourer in travelling twelve miles a day to and from his work, by telling him that the average distance of one inhabited place from another in the whole area of England, is not more than four miles.[2]

Dickens's novels, and the works of other social novelists, such as Mrs Gaskell, influenced many. So, in a different way, did the parliamentary Blue Books where quantitative and qualitative evidence was often combined. Whether through the work of the statistical societies, the social novelists, investigators like Mayhew, or the reports of Royal Commissions and parliamentary committees, more and more people came to be aware of the problems of the day and sought methods of dealing with them, so that the period should be remembered as much for the attempts at reform (however faltering or partial they may now seem) as for the awful problems themselves.

Individualism and collectivism

By any reckoning the welfare state is of recent origin. Many historians claim to see its beginnings in the Edwardian era, while others look back to an 'administrative revolution' in the 1830s and 1840s. It is a fit and proper activity for historians to hunt for origins, but the activity is not without its dangers, for hindsight can often lead the historian astray. The Poor Law, for example, although the most highly developed Victorian social service, proved to be a dead end. As Derek Fraser has observed, the Poor Law provision 'did not become the foundations of a more splendid edifice, but became ruins alongside which a welfare state was constructed'. This was because the Poor Law demanded what would eventually prove to be an unacceptable price, namely the social stigma of pauperisation which became abhorrent as social sensibilities became more refined. It became a weakened dinosaur, lingering on beside its fitter successors until 1948. Not that the sentiments upon which the New Poor Law was founded are all extinct yet. The individualism and moralism out of which it grew in the 1830s was echoed in much Conservative Party thinking of the 1980s and 1990s stressing as it does individual responsibility; while, in the minds of many, the idle and shiftless paupers of 1834 have their modern counterparts in the 'spongers' allegedly living on public assistance and the welfare services.

Some historians distinguish between the modern welfare state, which aims to provide services of a high standard to the whole population, and the nineteenth-century 'social service state', in which minimal services were provided for the poor, while the rest of the population provided for themselves. The social service state was also a 'tutelary state', in which those with power and property exercised tutelage, or guardianship, over those who had not. This might lead to attempts to exercise social control over the masses, but it did not necessarily have such sinister political overtones to its supporters. To them tutelage was merely an extension of the paternalism of the pre-industrial society. In such an interpretation, as F. M. L. Thompson suggests, the rulers 'were simply acting as the elders of one vast tribe, as the tutors and prefects teaching the rules of living in society'. In any case, the concept of social control is a matter of controversy among historians. It tends to cast the working class into an essentially passive role, waiting, like putty, to be moulded by their 'superiors'. It also tends to neglect the possibility that the workers were capable of establishing their own standards of behaviour (which could possibly even be identical with those of their middle-class 'controllers') and it appears to ignore the possibility that while those in power might wish to indoctrinate the working class, the members of that class might possess the means of inoculating themselves against the attack.

The idea of a social service state was based on individualism, but if individualism was the cornerstone of nineteenth-century social thought, at some time that corner was turned and *collectivism* came into view, whereby the state assumed a positive role, actively intervening in the affairs of its citizens for their own and for the general welfare. However, there is some controversy as to how this change came about. Rival models have been constructed, differing both in their mechanism and in their timing. There is also debate on the influence of theory, especially that of Utilitarianism, associated with the name of Jeremy Bentham (1748–1832). This aspect of the controversy centres around two issues: whether Benthamism leaned towards individualism or collectivism, and whether it had any great practical significance anyway.

It is certainly possible to exaggerate the role of individual thinkers. The tendency of intellectual history to concentrate on those individuals whose stature is still apparent today is one of its weaknesses, and parallels political history which has too often seen events in terms of the activities of 'great men'. Bentham was certainly a 'great thinker', but what he displayed in brilliance of thought he lacked in brilliance of literary style. His prose became so impenetrable that the essayist Hazlitt observed: 'His works have been translated into French – they ought to be translated into English.' Could such an individual have influenced many? Some historians, such as Oliver Macdonagh, have reacted against an interpretation of nineteenth-century social reform in which Bentham was central, and have argued that his influence has been grossly exaggerated. 'There is an obvious danger,' Macdonagh has argued, 'of *post hoc propter hoc* in, say, establishing the relationship of the doctrine of Utilitarianism to many, if not indeed most, "rational" or "useful" reforms.' Macdonagh argues that Benthamism had no influence on opinion at large, nor upon the great majority of public servants. He does however, accept that some administrators – and Chadwick was the prime example – were so influenced. Henry Parris, who takes a different view, holds that to have influenced one Chadwick was of more significance than influencing hundreds of rank-and-file public servants. He also argues that Macdonagh is mistaken in searching for an overt influence, for he claims that great numbers of people may be unconsciously influenced by the work of thinkers of whom they may not even have heard. Or, as Derek Fraser puts it: 'It has often been the case in the history of ideas that concepts discussed esoterically by experts become a simplified form of intellectual loose change of popular culture.'

What, then, were the ideas of Bentham, that they should have aroused so much controversy? The phrase indelibly associated with his name is 'the greatest happiness of the greatest number'. It assumed that self-interest is the only motivation behind human conduct, and that the achievement of pleasure and the avoidance of pain alone constitute that self-interest. The theory was wholly hedonistic, and made no allowance for the promptings of conscience or humane impulses such as generosity, mercy, compassion or self-sacrifice. A human being's whole existence was held to be guided by his or her pursuit of pleasure and eschewal of pain. Action was initiated by a demonstrable preponderance of 'good' results over 'bad' ones, which Benthamites claimed to be able to calculate by the 'felicific calculus' or 'moral arithmetic'. Bentham actually postulated a formula which included six categories of pleasurable or painful effect (intensity, duration, certainty, propinquity, fecundity and purity) with a seventh quality, number, added to the computation when more than one person was involved. Correctly weigh each factor, good and bad, place them on their respective side of the scales, and the heavier side determines action. The sole criterion was quantitative – so many units of pleasure against so many units of pain. That individuals might differ in their notion of happiness, or that they might prize values other than material ones, did not affect the calculation. According to Bentham, an action was 'conformable to the principle of utility . . . when the tendency it has to augment the happiness of the community is greater than any it has to diminish it'.

Did Benthamism support *laissez-faire* individualism or government intervention? Parris argues that this is a false antithesis. The question for nineteenth-century governments was where to draw the line. Sometimes the test of utility supported *laissez-faire*. The Corn Laws did not tend to the greatest happiness of the greatest number, so they were scrapped. At other times, Utilitarianism demanded intervention, as when the greatest happiness of the greatest number of railway passengers required that public regulation be imposed.

Parris put forward a model for changes in nineteenth-century social policy which derives from the writings of the nineteenth-century jurist, A. V. Dicey, who made a pioneering study of the relationship between law and opinion. Dicey had hypothesised a three-stage model:

1 legislative quiescence, 1800–30
2 period of Benthamism or Individualism, 1825–70
3 period of Collectivism, 1865–1900

Bentham obviously had a role in the transition from the first to the second stage, but who or what led to the second transition? Dicey could not point to an individual or individuals playing a similar role here; and he was, in fact, rather vague about the timing. Indeed, Parris has pointed out that Dicey acknowledged collectivist influences on housing legislation from 1851, on municipal trading from 1850, on public health legislation from 1848 and on elementary education from 1833. This was only three years after the first stage, of legislative quiescence, was held to have terminated! How could this be? Parris suggests that the second 'transition' as such never took place, and his alternative model postulates only two periods, with a dividing line at about 1830. Like Dicey he sees the first period as one of quiescence, but the second he sees as one dominated by Utilitarianism which, he claims, 'led to considerable extensions both of *laissez-faire* and of State intervention simultaneously'. He argues:

It would be absurd to argue that Bentham revolutionized the British system of government by power of abstract thought alone. His ideas were influential because they derived from the processes of change going on around him. He was working with the grain. But it does not follow that the same solutions would have been reached had he never lived.[3]

Parris does not deny that there was a change in the tenor of legislation after 1870, but he sees this not as the result of the adoption of a hypothetical philosophy of collectivism, but as the response to factors such as the Great Depression, the extension of the franchise, and pressure from the administration itself. Thus he (and not he alone) sees the development of governmental activity in the nineteenth century as a continuum rather than a dichotomy between individualism and collectivism.

After about 1870 the government did take a more positive role, as we shall examine in Chapter 11. In this chapter we are more concerned with the earlier period which we may still validly label an era of *laissez-faire*. During this period the classical economists never believed in a *total* absence of interference by the state. J. R. McCulloch put it thus in 1848: 'The principle of *laissez-faire* may be safely trusted to in some things but in many more it is wholly inapplicable; and to appeal to it on all occasions savours more of the policy of a parrot than of a statesman or a philosopher.' On another occasion he wrote that the economist or the politician who proposed to carry out the principle of self reliance 'to its full extent in all cases and at all hazards, would be fitter for bedlam than for the closet or the cabinet'. Government might intervene, then, but only to regulate. At no point did the classical economists envisage the state as having a positive role to play. Intervention was tolerable only so far as was necessary to ensure the fairest and fullest operation of the free-market economy, and in order to safeguard society against greater evils.

Laissez-faire was an ideal, for as John Stuart Mill claimed, 'Letting alone should be the general practice, every departure from it unless required by some good is a certain evil'. But men often profess to an ideal which their actions belie. Sidney Webb's description of the self-helping local politician, though written in 1902, well sums up this possibility:

> The individualist town councillor will walk along the municipal pavement, lit by municipal gas and cleansed by municipal brooms with municipal water, and seeing by the municipal clock in the municipal market that he is too early to meet his children coming from the municipal school, hard by the county lunatic asylum and municipal hospital, will use the national telegraph system to tell them not to walk through the municipal park, but to come by the municipal tramway to meet him in the municipal reading-room by the municipal art gallery, museum and library, where he intends to consult some of the national publications in order to prepare his next speech in the municipal town hall in favour of the nationalisation of canals and the increase of Government control over the railway system. 'Socialism, Sir,' he will say, 'don't waste the time of a practical man by your fantastic absurdities. Self-help, Sir, individual self-help, that's what made our city what it is.'[4]

Pressure for an increase of government intervention came from various sources. Once the state had acted, and appointed public servants to administer the law, a self-generating mechanism for growth in its activity was established. The number of civil servants increased greatly in the course of the nineteenth century. From 16,000 in 1780, they expanded to 54,000 by 1870. Of particular significance were the various groups of inspectors. Their impetus for greater public activity was not mere empire-building, but derived from their increasing professionalism and from the realisation that social problems were often much more complex than had originally been supposed. Pressure was also exerted by 'pressure groups' of one kind and another, and their development was a particular nineteenth-century phenomenon. On occasions the administrators and the pressure groups were directly linked, as when Chadwick founded the Health of Towns Association to put pressure on his political superiors.

Two other general points should be briefly considered before we move to a closer examination of the specific problems of poverty; public health, housing and the environment; crime and drink; religion; and education. These are the lingering fear of centralisation and the deeply felt belief in philanthropy and voluntary action.

When the government intervened, it was generally in a permissive or advisory capacity. Local authorities were told what they *might* do, and only rarely what they *must*. Individuals and institutions might be encouraged to act, but the state only rarely took the lead if they would not. Encouragement was tolerable, but direction from Whitehall aroused deep local resentments. The people on the spot, it was felt, knew the local problems better than any central administrator.

Furthermore, the men and women on the spot continued to tackle local problems through voluntary effort and philanthropic works. The nineteenth century was perhaps the classical period of organised charity. Sir James Stephen wrote in 1860: 'Ours is the age of societies . . . For the cure of every sorrow by which our land or our race can be visited, there are patrons, vice-presidents, and secretaries. For the diffusion of every blessing of which mankind can partake in common, there is a committee.' Stephen was a prominent Evangelical, and it has been argued that his co-religionists were every bit as influential in tackling nineteenth-century social problems as the Utilitarians.

The individual effort which went into charities, and the sums of money involved, were enormous. A survey in the early 1860s calculated philanthropic activity in London alone to amount to between £5.5 and £7 million annually. This compared with a total Poor Law expenditure for England and Wales of less than £6 million in 1861 and less than £8 million in 1871. Two decades later *The Times* noted that the income of London charities was greater than that of several independent governments, exceeding the revenues of Sweden, Denmark and Portugal, and of the Swiss Confederation, twofold.

The effectiveness of private charity varied from area to area. Some localities, especially the older towns with a long history of philanthropy and old-established charities, were abundantly provided for. Lichfield, for example, had, by the end of the century, nearly £4,000 to distribute annually among 8,000 inhabitants. Other areas − often newer, problem areas − were less fortunate. The motives which lay behind this philanthropic activity were varied. Sometimes ostentatious charitable activity might be a means to social distinction, and there were certainly many *nouveaux riches* in the towns who envied the paternal role of the squirearchy. Others, no doubt, were inspired more by fear and the desire to avoid unrest and disaffection. As Mark Twain put it: 'In all the ages, three-fourths of the support of the great charities has been conscience money.' Yet many were certainly moved by no cynical motives, but by a generous benevolence which must be set alongside the callousness which is often depicted as characteristic of the age.

The problem of the poor

In his introduction to a reprint of the Poor Law Report of 1834, S. G. Checkland describes it as 'one of the classic documents of western social history'. Fifty years earlier R. H. Tawney had summed up the Report as 'brilliant, influential, and wildly unhistorical'. That it was influential there can be no doubt; and it (literally) carried great weight, being supported by 13 folio volumes of evidence containing nearly 8,000 pages. It presented a mountain of data, and constituted the most detailed social investigation ever carried out in the British Isles at that time. Questionnaires had been sent out to each of the 15,000 parishes of England and Wales which administered poor relief. There was no compulsion to reply, and only a little over 10 per cent of the parishes (representing one-fifth of the population) did so. In consequence, armed with those replies which had been received, 26 Assistant Commissioners were sent to make personal enquiries, and they visited 3,000 places, about one-fifth of the Poor Law authorities. The report has been much criticised, but it has to be remembered that there was an almost total lack of experience of social investigation on this scale. Furthermore, the Commissioners were under government pressure to act with great speed. This they did. So much so that only six months elapsed between the circulation of the questionnaire and the despatch of the evidence to the printers; while the report itself was written before all the evidence had arrived, let alone been studied. Not, perhaps, that this worried the Commissioners too much. They knew what they were looking for; and they found it. So did the Assistant Commissioners, who were a dedicated bunch of amateurs who shared common presumptions and prejudices. Despite claims of objectivity and 'scientific' investigation, their evidence is impressionistic rather than quantitative. Attempts by historians such as Mark Blaug to rework some of the material in quantitative terms reveal that quite different conclusions could be drawn from it.

The report and the act were avowedly Benthamite. The Commission of nine, presided over by Charles Blomfield, the Tory Bishop of London, was dominated by two quintessential Benthamites, Nassau Senior and Edwin Chadwick. Between them they drafted the report along lines which, no doubt, they had previously determined. Senior was a prominent classical economist, and first holder of the Drummond Chair of Political Economy at Oxford. Better known is Edwin Chadwick, then aged 32 and destined to become one of the most controversial administrators of his generation. He was devoted to public service. One biographer commented: 'Edwin Chadwick belongs to that type of men the details of whose life add but little to our knowledge of their character. He *was* his public career.' However, his character was important, for his strong will and obstinacy cut short his career at the age of 54, and he was not recognised with a knighthood until 1889, the year before he died. The Hammonds felt that Chadwick's 'capable qualities were largely spoilt by the hard tone of his mind'. Eric Midwinter suggests that 'a Frenchman might see in him the combined gifts and faults of Colbert and Robespierre; an Englishman those of Thomas Cromwell and Stafford Cripps'. No one could argue that Chadwick was not influenced by Bentham, for he became his literary secretary in 1832, the very year in which the Poor Law Commission got under way.

The views expressed in the report also derived directly from contemporary ideas on individualism and moralism. The new opportunities afforded by the industrial revolution encouraged the economically successful to stress the autonomy of individuals and their right to the economic gains which their individual efforts might produce. Economic success gained moral approval, but economic failure was also seen in moral terms. This emphasis on the individual came at the very time that rapid social change imposed stresses on the mass of the population who had great need of group support. But the prevailing climate of opinion tended to withdraw this support when it was most needed. The Poor Law Commissioners made no systematic attempt to investigate the pressures which bore down upon the masses. They saw no need to examine the economy as a whole, nor to investigate the nature and extent of unemployment, or the general level of wages. Nothing, then, was present to temper the moral judgement made on individuals who failed to support themselves.

Strange as it may seem, the Poor Law was not concerned with poverty; for in the nineteenth century a distinction was drawn between poverty, which was seen as the lot of the majority of the people, and pauperism (or indigence), which was the inability of individuals to support themselves. Poverty was thought not only to be inevitable, but to have positive benefits – if not to the poor themselves, to society as a whole. Patrick Colquhoun, a friend and admirer of Bentham, put it this way in 1806:

> Poverty is . . . a most necessary and indispensable ingredient in society, without which nations and communities could not exist in a state of civilisation. It is the lot of man – it is the source of wealth, since without poverty there would be no labour, and without labour there could be no riches, no refinement, no comfort, and no benefit to those who may be possessed of wealth – inasmuch as without a large proportion of poverty surplus labour could never be rendered productive in procuring either the conveniences or luxuries of life.
>
> Indigence therefore, and not poverty, is the evil. It is that condition in society which implies want, misery and distress. It is the state of any one who is destitute of the means of subsistence, and is unable to labour to procure it to the extent nature requires. The natural source of subsistence is the labour of the individual; while that remains with him he is denominated poor: when it fails in whole or in part he becomes indigent.[5]

The purpose of the Poor Law, therefore, was to prevent the indigent from starving and to force the poor to stand on their own feet. William Rathbone, a Liverpool philanthropist, wrote in 1850:

> It is beyond the omnipotence of Parliament to meet the conflicting claims of justice to the community; severity to the idle and vicious and mercy to those stricken down into penury by the visitation of God . . . There is grinding want among the honest poor; there is starvation, squalor, misery beyond description, children lack food and mothers work their eyes dim and their bodies thin to emaciation in the vain attempt to find the bare necessities of life, but the Poor Law authorities have no record of these struggles.[6]

It was the resolution of so many to resist the stigma of receiving poor relief that explains the situation so startlingly revealed by Seebohm Rowntree two generations later: that beneath the surface of urban pauperism which ran at 3 per cent there lay submerged an impoverished 30 per cent of the population. While the Poor Law dealt with the pauperised, the impoverished were left to private charity. The inability of the Poor Law to deal with the overall problem was its greatest failing.

The attack on the Old Poor Law, and the principles of the New

The Poor Law Report of 1832–4 did two things. It mounted a remorseless attack on the existing Poor Law and it proposed far-reaching remedies. The Old Poor Law was held to have broken down, as evidenced by the rise in the cost of relief, from around £2 million in 1784 to approximately £7 million in 1832. By that date there were probably 1.5 million paupers out of a population of some 13 million. To contemporaries the rise in the cost of poor relief was dramatic, although to us it may seem less so. The gross national income in 1830 was around £400 million, so that the £7 million expended on the poor was less than 2 per cent of the whole. As poor relief was the only social service provided by the state this might seem to be a small price to pay for saving Britain from the revolution which must have seemed so imminent during the Swing riots. But contemporaries did not see it that way. The cost of the Poor Law had become intolerable, and something had to be done about it.

The main characteristics of the Old Poor Law are quite clear. First, it relied upon the parish as the unit of administration for it was believed that local people could more successfully distinguish the lazy from the deserving poor. The small size of the parish meant, however, that its finances were invariably feeble, while these generally had to be administered by unpaid, amateur administrators, although in the rapidly expanding industrial towns full-time salaried officials were increasingly employed. Assistant Commissioner S. Walcott, commented on the annually appointed overseers of North Wales he had encountered;

> As a body, I found annual overseers wholly incompetent to discharge the duties of their office, either from the interference of private occupations, or from a want of experience and skill; but most frequently from both these causes. Their object is to get through the year with as little unpopularity and trouble as possible: their successors therefore, have frequently to complain of demands left unsettled, and rates uncollected, either from carelessness or a desire to gain the trifling popularity of having called for fewer assessments than usual. In rural districts the overseers are farmers; in towns generally shopkeepers; and in villages usually one of each of those classes.[7]

A second characteristic was an adherence in theory, though not always in practice, to laws passed in the time of the Tudors and Stuarts; in particular the Elizabethan Act of 1601 (the famous '43 Elizabeth') and the Act of Settlement of 1662. The former act laid down that each parish was to be responsible for the maintenance of its own poor, that overseers were to be appointed annually, and a poor rate levied upon the inhabitants. The impotent poor were to be maintained, while work was to be provided for the able-bodied. The parochial basis of poor relief was reaffirmed by the Act of Settlement, which gave to the overseers, on complaint to a Justice of the Peace, the power to return any newcomer to the parish of his or her 'settlement' (generally the one where he or she was born) so that each parish would continue to support its own poor. These acts probably served the needs of the more static rural England of 1600 to about 1750, but the rapid economic changes thereafter meant that adjustments had to be made.

Third, there was great regional variation in the administration of the law, while many local practices subsequently became rationalised (and nationalised) through the statute book. By the end of the eighteenth century there existed a variety of expedients to deal with the problem of pauperism. In some areas a *labour* rate was adopted, whereby each ratepayer agreed to employ a certain number of labourers according to his poor-rate assessment. If he had no need of the labourers, he was required to pay to the parish the equivalent of their wages. Elsewhere, the *roundsman* system was employed, by which unemployed labourers were sent round the parish from one farm to another until they found someone willing to take them at a wage subsidised by the parish. The most widespread method (although not as widespread as the Poor Law Commissioners imagined) was the *allowance*, or *sliding-scale*, system. It was this which most shocked and distressed the Commissioners. 'Under the operation of the scale system – the system which directs the overseers to *regulate* the incomes of the labourers according to their families – idleness, improvidence, or extravagance occasion no loss, and consequently diligence and economy can afford no gain.'

In some respects the Poor Law Commissioners saw themselves as a conservative rather than a radical force. Repeatedly they referred to the need to return to the spirit of the Elizabethan Poor Law, and to set the poor to work. The principle on which they based their proposals was, however, pure Benthamism. All those able-bodied persons who required poor relief were to be given it – but only inside a workhouse, where conditions were to be 'less eligible' (i.e. more miserable) than those of the poorest independent labourer. This was the pleasure/pain doctrine in action. Those seeking relief would apply the 'felicific calculus', measuring the pain of the less-eligible workhouse against the pleasure of remaining outside, and only those genuinely destitute would pass in through the door. They would have proved the genuineness of their destitution by passing the 'workhouse test'. As Thomas Carlyle cynically commented: 'If paupers are made miserable, paupers will needs decline in multitude. It is a secret known to all rat-catchers.' He argued that the principle was no principle at all, but simply an attempt to sweep the problem of the poor out of sight. In that the New Poor Law attempted to deal not with the underlying causes of destitution but only with the symptom (namely the demand for relief) he was, of course, correct.

Workhouses themselves were nothing new, but the Commissioners heartily disapproved of the majority of those they found:

> . . . in by far the greater number of cases, it is a large almshouse, in which the young are trained in idleness, ignorance, and vice; the able-bodied maintained in sluggish sensual indolence; the aged and more respectable exposed to all the misery that is incident to dwelling in such a society, without government or classification; and the whole body of inmates subsisted on food far exceeding both in kind and in amount, not merely the diet of the independent labourer, but that of the majority of the persons who contribute to their support.

There were exceptions, one such. – Southwell in Nottinghamshire – being the model of the well-regulated workhouse which they proposed. Diet was to be wholesome, but plain and sparse. Regimen was to be strict, and inmates were to be classified into at least four groups: the aged and really impotent; children; able-bodied females; and able-bodied males. This entailed the separation of children from their parents, and husbands from their wives. While the latter practice found the support of the Malthusians, the break-up of families aroused the deepest resentment in the poor themselves.

In order to provide new workhouses where necessary, and to facilitate more efficient workhouse management, the Poor Law Report recommended that a central board should be empowered to combine parishes into unions. However, the Commissioners did not go so far as to recommend a national system of poor relief. This would have been inconceivable at the time for it would have broken with the centuries-old tradition that each area should maintain its own poor, and could only have been implemented in conjunction with a national poor rate. As it was, the advocates of local control found enough to complain about with such centralisation as was recommended.

Because the relief of the poor was to remain a local matter, the Law of Settlement was not to be abolished, even though it offended against many of the canons of contemporary economic thought, especially the belief in the operation of free-market forces. Although liberalised in the course of time, it remained on the statute book until 1948. The law was not always applied, for many employers could see that it was often better to maintain an unemployed labourer in the local 'pool', rather than return him to his parish of settlement. But the threat remained, and it has been suggested that the *fear* of removal — the 'settlement test' — was in many ways as effective as the workhouse test itself.

The implementation of the Poor Law Report

Within two months of its publication the main recommendations of the Poor Law Report were carried into law by the Poor Law Amendment Act of 1834. The actual programme of reform was implicit, for the only explicit provisions related to administration. The government, accepting the tenor of the report, was prepared to leave the principal questions of policy to a body of three Commissioners. In a way this was 'passing the buck', for a struggle which ought to have been fought by the government in Parliament now had to be fought by the Commissioners in the parishes. The Commissioners, a standing target for abuse, were known variously as the 'Three Bashaws of Somerset House', or the 'Pinch-pauper Triumvirate'. Chadwick had hoped to be a made a Commissioner, but had to be satisfied with the secretaryship, a post which he filled for 14 years.

The immediate task was to incorporate groups of parishes into unions, and the Commissioners started with the most heavily pauperised districts of southern England. There were scattered disturbances, but the episode of the Tolpuddle Martyrs ended the effective organisation of the farm labourers for a generation. With the support of farmers and landowners, and helped by good harvests, things went smoothly for a couple of years. By 1838, 13,427 of the parishes of England and Wales had been incorporated into 573 unions, but it was not until 1868 that the whole country came under the act. The unions were often hasty and rather arbitrary combinations, with the effect that few union areas still form the basis of any administrative function. However, the parishes and (until recent local government reforms) the counties still remain in evidence, despite Chadwick's contempt for them.

It was when the Commissioners sent their Assistants to the industrial north that the real storm broke, for in 1837 the relatively good times of the mid-1830s broke into a major economic depression. The workers were outraged by the new workhouses, or 'Bastilles', and they were supported by many officials, magistrates and ratepayers who argued that the workhouse was irrelevant to large-scale urban-industrial unemployment. What factory workers needed was short-term relief to tide them over periods of temporary unemployment until good times returned. For a while there was violent opposition to the new act, but with improvements in the economy, the attraction of rival causes such as Chartism, and the waning of the doctrinaire influence of Chadwick, resistance eventually died down. The psychological trauma of the workhouse was too deep-rooted to be eradicated, however.

The theory of the New Poor Law soon became clouded in practice, in some ways mercifully, in others less so. In the first place, experience of the Old Poor Law might have led to doubts about the ease of operating the 'well-regulated workhouse'. Many workhouse masters continued to be insensitive, petty or downright cruel. There were many workhouse scandals, some no doubt exaggerated, but others all too true. One of the most notorious was the Andover scandal of 1845–6, when it was disclosed that hungry able-bodied paupers, employed in crushing putrid bones for manure, had been sufficiently ravenous to gnaw them for the marrow. A Select Committee which was set up to look into the case developed into a virtual trial of the Commissioners who, in 1847, were replaced by a Poor Law Board, the President of which became a minister of the crown sitting in, and accountable to, Parliament.

5   The workhouse

The New Gruel Shops

Good people all I pray draw near that in this country
dwell;
Concerning these new workhouses the truth to you I'll tell.
Now no relief they give the poor if out of work they drop,
For by this Act, off they are packed to those new gruel shops.

Chorus
May Providence protect the poor while on the earth they
stop,
That none of them may have to go to these new gruel shops.

In England now like mushrooms they spring up from the
ground,
And they will cost poor Johnny Bull full many a thousand
pound;
He'll find this bill a bitter pill – it'll punch his belly
through –
It'll cost him many a thousand pound for making water
gruel.

The bedsteads there I do declare are made of iron strong;
The beds are filled with feathers fine, they're nearly two
yards long,
No grates are there I do declare or smoke your eyes to
torture;
For all the rooms are to be warmed by a pot of boiling water.

Each morning for their breakfast they're to have skilly
gruel;
Poor women will not be allowed to have a cup of tea.
Men from their wives will parted be, indeed it is no joke;
And no snuff must the women take, men neither chew nor
smoke.

For building these new workhouses some people did agree
Because they thought from poor rates the law would set
them free;
But now they find out their mistake they scratch their
wooden blocks
They do repent they did consent to build these new gruel
shops.

Now to conclude and likewise end these lines which I have
penned,
I hope there's no one present here my song it might offend.
Be kind unto the labouring poor who for your wealth do toil;
The Lord will surely bless you with the widow's cruse of oil.

feathers nearly two yards long horse hair.
skilly gruel prison gruel.

1   A broadside ballad on the Poor Law Amendment Act of 1834

Much has been written *about* the poor, but very little *by* the poor. However, we can learn a lot from folk songs. The ballad (1) comes from a broadside printed in Cheltenham. Such songs were originally transmitted orally. They had no particular author, but a 'collective authorship', for the words were altered as the song was passed on, and only those sentiments that were generally acceptable came to survive. The process of refinement came to a halt when a printer saw the commercial possibilities of publishing the song as a broadside. With which of the principles of the Poor Law Amendment Act does this song most take issue?

Pictures 2 and 3 both show the workhouse at Watford in Hertfordshire. The plan follows one of the models recommended by the Poor Law Commissioners, but only the ground floor is shown here. How far does the layout confirm the criticism of workhouse regulations in *The New Gruel Shops*? Does it offer any justification for the song's attack on the costs of the new system? Can the layout be used to support the argument that the Poor Law Commissioners were concerned with improvement? How would the provisions for education, sanitation and hygiene, for example, compare with those in most labouring districts at this time? What was the purpose of the cleansing ward?

The plan of the Watford workhouse shows wards for travellers. Picture 4 shows people outside a casual ward, which served the same purpose of providing a night's shelter in return for a stint of labour. Sir Luke Fildes reworked the picture from one he had drawn five years earlier for the *Graphic*, a newspaper which often pandered to the middle-class fascination with life among the 'the lower orders'. Like much *genre* painting, this is a morality tale. Is it possible to identify examples of the 'deserving' and 'undeserving' poor? What story might we be meant to read into the picture of the man on the extreme left, and what is the role of the policeman?

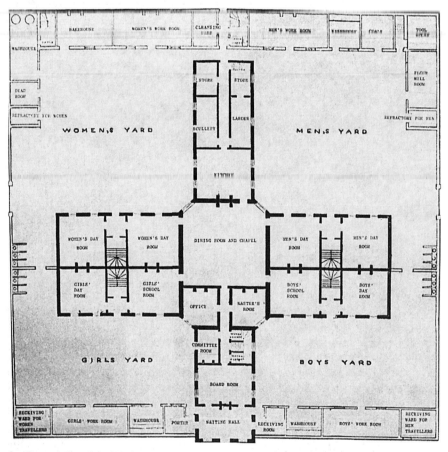

2   Ground plan of the Watford workhouse, 1838

3   The workhouse at Watford, built in 1838

4   'Applicants for Admission to a Casual Ward' by Sir Luke Fildes, 1874

5   'Christmas in a Workhouse',
    Hubert von Herkomer, 1876

6   1861 poster
    seeking ward-keepers
    for the Stepney
    workhouse

Picture 5 also appeared in the *Graphic*, in its Christmas issue of 1876. Hubert von Herkomer was a very popular late-Victorian artist. What story does his picture tell about workhouses? Is this accurate social information, or simply a Christmas tale of goodwill, to be enjoyed after a good dinner with one's family, or after reading *A Christmas Carol* (1843), or reciting the favourite parlour ballad, *It was Christmas Day in the Workhouse*?

The final picture (6) is an example of ephemera – printed items which were intended to have only a short life and which, therefore, were often not preserved. Does this give such items as posters and notices a special value as historical evidence? What does this poster tell us about the range of services carried out by the Poor Law authorities? Do pictures 4–6 suggest that a change in the main function of the Poor Law had taken place since the time of pictures 1–3?

IMBECILE
WARD KEEPERS
WANTED.

The Guardians of Mile End Old Town require the services of a MALE and FEMALE, to take charge of the HARMLESS LUNATICS in the Workhouse Infirmary. Candidates must be active, healthy, patient, without encumbrance, and between twenty-five and fifty years of age.

SALARY } MALE - - £25.
         FEMALE - £20.

With Board, Lodging, and Washing,
A MAN AND WIFE PREFERRED.

Applications in the Candidate's own hand-writing, marked on the outside "M." or "F.," as the case may be, stating age, and where previously employed, accompanied by THREE TESTIMONIALS, of recent date, must reach me before Twelve o'Clock on THURSDAY, 19th instant, on which day at Three, applicants must attend at their own expense. A selection will then be made, and the appointment take place at Six in the Evening, of the said 19th. No one need apply whose character for honesty, sobriety, and competency, will not bear the strictest investigation. Canvassing the Guardians is prohibited.

(By Order.)

E. J. SOUTHWELL,
Clerk.

Workhouse, Bancroft Road, Stepney, N.E.
7th December, 1861.

T. Perry, Printer, 111, Leman Street, Whitechapel.

Second, the attempts to abolish out-relief failed, in rural areas as well as in the towns. By 1842 most unions in the rural parts of England had been issued with an order which, with certain specified exceptions, prohibited outdoor relief of the able-bodied. This was followed in 1844 by a general order called the Outdoor Relief Prohibitory Order, again laying down that relief to able-bodied men and women was only to be given in the workhouse. This order applied only to the less populated districts, for it was apparent that such an Order would not only be ineffective in the more densely populated manufacturing regions, but would be positively inflammatory. There the Outdoor Labour Test Order of 1842 applied, under the terms of which the 'workhouse test' was to be paralleled by a monotonous and unpleasant 'labour test', work which had to be performed before out-relief to the able-bodied would be granted. However, the Assistant Commissioners, whose task it was to inspect the unions, were able to make only perfunctory half-yearly visits, and out-relief continued to be widely practised throughout the country. In 1846, for example, there were 1,331,000 paupers, of whom only 199,000 were 'in-paupers', leaving 1,132,000 paupers on out-relief. Of the gross total roughly one-quarter (375,000) were able-bodied adults. In theory, all of these should have been in the workhouse, but in fact only 82,000 were. A further General Order of 1852 failed to remedy the situation, and many boards of guardians used loopholes (such as sickness in the family) to continue to maintain the able-bodied outside the workhouse. Outdoor relief was cheaper, and could be supplemented by small earnings and private charity. In 1860, for example, paupers in the eastern counties cost 3s 5$\frac{1}{2}$d a week if taken into the workhouse, but only 1s 9d if relieved outside. The Lancashire cotton famine of the 1860s proved how inadequate the Poor Law was to handle mass industrial unemployment. It did, however, lead to the Public Works Act of 1863 which, though largely unsuccessful, broke new ground in empowering local authorities to borrow money cheaply in order to initiate public works schemes to provide employment. This was a clear acknowledgement that the assumption of the 1834 act that all able-bodied workers could find employment if they tried was a false one. The assisted emigration of paupers pointed in the same direction.

Third, while the vast majority of paupers, even able-bodied adult males, never saw the inside of a workhouse, those who did increasingly experienced conditions which were *not* 'less-eligible'. This basic tenet of the New Poor Law posed an insoluble dilemma. The condition of depressed urban workers and starving rural labourers was so low that it was hard, in a civilised society, to provide less agreeable conditions in the workhouse which were at the same time humane and decent. Moreover, so many of the able-bodied paupers remained on out-relief that work-houses came increasingly (but by no means exclusively) to house the aged, the sick, the mentally ill and the young. As early as 1841 the Poor Law Commission recognised the ideological problem:

> If the pauper is always promptly attended by a skilful and well qualified medical practitioner . . . if the patient be furnished with all the cordials and stimulants which may promote his recovery: it cannot be denied that his condition in these respects is better than that of the needy and industrious ratepayer who has neither the money nor the influence to secure prompt and careful attendance.[8]

The same consideration applied to pauper education, for the industrial training given to pauper children gave them a distinct advantage over children who were merely poor. Increasingly, then, the principles of 1834 were eroded. A spate of investigations into poverty between 1870 and 1901 did much to dislodge the idea that lack of means necessarily presupposed moral failings. The question of distinguishing the 'deserving' from the 'undeserving' poor came into greater prominence, and by the end of the century the Poor Law faced renewed attacks.

Public health, the environment and housing

If pauperism affected only those at the very lowest levels of society, public health and the environment were concerns to all. Disease was no respecter of persons. Albert, the Prince Consort, died of typhoid in 1861 at the age of 42; and in 1871, when he was 30, the Prince of Wales suffered a severe attack. Public–health problems affected the Victorians through their senses, and what the eye did not see the nose often smelled. The River Thames, its waters putrefied by masses of untreated sewage, stank unbearably in hot weather. The year 1858 was that of 'the Great Stink'. *The Times* reported that on 30 June officers in one of the corridors of the Houses of Parliament

> were suddenly surprised by the members of a committee rushing out of one of the rooms in the greatest haste and confusion . . . foremost among them being the Chancellor of the Exchequer [Disraeli], who, with a mass of papers in one hand and with his pocket handkerchief clutched in the other, and applied closely to his nose, with body half bent, hastened in dismay from the pestilential odour, followed closely by Sir James Graham, who seemed to be attacked by a sudden fit of expectoration; Mr Gladstone also paid particular attention to his nose, while . . . the other members of the committee also precipitately quitted the pestilential apartment, the disordered state of their papers, which they carried in their hands, showing how imperatively they had received notice to quit.

Rich and poor alike also endured the smoke which covered industrial towns, described in the case of Manchester in 1842 as 'an inky canopy which seemed to embrace and involve the entire place'.

While all suffered they did not, of course, suffer equally. It became increasingly clear from the beginning of the 1840s that urban conditions were more lethal than rural ones, and also that the areas of greatest poverty coincided with those of highest mortality. In 1842 the Poor Law Commissioners issued a 'Report on the Sanitary Condition of the Labouring Population', based upon a questionnaire sent to all the local boards of guardians, and upon the evidence of three eminent doctors, Neil Arnott, Thomas Southwood Smith and James Kay (later Sir James Kay-Shuttleworth, an educational reformer considered in more detail below). This report demonstrated the enormous difference not only between urban and rural death rates, but between the life expectancy of different social classes. Manchester statistics were placed alongside those of Rutland:

Table 5.1   Urban and rural death rates: Manchester and Rutland, 1842

Classification	Average age of death (years)	
	In Manchester	In Rutlandshire
Professional persons and gentry, and their families	38	52
Tradesmen and their families (in Rutlandshire, farmers and graziers are included with shopkeepers)	20	41
Mechanics, labourers, and their families	17	38

The man who drafted the report, which sold more copies than any previous parliamentary paper, was (have you not guessed?) Edwin Chadwick, who increasingly turned to public-health matters, especially as his relations with his masters, the Poor Law Commissioners, deteriorated. Under the Chadwick regime, said *The Times*, it was 'a perpetual Saturday night, with Master John Bull being scrubbed and rubbed and small-tooth-combed till the tears ran into his eyes, and his teeth chattered, and his fists clenched themselves with worry and pain'. The end of his reign, the paper concluded, demonstrated that 'we prefer to take our chance of Cholera and the rest, than be bullied into health'. That Chadwick was a bully is undoubted. Lyon Playfair, a member of the 1843 Royal Commission on the State of Large Towns, suggested that greater responsibility should be devolved on local authorities. Chadwick barked back: 'Sir, the Devil was expelled from heaven because he objected to centralisation, and all those who object to centralisation oppose it on devilish grounds!' Chadwick always felt that right was on his side. The infuriating thing is that it usually was; but not always. He was wrong-headed in his enthusiasm for the use of sewage as an agricultural manure, and he blindly refused to accept fresh medical evidence when it conflicted with his pet theories. He held to the 'miasmic' theory of disease, which suggested that epidemics were spread by the inhalation of odours caused by decaying animal matter. His solution was therefore to flush sewage away in narrow-bore earthenware pipes into the nearest river. The engineering was excellent, but the theory was wrong, as was demonstrated in 1854 when Dr John Snow proved conclusively that cholera was water-borne. Chadwick put his faith in engineering and centralised administration. His lieutenant and successor, John Simon, put his in preventive medicine and local management. Whereas Chadwick bullied, Simon cajoled. It is hard to say which was more effective.

Chadwick laid the foundations of modern sanitary reform. He was drawn into public health by the increasingly evident connection between poverty and disease, a relationship made clearer by the reports of the Assistant Poor Law Commissioners. He took the environmentalist position that poverty was caused by disease, and that disease was caused by factors over which, in the main, the poor had no control. Chadwick's report of 1842 led to the Royal Commission into the Sanitary Condition of Large Towns and Populous Districts, and to the formation of the Health of Towns Association (1844). This agitation in turn produced the Public Health Act of 1848. The whole process, from Poor Law to public health legislation, is an illustration of the process of 'feedback' within the administrative machine which the state was steadily expanding.

There was another reformer, however, and one which was perhaps even more powerful than Chadwick himself – cholera. As *The Times* commented: 'The cholera is the best of all sanitary reformers. It overlooks no mistake and pardons no oversight.' The disease was of Asiatic origin, first heard of in modern times in India in 1817. Not until 1884 was the bacillus isolated by the German chemist, Robert Koch. The disease spread from Asia to Europe. By the summer of 1831 it had spread as far as the Baltic ports, and in October struck Hamburg, a port in constant communication with Britain. The government, at that time preoccupied with the Reform Bill, took hasty precautions but nothing could keep out the dreaded disease. The port of Sunderland was the first affected, and within months it had spread to Gateshead, Newcastle, Glasgow and Edinburgh. By February 1832 it had struck London, where 5,300 people died before the autumn. Nothing like it had been known since the Great Plague of 1665. The disease struck people with terror, not least because of its appalling suddenness. Violent stomach pains, vomiting and diarrhoea were the symptoms, followed by a total collapse in which the body became cold, the pulse imperceptible, the skin wizened and blue. The victims sometimes died within hours, or days at the most. One in every two cases proved fatal.

In 1845 came reports from Afghanistan that cholera was on the rampage again; and there seemed something uncanny in the way that it spread once more across Europe. It hit Moscow on the very day of the sixteenth anniversary of the first attack. Britain was first struck on 22 September 1848. But by then the sanitary landscape had been altered by the Public Health Act, passed in the previous months. At least minimal precautions could now be taken.

The act was limited in scope and many of its provisions were permissive. For an experimental period of five years a Central Board of Health was set up, consisting of three members who included Chadwick and Lord Shaftesbury. In places where the death rate was more than 23 per 1,000 (just over the national average), or where 10 per cent of the ratepayers requested it, the Board was empowered to send an inspector, and then to authorise the town council to carry out the duties imposed by the act. Where there was no town council, the Board was authorised to set up local Boards of Health. In either case there were wide powers over drainage, building regulation, nuisance removal and water supply. Beyond these minimum require- ments there were wider powers, to provide parks or municipal baths, for example, but no local authority was required to adopt these. It was a weakness of the act that the power to appoint a Medical Officer of Health was permissive only, and did not become obligatory until the Public Health Act of 1875. Cheapness was one of the main advantages. Many areas had established Improvement Commissioners or suchlike bodies by private act of Parliament. But this could cost £2,000 or so, whereas the cost of setting up a local Board of Health was around £100. The act contained provision for inspection similar to that for the Poor Law, and the main sanction of the Central Board was its power to authorise loans. Even this degree of centralisation was excessive in the eyes of many local patriots. The Central Board came in for the usual degree of sniping, so much so that it was not renewed in 1853, but replaced by other less unpopular arrangements.

Public-health reform differed in one important respect from reform of the Poor Law. In the latter case there already existed a nationwide, statutory system capable of reorganisation. (The system was different in Scotland, where the law was not reformed until 1845.) Public health, however, had been the province of ad hoc bodies empowered by local acts. It was too much even for Chadwick to give public health the universality of the Poor Law, especially as vested interests were so great. Both public and private bodies were resistant to change. Local Improvement Com- missioners feared the loss of their powers; water companies wished to hang on to their revenues. Mill-owners felt under no compunction to reduce smoke emissions from their factory chimneys; and industrialists generally had more of an eye to profits than a nose for pollution. Nevertheless, the Public Health Act of 1848 showed that the government was prepared to do *something*, although a chaos of authorities remained.

If, as was suggested in Chapter 1, there is a danger in overemphasising the role of 'heroic' inventors and their macroinventions, there is equally a danger, when reviewing the history of public health, of concentrating excessively on the work of a few celebrated characters such as Chadwick and Simon, and upon the obstructions that prevented them from achieving more than they did. The death rate remained almost constant between 1848 and 1875, suggesting a lack of correspondence between reform and falling mortality. In the 1980s, however, the historian A. S. Wohl advanced our understanding of the problem by focusing on the actual achievements at local level, and upon the time-lag between the passage of legislation and its effective implementation. His approach shifted attention to the last quarter of the century, when mortality rates *were* falling. The key personnel then were not path-breakers at the top of the administrative hierarchy, but a growing body of professionals building an efficient system from the bottom. Foremost among these were the Medical Officers of Health, of whom there were 1,770 by 1899. They had their own journal, *Public Health*, first launched in 1888, and, by the end of the century, nearly 700 of them were possessors of the Diploma in Public Health. The Medical Officers of Health were supported by an expanding army of sanitary engineers and inspectors, and of public analysts (with a responsibility of examining the quality of local foodstuffs) who grew from seven in 1872 to 224 by 1882. Personal health, as well as public health was encouraged by the government, not least by the Medical Relief (Disqualification Removal) Act of 1885, which allowed people to enter Poor Law hospitals without suffering the indignity of disfranchisement which attached to paupers.

The relationship between public health and the environment was a complex one. The development of urban sewage systems did much to remove the causes of disease from towns – but most of the sewage was pumped directly into rivers. At the end of the century, London poured 150 million gallons of sewage a day into the Thames at the Barking and Crossness outfalls, and this constituted one-sixth of the total volume of river water. The houses that had their sewage removed in this way were heated by coal fires, which not only kept dampness and chills at bay, but enabled water to be heated for clothes and personal washing. Yet the fires spewed smoke into the air. In 1892 the Medical Officer of Health for Chelsea estimated that London consumed 7 million tons of coal a year, and shot 200 tons of soot into the atmosphere every *day*. It would only have cost around £3 to convert a house with five fires to burn coal more efficiently; but to make it compulsory would have entailed inspection, and in an era when the Englishman's home was his castle (provided that he was not one of the poor) the prospect of this was anathema.

Industrial pollution and health exhibited similar tensions. Industry polluted the air and rivers, yet provided many of the means (as well as the wealth) to improve health. Alkali works were double polluters, pouring hydrochloric acid into the air from their chimneys, and sulphurated hydrogen from their waste tips. Yet from these factories also came cheap washing agents which were essential to hygiene. The potteries were responsible for great clouds of smog, yet produced the sanitary wares and cheap sewage pipes that help to banish disease.

Some instances of pollution were as bizarre (and outrageous) as anything experienced in our own day. Brian Clapp gives many examples drawn from parliamentary papers. For example:

> In one of those telling illustrations that enliven some Victorian blue books, the royal commission reproduced in facsimile a letter written in Calder water sampled at a particularly unfavourable point – where the river received the contents of Wakefield's sewers. The water was strong enough to make a tolerable greyish ink. The author, an agricultural-implement maker, only regretted that he could not send a specimen of the odour of the ink as well.

The same Royal Commission (on Rivers Pollution) in its third report of 1867 described the inflammable Bradford Canal:

> Although it has usually been considered an impossible feat to set the Thames on fire it was found practicable to set the Bradford Canal on fire, as this at

times formed part of the amusement of boys in the neighbourhood. They struck a match placed on the end of a stick, reached over and set the canal on fire, the flame rising six feet and running along the water for many yards, like a will-o-the-wisp; canal boats have been so enveloped in flame as to frighten persons on board.[9]

Pollution control and care of the environment presented peculiar problems, and although many solutions were attempted, the results were anything but successful. In the first place it had to be demonstrated that what was offensive was also noxious. The gunpowder fumes which seeped from the Woolwich Arsenal were praised by some as a disinfectant against disease, while a whiff of air from the gasworks was thought to cure whooping cough. Robert Roberts, a Salford boy of the Edwardian era, must have been whooping-cough free in that case:

> The local gasholders, like vast iron dugs, bulging and sagging as they fed the town, dominated our neighbourhood . . . We grew up in their shadow and stench, breathing in more coal gas, it seemed, than oxygen. But the borough fathers sat proud, for had not Salford led the whole of mankind in the industrial use of gas?[10]

The borough fathers *would* sit proud, for industry paid the rates. Pollution and prosperity were seen as partners. Consequently, in the middle years of the century when environmental control was a matter of local by-law, it would have been an audacious authority that attempted to burden its industries with additional costs. What was needed was some national policy, but even then, as with the 1875 Public Health Act which consolidated the existing provisions against 'nuisances', the requirements of industry were deferred to. The act was weakened by the provision that no offence of creating excessive smoke was to be construed if industrial

> fireplaces or furnaces [were] constructed in such a manner as to consume as far as practicable, having regard to the nature of the manufacture or trade, all smoke arising therefrom, and that such fireplace or furnace has been carefully attended to by the person having the charge thereof.[11]

That 'as far as practicable', and similar phrases in other statutes, prevented any real progress from being made. Effective legislation had to wait until the late twentieth century, when pollution control and the protection of the environment came to be seen not as local, nor even as national issues, but as matters of global concern.

Matters of public health and the environment impinged most directly on the majority of people in the quality of their housing. Through the powers given to local authorities to regulate building, the Public Health Acts of 1848 and 1875 had important implications for the issue, but neither statute allowed for the provision of houses by the state. Housing was seen as a matter for private enterprise, to be governed by the laws of supply and demand. The problem was that in most nineteenth-century towns demand greatly exceeded supply, and overcrowding was the result. In the 1860s Liverpool's population per square mile was 66,000, giving each citizen little more than 5.5 square metres. The rapid expansion of urban population was not the only cause of overcrowding, for the economic pressures on urban land – from railways and business users, for example – entailed wholesale demolition which turned the screw on accommodation even tighter. The same was true of urban improvements, such as street widening. The effect of new building was expressed in a verse which appeared in *The Builder* in 1851:

> Who builds? Who builds? Alas, ye poor!
> If London day by day 'improves',

> Where shall ye find a friendly door,
> When every day a home removes?

The demand for living space was satisfied in a number of ways: by running down and sub-dividing existing houses and by using cellars; by constructing low-cost, jerry-built houses, often of the back-to-back variety; and by the expedient of the common lodging-house.

The facades of respectable or even grand houses could often hide appalling overcrowding. Robert Rawlinson, a prominent sanitary reformer, wrote in 1858:

> As towns increase there is an engulfing or lowering of whole streets and of entire districts of houses, built originally for the merchant and superior trades-man. Examine some of our great sea-ports and inland manufacturing towns, and it will be found that streets of houses originally erected for the 'merchant princes' are now in ruins . . . now the abodes of the improvident, the vagrant, the vicious, and the unfortunate . . .[12]

Such rundown areas were known as 'rookeries'. One such was the St Giles area of London. In 1847 the Statistical Society of London nominated a committee of three to survey Church Lane, which ran parallel with New Oxford Street, near its junction with Tottenham Court Road. In 1841 there were 27 houses in the street, accommodating 655 people. By 1847 they housed 1,095. Cellar dwellings were evident in most major towns. In the area of Greater Manchester in the 1830s a total of 40,000–50,000 people lived in such places; in Liverpool the number exceeded 45,000. Writing of the cellar dwellings of Manchester, Joseph Adshead observed in 1842:

> . . . it must be borne in mind that the cellars which are used as habitations by the poor have no other feature in common with the cellars attached to the middle-class of dwelling-houses than that of their being below the level of the street. They are most of them neither drained nor soughed. They are consequently damp – are always liable to be flooded – are almost entirely with-out the means of ventilation, having rarely but the outlets of door and window at the one side, and these almost hid below the level of the street.[13]

Back-to-backs, a widely adopted design for the cheapest terraced houses, had only one open face capable of admitting light. They shared a common back wall, stand-ing one on each side of it. Thousands were built in the first half of the century. Mid-Victorian Nottingham, for example, had at least 8,000, constituting about two-thirds of its total stock of houses. Out of 1,601 plans sanctioned in Bradford in 1854, 1,079 were for back-to-back houses, and though many towns banned them in the middle years of the century, Bradford and Leeds did not. The Leeds authorities should not be regarded as particularly backward, however, for they had confidence that this type of housing (which is very economical of land) was capable of incorporating improvements. Indeed, the last back-to-back was built in Leeds as late as 1937. F. M. L. Thompson has observed that 'the more modern ones continue to be lived in in the 1980s, some of them much sought after by the professional classes'.

Then there were common lodging-houses where a bed of sorts might be had for 2d or 3d a night. A report produced by the Leeds police in 1851 identified, in a half-circle drawn at a radius of a quarter of a mile from the parish church, 222 lodging-houses. They accommodated 2,500 people, averaging two-and-a-half persons to each bed and four-and-a-half persons to each room.

Such conditions were damnable, but as historians we are called upon to understand rather than condemn. The prevailing ethic that everything had to pay meant that those who could afford least got least. Work that was shoddy and nasty might not be dishonest. It might be a perfectly honest job at the price. The problem of providing improved dwellings at a rent which the poor could afford bedevilled most of the philanthropic activity in the field of housing, of which there was much. The aim was to set an example, but the principle example set in practice was that good, cheap housing did not pay. Rents were necessarily higher than could be afforded by those below the artisan class. In the 1880s improved dwellings attracted more curates and policemen than unskilled casual labourers. Yet, while the high rents kept out the 'degraded classes', the rules of many improved dwellings were themselves degrading to the artisans and others who could afford them. In the well-known Peabody dwellings, for example, tenants had to be vaccinated, were not allowed to keep dogs or hang out washing, were forbidden to paint or paper their rooms, or to hang pictures on the walls, and had to be in by 11 p.m., when the outside doors were locked and the gas turned off. The historian, Donald Olsen, says of the model block dwellings: 'Grim, bleak and forbidding, they resist even today our tendency to assimilate all aspects of Victorian culture in a warm, nostalgic embrace. The young and trendy may eagerly move into transformed rows of labourers' cottages, but there has been no comparable rush into Peabody Buildings.'[14]

It is clear that philanthropy did little to solve the total housing problem. One prominent reformer, Octavia Hill, admitted that the total number housed by philanthropy between 1845 and 1875 was 26,000, which amounted to little more than six months' increase in the population of London. It has even been argued that private philanthropic effort, by putting forward an inadequate solution, delayed the introduction of the only adequate one – the state provision of housing. On the other hand, the relative impotence of philanthropic housing societies offered an irrefutable argument for state action. This came late. The first real housing act, the 1868 Artisans' and Labourers' Dwellings Act (the first of three 'Torrens's Acts') enabled local authorities to compel an owner to demolish or repair an insanitary home at his own expense. The Cross Act, dating from 1875, enabled local authorities to make compulsory purchases for redevelopment schemes involving the erection of houses for sale. Both sets of legislation were permissive, and neither provided for drastic action. Even the 1890 Housing of the Working Classes Act achieved little. It empowered councils to deal with unhealthy areas, purchase land compulsorily and erect new houses, but only the London County Council made a start with the use of the new powers. Council housing remained a long way in the future.

Crime and social order

In 1844 Friedrich Engels claimed that social war was being waged by the British working class, and that the symptom was a rising crime rate:

> The clearest indication of the unbounded contempt of the workers for the existing social order is the wholesale manner in which they break its laws. If the demoralisation of the worker passes beyond a certain point then it is just as natural that he will turn into a criminal – as inevitably as water turns into steam at boiling point . . . Consequently the incidence of crime has increased with the growth of the working-class population and there is more crime in Britain than in any other country in the world . . . There can be no doubt that in England the social war is already being waged . . . . The criminal statistics prove that this social war is being waged more vigorously, more passionately and with greater bitterness every year.[15]

Although his ideological viewpoint was different, the Tory Sheriff of Lanarkshire, Sir Archibald Alison, writing in the same year as Engels, saw the same evidence of rising crime:

> It is difficult to say what is destined to be the ultimate fate of a country in which the progress of wickedness is so much more rapid than the increase of the numbers of people . . . Meanwhile, destitution, profligacy, sensuality and crime advance with unheard of rapidity in the manufacturing districts, and the dangerous classes there massed together combine every three or four years in some general strike or alarming insurrection, which, while it lasts, excites universal terror . . . The vast preponderance of crime is to be found in the manufacturing or densely populated districts.[16]

Allegations of rising crime rates are not unknown in our own day, and there are certain similarities between the alarm shown in the two periods, a century or more apart. In the first place, spectacular crimes, publicised by the press and used by politicians and others to boost their campaigns for tougher policing or punishment, can easily lead to 'moral panic'. Modern examples will speedily spring to mind, but examples from the nineteenth century would include the garroting panic in the summer of 1862 (after the street robbery of Hugh Pilkington MP) and the panic over Jack the Ripper and the Whitechapel murders in 1888. Although the latter murders were confined to an area of roughly one square mile in the East End of London, alarm spread throughout the country. Second, it has to be remembered that the state creates crimes with its laws, and can abolish them by repealing those laws. Such alterations of the law result from economic, social and political change, and also from technical change – as witnessed, for example, by the development of new crimes relating to the motor car or the computer. Individuals may question the legitimacy of such legal changes. When employers attempted to clamp down on petty pilfering, they were attacking a practice which many workers considered to be a traditional system of 'perks'. To continue the practice might be considered by the perpetrators as an act of social protest rather than criminality, in the same way that poaching was considered by many to be a non-criminal act. A third similarity between the two periods lies in the continuing debate about the nature of the evidence of increases (or decreases) in criminal activity.

Criminal statistics stretched back before 1815, but the present series of Judicial Statistics commenced only in 1856–7. They could provide ammunition for a variety of views. In 1892, for example, there was a discussion on the crime rate in which the same statistics were used by the chaplain of Wandsworth Prison to demonstrate that crime had increased; by the chairman of the Prison Commissioners to show that it had decreased; and by the chief constable of Staffordshire to support his view that it remained substantially unchanged!

So unreliable are the figures that the historian J. J. Tobias, in an important study first published in the 1960s, rejected them altogether, and worked instead from a variety of impressionistic reports, such as views expressed in parliamentary papers, or by reformers, magistrates, policemen, journalists and a wide range of other contemporary commentators. He has not gone unchallenged, however. David Philips has argued, for example, that as the contemporary commentators had themselves frequently based their opinions on the figures, the historian might as well use them at first hand, however inadequate they might be. For if the figures are faulty, a conclusion based on them in the 1850s (which is what Tobias is using) is no more valid than one drawn in the 1960s.

The figures certainly *suggest* that crime was on the increase. Between 1805, when comprehensive records began, and 1848, the numbers committed for trial for indictable offences in England and Wales increased more than sixfold, from 4,605 to 30,349; and the numbers convicted more than eightfold, from 2,783 to 22,900. But these figures do not, of course, indicate the amount of crime actually committed; they only reveal changes in the number of crimes detected and brought to trial. Several factors make it probable that more criminals were in fact brought before the courts, especially changes in the method of prosecuting offenders and the development of a more efficient policing system.

In the early nineteenth century the English legal system relied on private prosecution, whereby the victims of offences had the responsibility of bringing offenders to trial. Various factors deterred potential private prosecutors, the chief being the time and expense involved. Furthermore, until the death penalty had been repealed for all offences against property (not completely until 1837) there might be a reluctance to invoke the law at all. Other potential prosecutors were no doubt deterred by the fear of retaliation by the offender or his associates. Between 1752 and 1826 reimbursement of expenses for prosecutors and witnesses was gradually extended, while the Criminal Justice Act of 1855, by making petty thefts capable of a summary trial by magistrates made actions in such cases both cheaper and speedier. Improvements in policing must also have affected the crime figures as more offenders were detected, and as the police gradually took over the burden of prosecution. This had become the norm by 1860, and the police continued to prosecute the majority of criminal cases until such powers were passed to the Crown Prosecution Service, which was established for England and Wales in 1985.

Before the setting up of professional police forces in the nineteenth century, the traditional police authority throughout the country was the parish constable, an annually appointed, unpaid office, filled in rotation – although more and more paid deputies were employed. Not until 1872 was the ancient obligation on parishes to appoint a constable repealed, but for some time the office had been a mere formality. Parish constables had their limitations, but they should not be taken for the illiterate figures of fun they are sometimes depicted as having been. When they could rely on community support they could be very effective, as is indicated by the extent to which the system worked in many areas until the 1840s without a complete breakdown in law and order.

As with other social problems, urban conditions revealed the flaws in the system. But whereas London had lagged behind in questions of poverty and public health, it was the capital which led the way with police reform. The legislators, of course, were face to face with London's problems. Pressure from West Indian merchants (who had an effective lobby in Parliament) was strong, as their goods were regularly pilfered from ships on the Thames. The result was the setting up of the Marine Police Establishment in 1798. The government also supported the famous Bow Street Runners. Further extension of a police force, however, depended on striking a balance between, on the one hand, greater protection, and on the other, a feared loss of freedom. The Select Committee on Police of the Metropolis reported in 1822:

> It is difficult to reconcile an effective system of police with that perfect freedom of action and exemption from interference, which are the great privileges and blessings of society in this country; and Your Committee think that the forfeiture of such advantages would be too great a sacrifice for improvements in police, or facilities in detection of crime, however desirable in themselves if abstractedly considered.[17]

The year of Catholic Emancipation (1829) saw the passage of the Metropolitan Police Act, which established the first paid, uniformed force for the London Metropolitan area, and which broke new ground by transferring powers from the local to the central authority, the Commissioner being directly responsible to the Home Secretary. The Municipal Corporations Act of 1835 made it obligatory for all incorporated boroughs to set up police forces; and the County Police Acts of 1839 and 1840 permitted but did not compel counties to do the same. By the 1850s 30 counties (including Yorkshire) still had no regular police force, and it took the County and Borough Police Act of 1856 to compel them to act. Three Inspectors of Constabulary were appointed, and forces certified to be efficient qualified for a Treasury grant of one-quarter of the cost of pay and clothing. The legislation took some time to become implemented at local level, and for a while there existed two parallel systems of law enforcement, the new police and the old parish constables, frequently with friction between them.

The crime which police forces were up against was largely crime against property, about 90 per cent of all indictable offences dealt with falling into this category. By today's standards murder and manslaughter were not extensive, and there were few motiveless or perverse crimes of violence. David Philips's studies of the Black Country between 1835 and 1860 suggest 'a rough society with a degree of personal violence, but not a society in which the criminal violence generally extended to the taking of life. The chance of being killed in an accident in a mine or factory was much greater for most of the population'.

There are three further points we might consider: did those who committed offences against property see their actions as criminal; were the bulk of offences committed by a 'criminal class'; and how far were there cyclical trends in crime?

Whereas crime may be technically easy to define, in practice there are difficulties. An act which might be considered criminal if committed by one person may not be considered so if committed by another. In 1862 Henry Mayhew visited the House of Correction, Tothill Fields, and wrote:

> Here we find little creatures of six years of age branded with a felon's badge – boys, not even in their teens, clad in prison dress, for the heinous offence of throwing stones, or obstructing highways, or unlawfully knocking on doors – crimes which the very magistrates themselves, who committed the youths, must have assuredly perpetrated in their boyhood . . . Suppose you or I, reader, had been consigned to such a place in our school-boy days, for those acts of thoughtlessness which none but fanatics would think of regarding as crime.[18]

In addition to class differences, distinctions were made between types of theft. Many urban workers claimed what amounted to a traditional right to take 'perks' from employers' property. Philips demonstrates that in the areas, and for the periods he has studied, 28.2 per cent of all committals for larceny, and 22.2 per cent of committals for all types of offence were in the nature of 'industrial thefts', frequently of waste materials or other items low in value. The number of convictions for this type of offence went up between 1835 and 1860, largely, he argues, because magistrates (who increasingly included coal and iron masters in addition to the local gentry) made a determined effort to stamp out the practice.

Pilfering continues to this day, of course, and is committed by many people who would not regard themselves as criminals. There is controversy as to whether crime in the nineteenth century was committed by 'ordinary' citizens or by a 'criminal class'. Many contemporaries argued that there was such a class, and J. J. Tobias, who accepts this view, quotes a number of them. The Revd W. D. Morrison, for example, was a prison chaplain who wrote in 1891:

> There is a population of habitual criminals which forms a class by itself. Habitual criminals are not to be confounded with the working or any other class; they are a set of persons who make crime the object and business of their lives; to commit crime is their trade; they deliberately scoff at honest ways of earning a living, and must accordingly be looked upon as a class of a separate and distinct character from the rest of the community.[19]

Philips takes a different view. The dramatic picture of crime which Tobias gives may have been true of large and rich cities like London, but his researches into crime in the Black Country (which is probably more representative of industrial Britain as a whole) lead Philips to conclude that most crime was 'prosaic and un-dramatic; involving small amounts being stolen, squalid robberies, burglaries and assaults'. Likewise, most offenders were not professional criminals, but poor men and women committing largely unplanned crimes.

Philips and Tobias also disagree on the extent to which criminal activity was affected by the trade cycle. Tobias argues that 'on the whole . . . there is little ground to think that the immediate pressure of want was a major cause of adult crime, or that cyclical changes in this pressure altered its level'. Philips, basing his views on the work of V. A. C. Gatrell and T. B. Hadden, argues that in times of depression, property offences tended to rise, and offences of drunkenness and assault tended to fall, while these trends were reversed in times of prosperity. In other words, distress was likely to drive more people to theft, while prosperity meant that more could be spent on drink.

In the eyes of many, crime and drink were inextricably linked. The amount of alcohol consumed in the nineteenth century was staggering. Temperance workers (admittedly not the least biased of sources) assessed the total amount drunk at over £67 million in 1830 and nearly £81 million in 1850. This averaged nearly £3 per person per annum, or more than a labouring family of five or six would pay in rent. The peak years were 1875–6. In 1875 the official figures for spirit consumption (which exclude, of course, the product of illicit stills) showed an average consumption of 1.3 gallons (6 litres) of spirits per head of the population. The following year saw the peak in beer consumption, when the average amount drunk was 34.4 gallons (156 litres). When we remember the calculation of these averages includes the temperate and teetotal, infants as well as adults, and women as well as men, we can appreciate that the intake of some people must have been enormous. All social classes drank, of course, and the opponents of licensing restrictions often pointed out that the rich could drink in the comfort and privacy of their own homes, but there can be no denying that there was justification in seeing drink as a lower-class problem. Drink clearly brought wretchedness to many, and was, perhaps, the most significant cause of self-imposed poverty. We would be wrong, therefore, to consider temperance reformers as a gang of kill-joy puritans. How is the addiction to drink to be accounted for? Numerous factors were involved, some more obvious than others. Drink brought temporary relief from their miseries to many a man and woman. As the Earl of Derby commented in 1871:

> . . . if a man or a woman has to live in a hole where cleanliness and decency are impossible, you must not wonder if they try to drown – I will not call it their misery, but their discomfort, in drink.
>
> There is a kind of action and reaction in this matter. Crowded lodgings and poisoned air produce the craving for stimulants, and drunken homes keep the family from ever moving into a more respectable home.[20]

Or Robert Roberts, brought up in the slums of Salford:

To the great mass of manual workers the local public house spelled paradise. Many small employers of labour still paid out their weekly wages there. In the main fetid dens, they held an attraction with which nothing in present-day society can quite compare. After the squalor from which so many men came there dwelt within a tavern all one could crave for – warmth, bright lights, music, song, comradeship, the smiling condescension of the landlady, large and bosomy, for ever sexually unattainable, true, but one could dream, and her husband (the favoured called him by his first name), a man of the world dispensing wit and wisdom – and Tory politics too, of course: publicans were Tories almost to a man, and the party's self-appointed agents. But above all, men went for the ale that brought a slow, fuddled joy. Beer was indeed the shortest way out of the city. Then, driven at nearly midnight into the street, their temple shuttered and barred, the company lingered on, maudlin, in little groups, loath to face a grim reality again.[21]

It was expected that a man should drink, and there were many social pressures on him to do so. Drinking customs were woven into the fabric of working-class life. At fairs and markets, bargains were sealed with a drink, while tradition demanded a bout of drinking on particular occasions, such as the completion of an apprenticeship. The public house was also a form of job centre, and the teetotal worker (especially if he was a *casual* worker) cut himself off from one of the principal exchanges of employment information, if he refused to enter. It hardly needs saying that the public house was a male preserve. Women, who were better able to see the miseries caused by drink, were more likely to be on the side of the reformers.

The tenacious way in which workers clung to traditional customs was an assertion of their independence, and presented particular problems for temperance reformers. A number of strategies were employed. Successive legislation placed restraints on drinking hours and on children in public houses. A second line, pursued without success by the United Kingdom Alliance (a temperance society founded in 1853) was local option, whereby local authorities would be made free to ban the drink trade from their localities. Third, the would-be abstainer could be encouraged to insulate himself from temptation, by 'signing the pledge' and joining a group of like-minded men meeting perhaps in a Temperance Hall or coffee house, while his children might join the Band of Hope. However, dramatic inroads into the drink problem would not be made until working-class domestic conditions improved sufficiently for the home to become for them, as it was for the middle class, a place of comfort. That came about with the rise in material living standards at the end of the century.

Religion and education

The problems of drink, crime and pauperism, and the danger of unrest provoked by the appalling living and working conditions of the labouring poor, led the middle and upper classes to search for palliatives or more general agencies of reformation and social control. Two such agencies were organised religion and education. In many respects the two were linked. Voluntary societies organised by the churches provided the bulk of elementary education in the nineteenth century, while the rivalry between denominations over the control of a national system of education held up the state provision of elementary schools for generations.

The stereotyped view of nineteenth-century Britain dominated by religion falls down when it comes to the working class, the mass of whom remained alienated from both church and chapel. This was true in the countryside as well as in the towns, although indifference to church-going was much more marked there. The prominent Nonconformist Edward Miall wrote in 1849: 'The bulk of our manufacturing population stands aloof from our Christian institutions . . . an immense majority of those who in childhood attend our Sabbath schools, neglect throughout the period of manhood all our ordinary appliances of spiritual instruction and culture.' Yet there was seen to be a particular need for religious influence in the growing towns. A popular religious novelist wrote: 'Adam and Eve were created and placed in a garden. Cities are the result of the fall.'

There were several reasons why organised religion proved so unattractive to the working class. In the first place, there were not enough churches, for church-building failed to keep pace with the growth of urban population. For example, it was estimated in the early 1850s that if every seat in all the churches and chapels of Shoreditch were occupied on a Sunday, more than 80 in every 100 inhabitants would still be unprovided for. Everyone agreed that more churches were needed, but coupled with the cost of building them was the problem of their maintenance. This was one of the consequences of the separation of the classes in Victorian cities, while there was no provision (such as exists now) for the churches in richer areas subsidising those in poorer ones. The inhabitants of the slum districts themselves proved to be hostile. When, in 1839, the first of Bishop Blomfield's churches was built in Bethnal Green, a canvasser for sixpences was told by some of the inhabitants that they would gladly give him a shilling to hang the Bishop but not sixpence to build a church. What they wanted was food, not churches, they said.

When churches were built the majority of the labouring population still stayed away. Clothes were much discussed, for it was said that many could not come as they had nothing to wear. More women attended than men, it was argued, because at least they could cover their shabbiness with a shawl. This was just one symptom of the social gulfs which the churches failed to bridge and which proved so irksome. As Horace Mann put it: 'Working men, it is contended, cannot enter our religious structures without having pressed upon their notice some memento of their inferiority.' If they did enter a church, much that they heard therein they would find uncongenial. Jenifer Hart has made a content analysis of a cross-section of Anglican sermons delivered between 1830 and 1880, and she demonstrates their use as a vehicle for social indoctrination. Charles Kingsley, in the mid-Victorian period, was well aware of the problem. He believed that many well-meaning people antagonised the poor by using 'the Bible as if it were a mere special constable's handbook – an opium-dose for keeping working beasts of burden patient while they were being overloaded'.

Methodism had greater success in reaching the working class. For a start it was essentially a layman's religion. In addition to its full-time ministers (who super-intended a number of chapels in a circuit) there was an army of lay workers. In 1850 they numbered 20,000 local preachers, over 50,000 class leaders, and thousands of trustees, stewards, prayer leaders and Sunday-school teachers. It is difficult to say how many of them were working men and women or, if so, from the ranks of the artisans. Methodism was divided into 'connexions', the social composition of which varied. The Wesleyans were predominantly middle class; the Primitive Methodists distinctly working class. It is certainly true that a great many working men gained experience of leadership and public speaking in the chapel, a debt which a number of trade union leaders were only too prepared to acknowledge.

Some of the lack of interest in organised religion was no doubt due to infidelity, the loss of religious faith, but much, too, was simply due to apathy and the desire to relax on Sunday after a week of grinding toil. Various personal jobs had to be done on this day while, as one man put it, 'only working men can thoroughly appreciate or understand all that is embodied in that chiefest pleasure of the working man's Sunday, "a quarter in bed" '.

While so much missionary activity was directed overseas, it became apparent to many that there was a vast field for missionary effort at home, a view reinforced by the results of the Religious Census of 1851. Some clergymen did take up the challenge. A. C. Tait, Blomfield's successor as Bishop of London, preached to omnibus drivers at Islington, to costermongers in Covent Garden, to railway porters from the footplate of a locomotive and to gypsies upon the common at Shepherd's Bush. The Catholic Archbishop, Henry Manning, administered the pledge among the drunkards on Clerkenwell Green. Revival meetings were held and mission halls set up. Sankey and Moody, American evangelists with a fine line in rousing hymns, arrived in Britain in 1873 and returned in the following decades. Perhaps the new militancy is best illustrated by the Salvation Army, established by William Booth in its present form in 1878. Its motto was 'Through Blood and Fire', and it was said of Booth that when he spoke of fire and brimstone he evoked them so convincingly that a smell of sulphur almost assailed the nostrils. But the Salvation Army was a cheering presence. Booth never accepted the Victorian idea of the 'deserving poor', for his view was that if a man was poor he *was* deserving. The social work of the Salvation Army was extensive, but was seen as a means of access to the soul, and salvation was what Booth was concerned with.

It is clear that all this effort failed drastically to alter the picture. As the Bishop of London, A. F. Winnington-Ingram, commented in 1896: 'It is not that the Church of God has lost the great towns; it has never had them.' Great strides had been made in church-building, but the increase in population outstripped this. If the Religious Census of 1851 showed that Britain was no longer a Christian country, it certainly had not become one again by the end of the century. 'British Christianity,' wrote Edward Miall, 'is essentially the Christianity developed by a middle-class soil.'

The class divisions which were apparent in religion were equally apparent in education. Article 4 of the Education Code of 1860 defined elementary education as that 'suited to the condition of workmen and servants'. Like the Poor Law, therefore, public elementary education was a service designed by one class for another, and it served particular social ends. Public school education, as we have seen, was an education in leadership for boys of the middle and upper classes. For its part, elementary education was designed as one in followership for the masses. A characteristic early nineteenth-century view of education was that of the Evangelical clergyman, John Venn. The pupil, he said, 'may by education be endued with qualities friendly to the growth of Christianity. His mind may be enlightened by knowledge instead of being darkened by brutish ignorance. His conscience may be awakened instead of being seared by insensibility. He may be made attentive, docile, submissive, rational; instead of being thoughtless, obstinate, intractable, void of understanding'. Attention, docility, submissiveness and reasonableness were seen as qualities desirable in the poor.

At first there were conflicting attitudes to education, some arguing that to educate the poor would encourage restlessness and a desire to subvert the social order. 'What produced the French Revolution?' asked one MP rhetorically; and the answer he gave was 'Books!'. A writer of 1763 denounced charity schools thus:

The charity school is another universal nursery of idleness; nor is it easy to conceive or invent anything more destructive to the interests and very foundation principles of a nation entirely dependent on its trade and manufactures than the giving an education to the children of the lowest class of her people that will make them contemn those drudgeries for which they were born.[22]

By the 1830s, however, fear of educating the poor had been surpassed by a greater fear, that of either allowing them to remain ignorant or of letting the control of their education fall into dangerous hands. As the Assistant Poor Law Commissioner James Kay-Shuttleworth put it in 1838: 'The state had the most positive and direct interest in adopting measures to prevent the rearing of a race of felons and prostitutes . . . [it had] the duty of rearing these children in religion and industry, and of imparting such an amount of secular education as may fit them to discharge the duties of their station.'

The reports of the Poor Law Commissioners frequently referred to the need for education, as did those of the Factory Inspectors, while the Prison Inspectorate, founded in 1835, almost instinctively turned to moral and religious education to stem a rising crime rate. It was in this decade that state aid to education had its tentative beginnings, but there was a rapid build-up of the education service long before the first state elementary schools were established in 1870. By 1860 the Education Department had become one of the biggest civil establishments of the state, its staff of 127 including the largest inspectorate yet in existence, and controlling an annual expenditure of nearly a £1 million. Indeed, the vote for Education, Science and Art in the financial year 1860–61 constituted a fifth of the total civil estimates.

Before we trace the development of the public provision of elementary education, two points need to be made. First, while it is not hard to produce evidence that the policy of the educators (at least in the early stages of industrialisation and urbanisation) was to use education as a means of social control, is there convincing evidence that the policy worked? To answer this we would need to know how those for whom schooling was provided reacted to it. David Hamilton quotes an exchange between an Education Commissioner and a skilled workman in 1861:

> 'What would you have your son taught?' I asked an intelligent carpenter. 'Reading, writing, cyphering, drawing, algebra, Euclid – anything that he can learn until he knows his trade.' 'But', I said, ' What can be the use of such knowledge to your son if he means to be a working man?' To which the man answered with an air of considerable dignity, 'How do I know, Sir, what my son may become.'[23]

Such a man had wider aspirations for his children than had the providers of the schools. There are other pointers as to the way the working class felt about public elementary education. Studies of school attendance show how interrupted and short-lived was the experience which many children had of schools, as they and their parents bowed to various social and economic pressures. It is also clear that there existed a much more flourishing working-class private provision of schools in the nineteenth century than is sometimes supposed. It has been estimated, for example, that there were twice as many private as public schools for the working class in 1851, and that one-third of all pupils went there. These schools, condemned by government inspectors and middle-class reformers, are now being rehabilitated by historians. Standards may have been higher than was hitherto believed. More to the point, significant numbers of the working class clung to them (despite their fees) because they obviously provided what they wanted – teachers who were working people like themselves, promoting a culture that was part of their own. *They* controlled the schools, which were thus schools of the people rather than schools for the people. Furthermore, even those who attended schools designed for the people were subject to other socialising influences, such as the family and the peer group. Social control, therefore, however much desired by those in power, may not have been nearly as great as they would have wished. It could be argued that public schools were much more efficient socialising agencies, for these were 'closed communities', where the inmates were kept away from other influences during their formative years.

Second, the issue of literacy and industrialisation raises questions relating to the conflicting needs of the individual and of society, a matter of concern in any age. It is clear that industrialisation took place in Britain without the aid of an education explosion. The literacy requirements of industry were low, and evidence suggests that in the industrial north literacy rates actually fell in the early years of industrialisation. But it has been argued that, as an Arkwright water-frame mill and a National School cost roughly the same, what may have been a social deficiency was economic efficiency; resources were being allocated where they were most urgently needed. Not until the 1860s did deficiencies in education become a matter of serious concern, as Britain faced competition from overseas in industries which had become more technically sophisticated.

The administrative machinery of the state was geared not to the direct provision of education, but to the aid and direction of schools provided by voluntary religious bodies. Education represents a supreme example of voluntary, philanthropic action which was noted at the beginning of this chapter, and illustrates the weaknesses as well as the strengths of the system. The voluntary societies' concern with education failed to cover the country with schools, but the denominational rivalry between them acted as a brake on state provision. By the beginning of the nineteenth century the Church of England could no longer claim to represent the whole population. Nonconformity represented a large and influential minority who resented the claims of the established Church to control education. Both sides were agreed that religion constituted an essential element in the education of the masses, but they clashed over purely denominational issues. The relations between Church and state on the education issue remained one of the dominant themes of the nineteenth century.

There had been much educational activity in the eighteenth century, which had seen an enormous expansion of charity schools and Sunday schools. At the forefront of the charity school movement was the Society for Promoting Christian Knowledge, founded in 1699, which helped to form or reform over 1,500 schools within its first 35 years. The curriculum of the charity schools reflected their aims. Reading was based on the Bible or the Prayer Book; writing was only to be taught when the child could read competently well (for why did the poor need to write?); and arithmetic was the last skill to be tackled, and was confined to the first four rules.

Great numbers of children were not in a position to avail themselves of even this limited educational programme, for child labour – whether at home, in factory and mill, or on the farm – effectively prevented many from attending school during the week. It was to counteract this difficulty that the Sunday school movement began. Although he was not the inventor of Sunday schools, the movement is usually associated with the name of Robert Raikes, a newspaper proprietor of Gloucester, who opened his first school in 1780. It was as a propagandist that Raikes was most important, and the account which he wrote in his own paper soon went the round of others, as was typical in a period of scissors-and-paste journalism. By 1795 nearly 250,000 children attended Sunday schools, and when the Sunday School Union (an interdenominational body) was formed in 1803 there were 7,125 Sunday schools with 88,860 teachers and 844,728 pupils. Sunday schools were ubiquitous, and their historian, Thomas Laqueur, has claimed that they represented the 'single experience common to the children of an agricultural labourer in Bedfordshire, of a stockinger or handloom weaver in the Midlands, or of a factory operative in South Lancashire'.

The success of the Sunday schools (some of which extended their activities to weekday evenings) helped pave the way for the next stage of development, weekday schools run on the monitorial system, which was ideally suited to the factory age. As one writer commented, it represented 'the division of labour applied to intellectual purposes . . . The principle in schools and manufactures is the same'. The poet Coleridge approvingly referred to the system as 'this vast moral steam engine' Under the monitorial system the master taught the older children who passed on what they had learnt to the others. Thus, the master drilled the monitors, and the monitors drilled their groups. The degree of order no doubt varied, although one monitor later recalled 'the babel was such that I remember one occasion trying if I should be heard singing "Black Eyed Susan". I sang and no one noticed me'. The schools did provide a modicum of education, although dissatisfaction with the quality of teaching meant that they rapidly fell from popularity after the death of one of the pioneers of the system, Andrew Bell, in 1832. Their main importance was that they spawned the two major voluntary societies of the nineteenth century. Nonconformist supporters of Joseph Lancaster (another pioneer of voluntary schools) formed a society in 1808, renamed in 1814 the British and Foreign Schools Society. Not to be outdone, Bell's Anglican supporters formed in 1811 the National Society for the Education of the Poor in the Principles of the Established Church throughout England and Wales.

The National Society was a powerful body. With a committee composed of the Archbishops and Bishops of England and Wales it was, in effect, the education committee of the Church of England. Both societies established schools throughout the country, with the National Society well in the lead. Their statistics (which include Sunday schools) reveal a phenomenal rate of growth:

Table 5.2   *Numbers of Church schools and children attending, 1812–30*

Year	Schools	Children
1812	52	8,620
1813	230	40,484
1815	564	97,920
1830	3,670	about 346,000

There are no similar statistics for the British Schools, but a return of 1851 gave the number of Church schools as 17,015, with 955,865 children; and the British Schools as 1,500 with an estimated 225,000 children.

At first the voluntary societies were self-financing, but increasing urgency in the 1830s led to support for government aid. In 1833 a grant of £20,000 was voted in aid of school-building, to be divided equally between the National and the British and Foreign Schools Societies. Sums would only be paid, however, when at least half the total cost of a school building had been raised by private subscription. The grant was renewed annually until the end of 1838, by which time the shortcomings of the system had become manifest. There was no approved design for schools (the National Society had reported in 1816 that 'a barn furnishes no bad model, and a good one may be easily converted into a school'). Nor was there security for efficiency of instruction or even for the maintenance of the fabric; while the poorest areas, where needs were greatest, were least able to put up their share of the building costs.

In 1839, therefore, the government attempted to go further. A system of grants, to be allocated according to need, and to be administered directly by the state was proposed, the agency being a new Committee of the Privy Council, employing the shock troops of administrative reform, a body of government inspectors. In addition, it was proposed to establish a number of training colleges for teachers on an inter-denominational basis. The Anglican establishment immediately rose up against the proposals. The young Gladstone was one of the leaders of the opposition movement in the House of Commons (where he was supported by Disraeli); and in the House of Lords the entire bench of Bishops, stirred on by Blomfield, Bishop of London, mounted an attack. So powerful was the opposition that much of the scheme was surrendered. The plan for training colleges was abandoned, and by a 'Concordat' with the Archbishop of Canterbury, it was agreed that no inspector of National Schools would be appointed without the approval of either the Archbishop of Canterbury or York. Inspectors, once appointed, were to report to the Archbishop of the province, and to the Bishop of the diocese as well as to the Committee of the Privy Council. Finally, grants were to continue to match local effort, a provision which maintained the privileged position of the more numerous and financially stronger Church of England schools. Between 1839 and 1850 the National Society received 80 per cent of all government grants to elementary education.

If the events of 1839–40 demonstrated the strength of the Anglicans, then those of 1843–4 showed that of the Nonconformists. Having seen the power of the Bishops in the House of Lords in 1839–40, the precaution was taken, when presenting Sir James Graham's Factory Bill of 1843, of seeking their prior approval to clauses which effectively gave Anglican clergy control of proposed factory schools. Indeed, the Bishops were shown the bill even before it went to the Cabinet. Naturally, the Bishops approved of it. Equally naturally, the Nonconformists did not. Thirteen thousand petitions with 2 million signatures poured into the House of Commons, and by the beginning of 1844 the educational clauses of the Factory Bill were dropped. While this battle was being waged, the British and Foreign Schools Society was fighting another with the Committee of the Privy Council; it demanded equal control over the inspectors sent to its schools as the National Society and the Bishops enjoyed. This point was conceded by November 1843. The two sides in the denominational controversy thus reached a stalemate position from which they were not budged for another generation.

The initiative was firmly with the voluntary societies, who were given a further lease of life by Minutes of the Committee of Council issued in 1846 under the inspiration of Kay-Shuttleworth, who had transferred from the Poor Law Commission to become secretary of the new education committee formed in 1839. In the late 1830s Kay-Shuttleworth had experimented with the training of teachers at the workhouse school at Norwood, and with the failure of the government to secure state training colleges he had opened one of his own at Battersea in 1840. The financial strain became too much for him, and in 1843 the college was taken over by the National Society. Inspired by this example, the Church embarked on a campaign of building training colleges, with the result that by 1845 there were 22 Anglican colleges containing 540 students. However, whereas patrons could be found by the voluntary societies to support a local school, funds were not so forthcoming to support training colleges which did not carry such immediate local benefits. Both Anglicans and Nonconformists, therefore, found it difficult to maintain a steady supply of trained teachers.

The Minutes of 1846 passed most of the cost of training teachers on to the state. The pupil-teacher system which was adopted was, in effect, a form of apprenticeship. In schools which gained the approval of one of Her Majesty's Inspectors (HMIs), children of 13 years of age could be apprenticed to a teacher for five years. During that period they were to do some of the teaching, guided by the teacher, and were to receive additional instruction from him. At the end of each year their work was to be examined by the HMIs, upon whose satisfactory report both pupil-teacher and teacher received grants. At the end of their apprenticeship, pupil-teachers presented themselves for the Queen's Scholarship examination. Those who did best received an annual grant enabling them to attend a training college for three years, while unsuccessful candidates who nevertheless reached a certain standard were awarded a Certificate of Merit which brought a special annual grant towards their salaries. A pension scheme was also introduced.

Lord Macaulay described teachers in 1847 as 'the refuse of all other callings . . . to whom no gentleman would entrust the key of his cellar'. Thanks to the Minutes of 1846 the status of the teacher was substantially raised. Some saw a danger in this, especially as the teachers, themselves drawn from the working class, were supposed to inculcate submissiveness in their pupils. The harsh regimen of the training colleges, where the diet was coarse, the discipline strict and where the students were required to undertake manual labour as well as pursue their studies, was designed to remind them not only of their origins but also of their future work among the poor. Such frugality had additional merits of cheapness. Thus, the Principal of the training college at York was able to claim that 'a well-trained schoolmaster can be manu factured for about £90', which compared favourably with the £100 required to train an infantryman in one of the foot regiments. Nevertheless, teachers were afforded a certain uneasy social mobility, out of the class of their origin but not fully into that of the class above. The position of the schoolmistress was particularly hard, as one HMI reported in 1861:

> It separated her very much from the class to which she had originally belonged, while it did not bring her socially into contact with a different class, and therefore she was very much isolated. She could not marry a labourer, nor an artisan who was not an educated man, and she was not very likely, generally speaking, to marry a person very much above herself.[24]

The annual grants instituted in 1846 made it almost impossible for the government to control expenditure. The parliamentary grant stood at £150,000 in 1851. By 1857 it had risen to £541,233. With the Crimean War costing nearly £78 million, there were demands for a reduction and for greater efficiency. In 1857, therefore, the Newcastle Commission was set up 'to inquire into the present state of education in England, and to consider and report what measures, if any, are required for the extension of sound and cheap elementary instruction to all classes of the people'. Their report, issued in 1861, acknowledged the progress which had been made, but found much to criticise. Attendance at school was low, and even in the inspected schools only a minority of children remained after 10 years of age, with the effect that, in the Commissioners' estimation, not more than a quarter of the pupils received a satisfactory education.

Out of their recommendations came the system of 'Payment by Results', instituted by the Revised Code of 1862. When Robert Lowe outlined the Revised Code to Parliament, he observed:

> I cannot promise the House that this system will be an economical one, and I cannot promise that it will be an efficient one, but I can promise that it shall be either one or the other. If it is not cheap, it shall be efficient; if it is not efficient it shall be cheap. The present is neither one nor the other . . . We do

not profess to give these children an education that will raise them above their station and business in life; that is not our object, but to give them an education that may fit them for that business . . .[25]

Henceforth, there were to be two conditions for the government grant (other than the building grant): attendance and results in an annual examination of reading, writing and arithmetic conducted in each school by Her Majesty's Inspectorate. The work was to be arranged in standards, and it was expected that a child would move up to the next higher standard each year. The code thus set minimum standards, although financial uncertainty created pressures in the schools which, in practice, tended to make them maxima.

In a sense the Revised Code provided for a 'core curriculum', and may be seen as a fore-runner of the National Curriculum of our own day. However, it is often condemned for its narrowness, although when the school managers argued (as they often did) that their grants would be cut, they were saying, in effect, that the expected standard was too high. The Revised Code had many positive features, not the least being the implication that the state would no longer subsidise schools which placed a higher premium on religious instruction than on basic skills of literacy and numeracy. It could be argued, therefore, that it paved the way for the 1870 Education Act which at last provided for state elementary schools.

It remains to be asked, however, whether the Revised Code fulfilled Lowe's promise – was it efficient or cheap? From a narrow point of view it was cheap. The grant, which had reached £813,441 in 1862, fell steadily to a low-water mark of £636,806 in 1865. Efficiency is harder to measure. Schools faced greater financial insecurity which placed inevitable pressures on the teachers who were sorely tempted to falsify registers in order to maintain their livelihood. At the same time, the work of HMIs was circumscribed and their relationship with teachers strained. Joseph Ashby of Tysoe in Warwickshire later recalled the Inspectors' visit to his village school:

> Two Inspectors came once a year and carried out a dramatic examination. The schoolmaster came into school in his best suit; all the pupils and teachers would be listening till at ten o'clock a dog-cart would be heard on the road even though it was eighty yards away. In would come two gentlemen with a deportment of high authority, with rich voices. Each would sit at a desk and children would be called in turn to one or other. The master hovered round, calling children out as they were needed. The children could see him start with vexation as a good pupil stuck at a word in the reading book he had been using all the year or sat motionless with his sum in front of him. The master's anxiety was deep for his earnings depended on the children's work. One year the atmosphere so affected the lower standards that, one after another as they were brought to the Inspector, the boys howled and the girls whimpered. It took hours to get through them.[26]

The Act of 1870 marked the beginning of the end of *laissez-faire* in education. When the Reform Act of 1867 was passed, Lowe observed: 'I believe it will be absolutely necessary that you should prevail on our future masters to learn their letters.' This cry, popularised as 'We must educate our masters', was accompanied by a belief that improved elementary education was vital if Britain were to maintain its economic position in the world, for only on this foundation could technical education be built. W. E. Forster pointed out when he introduced the bill:

Our object is to complete the present voluntary system, to fill up gaps sparing the public money where it can be done without, procuring as much as we can the assistance of the parents, and welcoming as much as we rightly can the co-operation and aid of those benevolent men who desire to assist their neighbours.

A national enquiry into school provision was proposed; and where a deficiency of inspected schools was proven, existing voluntary schools were to be given a year's grace to make it up. If they either could not or would not, a school board was to be compulsorily established, although a majority of ratepayers in any school district could demand a Board. Finally, voluntary schools were to be entitled to aid from the rates, provided they fulfilled certain conditions, especially that of the 'Conscience Clause', which allowed parents to withdraw their children from religious instruction of which they did not approve.

So great was the outcry of 'the Church on the rates', raised by the Non-conformists, that the provision for rate aid was dropped, and yet another compromise was substituted. Two complementary networks of Board and voluntary schools were instituted, with the Board schools having the greater potential for growth, leaving the voluntary schools in a permanent state of grievance.

The 1870 act made elementary education neither compulsory nor free. By-laws making education compulsory to the age of 10 were made obligatory in 1880, and the age was raised to 11 in 1893 and 12 in 1899. In 1891 parents were given the right to demand free education for their children, although fees in elementary schools were not finally abolished until 1918.

In the 30 years after 1870, a number of earlier assumptions about elementary education became untenable. In the first place, the idea that elementary education was merely for the labouring poor began to be questioned. Because of their sheer efficiency, increasing numbers of lower middle-class parents were persuaded to send their children to Board schools rather than to the small, private schools which they had previously used. Second, the idea (enshrined in the Revised Code) that elementary education consisted essentially of the 'three Rs' was increasingly eroded. By the 1890s the system of payment by results was abandoned, and the curriculum was broadened. Schools continued to be organised in 'standards', but the standardisation was breaking down. Standard VI had been the expected level of a 12-year-old child, but a clever boy or girl might race through all the standards by that age or even earlier, and in 1882 a new Standard VII was added. To make the teaching of these older, and brighter children more efficient, many school Boards established 'higher grade schools', bringing together all those children in the district for Standards V and above. Here, more time was spent on advanced subjects, and children were often presented for the examinations of the Science and Art Department (founded in 1853) which, though more difficult, earned a higher grant for the school. Higher grade schools were in a very grey area so far as the law was concerned. The pretence was maintained that they were doing work of an elementary level (for that was the only legal basis on which school Boards could raise a rate) but both parents and teachers knew that their important work was in the advanced subjects and that, to all intents and purposes, these were in fact *secondary* schools. And they were popular, with 25,000 children in them by 1895. Not only that, but they provided a more vocational curriculum than the secondary schools dominated by the middle classes. Some have argued that, had this system been allowed to develop, working-class parents, who had shown considerable enthusiasm for the schools, would have encouraged their children to stay on. Not only that, but the nation would have developed a system of secondary education more in tune with the needs of the economy. But it was not to be. The voluntary schools and private schools resented the competition of the rate-aided Board schools and, in the Cockerton Judgment of 1901, the district auditor declared the expenditure of the London School Board on its higher grade schools illegal. The final outcome was the passage of the 1902 Education Act, which abolished the school boards, and devolved powers over education to the multi-purpose local authorities, at the same time making explicit provision for the state provision of secondary education.

Notes

1 Quoted in B. I. Coleman (ed.), *The Idea of the City in Nineteenth-Century Britain*, Routledge and Kegan Paul, 1973, pp. 62–3.
2 Quoted in Kate Flint (ed.), *The Victorian Novelist: Social Problems and Social Change*, Croom Helm, 1987, p. 3.
3 Henry Parris, 'The nineteenth-century revolution in government: a reappraisal reappraised' in Peter Stansky (ed.), *The Victorian Revolution*, New Viewpoints, 1973, p. 55.
4 Derek Fraser, *The Evolution of the British Welfare State*, Macmillan, 1973, p. 104.
5 Quoted in Michael Rose, *The English Poor Law*, David and Charles, 1971, pp. 47–8.
6 Quoted in Derek Fraser (ed.), *The New Poor Law in the Nineteenth Century*, Macmillan, 1976, pp. 13–14
7 Michael Rose, op. cit., 1971, p. 62.
8 Derek Fraser, op, cit., 1976, p. 6.
9 B. W. Clapp, *An Environmental History of Britain*, Longman, 1994, pp. 74 5.
10 Robert Roberts, *A Ragged Schooling*, Fontana, 1978, pp. 19-20.
11 Anthony Wohl, *Endangered Lives: Public Health in Victorian Britain*, Methuen, 1983, p. 223.
12 Quoted in Geoffrey Best, *Mid Victorian Britain, 1851–1875*, Fontana, 1971, p. 30.
13 Quoted in Kate Flint (ed.), op. cit., 1987, p. 18.
14 Donald J. Olsen, *The Growth of Victorian London*, Batsford, 1976, p. 280.
15 Quoted in David Philips, *Crime and Authority in Victorian England*, Croom Helm, 1977, p. 13.
16 Ibid., p. 147.
17 Quoted in Francis Sheppard, *London 1808–1870: The Infernal Wen*, Secker and Warburg, 1971, pp. 34–5.
18 Quoted in J. J. Tobias, *Crime and Industrial Society in the Nineteenth Century*, Batsford, 1967, p. 57.
19 Ibid., p. 52.
20 Quoted in B. I. Coleman, op. cit., 1973, p. 157.
21 Robert Roberts, *The Classic Slum*, Penguin, 1973, p. 120.
22 Quoted in A. P. Wadsworth, 'The first Manchester Sunday schools' in M. W. Flinn and T. C. Smout (eds), *Essays in Social History*, Clarendon Press, 1974, p. 101.
23 David Hamilton, *Learning about Education: an Unfinished Curriculum*, Open University Press, 1990, p. 57.
24 John Hurt, *Education in Evolution*, Paladin, 1972, pp. 140–41.
25 Quoted in Eric Evans, *Social Policy, 1830–1914*, Routledge and Kegan Paul, 1978, pp. 96–7.
26. Gillian Sutherland, *Elementary Education in the Nineteenth Century*, Historical Association, 1971, p. 41.

Chapter six

The great Victorian boom

The Great Exhibition

On 1 May 1851 over half a million people crowded into Hyde Park, while a further 30,000 were pressed inside the vast iron and glass building of the Crystal Palace, all hoping to catch a glimpse of the queen when she came to open the Great Exhibition. The day was a brilliant success – and yet, only two weeks before, it had been publicly announced that the opening would be in private. This had aroused a furore, *The Times* thundering, 'The Queen is not Lady Godiva'. There were real fears for the queen's safety: the previous July she had been violently attacked by a half pay officer of the Hussars, the son of a former High Sheriff to boot; and people asked what the populace might do if even a gentleman could lay hands on Her Majesty. The events of 1848, both at home and abroad, were fresh in people's minds, while the presence in London of the French socialist Louis Blanc and the Italian republican patriot Giuseppe Mazzini (not to mention Karl Marx, though few people noticed him), led some to believe that the Red Revolution was about to start. The 'Official Report of the Exhibition' was quite frank about the fears:

> The recent revolutionary movements on the Continent, the freedom of access to this country to men proscribed in their own, and the temptations to the increased activity of our own disorderly population, were considerations pregnant with doubt if not apprehension, and since they were expressed by public men they increased rather than allayed the general fears.

As a precaution, therefore, a thousand men were added to the Metropolitan Police and the number of troops stationed round London was doubled. There were other causes for unrest. The country had been seized by a fit of anti-Catholicism when, in September 1850, the Pope had restored the hierarchy of English Roman Catholic bishops, and had made Nicholas Wiseman both a cardinal and Archbishop of Westminster. Guy Fawkes night that year was celebrated with an intensity of feeling not often seen. The Whig government of Lord John Russell introduced fresh legislation against the Catholic Church which led to a constitutional crisis in February 1851. Although he remained in power, his position was precarious. The Great Exhibition came at a fortunate time, therefore, and as Disraeli claimed, it was 'a godsend to the Government . . . diverting public attention from their blunders'.

In March 1851 the *Illustrated London News* published a song for the Great Exhibition, entitled 'The Festival of Labour', and written by two popular song-writers, Charles Mackay and Henry Russell, the Andrew Lloyd-Webber and Tim Rice of their day. The first verse ran thus:

Gather, ye Nations, gather!
From forge, and mine, and mill!
Come, Science and Invention;
Come, Industry and Skill!
Come, with your woven wonders,
The blossoms of the loom,
That rival Nature's fairest flowers
In all but their perfume;
Come with your brass and iron,
Your silver and your gold,
And arts that change the face of earth,
Unknown to men of old.
Gather, ye Nations, gather!
From every clime and soil,
The new Confederation,
The Jubilee of toil.

These were to be the keynote of the Exhibition – the Gospel of Work and the Gospel of Peace. Martin Tupper's 'Hymn to the Exhibition' (translated into 24 languages, including Ojibway) made a similar point:

The triumph of the Artisan has come about at length,
And Kings and Princes flock to praise his comeliness and strength.

While there is evidence that some workers speedily formed the opinion that the Exhibition was no more than an opiate, intended to wean them from politics, others lent it their support by participating in the local committees set up to select exhibits. There was much activity in the provinces, for while this was to be an international exhibition, the opportunity to display Britain's national economic strength was not to be ignored. 'We strive not for dominion,' (ran another verse of 'The Festival of Labour') 'Whoe'er the worthiest be, Shall bear the palm and garland, And crown of Victory.' But Britons had no doubts as to who the worthiest would prove to be.

The Great Exhibition owed its success (despite considerable initial opposition) to three men: Henry Cole, Prince Albert and Joseph Paxton. Cole was a civil servant with a taste for the arts who had organised previous exhibitions, sponsored by the Royal Society of Arts, in 1847 and 1848. Prince Albert, however, persuaded Cole that the third exhibition should be international in scope, and it was he who chaired the Royal Commission set up to organise it. Paxton, so much the epitome of self-help that it is surprising that he does not feature in Samuel Smiles's work, came late on to the scene. The son of a small farmer, he became head gardener to the Duke of Devonshire at the age of 23. At Chatsworth he performed wonders, engineering the highest gravitational fountain in existence and building a vast greenhouse for the Duke's rare Victoria Regia Lily. He went from success to success, and it was said of him that 'he grew money as successfully as he grew flowers or trees'. It was only after the Building Committee of the Royal Commission had received and rejected 254 plans, and after they had produced a yet more ghastly one of their own, that Paxton produced his. From his first doodle, drawn during a meeting of the directors of the Midland Railway, of whom he was one, it took Paxton just seven days to prepare detailed drawings of a glass and iron building, breathtaking in its originality. A timely 'leak' to the *Illustrated London News*, and the felicitous choice (by Douglas Jerrold of *Punch*) of the title, 'Crystal Palace', ensured that the plan would be accepted.

The whole conception was a masterpiece of prefabricated design. The overall length of the building was 1,848 feet (563 metres), or just over the combined length of five football pitches. The area to be covered was 19 acres (7.7 hectares), or six times the area of St Paul's Cathedral. And the contractors had only 22 weeks to complete the job. Over 2,000 iron girders were required, each being tested on site; there were more than 3,000 iron columns, and over 6.5 hectares of glass in what were, for those days, exceptionally large panes. At the height of building work there were 2,260 men on the site, aided by a battery of machines. Some 205 miles of sash bar were mechanically produced, while mortice-cutting machines could cut seven or eight mortices in the time taken to cut one by hand. The sash bars were 'machine-painted' by being dipped into troughs and then passed through bristle-padded jigs which wiped off the surplus paint. Pickfords' vans plied between Euston Station and Hyde Park, delivering 50 tons of girders and columns every day, only 18 hours elapsing between despatch from the foundry at Smethwick and erection in London. The Great Exhibition was a supreme monument to Victorian engineering, and to their ability to get things done quickly if they so desired. However, the wide-spread adoption of these construction techniques were long delayed. The first steel-framed buildings were erected in the USA some two decades before the first sub-stantial British building was put up; and even in the middle of the twentieth century, few buildings had as many factory-made parts as went into the Crystal Palace.

If the Crystal Palace itself was a masterpiece of functional design, much of the ten miles of exhibits did no more than illustrate misplaced Victorian ingenuity and execrable middle-class taste. As the writer, Leigh Hunt observed, 'it was a Bazaar!'. Charlotte Brontë agreed:

> It may be called a bazaar or a fair, but it is such a bazaar or fair as Eastern genii might have created. It seems as if only magic could have gathered this mass of wealth from all the ends of the earth – as if none but supernatural hands could have arranged it thus, with such a blaze and contrast of colours and marvellous power of effect.[1]

The French section was the largest foreign one, but while it revealed the brilliant craftsmanship and quality of design typical of that country it aroused little fear of industrial competition. Most of the German exhibits were described as 'not above mediocrity', while *The Economist* held that 'in machinery . . . the Germans appear very deficient'. The one exception which that journal noted was field pieces, and a cannon exhibited by a certain Herr Krupp, whose new steel works in Essen had been opened four years previously, aroused much attention. Most scorn, however, was poured on the contribution of the United States, for although (at its own insistence) that country had been allocated a space second only to that of France, it failed to fill it. As there was a shortage of hotel accommodation in London at that time, *Punch* suggested that the Americans should utilise their vacant space by letting it as lodgings:

> By packing up the American articles a little closer, by displaying Colt's revolvers over the soap, and piling up the Cincinnati pickles on the top of the Virginian honey, we shall concentrate all the treasures of American art and manufacture into a very few square feet, and beds may be made up to accommodate several hundreds in the space claimed for, but not one quarter filled by, the products of United States industry.

But if the American exhibits were lacking in quantity, they were not lacking in quality, for the United States had on display what were to prove some of the most significant exhibits of all. These included the precision-made, mass-produced Colt revolver; the McCormick reaper; the world's first lock-stitch sewing machine; a

6   Victorian engineering

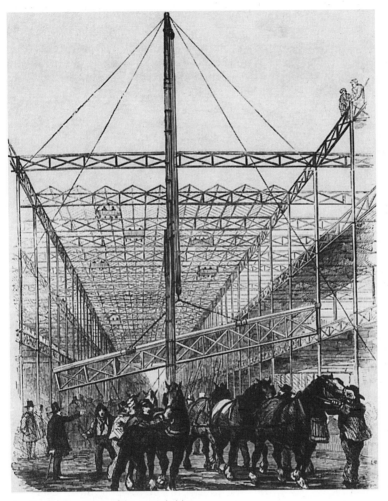

1   Raising the girders of the central aisle

All of the pictures in this section relate in some way to the Great Exhibition. Visitors to the Crystal Palace in Hyde Park in 1851 had ample evidence that British engineering had come a long way from the clumsy, mostly hand-built machines of the early textile mills. The far more sophisticated machines on display were made with machine-tools, created in the workshops of such men as Whitworth and Nasmyth. They were the products of a new class of workman, the skilled engineers whose importance to industry gave them the confidence to establish a 'New Model' Union in the year of the Exhibition.

Pictures 1–4 are from the *Illustrated London News* (*ILN*), a weekly magazine which gave its middle-class readers well-illustrated reports of current events. Before the advent of press photography, *ILN* sent an artist to make a sketch, which was then copied by skilled engravers in the studio. The finished pictures were thus one stage removed from the work of eye-witnesses. Does this in any way affect their validity?

2   Building the Crystal Palace: a sash-bar grooving machine

3   Glazing the roof of the Crystal Palace

The Crystal Palace was itself a marvel of engineering skill. Picture 2 shows a sash-bar grooving machine, while picture 4 shows a huge metal punch. The roof gutters were so designed that the glaziers could run their trollies along them, as can be seen from pictures 1 and 3. How far does the first picture suggest, however, that not all processes had been mechanised at this time? And do pictures 2–4 reveal limitations to the effectiveness of contemporary safety legislation?

4   Metal punching machine

Pictures 5 and 6 (see p. 172) come from the official catalogue of the Exhibition. The express locomotive was built by the Liverpool firm of Bury, Curtis and Kennedy. Edward Bury (nicknamed 'Vulcan') had built the locomotives for the London and Birmingham Railway in the 1830s, but they were puny compared with this 32-ton model. Does this engineering drawing convey a different impression of the locomotive than would have been given by a photograph?

5   Crampton's Patent Express Engine

The power-loom gallery (6) would be the nearest that many middle-class men and women would ever get to the inside of a mill. Is it likely that the Exhibition was as spacious as it is shown here? What features of the Great Exhibition does this particular illustration imply?

Penn and Sons (7) were an important marine engineering firm who had built the engines of the *Great Britain*, and entered several exhibits in the Crystal Palace. What limitations of contemporary photography are suggested by the composition of this picture; and who are the men in top hats likely to be – managers or customers?

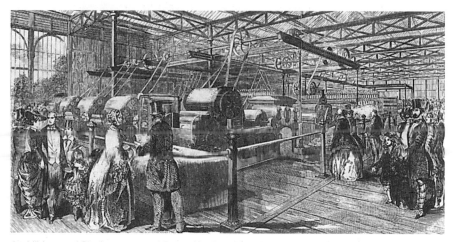

6   Hibbert and Platt's cotton machinery, showing power looms in the front and throstles and mules in the rear

7   The Deptford works of Penn and Sons, building marine engines in the 1860s

display of rubber products by the Goodyear Company; and a new refrigeration process. Not all were blind to the American potential for industrial growth. *The Economist* predicted that 'the superiority of the United States to England is ultimately as certain as the next eclipse', although, as Sir John Clapham pointed out, it did not say how long the ultimatum had to run.

Over 6 million people attended the Great Exhibition, many visiting London for the first time, and travelling by railway excursion trains. The railway companies did a brisk trade, the receipts of the eight companies with London termini for the 22 weeks of the Exhibition being 27.6 per cent higher than in the corresponding period of 1850. Four million of the visitors came on the 'shilling days' when the entrance fee was low enough for the skilled workman and his family to be present. This was considered quite remarkable, as the *Illustrated London News* made clear:

> Such multitudes never before met in such an area, or in any covered area since the world began; and we may justly boast of the good sense and the good temper, of the head and of the heart of the British people, who upon this as well as upon former occasions have shown themselves a multitude without becoming a mob.

It was the shilling visitors who ensured the financial success of the Exhibition. A profit of £186,437 was made, out of which the South Kensington museums were founded, and various education grants made, some continuing to this day. Paxton was given £5,000 and a knighthood. The building itself was taken down and removed to Sydenham, where it was reopened in 1859. Here it remained until destroyed by fire in 1936.

The Gospel of Peace which was proclaimed at the Crystal Palace had a short life. Even while the Exhibition was open, Britain was at war with the Kaffirs. Colonial wars were far away, and were becoming less troublesome all the time as a result of the very technology which the Great Exhibition was celebrating. Nearer home, in December 1851 Louis Napoleon engineered his coup in France, during which 12 people were draped with a carpet exhibited at the Great Exhibition and were shot down. Two months before the Crystal Palace reopened at Sydenham, Britain was plunged into the Crimean War. The British were equipped with a new rifle – produced on American machines purchased in 1853 from an exhibitor at the Great Exhibition.

What of Britain's economic domination of the world? Exports, which had been valued at only £53 million in 1848 (and that only £1 million or so above the 1815 figure) were worth £122 million in 1857 and £136 million in 1860. In little more than a decade after that the figure doubled again. But historians are now inclined to question the idea that in the third quarter of the nineteenth century Britain was the '*Workshop* of the World', for Britain's trading base was built largely upon coal and unskilled labour, with textiles as the major export sector. The complacency of 1851 was not to last for long. In 1847, as though anticipating the jeers directed at American industry, Walt Whitman had written

> Yankeedoodledom is going ahead with the resistless energy of a sixty-five-hundred-thousand-horse-power steam engine . . . Let the Old World wag on under its cumbrous load of form and conservatism; we are of a newer, fresher race and land. And all we have to say is, to point to fifty years hence and say let those laugh who win.

In 1897, as we shall see in Chapter 11, a great many British businessmen were *not* laughing.

Railways and inland transportation

The Victorian period has frequently and aptly been described as 'The Railway Age'. The Victorians themselves certainly saw the coming of the railways as a demarcation line between past and present. The novelist Thackeray was nearly 50 in 1860, when he wrote:

> Your railroad starts the new era, and we of a certain age belong to the new time and the old one . . . We elderly people have lived in that pre-railroad world, which has passed into limbo and vanished from under us. I tell you it was firm under our feet once, and not long ago. They have raised those railroad embankments up, and shut off the old world that was behind them. Climb up that bank on which the irons are laid, and look to the other side − it is gone.[2]

Not all were happy with the change. Colonel Sibthorp, arch-enemy of the Crystal Palace, exclaimed, 'I hate these infernal railways as I hate the devil'. The balance of opinion, however, inclined the other way; and though not the most impartial observer, a director of the Great North of England Railway voiced the view of many when he exclaimed that, 'nothing *next to religion* is of so much importance as a ready communication'. This is just what the railways provided, although the extent to which other forms of transport had developed should not be underrated.

Between 1760 and 1830 over 3,000 miles of canals and improved river navigation were constructed, rising to a peak in 1858 when there were some 4,250 miles open. In the middle decades of the century more than 25,000 barges were employed, competing with the railways for the carriage of a wide range of bulky commodities. In the early 1840s it is estimated that the canals carried between 30 and 35 million tons of goods annually; and as late as 1872 a prominent businessman from the Potteries claimed that, where they were free from railway control, canals could 'not only hold their own against the railways but beat them both in rate and in time of delivery'.

Not only did the inland waterway system reach its maximum mileage after the coming of the railways, but most canals also carried their greatest volume of traffic after the appearance of a railway in the district. For example, on the Leeds and Liverpool, the Leicester Navigation, and the Kennet and Avon Canals maximum tonnages were carried in the late 1840s; while on the Shropshire Union, the Staffordshire and Worcester, and the leading Welsh canals the peak was not reached for at least another decade. Various factors account for this: the goods traffic of railways developed comparatively slowly, while their competition forced down canal rates which, for a time, attracted more traffic to the waterways.

Gradually, however, the relative prosperity of canals declined. Although they carried more goods than the railways in the mid-1840s, they carried only a little more than one-tenth the tonnage of their rivals by 1898, by which time most canals were filling the humble role of feeder to a mainline railway rather than acting as a major artery of trade.

While many people condemned the railways for gobbling up their competitors − more than one-third of the mileage had passed under railway control by 1883 − the canals themselves were not free from blame. Britain had an inland waterways 'system' more in name than in reality. Canals had been built as a result of local initiative, and they came in all shapes and sizes. Difference in width and in length of lock hampered long-distance traffic. For example, the Leeds and Liverpool Canal could lock a boat of 76 feet (23 metres) from Liverpool to Wigan; between Wigan and Leeds only a 66-foot (20-metre) boat could travel; while at Leeds the canal joined with the Aire and Calder Navigation the locks of which could only accommodate a 53-foot (16-metre) boat. As late as 1913 a manufacturer had the choice of three canal routes between London and Liverpool; but on two of them he would have to negotiate tolls with nine separate companies, while on the third 10 companies were involved. At no time did the canals establish an equivalent to the Railway Clearing House to facilitate through traffic, nor did the companies throw up a counterpart to George Hudson, 'the Railway King', to bring together a national system under closer management. Instead they remained parochial in outlook and used the income of their golden years not to improve their service or standardise their facilities, but to enjoy monopoly profits or blindly to oppose the passage through Parliament of Railway Bills. Even when renewed interest in canals was shown at the end of the century (the Manchester Ship Canal was opened in 1894) the initiative came from the municipalities and commerce rather than from the companies themselves.

The transportation of goods by road had already been dealt a blow by the canals, for the cost differential was vastly in favour of the latter. In 1813, for example, there was no instance of the cost of canal carriage being above half the cost of land carriage. By the late 1830s there were nearly 127,000 miles of public road, but only 22,000 had been turnpiked, and many of these roads left much to be desired. Three generations of McAdam served the very progressive Metropolitan Turnpike Trust, a model authority responsible for managing all the principal Middlesex roads out of London, yet as late as 1856 not one-half of its mileage had been macadamised with broken granite. Even so, the roads were good by European standards. Whereas in the late 1860s France had less than three miles of metalled road per thousand of population, and Prussia a mere two and one-third miles, the corresponding figure for the United Kingdom was five miles.

In the early railway age many people expected the iron horse to drive the horse of flesh and blood from the roads, and some modern historians have reinforced the impression of a rapid decline of road transport. In fact, the horse still had an important part to play and the decline, when it came, was relative rather than absolute. Between 1851 and 1900 goods carried by rail increased from 60 million to 410 million tons, while those carried by carts, wagons and vans increased from 106 to 671 million tons.

The death-knell was certainly sounded for long-distance coach traffic. By the 1830s it was estimated that there were 3,000 coaches on the road, and that a person had 1,500 opportunities of leaving London daily. Each day 54 coaches went to Manchester, and 40 to Birmingham. Against the railway these coaches could not compete, although some of them put up a good fight. In the spring of 1838 the *Wonder* left Euston just as the Birmingham train departed, and waited 20 minutes for it at the other end. Such efforts could not be kept up for long, and even the cutting of fares offered only a temporary respite. The mail coaches of the Bath Road, which had pioneered that form of transport, ceased running when the Great Western Railway was opened from Paddington to Bristol in June 1841; and the mail-coach era came to an end on 6 January 1848 when the last of the old London coaches (from Norwich and Newmarket) were taken off the roads.

The four-horse coaches had contributed more than any other type of vehicle to the revenue of the turnpike trusts, and the withdrawal of services from the through routes was largely responsible for the decline in toll revenue of one-third between 1837 and 1850. By the middle of the 1860s a witness before the Select Committee on Turnpike Trusts asserted that 'all turnpike roads had ceased to be national roads, and had become purely of a local character'. Yet local traffic was actually fostered by the railways for, as F. M. L. Thompson has observed:

Without carriages and carts the railways would have been like stranded whales, giants unable to use their strength, for these were the only means of getting people and goods right to the doors of houses, warehouses, markets, and factories, where they wanted to be.[3]

Some of the big coach proprietors went over to the enemy camp. William Chaplin and Benjamin Horne operated the largest coaching business in England, bringing in a revenue of £500,000 a year; but they saw which way the wind was blowing and in return for an agreement to take their coaches off the road they secured the goods agency for the London and Birmingham Railway. Likewise Pickfords, which had run a profitable goods service of its own between London and Manchester from 1818 to 1825, opened the first railway goods station in London for the same company.

The census returns give some idea of the continued importance of the roads. In 1851 some 34,306 railway labourers and 14,559 railway officers, clerks and stationmasters were listed; but so too were 56,981 carmen, carriers and draymen; 29,408 horse-keepers, non-domestic grooms and jockeys; and 16,836 non-domestic coachmen, guards and postboys – not to mention those who serviced the tens of thousands of private carriages, and the whole armies of coach-builders, wheelwrights, blacksmiths or saddlers.

Finally, there was the extensive coastal shipping trade, facilitated by the remarkable length of Britain's coastline in relation to the land mass. As late as 1862 it was reckoned that the freight rates from three-fifths of the country's stations were affected by the potential competition of transport by sea. So great was the tonnage of goods carried by coastal shipping (over 12.5 million tons in 1847) that it actually exceeded that from overseas trade until 1906. This supremacy was maintained by the more rapid introduction of steamships, of which 188 were in service by 1821 and 639 by 1853. Coastal steam tonnage had surpassed that of sailing ships by 1866, well before that point was reached with overseas shipping.

A wide variety of goods was carried round Britain's coasts, although the majority comprised commodities with a comparatively low value but high bulk, such as raw materials and agricultural produce. The tonnage of coal exceeded that of all other produce combined, and it was not until 1867, when over 3 million tons was carried coastwise, that railborne coal exceeded that of 'sea coal' for the first time. The importance of this trade led to harbour improvements on Tyneside, Teeside and the Wear; and in South Wales, where river mouths were widened and wet docks opened at Llanelly in 1828, Cardiff in 1839, Newport in 1844 and Swansea in 1852.

It was the collieries which witnessed the birth of the railways. From November to April the prospect of gales on the east coast kept the sailing colliers in harbour at the same time as the roads from the pits were turned to quagmires. There was plenty of room at the staiths, or wharfs, to stock-pile coal for shipment in the spring, but the problem was to get it there from the pits. To solve this difficulty, wooden railways were laid down in the colliery districts from the early seventeenth century. By the beginning of the nineteenth century, iron-railed tramways were well established in the colliery districts, prompting a minor (and, as it happens, a miner) poet to pray:

> God bless the man wi' peace and plenty,
> That first invented metal plates.
> Draw out his years to five times twenty,
> And slide him through the heavenly gates.

Ironically, the canals were also instrumental in railway development, laying tracks as feeders or as temporary links, such as that used by the Grand Junction Canal while the tunnel from Stoke Bruerne to Blisworth was under construction. By 1811 South Wales was estimated to have nearly 150 miles of railway 'connected with canals, collieries, iron and copper works', while it was said that Tyneside had 225 miles before the Stockton and Darlington Railway was opened in 1825. That was not the first public railway, credit for which must go to the Surrey Iron Railway, which ran from Croydon to the Thames at Wandsworth, and was opened in 1803. Neither was it the first passenger railway, for the Swansea and Oystermouth Railway of 1807 bears that palm. However, the Stockton and Darlington Railway, of which George Stephenson was the engineer, drew together numerous strands of earlier development and employed steam locomotives from the first, although horses and stationary engines were also used. Yet, outside its immediate neigbourhood, it at first aroused little interest, and even in the next county the *Yorkshire Gazette* only devoted eight lines to the opening ceremony.

A modern railway has been defined as a publicly controlled means of transport combining the four features of specialised track, mechanical traction, the accommodation of public traffic and the conveyance of passengers. The first under-taking to satisfy all these conditions was the Liverpool and Manchester Railway, opened in 1830. From the beginning both passengers and goods were conveyed solely by steam locomotive; Stephenson's *Rocket*, with its multi-tubed boiler, having greatly increased engine efficiency. This railway also connected two of the most important cities in the country, with a combined population of 350,000 and strong trading links. Manchester textile manufacturers depended on the cotton imported through Liverpool, but as the railway prospectus declared, 'Merchandise is frequently brought across the Atlantic from New York to Liverpool in twenty-one days; while . . . goods have in some instances been longer on their passage from Liverpool to Manchester'. The canal companies had held the two cities to ransom, and the new railway was promoted in direct competition with them. The line was also a triumph of civil engineering. Chat Moss, a 12-square-mile peat bog, had to be crossed, yet it was so spongy that the surveyor was unable even to set up his theodolite. Furthermore, the entry into Liverpool required the blasting of nearly 400,000 cubic metres of rock through Olive Mount.

In the next half-decade four major lines were projected. The London and Birmingham, and the Grand Junction (from Birmingham to Warrington, where a connection was made with the Liverpool and Manchester) both successfully resubmitted parliamentary bills in 1833, while the London and Southampton was authorised in 1834, to be followed the next year by the Great Western. These formed the first trunk lines out of London, and together totalled 380 miles, as against the 30 miles of the Liverpool and Manchester Railway.

The launching of these trunk lines led to Britain's first railway boom when, between 1836 and 1837, 1,500 miles of new railway were authorised by Parliament. By 1843 there were more than 2,000 miles of railway in operation; and the good harvests of 1842 and 1843, coupled with Peel's reduction of tariff duties, set the scene for the mania of 1844–7, which greatly overshadowed that of the previous decade. The country was gripped by a speculative fever. A stockbroker recalled: 'A solicitor or two, a civil engineer, a Parliamentary agent, possibly a contractor, a map of England, a pair of compasses, a pencil and a ruler, were all that were required to commence the formation of a railway company.'

In the three parliamentary sessions of 1845–8 some 650 Railway Acts were passed, authorising the construction of nearly 9,000 miles of line. Not all were built. In 1850 it was found necessary to pass legislation by which projected railways might be abandoned and companies dissolved, and over 3,500 miles were given up in this way. The mania was not totally wasteful, and a network was laid down quickly. By 1852, 7,500 miles were open, and few important towns, with the exception of Hereford, Yeovil and Weymouth, remained unserved. Philip Bagwell has made the point that 'at least in respect of railways north of the Thames there is a remarkable degree of similarity between the railway map of 1852 and that envisaged by Dr (later Lord) Beeching under his 1963 scheme for the rationalisation of the railway network'. By and large the railways promoted after the 1850s comprised branch and feeder lines which pushed the total mileage up to 23,441 by 1912. There were, however, some spectacular engineering achievements in the last quarter of the nineteenth century, including the opening of the Severn Tunnel in 1886, and the Tay and Forth Bridges in 1887 and 1890.

Clearly the development of such a railway system had a great social and economic impact. Yet extravagant claims have been made for the effect of railways on economic growth, not only in Britain but in places like the United States and Russia. Railways made their presence felt in a very physical sense; they were new, and they inspired an exaggerated response. Yet the overall relationship between railways and economic growth differed from one economy to another. In countries such as the United States, where there were vast tracts of unsettled territory, railways might be said to have served a *developmental* function; they were promoted in anticipation of traffic building up as settlement proceeded. In Britain, on the other hand, the railways were *exploitative*, and were constructed to convey passengers and freight already there, and already being served by existing transport facilities, albeit less efficiently.

It is worth pausing at this point to consider a group of historians whose work is referred to at various points in this book. Known as the New Economic Historians, their approach is now rather less new than it was 20 years ago. Donald McCloskey, a leading member of this school, defines them thus: 'A cliometrician is an economist applying economic theory (usually simple) to historical facts (not always quantitative) in the interest of history (not economics)'. Although, as McCloskey is right to point out, the New Economic Historians do not confine themselves to quantitative evidence, they do lay great store by it. While no conclusion drawn from statistical evidence can be better than the statistics themselves (and many sources of such material are non-existent or are faulty), the emphasis on what can be measured does help us to guard against the exaggerated claims that may otherwise be made.

But it is the theoretical approach the cliometricians take that makes their work so interesting. One important technique is 'counterfactual analysis'. This is an analytical tool for understanding events by trying to determine what a situation might have been like had those events not taken place. This is not as outrageous as it might seem, for statements about what did happen in the past frequently imply statements about what did not. The cliometricians attempt to *measure* the differences. For example, it is perfectly possible to imagine a Britain of 1865 in which railways did not exist. If we could measure what the economy might have been like in that situation, we would be in a much better position to state what contribution railways actually did make. One theoretical device for doing this is 'social saving'. G. R. Hawke and J. P. P. Higgins, leading historians in the field of railways, describe it thus:

> The social saving . . . is measured as the difference between the actual cost of the transportation services provided by the railways and the hypothetical cost of those same services in the absence of the railways using the best available alternative source of transport services. If the prices used accurately

reflect resource use, this also measures the difference in national income with and without the railways, given that the economy is not allowed to adjust to the absence of railways (by, for example, relocating economic activity so that less transport is required for a given level of total output).[4]

Using such techniques, Hawke's conclusion is that in 1865 railways could not have been sacrificed without the need to compensate for a loss in the order of 11 per cent of the national income. If this is true, it shows that railways did indeed play an important part in the development of the British economy, but not such a large part that (as is the view of Eric Hobsbawm, for example) they almost single-handedly baled out a capitalist system on the verge of crisis in the 1840s.

The conclusions of cliometricians should be accepted with no less caution than those of any other historian. Derek Aldcroft points to one cause of concern:

> There is the question of what might have happened to alternative modes of transport in a non-rail situation. Hawke does not, for example, hypothesise what might have transpired in a world without railways, as Fogel did for the United States. We can reasonably assume that alternative transport modes would not have remained static. More resources would no doubt have been devoted to improving waterways, coastal shipping and road transport. Feasible extensions to existing networks and improvements in efficiency could have resulted in falling costs and therefore offset some of the gains from the railways. This is less fanciful than it might appear at first sight. For example, by the early 1830s steam carriages had been developed to the point where they offered one of the cheapest and quickest forms of travel over short distances. Had the railways not appeared, it is conceivable that even greater improvements in road transport would have subsequently transpired.[5]

Not every question relating to the railways can be (or has yet been) interpreted by the methods of the New Economic History, and for many questions we still need to rely on the kind of 'qualitative', literary evidence that historians are used to handling. For convenience, we will examine the economic impact of railways through four aspects: promotion and construction; the provision of transport services; the impact on other industries; and the importance of railways as an industry in their own right.

George Stephenson once remarked that engine and road were like man and wife, for the two went hand in hand. Thus, all the while locomotives were small and lacking in power, gradients had to be slight. Experiments in 1833 showed that a locomotive which could draw 67 tons on the level could draw only 15 tons on an incline of 1 in 100. Thus, in the early days (when most of the main lines were built) vast earthworks were required in order to keep gradients to a minimum. The Great Western, for example, was a mammoth feat of civil engineering which, with its mean gradient only 1 in 1,380, came to be known as 'Brunel's Billiard Table'. A former President of the Institution of Civil Engineers once observed that he had often thought that the railway navvies were unconsciously preparing the way of the Lord by exalting valleys, lowering mountains and hills, making crooked places straight and rough places plain (*Isaiah 40: 3–4*). On the London and Birmingham Railway alone some 4 million cubic feet (113,000 cubic metres) of earth were moved, enough, it was calculated, if spread in a band one foot high and one foot broad, to go round the equator more than three times.

To construct these works vast armies of men were organised by the great contractors such as Thomas Brassey and Samuel Morton Peto. Between 40 and 50 men were employed upon each mile of line, so that in 1839, when at least 1,000 miles were under construction, the number of men employed must have been around 50,000 or 1 per cent of the occupied male population. Their total wages for the year would have come to £2 million–£2.5 million. At the height of the mania in 1847 well over 250,000 men, or 4 per cent of the occupied male population, were thus employed, and their wages bill, in the region of £16 million constituted nearly 3 per cent of the national income. The increase in effective demand which this represented was important to the economy, although concentrated in a very short period, while the effect in areas through which the lines passed must have been particularly great.

In addition to the huge armies of men, the construction of the railways consumed vast amounts of capital, and it seems inescapable that the railways played a major part in pushing up the rate of investment to around 10 per cent of the national income by the middle of the century. As *The Economist* commented in 1845: 'Railway property is a new feature in England's social economy which has introduced commercial feelings to the firesides of thousands.' The London Stock Exchange, which had previously been concerned largely with government bonds and the stock of the historic chartered companies, was greatly stimulated. Many provincial stock exchanges were opened, such as those at Glasgow and Edinburgh in 1844, and others at Leeds, Bristol, Birmingham and Leicester in the following year. The invest-ment press also expanded, with *The Railway Times* launched in 1837, the 'Railway Monitor' section of *The Economist* in 1845, and many others. British investors seem to have acquired a liking for public utility securities; and when the period of major construction in Britain ended, they turned their attention overseas rather than seek alternative investments at home, as we shall see in Chapter 7.

The carriage of goods by the railways developed more slowly than might be imagined. In 1842, 12 years after the opening of the Liverpool and Manchester, only a little over 5 million tons of merchandise were carried on the railways of the United Kingdom, and of this, 4 million were coal. Five years later the figure had risen to 17 million tons, of which 10 million were coal. The majority of revenue still came from passengers, whose share was not overtaken by freight until 1852. It would thus appear that the reduction of transport costs did not have an overwhelming impact on industry, and the effect which it did have seems to have operated as much through forcing down canal rates as from attracting traffic to the new form of transport.

The establishment of the Railway Clearing House in 1842 greatly facilitated the through shipment of goods, and in the course of time a great variety of merchandise came to be distributed by the railways. In his book *Stokers and Pokers* Sir Francis Bond Head gave a vivid description of London's Camden Goods Station in 1849:

[The] picture altogether is really astounding. For from one side of the platform a set of active porters are centripedally wheeling from different spring-waggons innumerable packages to the recording clerks, as eagerly from these clerks (whose duty it is to record the weight of every article, and to affix to it the Company's printed charge for conveyance to its address) other porters, equally active, are centrifugally wheeling other packages to various railway vans, which, as fast as they can be filled, are drawn away from the despatching side of the platform, and immediately replaced by empty ones. One set of porters are wheeling to a recording clerk a waggon-load of raw silk, valued at £9,000, from China, which, via the South-Western Railway, has just arrived from Southampton to go to Macclesfield to be manufactured; another set, Russian tallow, in casks; others, draperies; another set, yarns for Gloucester; one porter has on his truck a very small but heavy load of iron or lead; another, with comparative ease, is wheeling through the crowd a huge wool-bag, large enough to contain, if properly packed, a special jury. Here comes a truck of mustard, in small casks, followed by another full of coffee; there goes a barrow-load of drugs – preceding a cask of spirits, which, to prevent fraud, has just been weighed, tapped, gauged, and sampled; also several trucks full of household furniture; the family warming-pan being tacked round the belly of the eight-day clock, & c. This extraordinary whirl of business, set to music by the various noises proceeding from the working of the steam-cranes, steam-doller [trolley used to transport freight along platform], steam-capstan, common cranes, and other machinery about the platform – from the arrival, turning, backing, and departure of spring-waggons beneath it – from the rumbling of porters' trucks crossing the platform, as also of the railway vans as, laden with goods, they are successively rolled away – forms altogether, we repeat, a scene which, though rarely visited, is astounding to witness, and which, we are sensible, we have but very faintly described.

The greater speed and reliability of the transit of goods by rail meant that the shopkeeper, merchant or manufacturer could rely on a quick replenishment of stocks, so that capital could be diverted from storage and ware-housing to more profitable purposes; while the reduced risk of being caught out with large stocks of unwanted goods no doubt encouraged businessmen to be more amenable to changes in fashion.

Railways were voracious consumers of the products of other industries, although it is important to retain a sense of proportion. All the steam locomotives in the country, for example, consumed less than 2 per cent of the national production of coal, and improvements in engine efficiency meant that the increase in the number of locomotives led to a less than proportionate rise in demand. There was an indirect effect of course. Urbanisation, to which the railways contributed, led to an increased domestic consumption, while there was a derived demand for coal to produce metal and bricks needed for railway contracts.

In 1845 as many as 740 million bricks may have been used in railway construction, representing one-third of the total output. The Kilsby tunnel alone had used 36 million ('sufficient', the lover of useless statistics will note, 'to make a good footpath from London to Aberdeen (missing the Forth) a yard broad').

That the railway consumed large quantities of iron is self-evident; why else should the French call it a *chemin de fer*, or the Germans, *eisenbahn*. Whereas improved design proportionately reduced the demand for coal, the increased weight of locomotives, and of the rails and chairs to carry them, multiplied the demand for iron. In the early days about 53.5 tons of iron went into the rails and chairs of each mile of single track, but by 1841 this had risen to 156 tons. Making allowance for double track and sidings, each route mile must therefore have required 300 or more tons of iron. From 1846 to 1850 therefore, when 4,000 miles of line were opened in the British Isles, and about 2,500 locomotives (each weighing around 25 tons) were running, making allowance for the iron used for rolling-stock, bridges, buildings and signals, one cannot suppose that less than 1.5 million tons were consumed. This was more than the total output for 1844. B. R. Mitchell has estimated that permanent way alone consumed 18 per cent of the United Kingdom output of iron between 1844 and 1851, the South Wales industry receiving the greatest boost. Certain difficulties face the historian seeking precise quantification of the impact of railways on the iron industry. Private goods wagons, provided by traders rather than the railway companies, clearly constituted part of railway demand, yet there is no way of estimating their numbers with any degree of accuracy, although clearly they were considerable. While this factor must raise railway demand, *net* demand was reduced by the scrap metal which the railways themselves produced. Wray Vamplew has calculated that if half the rails lifted from main lines and sidings in Scotland were immediately sold for scrap, and the other half had a further active life of (say) 10 years, then towards the end of the nineteenth century around 70,000 tons of scrap rail was being sold annually. This was equivalent to 6 per cent of total production and over 80 per cent of the Scottish railways' demand for pig iron. In other words, at that time the Scottish railways were producing a very large proportion of the iron they required, although they did not, of course, convert it themselves.

The railways created an entirely new section of the British engineering industry, consuming perhaps one-fifth of the total output of the industry as a whole between 1844 and 1851. A single locomotive was said in 1852 to contain no fewer than 5,416 separate components. Much of the work was done by hand. At the Great Western works in Swindon in 1852 there were two Nasmyth steam hammers, but no fewer than 176 blacksmiths' hearths for forging the smaller parts; while at the Wolverton works of the London and Birmingham there was practically no machinery at all in the early 1840s. The engineer, J. G. H. Warren, described the equipment at Robert Stephenson's works when he was an apprentice there:

> It is scarcely credible, but it is a fact, that there was not a single crane in Robert Stephenson's shop in 1837. There were shear-legs in the yard, by which a boiler could be lifted on to a truck, and there were portable shear-legs in the shop, by the skilful manipulation of which, at no little risk of life and limb, wonders were done in the way of transmitting heavy loads from one part of the shop to another. And the only steam-engine in that which was the most important locomotive shop in the world of that day, was a vibrating pillar engine, with a single 16-inch cylinder and 3ft stroke. The heaviest planing machine in Robert Stephenson's works in 1837, weighed probably not more than 3 tons.[6]

The bigger railway companies operated their own workshops, so the independent engineering firms increasingly looked abroad for orders, almost £1 million worth of locomotives alone being exported annually by the 1860s.

Agriculture, as well as industry, felt the presence of the railway. The farmer's transport costs for feed, fertilisers, seed and implements were greatly reduced, and he became better placed to take advantage of the growing urban demand for perishable foodstuffs, although James Caird pointed out that many farmers proved resistant to change. By the 1880s a city like Manchester could draw upon spring cabbages from Evesham and Lincolnshire; broccoli and cauliflowers from Northamptonshire, or even France; potatoes from Lancashire, Yorkshire, Lincolnshire and Jersey; carrots from the Midlands and France; cucumbers and onions from Bedfordshire; soft fruit from Kent; and imported apples from Liverpool. There was a vast increase in milk shipments, especially after the cattle plague of 1866 decimated the insanitary town dairies of London. In that year some 32 million litres of milk, shipped from 220 country stations, were brought by rail to London, the figure rising to 91 million litres a year by 1880. The transportation of livestock was also revolutionised, as the *Journal of the Royal Agricultural Society* observed in 1858:

> Fifteen years ago there was no railway communication between Norfolk and London. Cattle and sheep for the Smithfield Monday market had to leave their homes on the previous Wednesday or Thursday week. Such a long drift, particularly in hot weather, caused a great waste of meat. The heavy stall-fed cattle of East Norfolk suffered severely. The average loss on such bullocks was

considered to be 4 stones of 14 lbs, while the best yearling sheep are proved to have lost 6 lbs of mutton and 4 of tallow; but beasts from the open yards and old sheep, with careful drovers, did not waste in like manner. Stock now leave on the Saturday and are in the salesman's layers [enclosures or large sheds] that evening, fresh for the metropolitan market on Monday morning. The cost of the rail is considerably more than the old droving charges; but against that there is the gain of 20s a head on every bullock a Norfolk farmer sends to town, to say nothing of being able to take immediate advantage of a dear market.

Finally, it must be remembered that railways represented an industry in their own right. By 1847 the permanent staff of British railway companies numbered 47,000, rising to 112,000 by 1860 and 275,000 by 1873. These numbers embraced clerical workers, skilled craftsmen and unskilled labourers, all fitted into a highly bureaucratic structure. As employers, the railways have been likened to the army, and the relationship was more than a sartorial one:

When men joined the railway they entered the 'Service'. They worked for a company and wore the uniform and livery of that company. The officials of the company were termed 'officers' and 'superior officers'. Trains carrying such personnel were termed 'officers' specials'. A man did not go to work; he went on 'duty'. His position was a 'post', and when he left that 'post' he was 'relieved'. If he failed to report for duty, or left his post without permission, he was 'Absent without Leave'. If he offended against company rules (for instance by smoking on the foot-plate) he was put on a 'charge' and subject to a fine, to suspension from duty, or to loss of rank. No appeal was allowed. A railwayman worked to a roster or a rota. He was obliged to obey without dissent, those persons appointed 'above' him. 'Service', punctilio, and absolute obedience to rule were drilled into him.[7]

In fact the railway companies were early examples of the vast modern corporation, pioneering new business and accounting techniques, but also impinging on the lives of their employees in a host of ways. At its most extensive, 'company paternalism' embraced sick pay and retirement schemes, company housing, health and welfare services, libraries, social clubs, baths and recreational facilities.

If the economic impact of railways is difficult to quantify, the social influence is even more diffuse. The fundamental effect is, of course, very easy to see − travel became a lot easier. As Sydney Smith observed in 1842:

Railroad travelling is a delightful improvement of human life. Man is become a bird; he can fly longer and quicker than a Solan goose. The mamma rushes sixty miles in two hours to the aching finger of her conjugating and declining grammar boy. The early Scotchman scratches himself in the morning mists of the North, and has his porridge in Piccadilly before the setting of the sun . . . Everything is near, everything is immediate − time, distance, and delay are abolished.[8]

The Duke of Wellington was at first opposed to railways, fearing that they would encourage the workers to 'move about'; while John Stuart Mill recognised in 1852 that 'railways enabled them to shift from place to place, and change their patrons and employers as easily as their coats'. The early railways were certainly built at a time of political unrest, and anomalies of the franchise became more visible. When the Liverpool and Manchester Railway was opened, passengers on their way to Manchester (which had no MPs) passed the insignificant village of Newton (which had two). As a contemporary remarked: 'Parliamentary reform must follow soon after the opening of this road.'

Journey times were greatly reduced. By the Great Western, Sydney Smith could get to London from his West Country parish in six hours, whereas before he had been obliged to spend two nights on the road. News also travelled faster. Before the railway age, London daily newspapers with a national reputation were distributed mainly by post, a mere 40,000 or so leaving the capital in this way in the 1830s. Special trains, carrying newspapers at low rates, extended their distribution, and by as early as 1848, W. H. Smith & Son was getting London papers to Glasgow within 10 hours. The railway and the telegraph also went hand in hand. In 1854 eight of the 17 metropolitan offices of the Electric Telegraph Company were at railway termini, while the country telegraph office was almost invariably at the railway station. Commercial news, such as share and commodity prices, shipping news, weather reports and other information of a public nature were communicated by the company throughout the kingdom.

Railways helped transform the look of towns. Local building materials were used less and less, and were replaced by rail-borne Welsh slate, Bedford bricks, Baltic timber and Scottish granite paving-stones. Yet the influence which railways had on town development varied, and it is too easy to ascribe to the railway much growth which might be explained by other factors. Some towns clearly depended on the railways for their livelihood, having been built by the companies. The new town of Swindon resulted from the decision of the Great Western Railway in 1840 to site its principal locomotive depot there. After 1846 locomotives were also built there in increasing numbers, and a mill for rolling rails was added in 1861. Employment in the works rose to 4,000 by 1875 and 14,000 (plus 5,000 foot-platemen) by 1905. Crewe did not exist in 1841, the area which it was to occupy then comprising the two small parishes of Monks Copenhall and Church Copenhall, with a combined population of 747. The place grew rapidly after the Grand Junction Railway established a locomotive and carriage works there, and by 1901 it had a population of 42,074.

Other towns, while not the creation of companies, expanded phenomenally after the coming of the railway. Middlesbrough was such an example. 'When the railway was opened in 1825,' wrote Samuel Smiles, 'the site of this future metropolis of Cleveland was occupied by one solitary farmhouse and its outbuildings. All around was pastureland or mudbanks; scarcely another house was within sight.' The original intention was to open a port for the shipment of coal, but the discovery of vast iron deposits in the Cleveland Hills led to the establishment of the local iron industry. The first blast furnace was blown in 1851, and within 10 years there were 40. Meanwhile the population of the town grew to 19,416 in 1861 and 91,302 in 1902. Middlesbrough's great growth spurt took place at roughly the same time as the gold discoveries in California and Australia, leading Asa Briggs to describe the town as 'the British Ballarat'. It was the unlocking of raw material deposits which also led to the growth of Barrow, a village of 150 inhabitants before the Furness Railway opened there in 1847 to export iron ore. The opening of ironworks in 1859, and steelworks from 1865, together with shipyards after 1897, encouraged the growth of population from 3,135 in 1861 to 63,770 in 1911. Appropriately, Barrow Corporation met in the railway offices before the Town Hall was built. Not all the towns which owed their rise to the railways were industrial. Windermere did not exist before the railway reached there from Kendal in 1847; while Eastbourne was planned and largely built by the Duke of Devonshire (who also developed Barrow) after the opening of the railway in 1849. British seaside resorts in general gained from the railway, which helped to establish the tradition of the holiday by the sea. Seaside towns strove hard to gain a rail connection with London or one of the great industrial centres. Bournemouth was not successful until 1870, but in the following decade the population grew from 5,896 to 16,859, and it had reached 78,674 by 1911. Not that all seaside resorts welcomed the railway. Derek Aldcroft records:

> As early as 1845 one local historian lamented the fact that the railway had robbed Scarborough of its 'genteel exclusiveness and brought a new host of invaders who are inhabitants of murky and densely populated cities seeking to restore their sickly frames to health and vigour by frequent immersions in the sea'.[9]

The impact of the railway on other towns and cities is less easy to measure. In major cities the railways acquired vast tracts of land for their passenger and goods termini. J. R. Kellett, the leading historian of the subject, has estimated that by 1900 the percentage of the central zone owned by railways represented 5.3 per cent in the case of Birmingham; 5.4 per cent of London; 7.3 per cent of Manchester; 7.6 per cent of Glasgow; and 9.0 per cent of Liverpool. In London about 325 hectares of central land (an area sufficient for a fair-sized town in itself) was taken for railway use in the course of the nineteenth century, while H. J. Dyos calculated that 76,000 people had been displaced between 1853 and 1901. The hope had been that railway access might be coupled with slum clearance, and that the lines might 'ventilate' the disease-ridden slums. In the majority of cases this did not happen. As *The Times* commented in 1861:

> The poor are displaced, but they are not removed. They are shovelled out of one side of the parish, only to render more overcrowded the stifling apartments in another part . . . But the dock and wharf labourer, the porter and the costermonger cannot remove. You may pull down their wretched homes: they must find others, and make their new dwellings more crowded than their old ones. The tailor, shoemaker and other workmen are in much the same position. It is mockery to speak of the suburbs to them.

As the railway lines carved up the cities, distinct social zones were created, with development 'on the wrong side of the tracks' blighted for the foreseeable future.

Almost alone among the modern industrial nations, Britain left the development of its railways to private enterprise. Its network was completed swiftly, but at a high cost and with a lack of system. For example, the standard gauge of 4'8½" was not established by Parliament until 1846, by which date Brunel had completed the Great Western using what he regarded as the superior 'broad gauge' of seven feet. Technically he may have been right (he often was); but commercially he was wrong, for his rugged individualism necessitated a costly transhipment of goods for through traffic. Not until 1892 did the Great Western finally abandon the broad gauge.

Lines were promoted individually and often in competition with one another. Solicitors, counsel, land and law agents, as well as engineers and contractors all hoped to gain from piecemeal development; while Parliament was wedded to a private bill procedure which considered each case on its merits. The attempt by Gladstone to establish a Railway Board, under Lord Dalhousie, to examine all proposals for new promotions or amalgamations was a failure. The government gave it inadequate moral and financial support, and it struggled on only from 1845 to 1848.

There was a strong 'railway interest' in Parliament to protect the companies. By 1847, 178 MPs were directors of railway companies, and the peak came 20 years later when there were 215. At first the attitude of the state was to hold only a watching brief. The only precedent was that of the canals; and as they had frequently abused their powers it was feared that the railways would do the same.

The spectre of monopoly power haunted Parliament for the remainder of the century, although little was done to lay the ghost. Allegations of monopolistic practices by the London and Birmingham Railway led to the setting up of a Select Committee on Railways in 1839. The method (not abandoned till 1845) which had been adopted to control the canals was to prevent them from acting as carriers on their own water-ways. Instead they had been obliged to rely on tolls collected from independent carriers whose rivalry, it was supposed, would keep freight rates down. Such a system would not work on the railways, and the Select Comittee reported:

> [The] payment of legal tolls is only a very small part of the arrangement necessary to open railroads to public competition; any person with the mere authority to place an engine or carriages on a railway would be practically unable to supply his engine with water, or to take up or set down his passengers . . . The safety of the public also required that upon every railway there should be one system of management under one superintending authority. On this account it is necessary that the company should possess a complete control over their line of road although they should thereby acquire an entire monopoly.[10]

Two acts did follow the Select Committee, however. In 1840 the Railway Regulation Act was passed, which obliged companies to notify the Board of Trade of the opening of all lines, which would then be inspected. In addition, by-laws had to be submitted, together with toll, rate and accident figures. The concern over accidents was not misplaced, as they were of frequent occurrence. *Punch* went so far as to suggest that each passenger should carry a 'Railway Pocket Companion, containing a small bottle of water, a tumbler, a complete set of surgical instruments, a packet of lint, and directions for making a will'. Accidents to employees alone were sufficient to make railway employment the third most dangerous trade, surpassed only by coal mining and the merchant service. Many accidents were avoidable, and were the result of careless operating, or attempts at economy by cutting safety measures to a minimum, or working railwaymen for excessively long hours. A second act, passed in 1842, allowed the Board of Trade to postpone the opening of a passenger railway until satisfied as to its construction. The Board could not make regulations, but from 1858 onwards 'Requirements' were issued, outlining the basis upon which the Board proposed to use its discretionary powers. These two acts improved safety, but in the opinion of a Select Committee of 1872, they 'contained nothing which had any effect in checking or regulating monopoly'.

A further Regulation of Railways Act, better known as the Cheap Trains Act, was passed in 1844. The act required new lines to provide at least one 'Parliamentary Train' a day in each direction, stopping at all stations, and conveying third-class passengers in covered coaches for not more than one penny a mile. More sweeping proposals (including nationalisation) had been made; but the bill was emasculated in Parliament. As finally passed, it provided for state purchase only of lines sanctioned after the act, and then only after 21 years had elapsed since the passage of *each* authorising act. As this excluded the 2,300 miles of railway already sanctioned (which included most of the main trunk lines) the acquisition of the rest became impracticable.

Numerous attempts were made to regulate railway rates. The early Railway Acts included clauses specifying for each individual company the maximum charges which might be made, but nothing was done to prevent discrimination below the maximum. Not until the passage of the Railway and Canal Traffic Act of 1854 were railway and canal companies forbidden 'to make or give any undue or unreasonable preference or advantage to or in favour of any particular person or company or any particular description of traffic in any respect whatsoever'. Aggrieved persons might take action before the Court of Common Pleas, but the law was weak and easy to evade. In 1873 responsibility for hearing complaints was transferred to a Railway Commission but this, too, lacked teeth; one contemporary authority observing that it had 'power enough to annoy the railroads but not power enough to help the public effectively'. In 1888 the Commission was reorganised as the Railway and Canal Commission; and the railway companies were given six months to draw up a new classification of goods and a new schedule of maximum rates and charges. The former task was accomplished relatively easily, but rate-fixing was more difficult. So little time was given to produce the special rates *below* the maximum, that when the new law came into effect on 1 January 1893 the companies decided to raise all their rates to this level. Many shippers now found to their horror that they were actually paying appreciably more than before. Such was the outcry that in 1894 legislation was passed which provided that if any trader complained that the rate he had been charged since 1 January 1893 had been unduly raised, the burden of justifying the increase before the Railway and Canal Commission rested with the railway company. There were two unfortunate results of this act. Companies became reluctant to pass on economies in operating costs to the customer for fear that, if costs rose again, they would be prevented from raising their rates; and as wages formed an appreciable part of such costs, the attitude towards the railway trade unions hardened.

There was a considerable concentration of the control of railways by the end of the nineteenth century. In 1881 there were 351 companies, but this number was reduced to 233 by 1906, mainly through absorbtion. This increase in scale did not always lead to greater efficiency, and in fact productivity tended to deteriorate rather than improve. There were several reasons for this. Many companies were reluctant to innovate or to improve their methods of working; many later extensions were located in areas of thin traffic; and competition between the larger companies often took the form of adding expensive service 'frills' in order to woo customers.

Shipping

The development of British shipping in the nineteenth century is hardly less important than that of railways, for not only was shipbuilding a major industry, but the revenue from shipping was one of the country's most important 'invisible export' earnings. For example, between 1851 and 1855, when the average excess of imports over exports was around £33 million, net shipping revenue of about £19 million did much to redress the balance.

In the first half of the century British shipping faced a serious challenge from the Americans who, in 50 years, contributed as much to the sailing ship as had the whole world in the previous 300 years. The Americans possessed abundant raw materials, and they built cheap, well-designed ships. British shipyards tended to be small, and conservative in their practice; and their prices were appreciably higher than those of their major competitors. In the 1830s American and Scandinavian yards were building at £5–£8 10s a ton, while Thames shipbuilders were charging £13–£14.

The British response to this foreign challenge did not gather full momentum until the 1840s. By that time a partial revision of the tonnage laws had done away with certain fiscal impediments to the construction of broader and more stable vessels; and the repeal of the Navigation Acts in 1849 removed protection from British shipping, which further stimulated the shipbuilders. A small group of British ship designers and builders began to wrest technical superiority from the United States, and their efforts placed Britain in a very strong position to respond to the challenge of the sleek American clippers. This progress was partially sustained by the patenting in 1850 of composite construction, in which iron frames were covered with wooden planking sheathed in copper, thus avoiding the fouling of the hull by marine growth, which was the great drawback to iron ships. By such means British shipbuilders tipped the scales back in their favour in the 20 years from the mid-1830s. By 1855 Britain was again in a strongly competitive position.

Total iron tonnage built did not exceed wooden tonnage until 1860, although 61 per cent of steamer tonnage had been built of iron 10 years before. The two problems of iron construction were fouling by marine growth and magnetic variation. Fouling greatly reduced a vessel's speed, and could result in costly periods of time spent cleaning. Southampton pilots, for example, found that during the spring and summer they had to lay up their vessels on shore once a fortnight to scrub off weeds and growth. The problem was hard to solve, which was not the case with compass deviation which proved easy to neutralise. Compass error was widely blamed in 1846 for the running aground in Dundrum Bay on the coast of Ireland of Brunel's ship, *Great Britain*. Yet, ironically, the grounding for a year and eventual salvage of that ship in 1847 helped demonstrate the great strength of iron frames and plates.

The transition from sail to steam was very slow. The 1860s marked the zenith of the sailing ship, the famous *Thermopylae* and *Cutty Sark* not being launched till 1868 and 1869 respectively. With no stops for coaling, no fuel bills and no engine repairs or long overhauls, it is not surprising that owners were able to compete successfully against the steamship companies. By 1866 British steam tonnage was 750,000, but tonnage under sail was over 4.5 million. The opening of the Suez Canal in 1869 was one of the decisive factors in the changeover, for its successful navigation required a controlled power such as the sailing ship could not command. Even so, parity between steam and sail was not reached until the 1880s.

Although many countries experimented with steam vessels, Britain alone made a sustained effort to develop ocean-going steamships, to which a stimulus was given by the interest of coastal shippers and companies plying on the short sea routes. Seasickness was a Victorian nightmare but the early introduction of steamers on the Continental and Irish crossings did something to lessen the evil. Of greater significance to the reconquest of the Atlantic trade was the stimulus provided by the British government's policy of awarding contracts for carrying the mail, for these subsidies helped to offset fuel costs. The problem is indicated by the fact that when Cunard won the Atlantic mail contract offered by the government in 1838, he did so with his steamer *Britannia* which needed 640 of its total carrying capacity of 865 tons just to carry its own fuel.

The search for greater efficiency in the use of fuel remained a major problem for the development of the successful steamship. Auxiliary steamers (which carried sail as well as a steam-engine) were only a partial solution, for as an alternative to the 'pure' steamer they failed to give sufficient extra speed to warrant the increased cost. A solution to this and to many other problems was offered by Brunel, who noted that while the carrying capacity of a hull increased as the cube of its dimensions, its resistance, or the power required to drive it through the water, increased only as the square of those dimensions. Build a ship big enough and the problem would disappear. Brunel therefore set to work on the *Great Britain*. This ship 'could be likened in technological advance to the supersonic Concorde of today', claims Ewan Corlett, the naval architect largely responsible for having the hulk towed back in 1970 from the Falkland Islands to its original dock in Bristol. Launched in 1843, it was the first ocean-going ship driven by screw; the first with remote-indicating electric log; the first capable of lowering all masts in a head wind; first with a double bottom; first with watertight bulkheads; and progenitor of the Nasmyth steam hammer. Brunel did not stop there, and in 1851 conceived his 'Crystal Palace of the Sea', a ship to be six times the size of any competitor, with screws, paddle-wheels, six masts carrying over 5,400 square metres of canvas, and a cargo capacity of 6,000 tons. The *Great Eastern*, as it was called, was built on the Thames, and was so long (approximately 192 metres) that it had to be launched sideways into the river. Crowds massed to witness the event on 3 November 1857, but the ship refused to budge, and it eventually took three months and £120,000 to get it afloat. For Brunel, 'it was a simple, if stern, conflict between a Victorian father and the recalcitrance of a monstrous child. He won'. Like many of Brunel's ventures, the ship was a technical triumph but a commercial failure, partly because he had grossly underestimated the coal required to fuel its 6,600 hp engines. Its passenger-carrying capacity of 4,000 (twice that of the *Queen Mary* of 1936) greatly exceeded the demand at that time. Had it been conceived 10 years later and been fitted with the compound steam-engines then coming into use, it might have been successful – especially if employed on the Australia run as originally intended. Instead it made four publicity voyages across the Atlantic, settled down to less glamorous work as a cable ship, and ended its days as a show boat on the Mersey.

Developments in steel-making after 1856 enabled steel boilers to be built capable of pressures three times as great as those common in the early 1850s. Compound engines, using a high- and a low-pressure cylinder, came into use in the next decade, and led to a fuel saving of nearly 60 per cent. At about the same time the problem of boiler corrosion, arising from the use of salt water, was solved by the development of an effective marine condenser. Then came the triple-expansion engine, first employed on the *Aberdeen* in 1881, bringing fuel economies which could at last drive the sailing ship from the sea. In 1887 the scientist and politician, Lyon Playfair, wrote:

> Not long since a steamer of 3,000 tons going on a long voyage might require 2,200 tons of coal, and carry only a limited cargo of 800 tons. Now, a modern steamer will make the same voyage with 800 tons of coal, and carry a freight of 2,200 tons. While coal has thus been economised, human labour has been lessened. In 1870 it required 47 hands on board our steamships for every 1,000 tons capacity. Now only 28 are necessary.[11]

The zenith of British domination of world shipping was probably the decade from 1880 to 1890. In 1883, for example, all but 10 of the 138 steamships of over 4,000 gross tons afloat were British, as was 79 per cent of merchant tonnage launched between 1892 and 1896. By 1890 Britain had more registered tonnage than the rest of the world put together, and even in 1910 over 40 per cent of tonnage entered and cleared in world trade was British. Shipping and shipbuilding enjoyed a symbiotic relationship, and the high domestic demand for ships enabled yards to specialise in particular types of vessel and to maximise the use of their capital assets. The enormous demand for steel enabled shipbuilders to obtain it cheaply, and by 1901 British yards had a 10 per cent cost advantage over their German rivals. Foreign yards were equipped with more up-to-date technology (more hydraulic, pneumatic and electric power, for example), but while it may have been modern, it was also expensive. Foreign yards, in fact, tended to be *over*capitalised. What the British possessed was the superior skill of both workers and managers. The record was impressive, and shipping and shipbuilding represents one of those few sectors of the economy where Britain undoubtedly kept its lead after 1870.

Coal

George Stephenson once observed: 'The Lord Chancellor now sits upon a bag of wool; but wool has long ceased to be emblematical of the staple commodity of England. He ought rather to sit upon a bag of coals, though it might not prove so comfortable a seat.' It was its strategic position within the economy which gave coal its significance, for coal-mining itself accounted for under 1 per cent of British national income at the beginning of the nineteenth century and only 6 per cent even at the end. As an export it represented less than 5 per cent of the total value until the 1870s, rising to 10 per cent at the beginning of the twentieth century. As an employer of labour it ranked only eighth in 1851, rising to sixth place in 1871, although on each occasion the number of miners trailed behind that of the milliners and dressmakers. It was also relatively unaffected by technology, certainly as far as the actual hewing of the coal was concerned, for even by 1900 only 2 per cent was mechanically cut.

A steadily increasing demand pushed up production from an estimated 11 million tons in 1800 to nearly 16 million in 1816, and almost 22.5 million tons in 1830. The industry then entered upon its most rapid period of growth, output more than quadrupling by 1865, when the figure was 98.2 million tons. By 1895, with an output of 189.7 million tons it had nearly doubled again, the zenith being reached in 1913 when 287.4 million tons were raised, a figure never to be exceeded.

The increase in population, coupled with the reduction in transport costs, greatly expanded the domestic demand for coal, of which enormous quantities might be consumed. Fuel remained a major item of expenditure in many households and when, in the 1840s, the new enclosed kitchen range, the 'kitchener', was introduced, its consumption of only one and a half tons a month was regarded as a great economy in comparison with the open range. According to its household accounts, one ton of coal *daily* was the winter consumption of one northern country mansion; and it is not surprising, therefore, that some country houses employed miniature railways to transport their fuel.

By the middle of the nineteenth century probably about one-third of all coal raised was used in the metallurgical industries, but although the smelting demand was among the highest, technical advances within the iron industry prevented it from keeping pace with the output of pig iron. In 1828 James Neilson discovered the advantages of forcing a blast of hot air into the furnace, thus making it possible to make a ton of iron with only one-third the amount of coal previously required. The higher temperatures also made it possible to use raw coal rather than coke, which greatly benefited Neilson's compatriots, for Scottish coal did not coke well. Other fuel economies were to follow. Early painters of the industrial revolution had been fascinated by the infernal quality of blast furnaces at night, as the sky was lit up by the burning waste gases. Exciting though this may have been, it was also extremely wasteful; and when from mid-century the French practice of using the waste gases to preheat the blast was adopted, even greater savings in coal could be made.

The demand for coal to raise steam probably had a greater impact on the balance of production between individual British coalfields than on total output, although the percentage required for steam navigation increased from 1.5 to 12.5 between 1840 and 1887. Welsh coal was particularly favoured for this purpose. In comparison with coal from Newcastle it lit easily, blew up steam rapidly, left little ash and made little smoke. The last point was of great significance to British (and other) admirals who did not want the position of their warships to be betrayed by belching smokestacks.

Large quantities of coal were also demanded by the gas, and later by the electricity, industry. The introduction of gas lighting owes much, as does steam power, to the firm of Boulton and Watt, for the first successful attempt to use coal gas on a large scale was made by the manager of their Soho works, William Murdock. He installed a gas-making plant large enough to light the entire works; and to celebrate the Peace of Amiens in 1802 he floodlit the façade of the building with gas flares, a feat which excited much wonder and admiration. (In London, incidentally, the French ambassador arranged lamps in front of the embassy spelling the work 'Concord'. The illiterate crowd, reading this as 'Conquered', nearly started a riot!) Strangely, Boulton and Watt did not exploit their strong position and the initiative passed elsewhere, especially after 1805 when an employee, Samuel Clegg, left to start his own business. Clegg installed gas lighting in a great many factories and mills, and made many technical innovations including the development of the gasometer. He later teamed up with a German immigrant, F. A. Winzer (later anglicised to Winsor), who in 1807 arranged for the lighting of part of Pall Mall, a publicity stunt which helped arouse interest in his Gas Light and Coke Company, floated five years later. In 1814 the parish of St Margaret's, Westminster, was lit by gas; and by December 1816 London had 26 miles of gas main. This had increased to 122 miles by 1823 and 600 miles by 1834. By 1823, 52 English towns were lit by gas and by 1859 the country possessed nearly 1,000 gasworks. Although the gas cooker had appeared by the time of the Great Exhibition, the initial emphasis was almost entirely on lighting, which cost only one-third or even one-quarter as much as the same amount of illumination provided by oil. The social effect of this, while not capable of quantification, was clearly enormous. The lighting of factories allowed for a longer working day; the habit of reading was encouraged; streets became safer – indeed, when Manchester acquired gas street-lamps in the 1830s they were run by the police, while one London company seems to have owed its existence to the desire to eliminate muggers from the Whitechapel Road.

The gas industry, in turn, produced many by-products, such as ammonia, naphtha and crude tar. Ammonia provided a valuable artificial fertiliser (although chemists became convinced of its value much earlier than did farmers). Naphtha was discovered by the Glasgow chemist, Charles Macintosh, to be an excellent solvent of rubber, making possible the production of waterproof material, and thence the raincoat which bears his name. Crude tar, however, still accumulated at an embarrasing rate, and became a drag on the market. The navy experimented with the use of coal-tar for the preservation of ropes and timber, but it was foulsmelling and considered a health hazard. Railway sleepers were treated with tar, and later with creosote which was vacuum-forced into the timber. Although such uses as these were found, little effort was made to extract identifiable chemicals from tar until the 1860s. The slow exploitation of this raw material was partly due to the lack of an adequate theory of chemical structure, and also to the narrow profit margins. By mid-century, however, the chemical industry was poised for take-off, the goal being the production of artificial dye-stuffs. The founder of the industry was W. H. Perkin, but while Britain produced the theory, the practical benefits were largely reaped elsewhere, particularly in Germany. The fortunes of the chemical industry seemed symptomatic of a decline in British competitiveness, a topic to which we shall return in Chapter 12.

As the demand for coal from all these varied sources increased, so the size of many colliery undertakings expanded, while mines themselves became deeper. It was common opinion about 1830 that the 1,200-foot (about 365 metres) line would prove the limit of profitable working, but many pits soon went below this. The basic problems of mine drainage had been solved by the introduction of the steam pump at the turn of the century, but those of ventilation and haulage remained. Adequate ventilation was of paramount importance, both to circulate fresh air to the miners and to minimise the risk of explosion. In the deeper pits there was always the possibility of fire-damp, a highly explosive mixture of methane and air. The introduction of the Davy safety lamp was only a partial solution for, as one of the Mine Inspectors reported in 1851:

> The prevailing notion among miners is that the lamp is infallible; and the majority of them have yet to learn that under certain conditions, defined by its illustrious inventor, it ceases to be what they have hitherto believed it . . .
>
> The Davy lamp is usually adopted, but it is disliked by the miner on account of the feeble illumination yielded by it; and to obtain a better light he is sometimes tempted to take off the gauze, and by so doing he jeopardises his own and his fellow workmen's lives.[12]

Mine explosions continued to be a serious hazard, but the major disasters (like that at Oaks Colliery in 1866, when 334 miners were killed) should not blind us to the regular death toll from accident and illness. In the middle of the century about 1,000 miners were killed annually in accidents, while many others died from respiratory disease. Miners were 'mashed up at 40 or 45', and had a life expectancy in 1844 of only 49 years.

Not only was the vast majority of coal cut by hand, from seams which ranged from the famous 'ten-yard seam' of Staffordshire down to others so narrow that the miner had to crawl out to reverse his pick; but much was also hauled by hand. Underground pit ponies were employed in increasing numbers (there were 11,000 of them in 1851 and 70,000 in 1911); but earlier in the nineteenth century it was often women and children who did the work. Although the employment underground of women and of boys under 10 was forbidden by the Coal Mines Act of 1842, difficulties of administration and ease of evasion prevented effective enforcement for many years, and the Mines Inspector, H. S. Tremenheere found women still employed underground in 1851.

Iron, steel and engineering

The structure of the Crystal Palace contained about 4,500 tons of iron, of which about 700 tons was wrought and 3,800 tons cast. Hardly any steel at all was used in the building, for the day of steel had not yet arrived. Indeed, in 1850, when over 2 million tons of iron were made in Great Britain, a mere 60,000 tons of steel were produced. Iron reigned supreme, and its output leapt up. By 1830 about 2,000 tons were produced every working day (650,000–700,000 tons a year); by about 1835 production touched the 1 million-ton mark; 1.5 million tons was probably reached by 1840–41; and by the end of the century about 8.5 million tons a year were produced.

The Victorians seemed to find no end to the uses to which cast iron could be put, as a glance at the catalogue of the Great Exhibition will show. Even as early as the 1820s the adaptability of the material was noted in the song, 'Humphrey Hardfeatures' Description of Cast-Iron Inventions':

> Since cast-iron has got all the rage,
> And scarce anything's now made without it;
> As I live in this cast-iron age,
> I mean to say something about it.
> There's cast-iron coffins and carts,

There's cast-iron bridges and boats,
Corn-factors with cast-iron hearts,
That I'd hang up in cast-iron coats.
We have cast-iron gates and lamp-posts,
We have cast-iron mortars and mills, too;
And our enemies know to their cost
We have plenty of cast-iron pills, too.
We have cast-iron fenders and grates,
We have cast-iron pokers and tongs, sir;
And we soon shall have cast-iron plates,
And cast-iron small-clothes, ere long, sir.

Cast iron, while capable of being moulded into the most complicated shapes and being strong when *compressed* (for example when used as a column) has a low *tensile strength* (a load stretching it will tend to pull it apart). This brittleness is due to the high carbon content (up to 3 or 4 per cent). If virtually all the carbon is removed (down, say, to about four parts in a thousand) wrought iron is produced. This cannot be moulded, but has a high tensile strength, can be hammered or rolled into shape, and is easily welded. Steel is more difficult to define because it can take so many forms, but fundamentally it is an alloy of iron, carbon and other elements, containing less carbon than cast iron but more than wrought iron. For nearly all purposes steel has been proved superior to iron, but its manufacture remained a small-scale and laborious process in which no notable improvement had been made since the Huntsman crucible process of the mid-eighteenth century. By the middle of the nineteenth century, steel cost around £50 a ton, while pig iron cost only around £3–£4 a ton, in consequence of which the demand for a malleable iron was met by wrought or 'puddled' iron. Henry Cort's puddling process of 1784 has already been described in Chapter 1, but it made the puddler one of the key industrial workers of the next 100 years. Sir George Head, visiting the Low Moor Ironworks near Leeds in 1835, likened the working conditions to an inferno:

Athletic men, bathed in perspiration, naked from the waist upwards, exposed to severe alternations of temperature, some, with long bars, stirring the fused metal through the door of the furnace, whose flaming concavity presented to the view a glowing lake of fire – were working like Cyclopes. By continued and violent applications of strength, visible in writhing changes of attitude and contortions of the body, raking backwards and forwards, and stirring round and about the yielding metal, they contrived to weld together a shapeless mass gradually increasing in size till it became about an hundred pounds weight; this, by a simultaneous effort of two men with massive tongs, was dragged out of the furnace, radiant with white heat . . . Now subjected to the blows of a ponderous hammer, it was wonderful to mark the vigour and dexterity with which the men contrived to heave the mass round and round at every rise of the hammer . . . while the fiery ball was now turned one side, again the other side uppermost, with the same facility apparently to the operators as if it had been a horseshoe.[13]

So arduous was the work that in the late 1860s the life expectancy of puddlers in Sheffield was a mere 31 years. Yet puddling proved difficult to mechanise, for while machines could be made to stir the molten metal, only the human eye and touch could separate out the solidifying, decarburized metal. The whole process has been likened by David Landes to cooking, for it requires 'a feel for the ingredients, an acute sense of proportion, an "instinct" about the time the pot should be left on the stove'. In 1886 a Royal Commission was told that fully half of the iron (including steel) required in a malleable form continued to be made in the puddling furnace. Wrought iron is still made for certain specialised purposes, although much of the iron thus described (that used in modern ornamental gates, for example) is in fact mild steel.

It was the Crimean War, rather than the peaceful Great Exhibition, which indirectly led to the advent of cheap steel. Sir Henry Bessemer (he was knighted in 1879) was a professional inventor who devised a new method of type-founding; invented a type-composing machine; devised a method of making imitation Utrecht velvet; lead pencils from waste plumbago; and bronze powder by a secret process which afforded him a considerable income. The imperfections of the artillery used in the Crimean War led him to investigate the rifled cannon. He received little encouragement from the War Office, although the French were sympathetic to his ideas. Everything depended, however, on the ability to produce a metal for the gun barrels strong enough for Bessemer's heavy projectiles. Although he was no metallurgist, he started on a series of small-scale empirical experiments which resulted, 18 months later, in his paper, 'The Manufacture of Malleable Iron and Steel Without Fuel', delivered to the British Association in August 1856. The fuel to which Bessemer referred was that used in puddling, and in the processes by which small quantities of steel could be made. His original plan was to run molten iron straight from the blast furnace into a 'converter'. Here he would burn away all the chemical impurities (mainly carbon and silicon) if he wanted wrought (malleable) iron, and to burn out all but the appropriate amount of carbon if he wanted steel. The novelty of his process was to force air, in great quantities and at great speed, up through the molten mass, raising the temperature to such a degree that the mass of iron was kept perfectly fluid, while the carbon and silicon were rapidly burned away.

Within weeks of publishing his paper, Bessemer received £27,000 in licence fees from ironmasters anxious to use the new methods. But try as they might, their efforts resulted in disastrous failure, and what had been announced as an outstanding discovery was now denounced by The Times as 'a brilliant meteor that had flashed across the metallurgical horizon, dazzling a few enthusiasts, and then vanishing forever in total darkness'.

Had Bessemer been a metallurgist he would not have announced victory when the battle was in fact only half won. In his own experiments he had, quite fortuitously, used a Blaenavon pig iron made from one of the very few British ores that is almost entirely free from phosphorus. When repeated with phosphoric iron, his process failed to remove this impurity which, even in quantities as small as seven parts in 10,000, makes an iron which is non-malleable. Bessemer therefore began to look for a suitable nonphosphoric ore, finding what he wanted in Cumberland haematite and in ores imported from Spain and Sweden. Furthermore, the first Bessemer steel was brittle and contained many airholes. The problem of removing this excess oxygen was solved by R. F. Mushet, the son of a Scottish metallurgist, and owner of a small ironworks in the Forest of Dean. Mushet knew that oxygen has a particular affinity for manganese and therefore that the addition of a suitable quantity of spiegeleisen (an alloy of manganese and iron) would have a degasifying effect and would allow the oxygen to pass off in the slag as manganese oxide. This solution was not a complete one, however, for spiegeleisen is rich in carbon, and could therefore be used only in the production of steel with a high carbon content. A third difficulty was solved by Bessemer himself. The first converter had been fixed, and could not be stopped during the blast for fear of clogging the airholes. But in order to secure exact results the process had to be capable of being stopped and restarted at will.

Bessemer therefore swung the converter on an axle, so that when tilted the air pipes led in above the surface of the molten metal.

There was no mushroom growth in the production and use of steel. Although the price was reduced by the Bessemer process (Bessemer's quotation for high-class tool steel was £42 a ton as against £50–£60 by the old methods), steel still cost much more than iron. Bessemer charged a high price for patentee's licences, which settled down to £1 a ton on steel rails and £2 a ton for other purposes. The fee, together with the relatively expensive phosphorus-free raw material, made steel rails and plates much dearer than their competitors. The steel/iron rail price ratio was 2.65 to 1 in 1867, but fell to 1.50 to 1 in 1871, and to 1.16 to 1 by 1875. However, until long endurance tests had been completed there was no knowing that the dearer steel would still prove economical, and with so much capital and human skill locked up in puddling (in which Britain had undisputed eminence) attitudes remained conservative.

It was in the 1870s that rapid strides in the use of steel were made. Now, steel rails, the life of which were perhaps 30 times that of iron ones, were widely adopted by the railways. In 1872, for example, the North Eastern Railway used steel rails only at points and crossings, but by 1877 it had ceased to order iron rails at all. In that year, too, the Board of Trade for the first time authorised the use of steel for bridge-building. Shipbuilding witnessed similar changes. In 1847 iron ships had been so rare that Lloyds had made no regular rating for them. As that material only came to be generally adopted in the 1850s and 1860s, it is not surprising that there was a reluctance to experiment with yet another new material. The Admiralty was conservative, but the launching of two steel despatch vessels, HMS *Iris* and HMS *Mercury*, 1876–8, marks the moment of rapid change. In 1880 Lloyds' surveyors inspected 35,000 tons of steel shipping; and in 1885 a tonnage of 166,000 (which still has to be compared with an iron tonnage of 934,000).

Technical developments did not stop with Bessemer. Sir William Siemens was one of the founders of the great firm of Siemens Brothers, famous for the development of the electric telegraph and electrical power industries. William's elder brother, Werner, exhibited many electrical instruments at the Crystal Palace while William, on moving from his native Germany to England, was employed by Fox, Henderson & Company, the contractors for that building. Like Bessemer, Siemens had many inventions to his name, but none was more significant than his development of the regenerative open-hearth furnace. In Siemens's furnace a current of burning gas heated the firebrick labyrinth of the regenerative chambers. Through them passed the next incoming currents of gas and air, sucking in heat, and burning at a higher temperature than the first current, and so on. Far greater temperatures than previously possible could now be achieved. The furnace was first used in 1861 for the making of glass by Chance Brothers, the Smethwick firm which had supplied the panes for the Great Exhibition. From the first, however, Siemens had argued that his furnace could be used for steel-making, but early experiments were a failure. Then, in 1865, two French ironmakers, Pierre and Emile Martin, successfully made cast steel by melting scrap steel in a bath of molten pig iron on a Siemens open hearth. The Bessemer converter could not accommodate cold scrap, and the process was so fast (a 'blow' took about half an hour) that it could not be so accurately controlled as in the open hearth, where the process might last anything from six to 12 or 15 hours. This flexibility was of great importance as new alloy steels came to be adopted. The perfect control of gaseous fuel, and hence the temperature of the open-hearth furnace, enabled the steel-maker to work very exactly. Ore was fed in to keep the 'boiling' constant, the contents were sampled at intervals, and at the right moment the molten mass was 'physicked' with manganese or other alloy. The process was placed on a commercial footing in 1869 at the Swansea works of the Landore Siemens Steel Company, and by the end of the century three-quarters of Britain's annual output of nearly 5 million tons of steel was produced by the open-hearth method. The last two Bessemer converters in Britain went out of production early in the 1970s.

The problem of phosphoric ores remained unsolved until 1879, when a solution was finally found by Sidney Gilchrist Thomas, a London police court clerk, and his cousin, Percy Gilchrist, a Blaenaven chemist. Their experiments led to the discovery that in existing furnaces the phosphoric acid produced from phosphoric ores would not combine with the acidic silica lining of the converters. The solution was therefore the simple one of fitting a basic (alkaline) lining, and they chose a form of limestone known as dolomite. The basic lining drew off the phosphoric acid, leaving a pure steel, and producing a useful by-product – 'phosphoric slag' – valuable as an artificial fertiliser. Once again, however, British manufacturers proved conservative, although the method was eagerly taken up in Belgium, France, Germany and the United States, where phosphoric ores were abundant. Britain's dominant position in world iron and steel production thus became threatened for the first time.

Alongside the developments in iron and steel went expansion of the engineering industry. The successful engineer was one of the great Victorian folkheroes, whose popular appeal ranged from the highest to the lowest in the land. In *Lives of the Engineers* (1862) Samuel Smiles lavished praise on the leaders of technical enterprise. The queen gave Prince Louis a copy when he married Princess Alice, while Richard Tangye (the engineer who provided Brunel with the hydraulic rams which eventually floated the *Great Eastern*) gave one to each of his apprentices. The book's stress was on the virtues of independence, thrift, free enterprise and, of course, self-help. Smiles lauded George Stephenson, the offspring of a colliery engineman, and his son Robert, who became the first engineering millionaire. Brunel, who was not of humble origin and therefore did not prove the point Smiles wished to make, was neglected. So too was Trevithick, the real inventor of the steam-engine, who did not *persevere*, and who died in poverty. What Smiles chose to demonstrate was that 'the character of our engineers is a most signal and marked expression of British character'.

It has been suggested that the history of British engineering reads very much like the *Book of Genesis*. There was an awful lot of begetting. Bramah begat Maudslay, Maudslay begat Whitworth, and so on. It is certainly true that through apprenticeship and 'learning' as an articled pupil much skill and many basic principles were passed from one leader to the next. Joseph Bramah (1748–1814) was the fount from whom flowed much engineering expertise. Among his many inventions was a foolproof lock, patented in 1784, and never picked until the year of the Great Exhibition, when an American locksmith succeeded after 50 hours' endeavour. So complicated was the lock that many machine tools were required for its commercial production, and to help produce these Bramah employed Henry Maudslay. Maudslay (1771–1831) eventually set up on his own, and in turn employed and trained many of the great names of nineteenth-century engineering, including Joseph Clement, Richard Roberts, Joseph Whitworth and James Nasmyth. Nasmyth (1808–90) described how Maudslay impressed upon his pupils the need for simplicity of design as well as 'get-at-ability':

> One point he often impressed upon me. It was, he said, most important to bear in mind the *get-at-ability* of parts – that is, when any part of a machine was out

of repair, it was requisite to get at it easily without taking the machine to pieces. This may appear a very simple remark, but the neglect of such an arrangement occasions a vast amount of trouble, delay, and expense.[14]

No doubt many readers, faced with the repair of some broken household appliance, would agree. Nasmyth's own great contribution was the invention of the steam hammer, which made it possible to forge far greater iron and steel castings than ever before. As Nasmyth justifiably claimed, 'The machine combined great power with gentleness. The hammer could be made to give so gentle a blow as to crack the end of an egg placed in a wine glass on the anvil; whilst the next blow would shake the parish!'

At the time of the Great Exhibition Joseph Whitworth (1803–87) was easily the chief machine tool-maker in Britain. He had 23 exhibits in the Crystal Palace, many more than any competitor. They included lathes, machines for planing, shaping, slotting, drilling, punching and shearing metal. His greatest contribution was probably his crusade for standardisation. Screw threads were in a chaotic state. Whitworth collected samples from as many workshops as possible, and by taking the average of the measurements, put forward a proposal for screws of a standard angle of 55° between the sides of the thread, and a specified number of threads to the inch for different diameters. His recommendations became standard British practice in the 1860s, greatly facilitating the construction and maintenance of machinery of all descriptions. Whitworth went on to recommend standardisation in manufacturing items ranging from candlesticks to locomotives but with less success. For example, in addition to the basic difference over gauge, British railways showed a remarkable lack of standardisation; and as late as 1918 a government committee reported that there were over 200 different types of axlebox and 40 varieties of handbrake in use on wagons. Part of the problem was that very individuality and independence of engineers which Smiles had applauded. Many of them were contemptuous of ideas other than their own, while there was a tendency to admire the technical product rather than the technique of production. This differed greatly from the American experience, where mass-production methods were developed much more fully, and this depended, of course, on a standardised product.

As machinery spread, a greater quantity of goods could be produced with more accuracy and at a lower cost. The manufacture of wood screws is just one example; by 1875 two girls with two machines could turn out 24,000 a day, as compared with 20,000 a day by 20 men and boys in 1840. While the construction and maintenance of machines called forward a new breed of skilled engineering craftsmen, machines themselves replaced some skilled men with unskilled. To the employer this had certain advantages. Nasmyth, for example, claimed that his machine tools 'never got drunk; their hands never shook from excess; they were never absent from work; they did not strike for wages; they were unfailing in their accuracy and regularity'. But their expense might prove an inhibiting factor to the potential user. A steam sawing machine in 1850 cost £700 to install, but a pair of travelling sawyers could be hired to do a job for five shillings. As late as 1895 a steam saw-mill was blown up in the Forest of Dean, an example of Luddism of a much later date than we often imagine.

Engineers were among the elite of the labour aristocracy, and they jealously defended their craft skills. Until the end of the nineteenth century they proved successful in this, even when new machines such as the turret lathe came into use in the 1870s. Although these machines held up to eight cutting tools, and were capable of carrying out very complex cutting operations with only minimal supervision, it remained possible to absorb them into the engineers' craft framework. This was partly because the cutting tools themselves needed sharpening and accurate setting, and these tasks added to the engineer's skill. However, as machines were introduced with increasingly specific functions on a 'production line' they could be operated by semi-skilled men who were cheaper to employ than engineers who had completed a full apprenticeship. Disputes increased in the 1890s, culminating in the great engineering lock-out of 1897–8. This was the first major industrial dispute to be fought over the issue of managerial control – and the employers won. The pride and self-respect of engineers was greatly damaged, but this was not the only assault which they faced, as F. M. L. Thompson explains:

> Perhaps even more damaging to the craftsmen's sense of pride were the effects of the new special tool steels and the new grinding arrangements. With these, tool-sharpening itself became a specialized activity carried out by a specialist worker, and engineers found themselves deprived of some of their personal tools and of their individual responsibility for keeping them in good order. Employers assumed that the engineers were merely sulking over the loss of their customary grinding time, which had provided pleasantly sociable breaks from work. In fact, personal possession of the tools of the trade, and personal care of their condition, were the marks of the skilled tradesman – carpenter, joiner, plumber, or mason, no less than engineer – and emasculation of this was a direct emasculation of independence and status, a move towards stripping the artisan of both symbols and objects which distinguished him from other workers. Indeed, when a set of tools could well be worth between £30 and £40, the equivalent of well over one year's wages of most agricultural labourers, its possessor combined the independence of the petty capitalist with the position of wage worker.[15]

The organisation of industry and banking

Much of the stress in this chapter has been on technological developments, but it should not be thought that the prosperity of mid-Victorian Britain can be solely ascribed to such causes. There was a great growth in foreign trade, which will be discussed in the next chapter; and there was, too, a significant development of the organisation of industry and the country's banking system.

There had been little need for joint-stock organisation in the early stages of Britain's industrial growth; and although transport undertakings such as canals and railways invariably required corporate organisation, the scale of manufacturing industry did not necessitate joint-stock organisation until at least mid-century. The boom of 1824–5 resulted in the repeal of the Bubble Act; but it was not until 1837 that the Letters Patent Act was passed, giving to the President of the Board of Trade, as agent of the crown, the discretionary authority to grant certain powers of incorporation which could previously be obtained only by act of Parliament. The attitude still remained that incorporation should be a privilege rather than a right and only enterprises with certain characteristics – special risks, like many overseas mining companies; great size, like canals and railways; or need for widely extended responsibility, as an insurance – were likely to make successful applications. Many industrialists still considered joint-stock companies to denote irresponsible management, defective finance, or even fraud.

A Select Committee investigated the law relating to joint-stock companies in 1844 and, concluding that the development of this form of organisation was inevitable, recommended that Parliament should seek to control it. As a result the Joint Stock Companies Act was passed in the same year, by which any association of 24 or more members could register as a company, at first provisionally, and then fully, once the Registrar of Companies was satisfied as to its genuineness. The railway mania occurred soon after the passage of the act, and this did much to change attitudes towards joint-stock companies, for although many were unsound, on the whole investments were secure.

As the prosperity of the country increased, there came to be a mass of savings seeking profitable investment, but the failure of the act of 1844 to provide for limited liability acted as a deterrent, for any shareholder in a company was liable up to 'his last shilling and acre'. As the issue came to be more fully discussed there was growing criticism of the discretionary power to grant limited liability which had been one of the powers granted to the Board of Trade by the act of 1837. If the principle of limited liability was good, it was argued, then it should be available for all; if it was bad, then, as Robert Lowe put it, he would 'as soon think of allowing the Secretary of the Treasury to grant dispensations for smuggling or the Attorney-General licences to commit murder'.

In 1851 a Select Committee on the Law of Partnership recommended the granting of limited liability, and its merits were further discussed in a report by the engineers Joseph Whitworth and George Wallis, who acted as government commissioners to an industrial exhibition held in New York in 1854. As they reported:

> The Law of Limited Liability, which is now engaging public attention, is an important source of the prosperity which attends the industry of the United States. This law affords the most ample facilities for the investment of capital, and has led to a much greater development of the industrial resources and skill of that country than could have resulted under other circumstances for many years to come.[16]

At last an act of 1856 (following a clumsily worded act of the previous year) enabled any seven men to start a limited liability company, although banks were excluded until 1858, and insurance companies and discount houses until 1862. There was no great rush to form companies – a clear indication that absence of the corporate form had not been an inhibiting factor to manufacturing industry. The sober firm could always borrow from the bank, and ploughed-back profits, as in the early stages of industrial growth, still provided a majority of capital requirements. Not until the 1870s did manufacturers in general come to lose their former suspicions; but by the end of the century, with the exception of retail trade, joint-stock companies had become the characteristic form of business undertaking.

The trend towards joint-stock banking had its origin in Scotland, where the Bank of Scotland had lost its monopoly in 1716. New joint-stock banks gradually bought out their private competitors, and although private banks did not cease to exist in Scotland they became unimportant, with the exception of certain old-established houses in Edinburgh. As a result the number of separate banks diminished, but as they each had many branches the community continued to be well served, while small depositors and borrowers were afforded facilities unavailable in England and Wales.

By 1825 Scotland had fewer banks than Devon, and there had not been a single bank failure since 1816. The contrast between the soundness of Scottish banks and the instability of those south of the border was brought home by the financial crisis of 1825, when the country was said to have been 'within twenty-four hours of barter'. The crisis was the result of over-speculation in South America and at home (where one of the 624 new companies promoted was for a project to recover the treasure abandoned in the Red Sea when Moses led the Jews out of Egypt). In England and Wales 73 banks suspended payment and about 50 failed altogether. In Scotland, on the other hand, there were only two or three failures, and none among the older or fully developed joint-stock banks, nor among the banks of Edinburgh or Glasgow. As Sir John Clapham put it, 'the Country seemed almost immune to the virus'.

The lesson was not lost. Lord Liverpool, the Prime Minister, acknowledged the instability of a banking system based on small, privately owned local firms where 'any petty tradesman, any grocer or cheesemonger, however destitute of property, might set up a bank in any place'. In 1826, therefore, joint-stock banks were authorised outside a 65-mile limit from London, and the Bank of England was obliged to open branches in the provinces. At first the growth of joint-stock banks was slow, but there were 32 in England and Wales by 1833 and 115 by 1841. In the meantime the number of private banks diminished, either by conversion to joint-stock, by absorption or by closure. From a total of 321 in England and Wales in 1841, the number had fallen to 251 by 1886.

The charter of the Bank of England was renewed in 1833, but its privileges were further limited. The 65-mile limit was waived, and joint-stock banks were henceforward allowed in London provided that they did not issue notes. Financial crises still occurred (in 1836 and 1839) but both the City and Parliament were completely at a loss to determine the real nature of the problems involved or remedies possible. Two committees, in 1836-8 and 1840-41, amassed mountains of detailed evidence from which, observes one historian, 'the conscientious student of banking reforms could have deduced any remedy he cared, but which the Committees themselves found it impossible to digest'.

There were principally two schools of thought. The *Currency School* advocated a fixed relationship between the amount of gold in the country and the size of note issues, requiring the volume of notes to be decreased as gold flowed out of the country or increased as gold flowed in. It blamed the over-issue of notes by the country banks for the crises of the 1830s, and argued that by controlling note issue, booms and depressions in the value of money would in future be eliminated. It suggested, therefore, that the issue of notes should gradually be concentrated in the Bank of England, and also that this function should be separated from the Bank's commercial business. The *Banking School* held that the duty of the state was merely to ensure that banknotes were convertible to gold, in which case the size of the note issue might safely be left to the experience of bankers, and their expert knowledge of the needs of industry and commerce.

The Bank Charter Act of 1844 marked the triumph of the Currency School. The Bank of England was divided into a Banking Department and an Issue Department, and the note issue was to correspond exactly with the amount of gold held in its reserves, with the exception that there was to be a *fiduciary issue* of notes, to the value of £14 million, backed instead by government securities. This compromise was necessitated by the impossibility of requiring the Bank to purchase sufficient gold to back the notes already in existence. Other provisions applied to the note issue of the country banks (which in fact accounted for less than a quarter of the notes circulating at that time). No new privilege of note issue would be granted, but banks which already possessed the right would only lose it if they amalgamated or let it lapse. In such an event the Bank of England could increase its fiduciary issue by two-thirds of the lapsed issue. The number of note-issuing banks thereafter declined, only £250,000 of private notes remaining by 1910, and the last country bank to issue notes, Fox, Fowler & Co., of Wellington in Somerset, lost the right in 1921 when it amalgamated with Lloyds.

Curiously, the adherents of the Currency School had attached no importance to the circulating bill of exchange (a form of near-money) nor to the cheque, which was rapidly becoming a means of payment. Had it not been for these developments, and the discovery of fresh sources of gold (in California in 1849 and Australia in 1851) the rigidity imposed by the act would have been serious. Between 1848 and 1851 the aggregate addition to the commercial world's stock of gold was estimated to be an unprecedented 30 per cent, with perhaps 60 per cent of the gold entering Europe coming to Britain, causing a rapid augmentation of the reserves of the Bank of England.

Even so, the act failed to control financial crises, and on three subsequent occasions (one within three years of the act being passed) it had to be suspended. In 1847, 1857 and 1866 the Bank was permitted to lend beyond its legal limits, but the crisis of 1866 proved to be the last of its kind. Ironically, one of the most potent weapons of modern central banking, the variable Bank Rate, which exercises a control over general interest rates, came about almost by accident. The establishment of a separate Banking Department allowed the Bank of England to compete with the commercial banks for business. It immediately plunged into the discount market, but soon learned to stay out of the market and to act only as a lender of last resort. It was this growing sense of responsibility and experience which allowed the Bank to regulate the money market with increasing effect, although it remained a private institution until nationalized in 1946.

Meanwhile, after a lull caused by the stringent conditions of the Bank Charter Act, the amalgamation of commercial banks and the development of branch banking went hand in hand. Private banks did not much favour the supervision involved in branch banking, and hence business was increasingly transferred to the joint-stock banks. By 1864 there were 1,000 bank branches, and 2,500–2,700 by 1886–7. From then on the five main joint-stock banks, Barclays, Midland, District, Martins and Lloyds pushed on to establish a national system of branches, sweeping up the private banks into their vast organisations. The last-named bank, for example, incorporated 164 different banks by 1923. By 1900 country banks were curiosities but the last, Gunner & Co., of Bishop's Waltham in Hampshire, was not taken over by Barclays until 1953.

Notes

1   Quoted in Humphrey Jennings, *Pandaemonium*, Andre Deutsch, 1985, p. 262.
2   Richard Altick, *Victorian People and Ideas*, W. W. Horton, 1973, p. 75.
3   F. M. L. Thompson, *Victorian England: The Horse-drawn Society*, Bedford College, 1970, p. 13.
4   Roderick Floud and Donald McCloskey (eds), *The Economic History of Britain Since 1700*, vol. 1, Cambridge University Press, 1981, pp. 237–8.
5   D. Aldcroft, 'The railway age' in Anne Digby, Charles Feinstein and David Jenkins (eds), *New Directions in Economic and Social History*, vol. 2, Macmillan, 1992, pp. 73-4.
6   Quoted in Ken Baynes and Francis Pugh, *The Art of the Engineer*, Lutterworth Press, 1981, p. 116.
7   Frank McKenna, 'Victorian railway workers', *History Workshop Journal*, Spring 1976, pp. 27–8.

8   Hesketh Pearson, *The Smith of Smiths*, Folio Society, 1977, pp. 265–6.
9   D. Aldcroft, op.cit., 1992, p. 76.
10 Quoted in Philip Bagwell, *The Transport Revolution from 1770*, Batsford, 1974, p. 171.
11 Quoted in W. H. B. Court, *British Economic History, 1870–1914*, Cambridge University Press, 1965, p. 165.
12 Quoted in Brian Lewis, *Coal Mining in the Eighteenth and Nineteenth Centuries*, Longman, 1971, p. 109.
13 Quoted in Raphael Samuel, 'The workshop of the world', *History Workshop Journal*, Spring 1977, p. 43.
14 Quoted in P. W. Kingsford, *Engineers, Inventors and Workers*, Edward Arnold, 1964, p. 137.
15 F. M. L. Thompson, *The Rise of Respectable Society*, Fontana, 1988, p. 233.
16 D. H. Flower *et al., In Search of America*, vol. I, Holt, Rinehart and Winston, 1972, p. 373.

Chapter seven

Britain and the world

The opening up of the world

The contemporary world is sometimes depicted as a 'global village' – a term which aptly describes the interrelatedness of our lives. What affects the welfare of a nation in one part of the global village affects the rest, and news is spread as quickly as any village gossip can manage. An earthquake, a famine or a war anywhere on the planet will be reported rapidly, often within minutes, on our radios and television screens, and in our newspapers. It is easy to forget how recently all this has come about. To take one example: only a little over a century and a half ago Britain and the United States were at war, and on 8 January 1815 a battle took place for the control of New Orleans. Much damage and loss of life was caused – but neither of the commanders of the opposing armies knew that peace had been signed more than two weeks previously. The news had not yet reached them.

All this was to change with the development of the telegraph. W. F. Cooke and Charles Wheatsone produced the first practical electric telegraph in 1837. In the same year the American, Samuel Morse, devised the code which bears his name, and in 1844 he built the first telegraph line from Baltimore to Washington. The very first message was the grandiloquent, 'What Hath God Wrought!'. Morse had earlier said: 'If I can succeed in working a magnet ten miles I can go round the globe.' And that the telegraph soon did. By 1870 President Grant in Washington was able to inaugurate a new telegraph link by receiving a message from Lord Mayo, Viceroy of India, telegraphed from the vice-regal summer residence in the Himalayas only a few minutes before. Within another decade the whole world, with the exception of the Pacific, was covered by the telegraph. Sir John Clapham observed:

> It was not yet possible to telegraph to Honolulu, Iceland, New Guinea or Tierra del Fuego. Nearly every other place of real importance not in the heart of China could be reached overland or under the sea. The world, on the economist's projection, had shrunk into a single market. The final process of shrinkage had only taken about fifteen years and the greater part of it had been done in less than ten.[1]

Buyers and sellers in all continents were, for the first time in history, placed in direct contact with each other; and merchant fleets, in constant touch with their homelands, were moved about like pieces on a chess-board wherever need and profit dictated. Between a fifth and a quarter of Britain's merchant tonnage was directed around the world by cable from London, and never touched home shores from one year to the next. Such were the economies introduced by the telegraph, by finding cargoes for empty vessels to carry, that the capacity of the world's shipping fleet was greatly expanded without a single extra ton being built.

The late nineteenth century witnessed a revolution in communications. William Woodruff writes: 'Breakwaters, ports, harbours, lighthouses and other shipping aids were created or improved upon in every part of the world; roads, tunnels, and bridges were built in every continent. International agreements were generally evolved by the western nations in an attempt to create a unified world economy.'[2] As instances of the latter he cites the International Telegraph Union of 1865, the Universal Postal Union of 1875 and the many agreements to regulate traffic on the high seas. The Suez Canal (opened in 1869) reduced the sea journey from London to Singapore by almost one-third, and that between London and Bombay by more than two-fifths. Bombay was brought 3,000 miles closer to New York, and Melbourne 1,000 miles closer to London. The Panama Canal (opened in August 1914) effectively moved Cape Horn 5,000 miles to the north, cutting the distance between New York and San Francisco by three-fifths and between San Francisco and Liverpool by two-fifths. If distances by sea were reduced, so were those by land, for at the heart of the opening up of the world to trade lay the railway.

Table 7.1   Development of world's railway mileage, 1840 and 1920 (in thousand miles and in percentage of world total)

Continents and countries with largest percentages	First steam line opened	1840		1920	
		Mileage	%	Mileage	%
World	1825	5.49	100.0	674.89	100.0
Europe	1825	2.54	46.3	159.97	23.7
Great Britain	1825	1.48	27.0	20.33	3.0
France	1832	0.26	4.7	25.85	3.8
Germany	1835	0.34	6.2	35.85	5.3
Belgium	1835	0.21	3.8	3.05	0.5
USSR	1837	0.02	0.4	44.49	6.6
North America	1830	2.83	51.5	292.16	43.3
USA	1830	2.82	51.4	252.87	37.4
Canada	1836	0.02	0.4	39.29	5.8
Latin America	1837	0.10	1.8	62.91	9.3
Brazil	1854	–	–	17.73	2.6
Argentina	1857	–	–	21.18	3.1
Asia	1853	–	–	62.06	9.2
India	1853	–	–	36.74	5.4
Africa	1854	–	–	27.16	4.0
South Africa	1860	–	–	10.12	1.5
Australasia	1854	–	–	26.14	3.9
Australia	1854	–	–	23.12	3.4

Source: William Woodruff, 'The emergence of an international economy, 1700–1914' in Carlo M. Cipolla (ed.), The Fontana Economic History of Europe, vol. 4, Fontana, 1973, p. 690.

Mileage alone does not tell the whole story of course. Many lines were speculative, like some of those in Australia which were built 'to country racecourses that had hillbilly races twice a year', and showed little profit for a long while. On the other hand even short lines, like the 450 miles which Argentina had in 1870, could have strategic importance in opening up virgin territory. Always there was the *expectation* of profit, and of profit flowing into the hands of Europeans for, with the exception of Japan's, most railways were built to serve western needs. Great Britain played a key role in world railway development, contributing brain and brawn, capital and often the equipment and rolling-stock. Indeed, overseas railway-building exhibits the three facets of international economic relations which we shall examine in this chapter: the export of goods, the export of capital and the export (if we may use that word to describe emigration) of men and women.

Overseas railways had a great attraction for British investors, and by 1913, 41 per cent of Britain's overseas holdings were in railways (including 16 per cent in American railways alone). Frequently, the funds returned to Britain for the purchase of rails and locomotives, with a consequent multiplier effect. British engineers often planned the lines and British navvies often built them. As early as 1841 the Paris-Rouen railway was constructed by British labourers who elicited the admiring cry, '*Mon Dieu, ces Anglais, comme ils travaillent!*' ('My God! How these Englishmen *work!*'). In 1852 the *Railway Times* felt that British railway contractors were engaged 'on a kind of knight errantry to supply railway deficiencies all over the world'. The image was an apt one, for the great contractors, like Thomas Brassey, did indeed resemble medieval barons, at the command of vast armies which had to be kept employed or else they would disperse. Brassey gobbled up work. In a working life of 35 years he undertook 170 different contracts, involving 8,000 miles of railway. At one time he had simultaneous contracts for railways and docks in all five continents, and with the exception of Greece, Albania and Finland, he was to give every country in Europe a specimen of his workmanship.

Better communications increased trade; growing trade stimulated more efficient transport. Whichever was the causal factor (and clearly both effects were at work) world trade rocketed in the nineteenth century, soaring by 1913 to over 25 times that of 1800 (from £320 million to £8,360 million). Britain secured the lion's share of this increase. It consistently accounted for more than one-fifth, and sometimes more than one-quarter between 1850 and 1875 – the years of the mid-Victorian boom – and even though its lead fell thereafter, it still remained in 1913 the world's greatest trading nation.

The coming of free trade

Foreign trade exerted a major influence on the British economy throughout the nineteenth century, but especially after 1840 when the country moved increasingly away from self-sufficiency. A larger proportion of necessities, both for the consumer and the industrialist, was imported, and a wider range of home-produced goods came to contain imported raw materials. More and more communities, therefore, found their prosperity bound up with the state of foreign trade. With an export industry in their midst, or one producing for the home market but using imported materials, and with a shopping basket increasingly filled with foreign food, more and more people became affected by the vagaries of world trade. In the middle years of the century export markets were in an expansive condition, which more than anything else perhaps contributed to the general air of prosperity of those years. Britain basked in the warmth of free trade – which had taken more than two generations to arrive.

Free trade between the nations of the world came to be seen as part of God's plan, as Goldwin Smith observed in his 1859 inaugural address as Regius Professor of Modern History at Oxford:

The laws of the production and distribution of wealth are not the laws of duty or affection. But they are the most beautiful and wonderful of the natural laws of God . . . Silently, surely, without any man's taking thought, if human folly will only refrain from hindering them, they gather, store, dispense, husband, if needs be, against scarcity, the wealth of the great community of nations . . . They call on each nation with silent bidding to supply of its abundance that which the other wants; and make all nations labourers for the common store; and in them lies perhaps the strongest natural proof that the earth was made for the sociable being, man. To buy in the cheapest and sell in the dearest market, the supposed concentration of economic selfishness, is simply to fulfil the command of the Creator, who provides for all the wants of His creatures through each other's help; to take from those who have abundance, and to carry to those who have need. It would be an exaggeration to erect trade into a moral agency; but it does unwittingly serve agencies higher than itself, and make one heart as well as one harvest of the world.

The climax of free trade came in 1860 with Gladstone's budget and the Cobden treaty with France; but the principles had been expounded by Adam Smith in *The Wealth of Nations* published 84 years previously, in 1776. Within 20 years the book had run into eight English editions, and it was translated into several languages. Yet little was done to translate speculation into action, and 70 years passed between the publication of *The Wealth of Nations* and the ritual victory of 1846, when the Corn Laws were repealed. This is not to say that there was no interest in free trade during this period. Attitudes began to change after the Napoleonic Wars for a number of reasons. Manufacturers (especially of cotton textiles) began to feel greater confidence in their ability to compete in domestic and foreign markets, and Manchester became the Mecca of free trade. Second, the assumption that Britain could continue to be self-sufficient began to be questioned in the 1820s, when the rising population and growing employment problem led many to believe that agricultural imports should be encouraged in return for Britain's exports of manufactures. Third, disruption of trade in the Napoleonic Wars and the War of 1812 with the USA increased pressures to move towards a freer trade in the world's markets. This lay behind the successful attack on the East India Company's trading monopoly with India in 1813, and also underlies the more liberal attitude to economic affairs of Tory governments in the 1820s. This manifested itself in a variety of ways, including the revision of the Navigation Laws in 1822 and 1825; the inauguration of reciprocity treaties in 1823; repeal of the laws prohibiting the emigration of artisans in 1824; and a reduction and codification of tariffs between 1825 and 1826. Although these moves had a basis in classical economic theory, the attitude of the government was essentially pragmatic, and responded to particular pressures.

The road to free trade was a stony one, and there were several reasons why it proved so long. In the first place there was a technical problem. Tariffs occupied a central position in the national finances. In 1830, for example, they produced 43 per cent of the government's annual revenue (or as much as 75 per cent if taken together with the excise). The only alternative source of revenue was the income tax, which had produced 22 per cent of the total at the time of its abolition in 1816. To revive it would prove an unpopular measure. There was a second and more fundamental problem, however, arising from the wider economic, social and political implications of free trade. Commercial policy was bound up with the painful process of readjustment being faced by an evolving industrial society. The Corn Laws highlighted the problem. Agriculture was economically important (in 1815 it contributed a third of the national income and employment); but it was also socially important – as the basis of aristocratic power. Therefore free trade would seemingly demote agriculture by implying an ultimate reliance on foreign food, and it would strike at the roots of the traditionally dominant classes. If the landowning classes feared that they would lose by free trade, who was it predicted would gain? Certainly those manufacturers who used imported raw materials and wanted the duties abolished, also those in the exporting industries who wanted foreign exchange to be placed in the hands of their overseas customers. And the workers? There was some doubt about this, for some industrialists and commercial men argued that free trade would yet further expand British trade because lower food costs could be used to justify wage reductions which would reduce production costs still more. Many Chartists and working-class radicals therefore saw free trade as the work of rapacious mill-owners, especially as it was intellectually associated with *laissez-faire* liberalism which had proved hostile to factory legislation, trade unions, and state intervention to alleviate urban squalor.

To these two points we may add two others; one domestic and the other of international scope. In the 1830s, when the tide of free trade began to run more strongly, Parliament was absorbed with such major constitutional problems as its own reform and that of the municipal corporations. Internationally (although this was to be more significant in later years) free trade and protection have to be seen in their political context, as weapons in the armoury of international rivalry, or forces for cooperation and integration, as in the case of the German *Zollverein* and those attempts by certain British politicians to bind the empire by tariffs and imperial preference. Free trade, therefore, raised political and social issues as well as economic ones.

In order to follow through the stages by which free trade came about, we can conveniently begin in the late 1830s when protection came to be blamed for the stagnation in trade of that decade. Under mounting pressure, the government agreed in 1840 to the setting up of a Select Committee on Import Duties. The instigator of the committee was the radical free-trader, Joseph Hume, who is alleged to have exclaimed exultingly that 'the battle for Free Trade is about to be *won*'. His confidence was not entirely misplaced for the Committee was rigged. Hume had the chief say in nominating its members and packed it with free-traders. Most of the evidence was given by the dedicated free-traders of the Board of Trade, these being the days before the tradition of a politically impartial civil service had developed. And just to clinch the matter, the meetings were held in the summer months, when the London 'Season' was over and most landowners might be expected to be away on their estates. The Committee proved an excellent exercise in persuasion. Lucy Brown, who has made a special study of the role of the Board of Trade in the free-trade movement observes, 'witnesses . . . were not so much examined as invited to give prepared propaganda lectures'.

The Committee concluded that the mass of import duties needed simplification, and that this could be achieved without diminishing the revenue. It demonstrated that out of a total customs revenue of nearly £23 million in 1839, £21 million was raised on 10 commodities, and the remainder on 1,142 – such petty amounts proving 'merely vexatious'. Further propaganda poured out from the Anti-Corn Law League, the exploits of which have been described in Chapter 4.

The depression which had seen the rise of the League also led to a budget deficit, which foreshadowed the collapse of the Whig government. In September 1841 Sir Robert Peel was returned to office with a substantial majority and strong support from the country. His first budget (1842) was nevertheless cautious. There was an all-round reduction of duties, those on raw materials being lowered to 5 per cent, for example, and those on manufactured goods to 20 per cent. A bolder stroke was the reintroduction of income tax at the rate of 7d in the pound on incomes over £150, which not only made up the loss of customs revenue but produced a small budget surplus. The tax was imposed for three years. It has never been repealed. As prosperity revived in the next four years Peel was able to go further, and in 1845 a renewal of the income tax permitted the repeal of duties on 450 articles and the lowering of many others. The symbolic free-trade victory of 1846, when Peel split the Conservative Party, did not reverse the trend, for the Whigs carried the movement forward. The Navigation Acts were repealed in 1849, and gradually, as the budget permitted, duties were repealed or abolished. The climax came in 1860 when the number of articles liable for duty (1,146 in 1840) was reduced to 48, of which all but 12 were revenue duties on luxury or semi-luxury items. Paradoxically, the growth of Britain's foreign trade was so great that even these minimal duties brought in almost as much revenue as all the duties of the first half of the century. Between 1840 and 1870 customs receipts averaged £22 million; when at their lowest, in 1890, they produced £20 million. The big difference was in their proportion to the total public revenue, for customs revenue fell from 46 per cent of the total in 1840 to only 25 per cent in 1880.

The balance of payments in the nineteenth century

In 1965 James Callaghan, Britain's Chancellor of the Exchequer, was asked by an earnest American reporter: 'Why do you have balance-of-payments problems now, when you didn't have them fifty years ago?' To which Mr Callaghan replied with some feeling, 'There were no balance-of-payments problems fifty years ago because there were no balance-of-payments statistics'. It was a neat answer, but he was wrong on both scores; there was a problem (or, at least, a serious potential one), and there were statistics which revealed it (if you were willing to see). Most Edwardians were not, and did not bother their heads too much about the matter.

In so far as the figures could mask the problem, Mr Callaghan was no doubt justified in his comment. P. A. Cottrell, a historian who has made a special study of Britain's overseas investment in the nineteenth century has written that 'the construction of the balance of payments accounts for the nineteenth century is a heroic if not Herculean task'. The problem is most acute for the first half of the nineteenth century, for while details of the current costs of exports had been collected by customs officials since 1798, the actual costs of imports at current prices were not recorded until 1854. Prior to that, imports were set down at 'official values' based on fixed prices. These were those prevailing in England and Wales in 1694 although, just to make the situation that little bit more complicated, the figures for Scottish trade were based on 1755 prices, and those of Irish trade on the prices of 1801. As time passed, the actual price of imports increasingly came to differ from the notional prices with the result that the official statistics came seriously to misrepresent Britain's actual trading position.

Before we look at the trading problem itself, we ought briefly to clarify the principal terms involved in a discussion of a country's foreign trade. These are the *balance of payments*, the *balance of trade* and the *terms of trade*. The balance of payments is the balance of a nation's income and capital from abroad, and its outgoings to foreign countries. This balance consists of *visible* and *invisible* items. On the credit side the visible items include the exports of merchandise (including imported goods which are re-exported – where, in effect, the country is acting as a wholesaler or processor). On the debit side the visible items consist of imports of goods. Taken by themselves, the balance between the visible items – between imports and exports of goods –

constitute the balance of trade. When the prevailing economic theory had been mercantilism, it had been this balance which concerned people most, but it came to be seen that a country could be prosperous with an unfavourable trade balance. This would be so if a favourable balance of invisible items more than compensated for a deficit on the balance of trade. The invisible items on the credit side consist of the income from services afforded to foreigners, such as shipping or insurance; remittances by emigrants; personal expenditure within the country by foreigners (such as tourists); and income, in the form of interest or dividends, arising from investment abroad. The debit items are the converse of these. The balance of payments implies multilateral trading and a world settlement of accounts. Thus the balance of trade between particular countries does not usually balance. Throughout the nineteenth century, for example, British exports to India, coupled with the re-export of Indian merchandise, greatly exceeded Britain's imports. This can work, because deficits in the dealings with one country can be offset against surpluses with another. Any overall surplus or deficit is made up by the transfer of bullion or by lending and borrowing. In the nineteenth century Britain was the world's greatest lender.

The balance of trade reflects two things: the actual volume of goods exported and imported, and also the relationship between their prices. The latter constitutes the terms of trade. If they move in a country's favour (i.e. the prices of exports go up relative to the prices of imports), fewer of its exports have to be sold in order to obtain a given quantity of imports. If they move against a country, then the reverse is the case.

The artificial way in which early nineteenth-century statistics were presented misled people as to the state of Britain's trade. It used to be held that the newly industrialised textile trade released a flood of cotton goods, the export of which enabled a steadily mounting surplus on the balance of trade to be created. Revision of the statistics, however, has led historians to believe that at no time in the nineteenth century did Britain have an export surplus. During Britain's industrial primacy most of its imports were of raw materials and foodstuffs, for which there was a fairly inelastic demand. Although there was an intermittent cheapening of these imports, it was not until the latter part of the century that new techniques and, more particularly, transport improvements brought the prices of primary products substantially down. On the other hand, Britain's exports (of which textiles remained the dominant one) became progressively cheaper as the technological revolution continued. The terms of trade, in other words, moved against the country, and it had to sell more and more abroad in order to obtain its imports. In fact, compared with 1810, Britain had to sell twice the volume of exports in 1860 to obtain the same imports. That there was little concern about this reflects the obscurity of the statistics, but also the power of invisible items to reverse the deficit on the balance of trade and convert it into a surplus on the balance of payments. In the first quarter of the century Britain's income from services alone, without the aid of income from overseas investments, more than covered the deficit. Between 1825 and 1850 it did not quite do so; and after 1875 it was normally no longer adequate. As the century progressed, therefore, the deficit was increasingly made up, and the surplus produced, by the earnings of the country's overseas investments.

The course of Britain's balance of payments between 1850 and 1913 is outlined in Table 7.2.

Shipping was by far the most important of those services which contributed to invisible earnings, for it provided about two-thirds of the total. Net earnings from shipping rose from an annual average of £18.68 million in the period 1851–5 to £60.32 million in 1881–5, a peak of just over £100 million being reached in the

Table 7.2   Britain's balance of payments, 1850–1913 (in £ m)

	1850	1870	1900	1913
Exports	83.4	244.1	354.4	634.8
Imports	103.0	303.3	523.1	768.7
Balance of commodity trade	−19.6	−59.2	168.7	−133.9
Net invisible earnings	+31.2	+112.1	+212.7	+367.8
Surplus on current account (excluding capital and bullion movements)	11.6	52.9	44.0	233.9

Source: *Abstract of British Historical Statistics*, Cambridge University Press, 1971.

years prior to the First World War. By 1912 British ships carried 92 per cent of the inter-imperial trade, 55 per cent of the trade between the empire and foreign countries, and 30 per cent of the inter-foreign trade. In addition to this were the earnings from an expanding passenger traffic, swelled by the European upsurge of emigration.

As well as the income from shipping, there was that from financing and insuring much of world trade. Well over one-half of Britain's total foreign trade was shipped, serviced and financed from Britain, for in the foreign markets which were being opened up much of the enterprise was British. London became the major centre for marine insurance and the phrase, 'A1 at Lloyds', passed into the language. But London also became an international centre for insuring against other than marine risks. In 1879, for example, 23 per cent of all life cover in Canada and 18 per cent of the fire cover in the United States depended on policies issued by British companies. The San Francisco earthquake and fire of 1906 (an insurance company's nightmare if ever there was one) led to claims of over £10 million, but not one company failed to honour its obligations.

The comfortable surpluses on the balance of payments masked several potential weaknesses within the British economy. All the constituents of its invisible income depended on the maintenance of a high level of world trade and were therefore vulnerable to protectionist policies, which also put pressure on exports. The American tariff wall was built up higher and higher from the 1860s, while European tariff barriers were erected in the following decade – in Russia in 1877, in France in 1878 and in Germany in 1879, for example. British exporters not only found it harder to sell to these countries, but they also faced competition in their remaining markets from the industries which these tariffs were designed to protect. The changing composition of Britain's exports exemplifies the problem. The proportion of manufactured goods fell from about 90 per cent in the prosperous mid-Victorian years to about 75 per cent in 1911–13. This was largely due to expanding coal exports, which helped to supply the needs of the newly industrialising powers. Coal exports constituted about 9 per cent of the total in the early years of the twentieth century as against 2.5 per cent 50 years before. This trade was of great advantage to Britain's tramp shipping, for no other country enjoyed a bulky two-way traffic to the same degree.

Textiles continued to be the most important of the manufactured exports, four-fifths of the cotton textile production of the United Kingdom going abroad in 1913. It was said that Manchester produced sufficient for the home market before breakfast, and spent the rest of the day producing for export. As a share of total exports, textiles as a whole fell from a little over a third in 1831 to rather less than a third in 1913. In contrast to this fall, there was an increase in the export of certain engineering products (machinery, railway equipment, etc.) to just under 10 per cent in 1911–13 from less than 5 per cent in 1857–9, a rise occasioned by the spread of industrialisation overseas.

To what extent did exporters fail to maintain Britain's early industrial lead? They certainly came under contemporary criticism, and have incurred the censure of some historians. Manufacturers were alleged to have paid less attention than their competitors to the need to adapt the goods to local tastes and requirements. The market of British needles in Brazil, for example, is said to have been lost because the Brazilians did not like the black paper in which they were wrapped by the British, and turned instead to inferior German needles, wrapped in red paper, which captured the entire market. E. E. Williams, in *Made in Germany* (1896), quoted many such examples of slipshod commercial practice. The trade in kitchen knives to Serbia was allegedly lost because the Germans, but not the British, were prepared to supply the type of handles which the locals required; that in kerchiefs to Russia because Russian women liked them square while Lancashire only produced them oblong. Exporters were criticised for employing too few commercial travellers and for insisting on conducting business (and sending out catalogues and other promotional literature) only in English, and quoting English weights and measures. Stephen J. Nicholas, however, has questioned the accuracy of this picture:

> Special commissioner T. Worthington wrote from Argentina [in 1898] that 'not very much is heard now of English travellers being without a knowledge of the language of the country', and from Brazil that 'the idea that English shipping houses or manufacturers do not employ competent travellers with a knowledge of the language is, I believe, incorrect'. The evidence from the business archives of British firms presents a similar picture. The travellers for the Ipswich agricultural machinery makers, Ransomes, were qualified engineers who spoke Russian, French and Spanish. The European traveller for Huntley and Palmer, the Reading biscuit manufacturer, spoke French, German, Danish, Norwegian, and Swedish. American commerce reports repeatedly praised the English traveller as competent, hardworking, and knowledgeable of the local language and customs. According to one American report, 'one of the secrets of the success of German manufacturers in the [South African] market has been the employment of English travelling salesmen.[3]

Exporters tended to blame the British consular service, which was alleged to do less for British commercial interests than other countries' consuls did for theirs. D. C. M. Platt has argued that many of these latter criticisms were unfounded. The commercial community was unsure of what kind of information it wanted, while those who through their own enterprise had secured a foothold in a lucrative market did not want the opportunities broadcast to their competitors. Many failed to make use of the services which the consuls did provide. An under-secretary at the Foreign Office told the House of Commons in 1895 that a great deal of valuable information was lost by the failure of all but a minority of British merchants even to consult the consular reports, and he suggested that the spokesman for the Chambers of Commerce (who was making the complaint) would considerably benefit the cause he represented 'by increasing the reading capacity of his clients'. After 1886, however, commercial intelligence became more freely available through the *Board of Trade Journal*.

W. Ashworth argues that some of the complaints against British exporters may have been justified, but concludes that 'the deficiencies of British foreign trade at this time probably came less from slipshod commercial practices than from the limited range of commodities which were available for export'. This problem is one to which we shall return in Chapter 11.

While the rise in Britain's exports was curbed by the growth of protection abroad, its free-trade policies put no restraints on rising imports. The proportion of food-stuffs imported increased in the 1870s to reach that of raw materials. Of greater significance, perhaps, was the rapid growth of imported manufactured goods at the end of the century. The pattern of imports which emerged between 1900 and 1913 was one in which roughly 40 per cent consisted of foodstuffs, another 40 per cent of raw materials (of which a considerable quantity, together with some foodstuffs, were re-exported) and 20 per cent of manufactures.

The growth of imported manufactures reflects Britain's changing position within the world economy, and the growing industrial might of other nations, especially Germany and the USA. The label 'Made in Germany', which in the 1880s had been one of contempt, soon became one of alarm:

> The phrase is fluent in the mouth: how universally appropriate it is, probably no one who has not made a special study of the matter is aware. Take obser-vations, Gentle Reader, in your surroundings . . . You will find that the material of some of your own clothes was probably woven in Germany. Still more probable is it that some of your wife's garments are German importations; while it is practically beyond a doubt that the magnificent mantles and jackets wherein her maids array themselves on their Sundays out are German-made and German-sold, for only so could they be done at the figure . . . The toys, and the dolls, and the fairy books which your children maltreat in the nursery are made in Germany: nay, the material of your favourite (patriotic) newspaper had the same birthplace as like as not. Roam the house over, and the fateful mark will greet you at every turn, from the piano in your drawing-room to the mug on your kitchen dresser, blazoned though it be with the legend, A present from Margate. Descend to your domestic depths, and you will find your very drain-pipes German made. You pick out of the grate the paper wrappings from a book consignment, and they also are 'Made in Germany'. You stuff them into the fire, and reflect that the poker in your hand was forged in Germany. As you rise from your hearthrug you knock over an ornament on your mantelpiece; picking up the pieces you read, on the bit that formed the base, 'Manufactured in Germany'. And you jot your dismal reflections down with a pencil that was made in Germany . . . You go to bed, and glare wrathfully at a text on the wall; it is illuminated with an English village church, and it was 'Printed in Germany'. If you are imaginative and dyspeptic, you drop off to sleep only to dream that St Peter (with a duly stamped halo round his head and a bunch of keys from the Rhineland) has refused you admission into Paradise, because you bear not the Mark of the Beast upon your forehead, and are not of German make.[4]

A little later on came the so-called 'American Invasion', the first effects of which were felt in 1896 when large numbers of American bicycles were imported, together with machinery for their manufacture in Britain. Typewriters were another important item, and in 1898 even locomotives were imported from the USA – a bitter pill for the country which had been the birthplace of the railway. The most remarkable expansion was in imported footwear, which increased from £11,000 in 1896 to over £1 million in 1900. Improvement in American domestic demand and stagnation of trade in Britain soon caused all these imports to be reduced, and the 'invasion' was not repeated again before the First World War; but nevertheless it constituted a straw in the wind.

In the circumstances it was not unnatural that the principles of free trade should come to be questioned, and in 1881 a Fair Trade League was formed. Its idea of 'fairness' was to demand the imposition of moderate tariffs on foreign manufactures, which would be removed from the goods of any country as soon as it agreed to admit British goods free. The ideas never came to be applied, and it is not certain that the tariff would have been of any help to the British economy, for it might have further delayed the reorganisation required by industry, and the losses caused by the disruption in the pattern of international settlements would almost certainly have been far greater than any gains. The complicated pattern of multilateral trade in 1910, and Britain's balance of payments in that year are shown in Table 7.3 and Figure 7.1.

Table 7.3   Britain's balance of payments, 1910 (in £ m)

Debit		Credit	
USA	50	India	60
Continental Europe	45	Australia	13
Canada	25	Japan	13
Straits Settlements	11	China (incl. Hong Kong)	13
South Africa	8	Turkey	10
New Zealand	4	Uruguay	6
Argentina	2	British West Africa	3
Total	145	Total	118

Figure 7.1   World pattern of settlements, 1910

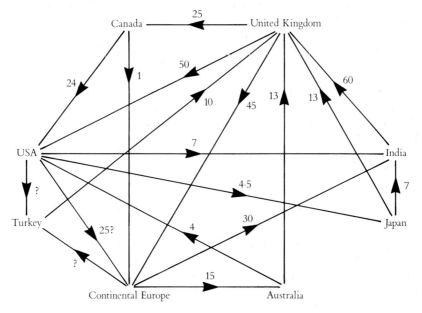

Source: S. B. Saul, *Studies in British Overseas Trade, 1870–1914*, Liverpool University Press, 1960, p. 58.

The arrows point to the country of each pair having a surplus with the other, and therefore indicate the direction of the flow of settlement. For example, Britain's visible and invisible imports from the United States exceeded its exports by £50 million. The deficit in Table 7.3 of £27 million represents small receipts from a number of other countries and also indicates an underestimation of income from some of the countries shown. One or two points are immediately apparent, in particular Britain's dependence on a high level of multilateral trade; but it will also be noted that Britain had increasingly become dependent on the less developed countries. These less sophisticated markets still had a demand for Britain's staple exports such as textiles, and they also required basic capital goods from Britain in order to bring about their own industrial development. British exporters came to be squeezed out of the wealthier markets which demanded a new range of imports, often provided by foreign competitors. This reveals one of the fundamental weaknesses of the economy, which was failing to innovate and to develop new export lines, an issue to which we shall return in Chapter 11.

It could be argued that the ease with which Britain was able to enter the markets of the empire dulled the initiative of exporters who otherwise would have been forced to become competitive. It is easy to see why India was the jewel in the imperial crown, for by 1880 probably one-third of Britain's deficit was covered by receipts from India, the proportion rising to nearer one-half by 1910. The overwhelming majority of India's imports came from Britain (80 per cent in the 1870s) and it not only paid regular dividends on the very large investments made there, but was also the source of remittances made by administrators and soldiers. The safety of India, therefore, which loomed so large in political decision-making, was a matter of economic necessity.

So long as the world economy was expanding, and the delicate mechanism of international settlements continued to operate, Britain was able to balance its accounts. Should this fail to happen, Britain would face unavoidable problems – as became all too clear after the First World War.

The export of capital

One of the main items which enabled Britain to balance its international accounts before the First World War was the income (in the form of interest and dividends) which it received from its overseas investments. Britain's 'export' of capital reached gigantic proportions in the four decades prior to the First World War. Its overseas investments were valued at £700 million in 1870, £1,500 million by 1885, £2,400 million by 1900 and a staggering £4,000 million by 1913. In that year about 7.5 per cent of the national income was invested abroad. By way of comparison, in 1947, at the height of the Marshall Plan, the United States strained to achieve a level of foreign investment at 3 per cent of the national income; while in the 1960s (which the United Nations dedicated as a 'Development Decade') the industrial nations found it hard to devote a mere 1 per cent of their national income to development aid.

Although Britain had raised a few foreign loans in the eighteenth century, organised lending began only after the Napoleonic Wars, when the Barings raised a £10 million loan to provide for the French war indemnity and the Rothschilds floated loans for Russia and Prussia. The success of these two banking houses in securing loans for the legitimist regimes of Europe, encouraged by slack trade at home in the early 1820s, led directly to the speculative mania of 1824–5, which was fuelled by the financial arrangements of loan issues. Investors were not required immediately to pay in full, but were obliged only to make a down payment or initial 'call' of 5 or 10 per cent of the holding they intended to take up. For a small initial payment, therefore, a handsome profit could be made by a rise in the price of the shares or bonds. For example, investors could acquire a title in £400 shares of the Real del Monte mine for an initial call of only £50, but they quickly rose to a premium of £550. The skill came in anticipating the bursting of the bubble and selling at a profit beforehand.

The speculative boom of the early 1820s, when capital exports probably reached an overall peak for the first half of the century, witnessed a switch of the centre of interest from Europe to the emerging republics of Latin America. Their governments proved eager to encourage borrowing, and British investors were equally eager to lend. There was the hope that Latin America would provide permanent markets for British goods, independent of the hostile tariffs of the United States and Europe, and it was expected that the introduction of the steam-engine would lead to a new era of highly profitable mining. The latter hopes were not realised: of seven mining companies floated in Mexico, for example, six actually commenced working, but only one had survived by 1850. Altogether, loans of £17 million were raised for Latin-American countries between 1824 and 1825, and joint-stock companies with a nominal capital of £35 million were floated to operate in the new republics. Most of the loans were for unproductive purposes, being raised by governments, for example, 'to secure a ship or two as an appropriate background for their respective admirals'. The countries lacked the resources to repay interest, let alone the capital sums, with the result that by the end of 1827 all the republics were in default. The response of British investors was to turn elsewhere for investment opportunities. This tended to be the pattern. Speculation would be concentrated in a particular region but default or disappointment would send the speculator in search of richer prizes elsewhere.

In the second quarter of the nineteenth century British capital began to flow into overseas railway building, and this remained a major field of British investment right down to the First World War, 41 per cent of all funds invested abroad being in railways in 1913. In the 1830s, when canals and railways were first being constructed in the United States, it was to the Old World that the builders looked for finance, and to Britain in particular. By 1836 over £90 million had been invested in canals and railways in the north-eastern states, of which more than half was guaranteed by public funds, the bulk of the capital being raised in Britain. The United States, however, proved hardly more reliable than Latin America, and by 1841 nine states were in default on their loans. Not until the early 1850s were American securities taken up again, encouraged by the discovery of gold in California, and the collapse of the British railway mania which left ironmasters eager to seek new markets for rails. American railways subsequently came to dominate the market, and in 1899 British investors probably held between a fifth and a quarter of the capital of American railways. By 1914 the value of American railway securities held in Britain was £620 million, or approximately 16 per cent of its total overseas investments.

Lending to South America, which had slumped after the mania of 1824–5, revived with the establishment of a new and stable government in Argentina in 1865. Within a decade, £23 million of British capital had been invested there, rising to £175 million by 1890. Over-confidence, however, led to an over-extension of lending on unsound projects which Barings, the leading brokers in the field, had backed without adequate investigation, with the result that the 'Baring Crisis' of 1890 stopped all Argentinian loans, and shook the confidence of overseas investors for more than a decade. The scale of lending in the 1890s was reduced, but was particularly concerned with South Africa and Rhodesia, where there were mining booms in diamonds, gold and copper. S. G. E. Lythe writes: 'The "Kaffir Circus" –

that part of the London Stock Exchange which specialised in South African securities – revolved at exciting speed especially in 1889 and 1892, and then slowed down to cool its overheated bearings.' When the flow of capital revived after 1900, the white dominions – Canada, Australia and South Africa – were the favoured market, and by 1913, 37 per cent of Britain's overseas investments were there, with a further 10 per cent in India bringing the empire's share to almost half.

It is clear, as Cottrell observes, that 'foreign lending in Britain was catholic in scope throughout the nineteenth century, but at any point of time tended to be concentrated both upon particular geographical areas, and forms of debt'. Various factors influenced the choice which investors made. The prospect of a higher profit was naturally a major element in decision-making. In the 1870s, for example, United States government bonds offered an average yield of 7.5 per cent, as against less than 4 per cent on British government Consols. The average yield on British railway stock was a little over 4 per cent, that on United States rails 9.3 per cent, South American rails 8.1 per cent, and Indian rails (which were guaranteed) 6.3 per cent. However, the price of a security on the London market was not always a reliable guide to its probable yield, and there could be great ignorance even about the location of overseas investments. H. S. Ferns, who has made a special study of Argentina, writes:

> The investors in Argentine bonds did not know and could not know how the money they lent would be spent. Judging from some of their letters addressed to the public press, to the Foreign Office, and to the various committees established to handle the interests of investors, their level of information was extremely low. Some of them confused Argentina with Chile and even Mexico. The distinction between the Province of Buenos Aires and the Argentine Republic was too subtle for most. One dissatisfied investor in Argentine railways appears to have believed that the Buenos Aires Great Southern Railway, of which he owned a small part, was in Brazil. Indeed the name of a banking firm like that of Baring Brothers or Murietta & Company meant more to investors than the names Argentina or Buenos Aires. Their decision to handle Argentine business was a certificate of reliability and a substitute for knowledge, initiative, and enterprise.[5]

Initially, the banks and other finance houses made their decisions to market loans on fairly reliable information and with sound judgement, although standards deteriorated in the 1880s, as the Baring Crisis of 1890 was to make clear.

In addition to the interest or dividends expected to arise from the investments themselves, some investors and financiers had other commercial expectations. The concentration of British investment in Louisiana in the 1820s and 1830s, for example, was directed towards the development of its cotton exports, a vital raw material for British industry. Investment in American railways showed a similar discrimination in favour of British trading interests. The transcontinental railways which linked the Midwest with the Pacific Coast proved relatively unattractive, British investors being more interested in those lines which tapped the wheat belt and the hog and cattle areas of the Chicago hinterland.

There was also a link between the export of capital and the export of capital goods. Much of the money invested in railways flowed back to Britain to purchase rails and rolling stock, perhaps a third of all capital invested in Indian railways returning in this way, for example. So long as Britain was the only effective supplier of such goods the linkage was strong, but after 1870 it is more difficult to trace such linkages, and they cannot be taken for granted. Loans were not usually tied, and borrowers could spend the money how and where they liked. Britain might raise the capital for a foreign railway, but the locomotives might be purchased from Belgium, say, or from Germany. The relationship between overseas investment and British exports was, in the main, indirect and resulted from the stimulus to long-term economic growth. Money raised in London might be spent on American or German goods, but part of the increase in the national income of these countries is likely to have been spent on imports from Britain. Such are the complexities of multilateral trade.

Certain aspects of the export of capital in the nineteenth century remain highly controversial. There is, for example, the debate over the contribution of overseas investments to imperialism, Lenin having argued that it was the quest for outlets for capital which led to this phenomenon. There is also controversy over the effects of overseas investment on the British economy as a whole. It has to be remembered that the number of investors was small, and that they made their investment decisions in the hope of *personal* rather than *national* gain. If the non-investing public benefited, it was more by accident than design. The export of capital – by developing the primary producing countries and lowering freight rates through improved facilities – had some effect on the price of British imports of raw materials and food. The fall in the price of imported foodstuff was the major factor leading to a rise in real wages during the last quarter of the nineteenth century. This period, therefore, saw what A. K. Cairncross described as 'a rare coincidence of interests' between workers and capitalists. But it was a coincidence and, after 1900, in spite of overseas lending on an unprecedented scale, the cost of imported foodstuffs rose and real wages either stagnated or declined.

It has been argued that the social benefits would have been greater if some of the capital invested abroad had been diverted to social investment at home – in housing, for example, or in schools and hospitals. But there is no certainty that, had there been no foreign investment, resources would have been diverted in this way, for to some extent the expectations of profit which investment raised also created the resources which sought to realise them. These resources might not have been diverted to home investment if the overseas opportunities had not existed. Those with a surplus of income might just as easily have used it on conspicuous consumption, by buying more comfortable houses, for example, or living more lavishly.

Some of the investments abroad clearly stimulated a demand for exportable goods, but an equivalent demand might have been stimulated by home investment. Here lies the crux of the matter. To what extent did the export of capital starve British industry of needed investment? It has to be remembered that fixed capital in industry remained small. For example, even in the cotton industry (the largest manufacturing industry and one employing 500,000 workers) the total capital in the mid-1870s was only about £100 million. Much of industry was labour- rather than capital-intensive. The really big consumers of capital were transport undertakings – railways in particular. It was when the British network was coming to completion in the 1870s that the great expansion of overseas investment began. As the shipowner and merchant, Russell Rea MP put it in 1909, when it was suggested in a parliamentary debate that capital ought to be invested at home rather than abroad: 'We have built a vast and profitable system of railways in Argentina. Would my Honourable Friend have preferred to duplicate the Great Western System?'

Most industrialists did not seek to raise capital publicly, for the representative manufacturing concern was the family firm in the form of a partnership or a private limited company. Ploughed-back profits, bank loans and trade credit continued to meet most financial needs. There was a strong resistance to raising capital through the stock market, for this would reduce family control over the undertaking. There is little evidence of those who actively went out to get capital finding undue difficulty. But there is *some*, as Sidney Pollard has observed:

> Occasionally a single flash may light up a whole scene. Such may be the case of Fred Hopper, bicycle manufacturer of Barton in Lincolnshire, His was a highly successful firm founded in 1896, which was kept technically up-to-date in its equipment as well as its product, employing 400 in 1905 and 800 in 1912, capturing important export markets and developing from pedal to motor cycles and, in 1912–13, to a cycle car. More remarkably still in such a volatile industry, it paid dividends of $7\frac{1}{2}$ per cent a year or more. Here, if anywhere, was an object within a growth industry worthy of support by a capital market interested in British prosperity. Yet, once it had exhausted the partners' own and the company's ploughed-back savings, the firm was in constant financial difficulties for lack of capital for expansion; no financier was willing to provide it with funds. Successive attempts to obtain capital from the London capital market, from the bank, from insurance companies and building societies all failed, and by 1913 the firm had gone into liquidation . . . How representative is the Hopper example? Was it unique, unusual, typical? We do not know. But until we do, it will be hazardous to maintain that the flood of foreign investment was not in any way at the expense of industrial growth at home.[6]

Emigration

In the century between 1815 and 1914 a total of nearly 17 million people emigrated from the United Kingdom, of whom approximately 80 per cent went to the United States and Canada. The total number was almost as great as the country's population in 1815, and well over a third of the population of 1911. Emigration was not solely a British phenomenon, of course, for although Britain's share was the largest (if we include Ireland) it formed part of a worldwide migration of population. Much of this movement of people can be seen in terms of a shift of population from the country to the towns. In many instances this was purely an internal movement but in others it involved a shift of population from the rural areas of one country to the urban areas of another. This can be seen particularly in the case of the United States which was the most popular goal. American industries, based in rapidly expanding cities, absorbed hundreds of thousands of European peasants. Some immigrants had cherished the hope of free or cheap land of their own to farm, but found themselves trapped in the cities; others were quite content to enjoy the blandishments of city life, unknown at home.

There is some debate as to whether emigrants were 'pushed' from their home-lands or 'pulled' to their adopted countries. With certain exceptions the distinction is rather artificial so far as individual motivation goes. However, of all the emigrants from the United Kingdom in the nineteenth century, two groups stand out as having been 'pushed' abroad, namely the Scots who fell victim to the breakdown of the Highland economy, and the Irish who fled the harsh realities of peasant life, especially after the potato famine. Not that all emigrants from these countries were destitute, for among the Scots in particular it was often the aspiring element among the farming class who left, while many Irish emigrants were small tradespeople.

The Highland economy was a subsistence economy which came under increasing pressure in the first half of the nineteenth century. The growth of population put strains upon it which it was unable to bear. Crofters came under increasing pressure, while the kelp-burning industry was ruined by the removal in 1827 of the duty on barilla, an alternative source of soda. Until 1845 there was no Poor Law in Scotland,

and at first the government attempted to keep the population employed through such public works schemes as the construction of the Crinan and Caledonian canals and the building of roads. Inevitably, emigration was seen by many as an effective method of relieving the pressure. Many landowners assisted their tenants to emigrate, and in 1851 the Skye Emigration Society, soon to become the Highlands and Islands Emigration Society, was established to facilitate the movement of people. The society particularly encouraged emigration to Australia, where there was a great demand for sheep-rearing skills, especially after the discovery of gold led to a mass desertion from the sheep stations.

Ireland presents an even more striking example of 'push' factors at work. The population of Ireland in 1788 is estimated to have been 4,389,000; in 1841 it had reached 8,175,000; but by 1911 it had fallen to 4,390,000, presenting one of those rare instances of a country suffering an absolute decline in numbers. Between 1841 and 1851 alone the population declined by more than a fifth. Many Irish people came across the channel to the British mainland, the number of Irish-born almost doubling there between 1841 and 1861. Many more went to the United States, where they flocked to the cities of the east coast such as Boston and New York. The pressures on Ireland were similar to those on Scotland, although the potato famine was a disaster of unique dimensions. There were, too, other factors at work. In 1822 some 2 million Irish spoke only Gaelic; by 1861 fewer than 164,000 did so. The breakdown of the language barrier meant that more people were released from isolation, and as they learned to read they found a voluminous emigrant press to lure them abroad.

The motivation of English and Welsh emigrants is more complex, although destitution and ambition both played their part. The prospect of a higher living standard was the big attraction. An emigrants' guidebook of 1830 observed: 'Artisans receive better pay in America than in Europe, and can live with less exertion and more comfort.'

The bulk of emigrants, from Britain as well as elsewhere, were peasants or agricultural labourers with no particular skills at their fingertips. This is not to deny that their labour was essential to the economic development of their host countries. However, the spread of industrialisation was greatly encouraged by the emigration of skilled men who were often able to establish industries in their new homelands. Parliament, afraid that Britain's industrial lead might be eroded in this way, had passed a series of acts between 1719 and 1799 designed to prohibit the emigration of skilled artisans and the exportation of machinery. The laws were not difficult to evade. John Cockerill, a member of a family which did much to industrialise Europe, claimed to have all the new inventions at his works at Seraing, near Liège, within ten days of their coming out in England. By 1825, when the laws prohibiting emigration were abolished (those on the export of machinery lasted until 1843) there are estimated to have been at least 2,000 skilled British workmen on the continent. They sometimes proved troublesome – a German machine-builder complained 'one must go easy with them since they actually talk of leaving if one fails to give them a smile' – but they were of vital importance as teachers, not only of skills but of industrial work habits. Many French metallurgists found that it took 10 years or more to train enough French iron puddlers to displace the British, not so much because they lacked the technical aptitude but because they lacked the ambition and the materialist drive.

Emigrants went where their skills or their labour were needed, although their choice was partly dictated by the cost of the journey. Thus the proximity of North America made it a more popular choice than Australia, even when transport costs in general fell. Emigrants also went where they had personal contacts, the letter from a

7   Emigration

1   'The Last of England' by Ford Madox Brown, 1856

Between 1815 and 1914, nearly 17 million people emigrated from Great Britain. The emigrants went to all parts of the world, although nearly 80 per cent went to the United States and Canada.

Ford Madox Brown's painting (1), 'The Last of England', was first exhibited at Liverpool in 1856. This was not an inappropriate choice of place, as Liverpool was one of the principal emigrant ports. The painting is dominated by the figures of the man and woman in the foreground, but we can see at least seven other people, and we can be sure that they all have a place in the artist's scheme. In what mood has Madox Brown depicted the foreground figures, and how does that mood contrast with the two men standing by the davit? In what ways is the artist suggesting that emigrants might have quite different feelings about leaving England? In this case we know precisely what the artist intended, because (in his biography) he has told us.

I have . . . singled out a couple from the middle classes, high enough, through education and refinement, to appreciate all they are now giving up . . . The husband is shielding his wife from the sea spray with an umbrella. Next them, in the background, an honest family of the greengrocer kind, father (mother lost), eldest daughter and younger children, make the best of things with tobacco-pipe and apples, &c., &c. Still further back, a reprobate shakes his fist with curses at the land of his birth, as though that were answerable for his want of success; his old mother reproves him for his foul-mouthed profanity, while a boon companion, with flushed countenance, and got up in nautical togs for the voyage, signifies drunken approbation. The cabbages slung from the stern of the vessel indicate, to the practised eye, a lengthy voyage; but for this their introduction would be pointless. A cabin-boy, too used to 'leaving his native land' to see occasion for much sentiment in it, is selecting vegetables for the dinner of a boatful.

James Collinson, like Ford Madox Brown, was associated with the Pre-Raphaelites, a group of artists among whose characteristics was a minute attention to detail. 'Answering the Emigrant's Letter' (2) depicts a cottage interior, where a family are replying to a letter, almost certainly from a relative. The map on the husband's lap indicates that the letter has come from Australia. Letters from relatives abroad were one of the principal means by which information about emigration was disseminated. The wife returns her husband's glance impassively. What thoughts, perhaps, are in their minds? The man in Collinson's painting holds the letter, but is there anything to suggest that he might be barely literate?

2   'Answering the Emigrant's Letter' by James Collinson

relative or friend being one of the principal advertisements of opportunities, and the remittance from abroad a major source of finance. This point is important, for as Wilbur Shepperson has commented, emigration 'was a self-imposed, personally arranged, and individually financed adventure'. There was some assisted emigration. What Clapham describes as 'official and officious organisations' were always at work to promote it, especially in times of gloom. The Poor Law Amendment Act granted powers to Boards of Guardians to raise money to assist emigration, and an average of 800–1,000 people were sent out each year between 1836 and 1845, after which the numbers greatly fell. The only really large-scale undertaking was that of the Colonial Land and Emigration Commissioners between 1847 and 1872, when 340,000 emigrants were given assistance. Three-quarters were sent out in 1847 and 1848, almost all to Australia, but a few to the Cape and the Falkland Islands. The Chartists and other radicals denounced such emigration as the transportation of the innocent, and there was certainly an illogicality in offering assistance to emigrate as a relief for internal distress while no assistance was given to those who wished to remain in Britain.

The 'innocents transported' in this manner included thousands of children, all of whom were poor, but not all of whom were 'orphans', as was often claimed. About 80,000 children were sent to Canada between 1868 and 1925, while children were shipped to Australia by Dr Barnardo's and other charities as late as 1967.

Trade unions also assisted emigration, for which the theoretical justification was afforded by the wage-fund theory, graphically (if crudely) put by Cobden: 'Wages rise when two masters run after one workman; wages fall when two men run after one master.' The emigration fund was a widespread feature of trade unions in the 1850s and 1860s, and the efficacy of emigration was not seriously questioned until the depression of the 1880s.

The impact of emigration on the British economy and British society is hard to pin down with any precision. In terms simply of population growth, net migration is the significant factor, i.e. emigration set against immigration or the return of former emigrants. In England and Wales in the 1840s there was a net immigration of well over 250,000 Scots and Irish. In the following decades there was a considerable net emigration from England and Wales, followed in the 1860s by a period of more equal balance. Between 1871 and 1911, despite a dramatic growth of immigration, especially of European Jews (of whom well over 100,000 settled in Britain before the First World War), there was a net loss of 2 million, although this was offset by the natural increase during the same period of some 18 million. But emigration must be seen in terms of quality as well as quantity. The emigration of skilled workers had an impact on world economic growth, not entirely to Britain's detriment, although it tended to lose the young and the active rather than the old and the apathetic.

Notes

1 Sir John Clapham, *An Economic History of Modern Britain*, vol. 2, Cambridge University Press, 1932, p. 217.
2 William Woodruff, 'The emergence of an international economy, 1700–1914' in Carlo M. Cipolla (ed.), *The Fontana Economic History of Europe*, vol. 4, Fontana, 1973, p. 689.
3 Stephen J. Nicholas, 'The overseas marketing performance of British industry, 1870–1914', *Economic History Review*, 1984, p. 493.
4 E. E. Williams, *Made in Germany*, 1896 (Harvester Press, 1973), pp. 10–11.
5 H. S. Ferns, *Britain and Argentina in the Nineteenth Century*, Oxford University Press, 1960, p. 330.
6 Sidney Pollard, 'Capital exports, 1870–1914: harmful or beneficial?', *Economic History Review*, 1985, pp. 501–2.

Chapter eight

The middle class

The range of the middle class

In the nineteenth century people talked a great deal about the middle class, for it seemed far more important than ever before. Much praise was lavished upon it for its supposed qualities. James Mill wrote in 1826:

> The value of the middle classes of this country, their growing numbers and importance, are acknowledged by all. These classes have long been spoken of, and not grudgingly, by their superiors themselves, as the glory of England; as that which alone has given us our eminence among nations; as that portion of our people to whom everything that is good among us may with certainty be traced.

To Brougham, speaking in 1831, the middle class represented 'the wealth and intelligence of the country, the glory of the British name'. Later in the century Joseph Chamberlain, screw manufacturer and statesman, declared: 'I belong to the middle class, and I am proud of the ability, the shrewdness, the industry, the providence, and the thrift by which they are distinguished, and which have in so considerable a degree contributed to the stability and prosperity of the Empire.'

The middle class also had its critics. Matthew Arnold pilloried the self-satisfaction of the 'Philistines' as he called them. In his book, *Culture and Anarchy* (1869), he wrote:

> . . . *Philistine* gives the notion of something stiff-necked and perverse in the resistance to light and its children; and therein it specially suits our middle class, who not only do not pursue sweetness and light, but who even prefer to them that sort of machinery of business, chapels, tea-meetings . . . which makes up the dismal and illiberal life on which I have so often touched.

Nowhere was this parochialism more apparent than among the lower middle class. Richard Church described the life of his parents, a Post Office sorter and a Board School teacher, in Battersea at the beginning of the twentieth century:

> Like most people at that time and in that walk of life [they] were grateful for small assurances: a safe job, a respectable anonymity, a local esteem. Outside that limit lay a dangerous unknown that included crime, genius, fame, notoriety and exalted rank. All the people who came to our house (few and infrequent) were of this persuasion, unanimous in their social and moral quietism. Behind my own parents' acquiescence in this lay an element of mystery, revealed only occasionally by oblique remarks and references, and by my father's perverse attitude towards the aristocracy and to all manifestations of ambition, or of pursuits larger than he could comprehend.[1]

Horizons were often limited, and Arnold mocked the middle-class man who 'thinks it the highest pitch of development and civilisation when his letters are carried ten times a day from Islington to Camberwell, and from Camberwell to Islington, and if the railway trains run to and fro between them every quarter of an hour'.

It was in the towns that the social structure was most complex, despite the absence (from the industrial towns at least) of the aristocracy. Although in such towns all who were not workers were middle class, the range of the latter was so great as to give great problems of definition. By the 1850s the middle-class stream was so broad that Bulwer Lytton could declare that it 'cannot be called a class, because it comprises all classes, from the educated gentleman to the skilled artisan'. The social historian might not agree that gentlemen and artisans were members of the middle class, but Lytton was right to emphasise the breadth of that class, which can be illustrated with examples drawn from fiction. At the top would be the Forsytes of Galsworthy's novels; or the Melmottes of Trollope's novel, *The Way We Live Now*, Mr Melmotte's career being based on that of George Hudson, 'the Railway King'. At the other end of the scale were the Pooters in the Grossmiths' *The Diary of a Nobody*. Mr Pooter, although prepared to go to ridiculous lengths to exert his social position, was by no means at the bottom of the middle class, for he was a fairly prosperous clerk, and there were many beneath him who might lay claim to inclusion, such as Bob Cratchit in Dickens's *A Christmas Carol*.

Those at the bottom of the lower middle class were extremely status conscious, and sought by all means in their power to mark themselves off from their 'inferiors'. Harold Perkin, however, springs to their defence. Referring particularly to the latter part of the century he writes:

> The lower middle class, whether clerks and shop assistants or shopkeepers and other business men, have had a poor deal from their chroniclers . . . Yet they were often the backbone of the burgeoning Sunday schools and other church organizations, sports clubs, youth clubs, the YMCA, the Salvation Army, and the Boy's Brigade, the Boy Scouts and the Girl Guides, of the university extension lectures and vocational evening classes, of the new constituency organizations of both major political parties, and even of the cadres of the Fab' ns and the ILP. They also produced probably more self-made men than the much larger working class, such as Sir Thomas Lipton, shopkeeper turned royal yachtsman, Lord Leverhulme, commercial traveller turned international soap and fats tycoon, Lord Northcliffe, office boy turned press baron, Lloyd George, solicitor's clerk turned statesman, Charles Booth, Liverpool shipping clerk turned shipowner and social investigator, Bernard Shaw, estate agent's clerk turned playwright, and H. G. Wells, pupil teacher and shop assistant turned novelist and pioneer of science fiction. At a less spectacular level, many were upwardly mobile in a more modest way . . . For the lower middle class, both the self-employed petty bourgeoisie and the employed white-collar division, was the traditional first step towards higher status for the ambitious sons and, increasingly daughters of the working class.
>
> This, paradoxically, is why they distinguished themselves so obsessively from the working class. They were, literally, trying to get away from them, in income, status, appearance, and physical residence. They did not always find it easy.[2]

Although the range of the middle class was immense, it comprised many groups who were either called into existence or greatly expanded by the growth of industry and trade. Such were the manufacturers and industrialists, many of whom had risen from humble origins. Indeed, the idea of the 'self-made man' was one of the key concepts of middle-class ideology. As industry expanded more and more people were needed to service production, either as clerks and office workers, transport workers, shopkeepers, dealers and tradesmen of all kinds, or people offering professional services.

In 1803 Patrick Colquhoun, the statistician, counted 30,000 'clerks and shopmen to merchants, manufacturers, shopkeepers, etc'. In 1861, 91,733 men (and virtually no women) were employed as clerks. By 1891 there were 370,433 men and 18,947 women; while by 1911, with 561,155 men and 124,843 women, clerks represented one of the largest and fastest-growing occupational groups. It was also a more diverse group than might at first be imagined. At the top end were clerks in banking and insurance (where over 40 per cent earned more than £160 a year by 1909) declining through central and local government, industry and commerce, to the railways, where only 10 per cent of clerks earned that sum. In the early years of the nineteenth century a clerkship might become the road to a job in management, but the opportunities for such upwards mobility declined as the scale of businesses grew.

Napoleon (and he was not the first) had described England as a nation of shopkeepers, and their numbers expanded also. Charles Booth noted that between 1851 and 1881 those who came under the head of 'dealing' had increased by 69 per cent, compared with a population increase of 39 per cent. This he claimed to have been due to a multiplication of small shopkeepers and street dealers, whose numbers rose from 547,000 to 924,000. The capital required to start a shop was often extremely small. Booth described a London shopkeeper in the 1890s whose shop cost only 40s and consisted of 'a wooden screen betwixt door and fire, two tables, a counter, small and large scales and weights, a good corner cupboard, and some odds and ends'. He paid 3s 6d a week in rent, spent less than 37s a week on stock, and took on average £2 15s. After a year the shopkeeper had amassed £25 in his bank. Shopkeeping was precarious, however, and the small shopkeeper increasingly faced the competition of multiple stores and, from the 1870s, a growing number of department stores. The pre-packaging of goods, and the growing prevalence of branded goods, also tended to degrade the shopkeeper's skill.

The growth of the professions was another striking phenomenon. Between 1841 and 1881 professional occupations trebled, compared with a two-thirds increase in the population as a whole. By 1887 the professions and public services constituted about one-sixth of all non-manual occupations. The industrial revolution added new professions to the traditional gentlemanly trio of the law, the army and the Church, including mechanical and civil engineering, public administration and accountancy. The status of professional men was rising, although recognition of professional status might prove a long and slow process. Architects and surveyors were not recognised by the Census Office as professions until 1881, and accountants had to wait until 1921.

Professional status set a man apart from the commercial middle class. Henry Byerley Thomson put it thus in 1857, in his book, *The Choice of a Profession:*

In point of social position the professions have vastly, the superiority over the business world. The man of business has, as a rule, no position in respect of his occupation. If *in society*, his position is the result of his wealth, his education or the accident of his birth, and breeding. He has not gained it by his mercantile pursuits, and he will not lose it should he abandon them. The member of the higher professions on the other hand, at once takes a place in society by virtue of his calling; the poor man of business is nowhere in social position, yet the poor curate is admitted readily to that coveted country society that the millionaire has even to manoeuvre for . . . The objects of a profession are nobler, more intellectual, of wider range, and confer more happiness than those of a business.[3]

How Thompson, who was no Benthamite, claimed to measure happiness is unclear, although the distinction which he drew is a real one. Harold Perkin speaks of the professions as 'the forgotten middle class', and has written of their crucial role in shaping modern society which has been permeated by a professional ideal:

A social ideal is a model of how society should be organized to suit a certain class or interest and of the ideal citizen and his contribution to it. Pre-industrial society was permeated by the aristocratic ideal based on property and patronage . . . Industrial society was permeated by the entrepreneurial ideal based on active capital and competition, on business investment as the engine of the economy run by the active owner-manager, ideally the self-made man who rose to wealth and influence by his own intrinsic worth and won out in open competition. The rival ideal of the working class, never achieved in practice, was the collective ideal of labour and co-operation, of labour as the sole source of wealth and co-operatve endeavour as the fairest means of harnessing and rewarding it, and of the worker's right to the whole produce of labour. The professional ideal, based on trained expertise and selection by merit, differed from the other three in emphasising human capital rather than passive or active property, highly skilled and differentiated labour rather than the simple labour theory of value, and selection by merit as trained and certified expertise.[4]

From the mid-Victorian period onwards, the range of occupations that became (in some respects at least) 'professionalised' was enormous, and deference came increasingly to be offered to 'the expert'. Society, argues Perkin, came more and more to be organised into vertical hierarchies of professions, the members of which competed for resources with each other. The keenest competition was between those public-sector professionals who were dependent on the state (mainly the vast armies called into being by the burgeoning welfare state) and the private-sector professionals who, with the gradual demise of the family firm, came to manage expanding business corporations. Perkin sees these divisions as a crucial element in Britain's industrial decline. George Bernard Shaw wrote in *The Doctor's Dilemma* (1906) that 'all professions are conspiracies against the laity'. As we shall see in Chapter 15, the Conservative governments of the 1980s largely concurred with this view, and the powers of many professional groups were curtailed in that decade.

Middle-class standards of living

However diverse may have been the occupations of the middle class, and however wide the variations of status within that class, there were many characteristics which bound the various sections together such as a common lifestyle which, if not actually enjoyed by all, was nevertheless aspired to. Crucial to this standard of living was a home of one's own and the enjoyment of domestic service; and an essential prerequisite was a steady income of at least a certain minimum, not derived from manual labour.

Middle-class incomes varied enormously. A minimum of around £300 a year was a figure frequently mentioned in the early Victorian period, but many incomes were appreciably above this figure. The fields of finance and commerce threw up some vast fortunes, including that of the self-made textile warehouseman and merchant banker James Morrison who, at his death in 1857, left £4 million–£6 million, making him the richest commoner of the nineteenth century. The insurance broker and Baltic merchant, Richard Thornton, boasted that his signature was 'good for three million' and left £2,800,000. Commerce and finance remained the most important element in Britain's wealth structure, with industrial fortunes – despite the industrial revolution – coming lower down the scale. Not that they were low. There were numerous industrialist millionaires, including Sir Robert Peel and Richard Arkwright, but the typical successful manufacturer appears to have left an estate in the region of £100,000 after mid-century. For example, Joseph Chamberlain, who had been so proud of his membership of the middle class, left £125,495 when he died in 1914.

Even excluding these vast fortunes, there were many others above the £300 norm, such as those of the 'upper middle class professional men and tradesmen' who were estimated by the statistician R. D. Baxter to be earning around £500 in the 1860s. At the same time many at the lower margin earned much less, including a great number of clerks and elementary schoolteachers who might receive as little as £60, a sum lower than that brought home by many of the 'aristocrats' of the working class.

As important as income to middle-class consciousness was expenditure, for a particular style of life characterised the group. High on the list of priorities was a house of suitable size and location. Until building societies entered upon their modern stage of development in the last quarter of the century, most middle-class houses were rented, an outlay generally considered to take up between a tenth and an eighth of total income. Renting rather than purchasing a house offered certain advantages. Those members of the upper middle class who associated with 'Society' required to follow 'the Season'. Here, social mobility involved geographical mobility, as the fashionable families migrated between London, the country and the sea. A different consideration applied on the divide between the middle class and the working class, albeit with a similar result. The anxiety which the lower middle class felt about their precarious status persuaded many of them to put a physical distance between themselves and the working class. This was one of the factors tending towards suburbanisation, as we shall see in Chapter 11; but the distance did not have to be great, for in many towns even adjacent streets constituted distinct social zones. A family whose fortunes prospered would expect to move to an area which more accurately reflected their enhanced status, and this might happen more than once. As Mrs Panton, a popular late-Victorian writer on household matters observed: 'Neighbourhoods alter so rapidly in character and in *personelle* likewise, that I cannot blame young folk for refusing more than a three years agreement, or at most a seven years lease.' Once again, therefore, social and physical mobility were related.

A London villa, with two drawing-rooms, breakfast room, large kitchen and scullery, three large and two small bedrooms, might rent at £45 a year at mid-century. The villa, preferably detached and in its own grounds, remained the town dweller's ideal. Most had to make do with a semi-detached villa or a terraced house, the former naturally being preferred, for it gave a greater impression of grandeur. Not until the 1890s, however, did suburbia stretch out far enough to embrace land sufficiently cheap to enable semi-detached or detached houses to come within the reach of the less well off. Nevertheless, as Geoffrey Best points out, although terraced houses were rarely *fashionable* outside mid-Victorian London (where the high cost of land made them the rule) they could undoubtedly be *respectable*. That was the main consideration. Charles Pooter was certainly satisfied with his terraced house:

My dear wife Carrie and I have just been a week in our new house, 'The Laurels', Brickfield Terrace, Holloway – a nice six-roomed residence, not counting basement, with a front breakfast-parlour. We have a little front garden; and there is a flight of ten steps up to the front door, which, by-the-by, we keep locked with the chain up. Cummings, Gowing, and our other intimate friends always come to the little side entrance, which saves the servant the trouble of going up to the front door, thereby taking her from her work. We have a nice little back garden which runs down to the railway. We were rather afraid of the noise of the trains at first, but the landlord said we should not notice them after a bit, and took £2 off the rent. He was certainly right; and beyond the cracking of the garden wall at the bottom, we have suffered no inconvenience.

After my work in the City, I like to be at home. What's the good of a home, if you are never in it? 'Home, Sweet Home', that's my motto.[5]

Although Pooter's servant, Sarah, was not much to speak of, she at least put her master into the servant-keeping class, the other essential mark of the middle-class man. Seebohm Rowntree, indeed, regarded the keeping of servants as *the* dividing line between the middle and working classes, binding the servant-keepers together irrespective of the number of staff each employed. That number again depended on income, with expected norms at different levels of wealth. Numerous household manuals advised on the appropriate establishment. In 1857, for example, in the *Manual of Domestic Economy*, J. H. Walsh counselled:

An income of £1,000, clear of all other expenditure, and devoted solely to housekeeping and rental, will afford the following servants: 1st, a butler, or manservant out of livery; 2nd, a coachman or groom, 3rd one or two house-maids; 4th, a cook; 5th, a lady's maid, or a nursery maid, or sometimes both . . . The income No 2. [this was his £500-a-year class] will only afford three servants, viz. 1st, a page, or a general manservant, or a parlourmaid; 2nd, a housemaid; and 3rd, a cook. This provides also for the keeping of a single horse or pony and carriage. If, however, the family is a large one, a young lady's maid must be kept for the purpose of making their dresses at home, and in that case a horse cannot be afforded . . . The income No. 3 [his £250-a-year class] will not allow even of the above domestics, and a maid-of-all-work must be the means of doing what is required, aided in some cases by a girl, or in others, by the younger members of the family . . . The income No. 4 [his £100-a-year class] is barely sufficient to provide what is required for the family in the shape of lodging, food and raiment, and therefore no servant can be kept, or at all events, only such a young girl as it is quite useless here to allude to.

Even 'such a young girl', if employed to do 'the rough', would enable a wife to be spared the indignity of soiling her hands. There was a steady stream of working-class girls prepared to enter domestic service until the end of the nineteenth century and even then, when the 'servant problem' became more acute, the daily help was an alternative to requiring the middle-class wife to do all her own housework.

Walsh alludes to another item of middle-class expenditure, namely the keeping of a carriage. In 1856 over 208,000 persons were carriage owners, and they constituted an important subgroup within the middle class – the 'carriage trade'. For some, such as doctors, the keeping of a carriage was a necessity rather than an ostentation. As a contemporary commented: 'A physician without a carriage . . . is looked upon with suspicion.' For others, however, the carriage was a status symbol akin to the twentieth-century motor car. However, the extension of cheap railway travel together with the urban omnibus and cab, made the keeping of a carriage less attractive as the century progressed, and many preferred to spend their income on other things, such as a holiday.

Middle-class ideals

The middle-class residence was more than just a house; it was a *home*. Here was a veritable Victorian cult. 'The Home,' wrote Samuel Smiles, 'is the crystal of society – the nucleus of national character; and from that source, be it pure or tainted, issue the habits, principles, and maxims which govern public as well as private life.' 'Home, Sweet Home', which Mr Pooter took as his motto, was the title of a song written by an American, John Howard Payne, and first heard in 1823. It was a phenomenal success on both sides of the Atlantic and became virtually a second national anthem of Victorian Britain. There were countless other poems, songs and magazine articles to feed the image of the cosy hearth. A German visitor to England in 1851 wrote: 'The damp cold of his native land doubles the Englishman's desire for a comfortable home.' Home was both private and comfortable; and the middle class much prized privacy and comfort, as witnessed by their heavily curtained windows and mightily over-stuffed furniture.

Enshrined in the home was the middle-class family. In the nineteenth century the middle class took the ancient institution of the family and invested it with new and distinctive qualities. In its ideal form it was considered a holy institution, aptly symbolised by the lavish and weighty family Bible. The novelist and Christian Socialist, Charles Kingsley, who was also an Anglican clergyman, held that 'fully to understand the meaning of "a father in heaven" we must be fathers ourselves; to know how Christ loved the Church, we must have wives to love, and love them'. The roles of husband and wife, as indeed of children and servants, were strictly delineated, and all were assured of their place in a hierarchical structure. The undisputed head was the husband. Unlike the working-class husband he was, unless he had sons of working age living at home, almost certainly the sole breadwinner, upon whose earnings the whole family was dependent. Wives were subordinated (legally as well as socially) to their husbands (see Chapter 10), as were children to their parents. In the idealised version all were happy in their allotted place, but in reality the home could subject its members to insufferable pressures.

Yet the middle-class ideal family set a pattern to both working class and aristocracy alike. Victoria and Albert, with their children gathered around them, were the very epitome of the 'middle-class family', a fact which Walter Bagehot considered to be of some constitutional significance in such an age of deference: 'A family on the throne is an interesting idea . . . it brings down the pride of sovereignty to the level of petty life.'

But Bagehot, too, could discern a less attractive side; the need of the family to 'keep up appearances', and to behave in a 'respectable' manner. The need to conform to an accepted code of behaviour could be crushing. Bagehot described its despotism:

> You may talk of the tyranny of Nero and Tiberius; but the real tyranny is the tyranny of your next-door neighbour . . . Public opinion is a permeating influence, and it exacts obedience to itself; it requires us to think other men's thoughts, to speak other men's words, to follow other men's habits. Of course, if we do not, no formal ban issues; no corporeal pain, no coarse penalty of a barbarous society is inflicted on the offender: but we are called 'eccentric'; there is a gentle murmur of 'most unfortunate ideas', 'singular young man', 'well-intentioned, I dare say; but unsafe, sir, quite unsafe'.[6]

Respectability, according to Geoffrey Best, was 'the great Victorian shibboleth and criterion':

> Here was the sharpest of all lines of social division, between those who were and those who were not respectable: a sharper line by far than that between rich and poor, employer and employee, or capitalist and proletarian. To be respectable in mid-Victorian Britain had the same cachet as being a good party man in a communist state. It signified at one and the same time intrinsic virtue and social value. The respectable man was a good man, and also a pillar of society. He might be poor, he might be rich; it really made no matter which.[7]

Certain set patterns of behaviour were marked down as respectable, and it was when these conflicted with economic circumstances that the strains of 'keeping up appearances' could become intolerable. The writer Edmund Gosse was born in 1849, and in his autobiography, *Father and Son*, described the tensions of his early home life:

> At the best of times, the money which my parents had to spend was an exiguous and an inelastic sum. Strictly economical, proud – in an old-fashioned mode now quite out of fashion – to conceal the fact of their poverty, painfully scrupulous to avoid giving inconvenience to shop-people, tradesmen or servants, their whole financial career had to be carried on with the adroitness of a campaign through a hostile country.

When, as was often the case, members of the lower middle class lived close to working-class areas, and when their incomes were so similar, the striving to keep themselves a cut above the manual workers was all the greater. Perkin tells of the wife of a Manchester clerk who told her son:

> No use being poor and seeming poor, always put on a good face outside . . . She would say, I must have the windows right because more pass by than come in. We had to dress to the public . . . Always give people a good impression.

And he describes the son of a Potteries insurance agent who came

> from the social stratum of those who 'would never go out without they was dressed up'; the local working people mocked such people with the phrase 'a fur coat but no breakfast'.[8]

The home, the family and respectability were not the only middle-class ideals to capture the nation's thought, for in the nineteenth century this class came to set the national tone. This happened despite the fact that the political power of the aristocracy remained entrenched for longer than has sometimes been supposed, and despite the fact that the middle class, while expanding in numbers, remained proportionately small. It accounted for only 10–20 per cent of the population at mid-century, and certainly fell far short of the 40 per cent or so which sociologists would discern today. Nor did the middle class succeed in establishing its own 'separate, permanent, potentially governing, parliamentary party' (to use Harold Perkin's words) to propagate its view. Not until 1918 did a Middle Classes Union appear, seeking to organise 'the unorganised middle, the section which is the butt, the buffer, and the burden-bearer when capital and labour are contending'. This association, directed against the growth of socialism, lacked impact; but it was not through associations, nor organisations, nor particular political parties that the middle-class voice was heard. This is not as surprising as it may seem, for it was the qualities of self-help, individualism and competition that the middle class suffused throughout society.

Competition was presented as both economically and socially beneficial. In the economy, competition balanced the market forces of supply and demand; it maintained profits at a remunerative level, neither so high as to exploit the consumer nor so low as to discourage enterprise. It also fixed wages at exactly the right level: low enough to provide full employment for all workers and to make it necessary for them to work full time to maintain their customary standard of living, yet high enough to give them subsistence. Within society it contrasted with the dependence and protection inherent in a paternal system, and stimulated individual independence, responsibility, self-respect and an ambition to rise in the social scale. Individual competition, energy and ability, rather than birth, patronage, or state aid, were the qualities which would enable any man to climb the social ladder.

From this belief arose the idea of the 'self-made man', one of the key ideas of middle-class mythology. It was, as Perkin says, a real myth, 'in that it had a sufficient basis in fact . . . to make it eminently plausible, while remaining utterly fictitious as a sociological explanation of the entrepreneurs as a class'. A long stream of 'instructive' and 'improving' literature, much of it in the form of magazines such as the *Penny Magazine*, the *Family Economist*, and the *Family Friend*, promoted the idea not only among lower middle-class people but among working men also.

Samuel Robinson, a manufacturer from Wilmslow in Cheshire published in 1854 his *Friendly Letters on the Recent Strikes from a Manufacturer to his own Workpeople*. The friendly advice he had to offer included the following:

> You would, indeed, have a just title to complain, if the road to fortune were not left as open to you as to others . . . But it is not so. Thousands of these very capitalists at whom there is so much railing have risen out of your own ranks. Thousands are so rising every day, and winning competence and wealth. None of you are witholden from trying for the same prizes. But to win them you will have to practise the same virtues by which others have won them: industry, frugality, temperance, activity, prudence, and self-denial – the disposition, I mean, to refuse yourself some present pleasure in order to secure some distant but much greater good. These are the conditions of your success, AND THERE ARE NO OTHERS.[9]

The bible of self-improvement, however, was undoubtedly Samuel Smiles's book, *Self-Help*, published in 1859. The book sold 20,000 copies in its first year, 55,000 by 1864, 150,000 by 1889, and about 250,000 by the time of Smiles's death in 1904. *Self-Help* was a masterpiece of propaganda, and represents one of the ways in which a middle-class ideal was spread throughout the whole of society. Smiles compiled an anthology of anecdotes relating to the lives of men throughout history and throughout the western world. Through individual striving each had made something of his life. Not all had become rich, but that was not the essence of his philosophy:

> Nothing is more common than energy in money-making, quite independent of any higher object than its accumulation. A man who devotes himself to this pursuit, body and soul, can scarcely fail to become rich. Very little brains will do; spend less than you earn; add guinea to guinea; scrape and save; and the pile of gold will gradually rise . . . To provide for others and for our own comfort and independence in old age, is honourable, and greatly to be commended; but to hoard for mere wealth's sake is the characteristic of the narrow-souled and the miserly . . . Far better and more respectable is the good poor man than the bad rich one – better the humble silent man than the agreeable well appointed rogue who keeps his gig. A well balanced and well stored mind,

a life full of useful purpose, whatever the position occupied in it may be, is of far greater importance than average worldly respectability. The highest object of life we take to be to form a manly character, and to work out the best development possible, of body and spirit – of mind, conscience, heart and soul. This is the end: all else ought to be regarded but as the means. Accordingly, that is not the most successful life in which a man gets the most pleasure, the most money, the most power or place, honour or fame; but that in which a man gets the most manhood, and performs the greatest amounts of useful work and of human duty.

However thrown together the anecdotal biographies may have been, the qualities which they were intended to exemplify are clearly displayed: perseverance, foresight, economy, punctuality, independence and individual effort.

The ramifications of individualism and self-help were wide. The desire to 'get on' wooed many an ambitious working man from more radical roads to improvement. An Anti-Corn Law League lecturer challenged a crowd of Chartist hecklers in 1840: 'Denounce the middle classes as you may, there is not a man among you worth a halfpenny a week that is not anxious to elevate himself among them.'

This middle-class ideal did not only influence the class beneath it, however, it conflicted with the landed view of society at many points. Any encumbrance to individualism had to be swept away. Thus patronage in all its forms came under attack. This led to the demand for open competition into the civil service, and the ending of purchased commissions in the army, two preserves previously maintained by and for the aristocracy. In commerce, free trade was demanded in place of protection and monopoly as symbolised by the Corn Laws. In industrial relations, it called for a free trade in labour, and the substitution of a contractual relationship between employer and employee for the personal relationship of master and servant. It even extended to religion, with the demand that the privileged position of the established Church of England should be abolished, so that each sect might 'compete' in equality with others.

The moral revolution and religion

Life in the eighteenth century was brutal and cruel. Pain and suffering were accepted among the commonplace things of life. For women, childbirth was a great leveller, sparing neither high-born lady nor low-born peasant. Dentistry and surgery presented ordeals which people today would find it hard to bear. Indeed, Lord Grenville wrote: 'Wonderful as are the powers and feats of the steam engine, the chloroform far transcends them all in its beneficent and consolatory operations.' Death, too, was common, often sudden, and owing to the primitive state of medicine, frequently painful. It is perhaps not surprising, therefore, that acquaintance with such hard facts of life should have had a hardening and brutalising effect.

Men did not shrink from inflicting pain on each other for sport, for honour, for justice or merely out of anger. Romance may have turned the highwayman and the smuggler into eighteenth-century heroes, but most were probably mean, petty, vicious and lacking in any saving grace. The forces of law and order were weak, and made up for their weakness with brutality. Newgate and Tyburn were among the sights of London; medieval punishments such as the pillory and flogging still flourished; and public hangings had all the trappings of a spectator sport. The death penalty could be imposed for a range of over 200 offences, including the theft of any article of more than 1 shilling in value. The deterrent effect was negligible; public executions were a

8   Victorian Sunday

1   *Sunny Sabbaths*   2   *Sunday at Home*

Many Victorians took very seriously the idea of the Sabbath as a day of rest. Children, if allowed to play with toys at all, were often confined to such 'Sunday toys' as the Noah's Ark. Sunday reading was also restricted in many households. *Sunny Sabbaths* (1) was one of many books of Bible stories, made attractive by coloured engravings, designed 'to brighten the Home on [the Sabbath] when work is suspended, by making the divine book more attractive to the youthful mind'. *Sunday at Home* (2) was a weekly magazine, of which there was a wide choice. In addition to a serial (here a story of the early Christians) there were Bible studies and quizzes, improving verse, and stories of missionary activity overseas.

favourite haunt of pickpockets (whose offence was a capital one), their favourite moment for a 'dip' being when the condemned man suffered 'the drop'. John Rule makes the point:

> From the moment the assize judge put on the black cap, to the fatal drop via the long procession from Newgate to Tyburn Hill, the state intended to enact an awful theatre before the lower orders. The problem was that the people turned it into a counter theatre and made a celebration of an intended humiliation.[10]

Bestial drunkenness was common throughout society, and the scenes which Hogarth depicted in 'Gin Lane' had their real-life counterparts. Gambling assumed gigantic proportions and sexual laxity was rife. Youths of noble birth were violently beaten by their schoolmasters, who countenanced a degree of schoolboy bullying which we should find intolerable. It is not to be wondered at that when they grew up they beat their wives, or took their pleasure in such cruel sports as prize-fighting and cock-fighting. Wantonness and brutality were evident at both ends of society. Patrick Colquhoun wrote:

> It is only those who pass their lives in vice and idleness, or who dissipate the surplus labour acquired by inheritance or otherwise in gaming and debauchery, and the idle life of paupers, prostitutes, rogues, vagabonds, vagrants, and persons engaged in criminal pursuits, who are real nuisances in society.[11]

Here speaks a member of the middle class, but it is possible that money-making, which often leads to vices of its own, leaves little time for the practice of others; and towards the end of the eighteenth century it was to the middle class that moral leadership passed.

'Between 1780 and 1850,' writes Harold Perkin, 'the English ceased to be one of the most aggressive, brutal, rowdy, outspoken, riotous, cruel and bloodthirsty nations in the world and became one of the most inhibited, polite, orderly, tender-minded, prudish, and hypocritical.' Most capital offences were abolished, the pillory went (in 1837), prisons were reformed and the barbarous treatment of lunatics subdued. Ox-driving, cock-fighting, and the baiting of bulls, badgers and bears were made illegal in 1833 and 1835. Duelling, hitherto an essential part of the aristocratic code of honour, declined. It is true that the Duke of Wellington, while Prime Minister, fought a bloodless duel in 1829, but in 1844 the army's Articles of War were amended to make an apology for insult permissible within the code of honour, and rendering an officer who took part in a duel, or who did not do his best to prevent one, liable to be cashiered.

If the Victorian middle class, to whom moral leadership passed, is accused of hypocrisy, it has to be remembered how close that period was to the eighteenth century, and how much debauchery and dissipation lay beneath the surface of society. Hippolyte Taine, a French commentator on the English, observed: 'What opportunities for sliding down the slippery slope, and how powerful the brakes, interior and exterior, need to be to hold them back!' It is not surprising that the brakes sometimes failed. New standards of behaviour could be difficult to maintain. D. C. Somervell has written: 'Hypocrisy is the shadow cast by idealism, and the higher the idealism the longer the shadow.' Yet new standards of behaviour did come to be expected, which makes the 'moral revolution' all the more worthy of closer examination.

That it should have happened when it did is interesting. For those who like dates, 1787 is a good one to pick, for that was the year in which George III issued a Proclamation against Vice and Immorality, which included blasphemy, sabbath-breaking, drunkenness, obscene literature and immoral behaviour. A more convenient date could hardly have been chosen from the historian's point of view, for it neatly begins the half-century leading to Victoria's accession in 1837. This is the period which Muriel Jaeger examined in a stimulating book, *Before Victoria*, where she showed the extent to which 'Victorian values' came to prevail before the queen ever came to the throne. We may take that very 'Victorian' character, Dr Thomas Bowdler, as an illustration. In publishing his *Family Shakespeare* in 1804, an edition in which 'nothing is added to the original text; but those words and expressions are omitted which cannot with propriety be read aloud in the family', he gave the nineteenth century a new literary genre, and the English language a new verb, 'to bowdlerise'. He died in 1825, if not a Victorian himself, at least a Father of the Victorians, to borrow F. K. Brown's phrase.

What, then, were the forces which brought about this transformation and which gave the Victorian era its particular moral flavour? The mainsprings are without doubt to be found in new religious movements. However low the spiritual temperature of the Church may have been in the eighteenth century there had yet remained some dedicated and fervent clergymen conscious of the need to rescue society from the depths into which it seemed to be plunging. They attributed the decline in morals to the want of a vital religion, a religion of the spirit rather than of superficial observance or outwardly decent living. To them, justification could be by faith alone. This was a return to the central thinking of the Reformation, and was a revival of many of the traditions of English Puritanism. Numerous clergymen and members of the laity felt the call to seriousness, including John Wesley who, together with a group of friends, founded the Holy Club at Oxford in 1729. From their observance of the method of study prescribed by the statutes of the university they became known as Methodists, a bantering title which stuck. Methodism spread by leaps and bounds from the 1740s onwards, much aided by Wesley's powers as a preacher. Before his death in 1791 he delivered over 40,000 sermons, generally travelling about 5,000 miles around the country each year. Although he had been ordained as an Anglican priest in 1728, Wesley had an ambivalent attitude towards the Church, and one Methodist in 1834 likened him to an oarsman who faced the Church of England while he steadily rowed away. The drift towards Nonconformity gathered speed from 1784, however, when Wesley felt impelled to ordain a Superintendent (in effect, a bishop) to serve the Methodists in the newly independent United States.

Many clergy, touched by the same religious movement, chose to remain within the established Church where, imbued as they felt themselves to be with the true spirit of the Gospel, they were known as Evangelicals. By the late 1820s, according to W. E. Gladstone, one-eighth of the Anglican clergy were Evangelicals, and at midcentury they made up between a third and a half of the clergymen of the Church of England. However, most of the leading figures of the Evangelical Revival – men like Wilberforce and Shaftesbury, and women like Hannah More – were lay people. A group of such men and women gathered around Henry Thornton, a celebrated banker living in Clapham, and they came to be known as 'the Clapham Sect'. The group had considerable influence, a wide range of interests and enjoyed great wealth. William Wilberforce, one of the most notable recruits, was the head of a large commercial house at Hull. He married the daughter of an Evangelical banker at Birmingham, and had an income (which, like other members of the group, he was prepared to use for the cause) of as much as £30,000 a year. It was Wilberforce who secured the Royal Proclamation against Vice and Immorality and who was the main driving force for a reform of manners. 'There is needed some reformer of the nation's morals,' he wrote, 'who should raise his voice in the high places of the land, and do within the Church, and nearer the throne, what Wesley has accomplished in the meeting, and amongst the multitude.' No one was better suited for such a mission than he, for he moved in the best circles and was a close friend of Pitt, and could see that by not affronting society it could be beneficially influenced. What some saw as the excesses of Methodism (at least in its externals) were therefore scrupulously to be avoided. 'There will be no capricious humours,' he wrote, 'no moroseness, no discourtesy, no affected severity of deportment, no peculiarity of language, no indolent neglect, no wanton breach, of the ordinary forms and fashions of society.' Their background and their behaviour gave the Evangelicals a sense of particular mission to the middle and upper classes. The Methodists saw their mission lower down the social scale.

It is of course with the abolition of the slave trade that Wilberforce's name is firmly linked. This was accomplished in 1807, the year which ironically saw the death of John Newton, the former slave-trader who became an abolitionist and an Evangelical clergyman, best known, perhaps, for his hymn, 'Amazing Grace'. The Clapham Sect had a positive zeal for reforming work, and there is a story of Wilberforce, chatting with Thornton at the end of the last debate of the anti-slavery struggle and asking, 'Well, Henry, what shall we abolish next?' The significant point is that the anti-slavery lobby adopted numerous expedients to excite public opinion. In order to bring their crusade to a successful conclusion they forged a new weapon, described by Kitson Clark as the weapon of 'organised moral indignation'. Pressure-group politics such as this put new power and influence into the hands of relatively humble people, and much of the moral fervour of the anti-slavery campaign went on to be deflected into the Anti-Corn Law agitation and other causes espoused by the middle class.

The influence of Evangelicalism throughout the Victorian age was enormous, yet, though Anglicans and Dissenters could find much common ground within the movement and captured much of the limelight, there were other influences at work. From Oxford in the 1830s developed a 'High Church' movement, in reaction to many of the characteristics of 'Low Church' Evangelicalism. The movement was led by John Henry Newman, John Keble and Edward Pusey, all Fellows of Oriel College. They countered the narrow, personal approach of Evangelicalism by stressing the continuity of the Church of England, which remained part of a universal Catholic Church. They stressed the importance of Church ceremonies handed down from the past, and their interest in ecclesiastical ritual, architecture and furnishings struck a rich chord in a society much influenced by Sir Walter Scott's medievalism and the Romantic Movement. The group gave publicity to their views in a series of *Tracts for the Times*, of which 90 were issued between 1833 and 1841, and from which came the title, Tractarians. These Tracts were significant for several reasons. They were works of considerable scholarship, and were aimed at the clergy rather than the laity. Their emphasis on the priesthood contrasts with the Evangelical movement in which clerical and lay elements were in greater balance. That the Tracts issued from Oxford meant that many undergraduates, destined for the Church, read them and helped to spread their influence. The most controversial tract was Tract XC, in which Newman put forward the view that the Thirty-Nine Articles, which formulated Anglican doctrine, were not substantially different from official Roman Catholic theology. The apparent taint of Roman Catholicism offended many people in the Church of England, but the Tractarians of the Oxford Movement did bring about profound and beneficial changes, especially by encouraging the clergy to greater devotion in their priestly duties, to deeper scholarship and to more vigorous pastoral care. In the second quarter of the century the devotion and character of Anglican clergymen showed a startling change for the better, so that even a Dissenter might write in

1851: 'We believe the Anglican clergy to be the most pernicious men of all within the compass of the church; but also the most sincere, the most learned, the most self-denying.'

From one direction or another, therefore, the Victorian period absorbed a religious atmosphere, manifested in a variety of ways. Religious literature flooded on to the market, as any rummager in a second-hand bookshop can tell. There was a vast output of hymns; one estimate, perhaps low, suggests an average of one new hymnal a year in the Church of England alone between 1830 and 1880. Both the Tractarians and the Evangelicals were prominent in hymnology. From the former came *Hymns Ancient and Modern*, first published in 1861, while Evangelicals wrote many hymns popular today, including 'Abide With Me', without which no Cup Final would be complete. The sermon, too, had great popularity and was, in G. M. Young's phrase, 'the standard vehicle of serious truth'. He noted: 'Old Sir Robert Peel trained his son to repeat every Sunday the discourse he had just heard, a practice to which he owed his astonishing recollection of his opponents' arguments and something, perhaps, of the unction of his replies.'

An enduring memorial to the age is the 'English Sunday'. Sabbatarianism is one of the least attractive aspects of Evangelicalism, for this crusade seemed to hurt only the poor and not the rich. In 1831 was founded the Society for Promoting Due Observance of the Lord's Day; and two years later Sir Andrew Agnew introduced a bill into the House of Commons which would have had the most swingeing effects. It would have made illegal 'any pastime of public indecorum, inconvenience or nuisance', and would have forbidden public lectures and speeches, the consumption of drink in hotels except by travellers, and the hiring of carriages (other than by clergymen and doctors). Further to impede travel, turnpike-keepers were forbidden to open their gates and lock-keepers their locks. The bill was only lost by six votes – an indication of the extent of the moral transformation – but agitation did not stop there. There was a vigorous campaign to abolish the running of trains on Sunday which, though unsuccessful, had some beneficial side-effects; the London and North-Western Railway, for example, opened a number of company schools financed from part of their Sunday revenues in response to the moral objection of some of their directors and shareholders. Even so, enough was closed, curtailed, or frowned on to make Sunday 'the fixed thing of amazement and terror to the foreign traveller.'

The failure to secure comprehensive legislation for the Sabbath was largely due to the fact that it cut across class lines in a clearly intolerable way, for the day of rest meant one thing for the middle class but quite another for the working class. Edward Miall, founder of the *Nonconformist* (alone among the leading Dissenting and Evangelical journals in discountenancing Sabbatarianism) saw the futility and hypocrisy of such legislation:

> Suppose the object aimed at could be compassed. Suppose all the means and opportunities of openly violating the Sabbath were cut off – every tavern and tea-garden shut – every vehicle prohibited – every avenue to pleasure barred – and every act expressive of contempt for the institution rendered impossible. What then? There would not be more religion – if by religion is meant sympathy with God, in the gospel of Jesus Christ – in consequence of the arrangement, than was before – not one single additional element of the social state upon which the eye of the Supreme could rest with approval. There would be nothing more than an imposing show without any corresponding reality – towards God a mockery – to the Churches a blind, concealing from them the actual spiritual condition of the world . . .[12]

What was the 'spiritual condition of the world'? Only one serious attempt was made to measure church and chapel attendance in the nineteenth century – the Religious Census of 30 March 1851 – and that hammered home what had already become clear to many clergymen and concerned laymen, namely, that the churches were basically middle-class institutions. The census revealed that not more than 54 per cent of possible worshippers (47 per cent according to the calculations of a recent historian) had attended church or chapel on that typical Sunday. To modern eyes the figure is impressive, but it deeply shocked contemporaries. It was clear to them, as it is to us, that the main absentees were the working class, whom both the established Church and most of the Nonconformist sects failed to attract. The census also showed that, despite regional variations, Nonconformist attendances slightly exceeded those of the Church of England, evidence of the great strides which Non-conformity had made during the previous half-century. Yet the extent to which Nonconformity was a 'middle-class movement' and the social composition of the different Dissenting denominations is open to question. Kitson Clark states: 'It seems probable that there were many members of the Church of England who were middle class, but there were singularly few members of the aristocracy who were Protestant Nonconformists.' David M. Thompson agrees: 'Nonconformity had no aristocrats and very few of the very poor. In this respect it differed from both Anglicans and Roman Catholics, who were represented in each group. The range of Nonconformity was from the respectable working man to the wealthy businessman or better pro-fessional man.'

Unitarians (regarded as 'sub-Christian' by most Trinitarians) and Quakers were probably the wealthiest groups and formed the 'aristocracy of Dissent'. Many of their members were merchants, businessmen, manufacturers and bankers. Congrega-tionalists, Baptists and Wesleyans were the main middle-class denominations. Con-gregationalists tended to contain the wealthiest manufacturers, Baptists were strong among small businessmen, while the Wesleyans abounded with shopkeepers. The Primitive Methodists, in both town and country, plumbed greater social depths and appealed to many artisans, small craftsmen and manual workers. There were dif-ferences in Nonconformist social composition in town and country, however, for in rural areas social stratification took place where there was more than one chapel; but where there was only one its social identity was defined in relation to the parish church. In Wales, all branches of Nonconformity embraced a greater social range. As the century progressed the social diversity of Nonconformity probably dimin-ished. Wealthier Nonconformists moved in wider circles, and many transferred from chapel to church. Kate Tiller gives the example of Edward Akroyd, the Halifax industrialist:

He was brought up a Methodist. His father had built a Methodist New Connexion chapel and Sunday school near their Haley Hill mills. Yet by the 1850s and 60s the son was a staunch Anglican, going so far as to have the bodies of his parents exhumed from the chapel burial ground and transferred to his newly built church (1856–9) of All Souls, Haley Hill. Such new churches (and many were built in this period) visually dominated the workplaces and homes of their builders' employees. Akroyd wanted 'every man, woman and child to feel that henceforth this is their church . . . and above all to show that interest by regularly attending its ordinances' . . . The effects of commer-cial success, accompanying changes in lifestyle, social connections, and political aspirations (he was elected MP for Halifax in 1865) contributed to Akroyd's switch to Anglicanism.[13]

Maintaining religious affiliation proved difficult for some members of the middle class as they moved to suburbs where their particular denomination might be unrepresented.

Matthew Arnold subjected middle-class Nonconformity to a withering attack in *Culture and Anarchy*, castigating its narrowness and provincialism. But there is an element of caricature in his writing. The chapel made a very positive contribution to the lives of thousands of people, culturally as well as spiritually. It is to Non-conformity that the love of choral singing owes a particular debt. In 1846 Alfred Novello published Handel's *Messiah* in cheap monthly parts, and there was an enormous demand for sacred music by mid-century. In July 1865 *The Musical Times* noted:

> In tracing the course of the widely spread love for sacred music, it must be remembered that Novello's cheap series of Oratorios not only supplied the demand which was caused by the constant performance of these works, but actually created a public of its own, by circulating, at the price of a common-place ballad, the entire Oratorios amongst the audience; so that, not only were they enabled to follow every note during the presentation of works, but a library of standard sacred music was almost unconsciously formed in thousands of homes, leading to the establishment of private and public choral societies, which have increased year by year.

It was easier for the likes of lower middle-class shopkeepers and working-class craftsmen to take an active role in chapel life than it was within the parish church, and there they might gain a confidence and a commitment which spilled over into their everyday lives. Thus was formed a spring of social and political action which contributed much idealism to Liberal and Labour Parties alike.

Middle-class education

Matthew Arnold met many members of the middle class (of which, of course, he was himself a member) in their capacity as managers of the elementary schools which he inspected, and it was on the subject of elementary education that most of his official writing was based. That term, together with 'secondary' education, had a different connotation in the nineteenth century and they denoted not so much chronological stages in a continuous process of education as types of education suit-able to different classes. Thus, elementary education was essentially education for the working class, while secondary education was that which was suitable for the middle and upper classes. Age did not really enter into the picture, for the determining factor in the type of education which a children received was not how old they were but the social class from which they came. This explains why the state concerned itself almost solely with elementary education and made no provision for secondary education until the beginning of the twentieth century. State provision of education smacked of charity, which it was far beneath the middle or upper class to accept. Not only did the state not provide secondary schools (or even elementary schools before 1870); there was no legal compulsion to have one's children educated at all. This applied even to the working class until 1880, with the exception of pauper children, who had to receive whatever instruction the guardians ordained, and factory children, who were required by the Factory Acts to receive part-time education.

The middle classes were therefore left to their own devices, and in an age when one paid for anything which was worth having, they bought education for their children wherever they wished or were able. But could they be trusted to buy wisely? Arnold argued that they could not:

The mass of mankind know good butter from bad, and tainted meat from fresh, and the principle of supply and demand may, perhaps, be relied on to give us sound meat and butter. But the mass of mankind do not so well know what distinguishes good teaching and training from bad; they do not here know what they ought to demand, and, therefore, the demand cannot be relied on to give us the right supply.

The idea that market forces should be allowed to determine educational provision (an idea taken up again by many radical Conservatives in the 1980s) was, in Arnold's view, foolish. 'Our middle class are nearly the worst educated in the world,' he wrote in 1861. It was not for nothing that he requested the Newcastle Commission in 1859 'to say to the Government, "Regard the necessities of a not too distant future, and organise your secondary education"'. Arnold was not the only contemporary critic of English middle-class education, but he was among the most eloquent, and his dismal view has been accepted by most historians.

The choice of school available to the middle class varied greatly. The most affluent members, as has been seen in Chapter 3, made use of the public schools, but the high fees of such institutions made them inaccessible to the great majority of middle-class parents. Instead they had to rely on the endowed grammar schools (many of which dated from the sixteenth and seventeenth centuries) and on a bewildering array of private and proprietary schools.

With a few exceptions the endowed schools were in an advanced state of decay at the beginning of the century. They had failed to respond to the new demands of industrialisation, although change was made difficult by the narrow statutes of many schools. In 1818 Nicholas Carlisle published his *Endowed Grammar Schools of England and Wales*, listing some 475 schools. Many failed to respond to his questionnaire – a symptom, perhaps, of their inefficiency – while 82 had either ceased to exist or had sunk to an elementary level. 'It is painful,' Carlisle wrote in his preface, 'to relate that many of our numerous and ample endowments have fallen to decay, by the negligence or cupidity of ignorant and unprincipled trustees.' In many places masters held sinecures, and endowments were misappropriated. Some masters drew their salaries, but admitted no children on the foundation, running instead a private school in the buildings. Other buildings were not used for educational purposes at all. Carlisle noted that the endowed school at Banbury was let to a textile manufacturer, while the schoolroom at Pocklington in Yorkshire was let to a local carpenter who used it as a saw-pit. The fortunes of Manchester Grammar School are indicative of the general decline; the population of the city almost doubled between 1770 and 1810, while decennial admissions to the school dropped from 548 to 288. Bristol Grammar School, which had 100 scholars in 1764, had none at all in the first decade of the nineteenth century.

The difficulties of reform were made clear by the case of Leeds Grammar School, which had reached its low-water mark in the 1790s. The trustees applied to the Chancery Court for permission to use part of the endowment for the teaching of modern subjects, including French and German, in addition to the classics which had previously comprised the whole curriculum. In 1805, however, Lord Eldon, the Lord Chancellor, declared that the case must stand by the facts rather than expediency. What the merchants of Leeds might desire or find useful must be subordinated to the declared intention of the founder. That intention had been to found a grammar school, and the Lord Chancellor accepted Dr Johnson's definition of such an institution as one 'for teaching grammatically the learned languages'. The school must therefore continue with its classical curriculum. It has been argued that this judgement held back the cause of reform for two generations, and nearly killed off half the grammar schools in the country. In fairness to Lord Eldon, however, it must be remembered that numerous grammar schools had ceased to be such and had become elementary schools, and while his decision had the effect of maintaining the classics as the core of the curriculum, it did not prevent the inclusion of more modern subjects provided fees were paid. In so far as such broadening of the curriculum led to this introduction of fees for subjects other than the classics, the status of the schools was increased, although they became more remote from the local poor for whom they had frequently been founded.

Private schools and proprietary schools were subject to no control whatsoever. Anyone who could afford a brass plate for the front door and an advertisement in the newspaper might open a school. Those who have read Dickens's *Nicholas Nickleby* and *David Copperfield* will have some idea what they could be like. Matthew Arnold read *David Copperfield* for the first time in 1880, and wrote that 'Mr Creakle's school at Blackheath is the type of our ordinary middle class schools'. This was the dismal academy of 'Salem House', with its 'alternation of boiled beef with roast beef, and boiled mutton with roast mutton; of clods of bread and butter, dog's-eared lesson books, cracked slates, tear-blotted copy-books, canings, rulerings, hair-cuttings, rainy Sundays, suet puddings and dirty atmosphere of ink surrounding all'. In *Friendship's Garland*, Arnold invented his own school, Lycurgus Academy, presided over by Archimedes Silverpump, PhD:

> Original man, Silverpump! fine mind! fine system! None of your antiquated rubbish – all practical work – latest discoveries in science – mind constantly kept excited – lots of interesting experiments – lights of all colours – fizz! fizz! bang! bang! That's what I call forming a man.

The lack of control over private education led to the growth of proprietary schools, often run on a joint-stock principle. King's College School was opened in 1829, University College School in 1833, the City of London School in 1837. These early schools were day schools, but the influence of Thomas Arnold at Rugby led to the growth of proprietary boarding schools similar to, but generally cheaper than, the public schools. To the latter they appeared a threat, leading Samuel Butler, the reforming headmaster of Shrewsbury, to lament that 'the traffic in joint-stock company schools is ruining, and will ultimately ruin, the old foundations'.

The Churches were active in the foundation of both day and boarding proprietary schools. Roman Catholic schools included Ratcliffe (1847) and Beaumont (1861); Nonconformists founded such schools as Queen's College, Taunton (1843), Bishop's Stortford College (1868) and The Leys (1875). The Quakers founded Ackworth in 1842. Anglican schools included Radley (1847), Bradfield (1850), and St John's School, Leatherhead (1851). It was an Anglican parson, the Revd Nathanial Woodard, who organised the most ambitious system of secondary schools. Woodard became curate of New Shoreham in Sussex in 1846. He was immediately impressed by the lack of educational facilities for the sons of local tradesmen and sea-captains. In 1848 he published a pamphlet, *A Plea for the Middle Classes*, in which he argued that it was wasteful to spend money on the education of the poor until the middle class was educated: 'By neglecting the employer you are, in the present pressure of civilization, hastening on a very general state of barbarism.' Woodard therefore urged the provision of 'a good complete education for the middle classes at such a charge as will make it available for most of them'; but he recognised the wide range of income within the middle class, and planned accordingly. His schools were therefore planned with particular groups in mind. The first, St Nicholas's, Lancing (1848) was for the sons of the gentry and the upper middle class. St John's, Hurstpierpoint (permanently established in 1853) was for the sons of well-to-do tradesmen, while St Saviour's (which moved to Ardingley in 1870) was for the 'poorest members of the middle class'. The fees and curriculum of each school were arranged according to his plan. Woodard had a genius for raising money – described by Gladstone as 'a perfect mastery of the machinery of philanthropic agitation' – and the Woodard Schools multiplied until, by the beginning of the First World War, they constituted the largest group of proprietary secondary schools in the empire. Some of the schools introduced modern subjects; otherwise Woodard was no educational innovator, his contribution being, in the words of his biographer, one 'of bricks and mortar rather than of intellectual inspiration'. However, when the Taunton Commission examined secondary education they suggested a threefold classification of schools very similar to Woodard's.

The Taunton Commission (or Schools Inquiry Commission, to give it its formal title) was appointed in 1864 with the task of examining all those schools which had been included neither in the Clarendon Commission on public schools nor the Newcastle Commission on popular education. Matthew Arnold was, it seems, invited to serve as Commissioner or alternatively as Secretary, but he preferred the post of Assistant Commissioner, with responsibility for enquiring into secondary education on the Continent.

The inquiry lasted four years and was the most exhaustive investigation ever made into English education. Private and proprietary schools as well as endowed schools were examined, and girls' as well as boys' schools were included. The Report, which ran to over 20 large volumes, was highly critical of the provision made for secondary education, which was shown to be hopelessly inadequate, especially in the areas of larger population. The Commissioners reported that 'the account given of the worst of the endowed schools must be repeated in even more emphatic language to describe most of the private schools' – of which there were over 10,000 scattered throughout the country. Proprietary schools, many of which were of recent origin, were, on the whole, shown to be better.

The result of the inquiry was to reveal 'that there are very many English parents who, though they are willing to pay the fair price of their children's education, yet have not suitable schools within their reach where they can be sure of efficient teaching'. Only a national system of secondary education, built round the nucleus of the existing endowed schools, would in their opinion adequately solve the problem. As a general principle they held that three grades of secondary school were necessary, based on the length of time that parents were willing to allow their children to remain at school. At the bottom end of the scale should be third-grade schools for those children (of artisans, small shopkeepers and the smaller farmers) who would leave at 14 or 15. It was here that the deficiencies in existing secondary education were most serious, and made worse by the large proportion of the population included in the group. Schools of the second grade would be established for those who would normally leave at 16, it being expected that 'many of the farmers, many of the richer shopkeepers, many professional men, [and] all but the wealthier gentry' would have sons filling this category. Schools of the first grade would be for the sons of the wealthiest members of the middle class, who would be expected to stay till they were 18 or 19, and would be prepared for entrance to the universities. The curriculum of all schools would be designed with the needs of the different scholars in mind, and would range from a liberal yet practical education in the third grade to an essentially classical education in the first-grade schools.

There was much evidence to support the Commissioners' view that 'social distinctions in education cannot at present be altogether ignored'. Arnold felt, however, that the weakness of the middle class derived from its lack of homogeneity. The professional middle class tended to be educated with the upper class. They were thus separated from the commercial and industrial middle class with whom they should have been on a social level and to whom they should give a lead. In 1868 he wrote in *Schools and Universities on the Continent*:

> So we have amongst us the spectacle of a middle class cut in two in a way un-exampled any where else; of a professional class brought up on the first plane, with fine and governing qualities, but without the idea of science; while that immense business class, which is becoming so important a power in all countries, on which the future so much depends, and which in the leading schools of other countries fills so large a place, is in England brought up on the second plane, cut off from the aristocracy and the professions, and without governing qualities.

Arnold hoped for a more homogeneous middle class through an improvement in education, but that homogeneity, as we have seen, did not come about.

The Taunton Commissioners proposed drastic administrative changes. The powers of the Charity Commissioners to deal with school trusts should be enlarged; they should have a representative in all regions or counties, who should be a member of all school trustees, and with the help of local nominees or representatives should plan the educational resources of the region according to its needs. Parishes and towns should be empowered to levy a rate to support schools of the third grade, or of the second grade if they acted in conjunction with each other. The commissioners also recommended a regular system of inspection and examination, of which private schools, if they wished, should be allowed to avail themselves. The Oxford and Cambridge Local Examinations (started in 1858) and those of the College of Preceptors (1853) already existed, but these tested a few selected pupils rather than the school as a whole.

Very little of this was taken up. As W. F. Connell comments: 'Out of the moun-tainous report . . . there eventually emerged the mouse of the Endowed Schools Act, 1869.' But many people are frightened even of mice, and the limited provisions of the act were themselves the subject of controversy and alarm. The government abandoned the proposal to establish local authorities for secondary education, and a bill embodying the recommendations about examinations and the setting up of a body for the registration of qualified teachers was dropped under the pressure of other legislative business. It has to be accepted, however, that there was less than full enthusiasm for a professional register of teachers, partly because the jealousy between secondary and elementary teachers, who catered for different social classes, was so strong.

The Act established three Endowed Schools Commissioners who were em-powered to draw up schemes reforming the 1,448 schools which came within the terms of the act. In many cases they applied endowments to girls' schools, where the original founders had not specifically confined their benefaction to the education of boys. A more questionable activity was the transfer of endowments away from working–class education to that specifically for the middle class, by abolishing free places. It was argued that working–class education was covered by the 1870 Education Act, and the provision of a few scholarships satisfied the middle-class conscience and fitted well with its ideal of free competition. The work proceeded slowly, and even by 1895, when the Bryce Commission of Secondary Education reported, over one-third of the schools remained untouched.

Events followed a different pattern in Wales and Scotland. The state of secondary education in the Principality had been investigated by the Taunton Commission, and the ensuing Endowed Schools Commissioners prepared a number of schemes for improvement of specific trusts. The great wave of political and national consciousness which followed the 1867 Reform Act led to the call for special consideration, however, and after the general election of 1880 the government felt compelled to appoint a Departmental Committee under Lord Aberdare 'to inquire into the present condition of Intermediate and Higher Education in Wales'. An appalling situation was revealed. Out of a total population of 1,570,000 in 1881, only 4,036 boys in Wales and Monmouthshire received secondary education, and there were only three endowed schools for girls. The problem was partly one of non-attendance, for of the 2,846 places in endowed grammar schools for boys, only 1,540 were taken up. Many of these schools were situated in areas remote from large towns, however, while there was Nonconformist prejudice against schools which were Church institutions, and nationalist prejudice against the many schools with English headmasters who showed little sympathy for the Welsh language and culture. The report was enthusiastically received and resulted in the speedy establishment of University Colleges at Cardiff in 1883 and Bangor in 1884. In 1889 the Welsh Intermediate Education Act was passed, which embodied the recommendations of the Aberdare Committee. Joint education committees were created for every county and county borough. These were empowered to submit schemes for secondary and higher education and, taking into account any endowments which might be used, were granted the power to levy a rate of $\frac{1}{2}$d in the pound which would be balanced by an equivalent Treasury Grant upon inspection of the schools. The act was speedily enforced, and by 1898 the county schemes covered 96 schools of which 79 were new creations.

The Taunton Commission sent Her Majesty's Inspector D. R. Fearon to Scotland to report on secondary education there. On the whole he liked what he saw, and admired especially the more democratic nature of Scottish secondary education:

> Such difficulties as those which often beset the promoters of English secondary education and primary schools, viz. that employers will not mix with the employed; that the man of £500 a year looks down on the man of £80 or £100 a year; that the 'genteel' refuse to use the same schools as the 'respectable', while the 'respectable' dislike to associate with the 'humbler classes', &c. appear to me to be much less prominent and troublesome in Scotland.

The reasons were complex, although one factor was that 'the wealth of the Scotch people has not yet outgrown their civilization'.

At the same time as the Taunton Commission was sitting, the Argyle Commission was making a specific review of the whole field of Scottish education. Its report, published in 1867, revealed that a somewhat higher proportion of Scottish children was receiving secondary education than in Prussia, over twice as many as in France and six times as many as in England. The report led to the passage of the Education (Scotland) Act of 1872, a piece of legislation which was more comprehensive than the English Act of 1870, for unlike the latter (which dealt only with elementary education) the Scottish act covered both the elementary and the secondary fields. A Scottish Education Department was established as a central authority, while 984 popularly elected school boards were established to become the local authorities responsible for both elementary and secondary education, a situation not achieved in England until 1902. Scotland also led the way with a Leaving Certificate, introduced in 1888; the English equivalent did not appear until 1917.

The Scottish universities were far more popular institutions than elsewhere in the British Isles, and were noticeably not the preserve of a single class. They might have their detractors, but they produced a large proportion of the nation's doctors, engineers, and other professionals.

Such scientific and technical experts came to be turned out by new English 'civic' universities towards the end of the century. In 1884 Owens College, Manchester joined with similar colleges at Liverpool and Leeds to form the Victoria University, dismembered in 1903–4 to become separate universities. The colleges at Aberystwyth, Cardiff and Bangor were combined into the University of Wales in 1893. Birmingham University received a charter in 1900, as did Sheffield in 1905 and Bristol in 1909, while at other provincial centres new university colleges offered external degrees of the University of London. These universities were in marked contrast to Oxford and Cambridge. They were strongly local, with funds often contributed by local industrialists, such as George Cadbury at Birmingham, and the Wills and Frys at Bristol. They also drew most of their undergraduates from the surrounding localities, and these young men and women (admitted on equal terms) were mainly the products of the reformed endowed schools and the new secondary schools established by local education authorities under the 1902 Education Act. The local background of the new universities was also reflected in their emphasis on such subjects as science and engineering. The expansion of education in these fields answered a crying national need. In 1903 Sir Norman Lockyer, in his presidential address to the British Association on 'The Influence of Brain Power on History', contrasted the 22 state-subsidised universities of Germany and 134 state and private universities in the USA with the 13 in Great Britain. Britain had fallen behind these two nations in its economic growth – a theme which will be taken up in Chapter 11 – and among the many culprits, one has to be the slow growth of English and Welsh secondary and higher education.

Notes

1   Richard Church, *Over the Bridge*, 1955, Heinemann, p. 162.
2   Harold Perkin, *The Rise of Professional Society*, Routledge, 1989, pp. 99–100.
3   Quoted in Barbara Dennis and David Skilton (eds.), *Reform and Intellectual Debate in Victorian England*, Croom Helm, 1987, pp. 70–71.
4   Harold Perkin, op. cit., 1989, pp. 3–4.
5   George and Weedon Grossmith, *The Diary of a Nobody*, 1892 (Penguin, 1971), p. 19.
6   Quoted in Walter E. Houghton, *The Victorian Frame of Mind*, Oxford University Press, 1957, p. 397.
7   Geoffrey Best, *Mid-Victorian Britain 1851–1870*, Fontana, 1971, p. 260.
8   Harold Perkin, op. cit., 1989, p. 96.
9   Quoted in Kate Flint, *The Victorian Novelist: Social Problems and Social Change*, Croom Helm, 1987, p. 80.
10 John Rule, *Albion's People*, Longman, 1992, p. 239.
11 Quoted in Harold Perkin, *The Origins of Modern English Society*, Routledge and Kegan Paul, 1969, pp. 276–7.
12 Quoted in David M. Thompson, *Nonconformity in the Nineteenth Century*, Routledge and Kegan Paul, 1972, pp. 140–41.
13 Kate Tiller, 'Religion in nineteenth century Britain' in John Golby (ed.), *Communities and Families*, Cambridge University Press, 1994, p. 168.

Chapter nine

The labour movement in the nineteenth century

Perspectives and problems

By 1819, according to E. P. Thompson, 'the British working class had already become – as it was to remain for a hundred years – perhaps the most "clubbable" working class in Europe . . . It seems at times that half a dozen working men could scarcely sit in a room together without appointing a chairman, raising a point of order, or moving the Previous Question'. He notes that even the Cato Street Conspirators of 1820, bent on plotting the assassination of the Cabinet, appointed one of their number as chairman, 'and took the questions of beheading Castlereagh and firing the Tower of London in proper form, with a vote upon the substantive motion'. In the course of the nineteenth century a vast number of working-class organisations came into being, some of which will be examined in this chapter. There were friendly societies and cooperative societies, trade unions and political parties, as well as a host of organisations to foster leisure and cultural activities, ranging from working-men's clubs to brass bands, and from debating societies and libraries to associations of pig, pigeon or dog fanciers.

It is tempting to see such organisations as trade unions as being more significant than pigeon clubs and, indeed, they may have been, although not to each and every individual. John Benson reminds us that it is possible to be a 'member' of a trade union in more ways than one:

> Even when workers did join a union, they did so with varying degrees of enthusiasm – it was possible after all to 'belong' to a trade union in as many ways as it was to a religious organisation. Membership did not necessarily imply commitment, and commitment itself did not necessarily mean that the union came to occupy a prominent place in the life of the individual member.[1]

He (or, less probably, she) might join a trade union in order to further the class struggle against the capitalists; or it might be because the union ran a funeral fund which provided for a 'proper' funeral. There is, in any case, a danger in any kind of history which deals excessively with institutions and bureaucracies – even if they be 'working-class institutions' – for the actual experiences of working people may be misinterpreted, or ignored altogether. Historical sources may be responsible for creating some misunderstandings for, as Raphael Samuel observes:

> . . . they can, of themselves, push work in a certain direction, and give it an unarticulated bias which has to be recognized if it is to be successfully resisted. The magistrate's clerk – or the police officer – guides the researcher on his journey into crime, the senior partner takes him by the arm when he looks at business, the temperance advocate leads him in and out of the pubs. Unless he is careful the historian may end up as their mouthpiece. Organizations can

swallow the historian up if he approaches their records unwarily, because they offer a ready-made subject for research, with all the materials perhaps to hand . . . The researcher may begin by wanting to find out about a group of workers and end up – like historians of the miners – writing about their union executives instead; or embark on an inquiry into, say, mid-Victorian prostitution, and finish up by writing not about women (or even their clients) but about one of the agencies set up to deal with them, a rescue society or Josephine Butler's League. Administrative records have similar pitfalls since they are more informative by far about the administrators than about those whom they investigated or oppressed. It is much easier for the historian to write about nineteenth-century Poor Law administration than about the inner life of workhouses . . . There are shelf-fuls of books about factory legislation; not one about factory girls.[2]

Other sources may help to fill the gaps left by official and administrative records, and in recent decades historians have increasingly turned to them for an insight into the lives of working people. Historians like John Burnett and David Vincent have made more systematic use than heretofore of working-class diaries and autobiographies, while others have made great strides in the use of oral evidence. Paul and Thea Thompson, for example, conducted in-depth interviews with well over 400 people, born between 1872 and 1906, for a study of Edwardian Britain. No source is free from bias, of course. In the preface to his book, *Useful Toil*, Burnett writes:

> . . . the chief defect of the use of diaries and autobiographies as a source must be the self-selectivity of the 'sample'. To keep a daily journal or to write the story of one's life is, and was, at once atypical, especially for working class people to whom writing did not usually come easily. Often there was a particular motivation behind such memoirs, most commonly the author's belief that he had some important message for others which it was his duty to communicate. In the Victorian age this was often his personal triumph over difficulties and misfortunes, the classic account of a rise from humble origins to a position of honour and respectability through hard work, self-education, thrift and a concern for the betterment of mankind. Equally commonly it was the story of redemption from early sin, profligacy or drunkenness by divine grace, often experienced as a sudden act of conversion or salvation at a revivalist or temperance meeting. More recently, a main motivation has been to leave for one's children or grandchildren a record of a different age and society which, despite its material privations, had compensations which contemporary society seems to lack. Whatever his reasons, it is necessary to recognise that the autobiographer or diarist was engaging in an activity which set him apart from the majority of his fellow men, and that to this extent he was not a strictly representative figure . . .
>
> Differentials of literacy within the working class, and the extent to which an occupation was exciting or humdrum, are also reflected in the surviving records:
>
> There are more memoirs of skilled workers than of unskilled, more of upper domestic servants than of lower, more of school-teachers than of farm labourers . . . there are more accounts of miners, sailors, soldiers and steel-workers than of labourers, factory workers, house maids or dressmakers.[3]

Despite their defects such sources do establish some points at variance with the picture presented by bureaucratic sources. For example, Burnett concludes that workers wrote very little about *work*, and concludes that 'work, it seems, was not a central life-interest of the working classes'. Studies of folk-song similarly indicate a lack of preoccupation with work itself and reveal that, both within and without the workplace, a greater concern was for personal relationships with family and friends, workmates and social acquaintances.

A second point relates to trends within the labour movement, and attempts by historians to divide it into periods. The pioneering study in this field, which to this day remains a classic of painstaking research and interpretation, is Sidney and Beatrice Webb's *History of Trade Unionism*, originally published in 1894, but extended in 1920. The Webbs were Fabian socialists, dedicated to gradual and peaceful social change, and it was inevitable that their history should have been influenced by their political views. The Fabian interpretation of social history is akin to the Whig interpretation of political history, both schools giving weight to those events and institutions which appeared to lead to ends of which the historian approved, and playing down or ignoring those of which they did not. For the Webbs, the labour movement was moving towards its consummation in such organisations as the Trades Union Congress and the Labour Party. Phenomena such as Luddism and Owenite community-building (examined in Chapter 2), which appeared not to fit into this general scheme, therefore received short shrift.

The Webbs defined certain stages in trade union development which dominated historical thinking for generations. For example, it was they who coined the title 'New Model' to describe certain unions of the 1850s onwards. The significance of the New Model Unions has since been questioned. At the same time greater emphasis has been placed on the so-called 'New Unionism' that was assuming importance at the very time they were writing. The progress of organised labour was by no means even, and historians have attempted to explain the ebb and flow of trade union strength, and the swings between union activity and more general political activity. Two theories predominate: one stressing the swing of the pendulum between political and economic activity according to the degree of worker disillusionment first with one and then the other; the second focusing on the effects of the trade cycle. The pendulum theory sees working-class activity turning to politics in the years 1830–32 after failure of strikes in 1829–30. Disillusionment with the 1832 Reform Act caused a swing back to trade union activity and Owenite socialism, but the collapse of the Grand National Consolidated Trades Union in 1834 swung the pendulum again towards radical activity, leading to Chartism from which, on the whole trade unions remained aloof. When Chartism failed in the late 1830s and early 1840s there was a revival of trade unionism, followed by a swing back to Chartism in 1847–8. Chartism's collapse was in turn followed by the so-called New Model Unions of the 1850s. Relationships are also observable with the trade cycle, for trade union advances tended to occur in periods of full employment, when conditions were favourable, while political activity increased in slumps, when heavy unemployment inhibited union membership. While these links are demonstrable at certain times, they do not fit every event, and it is clear that reactions to fluctuations in trade varied between different sections of the working class – between the better-off artisan, for example, and those with little or no skill who were most vulnerable in times of depression.

This takes us to a third general point – the actual strength of different sections of the working class, and the extent to which there was a shared class consciousness. While few would disagree with the view that social class, as we understand it today, is a product of industrialisation, there is less consensus as to the period from which a working-class consciousness can be dated. Malcolm Thomis remarks:

. . . historians are now inclined to argue that it is at the end of the nineteenth century and the beginning of the twentieth century that new working-class traditions are becoming established and recognisable. It is then that not only political organisations and trade unions for unskilled workers begin to flourish but also a working-class sub-culture begins to appear with its various identifiable features such as the working-men's club, the Saturday football match, and the rites and celebrations associated with family occasions. Family bonds strengthen and community solidarity becomes possible as the state begins to assume some of the burdens associated with old age, relieving the strain on the family and local community. The term 'working class', it has been argued, might more properly be applied to the year 1900 than to the year 1800 . . .[4]

Crucial to the argument is the role of the 'labour aristocracy' and its relationship to the middle class on the one hand, and the working masses on the other. To what extent did these potential leaders of the working class 'sell out' to their 'betters', preferring respectability to militancy?

Finally, it has to be noted that working-class organisations and institutions could be of two kinds. Some opposed the capitalist system and sought to replace it with something else, such bodies being particulary active in the first four decades of the nineteenth century, as seen in Chapter 2. Others sought by self-help to work within the system and to improve their members' position within society as then constituted; but there remains an important distinction between this *corporate* self-help and the highly *individualistic* self-help of the middle classes, which was the kind that Margaret Thatcher was to applaud among her 'Victorian values'.

Friendly societies and cooperative societies

Friendly societies, cooperatives and trade unions represent three of the major organisations through which workers attempted to ameliorate their position within an increasingly industrial society. The movements are not always easily separable, a confusion which at times was deliberately exploited by the workers. For example, before the repeal of the Combination Acts in 1824, when trade unions were illegal, such associations were sometimes established under the guise of a friendly society. Such was the case of the Breeches Makers' Benefit Society which the radical Francis Place joined in 1790. Ostensibly it was 'for the support of the members when sick and their burial when dead', but he soon found that its real object was to support the members 'in a strike for wages'.

In terms of both chronology and total numbers, friendly societies were the pioneers. It was estimated in 1801 that there were over 7,000 friendly societies in England and Wales, with a membership of between 600,000 and 700,000, while a return made in 1815 put the known membership for Great Britain at 925,000. By 1850 there were probably 1.5 million, and by 1872, 4 million. Many of these people would have been members of burial clubs rather than full friendly societies. Even so, the 1872 figure represents four times the membership of trade unions at that date, and twelve times the membership of cooperative societies.

Friendly societies differed greatly in organisation, function and strength. On the one hand there were the small village clubs, each with its own emblem and customs. William Howitt, in *The Rural Life of England*, described a Club Day in 1838, although similar festivals lasted up to and beyond the Second World War.

I see the clubs, as they are called, coming down the village; a procession of its rustic population all in their best attire. In front of them comes bearing the great banner, emblazoned with some fitting scene and motto, old Harry Lomax, the blacksmith, deputed to that office for the brawny strength of his arms, and yet, if the wind be stirring, evidently staggering under its weight, and finding enough to do to hold it aloft. There it floats its length of blue and yellow, and on its top nods the huge posy of peonies, laburnum flowers, and lilacs, which our own garden has duly furnished. Then comes sounding the band of drums, bassoons, hautboys, flutes and clarionets: then the honorary members – the freeholders of the place – the sage apothecary, and the priest whose sermon says 'be merry' literally, for years, his text being on this day the words of Solomon – 'let us eat and drink, for tomorrow we die'; and then the simple sons of the hamlet, walking as stately and as gravely as they can for the nods and smiles of their neighbours who do not join in the procession, but are all at door and window to see them go by. There they go, passing down the shady lane with all the village children at their heels, to the next hamlet, half a mile off, which furnishes members to the club, and must therefore witness their glory. Now the banner and the gilded tops of their wands are seen glancing between the hedgerow trees; their music comes merrily up the hill; and as it dies away at the next turn, the drumming of distant villages becomes audible in half a dozen different quarters. Then come, one after another, the clubs of the neighbouring hamlets . . .

At the other end of the scale were the massive affiliated orders like the Foresters, with over 667,000 members in 1886, and the Manchester Unity of Oddfellows with over 600,000. There were highly centralised societies, like the Hearts of Oak and the Royal Standard, which operated simple insurance business, devoid of 'friendly spirit'. There were societies associated with particular trades, whose interests spread into the realm of industrial relations. And there were burial societies, designed to protect their members from the ultimate horror of Victorian England – the pauper's grave. Such clubs were particularly strong in Lancashire where, for example, 49,000 of the 80,000 inhabitants of the Poor Law Union of Stockport were insured for burial in 1853–4.

By and large, friendly societies served the two distinct ends of social welfare and social solidarity. The dividing line between survival and disaster was closer to the worker in the eighteenth and nineteenth centuries than today. Prolonged or chronic illness, injury at work or an early or unexpected death could destroy the fragile security of the working man's family, and it was to guard against such disasters that men joined friendly societies. Such social welfare activities were greatly encouraged by the middle classes, for if workers made their own provision against ill-health and unemployment, the burden was removed from the community at large. It was, of course, felt desirable that such associations should be adequately supervised, and to this end a Registrar of Friendly Societies was created in 1846. He came to be described as 'minister of self-help to the whole of the industrious classes', for his administrative functions eventually covered not only friendly societies but also trade unions, savings banks, building societies, and cooperative societies.

Less middle-class sympathy was shown to the social solidarity aspects of the friendly societies, many of which were real societies of friends, much of whose social life revolved around the branch or lodge, with convivial 'box nights' when the funds were counted, monthly meetings at the public house or more elaborate dinners and annual festivals. The Revd Thomas Becher, Prebendary of Southwell, calculated with a sigh in 1823 that all told there would be no less than 190,170 friendly society meetings a year, which, at 6d per head per meeting meant 'that £347,039 a year was thus improvidently spent in ale-houses by the laborious classes'. Such complaints continued, but to little effect. Geoffrey Crossick has noted that in the Deptford, Greenwich and Woolwich areas of Kentish London of which he has made a special study, all but one of the 85 registered societies met in a public house between 1855 and 1870.

The decision of the Rochdale Pioneers in 1844 to pay dividends on purchases marks the transition from the community-building phase of cooperation to that of self-help. As one cooperator put it in the 1860s: 'Modern Co-operation . . . is the working man's lever by which he may rise in the world.' By 1872 there were 927 cooperative branches and 300,000 members, and the turnover of the societies was nearly £10 million. In the following year the North of England Co-operative Wholesale Society (established in 1864) was renamed the Co-operative Wholesale Society (CWS); by 1913 the CWS had 40–50 productive enterprises of its own (from biscuit and corset factories to fruit farms) and supplied the retail stores with many overseas foodstuffs which it imported directly. An annual congress of societies existed from 1869, and in 1890 the Co-operative Union was founded 'to promote the practice of truthfulness, justice, and economy in production and exchange'. Women's role in the movement was extended with the formation of the Women's Co-operative Guild in 1883, which expanded from 50 members at the start to 44,500 by 1919 and 67,000 by 1931.

The development of trade unions

The trade union movement was a response to fundamental changes in the structure of society and the economy rather than simply the result of the congregation of workers in factories, as is sometimes argued. The pioneers were not factory workers, but were mainly skilled artisans anxious to maintain their status and their standard of living in a rapidly changing world. Such men were better able than many to organise. Their skill gave them a scarcity value which allowed them to put pressure on employers, while their earnings were such as would allow them to pay a union subscription. In addition, they possessed in their ranks a greater proportion of literate persons who might be expected to possess organisational skills. Shoemakers had something of a reputation as agitators, and Henry Mayhew wrote of them that they were 'a stern, uncompromising and reflecting race . . . [and] are distinguished for the severity of their manners and habits of thought, and the suspicion that seems to pervade their character'.

Not unexpectedly there were marked regional differences in trade union organis-ation, with craft unionism finding much of its strength in the south, and general unions of factory workers being more characteristic of the north. Even there, the skilled workers took the lead, as in the cotton mills where the élite mule spinners played a particularly active role.

Early trade unions were small. Before the 1820s they were usually organisations of single crafts in single towns, with fewer than 500 members, and very likely with friendly society functions in addition to their trade interests. They were also weak, but their weakness sprang from economic conditions rather than from legal repression. Wage levels were never high enough to allow large funds to be accumu-lated, and even a minor strike could ruin a union for years. Many small, newly established masters entered trade as industry grew apace, and they often undercut in price, overworked their employees and broke apprenticeship agreements. Any downturn in the economy revealed trade union weakness. However, John Rule warns us against over-emphasising the frailty of the early unions. He notes:

> . . . the surviving documentation of intermittent eruptions is interpreted as indicating ephemerality. But continuous association need not imply permanent formal organisation. Members of a trade regularly brought together in workplace or community could acknowledge regular leaders and develop and insist on customary work practices without embedding any of this in formal regulations and procedures. Such a collective presence may have been submerged at times, but did not necessarily disappear. It would not disappear . . . When [the] need arose there is clear enough indication of the availability of collective response from a continuing association which does not always need to have been preserved as a formal organisation.[5]

The Webbs regarded the Combination Acts of 1799–1800 as a 'far-reaching change of policy', but it is now felt that their impact is easily exaggerated. Even before they were passed a substantial body of common law prevented men from combining 'in restraint of trade', and there were over 40 statutes aimed at particular occupations. The large number of acts indicates both a growing problem and the willingness of Parliament to support the labour policy of employers. What was new was that the Combination Acts applied to workmen *as a class*.

The Combination Acts of 1799 and 1800 did not make illegal what had been legal before. Instead, they represented an attempt at administrative reform. Indeed, the new penalties were mild – three months' imprisonment (or two months' hard labour) as against seven years' transportation under the existing law. The acts, by providing for summary conviction, made prosecution easier, but in fact few prosecutions took place. Malcolm Thomis has shown that in Nottingham, for example, at least 50 illegal unions existed during the years of the acts, at least 15 strikes took place, but there were no more than five prosecutions. The Combination Acts did remain something of a threat. As John Rule points out: 'Use of the law was capricious, so unions operated in a context of risk rather than of full and constant constraint.' In 1801, for instance, some of the workers at Messrs Bulmer's shipyard at South Shields sent an anonymous letter to their employer in the course of a strike:

> You Bulmer, if you do not give the carpenters a *guinea* [21 shillings] a week as sure as Hell is hot O before winter is done you must be shot O . . .

It was not difficult to identify some of the striking workmen who, when threatened with prosecution under the Combination Acts, publicly apologised and promised good behaviour in the future. For more serious offences the common law, with its heavier penalties, continued to be applied.

The law exhibited a strong class bias. In 1824 Mr George Ravenhill, a hat manufacturer, gave evidence to the Select Committee appointed, in part, to consider the Combination Acts:

> I believe as far as I can recollect it, that the masters considered the combination, on the part of the journeymen, to be illegal, and that they in consequence determined to prosecute the men for the combination . . .
>
> Then you and the other masters acted under the impression, that it was legal for you to combine to prosecute the men for demanding higher wages, though it was not legal for the men to combine to demand higher wages? – That, I believe, was the impression on the minds of the masters.[6]

9   Symbols of unity

1   Membership certificate of the Amalgamated Society of Engineers, first issued in 1852

2   Membership certificate of the Amalgamated Society of Carpenters and Joiners, 1886

Trade union solidarity was symbolised in a number of ways, but nowhere more vividly than in the elaborate membership certificates of the nineteenth century, and the massive national and branch banners. These symbols, which constitute the heraldry of labour, combine a number of traditions, including the mysteries of the medieval gilds and the secret rituals of the years before unions became legalised.

The respectability of the later New Model Unions is reflected in their emblems. The membership certificate of the Amalgamated Society of Engineers (1) was designed by a noted self-taught artist, James Sharples, whose struggles were immortalised by Samuel Smiles in *Self Help*. This certificate, like others of its kind, displays craft pride, the dignity and worth of the job, and industrial confidence. Six scenes in miniature illustrate the variety of work undertaken by engineers, but alongside this narrative illustration are set numerous allegorical images. At the top is to be found the dove of peace, in a position occupied in many early emblems by the 'all-seeing eye' of providence, a symbol drawn from freemasonry. Beneath the dove an angel holds palms of glory above two engineers. The artisan on the right is receiving a certificate from the figure of Peace, while his colleague on the left is refusing to repair the broken sword offered up by Mars, the god of war. These figures are flanked by others illustrating the allegory of the rods, which symbolise that strength is to be found in combination.

The rods are also to be seen in the certificate of the Amalgamated Society of Carpenters (2). Here they are found providing a seat for Joseph of Nazareth, 'the most distinguished member of the craft and reputed father of the saviour'. Beneath his feet is the union's coat of arms, an almost exact replica of that of the joiners' gild. Columns frame a series of panels illustrating the friendly benefits of the union, while the centre panels show both a bridge arch being centred and the interior of a workshop. Of the latter it was written: 'all the incidents . . . have been carefully drawn on the spot from actual fact with almost photographic exactness'. At the base, like the supporters of a coat of arms, appear two craftsmen surrounded by the tools of their trade. This particular certificate was designed professionally by A. J. Wardby, an exhibitor at the Royal Academy in the 1840s, who also produced certificates for the masons, the bricklayers and the machinists.

Union membership certificates were private documents, designed to be hung in the member's home. The other great symbol of unity was the trade union banner, a very public statement of the union's presence. Picture 3 shows a parade to celebrate the release from prison in 1875 of five cabinet-makers sentenced for peaceful picketing. The leading banner is probably that of the United Society of Coachmakers; its defensive motto is typical of those of the New Model Unions. The two banners behind would appear to be the national banners of the Cabinet Makers. Such elaborate banners were expensive, and probably came from the workshops of George Tutill and Co., a London firm established in 1837 which produced around three-quarters of all trade union banners. New unions, or poor ones, had to settle for something less costly.

3   Demonstration of the London Trades Unions, 1875

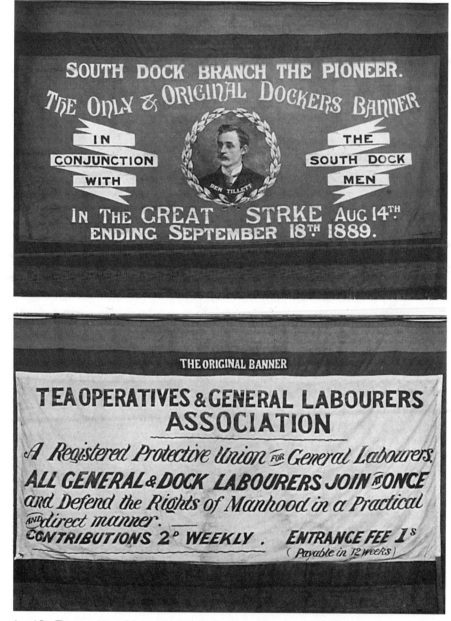

4 and 5   The two sides of the original banner of the Tea Operatives, 1889

Pictures 4 and 5 vividly capture the symbolic importance of banners, which could take on the ritualistic significance of a holy relic or a battle-scarred standard. During the Great Dock Strike of 1889 the new Tea Operatives and General Labourers Association produced a makeshift banner from a linen sheet. This reminder of a famous victory was later sewn to a new silk backing. The original banner was the work of amateurs, and concentration on the form of the letters no doubt accounts for the misspelling of 'strike'!

In fact, the acts of 1799 and 1800 did forbid combinations among the masters, but this aspect remained a dead letter. In 1811, in one of the few recorded actions against masters, evidence was brought before the magistrates that some Nottinghamshire hosiers had combined to reduce wages, but the authorities refused to take action.

Much credit for the repeal of the Combination Acts must go to Francis Place, 'the radical tailor of Charing Cross', although he was not alone in advocating reform. Place was no supporter of trade unions; indeed, he felt that combinations existed because of the law, rather than in spite of it: 'Repeal every troublesome and vexatious enactment, and enact very little in their place. Leave workmen and their employers as much as possible at liberty to make their own bargains in their own way. This is the way to prevent disputes.' Place was encouraged in his views by J. R. McCulloch, the Benthamite economist, and by the Radical MP, Joseph Hume, who in 1824 secured a Select Committee to inquire into matters affecting industry, including the Combination Laws. The committee was packed with supporters of repeal, and Place carefully rehearsed the workmen who were to appear as witnesses. In its report, the Select Committee endorsed the view

> That the laws have not only not been efficient to prevent Combinations, either of masters or workmen; but, on the contrary have, in the opinion of many of both parties, had a tendency, to promote mutual irritation and distrust, and to give a violent character to the Combinations, and to render them highly dangerous to the peace of the community.[7]

The committee recommended not only the repeal of the Combination Acts but an amendment to the common law to allow peaceful combinations. As a result, legislation was passed in 1824 which swept aside all statutes concerning combinations from the reign of Edward I onwards. Francis Place was sanguine about the result:

> Combinations will soon cease to exist. Men have been kept together for long periods only by the oppression of the laws; these being repealed, combinations will lose the matter which cements them into masses, and they will fall to pieces. All will be as orderly as even a Quaker could desire. He knows nothing of the working people who can suppose that, when left at liberty to act for themselves, without being driven into permanent associations by the oppression of the laws, they will continue to contribute money for distant and doubtful experiments, for uncertain and precarious benefits.[8]

He was soon to be proved wrong. Repeal was effected just at the beginning of a period of good trade and rising prices. This resulted in a great outbreak of strikes of which some were violent. The government quickly counterattacked, and it required great effort on the part of Place, Hume and their supporters to prevent the old laws being re-enacted. In the event, a compromise was reached. Repeal was upheld, but provisions against violence and intimidation were made much more stringent. The legal purposes of combinations were narrowed to questions of wages and hours of labour, and 'molesting' or 'obstructing' persons at work was forbidden.

Nevertheless, trade unions and strikes were no longer illegal as such, although the existence of unions was still precarious. For example, if (as frequently happened) union funds were stolen, no action could be taken unless the subterfuge of registering as a friendly society had been adopted. Despite this vulnerability, trade unions developed in the later 1820s in a remarkably ambitious way. Not only were national unions of particular trades established, but national general unions of all trades were attempted. The initiative came from the Lancashire textile industry.

Attempts at general union in Manchester and London in 1818 had been stillborn (a body with the grand title 'Philanthropic Hercules' had been established in the capital) but after a disastrous strike in 1829, delegates from the spinning trade met in the Isle of Man where, under the leadership of John Doherty, they established the Grand General Union of All Operative Spinners in the United Kingdom. The Webbs described Doherty as 'one of the acutest thinkers and stoutest leaders among the workmen of his time'. In Doherty's mind the spinners' union was part of a more ambitious plan. Thus in 1830 he founded in Manchester a general union of all trades which went under the name of the National Association for the Protection of Labour (NAPL). Twenty trades were represented at the inaugural meeting, and soon the number of affiliated societies rose to 150. The union's strength lay mainly in the Lancashire textile towns, although its net was, before long, spread further afield, and by 1831 it claimed a membership of 100,000. The resolutions establishing the union suggest its inherent weakness. Resolution 4 stated: 'That the funds of this Society shall be applied only to prevent reductions of wages, but in no case to procure an advance. Any trade considering their wages too low may exert themselves to obtain such advance, as they may think necessary and can obtain it by their own exertions.'[9] It was difficult to get one trade to support another, and even different sections of the same trade proved reluctant to offer mutual assistance. For example, the Lancashire spinners, engaged in a strike to prevent a reduction of wages, called on their fellow workers for support. But other English workers made only a partial response, while Scottish and Irish spinners failed to comply at all with the request. By March 1831 the strike had failed, breaking the spinners' union, and in consequence weakening the NAPL. A further nail was hammered into its coffin by the secretary absconding with the bulk of the remaining funds. By 1832 the NAPL had ceased to exist as a truly national and general union, and had broken up into a number of separate sections.

The years 1829–34 witnessed ferment in the working-class movement, and although it took a variety of forms, behind much (though not all) of the activity is to be found the influence of one man – Robert Owen. He was born in 1771 and died in 1858, and is one of the most fascinating characters of the nineteenth century. Growing up with the new industrial age, he was one of the first to see its evils. He was a prolific writer, producing over 130 tracts as well as numerous articles in his own periodicals. He was, however, given to repetition, what G. J. Holyoake, one of his disciples, described as 'a recurrency of anterior ideas'. Leslie Stephen, in the *Dictionary of National Biography*, wrote that 'Owen may be described as one of those intolerable bores who are the salt of the earth. To the Whigs and political economists he appeared chiefly as a bore'. Jeremy Bentham was blunt: 'He is always the same – says the same thing over and over again.' But the message, however endlessly repeated, was found highly persuasive by many people.

Owen was a mill-owner, and it was the solution of problems which faced him as an employer which occupied his attention: the creation of an efficient labour force in his factories; and the curse of unemployment and pauperism. The labour force at his New Lanark mills fluctuated around 1,400 to 1,500, making it the largest cotton mill in Britain. Wages were comparatively low, but were offset by superior welfare benefits. Owen provided housing at a reasonable rent, a contributory sickness and superannuation fund, free medical services, and a remarkably innovatory school for children. All of these and other facilities sprang from Owen's overriding belief in the importance of environment on the formation of character. Yet these measures were in no sense charity, for there could be no mistaking that New Lanark was, first and foremost, a profit-making enterprise. This side of his work therefore gained the support of the governing classes, as did – at first – his solutions to the problem of poverty. Gradually, however, the subversiveness of his ideas about community-building became apparent. Very quickly his rich friends deserted him, although his appeal to the working class increased and he became, in the words of Harold Perkin, 'a leader . . . chosen by his followers'. In an address sent to Owen by Sheffield trade unionists in 1834, Ebenezer Elliot wrote: 'You came among us a rich man among the poor and did not call us a rabble. There was no sneer upon your lips, no covert scorn in your tone.' Owen's influence was diffuse for, as J. F. C. Harrison, Owen's biographer, remarks: 'Owenism provided a kind of reservoir from which different groups and individuals drew ideas and inspiration which they then applied as they chose.'

The existing economic system set employer and workers – the providers, respectively, of capital and labour – on a completely different footing, as an articulate silk weaver observed to a parliamentary committee in 1835:

> In the dealings of capitalists with each other, they are generally the one as much in need of buying as the other is of selling, and they can either of them abstain from buying and selling if they consider improper terms are demanded of them. But how stands the case with the labourer? Labour is always carried to the market by those who have nothing else to keep or sell, and now, therefore, must part with it immediately, whether the price pleases them or not, or suffer privations, most likely severe want: labour is always purchased by capitalists, who can abstain from purchasing until they can have it on their own terms, without suffering either privation or want . . . Another [distinction] is that all kinds of commodities (capital or accumulations of the products of labour) having assumed a tangible, visible, substantial form, can be retained if an inadequate price be offered for them . . . many of them will keep any length of time without any damage at all. But how fares labour in this respect? The labour which I ought to perform or might perform this week, if I, in imitation of the capitalist, refuse to part with it, that is, refuse to perform it, because an inadequate price is offered me for it, can I bottle it? Can I lay it up in salt? In what way can I store it, that, in imitation of the capitalist, I may either get the same price for it, or a higher or lower price, as the case may be, at some future period?[10]

Under the prevailing system, the labourer was in an inherently weak position, but against this Owen set the *labour theory of value*, an idea supported by the economists, Adam Smith and David Ricardo. The theory postulated that the measure of the value of a commodity was the quantity of labour incorporated in its production. Owenites developed the 'orthodox' theory in such a way that only the productive labour of the worker counted, and capitalists and shopkeepers were cast in the role of parasites who could be dispensed with. In 1832 Owen opened in London a National Equitable Labour Exchange, soon to be followed by others at Birmingham, Glasgow and elsewhere. In such labour exchanges producers, whether cooperative societies or individual artisans, could directly exchange their products, dispensing with all middlemen. An entrance fee was charged on joining the exchange, and a small commission taken on every article deposited. A contemporary described the system thus:

> A tailor will bring – say, a waistcoat, or topcoat, say it cost four shillings for the cloth, etc. and six hours' labour; we give him a note to this amount; he turns round and sees a pair of shoes; they cost four shillings and six hours' labour; he

gives his labour note the same as we give a shilling over the counter; the shoes are taken away, and the note destroyed, because it ceases to represent real wealth.[11]

Labour notes were also used to give change. However, the system did not work well. The variety of goods produced on a cooperative basis was not large; and, unlike ordinary shops, the exchanges could not control their stocks to fit the demand but had to take what was brought to them. Goods which the exchange sold for less than the private tradesman were quickly disposed of; those which seemed high in price relative to the open market were naturally left unsold.

However, similar ideas did influence the building trades, which were undergoing changes threatening the independence of various building craftsmen. Local trade clubs had long existed among these craftsmen who now turned to national organisation. In 1827 a General Union of Carpenters was formed, and in 1831 the various crafts drew together into a federal body, the Operative Builders' Union. With a peak membership of over 40,000 it leapt to the forefront of the trade union movement. The union was governed by a 'Builders' Parliament' which, in 1833, took up Owen's ideas of cooperation on a grandiose scale. The plan was to take over the entire industry and reorganise it as a Grand National Guild, enthusiasm being such that plans were put in hand to construct a Guildhall in Birmingham to the design of Joseph Hansom (of cab fame). Master builders would be allowed to join the Guild as its servants; but if they refused, they would be forced out of the business, for no one would work for them. Such was the plan: the reality was somewhat different. The employers fought back with lock-outs and the hated 'document' – a formal renunciation of the union which men were forced to sign in order to get their jobs back. By the middle of 1834 the Operative Builders' Union was broken apart into its constituent elements. But its grandiose aims, as well as its federal constitution and its mouthpiece, *The Pioneer*, were taken over by the Grand National Consolidated Trades Union (GNCTU).

The GNCTU constitutes one of the most famous phenomena in British trade union history, coloured both by its associations with Owen and with the 'Tolpuddle Martyrs', and by its contemplation of the weapon of the general strike – the 'Grand National Holiday'. However, its significance has been exaggerated, and the Webbs' figure of 500,000 members at its peak was greatly inflated. Established at a London conference of trade union delegates in February 1834, it had faded away by the end of the year. The GNCTU had been formed largely in response to the Derby 'turn-out', a lock-out of workers in many trades, following a silk workers' strike in November 1833. The men decided to embark on cooperative production, and appealed to other unions for help. It was largely to organise this support that the GNCTU was formed, but after four months' struggle the workers were compelled to return to work on their employers' terms. A second blow was the arrest, a week after its formation, of the Tolpuddle Martyrs, and their subsequent trial and sentence. These six farm labourers, from the village of Tolpuddle near Dorchester, were sentenced to seven years' transportation under an act against the administration of secret oaths, originally passed to deal with the naval mutinies of 1796–7. Despite government fears, there was nothing sinister about such oaths which, along with elaborate ceremonial and regalia, brought some colour and drama into otherwise drab lives. The trial of the unfortunate labourers clearly showed how vulnerable unions were, despite the legislation of 1824–5. Agitation against the men's sentence culminated in a mass procession and demonstration in Copenhagen Fields, London, and the presentation of a petition containing 250,000 signatures. The demonstration had no immediate effect (the transported men had their sentences remitted in 1836) although it set a pattern for peaceful political agitation in the metropolis. The GNCTU achieved nothing, and was soon split by internal strains and dissension among its leaders.

The exaggerated membership figures which the Webbs ascribed to the GNCTU have tended to create a misleading impression of subsequent developments. There was no catastrophic collapse after 1834 as they suggested, for most of the tradition-ally organised craft societies remained in existence, although the trade depression between 1836 and 1842, with its burden of unemployment and wage reductions, put great pressure on labour. The disillusionment of workers was increased by the Poor Law Amendment Act of 1834, and attention was directed back to politics and, in particular, to Chartism.

The mid-Victorian labour movement

The extent to which there was a new movement among trade unions in the 1850s is a matter of some debate, for it is argued that there was a stronger thread of continuity with what had gone before than was once supposed. Again, it was the Webbs who termed unions such as the Amalgamated Society of Engineers (formed in 1851) 'New Model Unions', which they characterised as pacific institutions under con-servative leadership. These they contrasted with the radical, 'revolutionary' Owenite unions of the earlier period. But the Webbs are now felt to have overstated the novelty of the New Model Unions. The evidence indicates that the labour move-ment began to recover in the 1840s, and that unions like the Amalgamated Society of Engineers merely strengthened certain pre-existing characteristics of craft unions.

Nevertheless, the role of the New Model Unions warrants attention, for in the mid-Victorian period the old spirit of political and social revolution faded away, and trade union horizons narrowed somewhat. How far was this the result of a bourgeois plot to wean potential leaders of a radical movement away from the masses, cajoling them into abandoning general class aims in a selfish attempt to make the most of the system? This was certainly part of Lenin's explanation of why the revolution never came in Britain: bourgeois capitalists used their industrial power to buy off and neutralise a key section of the working class. While Marxist historians would argue that this was a betrayal of the struggle against capitalism, more conservative writers applaud this avoidance of revolutionary and utopian dogma in the interest of laying the foundations for legal, peaceful and constructive action. But did it happen?

In order to probe the question a little more deeply, it is necessary to examine some of the divisions within the working class and, in particular, the nature of the 'labour aristocracy' – that band of skilled artisans at the top of the wage-scale. Differ-ences of status between workers had long existed, sometimes at unexpected levels. Cobden, for example, cited the case of the chimney-sweep who refused to allow his daughter to marry a fish-and-chips seller on the grounds that the latter's origins were too lowly! Among craftsmen, also, there were strong status differentials. In *English Pleasure Carriages* (1837), William Bridges Adams, a master coach-builder, described the divisions among carriage artisans at the very beginning of the Victorian era:

> They are not an equal body, but one composed of classes taking rank one after another. In the carriage manufacture it is peculiarly so. The body-makers are the first on the list; then follow the carriage makers; then the trimmers; then the smiths; then the spring-makers; then the wheel-wrights, painters, platers,

brace-makers; and so on. The body-makers are the wealthiest of all, and compose among themselves a species of aristocracy, to which the other workmen look up with feelings, half of respect, and half of jealousy. They feel their importance, and treat the others with various consideration, according to their station. Carriage makers are entitled to a species of condescending familiarity; trimmers are considered too good to be despised; a foreman of painters they may treat with respect; but working painters can at most be favoured with a nod. A smith is considered quite unendurable; – a regular drunken, beer-drinking 'Ironsides'; and a plater is contemptuously denominated 'bead-sticker'. A wheelwright is held to be a kind of rough wood-chopper; and a brace-maker, a mere vulgar 'snob'. The other classes partake of the same feelings of caste in their various proportions. A body-maker is considered a 'good catch' as a husband for the daughter of an ordinary mechanic; and the carriage maker excites much anxious feeling on the part of mothers, who consider marrying to a carriage maker as important a matter as vulgar-minded mothers in the classes just above them consider 'marrying to a carriage'.

The real gulf, however, came between the skilled and the unskilled. Henry Mayhew noted this in 1862. 'The transition from the artisan to the labourer is curious in many respects. In passing from the skilled operative of the west-end to the unskilled workman of the eastern quarter of London, the moral and intellectual change is so great, that it seems as if we were in a new land, and among another race.'

At mid-century a skilled worker's earnings were more than twice those of an unskilled man, and he generally enjoyed greater security as well. The gender-specific language of the previous sentence is deliberate, for one of the noticeable features of skill is that it is a socially constructed concept. A sociologist of our own day makes this observation:

All occupational groups would like to be called skilled, since that is grounds for demanding high wages and is a source of social status. The very label 'skill' is a valuable resource which does not necessarily reflect the technical difficulty of a given job. It is significant that few occupations filled predominantly by women are called 'skilled'.[12]

Maxine Berg has remarked that 'the knacks, the deftness and the special application' with which women worked in many trades were regarded as 'female characteristics' rather than 'skill' – and were rewarded accordingly. As R. Q. Gray points out: 'In many industries, the "aristocrats" were men and the "plebeians" women.'

If labour aristocrats felt themselves to be above the mass of the working class, how did they relate to the class above them? Could a well-paid artisan be mistaken for a member of the middle class? Robert Roberts, that keen observer of life in Salford before the First World War, wrote: 'On Sundays the artisan in his best suit looked like the artisan in his best suit: no one could ever mistake him for a member of the middle classes.' A more pertinent question is whether the labour aristocrat *wanted* to be taken for a member of the middle class. How far did labour aristocrats identify with the middle-class ideology of, for example, hard work, self-help and respectability? There is much evidence that they did, although sometimes with subtle differences. They certainly valued their independence, and abhorred middle-class patronage. This was one reason why there was such a widespread desertion from Mechanics' Institutes once their management became dominated by the middle class. Robert Applegarth, the Carpenters' leader, wrote scathingly:

The fashion among a certain class of politicians is to treat the working man as a peg on which to hang any pet theory or crochet they may happen to have, or as a stepping-stone on which to walk in the direction of their own interests. Such persons dress up a dummy in their own fashion as a tailor dresses his block figure and call it 'the working man'. For this model man they are prepared to legislate, talk, write goody-goody style of books for his edification, tell him what he ought and ought not to do, in fact to do everything for him except one, to treat him as a rational thinking being.[13]

While some members of the working class accepted the ideals and attitudes which we associate with the middle class, it is quite wrong to think of these as being necessarily imposed from above; and there is an erroneous tendency on the part of some writers to see the working class as merely the passive receivers of standards and patterns of behaviour. F. M. L. Thompson puts this point clearly:

It is, indeed, unwarrantably condescending to the humble and anonymous masses to suppose that they were incapable of cultural development except as a result of instruction or coercion from outside . . . There is plenty of evidence that the respectable working classes wished to be respectable not because some middle-class pundit told them to be so, but because they liked it and disapproved of shiftless and sluttish ways. Similarly, the working classes did not need to be told by the middle class that family life was important, that honest toil was better than loafing, or that saving for a rainy day was sensible. Certainly, some middle-class commentators and reformers approved of the family, hard work, and thrift, and made great efforts to promote these things. This does little more than suggest a coincidence of purpose and of values on the part of some of the bourgeoisie and some of the working classes. It does not show that these values, and the institutions which embodied them, such as burial clubs and friendly societies, were alien imports imposed on an unimaginative or reluctant working class.[14]

Labour aristocrats had a keen desire for respectability, but it was one which went along with craft pride. Whereas the middle class looked down upon manual labour, artisans had a pride in the skill of their hands, and showed great scorn for 'pen-pushers' and 'counter-jumpers'. Their belief in self-help was also different, for theirs was of a communal variety, rather than the highly individualistic style of the middle class. Theirs was the self-help of the friendly society, the cooperative store and the trade union. Geoffrey Crossick, who has made a particular study of the labour aristocracy in Kentish London, gives a striking instance of this difference between artisan collective self-help and middle-class individualistic self-help. Samuel Smiles, the author of the bestselling book, *Self Help*, and apostle of that middle-class gospel, lived for 20 years at Blackheath, in the area which Crossick studied. He writes:

Not one occasion has been found upon which any working-class institution in the area sent him an invitation to dinners or festivals, or asked him to give addresses or speeches at meetings. Samuel Smiles might never have existed, let alone lived on their doorstep, for all the notice that the artisans of Kentish London appear to have taken of him.[15]

There was also a greater feeling for the community of neighbours. Indeed, the interviews conducted by the Thompsons of people born between 1872 and 1906 suggest that one of the sharpest single differences between the white-collar and skilled working-class families at that time lay in the degree of intimacy of their relations with neighbours.

Crossick concludes that the labour aristocracy absorbed sufficient of the dominant middle-class ideology of Victorian England to contribute to the stabilisation of society as a whole, but that they remained within the working class, and held to a value system with many working-class characteristics. They did not eschew radicalism, but theirs did not set employee against employer; they set the productive classes as a whole against the lazy and the privileged.

One final note of caution needs to be struck. While it is helpful to distinguish between a labour aristocracy and a wider group of largely unskilled workers, this is not the only division which existed. At certain times and in certain places, religious and ethnic divisions were important, as, for example, in the Lanark coalfield in the 1860s, where trade unionism was associated with Protestant 'Orangeism'.

If we turn to the New Model Unions, we can see that they shared certain essential characteristics, and consisted of a close combination of trade and friendly activities. A wide range of unemployment, sickness and superannuation benefits were provided, the payment of which required a high rate of contribution – around 1 shilling a week – which only the skilled artisans could afford. M. E. Rose reminds us that 'Provision of . . . contributory benefits by trades unions are now seen as a central feature of their work, and not as a mere smokescreen to disguise their industrial activities'.[16] As benefit funds grew large, leaders sought to protect them by avoiding strikes wherever possible. 'Never surrender the right to strike,' said Robert Applegarth, 'but be careful how you use a double-edged weapon.' George Odger, secretary of the Ladies' Shoemakers' Society, observed: 'Strikes in the social world are like wars in the political world; both are crimes unless justified by absolute necessity.' In fact the strike weapon never was surrendered. A more subtle weapon in the battle for advancement was thought to be education. The spread of literacy led to the growth of a vigorous trade union press, with well-produced periodicals such as the *Flint Glass Makers' Magazine*, which once advised its readers to 'get knowledge, and in getting knowledge you get power . . . get intelligence instead of alcohol – it is sweeter and more lasting'. The crafts tried to maintain the scarcity value of their skill by such devices as attempting to restrict apprenticeship, and by encouraging the unemployed artisan to go 'on the tramp, or, in the last resort, to emigrate'. E. J. Hobsbawm has argued that in fact workers with scarce skills failed fully to exploit their position, for they based their calculations on customary wages rather than what the market would bear. He argued that ironfounders and engineers before 1840 lived in a 'wonderful sellers' market', and could have demanded much more than in fact they earned. The lesson was eventually learned as artisans came to temper respectability with strength. A Manchester foundry owner wrote in 1868 that engineers were 'very nice people if they have their own way, but if they have not, they will fight, and they can fight anything and anybody, they are so strong'.

The Amalgamated Society of Engineers was forced into a trial of strength soon after its birth. In January 1852 the engineering employers locked out their men when they refused to accept systematic overtime and an increase in the number of unskilled men in the workshops. The lock-out lasted for three months, but despite generous financial help from men still at work, and from other trade societies, the union was defeated. The men were forced to sign 'the document', but taking the view that this was not binding (having been forced on them) many continued their membership, with the result that the union was not broken, but gradually built up its numerical and financial strength.

It must not be thought that the New Model Unions dominated the whole trade union movement. In many trades, both in London and the provinces, countless small societies still existed. In others, such as mining, district unions remained strong, while in cotton, a loose federal structure was adopted which contrasted with the amalgamation and centralisation of the craft unions. Those workers without the protection of a scarce skill demanded legislative redress of their grievances. The cotton workers pressed for an improvement of factory conditions and the limitation of hours of work; while the miners secured the passage of the Coal Mines Regulation Act in 1860, which improved safety measures, and protected the men from being cheated of their piece-rate wages.

In fact, all unions needed a more satisfactory definition of the law, for although they had ceased to be illegal in 1824, they still remained under many difficulties. In the 1860s, therefore, concerted action was taken to improve the workers' legal position. The body of law – significantly known as 'the law of master and servant' – which governed the relations between an employer and his employees was grossly unjust to the latter. An employer could give evidence against a worker or on his own behalf, but a worker could not give evidence against his employer, nor in his own defence. If an employee broke a contract of employment he could be sent to prison, whereas his employer was only liable to civil proceedings. Furthermore, magistrates developed the habit of threatening strikers with imprisonment for breach of contract if they did not immediately return to work. In the early 1860s it was claimed that over 10,000 cases came before the courts each year. As the law pressed most heavily in Scotland, it is not surprising that agitation for reform began there. In 1864 the Glasgow Trades Council convened a national trade union conference in London, which deserves to be regarded as a forerunner to the Trades Union Congress. A vigorous campaign was launched, petitions were drawn up, and MPs lobbied, with the result that a parliamentary committee was appointed in 1865. On the basis of its report, the Master and Servant Act of 1867 was passed. This remedied the worst abuses, although imprisonment (with or without hard labour) for up to three months could still be imposed for breaches of contract 'of an aggravated character'.

Events of that year conspired to put the unions under great pressure. In contrast to the respectable national unions of the New Model variety were the very small and narrow unions which predominated in the Sheffield cutlery trade. The trade was composed of many small, highly specialised firms, making it difficult for unions to organise. Consequently, arbitrary and violent methods of discipline were imposed on non-union men and upon backsliders. The sanctions were known as 'rattening', and frequently consisted of removing the offending workman's tools, or the drive-band of his machine. In more extreme cases it was known for a can of gunpowder to be placed in the trough of the victim's grinding wheel. There were numerous such incidents in 1865–6, culminating in an outrage in October 1866 when a workman's house was blown up. There was an immediate demand for an inquiry into the 'Sheffield Outrages' as they were called, but, realising that an investigation confined to such seedy matters would be detrimental to the movement as a whole, the London Trades Council successfully demanded an enquiry into the whole field of trade unionism.

There were other clouds on the horizon. In January 1867 the High Court delivered a far-reaching verdict in the case of Hornby v. Close. Since the Friendly Societies Act of 1855, trade unions had sought to protect their funds by depositing their rules with the Registrar of Friendly Societies. Under Section 44 of that act, a registered society could have disputes between its members settled summarily by the magistrates. The Boilermakers' Society was one of many unions which had registered, but when it proceeded against its Bradford branch treasurer for wrongfully withholding a sum of money, to its consternation the magistrates refused to act, on the ground that trade unions were *not* covered by the Friendly Societies Act. The High

Court upheld this view, further declaring that unions were so far 'in restraint of trade' as to be by nature illegal at common law. As Frederick Harrison, a staunch supporter of moderate unions, put it: 'In a word Unionism becomes (if not according to the suggestion of the learned judge – criminal) at any rate something like betting and gambling, public nuisances and immoral considerations – things condemned and suppressed by the law.' Thus, although no one could be prosecuted under the common law merely for forming or joining a trade union, the taint of illegality was held to exist, to the extent that the courts would neither sanction trade unions nor protect them. This was a body-blow, for anyone could make off with union funds and the courts would do nothing about it. A second adverse court decision (R. v. Druitt) came in June. In this action, against the journeyman tailors following a strike, the courts declared that even offering 'black looks' could be interpreted as illegal intimidation.

All this made the outcome of the Royal Commission vital. Trade unions rose in their own defence, but the leadership of the movement was disrupted. On one side were the 'Junta' (the Webbs' name, yet again!), which consisted of the officers of a number of New Model Unions who regularly met together in London. These included Robert Applegarth of the Carpenters, William Allan of the Engineers, Edward Coulson of the Bricklayers, George Odger of the Ladies' Shoemakers and Daniel Guile of the Iron Founders. They did not go unchallenged, for there was a rival group led by George Potter, a younger and more flamboyant man who had strong support both in London and the provinces.

It was the Junta which came to the fore. First, they sought to influence the membership of the Royal Commission. The government would not agree to a working man as commissioner, but they did accept the Junta's nomination of Frederick Harrison. With his presence, supported by Thomas Hughes, the Christian-socialist author of *Tom Brown's Schooldays*, the unions were sure of at least two friends out of the 11 members.

The conduct of the unions' case was left largely to Applegarth, who answered no fewer than 633 questions, many of them fed to him by Harrison and Hughes. His was the personality designed to win support for the unions, for, as the Webbs pointed out, one of his outstanding gifts was 'instinctively to make use of those arguments which were best fitted to overcome the prejudices and disarm the criticism of middle-class opponents'. The strategy was to divert attention away from the Sheffield Outrages and all forms of militant unionism, and to concentrate on the more moderate; and Applegarth and his supporters painted a picture of the unions as sober, businesslike and utterly respectable. The members of the commission fell for the bait, bringing in actuarial experts to show that the unions' friendly benefits could not be maintained in the long run. This kind of technical question the unionists were only too happy to discuss, for it kept the commissioners from probing too deeply into more contentious issues.

The Royal Commission produced both a Majority Report and a Minority Report signed by Harrison, Hughes and the Earl of Lichfield. So successfully did the trade unionists play their cards that even the Majority Report recommended that, under certain conditions, they should be made legal. Trade union funds should only be protected, however, if the union rules were free from such restrictive practices as the prohibition of piece-work or the limitation of apprentices and the use of machinery. Opposition was bound to be strong to these prohibitions, for the New Model Unions depended very much on such restrictive practices. The Minority Report suited them better, for it simply proposed that all legal discrimination against workers or trade unions should be repealed.

Not until February 1871 did the government introduce a bill. Legal recognition would be given to trade unions, and their funds might be protected by registration under the Friendly Societies Act. However, several penal clauses were included against all forms of 'molestation', 'obstruction' and 'intimidation', and even against peaceful picketing which had been legalised in 1859. In some respects the Junta were hoist with their own petard – if the unions were really as respectable as had been claimed, there could be no objection to such clauses. But objection there was; and a Trades Union Congress which met in March lobbied MPs for amendment to the bill. The government would agree to one compromise; the separation of the penal clauses into a separate bill. Thus it was that *two* acts were passed in 1871: the Trade Union Act, which legalised unions; and the Criminal Law Amendment Act which curtailed their actions. This was a gain of sorts for, in future, trade unionists would be able to concentrate their efforts on the latter act while accepting the former. The passing of this legislation marked the end of the Junta, for a parliamentary committee, which the Trades Union Congress (TUC) set up at its March meeting, could provide a more representative leadership. The Junta also lost Robert Applegarth when he resigned from his secretaryship of the Amalgamated Society of Carpenters. In May 1871 he was appointed to the Royal Commission on Contagious Diseases, thus becoming the first trade unionist ever to be offered such an appointment. But his union refused to allow him to attend the Commission's meetings during office hours. Concludes Henry Pelling: 'To be forced out of the movement in this way was a sad fate for a man who had contributed more than anyone else to making unionism acceptable to the public opinion of the upper classes.'

The Criminal Law Amendment Act soon began to bite – six gas fitters were sentenced to 12 months' imprisonment in 1872, while 16 farm labourers' wives were sentenced to short periods of hard labour in 1873 for 'intimidating' blacklegs. The failure of the Liberals to take further action favourably to amend the laws encouraged the parliamentary committee of the TUC to pursue a more independent line in the 1874 general election, and trade unionists were encouraged to give their vote to any Conservative candidate who gave more favourable replies to a series of 'Test Questions'. Working-class voters undoubtedly helped to defeat the Liberals and to return the Conservatives to power. At this election, however, two trade unionist candidates, Alexander McDonald and Thomas Burt (both miners) were returned to Westminster, fighting with Liberal support and becoming the first 'Lib-Lab' MPs, as they were called.

The new Conservative government speedily appointed a Royal Commission on the Labour Laws, but trade unionists feared that the whole question would be opened up again and that the Trade Union Act of 1871 might be placed in jeopardy. The parliamentary committee of the TUC therefore boycotted the Commission, which was rendered ineffective. However, when the government produced its draft legislation in June 1875 it was apparent that the principal demands of the unionists would be substantially met. The Master and Servant Act of 1867 was replaced by the Employers and Workmen Act (note the change of terminology) which made the penalty for breach of contract by either side the payment of civil damages. The Criminal Law Amendment Act of 1871 was replaced by the Conspiracy and Protection of Property Act. Henceforth the law of conspiracy was not to apply to trade disputes unless the actions complained of were criminal in themselves; and questions of intimidation and violence were left to the ordinary criminal law. Peaceful picketing was expressly legalised. This new-found legal status and legal indemnity in trade disputes protected the unions for the next generation, until it was seriously challenged in 1901.

New trends in trade unionism from the 1870s

In the years of the mid-Victorian economic boom, workers had (on the whole) tried to work within the framework of the capitalist economy, believing that, as Britain grew richer and richer, the lot of the working man would improve. The revolutionary fervour of the Owenite period waned, and the resignation of the workers led Friedrich Engels to dub England 'the most bourgeois of all nations', and to accuse the English proletariat of becoming more and more bourgeois. From 1849 until his death in 1883, Karl Marx lived in London (he did much of his research for *Capital* in the library of the British Museum); but so little known was he that *The Times* only heard of his death when its Paris correspondent telegraphed the news. It is true that the International Working Men's Association ('The First International') was formed in London in 1864, but only about 50,000 British trade unionists out of a total membership of 800,000, were affiliated, and it had little ideological impact on the British labour movement as a whole. The 'proletarian revolution' which Marx believed to be imminent showed no signs whatsoever of actually starting among the cautious, respectable trade unionists of this era. The prominent activist, George Howell, wrote of the First International: 'The attempt to engraft continental notions on English ideas is absurd and certain of failure – the talk about 'proletarians' and 'solidarity' is confusing to the English mind; they are big words which do not convey a single idea to the British workman.'

From the 1880s, however, the current of socialism ran stronger than ever, and although the socialists were small in number – perhaps 2,000 in the 1880s, and 20,000–30,000 in 1900 – their influence was widespread, especially in London and the north. Edward Carpenter, a leading activist, reflected in 1916 that 'the general teaching and ideals of the movement have permeated society in the most remarkable way, and have deeply infected the views of all classes, as well as general literature and even municipal and imperial politics'. There was Marxist socialism, with the Social Democratic Federation (SDF), founded in 1884. There was Fabian socialism, with the Fabian Society founded in the same year. There was a vigorous revival of Christian socialism at the end of the century. William Morris split the Socialist League away from the SDF in 1884, and in 1890 wrote *News From Nowhere*, a utopian socialist novel in which he condemned the uses made of machinery by capitalism and extolled the pride of the worker in his craftsmanship. Robert Blatchford reached out to others through his popular political journalism, especially in *The Clarion* which he founded in 1891. Yet all was not sweetness and light, and there were bloody riots in Trafalgar Square and elsewhere in 1886–7. There was an explosion of new unionism after the London Dock Strike in 1889. On the political front, 1892 witnessed the election of three independent working-class MPs, including Keir Hardie. In the following year the Independent Labour Party was formed. And the decision of the TUC in 1899 to encourage the election of independent working-class MPs led, in February 1900, to the formation of the Labour Representation Committee which, in turn, led to the Labour Party. It can be seen, then, that the middle years of quiescence were followed by an era of great activity.

When socialism returned to Britain, it was middle-class intellectuals who reintroduced it. In 1880 a wealthy Old Etonian, H. M. Hyndman, stopped off in Salt Lake City while on a tour of America. There he read a French translation of Marx's *Capital* (it was not available in an English translation until 1887), and was converted to its doctrines. Returning to England, he founded the Democratic Federation in 1881, which changed its name to the Social Democratic Federation three years later. At first Hyndman planned that his new organisation should support working-class agitation on the old Chartist lines; but by 1883 it had become a definitely socialist body, demanding such things as the nationalisation of banks, railways and the land, state-aided housing, universal free education and school meals, and the eight-hour day.

The SDF succeeded in recruiting many of the abler young artisans in London, including Tom Mann, a member of the Amalgamated Society of Engineers, who had experienced severe spells of unemployment. In 1886, at the age of 30, Mann published a pamphlet which conveyed an entirely new concept of trade unionism and castigated the established leaders of the movement:

> To Trade Unionists, I desire to make a special appeal. How long, *how long* will you be content with the present half-hearted policy of your unions? I readily grant that good work has been done in the past by the unions, but, in Heaven's name, what good purpose are they serving now? All of them have large numbers out of employment even when their particular trade is busy. None of the important societies have any policy other than of endeavouring to keep wages from falling. The true Unionist policy of *aggression* seems entirely lost sight of; in fact the average unionist of today is a man with a fossilized intellect, either hopelessly apathetic or supporting a policy that plays directly into the hands of the capitalist exploiter.[17]

A new movement was afoot which, unlike the New Model Unions, was no mere historian's label, for the distinctions between 'Old' and 'New Unionism' (as the new movement came to be called) were clearly evident to contemporaries. New Unionism involved not just the creation of new unions among workers previously unorganised, but a new spirit which pervaded old, established unions and newly founded unions alike. This spirit was reflected in a number of things: a more militant outlook; a greater readiness to employ coercion against non-unionists and blacklegs; and a tendency to look to Parliament to solve many of labour's problems. New Unionism was also characterised by an increased membership of low-paid, unskilled men, whose contributions were kept low and to whom only 'fighting' benefits were offered.

It is misleading, however, to think of New Unionism simply in terms of unskilled labourers. For a start, while the definition of 'labourer' varied from industry to industry, it would seem to exclude certain groups such as seamen, gas stokers, carters and tramwaymen who, although neither labourers nor unskilled, were swept up in the new movement. Second, Hobsbawm has demonstrated that while contemporary belief clung to a sharp division between 'skilled' and 'unskilled' and between 'artisan' and 'labourer', the facts suggested otherwise. There was a gradually ascending scale akin to our own division of 'unskilled', 'semi-skilled' and 'skilled'. The traditional division emphasised the difference between the genuine maker of things and the man who merely fetched and carried for him. 'Builders and engineers,' says Hobsbawm, 'boilermakers and tailors might still reasonably imagine that they were capable of making houses, machines, ships and clothes without the convenient, but not indispensable, help of the labourer; as a hotel chef could, at a pinch, produce a dinner without the help of the potato-peeler and bottle-washer.' But the conventional picture was made less and less real by every technical and industrial change. As methods involving a division of labour spread through a variety of industries, old distinctions of skill became increasingly unreal.

The response of the leaders of established craft unions was to attempt to reinforce the old restrictive barriers against intruders, rather than to spread unionism to men outside the charmed ranks. Hence, by the late 1880s, the excluded 'labourers' included an increasing number of men capable of being organised into unions, and who often possessed considerable bargaining strength. Many employers realised that modern factory methods made a stable labour force desirable, so that even the 'general labourer' came to have a 'special value'. When such men realised that by withdrawing their labour they could cause loss to their employers, the new unions had an increasingly large pool for recruitment.

It is often implied that the New Unionism sprang from the London Dock Strike of 1889, but although this gave a great fillip to the movement, there had been a number of attempts to organise workers outside the craft unions back in the 1870s. Joseph Arch's National Agricultural Labourers' Union of 1872 was part of this trend, and there were moves in other areas at about the same time. Many dockers came to be organised in the Labour Protection League which was founded in the East End of London in 1871. By April 1872 some 1,200 members had been enrolled, and rapid growth thereafter took the membership to a reported 30,000 in October. Not all were port workers, for included in the ranks of the union were builders' and engineers' labourers, dustmen and scavengers, and some coal porters and carmen. During the depressed years of the later 1870s the strength of the League was gradually worn away, although a foothold was maintained with some port workers such as the more skilled stevedores.

The downturn in the economy caused other new unions to suffer the same fate. The Amalgamated Society of Railway Servants (1871) shrank from over 17,000 to fewer than 6,000, pursuing narrow friendly benefit ends. The Amalgamated Miners' Association (1869) died out, and the Miners' National Union (1863) survived only in Northumberland and Durham.

Two factors brought about renewed growth: the revival of trade in 1887 and the efforts of socialist activists. The winter of 1885–6 was exceptionally severe, and February temperatures were the lowest for 30 years. Outdoor work was practically at a standstill, and distress was particularly severe in the docks and the building industry. A meeting of the unemployed in Trafalgar Square on 8 February attracted around 20,000, many of whom were provoked by the SDF into attacking property in the wealthy West End. Such were middle-class fears of revolution, that in the 48 hours after 'Bloody Monday' the Lord Mayor's Relief Fund for the Unemployed jumped from £3,000 to £80,000. Tension remained high, and 1887 witnessed 'Bloody Sunday', 13 November, when troops were called in to clear demonstrators from Trafalgar Square. J. W. Mackail, the biographer of William Morris, wrote: 'No one who ever saw it will ever forget the strange and indeed terrible sight of that grey winter day, the vast sombre-coloured crowd, the brief but fiery struggle at the corner of the Strand, and the river of steel and scarlet that moved slowly through the dusky swaying masses when two squadrons of the Life Guards were summoned up from Whitehall.' Morris himself wrote a moving 'death song' for a demonstrator who died from injuries received at the hands of the police that day:

> We asked them for a life of toilsome earning,
> They bade us bide their leisure for our bread;
> We craved to speak to tell our woeful learning:
> We come back speechless, bearing back our dead.
> Not one, not one, nor thousands must they slay,
> But one and all if they would dusk the day.

There were many links between socialists and the new movement in the unions. Eleanor Marx-Aveling (daughter of Karl Marx) was involved with the gasworkers, for example, and H. H. Champion, one-time Secretary of the SDF, who had stood trial after the 1886 riots, helped to organise the dockers. Champion was an individualistic ex-army officer described as 'the brains of the Dock Strike'.

It was Champion who suggested that Mrs Annie Besant, free-thinker and Fabian socialist, should take up the cause of the match-girls. The strike of London match-girls in 1888 had a significance out of all proportion to its small scale. The makers of lucifer matches were poorly paid, worked in appalling conditions, and were vulnerable to 'phossy jaw' (phosphorus necrosis) – a gangrene of the bone caused by the fumes of the phosphorus used in the matches. Mrs Besant drew attention to the girls' plight in her weekly journal, *The Link*, and did not hesitate to use the most emotive language in order to drum up support for them:

> Do you know that girls are used to carrying boxes on their heads until the hair is rubbed off and the young heads are bald at fifteen years of age? Country clergymen with shares in Bryant and May's, draw down on your knee your fifteen-year old daughter; pass your hand tenderly over the silky beauty of the black, shining tresses.[18]

Nearly 700 girls came out on strike against their employers (who were not the worst of the match manufacturers, by any means). With a fighting fund of £400, of which George Bernard Shaw was treasurer, and with public opinion on the girls' side, the employers were forced to give in after a fortnight.

Socialists also assisted the gasworkers to organise. The process of gas-making was a continuous one, with teams of men working arduous shifts of 12 hours (or 18 at the weekend changeover). Technical progress in the industry had been slow, so maintenance of the statutory gas pressure depended very much on the exertions of the stokers and firemen. Letting the pressure fall or, worse still, letting lights go out, was something the companies could not afford, especially in the early 1880s when they were anxiously watching the advances of a potential rival – electricity. Two factors had kept the gasworkers unorganised, although there had been a short flurry of activity in the early 1870s. First, work was extremely casual, for with a winter load three to five times greater than that of the summer, the winter labour force was double that of the summer months. Second, there was the weight of tradition which assigned stokers to the class of 'unorganisable' unskilled labourers.

Early in 1889 Will Thorne, a stoker at the Beckton gasworks in east London, launched the National Union of Gasworkers and General Labourers. Thorne, almost illiterate, was a member of the SDF, where he gained the support of fellow members, including Tom Mann, John Burns and Eleanor Marx-Aveling (who helped with the clerical work). Within four months the union had 20,000 members, and Thorne felt strong enough to put forward his demands for a three-shift system of working, which would reduce the basic working day to eight hours. To everyone's surprise the gas companies quickly gave way, giving the workers a victory which Mann declared 'put older and larger unions to shame'.

After the revolt of the gasworkers came that of the London dockers. Their labour was also casual; indeed, many men worked in the gasworks in the winter, when the trade of the port was slack, and became dockers in the summer months. In the age of sail, the availability of work in the docks depended very much on the wind. Henry Mayhew observed in the early 1860s:

> At one of the docks alone I found that 1,823 stomachs would be deprived of food by the mere chopping of the breeze . . . That the sustenance of thousands of families should be as fickle as the very breeze itself; that the

weathercock should be the index of daily want or daily ease to such a vast number of men, women, and children, was a climax of misery and wretchedness that I could not have imagined to exist . . .

He estimated that 12,000 persons depended on the docks for work, of which there was sufficient for 4,000. A generation later, in 1891, Charles Booth found 21,353 dockers regularly competing for work which he concluded would provide regular employment for 12,500 or, if sickness were taken into account, comparatively regular work for 16,000. Mayhew described the degrading nature of the scramble for jobs:

> As the hour approaches eight, you know by the stream pouring through the gates, and the rush towards particular spots, that the 'calling foremen' have made their appearance, and that the 'casual men' are about to be taken on for the day.
> Then begins the scuffling and scrambling, and stretching forth of countless hands high in the air, to catch the eye of him whose nod can give them work. As the foreman calls from a book of names, some men jump up on the back of others, so as to lift themselves high above the rest and attract his notice. All are shouting, some cry aloud his surname, and some his christian name; and some call out their own names to remind him that they are there. Now the appeal is made in Irish blarney; and now in broken English.
> Indeed, it is a sight to sadden the most callous to see thousands of men struggling there for only one day's hire, the scuffle being made the fiercer by the knowledge that hundreds out of the assembled throng must be left to idle the day out in want. To look in the faces of that hungry crowd is to see a sight that is ever to be remembered . . . Until we saw with our own eyes this scene of greedy despair, we could not have believed that there was so mad an anxiety to work, and so bitter a want of it among so vast a body of men.[19]

The growing use of steam in the late 1860s and 1870s affected the organisation of dock labour, for steamships imposed a quite different demand for casual labour from that of sailing ships. With sail, trade tended to be seasonal and, as such, could be predicted within rough limits. And when a ship came into port there was usually a certain amount of refitting to be done, with the consequence that unloading proceeded at a more relaxed pace. Men were generally hired by the day, and time was generally allowed off for beer in the morning and afternoon. Steamships might arrive at the docks at any time of the year, and their economic use required a speedy turn-round, measured in days rather than weeks. The dock companies therefore abandoned employment by the day; men were not engaged until they were needed, were paid by the hour and were paid off once the work was done.

A small strike had broken out in the West India Docks at the very moment of the gasworkers' victory, and it quickly spread, until the whole port of London was at a standstill. The men demanded 6d an hour (the 'dockers' tanner') instead of 5d; special payment for overtime; and a minimum period of employment of half a shift (four hours). With the exception of the more skilled stevedores who loaded the ships, the majority of dock workers at this time were outside any union. Only the small Tea Porters' and General Labourers' Union, founded by Ben Tillett in 1887, catered for them. However, during the dispute the strikers flooded in and Tillett, along with Tom Mann, John Burns and Tom McCarthy of the stevedores, set out to organise the fight. The dockers publicised their cause with enormous flair, and they quickly secured immense public sympathy – and cash. In this they were helped by their orderly behaviour, as well as by the revelations of Charles Booth's survey of the *Life and Labour of the People in London*, the first part of which had just been published.

A crisis was reached after two weeks, however, as blacklegs were brought in and as strike funds ran low. With some misgivings the leaders decided to call for a general strike, but the call was withdrawn when help came from an unexpected quarter – Australia. The dockers of Brisbane – where workers were better organised than in Britain – sent £150 for the strike fund. Although this initial sum was small, it gave the leaders fresh heart. Altogether, over £30,000 came in aid from Australia, a sum equal to more than half of the whole strike fund. The strikers held on until, after a month's stoppage, a settlement was secured by a committee of conciliation, which had among its members Cardinal Manning. All the major demands were granted, including the 'dockers' tanner' and overtime payment. A permanent dockers' union was established, with Tillett as secretary and Tom Mann as president, and by the end of November it had enrolled 30,000 members.

The London Dock Strike seemed to symbolise the New Unionism. It was the biggest dispute of the year, and almost 700,000 working days were lost. However, the next nine years saw 11 stoppages which were more substantial, including the miners' lock-out of 1893, which lasted four times as long as the London Dock Strike and cost 30 times as many working days. There was a great revival of union membership. From about 750,000 at the end of 1888, numbers rose to over 2 million in 1901.

Inevitably, the employers launched a counterattack which, together with a recurrence of depression in 1892, slowed down the initially spectacular growth. The gasworkers lost many of their gains, and in 1893 a seamen's strike at Hull, violent and lasting seven weeks, was soundly defeated. *The Times* wrote: 'At Hull, as elsewhere, the New Unionism has been defeated. But nowhere has the defeat been so decisive, or the surrender so abject.'

In fact, the New Unionism was far from defeated, although many unions abandoned their initial aim to be general unions of workers in different trades, and came to depend upon their foothold in particular industries or large works. They thereby came to recruit a more stable and regular type of worker than they had originally envisaged. However, the New Unionism still displayed important differences from the old. The leaders were often a generation younger than those of the old craft unions, and they remained more militant and aggressive. They even *looked* different, as John Burns noted:

> Physically, the 'old' unionists were much bigger than the new . . . A great number of them looked like respectable city gentlemen; wore very good coats, large watch chains, and high hats and in many cases were of such splendid build and proportions that they presented an aldermanic, not to say a magisterial, form and dignity. Amongst the new delegates not a single one wore a tall hat. They looked workmen; they were workmen. They were not such sticklers for formality or court procedure, but were guided more by common sense.[20]

Although the match-girls had won a noted victory in 1888, the general position of women in industry was weak. In 1885 the TUC accepted the principle of equal pay for equal work, although this had little practical effect. In 1895, 80 per cent of all women trade unionists were in the cotton industry. As Clapham commented: 'Outside Lancashire . . . the woman trade unionist was rather a curiosity.' She remained so until the First World War.

The spread of unionism to less skilled workers increased the importance o picketing during strikes, for whereas artisans were difficult to replace, the effectiveness of strikes involving unskilled workers depended on the strikers' ability to exclude blacklegs. Strikes therefore tended to become more violent, partly because employers (who were as unused as the workers to the new unions) were determined to smash them. Public opinion also waned after its peak at the time of the London Dock Strike, and *The Quarterly Review* came to describe the leaders of the New Unions as 'our national Mafia'.

The courts reflected the changes in public opinion, and a number of hostile decisions undermined the legal position of the unions. In a picketing case in 1899, one High Court judge declared: 'You cannot make a strike effective without doing more than what is lawful.'

The New Unionism did not leave the craft unions entirely unaffected; and their membership, too, increased. There were three reasons for this. First, temporary economic prosperity favoured their growth just as much as it did that of the new unions. Second, the success of the new unions encouraged non-union craftsmen to join the societies for which they were eligible. Third, unions in some industries opened their ranks to less skilled workers. The Amalgamated Society of Engineers, for example, faced with the introduction of new machinery such as the capstan- and turret-lathes manned by only semi-skilled machine-minders, reduced its entrance requirements in 1892, and the launching of an 'All Grades Programme' by the Amalgamated Society of Railway Servants in 1897 doubled its membership in the same year.

In some respects there was a closing of ranks towards the end of the century, which has led some historians to argue that it was then, rather than earlier, that a true working-class consciousness developed. Part of the cause is to be found in changes in the strata above. The expansion of white-collar occupations strengthened the lower middle class, while suburbanisation enabled such people to distance themselves from labour aristocrats, whose manual work they despised. With their aspirations curtailed, the labour aristocracy came increasingly to see that their political interests lay with those of the working class as a whole.

From Taff Vale to the First World War

The trade union legislation of 1871 and 1875 had been passed before the tide of New Unionism swelled, and legal decisions of the 1890s made the position of trade unions less and less clear. Matters came to a head with a court case in 1901. The South African War was then approaching its climax, and coal prices were running high. The railwaymen of South Wales therefore chose this moment to improve their lot and to gain union recognition. Attention was focused on the Taff Vale line, which was the essential link between the steam-coal collieries and the ports. Relations on this line had been bad for some time. Men claimed that uniforms due to them were not delivered and that 'they had to go around looking more like tramps than anything else'. Of more serious concern were charges that a signalman, who had previously led a movement for higher wages, had been victimised. The general manager of the line, Ammon Beasley, was, according to an impartial observer, one who 'loved litigation for its own sake'. When more than 1,000 men came out and secured the support (somewhat half-hearted) of the Amalgamated Society of Railway Servants, he prepared for battle. Professional blacklegs were called in, 400 summonses were issued against men who had come out without giving proper notice (of whom 60 were fined £4); two men were imprisoned for depriving a railway watchman of his hand lamp and whistle; and strikers in railway cottages were served with eviction orders. Beasley applied for an injunction, not just against the leaders, but against the union as a whole. It was granted; but then withheld by the Court of Appeal. However, the House of Lords (to which Beasley took the matter) restored the initial decision. There the five Law Lords agreed unanimously with the opinion of the Lord Chancellor, Lord Halsbury, that 'If the Legislature has created a thing which can own property, which can employ servants, and which can inflict injury, it must be taken . . . to have impliedly given the power to make it sueable in a Court of Law for injuries purposely done by its authority and procurement'. This decision opened the door for Beasley to sue the union for damages and, in December 1902, the union was obliged to pay the Taff Vale Railway Company £23,000. By the time the union had paid costs it faced a total bill of £42,000.

This was a crippling blow to trade unionism in general, and as neither the Liberal nor the Conservative Parties seemed willing to amend the law, many unionists were won over to the idea of independent representation for the working man. Before 1900 those trade unionists who sat in Parliament had almost invariably been 'Lib-Labs' – protégés of the Liberal Party. In February 1900, on a day of 'dreary, dripping rain', a Labour Representation Committee had been formed by the TUC, but the response from unions had been slight. The Taff Vale decision changed all this, and by 1903–4 a total of 165 trade unions had affiliated, with a combined membership of nearly a million. In the 1906 general election the Labour Representation Committee secured 29 seats in the House of Commons, and in the same year it changed its name to the Labour Party.

Not until after the general election was the report issued of a Royal Commission appointed by the Conservatives to consider the legal position of the unions. No trade unionist had been given a seat, and the unions had refused to give evidence. The report advocated not legal immunity for trade unions, but statutory recognition of them as legal entities, together with a separation of benefit funds from general and strike funds. Only benefit funds were recommended to be immune from actions for damages. The new Liberal government introduced legislation on the lines of the report, but the Labour Party, with full union backing, pressed for its alternative bill. The government gave way, and adopted Labour's bill which passed into law as the Trade Disputes Act of 1906. Section Four of the Act gave the unions indemnity against legal proceedings:

> An action against a trade union, whether of workmen or masters, or against any members or officials thereof on behalf of themselves and all other members of the trade union, in respect of any tortious act alleged to have been committed by or on behalf of the trade union, shall not be entertained by any court.

A 'tortious act' is any civil wrong (as distinct from a criminal act) other than a breach of contract. This section therefore placed trade unions in a privileged position at law, for their funds were protected against civil proceedings.

If the Taff Vale case had convinced trade unionists of the need for an independent Labour Party in Parliament, the Osborne Judgment of 1909 convinced many socialists of their need of trade union financial support. By a coincidence both cases involved the Amalgamated Society of Railway Servants (ASRS). It has to be remembered that political campaigns were expensive; and also that, before 1911, MPs were unpaid. Such facts pressed heavily on Labour, denied the support of wealthy backers as enjoyed by the Conservatives and Liberals. Many trade unions gave financial aid to the Labour Party, but a court action was taken by W. V. Osborne, a member of the ASRS who, as a Liberal, objected to the assistance which his union gave to

Labour. The case went to the House of Lords which decided, in 1909, that the support of a political party went beyond the powers granted to trade unions by the law. Not surprisingly, the unions reacted strongly to this decision; but not until 1913 was the Trade Union Act passed, restoring some of the lost ground. Henceforth, where a majority of members voted in favour of a political levy, a union could spend money on political purposes provided it was kept in a separate fund and individual members were free to 'contract out' of payment.

The years leading up to the First World War were ones of great unease, with trouble in Ireland and agitation by workers and women at home. Whether (as George Dangerfield suggested some 60 years ago in *The Strange Death of Liberal England*) there was any connection between the crisis areas remains controversial, although orthodox opinion tends to disparage the idea. Certainly, there were identifiable economic reasons why there should have been so much labour unrest. The rapid expansion of trade between 1909 and 1913 raised the expectations of trade unionists, while the reappearance of full employment strengthened those general unions which had survived after the rapid expansion of 1889–92. For example the Workers' Union, which enrolled just over 4,000 members within a year of its foundation in 1898, had only 4,500 members in 1910, but 143,000 in 1914.

There was, however, a new philosophy of militancy, in the form of syndicalism. This, said *The Times* in April 1912,

> is a banner which attracts the youthful and pugnacious and those who are tired alike of the older trade unionism, with its conciliation agreements, and of the older Socialism, with its politics. Syndicalism enlists the spirit of the one by advocating more complete organisation and greater solidarity, and that of the other by preaching the class war with the promise of a more speedy and vigorous campaign fought with the weapon so forged . . . All who march under the banner are not necessarily devotees of the cause or convinced believers in all or any of the doctrines it represents. Most of them are rather willing to give it a trial. Its hold is, therefore, indefinite and hard to gauge; but for the same reason its potentialities are great.

Syndicalism had its origins in France, where the philosopher Georges Sorel was its chief exponent; and it was influential in the United States where the Industrial Workers of the World (IWW) was established in 1905. Pledged to 'One Big Union' of all workers, the IWW advocated direct action to bring about social change. Syndicalist ideas were brought to Britain by Tom Mann, veteran of the London Dock Strike. He was away from Britain between 1901 and 1910, and while in Australia and New Zealand was confirmed in his view that industrial action offered a better hope for change than political activity. On his return he founded a monthly magazine, *The Industrial Syndicalist*, which ceased publication the following year when Mann became deeply involved in the seamen's strike. However, in 1912 he became associated with a new venture, *The Syndicalist*. In its issue of March–April 1912, Mann outlined the aims of syndicalism:

> Syndicalism means the control of industry by 'Syndicates', of Unions of Workers, in the interests of the entire community . . . The syndicalist of today . . . refuses to play at attempts at social reform through and by means of Parliaments, these institutions being entirely under the control of the plutocracy, and never tolerating any modification of conditions in the interest of the working class, save with the ulterior motive of the more firmly entrenching themselves as the ruling class . . . [The] object aimed at by the Syndicalists is

the control of each industry by those engaged in it in the interests of the entire community. This will be followed by the ownership of the tools and other means of production and transportation jointly by the industrial community. Strikes are mere incidents in the march towards control of industry and ownership of the tools of production. 'Sabotage', 'Ca'Canny', and irritation strikes are mere incidentals in the progress onwards . . . The watchwords are INDUSTRIAL SOLIDARITY and DIRECT ACTION. By these means we can and will solve unemployment, cure poverty, and secure to the worker the *full reward of his labour.*

Two months previously *The Syndicalist* had published an 'Open Letter to British Soldiers', urging them to cease 'being the willing tools any longer of the Master Class'. For this Mann and others were imprisoned under an Act of 1797, last used in 1804. There had already been violent scenes between troops and strikers, especially in South Wales where syndicalism had taken its firmest roots. In 1910 a miners' strike made 30,000 idle, and at Tonypandy troops with fixed bayonets were used against the strikers. Nevertheless, the strike dragged on well into the autumn of 1911, and in 1912 was followed by a national miners' strike which affected well over a million men throughout the country. In that year alone, 41 million working days were lost, compared with an average of 7 million over the previous 20 years.

The Miners' Next Step, published by the South Wales Miners' Federation in 1912, clearly stated syndicalist ideas in the context of militant unionism in the Welsh coalfields:

Alliances are to be formed, and trades organisations fostered, with a view to steps being taken, to amalgamate all workers into one National and International union, to work for the taking over of all industries, by the working men themselves . . .

It will be noticed that nothing is said about Conciliation Boards or Wages Agreements. . . . Conciliation Boards and Wages Agreements only lead us into a morass . . . the suggested organisation is constructed to fight rather than to negotiate. It is based upon the principle that we can only get what we are strong enough to win and retain.

The alliance of unions was one of the aims of the syndicalists and in 1910 Mann had founded the National Transport Workers' Federation which included dockers and seamen, but not railwaymen. The syndicalist model of 'One Big Union' was most nearly approached in Ireland, where James Larkin formed the Irish Transport Workers' Union which, in 1913, fought a ferocious battle with the Dublin employers. In Britain between 1913 and 1915 a Triple Alliance was formed between the Miners' Federation (870,000 members), the National Union of Railwaymen (268,000) and the National Transport Workers' Federation (163,000), by which they pledged common action. Dangerfield saw this alliance as 'clear evidence of the coming major conflict between Capital and Labour', averted only by the First World War. Most historians disagree, P. S. Bagwell arguing, for example, that 'only a small minority of the leaders ever considered that the purpose of the alliance was to bring about revolutionary change'. While the object of the alliance was to put pressure on the government as well as the employers, the immediate purpose was to secure an improvement of the wages and conditions of the workers concerned. This traditional aim was shared by the majority of trade unionists in 1914, and though some might talk of the General Strike, that event yet lay in the future.

However, Harold Perkin notes another feature of the pre-war industrial unrest:

The outstanding feature . . . was its upsurge from below, which took not only the government and employers but even the traditional trade union leaders by surprise. It was less surprising in the case of the 'New Unionists', the hitherto unorganized, or only occasionally and sporadically organized, workers like the dockers, the building workers or the Cornish clay miners. It was more surprising amongst the old unionists, the miners, railwaymen, textile workers, and West Midlands engineering and metalworkers, who had a long tradition of organization, negotiation, and, on a district or national scale, strike avoidance. Most of the strikes of the period began as 'wildcat' or unofficial strikes, often against the advice of the national union leadership . . . Many of the . . . strikes of 1910–14 displayed an instinctive fear and suspicion by the rank and file, by no means confined to politically conscious militants, that their union leaders were already *too* professional, *too* bureaucratic, *too* ready to see the employers' point of view and to respond to appeals to patriotism and 'responsibility' by members of the Liberal government.[21]

The world outside work: working-class patterns of leisure

At the beginning of this chapter it was suggested that work was not a central experience to the majority of the working class. This is not to say that *having* work was unimportant, for to be out of a job was to be cast adrift on a sea of insecurity. Work does not seem to have been valued as an end in itself, or as a satisfying experience *per se*. For most working men and women work and pleasure were strictly separated, the latter to be found among family and friends. Neighbourliness was a valued quality which contrasted strongly with the individualistic qualities of the middle class, who were far more likely to wish to 'keep themselves to themselves'.

Generalisations about the way people spent their non-working hours are bound to fail. There were many cultural differences: between workers in the north and those in the south for example; or between those of town and country. There were also a myriad of differences brought about by a person's individual circumstances or personality. Thomas Wright, a Manchester workman renowned for his missionary activities with ex-convicts, brought the point out vividly in 1867 in *Some Habits and Customs of the Working Class*:

Taking it for granted that the representative working men have tolerably comfortable homes, their methods of spending their Saturday afternoons will then depend upon their respective tastes and habits. The steady family man who is 'thoroughly domesticated' will probably settle himself by the fireside, and having lit his pipe, devote himself to the perusal of his weekly newspaper. He will go through the police intelligence with a patience and perseverance worthy of a better cause, then through the murders of the week, proceed from them to the reviews of books, and 'varieties original and select', take a passing glance at the sporting intelligence, and finally learns from the leading articles that he is a cruelly 'ground-down' and virtually enslaved individual, who has no friend or well-wisher in this unfairly constituted world save only the 'we' of the articles. This is generally about the range of a first reading. The foreign intelligence, news from the provinces, answers to correspondents, and 'enormous gooseberry' paragraphs, being left for a future occasion. By the time such first reading has been got through teatime is near – for an early tea, a tea to which all the members of the family sit down together, and at which the relishes of the season abound to an extent known only to a Saturday and a pay-day, is a stock part of a working man's Saturday. The family man, whom the wives of other working men describe to their husbands as 'something like a husband', but who is probably regarded by his own wife as a bore, and by his shop-mates as a mollicot – will go marketing with or for his wife, and will consider his afternoon well spent if he succeeds in 'beating-down' a butterman to the extent of three-halfpence. The unmarried man who 'finds himself', and who is of a scraping disposition, or cannot trust his landlady, will also spend his afternoon in marketing. Many of the unmarried, and some of the younger of the married men of the working classes, are now members of volunteer corps, workshop bands, or boat clubs, and devote many of their Saturday afternoons to drill, band practice, or rowing. When not engaged in any of the above pursuits, the men of this class go for an afternoon stroll – sometimes to some suburban semi-country inn, at others 'round town'. In the latter case, they are much given to gazing in at shop windows – particularly of newsagents, where illustrated papers and periodicals are displayed, and outfitters, in which the young mechanic who is 'keeping company' with a 'young lady', and upon whom it is therefore incumbent to 'cut a dash', can see those great bargains in gorgeous and fashionable scarfs marked up at the sacrificial price of 1s 11¾d. Those men who are bent upon improving their general education, or mastering those branches of learning – generally mathematics and mechanical drawing – which will be most useful to them, spend their Saturday afternoons in reading. Other men again, who are naturally of a mechanical or artistic turn of mind, and industriously inclined, employ their Saturday afternoon in constructing articles of the class of which so much has been seen during the last two years at industrial exhibitions; or in making, altering, or improving some article of furniture . . .

Although Wright's reforming zeal shines through in the above passage, his descriptions of different types nevertheless ring true. He described how added spice was given to simple pleasures by the week's hard toil and discipline which so many men and women endured:

On [Sunday] morning, when from force of habit the working man wakens at his usual time – I know several enthusiastic individuals who have themselves 'called' on that morning the same as any other, in order that they may make sure of thoroughly enjoying the situation – and for a confused moment or two thinks about getting up, he suddenly remembers him that it is Sunday, and joyously drawing the clothes tighter around him, he consumes time generally, and morning quarters in particular, and resolves to have a long 'lie in', and in many instances to have breakfast in bed. And on all these things the working man who benefits by the half-holiday movement can, when taking it easy on a Saturday afternoon, pleasingly ponder.

For only working men can thoroughly appreciate or understand all that is embodied in that chiefest pleasure of the working man's Sunday, 'a quarter in bed'.

There was the pleasure of visiting, and receiving friends, as the daughter of an Edwardian tin-worker from South Wales recalled: 'They'd knock the door and walk in, they were that real friendly, but they'd knock at the door in case somebody was having a bath, you know, by the fire . . . Every day there was somebody in and out. Oh, always a houseful, it was quite an open door for everybody.'[22]
Most leisure activity centred around the local community, for visits away from

home were a rarity. Paid holidays were unusual for manual workers before the 1880s, when the practice spread to a few enlightened employers, including local authorities and some of the railway companies. Annual holidays without pay were fairly common, especially in the north and Midlands, where wakes weeks became established. Blackpool became the northern working-class resort. Different towns staggered their wakes weeks, which not only enabled the resorts to cope with the numbers but meant that, at any one time, they were filled with people from the same town, and thus 'no one need feel isolated or lonely'. Seaside towns like Blackpool in the north, and Southend in the south, thrived on working-class visitors, but others went out of their way to deter such invaders, as F. M. L. Thompson describes:

> In some resorts, for example Eastbourne and Folkestone, respectable middle-class interests were so well entrenched in a local economy and society geared to a large resident community of the retired and invalid, as well as long-stay visitors, that the great unwashed were successfully excluded by the simple expedient of refusing to permit or provide any of the attractions demanded by trippers. No whelk stalls, no German bands, no nigger minstrels, no pleasure piers ruffled their sedate and stuffy serenity. All proposals to introduce trams were squashed, because these were a low-class form of transport. The working classes were not wanted in places like these, and they stayed away because there was nothing for them to do there.[23]

Workers who took holidays away from home were a minority until after the First World War, although Charles Booth reported in 1902 that among all classes in London, holiday-making was 'one of the most remarkable changes in habits in the last ten years'. The majority, if they went away at all, made do with excursions; a day by the sea; the brass band or chapel outing; the works' 'beano'; or a trip out to the country. Two factors were crucial to holiday-making: time and money; and many mass leisure activities had to wait until rising living standards gave the workers a little more to spend on non-necessities.

Although generalisations about the way the working class spent its free time cannot apply in the case of individual men and women, our knowledge of leisure has increased enormously in the last decade and a half. In addition to throwing light on particular leisure activities, historical research has centred around a number of interrelated questions. How far did industrialisation and urbanisation affect the people's leisure? Do attempts to promote 'rational recreation' and to check popular pastimes represent an aspect of social control? In what ways was leisure commercialised, and with what effect?

Many of the simple pleasures which Thomas Wright described were enjoyed by townspeople and countrypeople alike, but it would be strange indeed if industrialisation and urbanisation had no effect on leisure. In fact, they had a great deal, for urbanisation reduced the space available for leisure, while industrialisation (through rigid factory discipline) reduced the time. Urban land was at a premium, and much available space was taken up by housing and for commercial and industrial use. At the same time, enclosure of common land restricted access to many places previously used for a variety of games and gatherings. Free time was as important as free space, and the Short Time Committee complained in 1844 that 'Schools and libraries are of small use without the time to study . . . Parks are well for those who can have time to perambulate them, and baths are of little use to dirty people as do not leave work until eight o-clock at night'. The tyranny of time in the factory operated in a variety of ways. On the one hand, factory work demanded regular hours throughout the year, with the consequence that industrialisation witnessed a rapid decline in the number of public holidays to which people were legally entitled. As bank holidays were to become so prized by the workers, we can take the Bank of England as an illustration of the general trend. In the mid-eighteenth century the Bank closed for 47 holidays. By 1808 the number had declined to 44, and by 1830 to 18. In 1834, only four holidays were officially recognised – Good Friday, Christmas Day, 1 May and 1 November. What was officially recognised and what was unofficially taken are not, of course, the same; and there were many local holidays (such as fair days) which people continued to take off.

A second aspect of increased work-discipline is that work-time and leisure-time became more sharply delineated, so that leisure came to have an autonomous existence, in contrast to traditional society, where work and leisure were harder to separate out. With leisure given this new distinction, something of a battle ensued over the way it should be spent. F. M. L. Thompson has commented: 'It is ironical that so many Victorians, whose ruling ideology is supposed to have been dedicated to the pursuit of the greatest happiness of the greatest number, should have spent so much time trying to throttle the happiness of the people.' But did attempts to regulate working-class leisure constitute an attempt at social control by the classes above? There were certainly features of pre-industrial leisure which many factory owners and others might *wish* to eliminate. A disciplined workforce was required, and many traditional pastimes – football, boxing, bull-baiting and cock-fighting, for example (not to mention hard drinking) – were undisciplined and disorderly. This proved unacceptable to factory owners and threatening to the owners of property, for the crowd could easily become a mob. Ironically, the new police forces did not always take this view, although they had enormous discretionary powers in the field of public nuisance and threats to the peace. As they gained confidence in their ability to keep order, the police came to support 'harmless' outlets for popular energies, as is witnessed by the Home Office view, expressed in the 1880s, that fairs were 'innocent amusements of the poorer classes', not to be suppressed merely because they were no longer needed for trade. The police attitude illustrates the point that attempts to substitute 'rational recreation' for popular pastimes cannot be interpreted in narrow class terms. F. M. L. Thompson concludes:

> The lines of battle over popular enjoyments were drawn across class divisions: not middle class arrayed against working class, but puritans against indulgers, respectables against roughs. If popular leisure was enjoyed in more respectable ways in 1900 than it had been in 1800, this was more the result of the work of the entrepreneurs, and of changing ideas of what was considered respectable, than of the missionary crusades.[24]

The 'work of the entrepreneurs' was manifested in a variety of ways: for example, the provision of excursion trains; the rise of the music hall; the professionalisation of sport; and the growth of the popular press.

A writer of the 1860s claimed that 'not withstanding the comparatively low prices of admission to them, music halls are about the dearest places of amusement that a working man can frequent'. In our own day, when leisure is dominated by television, there remains a great nostalgia for this particular form of entertainment. Geoffrey Best describes the delights of the music hall to the Victorians:

> The music hall as they knew it was a place for eating and (more) drinking while you savoured the songs and studied the stars. It is for our purposes more interesting than most other recreational institutions, because it shows the Victorian city – which had, goodness knows, dark sides enough! – at its

brightest and best. It strongly suggests that for many of its humbler denizens it had rewarding aspects as well as grim ones, and that the two were taken together in the stride of a lively popular culture. Popular it certainly was, in most relevant senses. Its songs came straight from popular experience or aimed straight at the popular heart. Whether they were about figures of fun (mother-in-law, courting couples, lodgers, dominating wives, curates, swells, foreigners . . .) or aversion (rate-and-rent collectors, puritans, foreigners, bullies, snobs, seducers, hypocrites . . .), or of pathos (the heartbroken, the destitute, the abandoned . . .) or of admiration (royalty, heroes of the day, Jack Tar, Gladstone . . .); whether they were self-consciously patriotic or noble-hearted or virtuous or tragic, they were always on themes familiar and interesting to ordinary people. Its artistes seem virtually all to have had humble origins, and typically to have begun singing in bars, laundries, factories, shops. Its songs were the pop songs of the day, their topics could be highly topical, its stars became folk heroes and heroines.[25]

The 1890s marked the golden age of the music hall. All classes were attracted, and there was a sufficient variety of halls to cater for all tastes. However, with the advent of revue, ragtime and films, the halls declined rapidly from the early twentieth century, and though many staggered on to the late 1920s, most of the larger ones had been converted into cinemas or theatres for spectaculars.

Football was a traditional sport of the middle ages, but became virtually defunct as industrialisation made incursions into open spaces. It was brought back to life by the products of the public school, representatives of Eton, Harrow and other schools founding the Football Association in 1863. Many working-class clubs were formed under middle-class patronage and centred, for example, around the church or chapel. By the 1880s working men themselves were taking the initiative. Railway workers founded Manchester United, a group of cutlers created Sheffield United, and West Ham was started by Thames ironworkers. A symbolic date in the history of the game was 1883 when Blackburn Olympic beat the Old Etonians in the FA Cup Final. Thereafter, with a fiercely competitive game developing, and men going 'in the stands not to study and admire skill or endurance, but to see their team gain two points or pass into the next round', gentlemen and players drifted apart.

Popular newspapers were the means whereby football information and gossip was spread. By 1914 Britain was the leading newspaper-reading country in the world, with a daily sale of more newspapers per head than any other country. The great growth had been in the second half of the nineteenth century. Until 1855, when the newspaper tax was abolished, most daily papers cost 4d, but it was their dullness and unattractivenes, as much as their cost, which deterred working-class readers. The breakthrough came when newspapers were produced in a form which demanded little concentration, and which catered for a demand for entertainment and sensation. In 1881 George Newnes started *Tit-Bits*, a weekly paper which, as its title suggested, gave tit-bits of information and news. It also ran regular competitions, and was the first newspaper to offer free railway insurance to purchasers! In 1888 Alfred Harmsworth (later Lord Northcliffe) adapted the same formula in *Answers*. The editors declared: 'Anybody who reads our paper for a year will be able to converse on many subjects on which he was entirely ignorant. He will have a good stock of anecdotes and jokes and will indeed be a good companion.' The first issue included articles on 'What the Queen Eats', 'Narrow Escape from Burial Alive', 'How to Cure Freckles', and 'Why Jews Don't Ride Bicycles'. By 1892 *Answers* was selling 300,000 copies weekly. In 1896 came Harmsworth's greatest creation, the

Daily Mail, which soon had a circulation of almost 1 million a day. That was quite a momentous year for the mass media: Marconi arrived in London to sell his wireless inventions to the Post Office, and the first cinema show was presented in the West End. Their impact, however, had to wait until after the First World War.

Notes

1   John Benson, *The Working Class in Britain, 1850–1939*, Longman, 1989, p. 177.
2   Raphael Samuel, *Village Life and Labour*, Routledge and Kegan Paul, 1975, pp. xv–xvi.
3   John Burnett, *Useful Toil*, Allen Lane, 1974, pp. 11–12.
4   Malcolm Thomis, *The Town Labourer and the Industrial Revolution*, Batsford, 1974, p. 197.
5   John Rule, *Albion's People: English Society, 1714–1815*, Longman, 1992, pp. 203-4.
6   Quoted in Patricia Hollis (ed.), *Class and Conflict in Nineteenth-Century England, 1815–1850*, Routledge and Kegan Paul, 1973, p. 112.
7   Ibid., p. 114.
8   Ibid., p. 115.
9   Ibid., p. 166.
10 Ibid., pp. 47–8.
11 J. F. C. Harrison, *Robert Owen and the Owenites in Britain and America*, Routledge and Kegan Paul, 1969, p. 202.
12 Nicholas Abercrombie, Alan Warde, *et al.*, *Contemporary British Society*, second edition, Polity Press, 1994, p. 48.
13 Asa Briggs, *Victorian People*, Penguin, 1965, p. 181.
14 F. M. L. Thompson, 'Social control in Victorian Britain', *Economic History Review*, May 1981, p. 196.
15 Geoffrey Crossick, *An Artisan Elite in Victorian Society*, Croom Helm, 1978, p. 155.
16 M. E. Rose, 'Poverty and self-help: Britain in the nineteenth and twentieth centuries' in Anne Digby, Charles Feinstein and David Jenkins (eds), *New Directions in Economic and Social History*, vol. 2, Macmillan, 1992, p. 157.
17 Henry Pelling, *A History of British Trade Unionism*, Penguin 1963, p. 94.
18 Quoted in Asa Briggs, *Victorian Things*, Batsford, 1988, p. 204.
19 Francis Sheppard, *London 1808–1870: The Infernal Wen*, Secker and Warburg, 1971, p. 365.
20 Henry Pelling, op. cit., p. 104.
21 Harold Perkin, *The Rise of Professional Society: England Since 1880*, Routledge, 1990, pp. 178 and 183.
22 Paul Thompson, *The Edwardians*, second edition, Routledge, 1992, p. 116.
23 F. M. L. Thompson, *The Rise of Respectable Society*, Fontana, 1988, p. 292.
24 F. M. L. Thompson, op.cit., 1981, p. 204.
25 Geoffrey Best, *Mid-Victorian Britain, 1851–1870*, Fontana, 1979, pp. 236–7.

Chapter ten

Women in the nineteenth century

Gender roles in nineteenth-century Britain

When Queen Victoria came to the throne all women, of whatever class, were subject to laws which put them on a par with male criminals, lunatics and minors. Under the common law, married women had no identity apart from their husband's. The legal tag was that 'husband and wife are one person, and the husband is that person'. In practice this meant that a husband assumed legal possession or control of all property that belonged to his wife upon marriage, and of any property that might come to her during marriage. The law distinguished between real property (mainly freehold land) which the husband could not dispose of without his wife's permission (although he could control it and its income); and personal property, which passed into his absolute possession and which he could dispose of in any way he chose. Millicent Garrett Fawcett once had her purse snatched by a young thief in a London street. When the youth was brought to trial, she heard him charged with 'stealing from the person of Millicent Fawcett a purse containing £1 18s 6d, the property of Henry Fawcett [her husband]'. She later confessed: 'I felt as if I had been charged with the theft myself.'

The rights which a husband had over his wife's property were paralleled by his control over their children. Before 1839 the father had absolute rights over his children, and even the Court of Chancery found it virtually impossible to grant a mother access to them if her husband did not wish it. There were a number of notorious incidents in which this power was exercised. In one, a husband seized and carried away a baby as his wife was nursing it in her mother's house. In another the husband (while in prison for debt) gave his wife's legitimate child to his mistress. In yet another, the husband deserted his wife, claimed the baby born after the desertion (having already gained the custody of his other children) and left the mother to learn of its death from the newspapers.

The privileges on the wife's side were few. Her husband was responsible for her debts and for the civil wrongs (torts) she committed, both before and during their marriage; and, as they were one person in law, she could not be convicted of stealing from her husband nor (if her despair should become so great) of burning his house down.

The legal disabilities of women reflected a male-dominated society in which the sexes were ascribed particular roles. The ideal applied most fully to the middle class, and was well expressed by Tennyson in his 1847 poem, *The Princess*:

> . . . but this is fix'd
> As are the roots of earth and base of all.
> Man for the field and woman for the hearth:
> Man for the sword and for the needle she:

Man with the head and woman with the heart:
All else confusion . . .

The image of the 'active' male and 'passive' female was further developed by John Ruskin in his essay, 'Of Queens' Gardens' published in *Sesame and Lilies* (1865):

We are foolish, and without excuse foolish, in speaking of the 'superiority' of one sex to another, as if they could be compared in similar things. Each has what the other has not: each completes the other, and is completed by the other: they are in nothing alike, and the happiness and perfection of both depends on each asking and receiving from the other what the other only can give . . .

The man's power is active, progressive, defensive. He is eminently the doer, the creator, the discoverer, the defender. His intellect is for speculation and invention; his energy for adventure, for war, and for conquest, wherever war is just, wherever conquest is necessary. But the woman's power is for rule, not for battle – and her intellect is not for invention or creation, but for sweet ordering, arrangement, and decision. She sees the qualities of things, their charms, and their places. Her great function is Praise; she enters into no contest, but infallibly adjudges the crown of contest. By her office, and place, she is protected from all danger and temptation. The man, in his rough work in the open world, must encounter all peril and trial; – to him, therefore, must be the failure, the offence, the inevitable error; often he must be wounded, or subdued; often misled; and *always* hardened. But he guards the woman from all this; within his house, as ruled by her, unless she herself has sought it, need enter no danger, no temptation, no cause of error or offence. This is the true nature of home – it is the place of Peace; the shelter, not only from all injury, but from all terror, doubt, and division . . .

And wherever a true wife comes, this home is always round her. The stars only may be overhead; the glowworm in the night-cold grass may be the only fire at her foot; but home is yet wherever she is . . .

This, then, I believe to be – will you not admit it to be – the woman's true place and power? But do not you see that, to fulfil this, she must – as far as one can use such terms of a human creature – be incapable of error? So far as she rules, all must be right, or nothing is. She must be enduringly, incorruptibly good; instinctively, infallibly wise – wise, not for self-development, but for self-renunciation; wise, not that she may set herself above her husband, but that she may never fall from his side wise, not with the narrowness of insolent and loveless pride, but with the passionate gentleness of an infinitely variable, because infinitely applicable, modesty of service – the true changefulness of woman . . .

However, within this vestal temple of the home, the middle-class wife had less and less to do, for while the industrial revolution provided more work for working-class women, it took it away from their better-off sisters. In the traditional society wives had assisted their husbands in their businesses and professions in the same way that women participated in domestic industry. The wives of merchants and shopkeepers often managed the warehouse or shop and kept the accounts; farmers' wives took charge of the dairy and the smaller animals; the wives of doctors and lawyers would dispense drugs or write out documents. Rising living standards undermined these customs, and servants and clerks took over jobs from wives and daughters. The idea thus developed that a woman could not work and be a 'lady'. A correspondent to the *Englishwoman's Journal* wrote in 1866: 'My opinion is that if a woman is obliged to work, at once (although she may be a Christian and well bred)

10   Women in Victorian narrative painting

Insights into Victorian ideas about womanhood (and their views on many other issues) can be gained from narrative paintings, which proved so popular with the public. The story that a painting was intended to tell is often immediately apparent, but close inspection of the details usually provided further clues for the viewer.

Augustus Egg exhibited the three paintings which made up his series, 'Past and Present', at the Royal Academy in 1858. Together, the pictures tell of the consequence of a woman's unfaithfulness to her husband. The first in the series (1) shows the husband (whose silk hat suggests that he has just returned home) discovering the incriminating letter, while he grinds a portrait of his wife's lover underfoot. An apple, cut in half, reveals that it is rotten to the core, and the same theme is taken up in the painting (on the rear wall) of Adam and Eve being thrown out of the Garden of Eden. Another of the paintings, of a derelict hulk cast up on a beach, is entitled 'The Abandoned'. The children's house of cards is about to collapse, a portent of the collapse of this household.

Richard Redgrave painted five versions of 'The Poor Teacher', the first of which was exhibited in 1843. Two versions are shown here. What is our response to either version? Both show a governess dressed in mourning (but probably 'second mourning' i.e. more than six months have passed since the death occurred). She holds a black-edged letter in her hand. At her table is evidence of her solitary meal, while a pile of books suggests that she has marking yet to do. In picture 2 the music on the piano is 'Home, Sweet Home'. Both versions of the picture suggest the solitary and melancholy life of the governess. We know that the figures in picture 3 were added at the request of a purchaser, who objected to the forlorn loneliness of the governess. But what is the girl with the book thinking?

1   'Past and Present' by Augustus Egg, 1858

2   'The Poor Teacher' by Richard Redgrave

3   'The Governess' by Richard Redgrave

she loses that peculiar position which the word *lady* conventionally designates.' Margaretta Grey, aunt of the feminist reformer, Josephine Butler, captured vividly this feeling of 'genteel uselessness' in a diary entry of 1853:

It appears to me that, with an increase of wealth unequally distributed, and a pressure of population, there has sprung up among us a spurious refinement, that cramps the energy and circumscribes the usefulness of women in the upper classes of society. A lady, to be such, must be a mere lady, and nothing else. She must not work for profit, or engage in any occupation that money can command, lest she invade the rights of the working classes, who live by their labour . . . The conventional barrier that pronounces it ungenteel to be behind a counter, or serving the public in any mercantile capacity, is greatly extended. The same in household economy. Servants must be up to their several offices, which is very well; but ladies, dismissed from the dairy, the confectionary, the store-room, the still-room, the poultry-yard, the kitchen-garden, and the orchard, have hardly yet found themselves a sphere equally useful and important in the pursuits of trade and art to which to apply their too abundant leisure . . . But what I remonstrate against is the negative forms of employment: the wasting of energy, the crippling of talent under false ideas of station, propriety, and refinement, that seems to shut up a large portion of the women of our generation from proper spheres of occupation and adequate exercise of power . . . Life is too often divested of any real and important purpose.

When a middle-class woman expressed the necessity of 'getting on with her work', that work was likely to be decorative needlework such as embroidery or needlepoint. Or she might engage in 'Good Works', for ladies might sublimate their energies in charitable work, a sphere of activity in which the historian, F. K. Prochaska, has shown them to have exerted/considerable influence.

Denied the opportunity of undertaking paid employment, middle-class women were pushed back more and more into an ornamental role. It was their leisure rather than that of their husbands which signalled the family's membership of 'the leisured classes' while the richness of their dress and jewellery was evidence of the wealth of husband or father:

I saw her dancing in the ball. Around her snowy brow were set five hundred pounds; such would have been the answer of any jeweller to the question: 'What are those diamonds?' With the gentle undulation of her bosom there rose and fell exactly thirty pounds ten shillings. The sum bore the guise of a brooch of gold and enamel. Her fairy form was invested in ten guineas, represented by a slip of lilac satin; and this was overlaid by thirty guineas more in two skirts of white lace. Tastefully down each side of the latter were six half-crowns, which so many bows of purple ribbon had come to. The lower margin of the thirty-guinea skirts were edged with eleven additional guineas, the value of some eight yards of silver fringe, a quarter of a yard in depth. Her taper waist, taking zone and clasp together, I calculated to be confined by thirty pounds sterling. Her delicately rounded arms, the glove of spotless kid being added to the gold bracelet which encircled the little wrist, may be said to have been adorned with twenty-two pounds five and sixpence; and putting the silk and satin at the lowest figure, I should say she wore fourteen and sixpence on her feet. Thus, altogether was this thing of light, this creature of loveliness, arrayed from top to toe, exclusive of little sundries, in six hundred and forty-eight pounds eleven shillings.[1]

Such a woman was little more than a doll, and her home a doll's house. Although the image of the doll's house is associated with the playwright, Ibsen, Charles Dickens had used the phrase 15 years earlier in *Our Mutual Friend* (1864), where Bella Wilfer told her husband, 'I want to be something so much worthier than the doll in the doll's house'. Another image was that of the caged bird. Mary Wollstonecraft, a pioneer of the rights of women, had used it in 1792, in her book, *A Vindication of the Rights of Women*:

> Taught from their infancy that beauty is woman's sceptre, the mind shapes itself to the body, and, roaming round its gilt cage, only seeks to adorn its prison. Men have various employments and pursuits which engage their attention, and give a character to the opening mind; but women, confined to one, and having their thoughts constantly directed to the most insignificant part of themselves, seldom extend their views beyond the triumph of the hour . . . . Confined then in cages like the feathered race, they have nothing to do but to plume themselves, and stalk with mock majesty from perch to perch.

Over 100 years later Arthur J. Lamb wrote the popular music hall song, 'She's only a bird in a gilded cage', evidence of the enduring quality of the idea. That it should have lingered so long is partly due to the acceptance by many women themselves of the role ascribed to them, although recent historical research has suggested that the 'perfect lady' image was less typical of women in the home than it was on the printed page.

In 1851 Florence Nightingale bewailed the fact that 'women don't count themselves as human beings at all, there is absolutely no God, no country, no duty to them all, except family'. Queen Victora (perhaps the one woman in the country who could combine a public with a private role) was definitely not amused by those who sought to change the position in which society had placed woman: 'The Queen is most anxious to enlist everyone who can speak or write to join in checking this mad, wicked folly of "Women's Rights" . . . *with all its attendant horrors*, on which her poor feeble sex is bent forgetting every sense of womanly feeling and propriety . . . It is a subject which makes the Queen so *furious* that she cannot contain herself.'

If the woman's place was in the home, home was also the place where gender roles were learnt and shaped, as Michael Anderson makes clear:

> In middle- and upper-class homes, the gendered segregation of space, with different decorative styles (dark colours or panelled walls in the masculine study and billiard room, light flowery fabrics and wallpapers in the morning room), were a constant reminder of a segregated world. From earliest childhood, girls were dressed in ways which inhibited boisterous behaviour. Family ceremony (from religious observance led by the male head to who cut the Sunday joint of meat) supported these divisions. These were bolstered by material differences (for example, special food for the males in the household) and psychological expectations (girls would help with domestic duties from an early age while boys were usually exempt).[2]

Marriage was the end to which a girl was directed from birth. Education in the first half of the century was largely directed towards the attraction of a husband for, as Carol Dyhouse puts it, '[it] resembled (if it did not represent) a kind of decorative packaging of consumption goods for display in the marriage market'. Strong opinions on any matter might prove unmarketable so young ladies were trained to eschew them. The Schools Inquiry Commissioners reported in 1867 that parents believed that 'accomplishments, and what is showy and superficially attractive are what is really essential for them, and, in particular, that as regards their relations with the other sex and the possibilities of marriage, more solid attainments are actually disadvantageous rather than the reverse'. One Assistant Commissioner, estimating the amount of time spent on different subjects in girls' schools, concluded as follows: music, 25 per cent; 'miscellaneous information', including mythology, astronomy, botany, literature and history, 23 per cent; French and German, 16.5 per cent; and drawing, 6.5 per cent. The remaining 29 per cent was spent on subjects of lesser importance such as English grammar, writing, geography and arithmetic. Even parents of girls at schools run by reformers voiced criticisms. Dorothea Beale, principal of Cheltenham Ladies' College, the first proprietary girls' school founded in England, recalled a father who had grumbled, 'My dear lady, if my daughters were going to be bankers, it would be very well to teach arithmetic as you do, but really there is no need'. He sent his daughters to another school – but Miss Beale had the doubtful satisfaction of recording that the man died, leaving his daughters a fortune which they were ignorant to manage, and that they fell into 'pecuniary difficulties'. It was to prepare girls to *get* married that education was designed for, and there was little in it to assist girls to *be* married.

The 'surplus women problem'

What if a girl should fail to get married? The number of single women aged 15–45 rose from 2,765,000 in 1851 to 3,228,700 in 1871, with a rise in the surplus of single women of 72,500 to 125,000 (a 72 per cent increase in 20 years). In 1871 two-thirds of all women between 20 and 24 were single, and 30 per cent of those aged 24–35. For every three women over 20 who were wives, there were two who were widows or had never married. The 'surplus women problem', and the plight of the 'unattached female', greatly taxed the Victorians, the distress being felt more by the middle class, where the prohibitions on women working were stronger and where, according to the evidence, the disparity between the sexes was at its greatest. A number of factors, demographic as well as social, accounted for this sexual imbalance. There was a higher child mortality among boys, while emigration carried off far more men – 124,000 as against 41,000 women in 1861. There was also an increasing trend for men to postpone marriage. The requirement to keep his future wife 'in the manner to which she was accustomed' was too demanding for many young men as they embarked on their careers. It was necessary to keep up appearances, but as a letter to *The Times* put it in 1861: 'Girls are now so expensively, so thoughtlessly, brought up – are led to expect so lavish an outlay on the part of the husband, that, unless his means are unlimited, he must, to comply with the wishes of a modern wife soon bring himself to beggary . . . . Respectability may be too dearly purchased.'

At this point it is interesting to note that the financial pressures which might inhibit marriage also gave rise to a conscious desire to limit the number of children. J. A. Banks thoroughly explored the phenomenon in his *Prosperity and Parenthood*, published in 1954. He showed that the period up to the 1870s was one in which the middle-class standard of living was rapidly changing, and that although retail prices rose by only 5 per cent, something like 50 per cent more than the 1850 level came to be spent on what he called 'the paraphernalia of gentility', such as food, drink, dress, household requirements and domestic service. The material rewards were greater for those with smaller families. As the Royal Commission on Population put it in a historical survey published in 1949: 'In the individualistic competitive struggle, children became a handicap, and it paid to travel light.' Contraception became more widely practised as knowledge spread through books such as Annie Besant's *Law of Population*, which sold 35,000 copies within a year of its publication in 1878. Most people who practised contraception relied on withdrawal, abstinence or prolonged breast-feeding, which was believed to inhibit conception. Condoms had been known since the eighteenth century, and were manufactured in rubber (rather than the earlier animal intestines) from the 1870s, but they did not come to be widely used until the First World War when, from 1917, they were issued to the troops in France in an attempt to check the spread of venereal disease.

The superabundance of women inevitably led to changing attitudes for, whether they chose it or not, more and more women faced a future outside marriage. It was on the plight of single women that the majority of nineteenth-century feminists focused their attention, and their solutions included a reduction of the surplus by female emigration, and pressure for greater educational and occupational opportunities for those women who remained. Between 1862 and 1914 voluntary societies helped more than 20,000 women of various classes to emigrate to the colonies, although feminists had two minds about the movement. It could be seen as an attempt to remove an embarrassing problem from sight (rather like the transportation of convicts or orphans) or as a safety-valve which released the pressure for real reforms at home. The colonies needed working women such as domestic servants more than redundant middle-class ladies. Anti-feminists tended to argue that women who could not marry at home would find husbands in the colonies, even though it was pointed out that many men emigrated because they did not wish to marry or could not afford to,

At home attention was directed to the plight of the governess. The governess is a stock character in Victorian novels, and her situation was much discussed both in the learned journals and in the more frivolous pages of periodicals like *Punch*. So widely was their position discussed that Harriet Martineau, writing in 1859, suggested that readers were 'wearied . . . with the incessant repetition of the dreary story of spirit-broken governesses'. It may seem rather curious that so much attention was paid to them, for their numbers were comparatively small. In 1851 there were about 25,000 governesses in England, as against 750,000 female domestic servants and innumerable women toiling in factory and mine. What made the governess compel such consideration was the ambivalence of her situation, for she was neither a member of the family, nor a guest, nor yet a servant. Governessing was one way in which the unmarried daughters of 'failed' gentlemen or clergy could preserve a position in the middle ranks of society. A contributor to *The Quarterly Review* stated that 'the real definition of a governess, in the English sense, is a being who is our equal in birth, manners and education, but our inferior in worldly wealth'. Yet she could not be of equal status with the wife and daughters of the house for she was an employee. Pay, in fact, was notoriously low, but in recompense a governess was offered what the ideal of a lady demanded – a 'home'.

Attempts at reform involved a shift towards professionalism. In 1843 the Governesses' Benevolent Institution was formed to provide a placement service, temporary housing for those unemployed, insurance and annuities to the aged. In order that governesses might be better educated, Queen's College was established in London in 1848. Its purpose was to give governesses a training that would raise their self-esteem, make them better teachers, and increase respect for them. The school was open to ladies who were not governesses, for it was observed that 'Those who had no dream of entering upon such work this year, might be forced by some reverse of fortune to think of it next year'. In any case, it was argued that the training would prepare future wives and mothers better to perform their traditional roles. This increasing professionalism made it more difficult for the merely poor gentlewoman to enter the occupation; and if the position of governess was often filled by those who were moving down the social scale, as the century progressed it also came to be filled by those who were upwardly mobile – the educated daughters of farmers and tradesmen, for example – which further added to the social anomaly.

The reform of girls' education

Not every single woman in the middle class could be, or had any desire to be, a governess. Charlotte Brontë abhorred her 'governess drudgery', and would gladly have exchanged it for 'work in the mill'. Such a thing, of course, was out of the question, but a group of activists was concerned to widen women's proper sphere, and to this end concentratd much of their effort on a reform of girls' education. In this they achieved a great deal. They found themselves, however, in a difficulty (what we might call a 'Catch-22' situation). Reform would not come without agitation, and agitation was 'unfeminine' and would be sure to antagonise those with the power to grant reform! Many of the leading radicals appreciated the tightrope on which they walked. Elizabeth Garrett (later Elizabeth Garrett Anderson, Britain's first female doctor) wrote to Emily Davies as she was about to start her medical studies in 1860:

> Evidence is modifying my notions about the most suitable style of dress for me to wear at the hospital. I feel confident now that one is helped rather than hindered by being as much like a lady as lies in one's power. When my student life begins, I shall try to get very serviceable, rich, whole coloured dresses that will do without trimmings and not require renewing often.[3]

The campaigners demonstrated their femininity and ladylike qualities by getting male sympathisers to read their papers to learned societies and at public meetings. They took great care in arranging meetings in order to secure the fullest advantage – even if this meant packing audiences. At one meeting:

> Invitations were . . . sent to a number of Cambridge men, specially to those who were known to be opposed . . . The front row was carefully packed with well-dressed, good looking women, those who looked strong-minded or intellectual being relegated to the back . . . Elizabeth Garrett was allowed to sit in the front row, for she contrived to look 'exactly like one of those girls whose instinct it is to do what you tell them'.[4]

When Frances Mary Buss, headmistress of the North London Collegiate School for Ladies, gave evidence to the Schools Inquiry Commission (probably one of the first women to give evidence and to be cross-examined publicly by such a commission) it was noted that at one point there were tears in her eyes. As one of the Assistant Commissioners confessed: 'Nothing could have impressed the commissioners more than the evidence of competence applied to frailty.'

There are several ways that the education of girls can be approached, each depending on a different view of femininity and the natural needs of women. One approach may be called assimilation, and derives from a view that there are no differences between boys and girls, or that any differences which may exist are irrelevant to education. In 1865 Joseph Payne wrote in the *Transactions of the National Association for the Promotion of Social Science*, a journal in which women's education was much discussed:

Where we have to deal with a common mind, both the subjects taught and the mode of teaching must be in a great degree common. We are not teaching a different, but the same kind of human being. The mind has properly no sex. It is the mind of the human being, and consequently there must be of necessity a similarity in the instruction of both sexes.

A second approach sees girls as handicapped in comparison with boys, or as some-what deficient boys. There was much debate in Victorian times about the effects of education on the health of girls, who were looked on as having a fixed supply of energy which was drained away in any case by menstruation and childbirth. Henry Maudslay, a professor at University College, London, was one of the leading medical opponents of the development of girls' education. He wrote in the *Fortnightly Review* in 1874:

> The girl enters upon the hard work of school or college at the age of fifteen years or thereabouts, when the function of her sex has perhaps been fairly established; ambitious to stand high in class, she pursues her studies with diligence, perseverence, constancy, allowing herself no days of relaxation or rest out of schooldays, paying no attention of the periodical tides of her organization, unheeding a drain 'that would make the stroke oar of the University crew falter'. For a time all seems to go well with her studies; she triumphs over male and female competitors, gains the first rank, and is stimulated to continued exertions in order to hold it. But in the long run nature, which cannot be ignored or defied with impunity, asserts its power; excessive losses occur; health fails, she becomes the victim of aches and pains, is unable to go on with her work, and compelled to seek medical advice. Restored to health by rest from work, a holiday at the seaside, and suitable treatment, she goes back to her studies, to begin again the same course of unheeding work, until she has completed the curriculum, and leaves college a good scholar but a delicate and ailing woman, whose future life is one of more or less suffering.

Feminists, on the other hand, argued that 'a vacant mind revenges itself on the body', and pointed instead to a want of physical exercise, and to the dictates of fashion which could require a girl to hang 15–20 lb (about 7–9 kg) of material from a constricted 15-inch (38-cm) waist − 'a sort of portable prison of tight corsets and long skirts' as one historian described it.

George Romanes was a friend of Charles Darwin and a distinguished scientist who did much work on the mental faculties of animals and human beings. In 1887 he wrote that

> seeing that the average brain-weight of women is about five ounces less than that of men, on merely anatomical grounds we should be prepared to expect a marked inferiority of intellectual power in the former.[5]

Nearly 20 years earlier, J. S. Mill had shown the fallacy of such craniological studies, for he pointed out that if it were the case that there was a direct relationship between brain size and intelligence: 'A tall and large-boned man must be wonderfully superior in intelligence to a small man, and an elephant or a whale must prodigiously excel mankind.'[6]

The third approach to girls' education sees them as having completely different needs from boys, which have to be reflected in a curriculum with different emphases. Views on education, however, are very much tied up with views on social class. It has been argued that in the first half of the nineteenth century the education of middle and upper-class boys and girls was highly differentiated, but that of the working classes was designed without reference to sexual differences, but for some needlework taught to girls in order that they might make good wives or domestic servants. Working-class education was designed to inculcate the qualities of 'followership'; that of middle-and upper-class boys, that of leadership; while their sisters were trained to amuse and succour the leaders. Joshua Fitch, reporting to the Schools Inquiry Commission in 1864 after visiting many girls' schools, remarked that:

> above the age of twelve the difference is most striking. Girls are told that Latin is not a feminine requirement, mathematics is only fit for boys and she must devote herself to ladylike accomplishments . . . nothing is more common than to hear the difference in the future destiny of boys and girls assigned as a reason for a difference in the character and extent of their education, but I cannot find that any part of the training given in ladies' schools educates them for a domestic life or prepares them for duties which are supposed to be especially womanly. The reason why modern languages, which are especially useful in business, should be considered particularly appropriate for women, who spend most of their time in the home, is still one of the unsolved mysteries of the English educational system.

Depending partly on their views about the differences between male and female models, educational reformers took one of two lines. Some (such as F. D. Maurice, one of the founders of Queen's College and Anne Clough, who ran a school at Ambleside and went on to become first principal of Newnham College) accepted the prevailing notions of femininity, but attempted to provide girls with an education that would make them better wives, mothers and companions. Others, including Emily Davies, rejected the model and demanded equal educational and employment opportunities for women. Emily Davies poured scorn on Ruskin's description of male and female roles:

> We make the world even more puzzling than it is by nature, when we shut our eyes to the facts of daily life; and we know, as a fact, that women have a part in the world, and that men are by no means ciphers in the home circle – we know that a man who should be all head would be as monstrous an anomaly as a woman all heart – that men require the protection of law, and women are not so uniformly prosperous as to be independent of comfort and consolation – men have no monopoly of working, nor women of weeping . . .[7]

It was due to the persistence of Emily Davies and her associates that girls' schools were included in the terms of reference of the Schools Inquiry Commission (Taunton Commission). She believed that revelations concerning the inefficiency of existing schools would lead to improvements. The Commissioners certainly described middle-class girls' education as unsatisfactory, its particular defects being, 'Want of thoroughness and foundation; want of system; slovenliness and showy superficiality; inattention to rudiments; undue time given to accomplishments and those not taught thoroughly or in any scientific manner; want of organisation'.

The Commissioners' main contribution to girls' education was to show the need for well-endowed institutions. In 1869, when endowments for girls' education represented only 2 per cent of the total, there were only 12 endowed girls' schools, and none of them were outstanding. By 1895, 902 of the 1,448 endowments had been reformed, and there were 80 endowed schools for girls, as well as many proprietary schools such as those established by the Girls' Public Day

School Trust (founded in 1872) which had almost 40 schools and 7,000 pupils by the 1890s.

The particular contribution of Emily Davies was to the higher education of girls, although secondary and higher education were closely linked in the nineteenth century. Queen's College, for example, remained a school, while Bedford College, founded as a school in 1849, developed into a constituent college of the University of London. Emily Davies argued that the equal educational provision for girls which she demanded would only be secured by testing it against boys' education in equal examinations. She was the sister of Llewelyn Davies, one of F. D. Maurice's close supporters, and it was part of Maurice's philosophy at Queen's College that girls should be tested regularly in order that they be trained to disciplined study. Public examinations were a new phenomenon, but in the 1850s they were started for boys by the Royal College of Preceptors, the Royal Society of Arts and Oxford and Cambridge Universities. In 1862 Emily Davies began making informal enquiries at both Oxford and Cambridge regarding the attitude of the authorities to allowing girls to take their local examinations. The response from Oxford was discouraging, but the Cambridge authorities encouraged her to approach the local committees which administered their examinations. The fear of some local committees (that of Liverpool, for example) was that the admission of girls would lower the status of the examination for boys, but the London committee was prepared to allow a trial run, and 83 girls were entered. Not long afterwards the University of Cambridge officially and permanently opened its examinations to girl candidates, while Durham and Oxford shortly followed suit. The proportion of failures among the girls was initially high, but this forcefully demonstrated the urgent need for radical reform of their schools. At the same time the subjects required for the examinations encouraged girls' schools to align their curriculum with that of the boys. In 1869 Emily Davies opened a college for girls at Hitchin, a town midway between Cambridge and London, which allowed her to hedge her bets on which university would prove more accommodating. In 1873 she moved the college to Girton, a village which was a short but respectable distance from Cambridge. Her students were not admitted to degrees, but the authorities allowed her to make private use of the tripos papers. However, her single-minded devotion to educational equality brought her on a collision course with other reformers, such as Henry Sidgwick. He, along with others, was highly critical of much of the work at Cambridge but, despairing of persuading the university and boys' schools to change, hoped that an alliance with the new women's institutions would pave the way to general reform. This was not the view of Emily Davies. The university system might be bad, but equality demanded that girls' education should be just as bad as men's. It has to be admitted that she had a point, for a reformed system, if different from the norm and if tainted by association with women, was sure to be suspect. The immediate result was that Sidgwick and his supporters founded a second Cambridge college for women (Newnham) which, for a while, ran in competition with Girton.

In 1866 the University of London offered a special 'women's examination', but its separateness left it with no status in the academic world. However, in 1878 the university abolished its special examinations for women and opened every degree, honour and prize to them on equal terms with men. In 1880 Victoria University (the forerunner of Manchester, Leeds and Liverpool universities) admitted women to its degrees, as did Durham in 1895. However, Oxford did not admit women to degrees and full membership until 1919, and Cambridge did so only in 1947. Yet Oxford and Cambridge still retained an attraction for women even without the degree, because of the prestige which attached to anyone who had been to the ancient universities, with the result that some feminist historians have argued that the nineteenth-century reformers were more concerned with symbols than with the attainment of practical rights.

Women at work

The practical effects of education might be measured by the degree to which women's occupational horizons were widened. The proportion of women in the labour force remained remarkably constant in the second half of the nineteenth century, for they constituted 30.2 per cent in 1851 (the first year in which the census took detailed account of occupations), and 29.1 per cent in 1901. However, there was considerable change in the occupations in which women were employed, with new openings apparent for the middle and lower middle classes. We cannot be at all certain about the number of married women who worked for wages. The 1851 census counted 3,462,000 wives in Great Britain, of whom just over three-quarters (2,630,000) entered themselves as being of no specific occupation. Of those who stated an occupation, the largest groups were those wives of farmers, innkeepers and shopkeepers, but Edward Higgs has demonstrated that the census tended to underenumerate work done by women in the home. Those who helped their husbands when other domestic duties allowed, or who took in washing or needlework, probably did not look upon themselves as employed. At a guess, 500,000 wives may have fallen into this category, making a total of about two–fifths who were workers. The work of many women was spasmodic and diverse, which makes census classification particularly difficult. The working lives of most women outside the upper and middle classes was made up of a mixture of washing, cleaning, charring, as well as various sorts of work done at home in addition to the usual domestic chores.

Domestic service was the greatest employer of women, and a ready supply of working-class domestic servants was essential for the maintenance of the middle-class ideal of the perfect lady. The contribution of domestic service to the middle–class way of life is discussed more fully in Chapter 8. Domestic service for working-class girls was considered by some to be a particularly appropriate occupation. A writer in the *National Review* of April 1862 observed that female domestic servants

> discharge a most important and indispensable function in social life; they do not follow an obligatory independent, and therefore for their sex an unnatural, career: – on the contrary, they are attached to others and are connected with other existences, which they embellish, facilitate, and serve. In a word, they fulfil both essentials of woman's being; *they are supported by, and they minister to*, men. We could not possibly do without them. Nature has not provided one too many . . .

A rosy picture of the charms of domestic service was painted by J. D. Milne in *The Industrial and Social Position of Women* (1857):

> The situation of a domestic servant . . . . is attended with considerable comfort. With abundant work it combines a wonderful degree of liberty, discipline, health, physical comfort, good example, regularity, room for advancement, encouragement to acquire saving habits. The most numerous class of depositors in the Savings Banks is that of domestic servants. The situation frequently involves much responsibility, and calls forth the best features of character. Kind

attachment in return for honest service is not uncommon with the master or mistress; and an honest pride in the relation springs up on both sides and lasts throughout life.

In fact the situation was often very difficult, and servants were frequently treated with distrust and a total disregard for feelings. John Burnett has observed that 'an exact analogy is not easy to draw, but in the Victorian attitude to servants there was much in common with the attitude towards children, dumb animals and the feeble-minded; as God's creatures, all deserved kindness and consideration, but above all, they required authority, discipline, and the direction of the natural superiors'. The practice of giving and requiring references gave the employer almost feudal power, and the servant who 'lost her character' could never expect employment in a respectable home. Their free time was limited, and the lost of an independent social life was one of the many hardships they bore. A writer in *The Nineteenth Century* observed in August 1890:

> No amount of kindness, or even of genial companionship, on the part of master and mistress, can compensate them for being cut off from this independent social life. And what is offered to them instead? They are connected with the wealthier classes principally as ministering to their material well-being. They have a clear and complete view of their luxury. With their attention to their own comfort, with the ugly, squalid corners of their lives, with their bad tempers, with their efforts to keep up the appearance that convention demands, they are intimate. No people contemplate so frequently and so strikingly the unequal distribution of wealth: they fold up dresses whose price contains double the amount of their year's wages; they pour out at dinner wine whose cost would have kept a poor family for weeks. And of the amusements and occupations, of the higher interests and of the higher life of the leisured classes, of which comfort and ease and luxury is only supposed to be the basis, they have no share, and, probably, very little understanding. Cut off from their own general life, they remain spectators from the outside of that of others; and it cannot be said that its appearance is always elevating, or even intelligible, except from the standard of self-indulgence. What they gain by constant association with the wealthier classes are, principally, external qualities – politeness, a certain amount of outward refinement, a high standard of cleanliness for themselves and of comfort for others; sometimes they find a patron, but rarely a friend.

It was not surprising, therefore, that domestic service lost its attractiveness when other employment opportunities arose, and in 1902 it was remarked that, 'the young working girl of today prefers to become a Board School mistress, a post-office clerk, a typewriter, a shop girl, or a worker in a factory – anything rather than enter domestic service'. Women were engaged in other types of work servicing the home and the Victorian lady. Laundry work was often taken up when domestic service, for whatever reason, was left off. The 1851 census showed that the majority of general domestic servants were girls aged between 15–25, whereas the majority of charwomen, washerwomen, manglers and laundry-keepers were middle-aged and older. Many other women were involved in dressmaking and millinery, work with the needle having its high-class and its low-class ends. Dressmakers' and milliners' assistants were excessively overworked, and ill-health often forced retirement from the trade. During the Season an 18-hour day was the norm, and special orders for weddings or mourning, for example, entailed work continuing through the night.

The needle was the principal employment for women in London, and work in the sweated trades constituted one of the capital's major social problems. Thomas Hood drew the public's attention to the evils of sweated labour in his 'Song of the Shirt', written in 1843:

> With fingers weary and worn,
> With eyelids heavy and red,
> A woman sat in unwomanly rags,
> Plying her needle and thread –
> Stitch! stitch! stitch!
> In poverty, hunger and dirt.
> And still with a voice of dolorous pitch
> She sang the 'Song of the Shirt'.
>
> Work – work – work,
> Till the brain begins to swim;
> Work – work – work,
> Till the eyes are heavy and dim!
> Seam, and gusset, and band,
> Band, and gusset, and seam,
> Till over the buttons I fall asleep,
> And sew them on in a dream!
>
> Oh, Men with Sisters dear!
> Oh, Men, with Mothers and Wives!
> It is not linen you're wearing out,
> But human creatures' lives!
> Stitch – stitch – stitch,
> In poverty, hunger, and dirt,
> Sewing at once, with a double thread,
> A Shroud as well as a Shirt . . .

Working with black articles (especially black velvet) was particularly hard on the eyes and, all in all, we have to agree with Charles Dickens that the needle was 'a horrible little instrument of torture . . . to thousands of poor Englishwomen'. The evils remained, however, and a social investigator in 1900 found women stitching petticoats for 4d each, every one requiring hundreds of yards of stitching, three button–holes and two drawing-ribbons (which she had to supply). They sold in West End shops from 15s to 30s.

Much women's work was arduous in the extreme, and it says a great deal about the class system that the 'weaker sex' should have been allowed to toil as they did. In 1741 William Hutton, on his approach to Birmingham from Walsall, found a number of smithies on the road: 'In some of these shops I observed one or more females, stripped of their upper garments and not overcharged with their lower, wielding the hammer with all the grace of their sex. The beauties of their faces were rather eclipsed by the smut of the anvil. . .' Women were working in the same industry 150 years later, as the Royal Commission on the Employment of Labour made clear in 1893:

> Mr and Mrs Cole, man and wife, work together at spike nails . . . both use the oliver [a heavy hammer]. They expressed a strong opinion that 'women should be prevented by law from doing men's work' . . . With few exceptions, the homes I saw belonging to women who work either in factories or in home workshops are very nearly desolate . . . There is no home life at all . . . The

children are either 'minded' by little girls at 2s a week, or else they are perched on the warm heap of fuel or dangled in an egg box from the shop ceiling . . . all in the stifling vicinity of the forge . . .[8]

Although women were excluded from underground working in mines in 1842, many were not prepared to exchange this rigorous labour for the rigours of unemployment, and as late as 1850 at least 200 were found working underground in Welsh pits, some of them dressed as men. Work on the surface continued much later, despite several attempts, inspired by a mixture of motives, to stamp it out. Indeed, the Lancashire pit-brow lasses stopped work as recently as 1966, and it is worth noting that even today some women still work underground in the United States. There have always been those who argue that women should be free to do any work they wish, and it cannot be denied that the attitude of Parliament to unsuitable women's work was often one-sided. More often than not the decision was made to ban women from such work rather than to improve the conditions of men and women alike.

Inevitably, we know more about the attitudes of middle-class men and women to female employment than we do about those of the less articulate working class. There is some evidence that attitudes differed in different parts of the country and in different trades. Women workers in the textile trade valued their independence, and were inclined to delay marriage in order to prolong the enjoyment of a regular wage and factory fellowship. Married women, too, welcomed their return to the mill as a respite from home. Women in the textile towns could not conceive of confining their lives to home and children. As one commented: 'It 'ud give me the blooming "ump".' Such women sub-contracted many of their household chores such as washing and mending, while the preparation of food for the family was made easier by the spread of shops selling pies and peas, tripe or cooked cow-heel. Elsewhere middle-class ideals about the wife's domestic role and the husband's role as bread-winner filtered down to the working class; and as the social aspirations of working men rose, many felt that a wife who went to work constituted a slur on their capacities as male providers. It is ironic that towards the end of the century, when middle-class girls began to achieve an education undifferentiated from that of their brothers, the Board School curriculum was being shaped with greater emphasis on domestic economy and housecraft. This was partly because it was felt that an upgrading of housework would strengthen the home and solve a number of social problems, but also because it was hoped that the supply of trained domestic servants would be increased. In 1901 Seebohm Rowntree argued in *Poverty: A Study in Town Life* that the life of wives of better-paid workmen were as constricted as any to be found:

> No one can fail to be struck by the monotony which characterises the life of most married women of the working class. Probably this monotony is least marked in the slum districts where life is lived more in common, and where the women are constantly in and out of each other's houses, or meet and gossip in the courts and streets. But with advance in the social scale, family life becomes more private, and the women, left in the house all day while their husbands are at work, are largely thrown to their own resources. These, as a rule, are sadly limited, and in the deadening monotony of their lives these women too often become mere hopeless drudges.

Left alone while the husband was at work, the working-class wife was increasingly likely to be left there when he was not, for men tended to develop their own, separate recreations, either at the public house in the evening, or at football matches and races at the weekend. With a narrow education, and deprived of adult companionship, the life of the working-class woman was often stifling.

In some respects, then, the horizons of working-class women narrowed. On the other hand, those of middle-class women – especially single women – widened, as more and more occupations were opened to them. Whether this was the result of radical agitation or was simply a reflection of changes in the economy is debatable; but the view of Lee Holcombe is that 'the Victorian women's movement witnessed but did not cause the widening of the avenues of employment for middle-class women'. The impact of reformers was more instrumental in opening up some occupations than others. Medicine and nursing are examples of occupations where attitudes had to be changed before women could be admitted. Lorna Duffin sums up the arguments why, at mid-century, women were considered unsuitable for these professions:

> The first was based on class. In reply to an article in *Macmillan's Magazine*, *The Lancet* pointed out that the medical profession required that 'women must be drawn from the same rank as male physicians', that is, the middle classes. But these women were too refined, their sensibility and delicacy would not permit it. Working-class women, who had demonstrated their ability to cope physically, were excluded from medicine on the grounds of social class. These two objections, therefore, conclusively barred all women from medicine. In the second place the marital status of women would bar them from medicine. Medical women should be married because only these women would have sufficient experience of life in general to allow them to cope with the exigencies of medical practice. But married women could not be doctors because they would be 'inactive for some months annually'. In addition they 'will not be able to provide a restful home for men or cope with children'. Unmarried women could not be doctors because 'celibacy is not conducive to social success'. The threat from unmarried women was seen as the greater and the argument against them was extended. Apart from the fact that they would be doomed to spinsterhood since no one would want to marry them, celibacy is itself unnatural. If to be a doctor a woman needs to remain celibate then medicine for women is unnatural.[9]

On the other hand male doctors did concede that a place could be found for women in midwifery or nursing. Dr H. Bennet wrote in *The Lancet* in 1870:

> I believe . . . that there is a branch of our profession – midwifery – to which they might and ought to be admitted in a subordinate position as a rule.
> In France, and in many other parts of the Continent, this division of labour in Midwifery is fully carried out, and with great advantage to both parties – to the regular practitioner, who is relieved of part of his most arduous, most wearing and most unremunerative duties, and to the women who have a vocation for medicine, to gain a respectable living in the profession which they wish to practise . . .

Sophia Jex-Blake, a former teacher at Queen's College who had studied medicine in the United States, replied that Dr Bennet had given the game away – the most arduous, wearing and unremunerative parts of medicine were to be left to women! It was she who fought the real battle to admit women to the medical profession. She qualified at the University of Dublin in 1877, and worked with Elizabeth Garrett Anderson in founding the London School of Medicine, where women could be trained. Teaching hospitals were persuaded to take women medical students, and within a decade the battle had been won.

The story of Florence Nightingale and the development of the nursing profession is a familiar one. One eminent matron, reminiscing about her early days in hospital, recalled: 'The "nurses" were drawn from the lowest denizens of the surrounding neighbourhood, such as preferred sick-nursing to street-walking, and perhaps they were able to combine the two trades.' After her triumph in the Crimea, Miss Nightingale in 1860 founded the Nightingale School for nurses at St Thomas's Hospital in London, where a rigorous training was provided. By the end of the century all the leading hospitals in London and the provinces, and many smaller hospitals as well, had established training programmes for nurses, influenced very much by Florence Nightingale's ideas. By 1901 some 10,000 of the 64,000 nurses and midwives listed in the census would have been fully trained, the majority of the untrained being elderly widows. Nursing had become a career fit for ladies.

It was not so much the influence of reformers as changes in the structure of the economy that opened up careers in shop keeping and office work. In each of these occupations there was an expansion in the demand for workers accompanied by a degeneration in skill, a not unfamiliar pattern so far as women's work is concerned. At the beginning of the nineteenth century the characteristic figure in retail distribution was the small-scale trader who usually possessed only one shop, which he ran with the aid of his family and perhaps one or two helpers. He was a skilled craftsman dealing in a specialised and narrow range of goods, the quality of which he had to know intimately. He also had to do much processing of his goods himself; the grocer, for example, had to blend his own tea, roast his own coffee, and grind his own sugar. Little reliance was placed on advertising, and the tradesman supplied a regular clientele who sought him out for his skill, his honesty, the quality of his wares and his willingness to take a personal interest in his customers' requirements. Not only was there little demand for women in these circumstances, there was no great demand for shop assistants at all. The later nineteenth century saw a revolution in retail distribution, however, and shopkeepers more and more became dealers in standardised, mass-produced and 'branded' articles. This trend was accompanied by a great increase in both the number and the size of shops. In 1875 there were an estimated 295,000 shops in the country; and in 1907, 459,952. This represents an increase of 56 per cent, as against an increase in the population of the country between 1871 and 1901 of 43 per cent. This expansion created a demand for women shop assistants, and by 1914 they numbered close to 500,000, and were by far the largest single group of lower middle-class women workers in the country. It is difficult to imagine why shop work should have been so attractive, for conditions were hard and hours were long. The Factory and Workshops Act Commissioners reported in 1876 that shop hours ranged as high as 85, and a Select Committee of the House of Lords on Early Closing cited the same figure in 1901. The opening hours of shops depended upon their location, their size, the kind of trade and the class of the customer. Within the towns shops in central business districts tended to close earlier than those in residential districts. In 1886, for example, the factory inspector for the Sheffield district reported that in the centre of the city shops closed at 7 p.m. on weekdays and 9 or 9.30 p.m. on Saturdays, while in the suburbs the closing hours were 8 p.m. on weekdays and 10 or 11 p.m. on Saturdays. Small shops tended to stay open longer than larger ones, presumably because this was the only way they could compete effectively. In 1886 the hours of young persons were nominally limited to 74 a week, but it was not until 1913 that a maximum working week of 64 hours was established.

Clerical work underwent a similar transformation in the nineteenth century. In the early years a clerk might see a career stretching before him that would take him, once he had learned all aspects of the business, into the ranks of management.

However, as the size of businesses grew, clerical work became more and more fragmented, and there was a trend towards setting up separate departments, or groups of workers dealing with single aspects of the business, such as book-keeping, filing or records. There was a great increase in the overall demand for clerks, but the general standard of education necessary for clerical work declined. These changes had important implications for the employment of women. Many people asserted that women were temperamentally better suited to routine clerical work than were men, while women were probably more easily reconciled to the lack of opportunity for advancement, which increasingly became the characteristic of much clerical work. Certain new skills however, were speedily taken over by women. These included shorthand and the use of the typewriter. Remington typewriters were sold in England from as early as 1874, but it was in the next decade that typewriters made their real impact on the business world. Contemporaries likened typewriting to piano playing, and from the beginning it was almost exclusively a feminine occupation. The telegraph and the telephone provided other employment opportunities. By 1914 the Post Office was the greatest single employer of middle-class women in the country, and accounted for 90 per cent of women employed by the central government. In 1881 the census recorded 6,000 women clerks in private firms, rising to 60,000 by 1901, by which time there were a further 25,000 in government employment. By 1914 clerical workers ranked third (behind shopkeepers and teachers) in the list of occupations for middle-class women.

Although employment opportunities increased greatly, women generally lacked equality with men. Pay was lower and prospects for advancement more limited. A formal marriage ban on women teachers remained until 1944 (and in the civil service until 1946), and although equal pay in the civil service was formally accepted in 1955 (to be introduced over a seven-year period), sex discrimination in pay was not generally abolished until 1975. One of the factors which accounts for the continuing poor conditions of women workers was the weak trade union organisation, a reflection both of male exclusiveness and their own reticence. Margaret Bondfield, leader of the shop workers (who became Britain's first woman Cabinet minister in 1929) wrote in 1900:

> . . . the largest proportion of women wage-earners do not organise [because] . . . they look upon it as a temporary occupation to be superseded by marriage! They fail to see any need for bothering themselves about the wages and general conditions obtaining in their trade . . . Until girls are taught independence and a trade . . . women wage-earners in the aggregate will remain where they are today – outside the ranks of Trade Unionism.[10]

As another union leader put it: 'Trade unionism means rebellion, and the orthodox teaching for women is submission.' Membership trebled between 1884 and 1900, during which period public attention was focused on the plight of the female wage-earner by the Royal Commission on Labour, and by the much publicised strike of the match-girls in 1888. By 1906, 167,000 women were trade unionists (of whom 143,000 were in the textile unions), and by 1914 that figure had doubled.

The reform of women's legal position, and the suffrage question

The reform of the legal status of women (which has yet to be fully accomplished) took three major forms: reform of the property rights of married women, the custody of children, and divorce. In addition, we may include the suffrage question, although a full discussion of this is more appropriate to a work on political history.

It often happens that a *cause célèbre* aids reform, and such was the case of Caroline Norton, granddaughter of the playwright Sheridan and, in her younger days, a celebrated society beauty. She was unhappily married and left her husband, whereupon he took their children from her and, in 1830, unsuccessfully sued Lord Melbourne for adultery. Although the case was thrown out by the jury, Mrs Norton was unable to clear her name; nor could she sue her husband for divorce on the grounds of cruelty, for she had 'condoned' his behaviour having, on a previous occasion, received him back. In order to support herself she took to writing, but of her earnings from this her husband repeatedly tried to obtain possession. However, one of her early polemical pamphlets helped to secure the passage of the Custody of Children Act of 1839, which gave mothers certain limited rights to their children. The principal provision was that an 'innocent' mother might have custody of any children up to the age of seven. Not until 1873 was the age of custody raised to 16; but from 1886 the welfare of the child rather than the supposed guilt or innocence of the parents was made the determining factor in custody cases.

The case of Mrs Norton inspired Barbara Leigh Smith (later Leigh Smith Bodichon), who was to have a distinguished career in the women's movement. In 1854 she published a pamphlet, *A Brief Summary, in Plain Language, of the Most Important Laws Concerning Women*, which aroused considerable public interest and aroused the attention of the Law Amendment Society. The first known feminist committee organised a national petition which secured 26,000 signatures, but a bill introduced in 1857 was swamped by the Divorce Bill which was passing through Parliament at the same time. The Divorce Act of 1857 secured certain property rights for women: in particular, a woman who obtained a judicial separation or was granted a protection order on grounds of desertion by her husband, was to have all the rights of an unmarried woman with respect to property. However, the main concern of the act was to make divorce easier for men. Previously, it had required an expensive private act of Parliament, but thereafter a new Court of Divorce and Matrimonial Causes was empowered to grant men a divorce on the grounds of the wife's adultery. More than this was required for a woman to end an unsatisfactory marriage, for she also had to prove desertion, cruelty or the committing of an unnatural offence. By the 1860s there were 150 divorces a year, rising to 600 a year by 1890. But not until 1923 could a woman obtain a divorce on the same grounds – of simple adultery – as a man.

After the passage of the Divorce Act of 1857 the cause of property law reform languished for a decade, only to surface again when the suffrage question was taken up in the late 1860s. In 1867 John Stuart Mill introduced an amendment to the Reform Bill that would have extended the franchise to women on the same terms as men. His amendment was defeated, but his speech made a profound impression. In it he made much of women's property disabilities, drawing attention to the means whereby the upper classes managed to get around the law:

. . . the wife's position under the common law of England is worse than that of slaves in the laws of many countries: by the Roman law, for example, a slave might have his peculium, which to a certain extent the law guaranteed to him for his exclusive use. The higher classes in this country have given an analogous advantage to their women, through special contracts setting aside the law, by conditions of pin-money, etc: since parental feeling being stronger with fathers than the class feeling of their own sex, a father generally prefers his own daughter to a son-in-law who is a stranger to him. By means of settlements, the rich usually contrive to withdraw the whole or part of the inherited property of the wife from the absolute control of the husband; but they do not succeed in keeping it under her control; the utmost they can do only prevents the husband from squandering it, at the same time debarring the rightful owner from its use . . .[11]

In fact, only one wife in 10 was able to benefit from this type of settlement, which was administered under the rules of equity in the Court of Chancery. Bills were introduced in 1868 and 1869; and in 1870 the Married Women's Property Act was passed which allowed women to retain their property or earnings acquired after marriage. However, the law 'bristled with anomalies and absurdities', and not until 1882 was the husband's automatic right to his wife's property on marriage finally removed.

The Victorian age was one which saw sweeping changes to the English legal system, and reform of the antiquated system of courts culminated in the great Judicature Act of 1873. This act consolidated all existing superior courts into one Supreme Court of Judicature, and the conflict between equity and the common law was at last resolved. When reform of the property laws came, therefore, it was by the application to all classes of women of the equitable provisions and remedies once confined to women of the wealthier classes. Yet it still took 25 years for the law to be changed effectively. Between 1857 and 1882, 18 Married Women's Property Bills were introduced in Parliament. All were private members' bills, and their fate depended on the attitude of the government and the pressures of parliamentary business. Feminists argued that this proved that women needed the vote in order to bring pressure to bear on Parliament in support of their interests.

Almost every year from 1869 a private member's bill was introduced to give women the vote, but neither the Liberals nor the Tories were prepared to make women's suffrage a government question. Successive Liberal leaders were afraid that a household suffrage would only enfranchise well-to-do single women who would be drawn to the Tories. Liberal backbenchers, however, were friendly to the movement. It was the reverse with the Tories, whose backbenchers were hostile although the leaders were in favour of reform. Forty years of public meetings, petitions and publicity in favour of women's suffrage was succeeded by militant action when the Liberals achieved power in 1906. Mrs Pankhurst's Militant Suffragettes took to window smashing and arson. Imprisoned suffragettes went on hunger strike and were forcibly fed, until the infamous Cat and Mouse Act of 1913 allowed for the release of prisoners severely debilitated by hunger striking, and then rearrest once their health improved. It is impossible to tell whether the campaign would have achieved its goal, for when war broke out in 1914 the hatchet (which had literally been thrown at Asquith, the Prime Minister) was buried. The war was to have an enormous impact in breaking down the rigid divisions between what were considered male activities and what female. It was in its aftermath, as discussed in Chapter 12, that women at last won the vote.

Experience this century has shown how limited have been the gains to women even from such an important step forward as enfranchisement. While women obtained formal legal and political rights, they remain strikingly absent from positions of public power and authority. At the 1992 general election, women won only 9 per cent of the seats in the House of Commons, giving Britain one of the lowest proportions of women in its national elected legislature of the whole of western Europe. Likewise, women held a very small proportion of appointments on public bodies. In 1984, the government appointed 31,172 men to public bodies, compared with 7,233 women. Even the National Health Service, with 79 per cent of its workforce female, employed women in only 17 per cent of the unit general manager posts, and only 4 per cent of the district and regional general manager posts. The struggle for equal opportunities has not ended.

Notes

1 'The cost of a modern belle' in *The Family Friend*, September 1858, quoted in J. A. Banks, *Prosperity and Parenthood*, Routledge and Kegan Paul, 1954, pp. 97–8.
2 Michael Anderson, 'New insights into the history of the family in Britain' in Anne Digby, Charles Feinstein and David Jenkins (eds), *New Directions in Economic and Social History*, vol. 2, Macmillan, 1992, pp. 134–5.
3 Quoted in Patricia Hollis, *Women in Public: The Women's Movement 1850–1900*, Allen and Unwin,1979.
4 Sara Delamont and Lorna Duffin (eds), *The Nineteenth-Century Woman*, Croom Helm, 1978, pp. 145–6.
5 Quoted in Dale Spender (ed.), *The Education Papers*, Routledge and Kegan Paul, 1987, p. 11.
6 Quoted in Joan Burstyn, *Victorian Education and the Ideal of Womanhood*, Croom Helm, 1980, p. 79.
7 Quoted in Patricia Hollis, op. cit., 1979, p. 10.
8 Ibid., p. 81.
9 Sara Delamont and Lorna Duffin (eds) , op. cit., 1978, p. 50.
10 Quoted in Patricia Hollis, op. cit., 1979, p. 121.
11 Quoted in Margaret James, *The Emancipation of Women in Great Britain*, Edward Arnold, 1972, p. 13.

Chapter eleven

A new era dawns, 1870–1914

Great Britain and its competitors

In the middle of the nineteenth century, the economic running in the world was being made by a small group of islands perched off the coast of north-western Europe. At the end of the following century the running was again being made by a group of offshore islands, but this time half a world away off the coast of mainland Asia. That the torch of economic advance should at one time have been held by Britain, and is now held increasingly by Japan is in itself remarkable, for neither is a nation of great size. Paul Kennedy makes an interesting comparison between the two countries:

> While Japan does not have much in the way of *hard* power (tanks, aircraft), it possesses a growing amount of *soft* power, or nonmilitary influence, as can be seen in its enhanced position within the IMF and World Bank, its acquisition of Hollywood studios and European computer firms, the size of the Tokyo stock market, and the fact that Japan is now the world's largest donor of foreign aid, so that many developing countries now look to Tokyo for assistance, loans and investments. As politicians from developing countries hasten to Japan, a rising flood of Japanese businessmen, tourists, manufacturers, and capital penetrates most parts of the globe, in a manner reminiscent of Britain's mid-to-late Victorian expansionism.[1]

In the nineteenth century, of course, Britain had a great deal of what Kennedy calls 'hard power', with by far the world's largest navy and an army (although small by European standards) in excess of 230,000 men. That number does not include colonial troops, needed to defend an empire which, in 1897, the year of the queen's diamond jubilee, numbered 370 million people. In 1990 Britain's overseas dependencies had a population of 6 million, of whom 5.7 million lived in Hong Kong, which reverts to China in 1997, the centenary year of Victoria's triumphant jubilee. Whether or not the 1,800 residents of the Falkland Islands (who fall short of filling the Royal Festival Hall by 1,100 seats) will still be owing allegiance to the queen at that date remains to be seen, although a bloody war was fought in 1982 to ensure that they would. That conflict will come to be seen, perhaps, as a final fling in a century of unremitting imperial decline.

The mass of the people probably do not feel the decline of Britain as a world power in a personal way. Professor Barry Supple has suggested:

> . . . we should surely bear in mind that status as an imperial or world power does not of itself enhance the material welfare of the mass of the people. And it is, therefore, not at all clear that this aspect of decline has been of central concern to the majority of the population. . . No doubt it is in some sense

reassuring, even flattering, to be a citizen of a superpower. But for the men and women on the Clapham omnibus, work and income, social networks and quality of life – the prosaic essences of daily existence – take precedence over geopolitics and cartographical prominence in the ultimate calculation of welfare.[2]

There is an important difference, however, between decline in world political status and economic decline, for Britain's imperial decline has been *absolute*, while economic decline has been *relative*. There can be no doubt that Britain is far richer today than it was 100 years ago, and that the standard of living of its people has grown enormously. It is in comparison with the performance of its competitors that Britain has shown a relative decline. Perhaps such a decline was inevitable for, as Sir John Clapham wrote more than 50 years ago, when making a comparison between Britain and the United States: 'Half a continent is likely in course of time to raise more coal and make more steel than a small island, though the fact still surprised people between 1890 and 1910.' The more interesting problem may be to explain how Britain managed to hold sway for so long, rather than to explain its eventual decline. Nevertheless, there *are* questions to be asked. When did the relative economic decline of Britain set in, and was it as inevitable as the hard facts of physical geography might suggest? If it is concluded that it was not, then the historian is placed in the position of having to explain the causes of the changes which took place.

The problem to be analysed is complicated by the fact that the half-century before the First World War included the so-called Great Depression of 1873–96. This had contained within itself the more familiar 'short cycle' of boom and slump, but it is not clear that the period is of *particular* significance to the long-term slowing down of the economy. Debate continues as to the starting-point of this trend. In the 1950s the decade of the 1890s was favoured, but subsequent writers have pushed it back to the 1870s, and it has even been suggested that but for the distortion introduced by the recovery of the cotton industry after the American Civil War, retardation would be apparent from the 1860s. Again, the period 1873–96 does not constitute that of the greatest deceleration. This was much more evident in the years 1900–13, when the economy was probably growing more slowly than at any time since the industrial revolution. But it must be emphasised that it *was* growing.

It is mainly when comparison is made between Britain's performance and that of its competitors that the cause for alarm is revealed. Growing competition in world trade and the rapid industrialisation of such countries as Germany and the United States gave the impression that British economic supremacy was coming to an end, and that it had reached a 'climacteric' – a watershed in its economic development.

In 1870 Britain accounted for nearly one-third of the world's manufacturing output while its nearest rival, the United States, produced less than a quarter. By 1913, however, Britain had fallen to third place with only 14.1 per cent, while the USA and Germany respectively produced 35.3 and 15.9 per cent. A similar decline is apparent in its share of overseas trade. In 1880 Britain's overseas trade was twice that of its nearest rival, and although it was still out in front in 1913, Germany, in second place, was only just behind. And if we took account of American interstate trade – between California on one side of the continent and New York, 3000 miles away on the other side, for example – the United States would have become the world's greatest trading nation.

The historian who would attempt to explain the changes taking place in the British economy at the end of the Victorian period must proceed with great caution. There is a danger of concentrating our attention solely on areas of British 'failure' while ignoring more successful sectors of industry. In shipbuilding, for example,

British technical leadership and industrial power remained unchallenged. In the 25 years before the First World War, Britain built almost two-thirds of the new ships which were launched. In much light industry and food processing Britain also had a healthy record.

Even industry-wide comparisons can be misleading. The chemical industry is sometimes held up as an example of British 'failure'. This is undoubtedly true of some sections of it, although in fertilisers, soap and heavy inorganic chemicals Britain was often a match for its competitors. Likewise it remained fairly competitive in some of the older branches of the engineering industry, such as railway locomotives and rolling stock, and textile machinery. In 1914, for example, Platts of Oldham employed 12,000 workers, and had an output equal to the whole American textile machinery industry. The firm survived until 1982, going bankrupt in the recession of that time.

Lastly, the weakness of statistics must yet again be stressed. While the growing social awareness and expanding bureaucracies ensured that this period is better documented statistically than earlier ages, many statistical series give little more than a general indication of direction or quantity. Surrogate data often have to be used where the series the historian would like to use do not exist. For example, economic historians made much use of the statistical series produced by W. G. Hoffman, who deduced manufactured output from figures of raw material consumption or importation. The method, however, has flaws for the unwary. Hoffman was sometimes mistaken over the 'ingredients' which he used to make his deductions. For example, he estimated soap output solely from tallow, palm oil and coconut oil imports, ignoring (among other things) cotton-seed oil which was used from at least 1880. At the same time, technical improvements gave more soap for less material. Charles Feinstein has pointed to other sources of error:

> For instance, output of cotton or woollen cloth is measured by the corresponding supplies of yarn, because contemporary statisticians have left us figures for the yarn but not for the cloth. Similarly, output of machinery is measured by inputs of iron and steel, flour by supplies of wheat, furniture by imports of timber. The problem is that these and many other series make no adjustment for changes in the level of stocks held in ports and warehouses. They are thus likely to understate output in boom years if stocks of inputs were run down to meet unexpectedly large demands for materials. Equally, they may overestimate output in depression years if unwanted materials were added to stocks. Since there is very little information about stocks it will be extremely difficult to check this hypothesis, but that is a task which should now receive urgent attention. Until that is done, the extent and timing of the retardation of British economic growth will remain uncertain.[3]

The historical debate on the timing and dimensions of Britain's economic slowing down has been overshadowed by controversy over the factors which caused it. Basically, the possible causes can be classified under two headings, economic and sociological, although the former can be subdivided into those which are *theoretically* possible, and those which fit the discernible economic facts of the period. In practice it can be extremely difficult to disentangle the causes. However, there may be theoretical arguments which postulate a model of economic growth in which deceleration becomes inevitable in a mature economy. The 'early start' hypothesis is such an explanation. Then there are arguments which look to the actual historical situation and seek economic causes in a lower rate of technical innovation, a decline of exports, the character of capital formation, the effects of low profits on industry during the great depression and so on. The sociological arguments tend to blame the entrepreneur, the worker, or even society as a whole, alleging a loss of 'growth-mindedness' after the collapse of mid-Victorian optimism.

That Britain suffered from its early start is one of the explanations most frequently put forward. The argument is not as straightforward as it might seem, for the early starter ought to have greater resources to undertake new investment, and it should pay it as well as the newcomers to scrap old plant and invest in new. Admittedly, latecomers should be able to learn from their predecessors, avoid their mistakes, and take short cuts. Indeed, it was argued by entrepreneurs in both the British artificial silk industry and the glass industry that it paid to allow the foreigner to bear the costs of research and development, and then to pay royalties for a successful process. However, while the early-start hypothesis may explain the faster growth rates of latecomers, it does not explain how they *overtake* the first starter, as happened with much of British industry. In practice, of course, other influences come into play. The early starter may be made resistant to change by a variety of psychological and institutional factors. As early as 1915, for example, the American economist Thorstein Veblen observed that British industrialists were burdened with 'the restraining dead-hand of their past achievement'. Some historians have spoken in a similar vein (or artery?), describing the 'sclerosis' of British industry.

A more sophisticated variant of the early-start hypothesis is that of *overcommitment* to certain basic staple industries. This line of argument is based on the obvious fact that any expanding economy is a dynamic one, in which certain sectors are contracting while newer, more profitable ones are expanding. In other words, an expanding economy is also a *changing* one. It is argued that in late nineteenth-century Britain too many resources were locked up in the staple industries to the detriment of newer growth areas. This is an economic argument which, unlike the early-start hypothesis (which should apply to any mature economy) applies particularly to Britain, for there is no other case where so high a proportion of the economy's resources were tied up in such a narrow range of industries. The extent of overcommitment was indicated by the Census of Production of 1907 which revealed that coal, textiles, iron and steel, and engineering accounted for about 50 per cent of net industrial output, employed one-quarter of the occupied population, and supplied 70 per cent of Britain's exports. In contrast, industries in the growth areas (which included electrical goods, road vehicles, rayon, chemicals and scientific instruments) accounted for only 6.5 per cent of net industrial output, 5.2 per cent of industrial employment and 7.4 per cent of exports (reduced to 2.8 per cent if chemicals are excluded). Although the dangers of this overcommitment were discernible before the First World War, it was not until the collapse of the post-war boom that heavy structural unemployment and prolonged depression in those areas reliant on the staple industries indicated the costs of delayed readjustment.

H. W. Richardson, one of the early proponents of the overcommitment hypothesis, argued that it interfered with the growth of new industries in three main ways:

In the first place, it led to a scarcity of production facilities for these industries. Secondly, the long and unchallenged predominance of Britain's staple industries affected entrepreneurial psychology and lulled businessmen into making decisions and judgments based too much on past experience, which led to a misplaced emphasis on short-run as against long-run benefits. Thirdly, the institutional framework against which decisions are made was so moulded by the lopsided industrial structure that the adoption of new industries was less economic in Britain than abroad.[4]

We will discuss 'entrepreneurial psychology' and 'the institutional framework' shortly, but ought here to consider the starving of production facilities. Of these, three need examination: labour, entrepreneurs and capital. Richardson concluded that there is no evidence that the supply of labour to the newer industries was restricted, and this view still gains support. Although the rate of population growth slowed down, the absolute increase was sufficient to meet the demands of industry, largely because the occupied population became a larger proportion of the total population (36.5 per cent in 1881 and 40.6 per cent in 1911). Admittedly, the staple industries snapped up much of the labour (mining, for example, doubled its labour force between 1881 and 1911) but there is little evidence of newer industries suffering a labour shortage in the period before 1914. Furthermore, the heavy net emigration of the early years of the twentieth century does not suggest a general labour shortage. Nor does it look as though new industries were starved of efficient entrepreneurs. The decline of the family firm and the development of the business corporation accompanied by a belated spurt in technical education widened the pool from which managers might be selected. The progressiveness of some of the newer industries also suggests that they were not denied efficient entrepreneurs.

The heavy export of capital from the last quarter of the century has been blamed by some historians, who point to the preoccupation of the London capital market with foreign investment, to the detriment of domestic industry. However, as in the early period of the industrial revolution, retained profits and private sources of finance continued to be the principal sources of capital for industry. They accounted for three-quarters of capital formation in 1856 and for two-thirds of a much larger total in 1913. And there is much evidence that those who sought finance generally found it. By 1913–14, for example, the electricity supply industry had mobilised £66.5 million, while in 1896 the promoter Harry J. Lawson persuaded 550 investors to part with £100,000 in equity shares in the Daimler Motor Company even though, as Michael Dintenfass points out, 'the country had not yet seen the commercial production of even a single automobile'. Even if, as many historians are inclined to believe, the export of capital did not starve new industries of investment funds, it may have intensified overcommitment in indirect ways, for the opening up of markets by overseas investment had its strongest repercussions on staple exports such as cotton textiles and railway *matériel*.

Some historians have pointed to the absence from this country of large investment banks which, in the United States and Germany, were important in cradling many new enterprises from infancy to maturity. However, there were unsuccessful attempts to set up such banks in Britain in the 1860s and 1870s, and their failure suggests that there was no great demand for their services.

When we consider the 'institutional framework' of the economy, we have to remember that individual industrial processes are often so closely interlinked that advances in one sector are dependent upon changes in others. The extensive infrastructure of power and transport facilities constructed to meet the needs of industrial expansion resulted in a heavy dependence on coal, steam, gas and railways, which was an important factor in Britain's lag in road transport and electricity. In their turn other industries were blocked. The manufacture of both aluminium and carborundum (silicon carbide, an abrasive of strategic importance to the machine-tool industry) consumed enormous quantities of electricity, and was inhibited by the slow growth of that industry. Likewise the slow growth of the British motor car industry set back the rubber industry a decade behind that of the United States. The older industries presented various obstacles to change. The large output of 'old' goods led over the years to substantial cost reductions which encouraged fierce price competition so long as the production of 'new' goods remained at a high-cost stage. Thus the cheapness of gas inhibited the introduction of electricity, and that of cotton textiles checked the growth of a market for rayon before the First World War. Vested interests with political power, such as municipal gas undertakings, or the railway interest in Parliament could also obstruct innovation, as both the electrical industry and the automobile industry came to discover.

An argument favoured by some historians is one which stresses the slow technical development of British industry. The economist J. A. Schumpeter, in a classic study of the business cycle, placed technical innovation at the very centre of the process; but as major innovations such as steam, iron and steel, electricity and the motor car range over long periods of time, they seem more relevant to cycles of longer duration than the usual short trade cycle. It has been argued that the high growth rate of earlier years was sustained by a series of major innovations, particularly steam power and steel. By the 1890s, so the argument runs, the rate of expansion of these innovations had markedly declined. The railway network was virtually completed, and the transition from domestic industry to the factory system had also largely ended. In other words, it is alleged that Britain had almost literally run out of steam. The theory is an interesting one, marred only by the facts not fitting the case! The available statistics indicate that there were still ample opportunities for the extension of steam and steel. The latter had only begun to take hold by the 1880s, output more than doubling between the early part of that decade and 1895, and almost doubling again by 1910. It is true that the technology used was not always as advanced as that of Britain's competitors but that is not the point here. The statistics of steam power, although less adequate, tell a similar story. In 1850 the total of fixed industrial steam power in the United Kingdom was 500,000 horsepower, rising to 2 million in 1880 and over 9 million by 1907. The greatest concentration of steam power ever assembled was used in the construction of the Manchester Ship Canal in the early 1890s, including 58 Ruston steam navvies, 97 steam-excavators, 5 land dredgers, 194 steam cranes, 59 pile drivers, 212 steam pumps, 182 stationary steam-engines and 173 locomotives. Britain had not run out of steam! If anything, its brilliant steam engineers rested too long on their laurels, to the detriment of other forms of motive power.

Andrew Carnegie, the Dunfermline boy who emigrated to America with his parents, and became that country's foremost iron and steel manufacturer, wrote: 'Most British equipment is in use twenty years after it should have been scrapped. It is because you keep this used-up machinery that the US is making you a back number.'[5] It is true that over a wide spectrum of industry British technology did lag behind. David Landes has commented:

The worst symptom of Britain's industrial ills . . . was the extent to which her entrepreneurship and technology was defensive. She was no longer in the van of technical change; instead, even the best of her enterprises were usually being dragged in the wake of foreign precursors, like children being jerked along by important adults.[6]

With the possible exception of pottery, there was hardly a basic industry in which Britain retained technical superiority by 1914. In the words of Peter Stearns: 'Britain had taught her lessons well, but her pupils had taken over. The transformation, satisfying to a true educator perhaps, had not been part of the planned curriculum.'

Why the teacher should have become the pupil is an intriguing question. Attempts to answer it have emphasised a greater willingness by foreign industrialists to scrap outdated machinery, or the effects of different endowments of factors of production. American industry experienced labour shortages (both skilled and unskilled) and, so the argument goes, compensated for this deficiency by inventing labour-saving technology and capital-intensive techniques. Britain, on the other hand, enjoyed plentiful supplies of all factors of production with the possible exception of land. Thus A. J. Taylor has explained the slow introduction of machinery into the coal industry in terms of the availability of cheap labour. The same applied to other industries. By 1919 half the looms in the American cotton industry were of the automatic type, whereas Britain had only just begun to introduce them. But among all the possible factors of production, is a shortage of *labour* of particular significance to technical innovation? It is possible that at the time this was indeed the case. First, labour usually constituted a higher proportion of total costs than natural resources, possibly leading industrialists to deduce that it was the cost which could most easily be reduced, although this does not necessarily follow. Second, the response to a shortage of natural resources was a search for fresh sources of supply (guaranteed by colonisation, if necessary) rather than an incentive to resource-saving technology. Labour was comparatively difficult to 'import' (although there was an extensive migration of skilled and unskilled workers) but scarce raw materials might be imported from whichever they were in abundant supply. Finally, the available technical knowledge was more capable of solving problems of labour scarcity than natural resource scarcity; the former relies on mechanical engineering, which was relatively advanced. As J. D. Bernal put it: 'The typical inventor was usually a workman or amateur who contrived to find the most convenient arrangement of wheels, rollers, cogs and levers designed to imitate the movement of the craftsman at higher speed and using steam power.' Saving resources involved chemical and physical engineering of a sophistication frequently greater than that which was available at the time. Today, things are different, the response to the acute energy crisis being both a search for fresh sources of supply of traditional fuels and a search for alternative technologies.

If Britain lagged behind American technology because of its ample labour supply, why did it so often lag behind its continental counterparts whose labour supply was little less favourable than Britain's own? Abundance of fuel may provide one answer, for the evidence suggests that Britain's ample fuel supplies encouraged wasteful methods, in iron and steel production for example, which continental industrialists could not afford.

Only two years after the Great Exhibition, the Americans held their own Industrial Exhibition in New York, to which the British government sent distinguished commissioners, including the great engineer, Joseph Whitworth. The commissioners reported that in automatic machinery, 'the Americans showed an amount of ingenuity, combined with undaunted energy, which we would do well to imitate if we meant to hold our present position in the great markets of the world'. But British attitudes towards machinery differed greatly from those of the Americans; for in Britain machines were usually built to specification, whereas in the United States they were produced for a wide market. There was such an abundance of timber in that country that the enormous wastage resulting from the use of wood-working machines was accepted, whereas it was intolerable in Britain, which needed to import vast quantities of wood. In the United States a wide variety of machines was manufactured, of which an English expert wrote in 1873: '[They] are made in America at this time like boots and shoes, or shovels and hatchets. You do not, as in most countries, prepare a specification of what you need . . . but must take what is made for the general market.' American machines thus tended to be cheaper, and to this their comparative flimsiness also contributed. Americans seemed to be more optimistic about the possibilities of technical innovation and saw no object in building a machine to last 50 years when a better method might be discovered in another five. We should not make too much of this point, for many British manufacturers were capable of making flimsy machinery! And much of the 'heavy machinery' which they constructed had to be built heavy or it would not work. As S. B. Saul has observed: 'If a steam hammer was not built to last for ever, it would not work properly at all.' The same might be true of steam-engines, although the fact that six steam-engines installed in British breweries before 1800 were operational a century later is, claims Peter Mathias, 'one of the finest tributes to British engineers and one of the worst indictments of British industrialists'.

The readiness of manufacturers to adopt new technology was no doubt influenced by the size of the home market, for the bigger the market the greater the scope for mass-production methods. Both Germany and the United States had a larger population than the United Kingdom in 1870, and in both the rate of increase was greater in the following decades, as Table 11.1 shows:

Table 11.1   Population of the UK, Germany and the USA (in millions)

	1871	1911	% increase
United Kingdom	31.8	45.3	42.4
Germany*	41.0	64.9	58.2
USA*	38.5	91.7	138.1

*population figures for 1870 and 1910

What was even more important than mere numbers was the *nature* of the market, or what is sometimes called the 'social depth of demand'. The Americans and the Germans were more willing to purchase standardised products than the British, who were more likely to insist that goods should reach their own specifications. This applied to capital goods as well as consumer goods. In the steel industry, for example, standardisation proceeded more slowly than with Britain's competitors. In 1900 British steelmakers were manufacturing 122 kinds and sizes of channel and angle sections as a matter of course, while the Germans made 34 and the Americans 33. Not until 1903 did a degree of standardisation of steel beams come about. In the 1860s no fewer than 300 different classes of nail were being produced, with at least 10 different sizes to each sort, so that in all upwards of 3,000 different kinds of nail were on the market. *The Ironmonger* reported in 1878: 'Machine-made nails of certain kinds have largely invaded the market, but there seems no likelihood of machine nails superseding the general varieties now made by hand, for, considering the demand, it would not pay anyone to make these particular classes of nails by machinery.'

In Britain the demand for ready-made clothing was small. People either had their clothes made to measure, or they wore the cast-off clothing of other people. Not so in the United States, where one of the British commissioners to the New York Industrial Exhibition reported as early as 1854 that 'all classes of the people may be said to be well dressed and the cast-off clothes of one class are never worn by another'. It was in that country, therefore, that the sewing-machine was given its greatest industrial application. The Americans also pioneered new methods of mass-distribution. The mail-order business was developed by firms such as Montgomery Ward and Sears Roebuck in the 1870s and 1880s, while F. W. Woolworth pioneered the concept of the cheap chain-store after 1879, building an empire which, within 40 years, controlled 800 stores in the USA and 60 in Great Britain.

There is, of course, an element of 'heads we win, tails you lose' about all this. We condemn the British industrialist for not producing a standardised product, while at the same time charging him with failing to meet the particular needs and wishes of his export customers (see Chapter 7). We should not try to have it both ways, and we should remember the difficulties which the peculiarities of demand presented to manufacturers. Nevertheless, to some extent it was up to them to 'educate' the public into accepting articles of a more standardised nature, just as it was up to them to 'educate' their craftsmen, and to turn their attention away from technical perfection to the techniques of production. F. W. Lanchester, for example, one of the few British motor engineers to employ modern production techniques, described how reluctant craftsmen were to work to standardised instructions: 'In those days, when a body builder was asked to work to drawings, gauges or templates, he gave a sullen look such as one might expect from a Royal Academician if asked to colour an engineering drawing.' An example of an entire industry destroyed by craft conservatism is watch- and clock-making, centred on Coventry and at Prescot in Lancashire. In the late eighteenth and early nineteenth centuries its techniques had played an important role in the development of British engineering, but in the second half of the nineteenth century it was savaged by American and Swiss mechanised mass-production.

Finally, we come to the sociological and cultural arguments about retardation, which suggest that the phenomenon was rooted in the inadequacies of entrepreneurs or the obstructiveness of workers. Economic historians on the whole remain unconvinced by such arguments, for the picture of dynamic and energetic entrepreneurs urging Britain forward into the industrial revolution seems in too sharp contrast with complacent entrepreneurs holding back Britain's economic growth towards the end of the century.

There has been debate on what is called the 'third-generation argument' (a sort of sociological counterpart to the early-start hypothesis). The pioneering captains of industry, it is claimed, were obliged to devote their attention to their businesses in order to survive; but as they became established and their wealth accumulated, the second and third generations no longer strove to maximise profits but instead sought advancement for themselves in society, often by acquiring the trappings of gentility. According to the folklore, 'the third generation makes the gentleman'. This certainly happened in some cases – with, for example, the Boultons in engineering, the Marshalls in linen and the Strutts in cotton – but one can easily find examples where the third generation proved as enterprising as the first, while no one has claimed that Britain's financial and commercial dynasties suffered in a similar way.

Both industrialists and traders had their contemporary critics. One writer bewailed in 1906: 'The once enterprising manufacturer has grown slack, he has let the business take care of itself, while he is shooting grouse or yachting in the Mediterranean.' This is caricature, of course, as David Landes points out:

Contemporary observers emphasised the failures of British entrepreneurship and the imminent dangers of German competition much as a newspaper cries up the morbid aspects of the news. That was the way one sold articles or attracted the notice of officials in London. Besides, there is such a thing as fashion in opinions, and this was clearly one of the popular dirges of the day.[7]

Charles Feinstein reminds us that a distinction should be made between management and entrepreneurship:

The *manager's* task was to make rational decisions within an existing framework of markets and productive techniques. The *entrepreneur's* task was quite different. A successful entrepreneur was someone who could make changes in that framework – for example, by finding new goods to make, or new ways to produce or sell the product, or new structures for the firm or the industry. The tests for a manager might be rationality, but for the entrepreneur it was innovation. The good manager made rational decisions subject to existing constraints. The dynamic entrepreneur changes those constraints.[8]

With that distinction in mind, it has been argued that British entrepreneurs did show signs of weakness in the late Victorian period, but they did so not because of any cultural or social aberration, but because they failed to bring about the overhaul of institutional structures that would have transformed the economy. These institutional structures include the educational system, industrial relations, the capital market and the organisation of industry itself.

In 1885 most British businesses were owned and run by individuals or partnerships; by 1914 company ownership was usual, though private companies (which obtained limited liability without the public offer of shares, and which were legalised only in 1907) were more numerous than public ones. In 1885 there were 9,344 companies in the United Kingdom, rising to 62,762 in 1914, of which 77 per cent were private companies. Lacking the power of appealing to the public for funds, these private companies were often small with control firmly in family hands. The older partnership was a remarkably flexible form of association, and there were some great family firms such as Huntley & Palmer, Crosse & Blackwell and J. & J. Colman in the food industries, Pilkington Brothers in glass, and Harland & Wolff in ship-building. These giants were the exception, however, and the business unit often remained much smaller in Britain than in competing countries. Only one British steel firm in 1900 had an annual capacity of over 300,000 tons, whereas in Germany there were 10. The pre-war coal industry was characterised by a large number of concerns. In 1913, 3,289 collieries were being operated by 1,589 separate undertakings, each colliery employing on average 340 men. The number of companies was in decline in the early years of the twentieth century, but concentration had not proceeded as far as in the Ruhr, where the industry was coming to be dominated by about a dozen companies. Even in newer industries the unit remained small. In the motor car industry, for example, 393 firms had been founded by 1914, of which 280 had ceased to exist; and there was little attempt to combine in order to adopt more efficient production methods.

The long-term effects of the transition to company organisation were considerable. Where there is a large number of small firms, they have to rely on Adam Smith's 'invisible hand' of the market as the guide to making decisions about what to produce and how to produce it. The invisible hand, however, was a better guide to short-term decisions than it was to the formulation of longer-term strategies. Large corporations are better placed to take a longer view, and to forego present advantage for future gain. A more rapid transition to large-scale modern corporations would have had other advantages. An increase in scale would be facilitated which was often technically imperative and enabled financial reserves to be built up, either to finance further expansion or to give stability in times of bad trade. More precise accounting would have been encouraged, with the requirement of a compulsory audit, and professional accountants gaining an increasing influence in the making of business decisions. Indeed, the pool from which management skills might be drawn became wider as ownership came to be more separated from management. The other side of the coin was a greater impersonality in industrial relations. Robert Knight, the secretary of the Boilermakers' Society, wrote that 'the gulf between employers and employed was deeper, wider and more impassable than ever it was', and as early as 1879 the trade union leader George Howell complained of the tendency for the great majority of employers to look upon their work people as little better than 'mere machines for guiding machinery'.

The increase in scale which company organisation often entailed was further encouraged by an extension of combination among producers which almost invariably had the object of fixing minimum prices (at a time when prices were falling) or carving out spheres of influence. By the 1880s almost every trade had its trade association, which usually involved a 'gentleman's agreement' rather than formal sanctions. However, gentlemen's agreements generally illustrate that most men are not gentlemen, for if bad prices continued someone invariably broke the agreement and cut, while in the trade cycle upswing the more aggressive members often broke loose in order to free themselves from all restrictions. The more formal *trust* or *cartel* was more highly developed in Germany and the United States, but also took root in Britain. The institutional links which this involved might take a number of forms, including the exchange of shares or the creation of a common fund based on contributions from each member calculated on the basis of his share of total output.

These formal associations went beyond mere price-fixing and often included production quotas and agreements over profits. The most formal method of limiting the excesses of competition and price wars was outright merger or amalgamation. This could be achieved in many ways, such as simple purchase or the setting up of a 'holding company' to hold the ordinary share capital of each of the constituent companies and thus control them. The 'combine' then became a legal entity, not easily to be broken up. An example is the Salt Union, formed in 1888, which combined 64 firms (including all those in Cheshire) and controlled 90 per cent of British salt production. In 1891 the United Alkali Company drew together all 48 firms concerned with the production of soda by the ailing Leblanc process. When J. & P. Coats brought 14 competing firms together in 1897 to form the English Sewing Cotton Company, it gained a virtual monopoly of the British market as a step towards dominating the world market; and the Imperial Tobacco Company of 1901, which combined 13 firms to hold the British market against the Americans, went on in the following year to combine with its American counterpart in order to carve up the world.

Combines might involve either 'horizontal' or 'vertical' integration, the former encouraged by depression, the latter by boom conditions. Horizontal integration involved the combination – often under the pressure of adverse prices and profits – of firms competing in the same field. Rationalisation then became possible, together with economies of scale. Frequently these potential gains never actually materialised, although there yet remained the possibility of centralising research and other facilities and securing favourable rates from suppliers and shippers. Vertical integration was likely to come about as producers competed for raw materials, transport or markets. The aim was to embrace various stages of the production process, ranging up to the supply of raw materials and down to distribution. This type of integration became important in some sections of the food industry, for example, as well as in iron and steel where major concerns embraced orefields and collieries as well as their own transport fleets.

New directions for industry

The bicycle and motor car industries

The bicycle and the motor car were not only industries exhibiting the new technology and methods; they were of tremendous social impact. The origins of the British cycle industry go back to 1869 when James Starley reconstructed the Coventry Sewing Machine Company into the Coventry Machinists Co. Ltd, in order to obtain the powers necessary to carry out a French order for 400 cycles. The Franco-Prussian War frustrated his plans, and the company turned instead to the home market. The industry centred around Coventry, where the city's ancient ribbon and clock- and watch-making industries were depressed. By 1879, however, many of the 60 or so British firms manufacturing cycles were located there. The trade was as yet small, and only 700 persons were engaged in it in the Coventry and Birmingham area in 1881. The subsequent boom was due to a number of factors, not the least of which were sound entrepreneurship and dynamic marketing methods. The great breakthrough came in 1885 when John Kemp Starley introduced the safety model, incorporating the diamond frame and wheels of equal size, a great improvement on the 'ordinary' or 'penny-farthing' as it was popularly known. The pneumatic tyre followed in 1888. By that time there were about 400,000 cyclists in Britain, and as demand rose, manufacturers of cycles and components installed expensive mass-production machinery.

By 1891, 8,300 men were employed in cycle manufacture, and by the middle of the decade several firms employed around 1,000 men. The Coventry Machinists Co. became the Swift Cycle Company which was turning out 700 cycles a week in 1896. Two years later a rival firm, Humber, claimed a production of 1,000 a week. Attention soon turned to cutting the price and extending the market. By 1900, when Raleigh was marketing a serviceable machine for £10, the cycle at last came within the reach of the working class. Total output and exports continued to expand. Rudge increased its output from 9,000 in 1895 to 75,000 in 1906. By 1913 Britain exported 150,000 cycles, Germany 89,000 and the rest of the world hardly any at all.

Here, then, was an industry in which Britain achieved notable success, and one which had wider implications for British engineering. New techniques of milling and grinding were extended, and the production of weldless tubes developed. More important still was the development of machinery for the manufacture of ball-bearings, an essential component of modern machines, including the motor car. A number of the early British motor manufacturers entered the industry via the manufacture of cycles, including Humber, Rover, Singer, Star and Swift. James Starley, 'Father of the Cycle Industry', introduced the differential gear, essential to the motor car, and many other technical features were contributed by British engineers and inventors. Dunlop introduced the pneumatic tyre, Napier the six-cylinder engine and Lanchester alone contributed the epicyclic gear, accelerator, magneto ignition, pull-on hand brake, worm transmission gear, pre-selector control, cantilever springing and forced lubrication. The major developments in the petrol engine were almost all made on the continent, however; work in Britain was hampered by repressive legislation in force between 1865 and 1896, and passed at the instigation of the vested horse and railway interests, fearful of the impact of steam carriages on the roads. Before the so-called 'Red Flag Act' was repealed in 1896, no British car had been produced, the first car to be made on any scale being the German Daimler, built in Britain under licence from that year. British automobile engineers were caught unprepared by the removal of the restrictive legislation, although after 1900 they were beginning to make good after their late start. By 1913 they had an annual output of 34,000 vehicles, which was approximately three-quarters that of the French industry. Both were completely overshadowed by the American output, which reached 485,000 in 1914. By 1913 one person in 77 owned a motor car; in Europe the comparable densities were one in 165 in Britain, 318 in France and 950 in Germany.

The size of the home market was not the sole reason why car ownership was more widespread in the United States. Attitudes were important. L. T. C. Rolt has suggested that no illustration of the different philosophies of American and British manufacturers is clearer than a comparison of the Silver Ghost Rolls-Royce and the Model T Ford, the one a consummate example of conservative engineering craftsmanship, and the other a product of the most advanced machine tools in the world at that time. Ford introduced the Model T in 1908, and it remained in production until 1927, by which time 15 million had been sold throughout the world. His customers, declared Ford, could have any colour they liked – so long as it was black! Meanwhile, the Argyll Company of Glasgow gave the bodywork of their cars 30–35 coats of paint and varnish. Their magnificent finish was much admired – by those who could afford them. Such craftsmanship was not admired by Ford. One of his disciples wrote: 'As to machinists, old time, all round men, perish the thought! The Ford Company has no use for experience, in the working ranks anyway. It desires and prefers machine-tool operators who have nothing to unlearn, who . . . will simply do as they are told to do, over and over again, from bell-time to bell-time.' British manufacturers, on the other hand, clung to craft traditions. Henry Royce constantly held up the flow of production to make some trifling improvements to his cars, until banished to a research workshop. British output remained comparatively low. Before 1914 no British firm managed to exceed one car per man per annum. Wolseley, the largest, employed 4,000 men who produced 3,000 cars in 1913; and Austin, with about 1,900 workmen, must have averaged about the same. By the First World War the number of cars (both home-produced and imported) registered in Britain had risen to 265,000, but they remained the rich man's toy, and even then, as R. S. Sayers observes, 'the toy not of every rich man, but only of those with a taste for mechanical things and – in the early days at least – a streak of rashness'. The economic impact of the motor car was wider, of course, than just the output of new vehicles. In February 1914 *The Times* attempted to quantify the total effect:

> [The] annual expenditure on new purchases, large as it is, is completely dwarfed by the cost of running the motor-vehicles which are now upon the road. Motoring has built up an industry in the manufacture of tires which is almost as large as that of the car-building trade itself. The annual tire consumption approximates £14,521,000. Next to tires the cost of petrol and lubricating oil bulks heaviest in the motorist's expenditure. The fuel and oil bill works out at close on £8,500,000. Moreover the cost of repairs, renovations and periodical overhauls amounts to over six millions; while motoring brings into the Exchequer over one and a half million sterling in registration fees and licences, and the insurance companies benefit to nearly the same amount . . .
>
> Taking all of the heads of the expenditure of owners of motor-cars the benefit, directly and indirectly, to British labour aggregates £37,550,000. If the average of the wages and salaries of all engaged in the motor trade and its allied industries be taken as high as £100 per annum, this means that 375,500 people obtain their employment and that something like 1,000,000 of the population are supported by the industry of motoring.

The electrical industry

Despite the pioneering work of men like Michael Faraday, R. E. B. Crompton (a descendant of the inventor of the spinning-mule), Sir Joseph Swan and Sebastian de Ferranti, the British electrical industry lagged behind its German and American competitors. Electricity faced the competition of entrenched gas and steam industries, and in the slowly growing British economy could only expand by ousting them from their markets, whereas in more rapidly expanding economies a large untapped demand was there to be exploited. With basic industries located close to cheap coal, electric motive power was slow to gain a foothold, and it was not until the cost of electric motors for factory use fell in the early years of the twentieth century that the use of electric power expanded. By 1914 perhaps a quarter of the motive power used in mining and manufacturing was electric.

The domestic use of electricity also proceeded more slowly than abroad. The situation was the familiar one of chicken and egg. The promoters of electrical devices could not sell them because there was no cheap source of current. At the same time there was little urge to develop generators because there was no demand for the current. There was a false start with electric lighting in the 1880s when it failed to oust the much cheaper gas, which even in 1900 probably provided 10 times as much light as electricity. Here was an industry where standardisation was clearly a necessity, but progress was held up while the 'Battle of the Systems' was fought between the advocates of Ferranti's high-pressure alternating current and low-pressure direct current. As late as 1918 a Board of Trade Committee on Electric Power Supply reported:

> Owing to the chaos of different systems, and the absence of any attempt to standardise pressures and frequencies, co-operation between neighbouring authorities is difficult and expensive. In London, for example, there are seven railway and tramway systems which generate electricity for the purposes of traction at different frequencies – one at 50, two at $33\frac{1}{3}$, and four at 25 – thus rendering exchange of electricity between them impracticable except at the great expense involved in converting it. Again, there are in the area of Greater London 70 authorities who supply electricity to the public, and own some 70 generating stations, with 50 different types of system, 10 different frequencies, and 24 different voltages . . .[9]

Electric power made some headway with tramways; over 2,000 miles were built between 1897 and 1906, by which time horse trams had virtually disappeared. The central London underground railway network (the product largely of American initiative) was almost complete by 1907, but the electrification of steam railways proceeded slowly before the First World War.

It has been claimed that in an important sense the British electrical industry was not an industry of its own at all, but one which after 1895 was an offshoot of the American and German industries with an important fringe of domestic producers. The major American and German manufacturers established their own factories in Britain, and by 1914 three out of four major British companies were offshoots of foreign firms. British Westinghouse and British Thompson-Houston sprang respectively from the American firms of Westinghouse and General Electric, and Siemens derived from the German firm, Siemens and Halske. It is true that for much of the time Britain enjoyed a favourable balance of trade in electrical goods between 1880 and 1913, but this disguises the fact that much of the more technically advanced and sophisticated machinery was imported, while British exports were often of a less complex nature, and frequently went to the British empire or Latin

America, where tramway and electricity supply companies were often financed from London.

The chemical industry

Disraeli is credited with saying that the chemical industry is the barometer of a nation's prosperity. The glass was certainly falling at the end of the century. Up to the 1880s Britain led the field, but thereafter it declined and by 1913 had fallen to third place. However, the industry is complex, and competitiveness in particular fields varied considerably. In the manufacture of soda ash, used in the production of soap and glass, and for bleaching, Britain still took the lead; but Germany led in dyestuffs, and the United States in the production of superphosphates and sulphuric acid. Even minor industrial nations could dominate particular fields. Norway, for example, was the biggest producer of calcium carbide, used in the production of acetylene, a gas much used in lamps. We should not be too pessimistic about Britain's performance, therefore. It had marked successes and retained a strong position in soaps, paints, some fertilisers and heavy chemicals, coal-tar intermediaries and explosives. The largest explosives factory in the world was that of Alfred Nobel in Scotland, where the annual output was as much as 10,000 tons in the 1880s.

However, it is argued that British chemical manufacturers failed to follow up many leads and thus allowed overseas competitors to forge ahead. This is alleged in the case of alkali production, for example, where Britain clung to the older Leblanc process while others pushed on with the cheaper Solvay ammonia process. In 1874 world production of soda was 525,000 tons, of which no less than 495,000 tons were made by the Leblanc process; by 1902 it had risen to 1,800,000 tons, of which the Leblanc process provided a mere 150,000 tons. The once great British Leblanc soda industry did not finally close down until 1920, despite the clear superiority of the Solvay process, demonstrated in this country by the success of Brunner Mond (forerunners of ICI). That it lingered on for so long is due to several factors. There was undoubtedly a degree of inertia, with producers reluctant to scrap technically efficient but commercially obsolete plant. The Leblanc process (to which numerous technical improvements were made in mid-century) did produce by-products, such as hydrochloric acid (from which bleaching powder could be extracted) which could not be obtained from the Solvay ammonia process, and increasingly manufacturers turned to these and other more profitable diversified products such as fertilisers, laundry blue, sulphur and nitric acid. In *Made in Germany* E. E. Williams wrote in 1896: 'Unless you are wearing a blue shirt (perhaps not even then), and are clothed in homespun and home-dyed tweeds from the Western Isles of Scotland, you are safe in concluding that your every coloured article of apparel has seen the inside of an aniline dye-vat.' Many of the pioneering advances in the dyestuffs industry had taken place in Britain, such as the discovery of aniline mauve in 1856 by 18-year-old W. H. Perkin. But the technical advance was not exploited, and by the 1890s nine-tenths of the artificial dyestuffs of the world were made in Germany. In the 1880s its industry was around four times the size of Britain's; by 1913 it was 20–30 times as large. And when British soldiers went into action in France and Belgium in 1914 they wore uniforms dyed with German dyestuffs. Here, indeed, was complacency, for Britain's position was not inherently unfavourable. It possessed abundant supplies of raw material (in fact, it sent Germany many of the coal-tar derivatives from which the dyes were extracted), and its cloth-making industry constituted a large domestic demand. Indeed, in this area Britain's role was almost that of a 'colonial economy', exporting the raw materials and importing the finished product. Development of the dyestuffs industry would have aided the ailing

Leblanc soda industry, for it required large quantities of soda ash and hydrochloric acid.

The general failings of the British chemical industry are a serious indictment of its industrial enterprise, and illustrate a lack of interest in science, research and training. Michael Sadler observed: 'England, at least, hates the expert; Germany rejoices in him.' The difference in attitudes was illustrated by E. E. Williams:

> There is one factory at Elberfeld, where not less than sixty trained chemists form a part of the permanent establishment. These gentlemen have well-furnished laboratories at their disposal, and they receive a regular salary for what the English would call 'doing nothing' (but the German calls it 'Research'). They have no routine tasks in connection with the ordinary business of the firm: their work is simply to analyse and experiment day after day, and year after year, until one of them develops a new process, or a great use for something hitherto known as 'waste': when the fortune of his employers (in which he shares) is made. The Elberfeld Factory is no solitary instance; in Germany the Elberfeld system is the rule.

Similar examples could be found in the United States. Thomas Alva Edison, one of the world's greatest inventors, installed a team of researchers in his 'inventions factory' at Menlo Park, New Jersey, where they explored a wide range of practical ideas, contributing significantly to Edison's staggering list of 1,000 or more patents. Britain preferred to get by with 'practical tinkerers' using 'rule of thumb' methods in other industries as well as chemicals. There is a story, for example, of the manager of Dowlais ironworks who, in the 1880s, 'made the best guess he could as to the strength there should be, then multiplied by four, and the thing never broke' – although the weight, both structurally and to the pocket, was painful!

Britain's failure to establish a satisfactory system of scientific higher education was partly due to its slowness in setting up a system of adequate 'lower' education – elementary schools being the essential foundation to more advanced technical and commercial training. Just before the First World War Britain had only 9,000 full-time students compared with 58,000 in Germany, a figure it did not reach until 1938. It was alleged in 1916 that Britain had only 1,500 trained chemists, while four large German chemical firms which had played havoc with certain departments of Britain's trade employed 1,000 between them. The First World War was very much a 'scientific war' and provided the shock which brought about a belated change of attitude to research and development.

Light industry and retail distribution

The years of the Great Depression witnessed a revolution in the high street, where retail distribution was transformed, both in the sales outlets and in the goods sold. In light industry and food processing, Britain had an enviable record in these years, which also mark the rise of a number of entrepreneurs whose names have quite literally become household words: Sainsbury and Cadbury; Lilley and Skinner, and Freeman Hardy and Willis; and Boots the Chemists. Many of these companies operated on a large scale. Cadbury employed 6,000 people at its Bourneville factory in 1914, while Crosse & Blackwell (preserved foods), Bovril (beef extract) and Colmans (mustard) were among the largest British joint-stock companies at the beginning of the twentieth century.

Charles Wilson has complained that economists have for some reason found it 'doctrinally necessary to excommunicate . . . ready-made clothes and corsets, boots and shoes, newspapers, cheap jam and patent medicines'. The bicycle, he claims, just passes muster. In consequence he alleges that an obsession with retardation has led to the ignoring of spectacular strides in some sectors of the economy. While agreeing that British enterprise was effectively displayed here, Peter Mathias is forced to conclude that 'a major indigenous electrical engineering industry would have proved a greater long-term asset to the economy than a large, efficient jam-making or chocolate industry, of which the technology was relatively simple'. It is hard to disagree with this assessment, but while the light industries which Wilson extols may not have been of great strategic significance to the economy overall, they were of tremendous social significance, and should not be ignored.

Two things provided the basis for the growth of these industries. One was the cheap import of raw materials, ranging from cocoa for chocolate to wood pulp for newspapers. The other was the expansion of working-class purchasing power. During the prosperous years of the middle decades the lives of most Britons improved, but the improvement was much more striking during the 'depressed' years at the end of the century. Between 1889 and 1900 money wages rose by something like 15 per cent, while the trend of prices was downward until the outbreak of the Boer War, whereupon a sharp rise brought them back to the level of 1889. Between 1889 and 1900, therefore, real wages must have risen by well over 10 per cent, while over the longer period 1870–74 to 1910–13 per capita consumption rose by some 33 per cent. It is true that between 1900 and 1910 the national income did little more than keep pace with the growing population, with the effect that real wages are estimated to have fallen by about 10 per cent. This reduced standard of living would have been felt most acutely by those who remained in the same job, but as the period was characterised by a shift from lower-paid to higher-paid jobs (there was a mass exodus from agriculture, for example) most wage-earners were almost as well off at the end of the decade as at the beginning. A mass market developed, and the masses were the ones to benefit, despite the often patronising attitude of their betters. The mass press began with *Tit-Bits* in 1881, and the *Daily Mail* in 1896 (tartly described by the Prime Minister, Lord Salisbury, as 'written by office boys for office boys'). The *Daily Mirror* followed in 1903. Factory-made jams and pickles, or packets of custard powder and gravy were not welcomed in Belgravia or country-house kitchens, but proved a boon to the working-class housewife. The prejudice has died hard. Even today some people believe 'shop jam' to be inferior to any amateur effort, while Prime Minister Harold Wilson's alleged liking for a certain sauce gave cartoonists a field-day.

Retail trading changed in many ways. Before the 1870s, except in special circumstances such as the railway station bookstalls of W. H. Smith, multiple stores were very rare, but they gained a firm foothold in the following decades. In 1880 there were 1,500 multiple stores, and by 1900 over 11,500. In footwear, a trade with a strong craft tradition, one-third of the trade had been won by the factory-based multiple shoe shops by 1915. Retailing in general lost some of its element of skill, as shopkeepers less frequently had to select and price goods so that customers would come to trust them. More and more they came to stock branded goods which, apart from the physical handing over, had already been 'sold' by advertising, which manufacturers undertook on a much grander scale. Advertising loosened the purse-strings. In 1886 Jesse Boot, the founder of the chain of chemists, sent 200 of the new-fangled Post Office telegrams to selected Nottingham customers, urging them to buy his cheap sponges. In that year Lever Brothers spent £50 on advertising, but so astounded was the company by the success of the campaign based on Millais's painting, 'Bubbles', that it spent £2 million over the next 20 years. If Pears used 'high art' to advertise its goods, Thomas Lipton (whose grocery stores alone handled 10 per cent of the nation's sales of tea in the 1880s) adopted high-altitude advertising; he scattered leaflets from balloons to persuade people to patronise a newly opened branch; and if that failed, was up to painting his name on pigs driven through the streets, hiring elephants or employing brass bands to blow his trumpet for him.

Did the late-Victorian economy fail?

Enough has been said about the decades before the First World War to show that while there were areas of weakness, there were sectors of the economy which were highly efficient. Striking a balance between them is not easy, partly because notions of success or failure imply a target to be achieved. To use the language of the New Economic History, it is hard to construct a 'counterfactual' model of the British economy before the First World War against which the performance of the 'factual' economy can be judged. Such a counterfactual model, must be realistic, and suggest what the economy might reasonably have been expected to achieve, compared with its state at, say, the middle of the nineteenth century. A variety of elements would contribute to this target, including the notion that the economy should have responded to changing patterns of demand, and to the evolving pattern of world trade; that it should have used the most efficient techniques; and that output should have increased as rapidly as resources of capital, labour and raw materials might allow.

With hindsight it is easy to condemn the decisions made by British industrialists, and to argue that they were obsessed with short-run interests rather than long-term needs. It is also easy to argue that there should have been a greater and more rapid transfer of resources from the declining to the expanding sectors of the economy, but as Saul says:

> What reasons could there be for not investing in cotton mills in 1905 when profits expected and realised up to the war were comparable with any elsewhere? And if Britain was wrong to go on making steel rails because future demand was to be poor, were the countries of South America to go without? Were the world's steel-makers to say 'we will not make them for you; our crystal balls tell us that in twenty years demand will have collapsed'? Was it unwise to reap the advantages of favourable prices and satisfy the avid demand for coal from Europe even though the future problems this raised were acute indeed? Britain was surely right to develop these industries as she did . . .[10]

The staple industries depended heavily on exports, so an earlier concentration on predominantly home-demand newer industries would have placed a strain on the balance of payments and would almost certainly have resulted in a lower current real income than was actually achieved. Many contemporary decisions were less irrational or complacent than we might imagine. Take the slowness with which British coal-owners introduced mechanical coal-cutters, for example. By 1900 one-fifth of the American output of 240 million tons was mechanically cut, as against less than one-fiftieth of the British output of 225 million tons. However, Britain's narrow seams provided unfavourable geological conditions, while the abundance of cheap labour gave the coal-owner little incentive to instal labour-saving machinery, especially as such a course might require reorganisation throughout the colliery, and might lead to considerable industrial unrest. Likewise, the slowness of British cotton managers to adopt the ring spindle in spinning, and the automatic loom in weaving, can also be defended. To make yarn of any particular fineness (or 'count') the ring spindle required cotton of a longer staple than did the mule, and this increased raw material costs. Its advantage was that skilled mule-spinners could be replaced by unskilled (largely female) labour. In the United States, where there was a comparative scarcity of skilled workers, this made greater sense than in Britain, where the relatively large supply of skilled mule spinners did not offer labour savings sufficient to compensate for the increased raw material costs. Similar arguments apply to the automatic loom. Even had these machines been installed in large numbers, the collapse of the textile industry between the two world wars would not have been averted, and its eventual dismantling would have been even more painful.

More historians are now prepared to take an optimistic view than was once the case. Donald McCloskey argues that the picture was one of 'an economy not stagnating but growing as rapidly as permitted by the growth of its resources and the effective exploitation of the available technology'. Roderick Floud is substantially in agreement:

> Between 1860 and 1914 Britain certainly lost the predominant position which she had held as the leading or only manufacturing nation, [but] this was not because of deficiencies within the British economy. It stemmed, instead, from the increasing complexity of the international economy, and of the national economies within it. This brought to Britain a new role as a pivot of international trade and investment, which demanded adjustments within the domestic economy to enable Britain to carry out that role. Although some of these adjustments were difficult and painful, they were carried out sufficiently well to enable Britain to retain a commanding position in the world economy . . . Adjustments would have continued to be necessary, as the old staple industries of coal, cotton, iron and steel and shipbuilding lost their importance and were replaced by a wider spectrum of manufacturing and service industries. The advent of the First World War made it essential for these adjustments to be carried out rapidly, and the pain of the 1920s and 1930s was part of the price.[11]

The rise of the suburbs

The late nineteenth century witnessed changes in urban living, particularly the rise of the suburbs. Although most people have something definite in mind when they talk of 'the suburbs', the phenomenon is not easy to define with any precision. In 1944 the Ministry of Town and Country Planning classified urban types according to population density, their range extending from 'sparse rural' (with 1–50 persons per square mile) to 'dense urban' (with over 25,000 persons per square mile). Areas with a population density of 400–6,400 per square mile were classified as 'suburban and industrialised rural'. It would be quite unrealistic to apply these criteria (which were based on the 1931 census) to the nineteenth century. Kennington, in south London, would have been 'dense urban' by 1841, which it clearly was not, nor was Brixton 'urban' in 1851. Following the same criteria, the inner areas of London would have sunk back to 'suburban and industrialised rural' only a little later on. If population density is an unrealistic definition, so is that which sees suburbs in terms of their radius from an urban centre. In *Suburban Homes of London* (1878) W. S. Clarke observed that 'no mere formal radius of distance has been taken, as the adoption of any such hard-and-fast line was found inadvisable', and his London suburbs ranged from areas close in, like Brixton and Camden Town, and distant places such as Harrow (in Middlesex) and Woodford (in Essex). There were several reasons why suburbanisation advanced further from the centre in some directions

11A   Slums and suburbs

1   'Over London – by Rail' by Gustave Doré, 1872

'Over London – by Rail' (1) is taken from the book *London, A Pilgrimage* published in 1872 with text by Blanchard Jerrold, and engravings by the French artist, Gustave Doré. His vivid illustrations are frequently used in histories of the Victorian period. How realistic are they, and how far do they reflect artistic vision rather than historical accuracy? The pictures for *London* have to be seen in the context of Doré's work. He was best known for his illustrations of works of fantasy such as Dante's *Inferno* and Milton's *Paradise Lost*. There is a close affinity between Doré's nightmarish vision of London's East End and his vision of Hell. In the case of this picture, it has been suggested that any speculative builder who put as much unnecessary brickwork into his houses as is shown here would soon have gone bankrupt.

Are the illustrations from parliamentary papers any more accurate? Perhaps so, but they may not always be *representative*. The illustration of houses at Preston (2) appeared in the *Report of the Royal Commission on the State of Large Towns and Populous Districts*. It formed part of a report on Preston by the Revd J. Clay. It should be noted that he described these cottages as 'built upon a system so extraordinary as to deserve particular mention'. These 22 cottages backed on to a cesspool which ran between them and which was emptied twice a year. However, Clay wrote:

> It is right to state that the inhabitants of the cottages do not complain of annoyance from these reservoirs of filth; and, with the exception of one row of houses, the mortality does not appear to have been excessive. One woman expressed her great satisfaction at having removed from Albert Street to her present abode; it was 'so pleasant to hear the birds singing in a morning and to see the flowers growing in the spring'. It is, probably, owing to the freshness of the surrounding atmosphere which dilutes the miasmata from the 'pans' that the sickness of the district has not been greater; but if, as is probable, under the influence of the renewed activity in trade, the buildings should be extended, the circulation and supply of good air will be proportionately impeded . . .

It is probable, therefore, that conditions in many industrial cities were worse than this picture would suggest.

Picture 3 is in marked contrast. Those who could leave the infested towns did so, and suburbs developed for the more well-off. These villas at Camberwell were described as 'the tradesman's *beau ideal* of a suburban retreat'. They appear to be detached, but architects and builders were skilled at erecting semi-detached houses which had all the appearance of the more expensive and more desirable detached villa. Such suburbs depended upon the ability to commute, on foot or by omnibus, or using the rather dearer cabs shown in the illustration of Oxford Circus (4). This is one of countless thousands of photographs which were taken of Victorian cities. Do photographs have an objectivity which other illustrations lack? What effect was the photographer striving for? Did he aim to portray the bustle of the city? If so, did he set up his camera at a particularly busy time? Some photographs seem very contrived and posed. This one, on the other hand, seems to have been taken with a concealed camera. But we still do not know what the photographer's artistic intention was!

2   Houses at Preston in Lancashire, from a Royal Commission report of 1844

3   Villas at Herne Hill, Camberwell, 1825

4   The junction of Oxford Street and Regent Street, London, 1888

5   A street of terraced houses under construction, 1906

Come and see the "nests" the Birds are building at Harrow Garden Village!

Superior well-built Semi-Detached Villas are now being built in The Greenway (5 minutes Rayners Lane Station, Metro. and District Railway).

From   **£850.** Deposits arranged.

These Houses contain:—

THREE GOOD BEDROOMS (1) 16' 0" × 12' 0" | DRAWING ROOM 16' 0" × 13' 6"
(2) 12' 6" × 12' 0" | DINING ROOM - 12' 6" × 12' 0"
(3) 8' 0" × 8' 0" | TILED KITCHEN 13' 6" × 8' 0"
IDEAL BOILER AND GAS COOKER IN RECESS .. TILED LARDER AND EASY-WORK
CABINET .. GAS BOILER .. TILED BATHROOM .. SEPARATE W.C.
BRICK BUILT COAL HOUSE .. SPACE FOR GARAGE .. LARGE GARDENS

No road charges, law costs or stamp duties. Houses may be built to purchasers' own designs on selected sites.

B. D. BIRD & SONS

"Dunelm," The Greenway, Rayners Lane

6   A 1932 advertisement for suburban houses

Picture 5 was taken to illustrate an article in *Living London*, published in 1906. Notice how little house construction has been affected by technological change. Is there evidence here that the villa ideal has moved down the social scale?

Between the wars, rapid suburban development was facilitated by such factors as the development of the motor vehicle and the electric railway. The advertisement for houses at Rayner's Lane in Middlesex (6) comes from an annual published by the Metropolitan Railway. Note the continuing appeal of the term 'villa' and the lipservice paid to the concept of the garden village. Advertisements make valuable evidence, particularly of what was considered attractive in housing at any period.

than in others. Journey times differed with different transport facilities, while building estates were more readily available in some places than in others. One of the leading historians of modern suburbanisation, H. J. Dyos, recognised that 'the modern suburb is clearly less of a geographical expression than it is an attitude of mind and a species of social as well as of economic behaviour'.

The process, of course, was not new. Chaucer used the word 'suburbes', and Shakespeare talked of London's 'south suburbs at the Elephant'. The city walls of London were so confining (they enclosed only one square mile) that development soon spread beyond them, whereafter there were no physical barriers. This gradual decentralisation was stepped up dramatically in the nineteenth century. The population of the outer ring of London grew by 50 per cent in *each* of the intercensal periods between 1861 and 1891 and by 45 per cent between 1891 and 1901. Four of the fastest-growing areas in the country between 1881 and 1891 were London suburbs (Leyton, Willesden, Tottenham and West Ham); while 12 of the 17 districts with recorded growth rates of 30 per cent or more between 1891 and 1901 were in Greater London, including Ilford, which grew by 277.6 per cent. The trend was not unique to London. Most large towns had their suburbs, which often swallowed up what had once been separate communities, like the 'pleasant villages of Bootle and Aigburth' which wealthy Liverpudlians were moving to by 1859. The nineteenth century thus witnessed two distinct movements of population; centripetal forces threw people into the towns at the beginning of the period, while at the end centrifugal forces scattered them again.

In an influential book, *The Uses of Literacy* (1957), Richard Hoggart drew attention to the persistence of basically rural pursuits among modern urban workers, including pigeon-fancying, the keeping of whippets and greyhounds, and an interest in gardening and allotments. This is not perhaps surprising when one remembers the speed of urban growth and its recent occurrence, or the rural flavour of many towns (in London there were market gardens at Bermondsey and Rotherhythe in the 1850s, while Earls Court retained isolated farms even later in the century). A deeply rooted tension existed between town and country, exemplified by the view of the poet William Cowper that 'God made the country and man made the town'. He argued that 'close-pent man regrets the country', putting his finger on one of the mainsprings of suburban development, the attempt to get back to the country – or better still, to enjoy 'rus in urbe', the benefits of the country in the town. Of course there was an element of fantasy in this, and suburban man perhaps fell between two stools, being neither *urbane* nor exhibiting the qualities of the true-born English countryman. For a long time 'suburban' was a derogatory term. Mrs C. S. Peel, the author of *The New Home* (1898), a manual of middle-class domesticity, wrote: 'I must confess honestly that the suburbs of any large town appear to me detestable.' They had, she was prepared to allow, certain advantages, but these were mainly consolation prizes for 'those people who yearn for the pleasures of the country and who find the diversions in golf, tennis, bicycling, boating or gardening, and whom cruel fate prevents from living in the real country'. There is a large element of condescension in this view, of course, for suburbs clearly satisfied a pent-up demand from large numbers of people. F. M. L. Thompson has put forward the view that there is a connexion between 'physical expansion and cultural development', and suggests that the origins of modern suburbanisation are inevitably linked with evolving middle-class habits of privacy, domesticity and the separation of work from home.

There was another side of the coin. If suburbs represented the attraction of the country they also illustrated the repulsion of the city. Upper- and middle-class Victorians were terrified of the slums – as well they might be. Death rates were much higher in the central districts than on the suburban fringe. Consequently, as Dyos put it: 'The individual's retreat to the suburbs was often a personal solution to a collective sanitary problem.' Today's suburb could of course become tomorrow's slum, and development was often wave-like, with once prosperous suburbs decaying as population grew and the better-off moved yet further out. Dyos described suburbs as 'social transit camps' where people were frequently on the move, and he referred to 'social leap-frogging' and 'social zoning'. Distinct social zones, catering for particular income groups, did grow up, sometimes with physical differences which displayed the minutest social nuances. Even trees could play their part, with plane trees and horse-chestnuts shading the wide avenues of the well-to-do, while those of middle incomes lived beneath limes, laburnums and acacias, and the wage-earners made do with unadorned macadam.

The social character of a particular suburb was sometimes a chance afffair, determined by the first tentative steps at development, which might blight subsequent growth or might lead to a prestigious position. It could, however, be reinforced by restrictive covenants in bills of sale of land or building leases, or through the policies of railway companies. Thus Radlett in Hertfordshire, of which J. T. Coppock has made a close study, was protected by a *poor* railway service to London, which made it an unsuitable place of residence for those who had to be at their City desks early. In contrast, the liberal granting of cheap workmen's tickets by the Great Eastern Railway (keen to protect more valuable passenger traffic elsewhere) meant that solid working-class suburbs developed in north-east London. The inner city also came to be 'zoned', for here remained the 'residual working class' who became yet more isolated from the rest of the community.

Numerous factors governed the pace and direction of suburban growth. Most fundamental were demographic factors. As urban population grew, the central core of cities first came to be filled up. Then the central areas were thinned by demolition and clearance, either for commercial building, 'improvement', or under the impact of railways (see Chapter 6). At the same time, vacant areas in surrounding districts were filled up. As the population continued to grow, the outer suburbs were at last penetrated.

Which areas were penetrated first depended on the availability of land and the range of transport facilities. As land was sold piecemeal, so estates developed piecemeal, as a comparison between an old field map and a current street map of almost any town will indicate. Mostly, like Topsy, suburbs 'just growed', and in an altogether unplanned manner. Some suburbs *were* planned like Bourneville, outside Birmingham, commenced by George Cadbury in 1893, and New Earswick, the inspiration of another chocolate manufacturer, Joseph Rowntree of York. Ebenezer Howard, a stenographer and inventor of typewriter mechanisms, emigrated to the United States for a while, and was much taken there with Riverside, Illinois, now a suburb of Chicago. In 1894 in *Tomorrow: A Peaceful Path to Real Reform*, he put forward the idea of the garden city, a self-contained community of about 32,000 people, in which farming and industry would be combined, and in which the value added to the land by development would be ploughed back into the community. His ideas were the inspiration for the founding of Letchworth, Hertfordshire, in 1903. The plans for the town were drawn up by Barry Parker and his brother-in-law and partner, Raymond Unwin (who was to become a town planner of international repute). Much of the thinking behind the garden city was adapted (rather more economically) in the form of the garden suburb; and in 1906, Parker and Unwin went on to plan Hampstead Garden Suburb, the brain-child of Dame Henrietta

Barnett. She had come to the idea of the garden suburb after 20 years of working among the poor in Whitechapel, and she dreamt of a community where rich and poor alike could make their home, uplifted by the beauty of their surroundings. This side of Hampstead Garden Suburb was never realised, for it quickly became the preserve of middle-class intellectuals, artists and professional people. The rents of even the smallest cottages were too high for significant numbers of working-class people to afford them. Nevertheless, the garden suburb was to provide the architectural ideal to which many suburban developments aspired in the interwar period.

Rents were only one item which a person had to consider when contemplating a move to the suburbs, the other being the journey to work. Two factors were relevant here: cost and time. Thus the decreasing of the length of the working day was of vital importance. As one commentator put it: '[A man] is able to live in the suburbs, not so much because he has more wages as because he has more time.' Cost naturally remained important. The growth of suburbs four or five miles from the centre was influenced by the horse bus, the fares of which might come to about 5s or 6s a week. The 'man on the Clapham omnibus' became a symbol of middle-class respectability and common sense. Railway fares to the outer areas were higher. We should therefore be on our guard about exaggerating the impact of the early railways on suburban growth, especially as many of the main-line companies were primarily concerned with their long-distance traffic. Indeed, it has been argued (by John Kellet, for example) that the role of the commuter has been overstated. Suburbs generated a great economic activity of their own, so that even in twentieth-century suburbs, where commuting is more general, 75–90 per cent of the population may be genuine residents rather than dormitory dwellers. Outer suburbs tended to cluster around existing villages and small towns with a life of their own, while the dominant middle-class commuters of the period up to the 1880s released much potential for expansion through their demand for servants, and for shops and other services.

The eagerness of the railways to build up their traffic through cheap fares can also be exaggerated. Railways do not enjoy economies of scale in the same way as many other industries – indeed, there may be diseconomies of scale. Their services show seasonal fluctuations as well as fluctuations at different times of the day. Increased traffic can, therefore, lead to excess capacity of rolling-stock and staff for large parts of the day, a problem with which the transport authorities have even now to grapple. Nevertheless, experiments were made with workmen's trains, the Metropolitan Railway introducing a workman's fare as early as 1864. In the same year, in return for permission to build its Liverpool Street terminus in London, the Great Eastern Railway accepted the obligation to run a train each morning and evening from Walthamstow and Edmonton at a fare of 2d return. Although these trains barely paid their way, the company eventually ran far more than required by the act, going all out to 'zone' workmen in particular areas of north-east London. Giving evidence to the Royal Commission on the Housing of the Working Classes in 1884, the general manager of the Great Eastern described the impact of workmen's fares on Stamford Hill, Tottenham and Edmonton:

> That used to be a very nice district indeed, occupied by good families, with houses of from £150 to £250 a year, with coach houses and stables, a garden and a few acres of land. But very soon after this obligation was put upon the Great Eastern to run workmen's trains . . . speculative builders went down into the neighbourhood and, as a consequence, each good house was one after another pulled down, and the district is given up entirely, I may say, now to

the working man. I lived down there myself and I waited until most of my neighbours had gone; and then, at last, I was obliged to go.

By the end of the century, 19,000 people arrived at Liverpool Street each morning by workmen's trains; followed by another 35,000 on trains with reduced, but not workmen's, fares; followed in their turn by the regular season-ticket holders who travelled on trains arriving after 9 a.m. The Cheap Trains Act of 1883 compelled *all* companies to run workmen's trains, yet in 1901, 20,000 of the 27,000 workmen commuting on 2d tickets used the Great Eastern Railway, which became known as the 'Workmen's Line'.

There were other forms of cheap transport. The Tramways Act of 1870, which enabled local authorities to buy out private lines after 21 years, encouraged the growth of the street tram, while at the end of the century London began to develop its system of underground railways. Trams and other cheap forms of transport were seen as a solution to the slum problem, but there were many factors inhibiting the dispersal of workers to the suburbs. Basically, labour is *immobile*, a fact not fully appreciated until this century. A factory worker in a regular job explained in 1865:

I go to my factory every morning at six, and I leave it every night at the same hour. I require, on the average, eight hours' sleep, which leaves four hours for recreation and improvement. I have lived at many places on the outskirts, according as my work has shifted, but generally I find myself at Mile End. I always live near the factory where I work, and so do all my mates, no matter how small, dirty, and dear the houses may be . . . One or two of my uncles have tried the plan of living a few miles out, and walking to business in the morning, like the clerks do in the city. It don't do – I suppose because they have not been used to it from boys; perhaps, because walking exercises at five in the morning don't suit men who are hard at work with their bodies all day. As to railways and omnibuses, they cost money, and we don't understand them, except on holidays, when we have got our best clothes on.[12]

For casual workers there were further problems. They had to be on call, or had to be in a central position in order to be able to operate in different pools of casual labour. And for many there was a cultural attraction to the inner areas, a positive 'contagion of numbers', with 'penny gaffs', public houses, working-class amusements and cheap street markets. They enjoyed the community of neighbours. The lower middle classes of the suburbs preferred to keep themselves to themselves.

Towards the welfare state

Suburbanisation further isolated the very poor, to such a degree that towards the end of the nineteenth century poverty underwent one of its regular periods of 're-discovery' by better-off members of society. In 1883 the Revd Andrew Mearns, then secretary of the Congregational Union, and a group of Nonconformist ministers published *The Bitter Cry of Outcast London*, a pamphlet which attracted widespread attention. While others had worried themselves about the resistance to formal religion exhibited by the poor, Mearns argued that they had physical as well as spiritual needs, and that Christian missionaries would achieve little among them until something had been done to 'secure for the poorest the rights of citizenship; the right to live in something better than fever dens; the right to live as something better than the uncleanest of brute beasts'. His descriptions of the filthy hovels in which many of the wretched poor were forced to live, their condition worsened by the obnoxious nature of the 'sweated' trades at which many of them worked, might easily have been drawn from Chadwick's reports of 40 years earlier:

> Here you are choked as you enter by the air laden with particles of the superfluous fur pulled from the skins of rabbits, rats, dogs and other animals in their preparation for the furrier. Here the smell of paste and of drying match-boxes, mingling with the fragrance of stale fish or vegetables, not sold in the previous day, and kept in the room overnight. Even when it is possible to do so, the people seldom open their windows, but if they did it is questionable whether much would be gained, for the external air is scarcely less heavily charged with poison than the atmosphere within.[13]

In 1887 a Board of Trade report declared that some 20,000 workers in East London, many of them recent immigrants from eastern Europe, could be classified as sweated labour. This report led to the establishment of a Select Committee of the House of Lords which examined various sweated trades, including chain-making and the clothing trades. Sweating was difficult to define, but the Report summarised the evils which were associated with it:

1 A rate of wages inadequate to the necessities of the workers or dispro-portionate to the work done.
2 Excessive hours of labour.
3 The insanitary state of the houses in which work is carried on. These evils can hardly be exaggerated.

The earnings of the lowest classes of workers are barely sufficient to sustain existence.

The hours of labour are such as to make the lives of the workers periods of almost ceaseless toil, hard and often unhealthy.

The sweated trades represented the depths of oppressive treatment of workers which was common elsewhere in industry. In 1890 the Anglican Christian Social Union tried to prepare a 'White List' of manufacturers who paid and treated their workers well and whose products could be bought by Christians with a clear conscience. The list was so sparse that the idea had to be dropped.

Many clergymen did succeed in combining parochial with social work, among the most notable being Samuel Barnett, vicar of St Jude's, Whitechapel, in the East End of London, and a Canon of Westminster from 1906. Barnett (who often worked in collaboration with his wife, the afore-mentioned Henrietta) was one of the greatest social pioneers of his day who, in commemoration of his friend, Arnold Toynbee the economist, historian and reformer, founded Toynbee Hall in 1884. Just before he died in 1883, Toynbee expressed a feeling of guilt shared by many middle-class people when he told a working-class audience: 'We have neglected you; instead of justice we have offered you hard and unreal advice . . . we have sinned against you grievously . . . but if you will forgive us . . . we will serve you, we will devote our lives to your service.'[14] Toynbee Hall and the University Settlement Movement with which it was associated brought able young men face to face with the problems of the poor. George Lansbury, the Labour leader from nearby Poplar, suspicious perhaps of the whiff of philanthropic patronage, declared that the only permanent social influence of Toynbee Hall was to secure for its young men com-fortable posts in government service. There was some truth in this, but as the alumni included men like William Beveridge and Clement Attlee (Secretary of Toynbee Hall from 1910–11) any debt which they owed to Whitechapel was amply repaid.

One assiduous attender at Toynbee Hall lectures was Charles Booth, the properous

IIB   Dr Barnardo and photography

In 1867 Dr Thomas Barnardo opened his first 'home of refuge' for destitute children in Commercial Road, London. In that year the annual income of the charity was £215. When he died in 1905 his organisation had cared for 62,000 children, and had an annual income of well over £200,000. Among other methods of raising money, Barnardo turned to photography, setting up a department for that purpose in 1874. From about 1870, however, Barnardo had engaged a professional photographer to take 'before' and 'after' photographs of selected children. These were used in the charity's publicity material and were also produced as cards (1 and 2) which were sold in packs of 20 for 5 shillings. In 1877 Barnardo felt obliged to take action before the Court of Arbitration in order to put down rumours of 'artistic fiction' after allegations were made that the photographer sometimes exaggerated the look of destitution in the 'before' photographs in order to produce a more pathetic image. The court ruled against him in one instance, with the result that Barnardo abandoned the use of photographs for propaganda purposes, and confined them to use as a means of identification. The resulting photographs (3 and 4) are far more interesting to the historian. As the photographer no longer attempted to create any particular impression, we are left with a visual record of thousands of children in the state in which they were taken in from the streets.

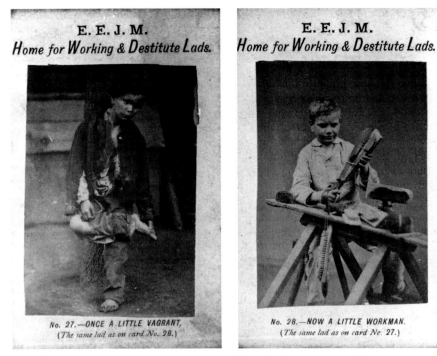

1 and 2   The same boy photographed 'before' and 'after' Dr Barnardo rescued him

3 and 4   Two children as Dr Barnardo found them

proprietor of a Liverpool shipping line who opened a London office in the 1880s. Booth interested himself in social issues, his enthusiasm strengthened by his relationship (through his wife) with Beatrice Potter – later Beatrice Webb – who collaborated with him on his major work, the 17-volume *Life and Labour of the People in London*, which took 17 years to complete. In 1885 the popular, somewhat leftist, *Pall Mall Gazette* published the results of a survey conducted in the working-class districts of London by the Social Democratic Federation (SDF) which claimed that 25 per cent of Londoners lived in abject poverty. Booth believed this figure to be exaggerated socialist propaganda, and he set out to disprove it. Instead he discovered that the SDF had underestimated, for he found that the proportion of East Londoners living in poverty was close to 35 per cent.

What made Booth's work all the more telling was that he did not set out to shock. As he wrote to one of his assistants: 'I am afraid we are sure to shock very many good people in the conclusions – the danger of hurting is rather to be found in the details necessary to support these conclusions. It cannot be entirely avoided, but must never be wanton.' His report, commented the *Morning Post*, was more valuable that 'an ocean of sensational writing'. *The Times* described it nevertheless as 'the grimmest book of our generation', and Beatrice Webb declared that it 'reverberated in the world of politics and philanthropy'. Booth did not entirely abandon a moralistic attitude towards poverty, but concluded, on the basis of information received from 4,000 poor people, that in about 85 per cent of the cases their poverty was caused by 'employment' (including low pay as well as lack of work) or 'circumstances' (large family and sickness). 'Habit' ('idleness, drunkennness and thriftlessness') accounted for only 15 per cent.

Booth's work related solely to London, which had become the 'shock city' of the late nineteenth century. The revelation by Seebohm Rowntree, a member of the chocolate-manufacturing family, that similar conditions were to be found in York, was all the more disturbing. Rowntree's *Poverty. A Study of Town Life*, which appeared in 1901, greatly extended people's understanding of poverty. He demonstrated the existence of a 'poverty cycle' which affected the majority of the working class. Poverty could first be expected in childhood and would continue until the individual or his brothers or sisters began to earn. A short period of relative comfort would follow, lasting into the early years of marriage. Then the family sank back into poverty until the children grew up and either left home or contributed to the family income. Finally, as they grew old and sick in later years, poverty would strike again. In addition, he drew a distinction between 'primary' and 'secondary' poverty:

> Families regarded as living in poverty were grouped under two heads:
> a) Families whose total earnings were insufficient to obtain the minimum necessaries for the maintenance of merely physical efficiency. Poverty falling under this head was described as 'primary' poverty.
> b) Families whose total earnings would have been sufficient for the maintenance of merely physical efficiency were it not that some portion of it was absorbed by other expenditure, either useful or wasteful. Poverty falling under this head was described as 'secondary' poverty . . .
>
> For a family of father, mother, and three children, the minimum weekly expenditure upon which physical efficiency can be maintained in York is 21s 8d, made up as follows:
>
> | | |
> |---|---|
> | Food | 12s 9d |
> | Rent (say) | 4s 0d |
> | Clothing, light, fuel | 4s 11d |

Almost exactly 10 per cent of the population of York fell in the former category, a further 17.93 per cent into the latter. Nearly 28 per cent of the people of York thus lived in poverty. Rowntree described what it was like to live at the 'poverty line':

> A family living upon the scale allowed for in this estimate must never spend a penny on railway fare or omnibus. They must never go into the country unless they walk. They must never purchase a halfpenny newspaper or spend a penny to buy a ticket for a popular concert. They must write no letters to absent children, for they cannot afford to pay the postage. They must never contribute anything to their church or chapel, or give any help to a neighbour which costs them money. They cannot save, not can they join sick club or Trade Union, because they cannot pay the necessary subscriptions. The children must have no pocket money for dolls, marbles, or sweets. The father must smoke no tobacco, and must drink no beer. The mother must never buy any pretty clothes for herself or for her children, the character of the family wardrobe as for the family diet being governed by the regulation, 'Nothing must be bought but that which is absolutely necessary for the maintenance of physical health, and what is bought must be of the plainest and most economical description.' Should a child fall ill, it must be attended by the parish doctor; should it die, it must be buried by the parish. Finally, the wage-earner must never be absent from his work for a single day.

Rowntree's ideas about the poverty line and secondary poverty were to have a great influence on social policy, as Michael Rose points out:

> . . . the concept of a poverty line remained enshrined in the existence of a minimum state welfare benefits level. Any increase in this, to meet rising living costs and standards, swelled the numbers defined as being in poverty. At the same time, the concepts of 'secondary poverty' provided support to those who thought that poverty was of the individual's own making. In this view, more careful management of a limited income should ensure that the family had enough to eat and was not, by absolute standards, poor.[15]

The writings of Booth and Rowntree present stark contrasts within British society. On the one hand was great wealth, displayed through what the economist Thorstein Veblen described as 'conspicuous consumption' – in 1896 Lord Rosebery (one of 12 men in England with an income from land of over £100,000) bought up every single out-of-season strawberry in the country for one meal, at a price which would have kept a family of four for more than a year. On the other hand; abject poverty. Lloyd George poured out his wrath on 'the Dukes': 'Oh these dukes, how they harass us . . . . a fully equipped duke costs as much to keep up as two Dreadnoughts, and they are just as great a terror and they last longer.'

Dreadnought battleships were, of course, necessary for the maintenance of imperial glory. And here lay a second contrast, that the nation which was bearing 'the white man's burden' in the colonies, turned a blind eye to the problems at home. Winston Churchill declared: 'I see little glory in an Empire which can rule the waves and is unable to flush its own sewers.' The Boer War (1899–1902) made the issues clearer still. Lloyd George, an ardent pro-Boer, commented bitterly: 'The country that spent two hundred and fifty million to avenge an insult levelled at her pride by an old Dutch farmer is not ashamed to see her children walking the streets hungry and in rags.' The war gave the nation a shock, for 40 per cent of the recruits (and in some areas as many as 60 per cent) had to be rejected as unfit, and although the minimum height for infantrymen had been lowered in 1883, it had again to be lowered in 1902. Such were the fears of national physical deterioration that an Inter-departmental Committee of the Home and Education Departments and Local Government Board investigated the matter, and in their report of 1904 made far-reaching recommendations (especially with regard to child welfare) which bore fruit under the Liberal government.

There are other ways in which wars (including the Boer War) result in increased attention being paid to social issues. During wars, higher tax levels are imposed and accepted, which results in a higher toleration of taxes in the post-war period which the government is free to direct towards welfare projects. At the same time, responsibilities for expenditure tend to be transferred from local authorities to central government, which thus secures a firmer basis for reform. Demands for reform arise partly from the increased awareness of social evils revealed, for example, by recruitment, and partly from a natural desire that the sacrifices of war should lead to a better society.

Motivation for reform is, of course, complex. The debate on physical deterioration was immediately relevant to the question of military recruitment, but there were also industrial recruits to be thought of, and social reforms therefore had an economic dimension. (It is interesting to note that Boy Scouts – one of the more enduring spin-offs from the Boer War – were originally required to promise to do their duty to their *employer*, as well as to God and the king.) The efficiency of the worker assumed a particular importance towards the end of the nineteenth century, as Britain faced up to increased foreign competition. The desire to find remedies was increased by the possibility that relative decline might become absolute decline.

Not surprisingly, it was to one of Britain's competitors – Germany – that many people looked for models of social reform, but that was not the only source of ideas. Australia provided the pattern for legislation to curb sweating (which in Britain came to be regulated by the Trade Boards Act of 1909); while New Zealand, where old age pensions were introduced in 1898, established a precedent for that reform.

Social investigation at home, and successful welfare reforms abroad, helped to establish a climate in which progress could be made. Lloyd George argued that a swing in public opinion gave strength to the Liberal reform programme, for his party had the good fortune to be 'carried forward on a tide of social pity that was only waiting for a chance of expression'. But the pity was tinged with economic self-interest, and with fear – of enemies abroad and of socialism at home. J. R. Hay writes:

> Socialism at this time was the great bogey, and Liberals alternated between fear and contempt for socialism as a doctrine. They feared its implications for the type of society they wished to preserve or create. They feared the consequences of their own failure to create that society, a socially responsible form of capitalism. They had little but contempt for what they regarded as socialism's over-simplification of economic and social processes and its nebulous utopianism. Liberals felt that socialism would result in the primacy of sectional interests, instead of a society where interests were balanced for the common good. So Liberals, even the most radical, were concerned to discriminate between their ideas of state action to liberate the faculties of the individual, and what they saw as the complete control of economic and social processes by the state.[16]

Of all the socialist groups, the Fabians were the most 'respectable' and middle class, and were described by their critics as 'gas and water socialists'. They were committed to a gradualist approach and, as Bernard Shaw (one of their members) put it, planned 'to make it as easy and matter-of-fact for the ordinary, respectable Englishman to be a Socialist as to be a Liberal or a Conservative'.

On the whole, ordinary respectable Englishmen, including those newly enfranchised members of the working class, continued to support the older parties. There is no evidence of a general working-class pressure for reform. Some working men and women argued that the reform of the economic and political system must take precedence over social reform. Others argued that economic reforms were justified, but that *social* reforms inevitably implied 'social control'. Yet others took a more pragmatic view and supported certain reforms while remaining indifferent to others. Harold Perkin makes another important distinction when he writes:

> 'Pressure from below' did operate in the sense that both the Conservatives and the Liberals wooed the working-class voter with social imperialist policies of social reform which *they thought* he wanted, but the actual measures offered by strong-minded politicians like Chamberlain and Lloyd George and self-confident administrators like Sir Robert Morant and William Beveridge were based on *their* criteria, not *his*, and the Liberal reforms were made *for* him, not *by* him.[17]

The Conservatives, in power from 1895 to 1905, based their electoral strength on the middle class, yet also managed to secure between one-third and one-half of the working-class vote. Working-class Conservatives voted as they did either from deference or for economic reasons, believing, as one put it, that 'there was plenty of work about when the Conservatives was in'. In the early years of the twentieth century, however, the Conservatives played into the hands of the Liberals. The Education Act of 1902 (sometimes called the Balfour Act, but in reality the brain-child of a civil servant, Robert Morant), which abolished the School Boards and provided public rate support for church schools, alienated the Nonconformists – the traditional power-base of the Liberals – like nothing had before. Second, the failure of the Conservatives to attempt to reverse the Taff Vale decision of 1901 threw the infant Labour Party into the arms of the Liberals, the two parties forging an electoral pact in 1903. There was, however, a limit to how far the Liberals could go to woo the working-class vote, for although they won electoral support from the trade unions, for financial support they still depended on the minority of well-to-do party members. They could not afford policies so radical as to alienate their wealthy backers. This has to be remembered when considering their landslide victory of 1906. Lloyd George hailed the result as 'a quiet, but certain, revolution, as revolutions come in a constitutional country', while the Conservative leader, A. J. Balfour declared, 'Unless I am greatly mistaken the election of 1906 inaugurates a new era'.

Nevertheless, while there was a heightened sense of awareness of social problems and a greater sense of urgency, no revolutionary ideas were put forward in the official election programmes, which tended to concentrate on the single issue of free trade. Campbell-Bannerman's premiership down to 1908 was relatively barren of social reform, although the Education (Provision of Meals) Act of 1906 and the act of 1907 which provided for medical inspection in state schools (and opened the door for medical *treatment*) were important steps forward. It is interesting to note that these early reforms applied to children, who were seen as a valuable national asset whose importance was increased by the falling birth-rate. It is also significant that the act of 1906 which provided free school meals for needy children did not impose any penalties on the parents. They were not disfranchised, as happened when resort was made to the Poor Law, and so a further step was taken along the road from individual to collective responsibility for social welfare.

The pace quickened when Campbell-Bannerman was succeeded by Asquith in 1908 and the leading 'New Liberal' radicals – Lloyd George and Winston Churchill – were promoted to the Treasury and the Board of Trade respectively. Lloyd George was in his mid-40s, and was the first Cabinet minister to have been born in poverty. Churchill, the aristocrat born in Blenheim Palace, was in his early 30s. Each had a flair for catching the mood of the times and of expressing it through brilliant oratory. 'The cause of Liberalism,' cried Churchill in 1906, 'is the cause of the left-out millions'; a battle cry which spurred them on in the next few years. The reforms of the Liberal heyday touched on many social and economic issues, of which the three most important were old age pensions, the relief of unemployment, and national insurance.

Old age pensions
The idea of old age pensions was not new, and a 21-year struggle took place before they became a reality. Charles Booth had advocated old age pensions which 'would lift from very many old heads the fear of the workhouse at the last'. So had Canon Barnett, who argued that pensions 'would be no more corrupting to the labourer who works for his country in the workshop than for the civil servant who works for his country at the desk'. There was a touch of Bismarck here, for he had argued that it was unfair to pension soldiers while allowing 'the veterans of industry to die in misery'. Germany introduced pensions in 1889, as part of the system of social insurance which Bismarck had been building up since 1883 as a bulwark against socialism. Joseph Chamberlain, the first Cabinet minister to concern himself with the problem of the aged, was much influenced by the German example. In 1893 a Royal Commission on the Aged Poor was set up which, in its report of 1895, recognised the extent of the problem but recommended no major change:

> We are of opinion that no fundamental alterations are needed in the existing system of poor relief as it affects the aged, and that it would be undesirable to interfere either by Statute or order with the discretion now vested in the guardians . . . since it is in our view of essential importance that guardians should have power to deal on its merits with each individual case. At the same time we are convinced that there is a strong feeling that in the administration of relief there should be a greater discrimination between the respectable aged who become destitute and those whose destitution is directly the consequence of their own misconduct . . .[18]

The distinction between the 'deserving' and the 'undeserving' poor, much stressed by middle-class agencies such as the Charity Organisation Society, was an obstacle to progress, as was the vested interest of the friendly societies, although they found it hard to conceal that increasing longevity of life put a strain on their resources. An important issue was whether pensions should be contributory or non-contributory. The friendly societies were doubly opposed to contributory pensions for few working men could afford to pay into two schemes, and the societies' income was bound to suffer. Furthermore, as Churchill pointed out, while unemployment, sickness and accident were 'vultures . . . always hovering around us', it was hard to persuade men to insure against old age which seemed far off. Thus it was that the Liberals put forward a scheme to be financed solely out of taxes. The budget surplus needed to finance the scheme came in 1908, whereupon Lloyd George pushed his Old Age Pensions Bill through Parliament. Pensions were to be paid to people over the age of 70 whose incomes did not exceed £31 a year, the maximum being 5s a week for those with an income of £21 a year falling, by units of 1s, until the maximum earnings of £31 a year was reached. An outcry in the House of Commons resulted in the throwing out of a scheme for a joint pension of 7s 6d to married couples, which had been put forward on the carefully documented grounds that two could live as cheaply as one. Although this meanness was avoided, the provision was meagre enough – Churchill likened it to 'a lifebelt'. Yet it was a lifebelt which many old people were happy to cling to. Old age pensions were the first national social service, and the only government department with the necessary local facilities for making payments was the Post Office. In *Lark Rise to Candleford* Flora Thompson, herself for some years a Post Office worker, described the impact on an Oxfordshire village:

> When the Old Age Pensions began, life was transformed for such aged cottagers. They were relieved of anxiety. They were suddenly rich. Independent for life! At first when they went to the Post Office to draw it, tears of gratitude would run down the cheeks of some, and they would say as they picked up their money, 'God bless that Lord George! (for they could not believe one so powerful and munificent could be a plain 'Mr.') and God bless *you*, miss!', and there were flowers from their gardens, and apples from their trees for the girl who merely handed them the money.

Ironically, it was the Lords who were among the sternest critics of the scheme, and whose objection to the People's Budget of 1909, whereby social services such as pensions would be financed by redistributive taxation (more likely to hit Conservative voters than the Liberals' own supporters), brought about a constitutional crisis.

Maurice Bruce sums up the significance of old age pensions thus:

> . . . the Old Age Pensions Bill introduced a new principle into social policy. Hitherto relief had been provided, as an act of grace, for all the needy from *local* funds and only after a test of destitution. Now for the first time payments were to be made, as of right, from *national* funds to a section of the needy, the elderly, within strict limitations of age and means, but with no test of actual destitution. Once the idea of pensions was accepted only national provision, as Asquith himself pointed out, was possible, for otherwise there would be the local variations and the difficulties about settlement which had plagued the adminis-tration of the Poor Law. The very ease with which the measure passed was, in fact, an indication of the general recognition of the inadequacy of the Poor Law and of the need for a new approach: as some stern critics complained, the pass was sold without a fight.[19]

The relief of unemployment

Unemployment is a concept with which we are now all too familiar, but Edwardians, like their predecessors, found it difficult, for the idea still lingered that there was always work for anyone who truly wished to find it. Experience increasingly cast doubt on this proposition, especially as prosperity at home was now so dependent on events abroad. As Churchill observed, the well-being of thousands could now be affected by events 'as independent of our control as the phases of the moon [and] as unpredictable as an Indian famine'. The nature of the problem was as much one of permanent *under*employment as one of temporary *un*employment, as men and women on the casual fringes of industry competed with each other for work which they obtained only spasmodically. Inadequate statistics made the extent of unemployment unclear. The Labour Bureau of the Board of Trade had started collating trade union statistics in 1886, but as only a minority of workers were members of trade unions the figures for unemployment which were produced underestimated the problem.

The issue could be broken down into two components. There was the problem of finding work, and there was that of insuring against unemployment when no work was to be found. John Burns (who advocated labour exchanges) railed against the loafer – 'the gentleman who gets up to look for work at mid-day, and prays that he may not find it'; but Will Crooks, a cooper who, like Burns, became a Labour MP, presented another side of the coin:

> It is a weird experience, this, of wandering through England in search of a job . . . You keep your heart up so long as you have something in your stomach, but when hunger steals upon you, then you despair. Footsore and listless at the same time, you simply lose all interest in the future . . .
>
>   Nothing wearies one more than walking about hunting for employment which is not to be had. It is far harder than real work. The uncertainty, the despair, when you reach a place only to discover that your journey is fruitless, are frightful. I've known a man to say 'Which way shall I go today?' Having no earthly idea which way to take, he tosses up a button. If the button comes down on one side, he treks east; if on the other, he treks west.
>
>   You can imagine the feeling when, after walking your boots off, a man says to you, as he jingles sovereigns in his pocket, 'Why don't you work.' That is what happened to me as I scoured the country between London and Liverpool, asking all the way for any kind of work to help me along . . . [20]

Despite opposition from some employers who felt that they would be the refuge of the work-shy, and from some workers who feared that they would be used to recruit blackleg labour during strikes, labour exchanges excited much support. William Beveridge (who had been sub-warden of Toynbee Hall in 1903–4) was Churchill's principal adviser at the Board of Trade, and he saw that the labour exchange was an indispensable counterpart to unemployment insurance, for only by 'signing on' would it be known that a man was unemployed. Beveridge wrote: 'The Labour Exchange thus opens a way of "dispauperisation" more humane, less costly and more effective than that of the "workhouse test" – the way of making the finding of work easy, instead of merely making relief hard.'

The bill to establish labour exchanges, which Churchill introduced in May 1909, contained only six clauses, and passed through Parliament with little comment, becoming law in September. Eighty-three exchanges were opened in February 1910, and by 1914 there were 430. Churchill is alleged to have said that 100 exchanges would be less costly and more effective that a new battleship, the prophetic truth of which became apparent when war broke out and they were used for recruitment purposes.

Unemployment insurance had to wait for two years after the labour exchanges were first set up, for Churchill could see that it formed one part of a national insurance scheme, and he therefore waited until Lloyd George's plans on health insurance were formulated. Unemployment insurance therefore constituted Part II of the National Insurance Act of 1911. The scheme was experimental, and was restricted at first to a small group of trades which were ordinarily well-paid (their members could therefore afford the contributions) but which were liable to severe unemployment during years of depression. These included building, shipbuilding, mechanical engineering, ironfounding, vehicle construction, and saw-milling. The 2.25 million men in these industries were to be compulsorily insured. As the success of the scheme depended on higher contributions than the individual workman could afford, and as employers also stood to gain, both parties were to contribute $2\frac{1}{2}$ d a week, the state undertaking to add a third of the total at the end of each year. In return the workman was guaranteed 7s a week when unemployed, qualifying for a week of benefit for each five contributions paid, up to a maximum of 15 weeks in any year. The scheme was significant more for what it represented than for what it achieved, for a low level of unemployment in the generally prosperous years between 1912 and 1914 did not put it to the test. The limited strain which it could bear was revealed in the dark days of unemployment after the First World War. What the treatment of unemployment *represented*, however, was yet another move away from a moralistic attitude to social problems. Churchill was opposed to men who had been dismissed for misconduct being debarred from benefit: 'I do not like mixing up moralities and mathematics.' He wanted relief to be based on actuarial (mathematical) rules rather than on a distinction between the deserving and the undeserving (i.e. moral rules). He was out-voted, in fact, and men dismissed for misconduct were debarred, but less for moral reasons than for the mathematical one that such risks could not enter any actuarial calculations.

Health insurance

The driving force behind unemployment insurance was Churchill – 'a signal instance', as Beveridge put it, 'of how much the personality of a single Minister in a few critical months may change the course of social legislation'. The driving force behind health insurance, on the other hand, was Lloyd George. He was much impressed by a visit to Germany in August 1905, and had a deep, personal experience of disease, for his own father had died of tuberculosis. This disease, commonly called 'consumption', was a great scourge which killed 75,000 every year, one-third of whom were in the prime of working life. Many people had no idea of the onset of the disease until it was well established in the lungs. In the course of a few months the serious symptoms developed, including severe coughing with expectoration, loss of weight, haemorrhage from the lungs, erratic temperature and general weakness. According to the books of one great friendly society, the average length of illness was over a year, but it might take two or three years before death ensued. Robert Tressell wrote of the oppressed conditions in his trade of house-painting during the Edwardian era. His novel, *The Ragged-trousered Philanthropists*, appeared posthumously in 1914 – three years after Tressell had died of tuberculosis. Frank Owen, one of the principal characters in the book, was also consumptive:

> One day, having nothing better to do, Owen was looking at some books that were exposed for sale on a table outside a second-hand furniture shop. One book in particular took his attention: he read several pages with great interest, and regretted that he had not the necessary sixpence to buy it. The title of the book was: *Consumption: Its Causes and its Cure*. The author was a well-known physician who devoted his whole attention to the study of that disease. Amongst other things, the book gave rules for the feeding of delicate children, and there were also several different dietaries recommended for adult persons suffering from the disease. One of these dietaries amused him very much, because as far as the majority of those who suffer from consumption are concerned, the good doctor might just as well have prescribed a trip to the moon:
> 'Immediately on waking in the morning, half a pint of milk – this should be hot, if possible – with a small slice of bread and butter.
> 'At breakfast: half a pint of milk, with coffee, chocolate, or oatmeal: eggs and bacon, bread and butter, or dry toast.

'At eleven o'clock: half a pint of milk with an egg beaten up in it or some beef tea and bread and butter.

'At one o'clock: half a pint of warm milk with a biscuit or sandwich.

'At two o'clock: fish and roast mutton, or a mutton chop, with as much fat as possible: poultry, game, etc., may be taken with vegetables, and milk pudding.

'At five o'clock: hot milk with coffee or chocolate, bread and butter water-cress, etc.

'At eight o'clock: a pint of milk, with oatmeal or chocolate, and gluten bread, or two lightly boiled eggs with bread and butter.

'Before retiring to rest: a glass of warm milk.

'During the night: a glass of milk with a biscuit or bread and butter should be placed by the bedside and be eaten if the patient awakes.'

Unable to afford the recognised treatment of prolonged rest and carefully controlled diet, many people poured money away on the many quack remedies which were advertised, like 'Tuberculozyne' ($2\frac{1}{2}$d worth of useless chemicals at a cost of £2 10s 0d); 'The Brompton Consumption and Cough Specific' (which resembled diluted treacle; its $\frac{7}{4}$d worth of ingredients cost the buyer 2s 9d); or 'Stevens' Consumption Cure' (which claimed to contain the magical, but utterly fictional, African herbs, 'umckaloabo' and 'chizitse').

The Poor Law Commission of 1905–9 described tuberculosis as 'the most pauperising of all diseases'. As a disease associated with environment it links with the nineteenth-century concern with *public* health, but its treatment, which called for the lengthy attention of a highly skilled medical practitioner, linked it to a growing concern with *personal* health, safeguarded by general practitioners backed up by consultants and hospitals. Tuberculosis was, of course, only one of many diseases with which the poor had to contend, while many suffered from the effects of industrial and other physical injuries and ailments.

Powerful interests, able to wield great political pressure, were involved in the struggle for health insurance. Foremost among these were the friendly societies and industrial assurance companies which insured against sickness. Only half the working population was covered, and not all of these received even the inadequate medical attention that was arranged on a contract basis. All of Lloyd George's persuasive powers were needed to steer a bill through Parliament, and he was forced to make many compromises. His proposals were introduced into the House of Commons in May 1911. A compulsory weekly levy of 4d per employee, 3d per employer and 2d from the state ('ninepence for fourpence') was imposed on all workers earning less than £160 a year, and on all manual labourers aged 16–60. In return the insured worker (but not his family) received medical treatment from a general practitioner with free medicine, sickness benefit of 10s a week for 13 weeks and 5s a week for the next 13 weeks, starting from the fourth day of illness, 5s a week disability benefit, and the right to treatment in a sanatorium. Women were to receive a maternity benefit of 30s. There was no unified health service. To placate the friendly societies and insurance companies, the payment of benefits was entrusted to 'approved societies'; to placate the doctors, medical treatment was to be supervised by local Insurance Committees, with medical representation. The doctors, in fact, with enhanced status and increased remuneration, were among the principal beneficiaries.

The health scheme had many deficiencies. There was no general hospital provision, no inclusion of the dependants of insured workers, and services continued to be fragmented. Lloyd George defended the scheme as an 'ambulance wagon', and in a speech at Birmingham, reported in *The Times* of 12 June 1911, he said,

> I never said this bill was a final solution. I am not putting it forward as a complete remedy . . . We are advancing on the road, but it is an essential part of the journey . . . This year, this Session, I have joined the Red Cross. I am in the ambulance corps. I am engaged to drive a wagon through the twistings and turnings and ruts of the Parliamentary road. There are men who tell me I have overloaded that wagon. I have taken three years to pack it carefully. I cannot spare a single parcel, for the suffering is very great. There are those who say my wagon is half empty. I say it is as much as I can carry. Now there are some who say I am in a great hurry. I *am* rather in a hurry, for I can hear the moanings of the wounded, and I want to carry relief to them in the alleys, the homes where they lie stricken, and I ask you, I ask the millions of goodhearted men and women who constitute the majority of the people of this land – I ask you to help me set aside hindrances, to overcome obstacles, to avoid the pitfalls that beset my difficult path.

If the health scheme was not a final solution, the same can be said of the whole package of Liberal reforms. Did they, as many historians have argued, lay the foundations of the welfare state? Some visionaries such as Lloyd George and Churchill certainly looked beyond individual pieces of legislation to a society in which the scourge of poverty would be eliminated. But the reforms made were (in many respects) very conservative, and stemmed more from a desire to protect the capitalist system against the threat of competition from abroad and socialist agitators at home. The reforms were therefore minimalist although, as J. R. Hay concludes, 'much of the legislation introduced was capable of extension in ways which would have made fundamental changes in the British economy and society'. Derek Fraser is of substantially the same opinion: 'Whatever historical perspective is used, one cannot escape the conclusion that Liberal social policy before the First World War was at once at variance with the past and an anticipation of radical changes in the future.' However, it would not be a Liberal government which continued the developments, but the Labour government after the Second World War.

Notes

1 Paul Kennedy, *Preparing for the Twenty-First Century*, HarperCollins 1993, pp. 142-3.
2 Barry Supple, 'Fear of failing: economic history and the decline of Britain' *Economic History Review*, August 1994, p. 446.
3 Charles Feinstein, 'Slowing down and falling behind: industrial retardation in Britain after 1870' in Anne Digby, Charles Feinstein and David Jenkins (eds.), *New Directions in Economic and Social History*, vol. 2, Macmillan, 1992, p. 169.
4 D. H. Aldcroft and H. W. Richardson, *The British Economy, 1870–1939*, Macmillan, 1969, p. 195.
5 Quoted in Michael Dintenfass, *The Decline of Industrial Britain 1870–1980*, Routledge, 1992, p. 12.
6 Quoted in D. H. Aldcroft and H. W. Richardson, op. cit., 1969, p. 128.
7 David Landes, *The Unbound Prometheus*, Cambridge University Press, 1969, p. 338.
8 Charles Feinstein, op. cit., 1992, p. 174.

9   W. H. B. Court, *British Economic History, 1870–1914; Commentary and Documents*, Cambridge University Press, 1965, p. 133.

10   S. B. Saul, *The Myth of the Great Depression, 1873–1896*, Macmillan, 1969, p. 46.

11   Roderick Floud and Donald McCloskey (eds), *The Economic History of Britain Since 1700*, vol. 2, Cambridge University Press, 1981, pp. 25–6.

12   H. J. Dyos and Michael Wolff (eds), *The Victorian City*, vol. 1, Routledge and Kegan Paul, 1973, p. 368.

13   Michael Flinn, *Readings in Economic and Social History*, Macmillan, 1964, p. 322.

14   Derek Fraser, *The Evolution of the British Welfare State*, 1973, pp. 125–6.

15   M. E. Rose, 'Poverty and self-help: Britain in the nineteenth and twentieth centuries' in Anne Digby, Charles Feinstein and David Jenkins (eds). op. cit., 1992, p. 154.

16   J. R. Hay, *The Origins of the Liberal Welfare Reforms, 1906–1914*, Macmillan, 1983, p. 36.

17   Harold Perkin, *The Rise of Professional Society. England Since 1880*, Routledge, 1990, p. 161.

18   Eric Evans, *Social Policy 1830–1914*, Routledge and Kegan Paul, 1978, pp. 167–8.

19   Maurice Bruce, *The Coming of the Welfare State*, Batsford, 1961, pp. 178–9.

20   W. H. B. Court, op. cit., 1965, p. 401.

Chapter twelve

Britain between the wars

Poverty or progress?

A powerful mythology has built up concerning the interwar years, a mythology with its roots in the period, but also one which has hardened into the political cliché of the world since 1945. At the 1951 general election the Labour Party urged younger voters to 'Ask Your Dad!' and contrasted conditions of that year with those of the pre-war days which were characterised as a time of 'mass unemployment; mass fear; mass misery'. A generation later, in the late 1970s and early 1980s, when unemployment was rising to fresh heights, there seemed to many people to be points of similarity rather than of contrast with the 1930s, the decade of 'the Great Slump'. The fear was that we had seen it all before.

The popular image of the interwar years is one of deepening depression at home and the rise of Fascist regimes abroad. Appropriate symbols range from the dole to the dictators, from the Jarrow March to the jackboot. Many of the epithets applied to the age have confirmed the popular conception. H. G. Wells wrote of the 'Fatuous Twenties' and the 'Frightened Thirties', the latter being described elsewhere as the 'Devil's Decade'. In 1940 the poet Robert Graves, together with Alan Hodge, published a social history of Great Britain between 1918 and 1939 which they entitled, *The Long Weekend*. The title may be interpreted in two ways. For some the period represented the waste and lost opportunity of a life without work, and for whom idleness (but hardly leisure) was enforced. For others, 'the Long Week-End' might conjure up suburban tennis parties on Saturday afternoons, or Sunday jaunts in their first motor car, down clear roads to still uncluttered beaches.

There are probably few periods in which our assessment depends so much upon our viewpoint, whether social or geographical. How people remember the interwar years depends very much upon who they were and where they lived. The picture you would get in Merthyr Tydfil would be very different from that in Maidenhead, Greenock from Greater London, and Jarrow from Coventry or Slough. In the autumn of 1933 the novelist J. B. Priestley travelled through England, publishing his account in the following year under the title, *English Journey*. Priestley, who was an acute observer, identified not one England, but three:

> There was, first, Old England, the country of the cathedrals and minister and manor houses and inns, of Parson and Squire; guide-book and quaint highways and byways England . . . But we all know this England, which at its best cannot be improved upon in this world. That is, as a country to lounge about in; for a tourist who can afford to pay a fairly stiff price for a poorish dinner, an inconvenient bedroom and lukewarm water in a small brass jug. It has few luxuries, but nevertheless it is a luxury country. It has long ceased to earn its own living. I am for scrupulously preserving the most enchanting bits of it,

such as the cathedrals and the colleges and the Cotswolds, and for letting the rest take its chance ... Then, I decided, there is the nineteenth-century England, the industrial England of coal, iron, steel, cotton, wool, railways; of thousands of rows of little houses all alike, sham Gothic churches, square-faced chapels, Town Halls, Mechanics' Institutes, mills, foundries, warehouses, refined watering-places, Pier Pavilions, Family and Commercial Hotels, Literary and Philosophical Societies, back-to-back houses, detached villas with monkey-trees, Grill Rooms, railway stations, slag-heaps and 'tips', dock roads, Refreshment Rooms, doss-houses, Unionist or Liberal Clubs, cindery waste ground, mill chimneys, slums, fried-fish shops, public-houses with red blinds, bethels in corrugated iron, good-class draper's and confectioner's shops, a cynically devastated countryside, sooty dismal little towns, and still sootier grim fortress-like cities. This England makes up the larger part of the Midlands and the North and exists everywhere; but it is not being added to and has no new life poured into it . . . The third England, I concluded, was the new post-war England, belonging far more to the age itself than to this particular island. America, I suppose, was its real birthplace. This is the England of arterial and by-pass roads, of filling stations and factories that look like exhibition buildings, of giant cinemas and dance-halls and cafes, bungalows with tiny garages, cocktail bars, Woolworths, motor-coaches, wireless, hiking, factory girls looking like actresses, greyhound racing and dirt tracks, swimming pools, and everything given away for cigarette coupons. If the fog had lifted I knew that I should have seen this England all around me at that northern entrance to London, where the smooth wide road passes between miles of semi-detached bungalows, all with their little garages, their wireless sets, their periodicals about film stars, their swimming costumes and tennis rackets and dancing shoes.

Having described these three faces of England, Priestley went on to describe a fourth, 'the England of the Dole':

It is a poor shuffling job, and one of our worst compromises. When I began to ask myself exactly what was wrong with it, faces and voices from that unhappy world returned to my memory. I saw again the old men who, though they knew they were idle and useless through no fault of their own, felt defeated and somewhat tainted. Their self-respect was shredding away. Their very manhood was going. Even in England, which is no South Sea Island, there are places where a man feels he can do nothing cheerfully, where gay idling is not impossible. But the ironist in charge of our affairs has seen to it that the maximum of unemployment shall be in those very districts that have a tradition of hard work and of very little else . . . You have only to spend a morning in the dole country to see that it is all wrong. Nobody is getting any substantial benefit, any reasonable satisfaction out of it. Nothing is encouraged by it except a shambling dull-eyed poor imitation of life. The Labour Exchanges stink of defeated humanity. The whole thing is unworthy of a great country that in its time has given the world some nobly creative ideas. We ought to be ashamed of ourselves.

Only a picture which includes all of these facets will approach the truth, for Britain between the wars presents an apparent paradox. Despite mass unemployment – at least 10 per cent of the insured workforce was unemployed in any year between 1921 and 1938 – the economy not only grew, but grew at a high rate compared with other periods, or other economies at that time. Whereas economic growth was slowing down in Britain in the decades before the First World War, the interwar years witnessed an acceleration of growth. For example, per capita income grew faster than at any time since the 1880s. Industrial productivity showed a remarkable break in trend. Between 1870 and 1913 the annual rate of growth was 0.6 per cent, and only 0.2 per cent in the 1900s. Between 1920 and 1938, however, the annual rate was 2.8 per cent. By 1938 total industrial production had risen 63 per cent above the 1913 level while between 1924 and 1935 output per head grew by one-third, which was more than in the Victorian heyday. It is true that Britain's export performance was poor, for exports contracted at a rate of 1.2 per cent per annum as against a 2.7 per cent increase between 1870 and 1913. Yet, on balance, the growth record shows the economy to have been far from stagnant.

When an international comparison is made, it is apparent that Britain's interwar growth record was relatively better than before 1914 or after the Second World War. In both of those periods it was at or near the bottom of the league table of leading economies, whereas between the wars its performance was above the general average. There was nevertheless a sense of lost opportunities. The Minority Report of the Macmillan Committee on Finance and Industry lamented: 'If we can do what we are doing with nearly a quarter of our industrial resources idle, what might we not do if they were all employed?' The committee estimated that the loss of output from 1 million unemployed men – the average in the good years – over a period of five years amounted to £1,000 million, assuming the net output per worker to be around £200. In other words, in the best years of the period the national income would have been £200 million per annum higher had the labour force been fully employed. It is the existence of these unemployed resources which justifies a pessimistic view of the economy between the wars.

The interwar economy is frequently explained in terms of declining 'old' staple industries and expanding 'new' ones, but such a distinction can be misleading, in part because some key industries (such as house-building and engineering) are difficult to classify in this way. Nor can the new industries be said to have dominated the top end of the productivity scale. Only two new industries – vehicles and precision instruments – experienced an above average growth in productivity, and the ranking of the top nine was timber, furniture, mechanical engineering, vehicles, building and contracting, non-ferrous metal manufacture, iron and steel, precision instruments and clothing. Increased productivity resulted from rapid technical progress (which was not confined to any particular group of industries) and from increased workforce efficiency. That efficiency had its price – unemployment – which certainly affected the basic industries more than the new ones. The cheapness of labour before the war may have delayed technical innovation, and certainly did in the coal industry, where mechanical coal-cutting was introduced much more slowly than in many overseas collieries. After the slump of 1921 there began a massive 'shake-out' of labour from the old staple industries and, with the introduction of unemployment benefits, many employers who had previously been paternalistic to their workforces were able to enforce redundancies more ruthlessly. Most basic industries were therefore able to raise their output and productivity at least modestly between 1920 and 1938. However, if the comparison is made with 1913 it is easier to speak of stagnation or decline. In general, the staple industries reached a peak in that year and, apart from iron and steel, output never again returned to pre-war levels. How significant, then, was the First World War to changes in the British economy, and to the new society which observers reported between the wars?

The impact of the First World War

The British Expeditionary Force (BEF) which crossed into France in August 1914 was not so very different from the army which had gone out to South Africa to fight the Boers or, for that matter, the one which had embarked for the Crimea 60 years before. Less than 10 years after that conflict, the American Civil War had pointed the way to the technological wars of the future, for on the battlefield appeared for the first time the combat repeating rifle, the portable telegraph, the machinegun and the balloon. (One British army manual current in the First World War contained the memorable instruction: 'Officers of Field rank on entering balloons are not expected to wear spurs.') British generals learnt their lessons slowly; the strategist Sir Basil Liddell Hart observing that, 'There is only one thing harder than getting an old idea out of the military mind, and that is getting a new one in'. In battle after battle between 1914 and 1918 waves of allied soldiers were to be scythed down by the machinegun which General Sir Douglas Haig described as 'a much overrated weapon'. Likewise Kitchener (the image of whose stern gaze and gloved finger on a recruiting poster persuaded many men that their country needed them) dismissed the tank as 'a pretty mechanical toy'. Despite the tank's major contribution to the allies' final offensive the dash and glamour of the cavalryman was not diminished, for as late as 1937 the official manual, *Cavalry Training*, devoted 23 pages to sword and lance exercises, while relegating the armoured car to a brief appendix.

Although the cavalry saw next to no action on the Western Front in the First World War, the horse remained the chief motive power of transportation. At the end of November 1918 the army possessed (in all theatres) nearly 750,000 horses and mules, and over 500,000 had perished on war service. However, even military conservatism gave way under mounting technical pressure. By the date of the Armistice, the army had in use 85,138 motor vehicles and 34,711 motorcycles. The internal combustion engine made possible the tank (2,818 had been produced by 1918) and enabled the war to be fought in the air as well as on land and sea. At the outbreak of war the British forces possessed 272 aircraft; by October 1918 the RAF had over 22,000 effective machines. Not only were there more military aircraft; there were striking improvements in performance. The aeroplanes which first went out with the BEF had a maximum speed of 80 mph, and a rate of climb from ground level of 300–400 feet (approximately 91–122 metres) per minute. The fastest machines of 1918 could reach 140 miles an hour and had a rate of climb of 2,000 feet (over 600 metres) per minute.

Great progress was also made with the field telephone and the radio, including the manufacture of radio valves. Invention and research were encouraged, and were given government backing on an unprecedented scale. The National Physical Laboratory had been founded in 1907, but received a paltry grant of only £7,000 per annum in 1914, plus some additional funds for aeronautical research. In 1916, however, the Department of Scientific and Industrial Research was set up which, later in the war, took over control of the National Physical Laboratory from the Royal Society. By the time the war was over the scientist, hitherto a somewhat suspect character, had acquired a new status. Many of the technical advances which the war encouraged were to have a permanent effect upon society (the motor vehicle and the radio are, perhaps, the prime examples) while the enormous demand for the paraphernalia of war was to have a marked effect upon the economy.

When Gladstone introduced his Crimean War budget into the House of Commons he had remarked that, 'The expenses of a war are the moral check which it has pleased the Almighty to impose upon the ambition and the lust of conquest that are

12   War and social change

The two world wars of this century resulted in significant social and economic change. They also generated vast quantities of propaganda material, and the historian has therefore to sort out the truth from the patriotic lie. Propaganda campaigns covered many activities, from recruiting to food and raw material saving, internal security and the boosting of morale.

Picture 1 is a recruiting poster dating from 1915. Its principal interest is that it was designed by Lord Baden-Powell, hero of Mafeking and founder of the Boy Scouts. It was described as 'a picture typifying the unity of all classes in the common aim'. Baden-Powell was an amateur artist. Philip Boydell, on the other hand, was a professional advertiser. He created the Squander Bug campaign for the National Savings Committee in the Second World War (2). There was a need to persuade people to save and to resist extravagant spending. Boydell's campaign, which featured numerous posters as well as press advertisements and cartoons, used humour as its principal ingredient.

Are YOU in this?

1   A 1915 recruiting poster designed by Lord Baden-Powell

2   The 'Squander Bug' savings campaign of the Second World War

3   First World War poster issued by the
    Ministry of Munitions, 1916

4   A woman at the wheel of a
    London tram, 1917

The effect of the world wars on women is discussed elsewhere in this book. In picture 3 the soldier's arm raised in farewell is echoed by that of the woman as she dons her overall preparatory to getting down to work. Many women did work which had previously been reserved to men, but there was some male resistance. Very few women drove trams (4). Although the number of women employed in municipal tramways rose from 1,200 in 1914 to 18,800 in 1918, most were clerks and conductresses. In the services, too, women tended to be confined to 'feminine' roles. On the poster for the Voluntary Aid Detachments (VAD) (5) only motor driving is not an established role for women. Things had not changed so much by the Second World War. The VAD poster happened to have been designed by a woman (Joyce Dennys). The cartoon (6) was drawn by a man. Is he suggesting that women were satisfied with their limited role? And to what extent do cartoons depend for their effectiveness on stereotypes?

How far is war compatible with feminine glamour? The use of cosmetics increased in the First World War, and the Icilma advertisement of 1915 (7) implies that it was a woman's first duty to appeal sexually to her man at the front. Compare this with the 1941 poster for the Auxiliary Territorial Service (8). It was felt that the women's branch of the army was not competing for recruits with the Women's Royal Naval Service and the Women's Auxiliary Air Force, and a vigorous recruiting campaign was started. This poster was withdrawn, however, after parliamentary criticism that the woman depicted (who became known as the 'Blonde Bombshell') was *too* glamorous.

5   First World War recruiting poster
designed by Joyce Dennys

6   Women still behind the typewriter in the
Second World War; a cartoon from *Punch*
22 March 1944

7   Glamour applauded in a 1915
advertisement in the *Daily Mirror*

8   Glamour condemned –
Abram Games's poster of 1941

9   Censored poster of 1942

Abram Games was one of the most notable of British graphic designers of this century. Altogether he produced over 100 posters for the War Office, several of which were censored. 'Your Britain, Fight For It Now' (9) was withdrawn after Churchill objected to the boy with rickets. The poster had been designed for distribution by the Army Bureau of Current Affairs, a remarkable organisation which fostered discussion by the troops. Churchill was very suspicious of this, writing that 'such discussions only provide opportunities for the professional grouser and agitator with a glib tongue'. Yet the Bureau did boost morale by keeping in the soldier's mind the need for, and possibility of social reconstruction which would follow military victory.

A most difficult task for the historian is to establish how people would have responded to pictorial and other material at the time it was produced. How might service men and women from different backgrounds have reacted to the two posters by Games which are reproduced here?

inherent in so many nations'. By the turn of the twentieth century many people argued that the enormous costs of modern war would act as a deterrent, and this was the message of Norman Angell's much-discussed book, *The Great Illusion*, of 1910. Angell attempted to demonstrate that war was economically absurd, but the events of 1914–18 were to show that nations were prepared to make the sacrifice of money as well as men. By 1915 the cost of the war to Britain was running at £3 million a day. On artillery shells alone the army spent £22,211,389 14s 4d in the Battle of Passchendaele in 1917, while the most expensive day was from noon of 28 September to noon of 29 September, when the army blasted off 943,847 rounds of ammunition at the Hindenburg Line, at a cost of £3,871,000.

War on this scale required unprecedented intervention by the government in the workings of the economy. Some steps were taken immediately. For example, under powers derived from an act passed at the time of the Franco-Prussian War in 1871, the government commandeered the railway network on 4 August 1914, the very day that war broke out. The railways were not truly nationalised, but were run as a unified system by a Railway Executive Committee which consisted of the general managers of the main companies, under the official chairmanship of the President of the Board of Trade. Considerable economies were made, through the pooling of wagons for example. In 1913 nearly 61 per cent of wagons in transit were running empty. By the end of the war the figure was around 20 per cent. So great was the success that many argued that railways should be permanently nationalised.

The extent to which the whole economy would be controlled by the government was not foreseen in the early stages of the war, just as it had not been foreseen that the fighting on the Western Front would not constitute a war of movement but would become a war of attrition, between armies bogged down in trenches. Success in that kind of war would come to the nation which most effectively mobilised its manpower and its industrial power. Gradually it became apparent that the free economic system, in the words of one contemporary economist, 'produced too little, it produced the wrong things, and it distributed them to the wrong people'. As the tentacles of government intervention extended, eventually two-thirds (or possibly more) of all employed workers were engaged in activities subject to government control. Sir John Clapham put the point vividly:

> As pressures increased in 1916–17, and . . . the unrestricted submarine attack on shipping of 1917 became painful, industry and commerce which had been reasonably free so far . . . had to accept more and more government super-vision, or self-regulation under instructions from Whitehall. The thing had begun gradually with the prior claims of the fighting department on the stocks and services of industry; it grew with the Ministry of Munitions; and ended with a complex system of controls, controllers, and 'priorities' which so covered the industries of the country that a man could not put steel into corsets – the corset of 1917 was full of steel – without a certificate from the Ministry of Munitions that it was necessary to support the backs of his women workers; and hairpins might only be made out of wire that the Admiralty did not want, 'fallen' wire which was not springy. When peace came, common bricks appeared to be under two or three separate controls . . .[1]

In May 1915 Colonel Charles Repington, military correspondent of *The Times*, sent back a disturbing report from France – British field-gunners could not operate effectively because of a shortage of shells. The matter soon became a crying public issue, and helped to precipitate both the formation of a coalition government and the creation of a Ministry of Munitions under David Lloyd George. The new ministry, which soon acquired powers to take over direct control of certain factories concerned with war production, had no traditions or established practices behind it, and was therefore an ideal instrument for direct government action. The nucleus of the new ministry were the twenty clerks of the Army Contracts Department. By the end of the war their number had swollen to 65,000 officials, controlling the work of 2 million workers in 250 government factories, mines and quarries, and another 1.4 million in 20,000 controlled establishments. The Ministry of Munitions assumed responsibility for the supply of aircraft to the forces, the development of agricultural machinery, the supply of fuel oils, and the manufacture and use of sulphuric acid, among other things.

A main aim of the government was to increase productivity in factories manufacturing war goods, and as the concentration of firms into larger organisations made control easier, business consolidation was encouraged. Mass production received a spur; it has to be remembered that the 'American system' of mass production, involving standardised, replaceable parts, had been pioneered by Eli Whitney in the manufacture of small-arms. Nearly 250,000 .303-inch machineguns, and about 4 million rifles were produced, and the tank had become a mass-produced weapon by 1918. During the first 12 months of the war an average of 50 aeroplanes was delivered each month; in the last 12 months the average was 2,700. Throughout the duration of the war the total number of military aircraft manufactured was 52,027.

Just as the inadequacy of undirected industry to produce war goods had not been anticipated, so the difficulties of British agriculture to feed the nation had been underestimated. A Royal Commission on Supply of Food and Raw Material in Time of War reported optimistically in 1905:

> We . . . regard the present variety of sources from which our supplies are drawn as likely to contribute to our advantage in time of war, since their wide geographical distribution must tend to minimise the risk of interference with our imports . . . Instead of deriving 62 per cent of our total annual imports of wheat and flour from a single source, we are at the present time drawing our main supplies from four countries in widely different parts of the world, namely, British, India, Russia, the Argentine, and the United States, which in 1904 sent us, respectively, 21 per cent, 19 per cent, 18 per cent, and 16 per cent of our total imports . . .
>
> It may also be said that the more numerous the neutral powers supplying our wants the less probable is the violation of International Law by our enemies. There is, therefore, a certain advantage to us in the fact that the supplies of our principal foodstuffs are drawn in a greater proportion from foreign countries than from the British possessions . . .
>
> We think that the effect of the naval and shipping evidence is conclusive as to the point that while there will be some interference with trade and some captures, not only is there no risk of a total cessation of our supplies, but no reasonable probability of serious interference with them, and that, even during a maritime war, there will be no material diminution in their volume . . .
>
> We do not therefore apprehend that any situation is likely to arise in which there would be a risk of the actual starvation of our population into submission.

Food prices quickly rose after the outbreak of war, but there was no great concern until the submarine menace became really threatening after the Battle of Jutland in May 1916. By April 1917 one out of four ships leaving the British Isles never came home. A convoy system was introduced to protect shipping, and steps were taken to boost home agricultural output, to distribute food more effectively and to conserve supplies. In February and March of 1917 a massive survey was undertaken to reveal the amount of new land that might be cultivated. Farmers were given instructions on methods of cultivation, and could be served with compulsory plough-ing orders. Those who disobeyed could be dispossessed, but the cooperation of farmers was encouraged by a Corn Production Act by which the government guaranteed minimum prices. In addition, 316,000 women labourers were supplied (many of them organised in the new Women's Land Army) and 22,000 men, of whom a large number were prisoners of war.

Rationing came very late, although voluntary rationing (put forward in a totally unrealistic scheme) was promoted from February 1917. It was not until 1 January 1918 that compulsory rationing began with sugar, soon spreading to meat, butter, margarine and nearly all important foodstuffs. Regulations already existed to control food waste. A Ministry of Food leaflet of 1917 had this to say to the public: 'One teaspoonful of breadcrumbs saved by each person in Great Britain per day represents 40,000 tons of bread in a year. One ounce of bread wasted by every person in the kingdom in one week equals 9,380 tons of bread – nine shiploads of bread.' Advice was bolstered with sanctions. A lady in Wales who gave meat to her St Bernard dog was fined £20; a furnaceman was fined £10 for showing his dissatisfaction with his dinner by throwing chips in the fire; and a farmer was fined the same sum for feed-ing to his pigs rock cakes which he had purchased cheaply from an army canteen. (Should they have been kept for throwing at the enemy?) Such a mass of food control orders poured from the Ministry that one MP weighed the issue of one day and found it to equal half a pound (225 grams).

Not only did rationing and other controls prevent starvation; there is evidence that the health of the nation improved, and Britons were fed infinitely better than their enemies, and somewhat better than most neutrals. An official report of 1918 confirmed that London schoolchildren in a poorly nourished condition made up less than half of the percentage of 1913, and similar results were exhibited at Birmingham, Bolton, Bradford, Bristol, Glasgow and Nottingham. A government attack on heavy drinking struck at another hazard to health. 'Drink,' said Lloyd George in February 1915, 'is doing us more damage in the War than all the German submarines put together.' Control of excessive drinking was exercised in a number of ways. New licensing laws cut down the opening hours of public houses, spirits and beer were reduced in alcoholic strength, and taxation was increased – so that by 1920 spirits cost four or five times what they had before the war. At Carlisle, close to the great munitions works at Gretna, the government acquired all the licensed premises save for two large hotels, and nationalised four breweries. The decline in heavy drinking was to be a permanent feature of British society, although the downward trend was reversed after the Second World War.

The war forced people to change their attitudes. Arthur Marwick writes: 'Ideas which could in pre-war years be laughed off as utopian fantasies denounced as con-trary to economic law, or displayed as evidence of the sinister intentions of socialism, had been put to work and had been seen to work.' A number of commentators made this point in the years after the war. In 1927, for example, four young Con-servatives (including Harold Macmillan) wrote that, 'The war period shattered pre-conceived economic notions, proved possible theoretic impossibilities, removed irremovable barriers, created new and undreamt-of situations'. The same applied to society. Writing in 1918, the social investigator, Seebohm Rowntree, observed: 'We have completely revised our notions as to what is possible or impossible. We have seen accomplished within a few brief months or years reforms to which we should have assigned, not decades, but generations.'

William Beveridge argued: 'The most general effect of war is to make the common people more important.' Not only were the masses required to exert greater efforts in their traditional role of industrial army, but they were also called to the colours in unprecedented numbers – the French poet, Paul Valéry, spoke of the infantry as 'the man in the street dressed as a soldier'. Britain had no tradition of conscript armies, but volunteers quickly flocked to the recruiting offices. In the first five weeks of the war 250,000 men joined up. One ex-artilleryman later recalled his own gesture:

> War had been declared and the following Sunday I went with a friend of mine into Shepherd's Bush Empire to see the big show there, and at the end of the show they showed the Fleet sailing the high seas and played 'Britons Never Shall Be Slaves' and 'Hearts and Oak', and you know one feels that little shiver run up the back and you know you've got to do something. I was just turned seventeen at the time and on the Monday I went up to Whitehall – Old Scotland Yard – and enlisted.[2]

By the end of 1914, 1,186,337 men had joined up, and by September 1915 the total was 2,257,521. Much of the public spirit which lay behind these astonishing figures was misplaced, for in the early days of the war recruiting was quite indiscriminate. Lloyd George declared in July 1915: 'We are suffering from the patriotism of the miners. A quarter of a million of them have gone into the fighting line. The demand for coal is greater than ever; the supply of coal is less than ever.' Statistics compiled at this time showed that a fifth of all miners had enlisted, while almost a quarter of workers in the chemicals and explosives industry and in electrical engineering had joined up. The armaments firm of Vickers suggested a system of badges to be worn by men on vital production work which would protect them both from the recruiting sergeant and from the attentions of young women with white feathers. The Admiralty, and later the army, took up the idea and a spasmodic movement began to keep certain men out of the forces.

However, undreamt of numbers of men were sacrificed on the Western Front. On the first day of the Battle of the Somme (1 July 1916), 20,000 British soldiers were killed: the equivalent of wiping out the population of Salisbury or Inverness at that time. At Passchendaele in 1917, 250,000 Britons were killed or wounded in an advance of five miles. In the face of losses such as these, many reserved men were 'debadged' or 'combed out', while attention was turned to conscription. Voluntary enlistment was given a last fling with the Derby scheme of 1915 which was a canny piece of political manoeuvring. Under this scheme, men were pressured to 'attest', i.e. to undertake that they would serve when called to do so. Priorities were then promised which would result in unencumbered men being enlisted before those whose work was of national importance, or who had stronger personal or family reasons for exemption. It was a clever tactical move on the part of the government. If enough men attested, the ideal of voluntarism would be preserved: if the scheme failed, the case for conscription would be irresistible. It failed. By the beginning of 1916 only 1,150,000 single men – out of a total of 2,179,231 – had attested. Conscription therefore followed in the spring. The calling-up for military service of a whole generation of young men revealed how unfit many of them were. Of 2.5 million men examined in 1917–18, only 36 per cent were passed as fit for full military duties. In this respect, little had changed since the Boer War.

The labour movement had shown great hostility to the idea of compulsory enlistment, fearing that military conscription would be followed by industrial conscription. The government needed the goodwill of trade unions and workmen generally, and it was not always easy to get. Much normal trade union activity was suspended,

although there was resistance in two areas: South Wales and Clydeside. A strike of
South Wales miners in 1915 brought them nearly all of their demands, while unrest
on 'Red Clydeside' saw shop stewards for the first time converted from minor trade
union officials into major spokesmen for rank-and-file members.

A realisation by ordinary men and women that their cooperation was essential to
the well-being of the country contributed towards a major social change – the
decline of deference and the spread of a mood of egalitarianism. The senseless slaughter
made men disillusioned with their leaders, while the death of so many young men
led to an alienation of the generations, movingly expressed by Wilfred Owen in his
poem, 'Parable of the Old Men and the Young':

> So Abram rose, and clave the wood, and went,
> And took the fire with him, and a knife.
> And as they sojourned both of them together,
> Isaac the first-born spake and said, My Father,
> Behold the preparations, fire and iron,
> But where the lamb for this burnt-offering?
> Then Abram bound the youth with belts and straps,
> And builded parapets and trenches there,
> And strètched forth the knife to slay his son.
> When lo! an angel called him out of heaven,
> Saying, Lay not thy hand upon the lad,
> Neither do anything to him. Behold,
> A ram, caught in a thicket by its horns;
> Offer the Ram of Pride instead of him.
> But the old man would not so, but slew his son,
> And half the seed of Europe, one by one.

The fitness of the aristocracy of birth and money to rule was questioned, while the
sight of bishops (exempt from danger) urging others to die and to kill, shook the
religious faith of many. This mood was captured by Siegfried Sassoon who, like
Wilfred Owen, served in the trenches:

> The Bishop tells us: 'When the boys come back
> 'They will not be the same; for they'll have fought
> 'In a just cause: they lead the last attack
> 'On Anti-Christ; their comrades' blood has bought
> 'New right to breed an honourable race,
> 'They have challenged Death and dared him face to face.'
>
> 'We're none of us the same!' the boys reply.
> 'For George lost both his legs; and Bill's stone blind;
> 'Poor Jim's shot through the lungs and like to die;
> 'And Bert's gone syphilitic: you'll not find
> 'A chap who's served that hasn't found *some* change.'
> And the Bishop said: 'The ways of God are Strange!'

The war created what Arthur Marwick describes as 'a strong breeze of egalitarianism'. Harold Macmillan, who later spoke of the 'wind of change' himself, felt that
breeze as a young officer in France. One of his duties was to censor the letters
which his men sent home. He wrote to his mother in 1915:

> Of all the war, I think the most interesting (and humbling too) experience is the
> knowledge one gets of the poorer classes. They have big hearts, these soldiers,

and it is a very pathetic task to have to read all their letters home. Some of the older men, with wives and families, who write every day, have in their style a wonderful simplicity which is almost great literature. And the comic inter-mixture of official or journalistic phrases – the kisses for baby or little Anne; or the 'tell Georgie from his daddy to be a good boy and not forget him' – is all very touching . . . And then there comes occasionally a grim sentence or two, which reveals in a flash a sordid family drama. 'Mother, are you going ever to write to me. I have written you quite ten times and had no answer. Are you on the drink again, that Uncle George writes me the children are in a shocking state?' . . . There is much to be learnt from soldiers' letters.[3]

Other factors also led to a blurring of class lines. Rationing led to a certain level-ling in diet, while the lowering of income-tax thresholds and the floating of war loans in small enough units to attract the working-class subscriber gave more people a direct financial stake in the country's affairs. In the year 1919–20 there were six times as many taxpayers as there had been in 1914, although shortly afterwards the number fell as the exemption limit was raised. Lest it be thought that the tide of egalitarianism flowed only in one direction, it has to be remembered that among the military decorations introduced in the First World War were the Military Cross, instituted for officers and warrant officers. If discharged with a pension, the holder of the Military Cross earned an extra sixpence a day (or threepence if non-European). For similar deeds, non-commissioned officers and men and women in the ranks were awarded the Military Medal, instituted in 1916, and not carrying a pension. The author possesses the Military Medal awarded to his great-grand-uncle, its historical interest being enhanced by the curt note which accompanied the medal when it was delivered through the post. No summons to Buckingham Palace for him. (The Victoria Cross, since its institution in 1856, has continued to be issued to officers and other ranks, without distinction.)

The war did not immediately give women a new status. Mrs Pankhurst, who for a decade had been waging war on the government, swung the Suffragette move-ment behind the war effort and insisted on women's 'right to serve'. A rally organised to this end brought 30,000 women on to the streets of London in July 1915. Until then there were no really striking changes as far as the mass of British women were concerned, and the contribution of most was confined to knitting woollen comforters for the men at the front, and engaging in similar social and charitable work. Two events thereafter created a demand for women's labour: the setting up of the Ministry of Munitions and the introduction of conscription for men opened up many new types of occupation. However, it was not until the last 18 months of the war that women were admitted into the armed forces in the Women's Army Auxiliary Corps, the Women's Royal Naval Service and the Women's Royal Air Force. Many people were surprised at the heavy work which women could accomplish, although this was due partly to an ignorance of the nature of much pre-war women's work. The work which women did in munitions factories could be extremely heavy and unpleasant, and carried hazards to health. The explosive used (TNT) could cause severely irritating symptoms and might lead to skin discolouration: women affected were jocularly called 'canaries'. There was also the danger of explosion – the most serious one at Silvertown in East London killed a dozen women – and altogether well over 200 deaths were caused in incidents up and down the country.

The introduction of women into engineering workshops required the abandon-ment of traditional labour practices, and resulted in 'Dilution' agreements with the trade unions whereby semi-skilled, unskilled and female labour was substituted for that of the skilled craftsman. Lloyd George, the Minister of Munitions, gave mixed assurances on the question of equal pay for women. He promised that there would be no sweated labour, but added that 'for some time women will be unskilled and untrained, and they cannot quite turn out as much work as men can who have been at it for some time'. Official wages rates, which came to accept equal pay, were enforceable only in 'national factories', and simply recommended elsewhere, and even the official rates were subject to conditions which meant that women generally earned less than men. There was thus a limit to the step forward made by women, illustrated also by the occupations which expanded most. Both in civilian occupations and in the forces women were largely confined to the 'feminine' jobs. One of the fastest growing occupations was clerical work, and the expansion of opportunities in commerce and administration helped in the rise of that new phenomenon – the business girl.

Women certainly gained in confidence during the war and a new self-pride was displayed in the growing use of cosmetics and in dress reform. The Land Army had helped lead the way here. As a contemporary song put it:

> Dainty skirts and delicate blouses
> Aren't much use for pigs and cows-es.

Not only were trousers worn for the first time, but skirts became shorter (being both practical for active work and economic of material).

Some saw such changes in women's behaviour as a moral issue, and the moral views of many people undoubtedly changed. The old certainties of Victorian England were no longer there, and the new standards of behaviour had sometimes painfully to be established.

The return to peace

From the outbreak of war to its close the British army and navy (together with the Royal Air Force, formed in 1918) lost at least 616,382 men. Over the same period 1,656,735 men were wounded, some so seriously that they would never work again. These figures do not include the dead and wounded of the dominions and colonies, Indian deaths alone amounting to 53,486, with a further 64,350 wounded. Most of the casualties were in the prime of their working life. For the first time since the Civil War of the seventeenth century there were also civilian casualties – totalling 5,611, including 1,570 deaths, the majority arising from air attack.

Such sacrifices left the desire, in politicians and people alike, that the post-war world would be so improved that the pain and suffering would be proved worthwhile. Modern total war became accepted only if it held out the prospect of a better world and a better life for its survivors. Walter Long, the President of the Local Government Board, in referring to the troops, said that 'to let them come home from horrible, water-logged trenches to something little better than a pigsty here would indeed be criminal . . . and a negation of all we have said during the war that we can never repay those men for what they have done for us'. The need for a reconstruction policy was appreciated quite early in the war, and in 1916 a Reconstruction Committee was established by the Asquith government, to be elevated by David Lloyd George to the Ministry of Reconstruction in July 1917. The Ministry made specific recommendations, but under Lloyd George reconstruction developed far-reaching, if somewhat vague, connotations. It was Lloyd George who, in a speech at Wolverhampton on 24 November 1918, asked rhetorically, 'What is our task? To make Britain a fit country for heroes to live in'. The war had been won (so it seemed, although there had only been an armistice and the German army had not been beaten in final battle); it now remained for the country to elect a government to win the peace. All three major parties played the reconstruction tune in their 1918 general election manifestos. Lloyd George's coalition government declared:

> The principal concern of every Government is and must be the condition of the great mass of the people who live by manual toil. The steadfast spirit of our workers, displayed on all the wide field of action opened out by the war – in the trenches, on the ocean, in the air, in field, mine and factory – has left an imperishable mark on the heart and conscience of the nation. One of the first tasks of the Government will be to deal on broad and comprehensive lines with the housing of the people, which during the war has fallen so sadly into arrears, and upon which the well-being of the nation so largely depends. Larger opportunities for education, improved material conditions, and the prevention of degrading standards of employment; a proper adaption to peace conditions of the experience which during the war we have gained in regard to the traffic in drink – these are among the conditions of social harmony which we shall earnestly endeavour to promote.

Asquith's election address for the Liberals argued: 'The war has cleared away a mass of obstructive prejudices and conventions, and with peace will come a realisable prospect of a new and better ordered society.'[4] The Labour Party manifesto stressed that 'the workers supplied the vast majority of our soldiers and sailors, and sustained the burden of war at home'.

There were practical reasons why stress was placed on the future, for it was not ideas of social justice alone which prevailed. War weariness and discontent provided the background to much publicised programmes in 1917, while the coalition and Liberal pledges of 1918 must be seen as an attempt to woo the workers' vote from the Labour Party, which emerged from the war with new vigour.

We have seen in an earlier chapter that the period after the Napoleonic Wars was one of social stress. So too were the years 1917–20, when there was a real danger of revolution. The Russian Revolution of October 1917 set off tremors throughout Europe, and in Britain there was a questioning of traditional authority. Although the coalition government won 473 of the 707 seats on the House of Commons at the general election, Labour greatly increased its vote, and in the same year adopted a definitely socialist policy of public ownership. There were disturbing police strikes in August 1918 and in May 1919; and in May 1920 British intervention against the Russian Bolsheviks led to the *Jolly George* incident, when London dockers refused to load a ship with munitions for Poland. In August a general strike was threatened to prevent Britain intervening when the Red Army moved against Warsaw. There was a high level of industrial militancy, of which Alan Bullock has written: 'The force behind this sudden outburst of industrial conflict derived not so much from particular claims over hours and wages (most of these were soon met) as from a pent-up, passionately felt demand for drastic change, an angry refusal to return to pre-war conditions.'

Part of the problem was the traditional one of reabsorbing large numbers of soldiers into civilian life after a major conflict; and the desire not to repeat the disasters following the Napoleonic Wars was one of the reasons for the original government interest in reconstruction. The Armistice had robbed the troops in the field of the symbolic fruits of victory, and hitches in demobilisation were sufficiently serious as to incite actual mutinies. At the beginning of January 1919, 12,000 soldiers in rest camps at Folkestone and Dover demonstrated against re-embarking for France, and 'soviets' were set up at depots in Kempton Park and Calais. Near Rhyl, five men were killed and 23 injured when Canadian troops engaged in two days of riot over delays in repatriation.

Many ex-officers also found it difficult to readjust to civilian ways. Some of the more violent of them joined the 'Auxis' or the 'Black and Tans', the notorious auxiliary units of the Royal Irish Constabulary who terrorised that unhappy country. The experience of others, particularly of 'temporary gentlemen', who had received commissions for the duration of the war, is expressed by George Bowling, the central character in George Orwell's novel, *Coming Up For Air* (1939):

> If you'd suggested to me then, in 1919, that I ought to start a shop – a tobacco and sweet shop, say, or a general store in some god-forsaken village – I'd just have laughed. I'd worn pips on my shoulder, and my social standards had risen. At the same time I didn't share the delusion, which was pretty common amongst ex-officers, that I could spend the rest of my life drinking pink gin. I knew I'd got to have a job. And the job, of course, would be 'in business' – just what kind of job I didn't know, but something high-up and important, something with a car and a telephone and if possible a secretary with a permanent wave. During the last year or so of war a lot of us had had visions like that. The chap who'd been a shop walker saw himself as a travelling salesman, and the chap who'd been a travelling salesman saw himself as a managing director. It was the effect of Army life, the effect of wearing pips and having a cheque-book and calling the evening meal dinner. All the while there'd been an idea floating round – and this applied to the men in the ranks as well as the officers – that when we came out of the Army there'd be jobs waiting for us that would bring in at least as much as our Army pay. Of course, if ideas like that didn't circulate, no war would ever be fought.
>
> Well I didn't get the job. It seemed that nobody was anxious to pay me £2,000 a year for sitting among streamlined office furniture and dictating letters to a platinum blonde. I was discovering what three-quarters of the blokes who'd been officers were discovering – that from a financial point of view we'd been better off in the Army than we were ever likely to be again. We'd suddenly changed from gentlemen holding His Majesty's commission into miserable out-of-works whom nobody wanted. My ideas soon sank from two thousand a year to three or four pounds a week.[5]

Demobilisation represented a running down of the war machine. Decontrol meant the same. Some decontrols came quickly: food coupons were abolished in May 1919 and bread rationing in August. A few wartime innovations remain little changed down to our own day: daylight saving by the institution of summer time (1916), and the limits placed upon the opening hours of public houses, for example. Most of the wartime regulations were dismantled within a year or two of the peace. The wartime controls which the government exerted over the economy and social life had been imposed because they were considered unavoidable, and did not represent an attempt at social engineering – changing the basic fabric of the country's institutions. Creating a 'Land Fit For Heroes', however, would necessitate fundamental change. On the one hand, the government was pledged to social reform. On the other, it was determined to take the country 'back to normalcy'. In the struggle between reform and reaction it was reaction which won, although there was nothing inevitable about this. It is true that the depression which followed the short post-war boom made things difficult, but, as Rodney Lowe has said in an article on the erosion of state intervention in Britain between 1917 and 1924: 'In these years, it must be remembered, reform was always as credible a response to depression as reaction.' He blames instead the political timidity of the Cabinet, and the absence of pioneering civil servants in the tradition of Chadwick and Kay-Shuttleworth. The demand for the nationalisation of key industries fell on deaf ears. Railways were returned to private hands in 1921 (although the Railway Act of that year established four large systems in place of the individual companies which had existed before the war). The fate of the coal industry remained a source of friction right down to the General Strike.

The short lived post-war boom (lasting roughly from March 1919 to April 1920), while insufficient to transform society, did allow labour to make significant gains. One of the most abrupt changes in working hours came in 1919 when, in a single year, the eight-hour day became normal, with enormous consequence to the quality of workers' lives. Even more striking were the political and social gains made by women – a case of the 'heroines' as well as the 'heroes' being remembered. An act of 1918 gave the vote to women over the age of 30 (and extended it to all adult males); not until 1928 did women receive the franchise at the same age as men. In 1919 the Sex Disqualification (Removal) Act swept away a number of legal barriers to women's advancement. Jury service was opened up to them, as was the magistracy and the legal profession. Qualified entry to the upper reaches of the civil service was allowed, and it was made clear that there was no legal bar to full membership of Oxford and Cambridge universities. In 1920 the section of the Larceny Act was abolished which assumed that a woman living with her husband could not steal from him. In 1923 the laws on divorce were amended; and in 1925 the presumption was swept away that a woman who committed a crime in her husband's presence did so under his coercion. However, the extent of these changes should not be exaggerated. The Sex Disqualification (Removal) Act lacked specific machinery for enforcement, and did nothing to safeguard the rights of women in private employment. Women's pay generally remained lower than that of men, while the removal of legal barriers frequently left other insurmountable barriers untouched. In 1919 the first woman MP took her seat (Lady Astor), but she waited two years before being joined by another. The number of women in the House of Commons remained small, for no party would give a woman a safe seat except in special circumstances such as the death of a husband who had held it, or some very strong local interest.

A return to peacetime conditions meant that a compromise had to be reached between the demands of 'normalcy' and those of 'reconstruction'. There was also a need to reach an international settlement while, at the same time, forcing Germany to make amends for the enormous losses incurred. In this field, too, much thought was reduced to the level of slogans, such as 'Hang the Kaiser!' What was not foreseen was that the consequences of the peace could be as disastrous (if not more so) as the consequences of the war, consequences which were not inevitable, but represented the decisions of politicians. The French took the lead in insisting that heavy reparations be imposed on Germany. Their driving force was the popular hatred of an enemy which had invaded them twice within 50 years. As they had been successful in paying a large forced indemnity to Germany after 1870, they were encouraged in their belief that the Germans could pay heavy reparations now. Reparations were like links in a chain. There existed a mass of interconnected war debts. Britain had lent substantial sums to its European allies and had, in turn, borrowed heavily from the Americans. A British proposal that it would demand payment from its debtors only to the extent that the United States demanded payment from it was vetoed by the Americans, whose hard 'business-is-business' philosophy was epitomised by

President Coolidge's remark, 'They hired the money, didn't they?'. Eventually a circular network of obligations was established. The Germans, forced to pay reparations to the European allies (so that they could in turn, settle their debts with the United States) found that they could best do so by borrowing – from America! This was fine until economic difficulties in the United States in 1929 brought the whole edifice of international payments crashing down. The result was economic havoc on a world scale, which greatly exacerbated the depression and encouraged the rise of the dictators.

Industrial change

In the last chapter it was pointed out that Britain in the late nineteenth century had a large share of its resources tied up in a narrow range of staple industries, and that this 'overcommitment' is held by some historians to have been a significant factor in its declining industrial performance. The full measure of that overcommitment was evident after the First World War, when Britain's basic industries had to accommodate themselves to the world depression which set in in 1921.

The staple industries had a number of factors in common. Their decline was largely caused by a collapse of export markets, coupled with a stagnating or, at best, a slowly growing home demand. The demand for their products was relatively inelastic; they suffered from the development of competitive substitutes; they faced growing foreign competition and national self-sufficiency; and they fell victim to increasing restrictions in trade. Added to these difficulties was the overvaluation of the British currency between 1925 and 1931, and labour unrest (especially in mining). The social problems caused by these distressed industries was exacerbated by the fact that they were highly concentrated in certain parts of the country, especially the north of England, Clydeside and South Wales.

The isolation of the coalminer impressed itself upon J. B. Priestley:

Nobody . . . goes to East Durham. The miner there lives in his own little world and hardly ever meets anybody coming from outside it. He sees far less of the ordinary citizen than a soldier or a sailor does. I have often heard people say that the miners are indifferent to the welfare of the country at large, caring for nobody but themselves. I doubt if this is any truer of them than it is of any other members of a trade or profession . . . But even if the charge were true, there would be every excuse for the miner. Indeed, I could not blame him if he detested the whole coal-burning public. He is isolated geographically. More often than not he lives in a region so unlovely, so completely removed from either natural beauty or anything of grace or dignity contrived by man, that most of us take care never to go near a colliery area. The time he does not spend underground is spent in towns and villages that are monuments of mean ugliness. I shall be told by some people that this does not matter because miners, never having known anything else, are entirely indifferent and impervious to such ugliness. I believe this view to be as false as it is mean. Miners and their wives and children are not members of some troglodyte race but ordinary human beings, and as such are partly at the mercy of their surroundings . . . Their environment must either bring them to despair – as I know from my own experience that it frequently does – or in the end it must blunt their senses and taste, harden the feelings and cloud the mind. And the latter is a tragic process, which nothing that calls itself a democratic civilisation has any right to encourage.

Peak coal output was in 1913, when 287 million tons were produced, a figure never again attained – not even in the war, when the domestic demand for coal was so high. Coal strikes in the United States in 1922, and the French occupation of the Ruhr in 1923 (in an unsuccessful attempt to enforce reparations payments) meant that the British coal industry was given a temporary boost, and it was not until 1924 that it became set on its long-term downward trend. The trough was reached in 1932 and 1933 (excluding the year of the General Strike) when output was less than 210 million tons (73 per cent of the 1913 output). Productivity within the industry increased, however. By 1939, 61 per cent of coal was cut by machines and 54 per cent respectively in 1913. In consequence, the workforce declined more than output: from a peak of 1.2 million in 1920 to 702,000 in 1938.

The root cause of the fall in output was the collapse of the export market, for exports (including ships' bunker coal) had accounted for a third of all output just before the First World War. A variety of factors led to this decline. Greater use of competitive fuels and progress in fuel economy affected foreign and domestic demand in similar ways. At home, for example, there was increased use of electricity. This admittedly gave rise to a demand for coal to power generating stations, but a fivefold increase in electricity was achieved with only a twofold increase in coal and coke consumption. The spread of oil-fired ships reduced foreign demand. Before the war the bulk of the world's mercantile shipping consisted of coal-burning steamships; by 1939 over half the world's mercantile fleet and almost all navies had changed to oil. Britain, which had previously supplied a large proportion of the world's bunker requirements, was hit particularly severely by this changed technology. Curiously, world consumption of coal did not decline, although its increase of 0.3 per cent per annum was much below the rate of 4.0 per cent before 1914. World production, however, rose by 0.7 per cent per annum between 1913 and 1937, meaning that there was considerable excess capacity in the world's industry. The resulting competition for markets had an impact on the British industry. Some countries, which had formerly been dependent on Britain, became self-sufficient; while others, for example Germany and Poland, exerted strong competition in former British markets such as the Baltic and the Mediterranean. Third, many countries, in the increasingly nationalistic climate of the 1930s, placed quantitative restrictions on coal imports which sometimes discriminated against British coal.

A number of attempts were made by British producers to regulate the market in the 1920s, but their voluntary nature resulted in only limited success. In 1930 the government intervened with the Coal Mines Act, which established compulsory cartelisation schemes (run by the owners) to allocate production quotas and fix prices for different grades of coal. In addition, a Coal Mines Reorganisation Committee was set up to promote amalgamations. The act proved a disappointment because of the opposition of the owners; excess capacity remained and there were only modest improvements in efficiency.

The most spectacular collapse of a great industry was cotton textiles, for before 1914 Britain had dominated international trade in cotton goods, providing 65 per cent of total world exports. At that time 80 per cent of Britain's output was shipped overseas. The development of the industry was checked during the war by labour shortages, reduced raw material supplies and restrictions on trade. Wool was in demand for uniforms, but little cotton found its way into any trench or on to any ship – or into the air (for linen was the fabric used to cover aeroplanes). Wartime conditions created a backlog of demand, and there was a violent boom in 1919–20, when large profits where paid to shareholders and cotton firms changed hands at greatly inflated prices. Many cotton firms became overcapitalised, and were to be weighed down with a burden of debt to repay at a time when they were least able to do so. When the boom broke the industry went into almost continuous contraction. Between 1912 and 1938 cotton production was halved.

British cotton exporters suffered heavy losses in every market except South and West Africa, the greatest decline occurring in the Far East. There were two reasons for this setback. Roughly one-third of the losses resulted from the increased competition in third markets by the Japanese industry; two-thirds are attributable to rapid increases of home production in former markets. The most painful loss was in India, which had been Britain's best customer. By 1938 India's domestic production of cotton goods had quadrupled, and British exports to India had fallen to only one-tenth of the pre-war level. Five years earlier J. B. Priestley had visited Blackburn, and had this to say:

The tragic word round there, I soon discovered, is *dhootie*. It is the forgotten *Open Sesame*. A *dhootie* is the loin-cloth of India, which even Ghandi does not disdain to wear, and it is also the name of the cheap cotton fabric from which these loin-cloths are made. Blackburn expected every man to do his *dhootie*. This fabric was manufactured in the town and the surrounding district on a scale equal to the needs of the gigantic Indian population. So colossal was the output that Blackburn was the greatest weaving town in the world. It clothed the whole vast mad peninsula. Millions and millions of yards of *dhootie* cloth went streaming out of this valley. The trade is almost finished. Few of them there now believe that it will ever return. Those firms that were able to survive the crash have made desperate attempts to find openings in the markets for the fine fabrics. Lancashire with its industrial resources, which have always kept pace with every new development in the industry, its long experience, its excellent workmanship, should be always able to sell its most expensive cotton fabrics, which must still be the best in the world. But this trade is limited; the prosperity of Lancashire was chiefly based on the gigantic output of cheap stuff for the East.

However efficient the Lancashire cotton industry might have been, it would not have been able to withstand the savage assaults on its export trade. But it was not efficient. Little investment was made in new plant and machinery and, as a result, the industry's equipment became steadily older and more inefficient. This failure to keep up with new technology is not hard to understand. Contracting markets are not conducive to re-equipment, while many firms had little to spend on new capital projects because of debts contracted during the post-war boom. Furthermore, new machinery was not only costly in itself, but often required the adaptation or re-building of workshops, and a large measure of cooperation between the fragmented parts of the industry.

From the late 1920s attention was focused on the need to reduce excess capacity. A number of voluntary schemes were drawn up which had some limited success. By the mid-1930s spindle capacity in the spinning section had been brought down to 44 million, compared with 59 million in 1920, but it was estimated that there were still 13.5 million spindles in excess of requirements. In 1936, therefore, the government intervened with the Cotton Industry (Reorganisation) Act, which imposed a compulsory levy on existing machines which financed the purchase and scrapping of surplus spindles. By 1938 the Spindles Board had managed to scrap nearly another 5 million spindles. By the outbreak of the Second World War the cotton industry was but a shadow of its former self. Output was about half what it had been before 1914, while cotton goods accounted for only 12 per cent of Britain's exports. Lancashire would never be the same again.

However, it was from the shipbuilding town of Jarrow that the hunger marchers descended on London. Shipbuilding was probably the most depressed of all industries between the wars. Apart from 1920 output never again reached the 1913 level of 1.93 million tons; while at the bottom of the slump in 1933 it was a mere 7 per cent of the pre-war level. Even in the peak (and freak) year of 1920, over 50 per cent of shipyard berths were empty, while in the slump of the early 1930s nearly all ship-building capacity was idle or under-used, and the unemployment average well over 50 per cent.

The problem was worldwide: there were too many ships chasing too little trade. Three factors were involved: the rapid increase in the size of foreign fleets, improvements in the technical performance of ships and a fall in the rate of growth of world trade. The post-war boom brought into existence more shipping than was required, and by 1923 there was 39 per cent more tonnage compared with 1913 to handle 6 per cent less seaborne trade. To make matters worse, there was a sharp contraction in warship building, naval orders having provided the industry with much work before the war. The average annual output of warships between 1911 and 1913 amounted to 132,633 tons, whereas in only seven of the inter-war years did it reach 50,000 tons, and only once did it surpass 100,000.

In the falling world market for ships British shipbuilders suffered from the nationalistic shipping policies of many countries anxious to protect maritime industries which had expanded during the war. Many foreign fleets were subsidised by their governments, with two results for British shipbuilders. In the first place, subsidies were usually dependent upon ships being built in national yards. Second, British shipowners who faced the competition of subsidised fleets proved less able or less willing to provide funds for fleet replacement, and so home orders were lower than otherwise they might have been. Not that British shipbuilders can be absolved of all responsibility for their difficulties. The British industry had reached supremacy in the age of steam, and there was a failure in the twentieth century to exploit the much more efficient diesel engine. Likewise, shipbuilders failed to reorganise the layout and equipment of their yards, and retained inadequate business as well as technical structures.

Little in the way of reform was achieved until the 1930s. In that decade shipbuilders benefited indirectly from subsidies paid to tramp owners, and from the 'scrap and build' schemes inaugurated in 1935, although the latter were something of a failure. There was no government scheme to tackle the main problem – that of excess capacity within the industry. Little rationalisation was effected until the industry established National Shipbuilders Security Ltd, which used a 1 per cent levy on the sales of participating firms to buy and scrap redundant or obsolete yards. By 1937, 28 yards, with a total capacity of more than 1 million tons, had been destroyed; but there was still a long way to go. In the event, however, the demands of the Second World War provided much-needed respite.

The depression in shipbuilding inevitably had a serious effect on the British iron and steel industry. However, that industry is difficult to classify, and in many ways it stands between the declining industries and the new and expanding ones. A demand for its products derived from both groups. It certainly underwent change; for example, the output of pig iron fell continuously between 1913 and 1937, a reflection both of the increasing shift from iron to steel, and a growing use of scrap in steel manufacture. The First World War saw steel production rise by nearly 2 million tons, but it fell back in the depression of the early 1920s. However, the 1913 output had been exceeded by 1924, and the 1918 output of 9.6 million tons had been regained by 1929. During the depression of the early 1930s, steel output was almost halved, but recovery was fairly rapid, and the industry reached an inter-war peak of 13 million tons in 1937. By that time the industry was working at practically full capacity.

Recovery was firmly based on the domestic market (the motor industry, for example, consumed vast quantities of steel); export performance remained poor. Improvements in the industry were certainly made, but as similar improvements were made to industries abroad, the gap between British and foreign producers remained, and may indeed have widened. While there were barriers to exports, there was also severe foreign competition in the home market. However, in 1932 a 33.3 per cent tariff was imposed, and imports fell sharply. The price that had to be paid for tariff protection was the reorganisation of the industry, which was set in motion by the establishment of the British Iron and Steel Federation in 1934. However, the Federation did little to improve techniques or to effect rationalisation, and although by the eve of the Second World War the industry was larger and more modern than it had been in 1913, it yet remained backward and inefficient in comparison with foreign producers.

Just as the basic industries shared certain common characteristics so, too, did the new industries, most of which recorded positive rates of growth. First, their expansion was based on the exploitation of new (or comparatively new) technology. Second, they were structurally different from the old industries, for output was soon concentrated in the hands of a few large producers, thus enabling mass production techniques to be employed. For example, the percentage of net output produced by the three largest units was 84 per cent in the case of the rayon and dyestuffs industry; 75 per cent in photographic apparatus, 73 per cent in rubber tyres and tubes; 66 per cent in electrical wires and cables and in aluminium; 48 per cent in electrical machinery; and 45 per cent in motor vehicle manufacture. The degree of concentration was much lower in the case of the basic industries, although the government sponsored moves in that direction. Third, the new industries were much less dependent upon the export market, and looked primarily to the domestic consumer for their sales. Only rarely did the proportion of production going to exports exceed 25 per cent, one notable exception being motorcycles, of which nearly two-fifths went abroad in the early 1920s. The world then rode the BSA, AJS, Royal Enfield, Rudge, and Triumph, but had not yet become familiar with the BMW, let alone the Suzuki, the Kawasaki or the Honda. Fourth, unemployment in the new industries was below the national average, and well below that in the old staple industries. Fifth, the new industries were for the most part located in the south or the Midlands.

The relocation of much of British industry was one of the most striking features of the inter-war period. The north had enjoyed two great assets in the nineteenth century – good rail communications and access to plentiful supplies of raw materials, especially fuel. The development of road transport and electrical power made industrial location much more flexible, and the market became a greater determining factor. Between 1921 and 1937 the population of Great Britain rose by 7.5 per cent, but in London and the Home Counties the increase was 18 per cent, while in the Midlands it was 11 per cent. Other areas expanded less than the national average, while Wales and the north east lost absolutely. As the south had such a large and growing population and a higher level of purchasing power, it was natural that growth industries, no longer tied to traditional forms of power and transportation, should concentrate in that region. Once such a process starts it becomes cumulative. New industries are established, incomes grow, population expands by migration and natural increase, and the market expands yet further. Concentration is again encouraged by the interdependence of many trades. For example, firms producing components for the motor trade tended to congregate around the assembly plants at Luton, Coventry and Oxford rather than in the north, for transport costs were thus reduced to a minimum. Social and largely subjective motivations may have influenced managerial decisions, such as a possible preference of managers and investors for life in the south of England. On the other hand, there is little evidence to support the allegation that the south was preferred because of weaker unionisation or a less well-established tradition of working-class solidarity; nor did the new industries as a whole make a greater use of female labour.

Typical of the new locations of industry was the Great West Road, leading out of London, down which J. B. Priestley commenced his English journey in 1933. Being Bradford-born, he had a clear idea of what a factory should look like ('a grim blackened rectangle with a tall chimney at one corner'). Those which he saw on the western outskirts of London were in marked contrast. 'These decorative little buildings, all glass and concrete and chromium plate, seem to my barbaric mind to be merely playing at being factories,' he wrote. What made them so different was the fact that dirty steam power, the motive force of the old industries, was replaced in the new factories by electricity.

The electrical industry was one of those which showed phenomenal growth. Britain's industrial and urban development had occurred in the days of steam and gas, the low cost of which hindered the adoption of electricity more than in those countries which developed later on which did not share the same natural advantages. By the early 1920s there were fewer than 1 million domestic consumers, and only about half the power requirements of industry were supplied by electricity as against 73 per cent in the United States and 67 per cent in Germany. Per capita consumption of electricity was very low: in 1926 it averaged 118 units compared with 900 in Canada, 700 in Switzerland, 500 in the USA, Sweden and Norway, and 140 in France and Germany. Power was generated by a large number of small, unconnected plants, each with its own frequency and voltage. In 1926 there were nearly 600 public generating stations, although about half the output was supplied by a mere 32. The inefficient methods of generating electricity meant that the cost was high. Not until 1926 was effective legislation passed to deal with the problem. In that year the Central Electricity Board was established, with monopoly powers over the production of electricity.

The Board did not own the generating stations, and its primary concern was to concentrate production into a number of efficient stations, while linking the stations and existing regional systems into a National Grid. Remarkable progress was made, and within six or seven years 4,000 miles of National Grid transmission line were constructed at a cost of roughly £29 million. Eventually, 98 per cent of the United Kingdom population were brought within the grid's orbit. Meanwhile the generation of electricity was concentrated in more efficient plants, with the result that by 1938 there were only 137 generating stations, of which 13 supplied half the total output. As a result of these organisational changes, accompanied by technical improvements, the average price of a unit of electricity was reduced by 1938 to about half the level of the early 1920s. By the outbreak of the Second World War, 26.7 billion kilowatt-hours were being generated as against 6.7 billion in 1925.

The Central Electricity Board regulated the production of electricity, but distribution remained in the hands of a welter of local authorities and electrical companies. Voltages remained chaotic. In the early 1930s as many as 45 different voltages between the range of 100 and 480 volts were being supplied to the consumer. Although some of the economies of improved supply were offset by the inefficiencies of distribution, the price of electricity fell and a mass market was created. In 1920 the number of consumers was only 730,000; by 1926 the number had increased to

1,768,000. By 1938 there were nearly 9 million. By that time nearly three-quarters of the homes of the country were wired for electric power. A wide range of domestic electrical appliances came on to the market: cookers, irons, vacuum cleaners, wash-boilers, washing machines, refrigerators and radios. Electric cooker sales trebled between 1930 and 1935; sales of vacuum cleaners doubled between 1930 and 1938. However, the market was by no means saturated by the end of the inter-war period, and many appliances were confined to the wealthier classes to whom they provided some compensation for the difficulty in obtaining domestic servants. Two which were more widespread than others were electric irons and, more particularly, radios. Sales of radios rose from just over 500,000 in 1930 to nearly 2 million at the peak of 1937, while the number of licences increased from 3 million in 1929 to around 9 million at the end of the 1930s.

The electrical industry had many branches, and its products ranged from heavy industrial plant to light consumer items. Not all branches of the industry reaped the same benefits from the electrical revolution, although the industry as a whole became competitively stronger than it had been before 1914. The cable-making section had always been strong, while the heavy section – covering machinery and generating plant – improved its position between the wars, partly because of the construction of the grid, but also because the construction of large items to individual specification suited traditional British skills. The position was weaker at the lighter end of the industry, where mass-production methods were more applicable. In the late 1920s imports of goods like radios, batteries, lamps, valves, refrigerators and vacuum cleaners flooded into the home market, mainly from America. Around 80 per cent of the vacuum cleaners sold in Britain were made abroad, one American brand leading many people still to talk of 'hoovering the carpet', irrespective of the make of vacuum cleaner they use. A number of factors helped the domestic appliance sector of the industry in the 1930s. Mass-production techniques developed, and imports were checked by the tariff. The import of vacuum cleaners, for example, fell from 140,000 to 13,000 between 1930 and 1935, by which time 97 per cent of sales were produced at home, compared with only 20 per cent prior to tariff protection.

While most branches of the textile industry witnessed stagnation or outright decline, one branch, rayon – an artificial fibre made largely from wood pulp – expanded rapidly. The chemistry of artificial silk had been known for several generations, but there were many problems before commercial production could be achieved. The old-established silk firm of Courtaulds began experiments and developed the viscose process, which helped Britain to gain the lead. By the early 1920s most of the technical problems in the manufacture of rayon had been eliminated, and expansion was well in hand.

Compared with around 6 million lb (2.7 million kg) in 1913 and 1920, British industry was producing over 52 million lb (23.5 million kg) by the end of the 1920s and, after an initial setback, there was almost continuous expansion in the following decade. In 1939 total output was almost 170 million lb (77 million kg). A fall in price, due largely to technical advance, was one of the main reasons for the industry's success, but the acceptance of rayon was encouraged by changes in fashion. Between the wars there was a shift towards lighter clothes for women, and towards lighter fabrics. By the late 1920s a woman's entire clothing might weigh no more than 1 lb (453 grams). Compare this with the 15–20 lb (about 7–9 kg) of material which the Victorian woman might hang from her waist (a part of the anatomy which women in the 1920s appeared to lack). Rayon also proved admirable for the manufacture of artificial silk stockings.

Courtaulds, together with British Celanese, dominated the industry; and the large size of these companies led to economies of scale. There was no guarantee that such economies would be passed on to the consumer, and the performance of Courtaulds was not above reproach. The achievements of the industry were remarkable, but not sufficient to prevent Britain from losing ground in comparison with other countries. After the First World War the United States became the leading producer of rayon yarn, and by 1929 both Italy and Germany had overtaken British output.

Rayon was originally used mainly for clothing. Technical improvements made it suitable for motor car tyre-cords. The motor industry attracted the products of many others, and was therefore particularly important to the economy. Before the First World War the British industry was in its infancy. Production was a mere fraction of that of the United States, and was lower than that of France. Of the 65,000 motor cars in use in 1907, 83 per cent had been imported. The war had several effects. The capability of motor vehicles was demonstrated: requisitioned taxicabs rushed French troops from Paris to the first Battle of the Marne, and B-type London buses ferried British Tommies from base areas to the front line. The home industry received a setback, however, for many motor manufacturers shifted over to making armaments or aircraft engines. Some went out of business altogether. The United States did not enter the war until 1917, and its motor industry expanded rapidly; production rose from 485,000 vehicles in 1913 to 2.2 million in 1920. By the time the British industry converted its plants to peacetime production the brief post-war boom was almost over, but recovery from the 1921 slump was fortunately very rapid. By 1922 output was almost double that of 1918, and for the rest of the decade there was almost continuous expansion. In the depression of the 1930s Britain did comparatively well and, with an output of 508,000 vehicles in 1937, it had become the world's second-largest producer. On average the home market took 80 per cent of annual production and, apart from a short period in 1924–5, that market received tariff protection from 1915 onwards. Except in the early 1920s there was little to fear from imports and by the late 1930s British manufacturers were supplying 97 per cent of the market. Although the industry was protected from imports, exploitation of the home market made demands upon manufacturers, who were required to become more efficient and to reduce the price of their vehicles. It has been argued that technical innovation and production methods were in advance of marketing strategy. William Morris (later Lord Nuffield) described in the journal *System*, in 1924, the advantages of subcontracting:

> There is no point in producing any article yourself which you can buy from a concern specializing in the work . . . Even at the present moment we have contracts running with at least 200 firms for various parts. At Oxford we merely assemble. However, we now make our own engines at Coventry, and bodies at our own works at Coventry. But our method of using outside services is, I believe, more thorough than is usual. To begin with, we buy our own raw material for the job; we fix up contracts, possibly with four or five firms up and down the country, to maintain that supply of raw material for us. We personally inspect the raw material before it is delivered from contractors; we settle the method of machining; we supply gauges, and in many cases we design the actual fixtures. The whole of the finished parts are delivered to us; they are tested on our own inspection benches, and then issued into our component stores. The firms working for us simply undertake a machining contract; we guarantee the material; we allow a percentage of scrap free; and we place long contracts, so that the financial liability of the concern is limited.

It will be argued that, with our large output, we could do the thing cheaper ourselves; that we are piling up transport costs, and so on. This is largely an illusion. The outside firm that makes perhaps only one important part, is probably making in even larger quantities than we should . . . Personally I believe that in a highly organized industrial country like ours there are great opportunities in many lines for the small, keen firm that will devote itself to highly controlled and standardized assembling of many types of goods.

Standardisation, however, was not a strong point with British motor manufacturers, despite the popularity of certain models such as the Austin Seven and the Bullnosed Morris. In 1939, for example, the six leading manufacturers produced roughly 350,000 private cars, but with more than 40 different engine types and an even greater variety of chassis and body models – greatly in excess of the number offered by the three leading American firms, which produced around 3.5 million. Even this comparatively lavish choice represented a degree of rationalisation. There were 88 British car-producing companies in 1922. By 1939 there were 33 producers, six of whom (Morris, Austin, Ford, Vauxhall, Rootes and Standard) accounted for nearly 90 per cent of the market, and three of these (Morris, Austin and Ford) for about two-thirds. As the output of each company increased, and as the number of models offered was reduced, so prices fell – by about half between 1924 and the mid-1930s. There were other factors which made ownership of a car more attractive. Running costs fell (petrol was 2d a gallon cheaper by the end of the 1930s than it had been in 1914); and vehicles became more reliable, with improvements such as better braking, windscreen wipers, self-starters and improved bodywork. The desire to own a car became a strong one, encouraged by the increasing mobility of the population, and by suburban housing developments away from existing transport facilities. By 1938 the number of passenger cars in the United Kingdom was 39 per 1,000 inhabitants, as against 194 in the United States, a figure not matched in the UK until 1967–8.

Motor manufacturing occupied a key position within British industry. By 1938 the industry employed 500,000 workers, sales amounted to £200 million, and the motor car contributed £90 million to government revenue, or one eleventh of the whole. Like the railways in the nineteenth century, the motor car consumed vast quantities of the products of other industries. The industry accounted for two-thirds of the country's consumption of rubber, and took approximately half the plate glass produced in Britain. Among the 7,000 or so components that a car might consist of were products made of iron, steel, aluminium, copper, brass, leather, rubber, timber and much more.

Unemployment

Of all the factors which tend to colour people's views of Britain between the wars, the greatest is undoubtedly unemployment. With the exception of 1927 (when it dipped to 9.7 per cent), at least 10 per cent of the insured workforce was unemployed in any year between 1921 and 1938, and the average level for the period was 14 per cent, or approximately one in seven. At the peak of unemployment between April and June 1921, and during the depression years 1931–2, the level exceeded 20 per cent. By way of comparison, around 12–13 per cent of the United Kingdom workforce was unemployed in the first half of the 1980s (an average of 13.1 per cent in 1984). Although the interwar period stands out as one of exceptionally high unemployment (the annual average, based on trade union figures, had been 4.5 per cent between 1880 and 1914), it is possible to exaggerate the change, because of the different basis on which the figures were collected. Before

1911 statistical information on unemployment is only available on the basis of returns made by trade unions which regularly paid unemployment benefit to their members. But since trade unions, particularly before 1900, contained a higher proportion of skilled workers than the workforce as a whole, and since skilled workers were less likely to be unemployed than unskilled, statistics based on trade union figures tend to understate unemployment. This tendency was reinforced by the fact that trade unions in industries prone to unemployment were less likely to pay unemployment benefit and were therefore not counted.

After 1911 the basis for unemployment statistics became unemployment insurance, payable under the National Insurance Act of that year to some 2.5 million workers in a narrow band of industries. By subsequent acts the coverage was extended, and from 1923 about 60 per cent of the working population were covered. However, workers in excluded categories were, on the whole, less prone to unemployment than insured workers; in other words, the official figures for unemployment relate to workers who were more likely to be unemployed than was the workforce as a whole. A check on the figures, based on information derived from the 1931 census, suggests that the percentage of the whole workforce unemployed was 15.5 per cent, compared with the official figure (based on the insured workforce) of 21.3 per cent. While the official figures *overstate* the percentage of workers unemployed, they *understate* the absolute figures, because unemployed people in uninsured occupations are not included.

Various factors affected the incidence of unemployment, including age, sex, occupation, skill and region. Men over 45 did not necessarily run a greater risk of becoming unemployed than younger men, but if they did lose their job, they found it more difficult to find a new one. Older men therefore generally faced longer periods of unemployment. Unemployment among women is a complicated issue. We have no way of telling how many unoccupied women would have been willing to seek paid employment at prevailing wage levels had it been available. Marriage bars, relaxed during the First World War, were reintroduced into many occupations, while in others there were social pressures which dictated that married women should be the first to lose their jobs. From the employer's point of view this did not always make sense, for many women continued to be paid lower than men for equivalent work. Some industries, dominated by female labour, suffered less from unemployment than male-dominated manufacturing industries, and there were many homes in which the bread-winning role was reversed. Occupation greatly affected the incidence of unemployment, for unskilled manual workers were twice as likely to be unemployed as skilled or semi-skilled men who, in turn, were more vulnerable than white-collar workers.

The most serious variations in unemployment were regional ones. Before the war unemployment rates had been higher in the south than in the north, while London's unemployment had been twice the national average. Between the wars the position was reversed. Taking an average of the eight years 1929–36, for example, unemployment in London and the south-east was roughly half the national level, while it was double the national average in northern Britain and in Wales. There could be great local differences, however. In 1929 Wigan had an unemployment rate of 23 per cent, whereas in Rochdale it was only 8.3 per cent. In the prosperous county of Essex, Chelmsford had a rate of 1.6 per cent in 1937, as against 36.4 per cent in Pitsea. Such local differences need not surprise us for, as in the case of regional variations, they were caused by the particular industrial structure of the places concerned.

Local and regional variations in unemployment are not hard to understand if we take account of some of the common categories of unemployment. *Seasonal* unemployment is common in any economy, and will apply to any occupation which follows a seasonal pattern of activity. *Frictional* unemployment is also to be expected, and represents workers who are in the act of transferring from one job to another. If changes in technology lead to a process being superseded by another which requires less labour or a different kind of labour, then *technological* unemployment may occur. And if whole industries contract because of technical or other change, then *structural* unemployment is the result. Finally, *cyclical* unemployment, on a temporary basis, occurs when the whole economy experiences a downturn in activity. The greater part of the interwar unemployment was structural, and resulted directly from the poor performance of the basic industries. As those industries were regionally based, so whole areas became depressed and suffered from a high proportion of men out of work.

In 1923 well over one-third of the insured population of areas such as Lancashire, the north-east of England, South Wales, the West Riding, Nottinghamshire and Derbyshire were engaged in coal, cotton, wool, shipbuilding and iron and steel. London and the south-east had only about 1 per cent of their insured population in such industries, while in the Midlands the insured population in these industries was 12 per cent. These regions, moreover, had more than their share of the expanding industries: 56 per cent of the insured population of London and the Home Counties were thus employed, as were 42 per cent of those in the Midlands, the national average being 38 per cent. The depressed areas fared much worse, the proportion of their insured workforce thus engaged ranging only between 17 and 28 per cent. The depressed areas thus had more than their share of the declining industries but less than their share of the expanding ones. Wales was hit particularly badly, and as a result of migration the Principality lost 450,000 people between 1921 and 1939.

It was not easy for men to move in search of work for, as one Londoner put it:

> You live on more than just what you get from your work. There is the fact that you're known in the neighbourhood and can find help tiding you over bad times. Then there is your family. It's pretty risky to move away and leave all that for a job that just might be a good one.[6]

The depressed areas, in particular, presented distressing scenes of men unemployed for long periods of time. The poet, Stephen Spender, wrote in his poem 'Moving Through the Silent Crowd':

> They lounge at corners of the street
> And greet friends with a shrug of shoulder
> And turn their empty pockets out,
> The cynical gestures of the poor.
>
> Now they've no work, like better men
> Who sit at desks and take much pay
> They sleep long nights and rise at ten
> To watch the hours that drain away.

Priestley was haunted by the sights he saw on his journey through England:

> I remembered then how, just after the Armistice, I had been sent to look after some German prisoners of war. They had a certain look, these prisoners of war, most of them had been captured two or three years before. It was a strained, greyish, faintly decomposed look. I did not expect to see that kind of face again for a long time; but I was wrong. I had seen a lot of those faces on this journey. They belonged to unemployed men.

Not just the unemployed man, but his wife and children were affected:

> Men folks were obliged to go out of doors, even if only to the Employment
> Exchange; this was a reason for washing and dressing-up. The women had not
> this incentive. Their outings extended little beyond the small shops at the corner
> of the street, and to these they could 'slip-down' without washing. To them
> there seemed little point in washing the children, as they just got dirty anyway.
> All this is highly regrettable and, quite apart from unemployment and bad housing
> conditions, many of the women, even if given the opportunity and money for
> improved standards, would find it an exceedingly difficult task to break away
> from their acquired habits. But we must face the fact that to live constantly on
> a depressed standard of living, where life is a hand-to-mouth existence, is, except
> for the bravest souls, to experience the bitterness of defeat. Incentives to do
> better things cease to influence individual conduct. The man or woman gradually
> becomes conditioned to lower levels of existence; powers of resistance are
> weakened until he (or she) gives way before the superior forces of poverty and
> drifts aimlessly along the current of life. And it is particularly the women, the
> wife with a number of young children, who reacts most tragically to this situation.

It was only natural that men should protest against such conditions. On Armistice
Day 1922 some 25,000 unemployed Londoners attached themselves to the official
ceremony. They carried at their head a large wreath inscribed: 'From the living
victims – the unemployed – to our dead comrades, who died in vain'. Traditional
labour organisations were not designed to cope with mass unemployment. Trade
unions were essentially organisations of men in work, and adapted neither in attitude
nor structure to deal with the jobless. Many unions faced a financial situation which
made it impossible to offer exemptions from union dues, or to offer membership to
the unemployed at a concessionary rate; and so it is not surprising that many men,
living on a subsistence budget, let their union dues lapse. The field was left wide
open, and into the gap slid the National Unemployed Workers' Movement (NUWM).
The NUWM was a militant movement having strong links with the Communist
Party, and was formed in 1921 when left-wing political movements were at their
height. The NUWM organised a number of hunger marches and other demonstrations, but its membership never approached 10 per cent of the unemployed and
it failed to develop as a mass movement. Wal Hannington, its leader (who was
arrested five times and served three terms of imprisonment), gave three reasons for
the limited success of the movement. First, he blamed the representatives of organised labour for failing to cooperate; second, he noted the fatalism of the unemployed, which tended to inhibit political activity; third, he claimed that the
unemployed were reluctant to accept unemployment as a permanent condition and
therefore regarded joining the NUWM as an admission of hopelessness. To these
must be added the widespread suspicion of its Communist connections.

The demonstrations of the NUWM represented a threat to public order. It is
significant, therefore, that the much publicised Jarrow March, the one hunger march
of the 1930s *not* organised by the NUWM, should have obeyed the rules, working
with the authorities rather than challenging them.

J. B. Priestley visited Jarrow in 1933, three years before the march took place. He
wrote:

> My guide-book devotes one short sentence to Jarrow: 'A busy town (35,590),
> has large ironworks and shipbuilding yards.' It is time this was amended into
> 'an idle and ruined town (35,590 inhabitants, wondering what is to become of

them), had large ironworks and can still show what is left of shipbuilding yards'. The Venerable Bede spent part of his life in this neighbourhood. He would be astonished at the progress it has made since his time, when the river ran, a clear stream, through a green valley. There is no escape anywhere in Jarrow from its prevailing misery, for it is entirely a working-class town. One little street may be rather more wretched than another, but to the outsider they all look alike. One out of every two shops appeared to be permanently closed. Wherever we went there were men hanging about, not scores of them but hundreds and thousands of them. The whole town looked as if it had entered a perpetual penniless bleak Sabbath. The men wore the drawn masks of prisoners of war. A stranger from a distant civilization, observing the condition of the place and its people, would have arrived at once at the conclusion that Jarrow had deeply offended some celestial emperor of the island and was now being punished. He would never believe us if we told him that in theory this town was as good as any other and that its inhabitants were not criminals but citizens with votes. The only cheerful sight I saw there was a game of Follow-my-leader that was being played by seven small children. But what leader can the rest of them follow?

A leader was found in the person of 'Red' Ellen Wilkinson, who became Labour MP for Jarrow in 1935. She led the Jarrow March, although the original idea came from a local councillor. Many hundreds of men volunteered for the march, out of whom 200 were chosen. After a huge non-denominational service, and with a blessing from the Bishop of Jarrow, the men set off on their 300-mile march on Monday 5 October 1936, 'Red' Ellen at their head. In the House of Commons, Ellen Wilkinson presented a petition containing 12,000 names but, although the Jarrow Crusade had received great publicity and was to enter into working-class folklore, it achieve very little in practical terms. And when the marchers got back home the Unemployment Assistance Board docked from 4s to 11s from the allowance of each of the marchers on the grounds that while they were on the march they were not available for work, had work turned up!

The most amazing thing about interwar unemployment is not so much the demonstrations against it as the general public acceptance of it. The majority of the electorate had a fatalistic attitude to the problem, while social investigators confirmed that the unemployed only rarely showed widespread or deep dissatisfaction with the existing political system, and generally appeared resigned to their fate. To contemporaries, unemployment was seen as only one of a number of economic problems, and other issues – such as the perceived need to balance the budget or the need to preserve the country's international financial position – were at times considered more important. At no time was there an overwhelming determination to deal with the problem of unemployment as such, although as the problem refused to go away, official attitudes inevitably changed. In the early 1920s the prevailing attitude was that unemployment *would*, in fact, go away unaided, for it was a widely held view that it was a cyclical problem which would disappear as soon as the expected upswing in the economy got under way. Before about 1927 the policies most commonly recommended were aimed at removing war-induced obstacles to the normal operation of the trade cycle, and included the settlement of war debts and reparations, and the removal of tariffs. Ad hoc emergency measures were adopted, the one exception being a determination to return to the gold standard. Only when that was shown not to resolve the unemployment problem were other measures adopted.

The theoretical basis for attitudes to unemployment derived from the classical economists, especially the French writer, J-B. Say (1767–1832). 'Say's Law' held that general unemployment was impossible, for 'supply creates its own demand'. Consequently, underconsumption or overproduction was impossible. Local pockets of unemployment might occur, but these represented the inability or unwillingness of the workers to move to where their labour was in demand, or because rigidities were introduced into the price of labour by, for example, trade union activity. According to Say, a natural adjustment of interest rates would bring the economy into that state of equilibrium which would keep fully employed all the resources of the community. Unemployment, therefore, tended to be regarded as more of a social than an economic problem, and was frequently regarded as 'voluntary', being caused by social issues such as idleness and drunkenness. Thus, for example, William Beveridge's classic book on unemployment of 1909 discussed the question almost without reference to government policy decisions other than those to do with social *administration*. He saw unemployment mainly as the effect of inefficiencies in the labour market mechanism, for which his solution was the setting up of labour exchanges.

Attitudes began to change in the 1920s when, for the first time, unemployment came to be regarded as an economic rather than a social issue. Several factors brought this about. Prior to the war, unemployment relief had been largely a matter of local authority and Poor Law expenditure, but unemployment insurance made it part of the national budget, and a large part at that. As there was so much pressure to balance the budget, it was inevitable that concern with unemployment should become allied to a concern with the national finances. Furthermore, it was acknowledged that Britain's exports – so vital to the nation's economic health – were largely produced by the industries which were experiencing such high unemployment rates. Here was a structural problem which required a solution, and in the later 1920s the view that unemployment was a cyclical problem gave way to the view that the very structure of British industry had to be tackled. Hence the attempts to 'rationalise' the staple industries, and to retrain and transfer labour from the old industries to the growth points of the economy.

Until the late 1970s it was generally accepted that the government should make a contribution to attempts to maintain a high level of economic activity, and debate centred around the most effective way for achieving this. In the interwar period, however, and again in the 1980s, there was more debate on whether the government could effectively intervene at all. One theory towards which the Treasury leaned between the wars was the rather primitive 'Capital Fund Theory', which argued that government expenditure on public works would merely divert capital away from private investors, without increasing the aggregate level of either investment or employment. There were plenty of 'theories' for the policy-makers to absorb. Round about 1930 the quip circulated that where five economists were gathered together, there would be six conflicting opinions – and two of them would be held by Keynes.

John Maynard Keynes's *General Theory of Employment, Interest and Money* was not published until 1936. His impact on government policy in Britain at this time was therefore minimal, for although he had consistently advocated expansionist policies since the early 1920s, his ideas were not fully worked out or generally understood until late in the interwar period. In the *General Theory* Keynes rejected the classical view that full employment would result naturally from market forces, given flexibility of factor prices. He argued that the level of total output (and employment) was determined by aggregate economic demand (consumption plus investment plus government spending). This might be less than was necessary to ensure full employment. In such a situation wage cuts (a classical economic solution) were likely to exacerbate the employment situation by reducing aggregate demand. The only solution, Keynes suggested, was through government intervention to encourage private investment by lowering interest rates, to raise consumption by budget deficits, and to increase investment through public works and the like.

Keynes, who was a Liberal, was not the only one to advocate government spending as a solution to unemployment. Although Ernest Bevin was one who suggested action along similar lines, the Labour Party, theoretically the party of the working class, was no more radical than the Conservatives. The party strongest in ideas was the Liberal Party. It was also the weakest in organisation: its grassroots had languished, for its great interest group, the Nonconformists, lost much of their driving interest in politics once education ceased to be a sectarian feud. The party also suffered from internal strains, apparent since December 1916 when Asquith had been overthrown by Lloyd George. The aim of the latter was to make the Liberal Party a party of ideas, and for years he financed from his own pocket enquiries into industrial and social questions by distinguished economists and sociologists. In March 1929 their conclusions were translated into a programme, *We Can Conquer Unemployment*. The central assumption of Liberal policy was clearly stated: 'At the moment, individual enterprise alone cannot restore the situation within a time for which we can wait. The state must therefore lend its aid and, by a deliberate policy of national development, help to set going at full speed the great machine of industry.' Vast public works schemes were outlined and, furthermore, were costed. The whole would be funded by a deliberate deficit. A massive road-building scheme would employ 350,000 men; 60,000 would be employed on housing; 60,000 on telephones, and 62,000 on electrical development. The programme immediately became the main topic of the 1929 election campaign, and the government took the unprecedented step of issuing a White Paper in order to refute it. The government's criticisms of the Liberal plan were not based solely on the narrow Treasury view that the budget must be balanced. Indeed, the historian Jim Tomlinson has shown that 42 of the 54 pages of the White Paper dealt with the objections of departments other than the Treasury, and he argues that many were cogent ones. For example, the inappropriateness of road-building as an instrument of rapid employment creation was pointed out.

At the ensuing election the Liberals increased their vote by over 2 million – from under 3 million to over 5 million – but they still won only 59 seats. The ruling Conservatives under Baldwin (whose election slogan was 'Safety First') won 260 seats; Labour won 287. Not wishing to give Lloyd George the credit for pushing him out (or keeping him in) Baldwin resigned, and the king sent for Ramsay MacDonald. MacDonald had tasted power as Prime Minister in the first Labour government of 1924. His Chancellor of the Exchequer then had been Philip Snowden, and he filled that office once again. Snowden's views on public finance were severely Gladstonian, and he declared that 'the function of the Chancellor of the Exchequer . . . is to resist all demands for expenditure made by his colleagues, and when he can no longer resist, to limit the concessions to the barest point of acceptance'. The members of the Cabinet were not inferior to many ministers of this century, but none (with the possible exception of Sir Oswald Mosley) were men of real intellectual flair, while their relative inexperience made them more inclined to follow the lead offered by their civil servants. It might be argued that Labour could have done more to tackle unemployment had the government not been a minority one. But to argue thus is to argue that Labour had positive plans, and that these plans were blocked by the Liberals who held the balance between the parties. Neither assertion is true. The King's Speech of 1929 outlined little that was positive in the way of action, and Baldwin dismissed it in one sentence: 'My government is going to think.' That the government did not think can be explained by the dilemma in which Labour found itself. The party had long-term plans - the introduction of socialism – but no short-term plans. (Keynes, it may be remembered, was of the view that, 'In the long run we are all dead'.) Robert Skidelsky has made the point that 'Socialism explained the past and promised the future: it had nothing constructive to offer the present'. British socialists found much Marxist thought unacceptable: bloody revolution was rejected (as the failure of the General Strike demonstrated), and instead reason would hold sway. Reason, however, takes time to produce results and, for the present, Labour was impotent. MacDonald declared in October 1930: 'So, my friends, we are not on trial: it is the system under which we live. It has broken down not only in this little island; it has broken down in Europe, in Asia, in America; it has broken down everywhere as it was bound to break down.' In other words, it was the breakdown of capitalism, not the failure of the government to act, which caused the suffering. Socialism was the one cure that Labour had to offer, but for this the government had no mandate. Mosley later derided the Labour government as 'a Salvation Army which took to its heels on the Day of Judgment'. The cures suggested by the other parties Labour could not accept. Labour's internationalism made it reject the Conservative solution of protection; the Liberal solution of public works was rejected partly because it smacked of the Poor Law, and partly because the schemes were considered on a narrow accounting basis which concentrated on 'paying the way' rather than 'priming the pump'. Throughout the period, therefore, Labour's prime concern was to secure for the unemployed relief *as of right*, since it was the fault of the system, rather than their own, that they were out of work.

   The introduction of unemployment benefit in 1911 was part of an insurance scheme, and as such was a logical extension of the nineteenth-century doctrine of self-help. The worker acquired certain rights on the strength of his contributions, but these rights were precisely defined. Only 15 weeks' benefit were allowed in one year, and each week's benefit required at least five previous contributions to the fund. By adhering to such rules it was calculated that the fund would be self-supporting over a number of years, even if there were deficits in particularly bad years. In fact, when the First World War broke out, the fund had a credit balance of over £3 million which, because of the high level of war-time employment, had risen to £15.2 million by the end of 1918. This seemingly healthy balance was no doubt one reason why the insurance scheme was extended after the war. In 1921 12 million workers were covered compared with the original 2.25 million. Bentley Gilbert has shown that unemployment insurance was extended by a series of concessions and expedients in the immediate post-war period. The government made 'out of work donations' to returning troops and civilian workers, and adopted dependents' benefits. Such subsidies conflicted with the insurance principle but concessions, once made, proved impossible to discontinue. In Gilbert's opinion:

> The decisions made at the end of the war put the British government into a trap from which it never succeeded in extricating itself until after the Second World War. It was caught between a limited programme it could afford but was not allowed by public political pressure to maintain and an unlimited one which the public seemed to want but which the leaders of the Government felt was beyond the nation's resources.[7]

The expanded system might have worked had unemployment remained at the pre-war rate. The 1920 Insurance Act assumed an unemployment rate of 5.32 per cent, but this was only about one-third of the rate which actually prevailed. Further-more, as we have seen, unemployment between the wars was different in its nature from most pre-war unemployment. The insurance scheme, hedged as it was with conditions as to length and availability of benefit, proved inadequate to the new needs and extra payments had to be paid to those who did not qualify under the 'normal' scheme. Various names were given to these payments at different times – 'uncovenanted benefits', 'extended benefits' and 'transitional benefits or payments'. Unlike the 'standard benefit', which was payable as of right, these payments might always be subjected to a means test or other check, and could be withdrawn. All that then remained was the Poor Law.

As the insurance funds were quite inadequate to pay the extra benefits, the question arose as to how they should be financed. The answer was by allowing the insurance fund to run up a deficit which was covered by government borrowing. In other words, an addition was made to the national debt. Almost everyone regarded this as somehow immoral. By 1931 the government was committed to finding about £80 million a year over and above its contributions under the insurance scheme proper, and this represented about 20 per cent of the gross national product. The reaction of the Labour government to these figures is examined below, in the context of the 1931 financial crisis. Suffice it to say at this point that benefits were cut and a formal means test was introduced. The means test aroused deep resentment. Once a man had exhausted his insurance stamps, he was turned over to the Public Assistance Committee which demanded to know details of all money coming into his house. If his son had a 3s a week paper round, or his wife had put a few pounds away in the Post Office, he had to declare it; and the Public Assistance man could vary his 'dole' accordingly. The test was an encouragement to the informer, the gossip and the writer of anonymous letters. It led to all sorts of unneighbourliness, and stimulated petty tyranny on the part of many minor civil servants.

The weekly rate of benefit varied throughout the period, generally between 15s and 18s, the average manual worker's wage being in the region of £3. The allowance for children started at 1s in 1921, was raised to 2s in 1924 and to 3s in 1936. As prices fell during the depression, the real value of allowances rose, but they were never sufficient to allow for anything other than a low standard of living, nor to raise even a small family above the poverty line as defined in numerous contemporary social surveys.

A number of studies were made of the effect of unemployment upon health, and in 1933 the Minister of Health claimed that 'there is at present no available medical evidence of any general increase in physical impairment, sickness or mortality as a result of the economic depression or unemployment'. Such official statements were regarded by many investigators as complacent. There was a strong correlation be-tween the depressed areas with high unemployment and regions with higher than average mortality rates. However, regional differences in the nation's health had been evident in the nineteenth century and continued after the Second World War when unemployment had disappeared. The provision of health services, however, continued to be deficient between the wars, despite the establishment of a Ministry of Health in 1919. Strictly speaking, the free services of a 'panel doctor' were avail-able only to the insured employee and not to his dependents, and there were con-siderable variations not only in the availability of panel doctors, but in the quality and range of services which they provided. In Manchester, for example, a panel doctor might have over 1,000 patients, while in Gloucestershire the figure was fewer than 700. In the worst position were those 'bad risk' men with congenital illness who were turned down by the approved societies. They were handled by the Local

Insurance Committees, and received the barest minimum of attention although they were the most in need. Hospital provision was one of the weakest parts of the health scheme. The 1929 Local Government Act empowered local authorities to take over Poor Law infirmaries as municipal hospitals but, outside London, progress was slow. Between 1921 and 1938 the public provision of hospital beds increased by only 4,000, to about 176,000, while voluntary hospitals provided a further 87,000.

Moments of decision: the gold standard, the General Strike and the 1931 financial crisis

The gold standard

Prior to the publication of Keynes's *General Theory*, and for most of the interwar period therefore, the national budget was not seen to be very different from the budget of a private company, a household or an individual. As with these micro-budgets, it was believed that the state should attempt to reach a balance. Preferably, taxation and spending should be minimised, and a small budget surplus should be aimed at for the purpose of redeeming the national debt. This view of public finance is described as Gladstonian, and supporters of it would have agreed with Gladstone's view that money should be left to 'fructify in the pockets of the people'. Such an attitude, based on ethics and political economy, had presented few problems before 1914, but was singularly inappropriate to the post-war period when government influence had become enormously enhanced, and a massive unemployment problem had set in. The balancing of the budget was also more difficult to achieve. The enormous cost of the war had been met less by taxation than by internal loans, raised at a high rate of interest. By the end of the war the amount of interest required to service the national debt exceeded an *entire* pre-war budget; and in the 1920s the servicing and redemption of that debt absorbed roughly 40 per cent of the annual budget. In the long run, the problem of the national debt was considerably reduced by repayments, funding and (after 1932) a cheap money policy; but throughout the interwar period debt management remained a serious budgetary constraint.

Another new problem was the substantially increased expenditure on social services, resulting both from the spending on housing and education, which had been key elements in the promised reconstruction after the war, and from the increased outlay involved in coping with those who were out of work. Public spending inevitably fell sharply immediately after the war, but it remained at roughly double the pre-war level, and there was no prospect of ever returning to that situation.

Despite these differences, successive Chancellors attempted to keep their budgets in balance, believing that this would safeguard the economy against inflation, would sustain business confidence, and would maintain the faith of foreigners in the currency. A tight rein had to be kept, and at those times when the economy took a particularly sharp downturn (when tax yields declined, and social service costs – particularly unemployment benefits – increased) severe cuts had to be made.

Such was the case in the early 1920s. The downturn in the economy in 1921 led to the establishment of a Committee on National Expenditure under the chairmanship of Sir Eric Geddes, a former Minister of Transport. The Committee's function was to suggest economies, and so draconian were the suggestions made that the proposed cuts immediately became dubbed 'the Geddes Axe'. The Committee proposed sharp cuts in the army and navy estimates, savage cuts in education and social services, and the abolition of certain government departments, including the Ministry of Transport. As K. J. Hancock has observed, this justifies confidence in the chairman as a poacher turned game-keeper! Even the government was aghast at the extent of the economies proposed, and the £86 million suggested was whittled down to

£64 million. The sacrifices involved were warranted, it was argued, because a soundly managed currency and economy would increase international confidence, and to the same end bankers and financiers pressed strongly for a return to the gold standard.

As we have seen in earlier chapters, Britain before the First World War was one of the world's chief trading nations, and London had been the financial and commercial centre of the world. International payments had been greatly facilitated by the gold standard, which contained three essential elements. First, there was a commitment to a fixed rate of exchange and free convertibility as between the domestic currency on the one hand and gold and all other currencies on the other. Second, there was a commitment to link the national currency to the national gold reserves. Third, there was the understanding that the total volume of world gold reserves should be determined by the price mechanism combined with the geological accident of gold discoveries. In theory, under conditions of free trade, the gold standard provided a mechanism whereby international exchange rates were automatically stabilised. International adjustments appeared to be made as under a natural law, free from the political manipulation of governments.

Britain went off the gold standard during the First World War, and its resumption after the war was seen by the Bank of England and the financiers of the City as a top priority. Towards the end of the war the government established a committee to consider the question, consisting mainly of bankers, and chaired by a former Governor of the Bank of England, Lord Cunliffe. The Cunliffe Committee urged a return to the gold standard, presenting it as in the national interest – but there can be no escaping the conclusion that it was primarily the interests of bankers and financiers that the proposal was meant to serve. The financial community of the City was narrow and inbred. In 1924–5, for example, at least 15 of the 26 members of the Court of Governors of the Bank of England were connected with overseas banking, and five with shipping and insurance. At most, only two could be described as industrialists.

In the view of the bankers it was essential that British probity be reasserted, and they therefore pressed not only for a return to the gold standard but a return *at the pre-war rate*, where £1 had been equal to $4.86. Changed economic conditions meant that the prevailing rate was much below this. Indeed, at its lowest point in 1920 the pound was equal to only $3.40. Not until 1925 did the market rate come within touching distance of the goal. The fall of the Labour government in October 1924, and the success of the Conservatives at the subsequent general election, led to a speculative landslide which pushed the rate up to $4.74. On 28 April 1925, therefore, the new Chancellor, Winston Churchill, put the nation back on the gold standard at pre-war parity.

The consensus view today is that the decision was a disaster, and many contemporaries came to the same view. Even Montagu Norman, the Governor of the Bank of England and a leading advocate of the gold standard, admitted in 1932: 'It was probably a mistake' (but, he added significantly, 'And still . . . I would do the same thing again'). The pound was a clear 10 per cent overvalued against the dollar, which meant that British prices were 10 per cent too high to sustain that rate. Equilibrium could be brought about in one of two ways. In explaining his decision to the king, Churchill wrote that the gold standard 'benefits all countries, but it benefits no country more than our crowded island with its vast world trade and finance by which it lives'. The hope was that the return to the gold standard would stimulate international trade and that world prices would be brought up to Britain's. This never happened. It was therefore the second force for equilibrium which had to operate: British prices – and therefore costs – would have to come down by 10 per cent. This imposed enormous strains on the economy. Sir Robert Kindersley, of the firm of merchant bankers Lazard Brothers, spoke for many financiers when he urged, 'We have got to take our medicine, and I believe that it is healthy that we should'. But, as Sidney Pollard has observed: 'The sacrifice and the medicine were to be the lot of the miners and the shipbuilders, the entrepreneurs and the unemployed.' Keynes was one who consistently spoke out against such views. In an article written immediately after the return to gold and entitled, 'The Economic Consequences of Mr Churchill' (a parody of a book he had written about reparations called *The Economic Consequences of the Peace*) Keynes wrote:

> The Chancellor of the Exchequer has expressed the opinion that the return to the gold standard is no more responsible for the condition of affairs in the coal industry than is the Gulf Stream. These statements are of the feather-brained order. It is open to Ministers to argue that the restoration of gold is worth the sacrifice and that the sacrifice is temporary. They can also say, with truth, that the industries which are feeling the wind most have private troubles of their own. When a *general* cause operates, those which are weak for other reasons topple over. But because an epidemic of influenza carries off only those with weak hearts, it is not permissible to say that the influenza is 'all to the good', or that it has no more to do with the mortality than the Gulf Stream has.[8]

There were two ways in which British costs might be cut. Industry might attempt to reorganise and rationalise production and distribution. This would take time, and required capital. But the need to attract foreign capital and to prevent a drain on gold meant that the government had to keep interest rates high. This has been likened to 'putting on the brakes when going uphill'. A quicker solution was to cut wages, which many argued were 'inflated' after the settlements reached between 1914 and 1920.

The return to the gold standard proved doomed to failure. For its successful operation, all countries have to make it work, but after the war there was a wave of economic nationalism and new tariff barriers. Reparations interfered with international payments, and the United States, the world's greatest creditor, did not (or did not know how to) play the game. America was unaccustomed to its new creditor role, and continued to behave like a good and punctilious debtor – selling much and buying little. Its high tariff prevented foreigners from paying in goods for its exports and loans, however. Instead, it acquired a vast hoard of gold. Here was one of the great mistakes made by British advocates of the gold standard. London had not been the financial centre of the world before the war because of the gold standard; the gold standard had worked because London had been the financial centre. And now that centre had moved to New York and Paris. No amount of British sacrifice could have made the gold standard work without the cooperation of France and the United States, and that cooperation was not there.

The General Strike, 1926

The return to the gold standard was a vital link in that chain of events which led up to the General Strike of 1926. That crisis developed out of a dispute in the coal industry, which was one which seemed to symbolise the struggle between capital and labour. Immediately after the return to gold, Keynes wrote of the miners:

> They are the victims of the economic Juggernaut. They represent in the flesh the 'fundamental adjustments' engineered by the Treasury and the Bank of England to satisfy the impatience of the City fathers to bridge the 'moderate gap' between $4.40 and $4.86. *They* (and others to follow) are the 'moderate sacrifice' still

necessary to ensure the stability of the gold standard: The plight of the coal miners is the first, but not – unless we are lucky – the last, of the Economic Consequences of Mr Churchill.[9]

The coal mines had been nationalised for the duration of the war, and in 1919 the miners voted by an overwhelming majority to strike for permanent nationalisation (with miners taking half the seats on the managing body), and for shorter hours and higher wages. Threatened with the strike and the possibility that the Triple Alliance between the miners, the railwaymen and the transport workers might be invoked, Lloyd George used that old tactic for gaining time – he appointed a commission, the Coal Industry Commission under Sir John Sankey. Mine owners and unions were represented equally on the Commission, which divided evenly on the question of nationalisation. Sankey cast his vote in favour, but the danger of a major strike had been averted and the government ignored the recommendation. The miners felt cheated; while the mine owners were furious that their escape had been so narrow. A three-week strike did take place in 1920, when the miners secured increased wages in return for higher productivity; and although the attempt to involve the Triple Alliance failed, the government was sufficiently alarmed to introduce the Emergency Powers Act. This enabled it to declare a 'state of emergency' and to govern by decree, as had been done during the war. This act gave the government the powers which it used in the coal dispute of 1921 and in the General Strike, five years later.

The mines were returned to private hands in 1921, whereupon the owners tried to impose wage cuts and longer hours. The miners, refusing to accept, were locked out by the owners on 31 March, the very day of decontrol. Once again the miners invoked the Triple Alliance. Once again it failed. The government declared a state of emergency; troops in battle order were sent to the industrial areas, and machine-guns were posted at pit-heads. On 15 April 1921 ('Black Friday'), the railwaymen and transport workers (who, unlike the miners, were relatively unaffected by the depression) withdrew their support. The embittered miners were forced to give way at the end of June, and had to accept lower wages under local (rather than the preferred national) agreements.

The fortunes of the coal industry improved in 1923, when there was a French occupation of the Ruhr and a miners' strike in the United States. British miners were thus able to secure an increase in wages. However, in 1924 foreign competition picked up again, while return to the gold standard in the following year hit exports. And so the mine owners again demanded lower pay and longer hours. The miners appealed to the TUC, which was then under left-wing control; and this, together with a collective sense of guilt left over from 'Black Friday', meant that their cry received sympathetic attention. At the request of the TUC the railwaymen and the transport workers agreed to place a total embargo on the shipment of coal. Faced by this threat, on what became known as 'Red Friday', 31 July, the government agreed to a temporary subsidy to maintain existing wages. At the same time it set up another enquiry, this time a Royal Commission under Sir Herbert Samuel. Asked why the government had given in, Baldwin later said, 'We weren't ready'. But the government made sure that it would be – next time.

The Samuel Commission differed from the earlier Sankey Commission in certain important respects. It included no representatives of the miners, and, although there were two businessmen on the commission, no one had any experience of the coal industry. The Commission's report, published in March 1926, favoured nationalisation of mining royalties, rather than nationalisation of the mines themselves; and it urged the amalgamation of pits, of which there were currently 2,500, owned by some 1,400 colliery companies. It also favoured immediate wage cuts, but not as drastic as those proposed by the owners. Many people, including some trade unionists, regarded the Commission's report as a reasonable compromise, but not so the miners. Their leaders, says Henry Pelling, were 'chosen for their obstinacy rather than for their negotiating skill'. That obstinacy (or resolution, depending on your point of view) is summed up by the war-cry of A. J. Cook, one of the miners' leaders, 'Not a penny off the pay, not a second on the day'. There was stubbornness on both sides. Lord Birkenhead, a government minister, observed that 'it would be possible to say without exaggeration that the miners' leaders were the stupidest men in England, if we had not had frequent occasion to meet the owners'. Samuel thought that his report gave the miners 80 per cent of what they demanded, but it was readily apparent that the elements which were favourable to the miners were all in the future, while those which were unfavourable would take immediate effect. The miners rejected the report, and prepared for a lock-out on 1 May, the day that the temporary subsidy would run out.

Since 'Red Friday' the government had been making elaborate preparations, and was now well prepared. An emergency organisation had been planned, and ten Civil Commissioners, with wide powers, had been appointed in case of unrest. Arrangements were made for an air courier service; for food convoys; for the use of naval stokers at power stations, and for the building up of stocks of coal, fuel and food. In addition, the government gave its blessing to a private body with a high-sounding name – the Organisation for the Maintenance of Supplies – founded in order to organise volunteers who were willing to work in the event of a national strike. The TUC had no such elaborate plans, and its main hope was for some reasonable compromise along the lines of the Samuel Commission's recommendations.

In the epic struggle which followed, it should not be thought that a monolithic government was locked in struggle with a monolithic TUC, for there were divisions on both sides. Stanley Baldwin, the Prime Minister, was a successful ironmaster, with a good record of industrial relations, and he believed in compromise and restraint. But there was also a group in the cabinet, of whom Winston Churchill was one of the more prominent, who wanted revenge for Red Friday. In the event of a general strike, Churchill and his supporters wanted the government to make a massive show of military strength. The labour movement was equally divided. Arthur Pugh, the chairman of the TUC, was described by a contemporary as a man 'who could have made a fortune as a chartered accountant', and the majority of the council inclined towards the right. J. H. Thomas, the secretary of the National Union of Railwayman, was a passionate negotiator, described by Julian Symons as one who 'negotiated as others play chess or bridge'. Such men were far from the rabid revolutionaries of Churchill's imagination, even if some grassroots trade unionists would have liked them to be.

The TUC was committed to support the miners (who were in fact locked out at the end of April) and on their behalf entered into last-minute negotiations with the government. A formula was arrived at, but before the agreement of the miners could be secured, the government broke off negotiations on 2 May, after the printers at the *Daily Mail* refused to print what they considered to be an objectionable leading article. The strike began at midnight on 3 May. The first wave of workers called out were those in printing, transport, iron and steel, gas, building and electricity. A second wave, including engineers and shipbuilders, were ordered out on 11 May. One and a half million men were involved, in addition to the million miners already out. Despite its lack of preparations, the TUC strike call was remarkably effective, and there was a high turn-out and high morale. Much normal industrial activity was brought to a standstill, but the fine May weather and the elaborate government pre-parations meant that essential supplies were maintained and normal life was kept ticking over.

The strategies adopted by the government and the TUC were very different. The government's approach was highly decentralised, with important decisions left to the locally autonomous Civil Commissioners. The TUC's approach (in intention if not in practice) was the reverse. An attempt was made to keep tight control over the strike, partly because of a fear that local 'councils of action' might go too far. In its bid to appear responsible, the TUC veered towards timidity. Postal and telegraph workers were not called out, and the permit system for transport, which was de-signed to let essential foodstuff through, was greatly abused as the TUC would not issue instructions to stop and search vehicles carrying its permits. In consequence, much other material was carried, to the detriment of the strikers' cause.

One of the more disturbing features of the General Strike was the evidence that it produced of the strong class divisions within British society. Lord Winterton, the Conservative MP appointed as Civil Commissioner for Oxfordshire and Bucking-hamshire, subsequently wrote:

> Men and women of all classes [i.e. the middle and upper classes] thronged to our . . . offices offering to drive cars, to move food and goods, or do any other work required. On the last day of the strike, I had 10,000 more volunteers than I could find work for. One lot of young wage-earners from a certain village asked to be sent as special constables to Glasgow . . . 'to have a crack at them dirty Bolshies on the Clyde'.

On 15 May the *Illustrated London News* reported:

> We felt that the heart of England must be sound when, for instance, we read a small paragraph stating that 'Mr C. E. Pitman, the Oxford stroke, is driving a train on the G. W. R. from Bristol to Gloucester', and another which said: 'The Headmaster of Eton (Dr Alington) and about fifty of his assistant masters, have enrolled as special constables'; or this: 'Lord Chesham is driving a train. The Hon. Lionel Tennyson is a "special". Mr Roger Wethered, the golfer, was yesterday working on a food convoy from the docks'; and again, of the volun-teer labourers loading sacks of flour at the docks: 'Most of them were young men – undergraduates, medical students and clerks. Many of them wore the sweaters and scarves of some well known school or club.' But perhaps the most encouraging fact of all was that at Plymouth, on May 8, the police played a football match with the strikers, and the wife of the Chief Constable kicked off.

That football match entered into folklore; but it is a myth that there was no violence. In a number of towns the police made baton charges, and the Home Office reported 1,760 arrests. The government made a great show of force. Warships were stationed in the Tyne, on the Clyde and Humber, and at Liverpool, Cardiff, Bristol, Swansea, Barrow, Middlesbrough and Harwich. Troops were moved into London in large numbers, and more than 200,000 'second reserve' police were mobilised in England and Wales alone. In addition, members of the Territorial Army were 'invited' to join a Civil Constabulary Reserve, based in drill halls, and with the promise that they would serve with their comrades as distinct units.

The government maintained that the General Strike was a challenge to the constitution, and mounted a propaganda battle through *The British Gazette*, a tem-porary newspaper run by Winston Churchill, who also tried (without complete success) to influence the radio coverage of the BBC. The paper of the TUC, *The British Worker*, was less successful as an organ of propaganda, and it can be argued that calling out the printers and preventing normal newspaper publication was a tactical error. The longer the government held on, the weaker the position of the TUC – its strike call had been seen as a weapon to impose the continuation of negotiations. But the government doggedly refused to negotiate while the strike was on, and there was a genuine fear that more militant elements within the labour movement would throw the country into a genuinely revolutionary situation. That the General Council of the TUC did not itself have such intentions is apparent from the abject nature of its surrender. After nine days the strike was called off on the pretext of a compromise formula put forward by Sir Herbert Samuel, a formula which the government declined to guarantee and which the miners openly rejected. Feeling bitterly betrayed, the miners remained on strike until the winter of 1926, when they were forced to admit total defeat.

The failure of the General Strike was a great blow to the morale of the unions, and membership fell into decline. In 1927 the government victory was consolidated by the Trade Disputes and Trade Unions Act which made general sympathy strikes illegal (an indication that they were not illegal before, as the government had claimed); and union contributions to the Labour Party were attacked by making it necessary for union members to 'contract in' to the political levy. Labour pledged itself to repeal the act when it came to power. That opportunity came after the 1929 election, but the repealing bill was abandoned under the combined opposition of the Conservative and Liberal Parties.

The 1931 financial crisis

The second Labour government had pressing foreign and domestic issues with which to grapple. Three months after it came to power the Wall Street Crash occurred, heralding the steady slide of the world economy towards the slump. There was a wave of bank crises. In America alone 1,345 banks collapsed in 1930, and as foreign loans were called in the banking crisis spread to Europe. In May 1931 the largest bank in Austria, the Credit Anstalt, failed, pulling down a number of German banks in its turn. As the loss of confidence widened, foreign investors rushed to withdraw their assets, and much of the strain fell upon London, as one of the few places still willing to grant accommodation. Between June 1930 and December 1931, London lost £350 million of foreign funds. Before the war a rise in the Bank Rate would have helped to staunch the flow of funds, but although it was now raised by two stages from $2\frac{1}{2}$ per cent to $4\frac{1}{2}$ per cent, the mood was such that this tended to confirm suspicions rather than to reassure. Foreign pressure on London was increased by the likelihood that the government would have difficulty in balancing its budget.

The worsening economic situation was reflected in rising unemployment. The position deteriorated in an alarming manner throughout 1930. In January, 1,521,000 were registered as unemployed; 1,761,000 in April; 2,070,000 in July; and 2,319,000 in October. By December there were 2.5 million unemployed. By July 1931 the figure was around 2.8 million.

A number of steps were taken to raise revenue. The 1930 budget increased income tax from 4s to 4s 6d in the pound, and raised surtax and death duty rates. More emphasis, however, was placed upon economy. In February 1931, therefore, Snowden appointed a Committee on National Expenditure under the chairmanship of Sir George May, the recently retired secretary of the Prudential Assurance Society. Of the remaining six members, two represented labour and four the business community. The function of the May Committee was similar to that of the Geddes

Committee 10 years earlier. But whereas the Geddes Axe prolonged a government, the May Committee's report helped to bring one down.

London's financial crisis was at full spate when the May Committee reported on 31 July 1931, the day *after* Parliament rose, thus forestalling immediate debate. The report painted a gloomy picture which struck a further blow to confidence. By April 1932, it was estimated, the budget would be in deficit by £120 million. Over remedies the Committee was divided. In a minority report the labour members argued that the burden should fall on increased taxation. The majority were only prepared to recommend that £24 million should be raised from this source. The remaining £96 million should come, in their view, from government economies. Cutting unemployment relief by 20 per cent would raise two-thirds of the necessary sum. A reduction of government 'waste', including a cut in pay for teachers, policemen and the services, would produce the remainder. The deflationary policies represented orthodox financial thinking. The as yet unorthodox Keynes described the report as 'the most foolish document I have ever had the misfortune to read'.

The publication of the report coincided with the worsening international situation. To prevent the drain on London's reserves a number of tactics were possible, including import controls, exchange controls, or the blocking of foreign funds. But, it was argued, to pursue any of these would be to admit that London was no longer able to act as the world's financial centre. It would therefore be better to ride out the storm by securing French and American loans. In order to secure these, a dramatic gesture would have to be made, and by one means or another the budget would have to be balanced. Foreign suspicions of a Labour government made such a gesture even more necessary. The Cabinet argued over the expenditure cuts for three weeks. There was some measure of agreement, but a split on the necessity of slashing unemployment benefits could not be resolved. On 20 August the TUC firmly rejected the cuts. Three days later the Cabinet finally failed to agree, and it was clear that the Labour government could not go on.

We need not here go into the political and constitutional controversy surrounding the subsequent formation of the National government. Snowden, who remained in office as Chancellor, introduced an emergency budget in the House of Commons on 8 September, in which he secured the balance which he so passionately desired. This was done by raising income tax to 5s in the pound, and cutting unemployment benefits and public salaries by 10 per cent. Yet all was in vain. In the middle of September 12,000 naval ratings refused to work in protest at the proposed pay cuts. Whether or not this action at the Invergordon naval base in Scotland was in fact a mutiny or not, it looked like one to foreigners – and the drain on gold reserves became a flood. The gold standard could not be saved, and Britain came off it on 19 September. Within 10 days sterling had depreciated by 18 per cent, and by the end of the year the rate of exchange had fallen to $3.40.

The abandonment of the gold standard proved something of an anticlimax. 'Hardly a leaf stirred,' says C. L. Mowat. However, it was a significant event for it marked the end of the attempt to revive the self-acting system of pre-war days, and heralded the first steps towards a managed currency and, eventually, a managed economy. In 1932 the government established the Exchange Equalisation Account (managed by the Treasury rather than the Bank of England), the purpose of which was to reduce the extent of fluctuation in the value of the pound, by buying foreign exchange when the pound was strong, thus damping any rise in its value; and selling when the pound was weak, thereby reducing the downward swing. This was not an easy operation, for slight cyclical variations had to be distinguished from longer-term trends, and the difficulty of making this distinction meant that 'smoothing' quickly became 'pegging'. However, currency management in the 1930s was somewhat easier than it subsequently became because no serious attempt was made to solve the unemployment problem, which has intimate links with foreign exchange rates.

Soon after the gold standard was abandoned, free trade, that other pillar of orthodox British economic policy, was given up. In the elections of 1906 and 1923 the electorate had shown its dislike of tariffs, and in 1930 over 80 per cent of all imports entered the country free of duty. Ramsay MacDonald's election manifesto on which a National government was returned in 1931 declared: 'The Government must . . . be free to consider every proposal likely to help, such as tariffs, expansion of exports, and contraction of imports, commercial treaties, and mutual economic arrangements with the Dominions.' As traders rushed to beat the tariff which now seemed inevitable, the government pushed through an emergency levy which, however, exempted imports from the dominions and colonies. A more considered tariff policy was worked out between 1932 and 1934. Early in 1932 a 10 per cent *ad valorem* tariff was placed on all imports other than food and certain raw materials, but higher tariffs could be imposed on the recommendation of the new Import Duties Advisory Committee. This in fact led to a 20 per cent tariff being imposed on most manufactured imports, with higher rates designed to protect particularly hard-pressed industries such as iron and steel. These duties did not apply to the empire, but were made the basis of an Imperial Preference scheme, negotiated at Ottawa in 1932. It is generally agreed that the dominions gained more from these arrangements than did Britain. Its exporters gained minor tariff concessions in dominion markets, in return for which Britain guaranteed free entry to most dominion products, the margin of preference being increased by imposing additional duties on certain goods imported from foreign countries.

The slow process of recovery which began in the 1930s seems to have owed little to protection, for one of the features of the inter-war economy was the decline in importance of international trade and the growth of the home market. Many of the pace-setters in the early stages of recovery were largely unconnected with overseas trade, such as building and retail distribution. Motor manufacturing, another growth industry, had been protected since 1915 (with a short break between 1924 and 1950). Many industries which received protection for the first time were old staple trades which contributed only marginally to recovery. However, a return to protection was one of the manifestations of increasing nationalism in the 1930s, and it would have been almost impossible for Britain to have remained a free-trading nation without suffering even worse unemployment than it did. Clement Attlee, who opposed protection, observed in the House of Commons that the Chancellor must have been working on the principle of 'when in Rome do as Rome does, and when in a lunatic asylum behave like a lunatic'. However, when the whole world has gone mad, the solitary sane man can be dangerously isolated.

If confidence in the British economy was shaken in the summer of 1931, it revived strongly in the first half of 1932, when there was a heavy flow of international funds into London. This made it possible to reduce the official rate of interest, and in June the Bank Rate was reduced to 2 per cent, where it remained until 1939. At the same time, some of the burden of economies were passed on to rentiers, as over £2,000 million of war loans (about one-quarter of the total national debt) were converted from 5 per cent to $3\frac{1}{2}$ per cent interest. Too much can be claimed for the era of 'cheap money' which ensued, with a general fall in interest rates. It has been suggested that this was a crucial factor in the housing boom of the 1930s, but the upswing was already under way before the reduction came, and building societies were in any case tardy in passing on the benefits of lower interest rates to their clients. What was perhaps of greater significance to businessmen was the more general certainty that favourable credit conditions would be maintained, whereas in the 1920s, as D. H. Aldcroft notes, 'the condition of the internal credit structure was balanced somewhat precariously on the pendulum of the gold standard'. The introduction of 'cheap money' was the result of an orthodox concern with reducing the interest burden of the public debt, and was certainly not part of a planned programme of expansion. Indeed, there was no such plan. Lip service might be paid to economic planning along Keynesian lines, or in the style of the American 'New Deal'. But British policy remained essentially in the mould of the 1920s, even though the events of 1931 had shown that the old system had clearly failed.

House and home

Between the wars building (including housing, commercial and industrial building) had a greater importance to the economy than at any other time in modern history. With an annual growth rate of 5.4 per cent between 1920 and 1938, it grew more rapidly than any other industry except vehicles. In many respects it could be argued that house-building, rather than industry, was the engine of economic recovery in the 1930s. The totals for house-building are shown in Table 12.1.

Table 12.1   House-building in Great Britain, 1919–39

	England and Wales	Scotland
Built by local authorities	1,112,505	212,866
Built by private enterprise with subsidy	430,327	43,067
Built by private enterprise without subsidy	2,449,216	61,444
	3,992,048	317,377
Total (Great Britain)	4,309,425	

Source: Royal Commission on the Distribution of the Industrial Population, in Sean Glynn and John Oxborrow, *Interwar Britain: a Social and Economic History*, Allen and Unwin, 1976, p. 227.

Over the whole period this represents an annual output of nearly 213,000, a larger number than had ever previously been built. In the five years ending 31 March 1939, house-building in England and Wales passed the 300,000 mark annually. That level was not reached again until 1954, and the record figure of 347,000 in 1936 was not again reached until 1965. The look of vast areas of the country was changed by this building boom, as is very evident today.

The boom had its roots in the First World War. The government first became involved because of the problems of housing the new industrial army of munitions workers. At Woolwich, which bore the initial brunt of the demand for munitions, the number employed rose from 10,866 in 1914 to 74,467 in 1917. The government also planned a vast munitions factory at Gretna, just north of Carlisle. Within a radius of 25 miles accommodation was initially estimated to be available only for 4,500. Gretna came to employ about 16,000. Housing at both these centres, and elsewhere, had therefore to be provided. Much consisted of temporary wooden huts and hostels, but as timber stocks fell and prices rose, the cost differential between temporary and permanent building diminished. Where it was thought that demand for houses would outlast the war the Treasury agreed to the building of permanent dwellings, and altogether 10,000 permanent houses were built on 38 different munitions sites throughout the country. The wartime shortage of materials had some unanticipated results, as the architectural historian, Anthony Quiney points out, in the context of the Eltham estate, built for workers of the Woolwich Arsenal:

> The houses were designed with intricately varied forms, using projecting bays, jetties, gables and dormers. They were built in a seemingly endless variety of materials, with combinations of timber-framing, tile-hanging, slate-hanging, weather-boarding, colour-washed rendering, pebble-dash, brick and stone. The immediate reason was to make use of whatever materials might become available during a period of acute wartime shortages, but the underlying intention was to demonstrate to the fullest the qualities of a progressive domestic style whose variety and rural character were believed to have a civilising effect on the inhabitants. Yet here lived the arsenal workers who produced the means of slaughtering regiments and regiments of massed soldiers. It was a strange meeting.[10]

The great pressure on housing forced up rent, and discontent was so strong on Clydeside that the government introduced the Rent and Mortgage Restriction Act of 1915 which, in effect, pegged rents at the level existing at the outbreak of war. This was intended as a temporary measure, but proved politically impossible to repeal in the post-war circumstances of inflation and housing shortage. One effect of the pegged rents was that the cheapest housing became uneconomic to build, and so the shortage became particularly acute for the lowest-paid workers.

The need to secure the active cooperation of labour during the war gave housing a particular urgency, while in the tense period following the Armistice it assumed an even greater significance in official attempts to damp down unrest. As the Parliamentary Secretary to the Local Government Board (one of the government departments with a special responsibility for the matter) put it in April 1919: 'The money we are going to spend on housing is an insurance against Bolshevism and Revolution.' However, if housing were to bear this counter-revolutionary burden, the new houses would have to be not only greater in quantity but also of a better quality than those in which the mass of working men lived. By building new houses to a standard previously reserved for the middle class, the government would demonstrate to the people how different their lives would be, and they might be persuaded that their aspirations could be met within the existing social order and without the necessity of revolution.

Just what quantity of homes would be required presented something of a problem, for a 'housing shortage' is a highly subjective concept which, depending on the criteria applied, can suggest any number of estimates. Thus, a report to the Ministry of Reconstruction in 1917 identified a need for 300,000 houses; in 1918 the Labour Party election manifesto demanded a million; and in 1919 the government talked of a programme to build 500,000. In fact, on the demand side alone, many factors come into play including the rate of formation of potential families, the level of income and the existence of institutions to solve the financial problem, and social convention.

The question of quality was tackled in the 1918 report to the Local Government Board of a committee chaired by Sir John Tudor Walters, MP. The committee boldly proclaimed that its object was so profoundly to raise the general standards of housing that houses built to their specifications would remain above acceptable minimum standards for 60 years. The report was thorough, imaginative and innovatory, but by no means unrealistic or utopian. It immediately became absorbed into government policy.

The government's ambitious plans were unfolded in two acts passed in 1919 known as the Addison Acts, after Dr Christopher Addison, President of the Local Government Board and, later, the first Minister of Health. The Housing and Town Planning Act required local authorities to survey their housing needs, and then to make plans for the provision, under the approval of the Minister of Health, of the requisite houses. All losses, above the proceeds of a penny rate (in effect a token sum), would be borne by the Treasury. Rents were to be set independently of costs, and were to be fixed in line with the generally prevailing level of working-class rents. The Housing (Additional Powers) Act was designed to stimulate private builders into greater activity, and offered a lump sum subsidy of £150–£160 to any builder who built a house not exceeding a specified size for sale or rent.

These acts to provide homes fit for heroes were themselves heroic, for the liability of the Treasury was effectively open-ended. Concern was soon expressed at the high cost of building, which was due partly to the general rise in prices and to inflation in the price of building materials in particular, these being forced up by the greatly increased demand. In Manchester, for example, houses which had cost £250 to build in 1914, cost £1,250 in 1920. Costs, however, were not kept as low as they might have been, for many authorities lacked experience in making housing contracts, while the limitation of local authority liability to the sum produced by a penny rate removed an incentive to keep the expense down.

In 1921 allegations of extravagance had discredited the Addison Acts, and all new approvals were stopped. By then, however, 214,000 houses had been sanctioned, and they were among the highest quality local authority houses produced between the wars. A brief period followed, between 1922 and 1923, when the government attempted to withdraw from the housing market, but in 1923 and 1924 the Conservative and Labour governments respectively framed fresh legislation, less ambitious than that of 1919, but confirming the permanent role of the government in the provision of houses.

In 1923 Neville Chamberlain introduced a new Housing Act intended primarily to encourage private enterprise building. A subsidy of £6 a house for a maximum of 20 years was offered to private builders or local authorities which built houses to a required minimum, but not exceeding a stated maximum size. The houses could be either sold or rented. Local authorities, however, could build only if they could convince the minister that it would be better for them to do so than to leave the task to private builders. At first the subsidy was offered only until October 1925, but it was later extended to 1929, although at a lower rate of £4 a house after 1927. Altogether the Chamberlain Act provided 438,000 houses over its six years of life, of which 363,000 were built privately.

In 1924, when the Labour Party took office for the first time, a new Housing Act was brought in by John Wheatley. As befitted a Labour measure, it was largely concerned with local authority housing. A subsidy of £9 a house for 40 years was offered (£12 10s in rural areas) to local authorities, provided the houses met the same standards as under the Chamberlain Act, and were let. Rents were to be fixed in relation to the prevailing controlled rents of pre-war houses. The Wheatley Act remained in operation until 1933 and produced a total of 508,000 houses, all but 15,000 provided by local authorities. The act brought the prospect of a house closer to large numbers of the working class, although there were still many who could not afford the rents.

The problem of the slums was left untouched by the Chamberlain and Wheatley Acts. Optimists argued that the problem would eventually solve itself, and that the slums would wither away through a process of 'filtering up'. This assumed that as new houses came on to the market from whatever source, those who could afford to upgrade their housing would vacate property into which those lower down the economic hierarchy would move. As the lower middle class exchanged inconvenient Victorian houses in the congested parts of towns for a semi-detached house in the suburbs, the older property would be released for renting by working-class tenants. In practice, the poorer working class were not aided in any significant way, for in the circumstances of the depression people were less mobile, both physically or economically. The poorest had no surplus cash for increased rent and were in many cases in arrears with their landlord, while the Rent Restriction Acts acted as a deterrent, for an empty house to which they might move would normally be decontrolled. In any case, filtering up could not work on the scale expected because the increase in the total number of houses, while very large, did not keep up with the rate of new family formation.

Many descriptions of slum property between the wars might well have been written in Victorian times. In 1935 Sir Ernest Simon described a slum district of Manchester (ironically known as 'Angel Meadow'):

> Angel Meadow is an extraordinary jumble of factories, warehouses, common lodging-houses, waste space where houses have been demolished, derelict houses, closed against habitation but left standing with their empty window-panes and in some cases cellars that are a happy home for rats, and in and amongst all these, houses that are still inhabited. Some warehouses and factories are derelict, but their high walls remain to darken the streets. Among those still in occupation are a printing works and a tobacco factory, the latter providing by far the most fragrant perfume of the area; factories for paper, gas-engines, umbrellas, hats, shoes, waterproofs (with a strong smell of rubber), ironworks, general goods warehouses, a number of smaller factories and coalyards and a glue factory, the stench from which is at times appalling. The gasworks on the edge of the area also makes an effective contribution to the mixture of smells that pervades Angel Meadow.
>
> The Irk is rich in colour and in perfume from the factories that lie farther up its banks. On a hot summer day existence in the houses nearest it must be almost intolerable . . . The fact is that the houses are for the most part completely worn out, and have reached a stage when effective repairs are practically impossible.[11]

The slums gave rise to two powerful myths: that they were run to the profits of rich landlords, and that they were made by the slum dwellers themselves. In *The Road to Wigan Pier* (1937) George Orwell noted that small landlords were worse than large ones:

> It goes against the grain to say this, but one can see why this should be so. Ideally, the worst type of slum landlord is a fat wicked man, preferably a bishop, who is drawing an immense income from extortionate rents. Actually, it is a poor old woman who has invested her life's savings in three slum houses, inhabits one of them, and tries to live on the rent of the other two – never, in consequence, having any money for repairs.[12]

Sir Ernest Simon commented on the second myth:

> It is often argued that the slum can never be abolished because it is the slum dweller that makes the slum. Those who hold this depressing theory believe that quite a considerable proportion of those who now live under bad and dirty conditions in the slums are under no circumstances capable of bringing up their

families decently . . . But the evidence of all experienced persons, as against the pessimist who asserts that the pig makes the sty, is that the proportion of those who do not respond to environment is small . . . In view of statements which have frequently been made as to the misuse which tenants who have not been accustomed to the use of a bath would be likely to make of it, the suggestion being that it would be used for the storage of coal or other articles, it is of interest to note that in none of the houses visited was it found that the bath was being utilized for any such purpose. In most cases the tenants highly appreciated the accommodation and conveniences provided, and one tenant went so far as to say that the bathroom in itself was 'worth half the rent'.[13]

The foundations of a slum clearance programme were laid by the Greenwood Act, passed by the Labour government in 1930 although, because of the financial crisis and the change of government in the following year, the scheme did not properly begin until 1933. Thereafter the government's housing policy concentrated on slum clearance, and the provision of ordinary working-class houses was left to private enterprise. The Greenwood Act introduced a Treasury subsidy specifically for slum clearance, relating it to the numbers of people displaced and rehoused. The aim was to prevent local authorities demolishing property without providing replacements and, by basing the subsidy on people rather than houses, to encourage the authorities to deal with the problem of large, poor families. The slum clearance programme was pursued with considerable energy. Up to 1939, 272,836 houses were either demolished or closed as unfit, and 265,000 houses or flats were built to replace those displaced. A further 23,600 houses were built under the Housing Acts of 1935 and 1936, which specified standards of crowding, and made it an offence to cause housing to be occupied at above specified densities per room.

Many of the new local authority houses were built on council estates and, as John Burnett says: 'The local authorities' housing policies . . . institutionalized for the working classes the process of suburbanization which the middle classes had followed since at least the middle of the nineteenth century, but developed what had been a largely unconscious process for the few into a planned policy for the many.'[14]

The interwar years were a golden age of suburbs and speculative building. Some 72 per cent of all houses in this period were built by private enterprise, and of these the vast majority were built for sale rather than rent. A mass market for home-ownership was created by low material costs and low interest rates together with a vast expansion in the activities of building societies. In consequence, the possibility of a mortgage spread from white-collar occupations to at least the higher-paid manual workers. In the 1930s repayments of around £1 a week bought a fairly standard three-bedroomed £650 house, the major difficulty for lower-income groups being the deposit rather than the repayments. In 1913, £9 million was advanced by the building societies on mortgage. By 1923 the amount had risen to £24 million, by 1935 to £530 million and by 1940 to £678 million. That figure represented advances to 1,503,000 borrowers, or one in eight of all British families.

Much suburban development depended upon transport improvement, and the development of bus and rail services, and of the Underground in Greater London, opened up vast areas for expansion. Between 1921 and 1937, 1.4 million people moved to outer London, the population of the central area falling by 400,000. The need to sell houses led developers to resort to all sorts of gimmicks, as Alan Jackson describes:

Son et lumiére can always be relied upon to attract night crowds. 'FREE TONIGHT! BRING YOUR FRIENDS TO SEE THE GREAT FIREWORKS AND SEARCHLIGHT DISPLAY

AT RUISLIP MANOR' invited George Ball in the *Evening News* of 30 September 1933. Either before or after the excitement, he clearly hoped some might be persuaded to commit themselves to a £450 'Manor Home'. His display was no doubt intended to outdo the great bonfires arranged by E. S. Reid to publicise houses at neighbouring Rayners Lane in 1930–2 . . . At Field End Lane, Eastcote, in 1936, Lanes announced that the whole estate would be lit up, 'the largest area floodlit outside London'.

This firm also offered in September 1936 free furnishings to 'all who buy who married or will be married in 1936' . . . Offers of furnishings, even furniture, over limited periods were fairly common in the hectic early thirties, when as much as £50 worth might be given away. Larger items were also used as bait. Refrigerators were among the more usual from 1932 onwards, sometimes supplemented by an electric cooker. Modern Houses Ltd, of the Joel Park Estate, Pinner (£895 to £1,500), set up the jackpot in 1935: with each house went an electric refrigerator, washing-machine and cooker, and seven electric fires.[15]

Increasing home-ownership and improved housing led to a renewed stress on domesticity, coyly expressed in the 1920s' hit tune, 'Tea For Two':

> Tea for Two and Two for Tea
> Just Me for You and You for Me Alone . . .
> Day will break and You'll Awake
> And Start to Bake a Sugar Cake
> For Me to Take for All the Boys to See.
> We will Raise a Family
> A Boy for You a Girl for Me
> Oh can't you See How Happy We Will Be!

Its banal (but rather engaging) words hint at a number of important truths. In the first place, the life of the suburban housewife could be very restrictive, although the deprivation was often self-imposed. Lack of social contacts led to boredom; there were often worries about money, and few married women had outside jobs. Housework could only fill part of the day, although the desire of manufacturers to sell new household durable goods led to advertising which emphasised the role of the housewife in home-making.

Second, the family which 'we will raise' was indeed likely to be small. The number of children born on average to women who married in the 1880s had been 4.6; and for marriages between 1900 and 1909 it was 3.37. In the early 1920s it was down to 2.38; by the second half it had fallen to 2.19. Behind these figures lies a growing use of contraception. During the First World War contraceptive sheaths had been issued to troops as a protection against venereal disease, but one effect was indirectly to teach many men about birth control. In 1918 Marie Stopes published *Married Love*, a classic piece of propaganda for birth control, and in 1921 she opened her first birth-control clinic. In 1930 the Family Planning Association was established, and by 1939 it had 66 voluntary birth-control clinics. Only a small proportion of the population ever attended such clinics or received any form of outside advice, for the subject was still taboo; and most would have discovered the techniques by gossip, common sense or perhaps a book. Why couples chose to limit their families is another question, although the argument put forward by J. A. Banks no doubt applied in this period, too. However, whereas the dilemma facing the Victorian middle-class couple was the choice between a child or a carriage, now it was between a baby or a Baby Austin.

When not engaged in baking sugar cakes (no doubt on a new gas or electric stove) or raising a family, the interwar couple, whether middle class or working class, had a range of new opportunities for leisure. Several factors brought this about, both social and technical. The working week, which was typically 54 hours for manual workers before the First World War, was reduced to about 48 hours in the course of 1919–20. Similarly, there was an increase in holidays with pay. Before 1914 manual workers did not usually have a paid holiday, but 2 million had such agreements by 1919, and 3 million by 1938. In that year a Holidays with Pay Act was passed, but the onset of war prevented the immediate application of the law to 10.75 million workers still not covered. Increased time available for leisure was accompanied by increased means as real wages rose until, by 1938, they were perhaps one-third higher than in 1913.

Technology provided new mass entertainments in the form of the radio and the cinema. Radio received a boost during the First World War, and there were approximately 200,000 receiving licences in 1923. By 1939 there were nearly 9 million. The direction which the medium took was strongly influenced by one man, John Reith, who became general manager of the British Broadcasting Company in 1922, and the first Director General of the British Broadcasting Corporation (BBC) on its foundation in 1927. Reith, 'a man with a mouth made almost sensuous by the warmth with which it murmured negatives', was a Scots Presbyterian from Aberdeen, who has been described as 'the Napoleon of broadcasting.' He ran the company and later the Corporation with an iron hand. Language and pronunciation were strictly controlled, and on one occasion two popular cross-talk comedians were hauled over the coals for letting slip the word 'Damn'. When next they broadcast, they repeatedly referred to two Dutch cities as 'Rotter' and 'Amster', not wishing to risk, they said, further trouble by uttering the names in full! On Sundays the programmes were gloomily puritanical, and many people switched over to Radio Luxemburg and Radio Normandie, stations which offered popular music and variety turns sponsored by advertisers. A mains radio set cost around £25 in 1930, but a cheap one-valve battery model could be bought from £2 10s upwards, while a crystal set (simple to use but with a limited range) might be had for around 10s 6d. The potential of television, on the other hand, was only slowly recognised. John Logie Baird transmitted the first recognisable pictures in 1925 (three years before he made the first video-recordings) but it was a rival system which the BBC adopted in 1936 when it began its first regular transmissions from Alexandra Palace in north London. Audiences were small, and they remained so until 1939 when war stopped transmissions. They were not resumed until 1946.

The cinema enjoyed far greater success as a visual entertainment. By 1939 it was easily the most important form of mass entertainment, and something like 20 million tickets were sold each week. In 1926 there were around 3,000 cinemas, and in the next decade cinema-building averaged 160 a year. By 1939 Britain had 4,300 cinemas, many with exotic decor, plush seating, mighty Wurlitzer organs and luxurious-sounding names like the Ritz, the Empire or the Rialto. In Liverpool in 1937 it was found that at least 40 per cent of the population visited a cinema once a week, while 20 per cent went twice or more.

In 1937 E. W. Bakke, an American investigator, described in *The Unemployed Man* how the cinema offered an escape from the realities of life:

[The] continuous appeal of the movie is that it satisfies the desire for new experience and a glimpse of other worlds and at times an escape from the present environment. This satisfaction is doubly important to the man whose world is severely limited because of the smallness of income or the total absence of earned income because of unemployment. At work and at home his activity and thought must run in rather straight grooves. Very often these grooves pass through some very unpleasant territory. But at the cinema, all of these limitations drop away and for three hours he rides the plains of Arizona, tastes the night life of Paris or New York, makes a safe excursion into the underworld, sails the seven seas or penetrates the African jungle. Famous comedians make him laugh and forget his difficulties and discouragements.[16]

It was not just the unemployed man who enjoyed the cinema, of course, and many children must have attended with far greater enthusiasm than they attended school. For a start, the building was generally much more attractive, for school design between the wars was a rather drab affair, with architects under constant pressure to make economies.

The 1918 Education Act raised the school leaving age to 14 and, among other things, provided for compulsory day-continuation schools for those in employment aged 14–18. However, the expenditure cuts of 1921 played havoc with the act, and the raised school-leaving age was the principal provision to survive. Many employers remained unenthusiastic about youth-training, and it was only in Rugby, a town with a number of important engineering works (where owners and managers were supportive of the idea), that day-continuation schools survived.

The majority of children continued to receive the whole of their education in an elementary school. The concept of secondary education as a separate *phase* of education was gaining the acceptance of educationists, and there were obvious failings in the 1902 Education Act. The highly selective grammar schools which that act had set up proved incapable of offering places to all those who wanted them or were capable of taking them. Even though scholarships were available, many working-class families could afford neither the uniform nor the loss of earnings which acceptance of a grammar school place implied. In Bradford, for example, it was discovered that more working-class children refused places than accepted them. Melvyn Bragg quotes an interview with Henry Fell, who was born at Wigton in Cumberland in 1915:

The Headmaster said, Henry I think you should try and go on for the scholarship for the Nelson Thomlinson, the Grammar School – the Nelson School as it was called then, he said, I think you could pass your exam for the Nelson School. Well I thought, Well that might be all right but I wasn't really keen to go in Nelson School. It was in my mind if I could get a job when I was fourteen and earn some money it would be a big help to me mother with being the oldest of the family and I would rather have pleased my mother than help anyone else in the world, so I thought it over. But anyway he would persist in putting my name down to sit this exam for the Nelson School and there was about six of us sat it. And I was really bothered about it, I had a feeling I might pass and I thought if I pass I know the scholarship's free but you got to have better clothes and there's a bit of uniform to buy and there's books and schoolbag and even though I knew me mother would somehow manage to get the money someway honestly as she always did I didn't feel like imposing on her any more so I deliberately made some mistakes in the exams.

I made pretty sure I wouldn't pass and I always remember after the exam Mr Scott, the Headmaster, said, Well I don't know, Henry, what you been thinking about, it must have been nerves he said, for I was sure you would pass, he said, you've been the brightest boy in my class – we were in his class – he used to take a class but I didn't let on, I didn't tell him that I had deliberately put some wrong answers down. And unfortunately as time got near when I was drawing to fourteen and I had to leave school I felt such a desire to go on learning more and I didn't want to leave school . . .[17]

In 1922 R. H. Tawney published *Secondary Education for All*, in which he advocated that 'all normal children, irrespective of the income, class, or occupation of their parents, may be transferred at the age of 11+ from the primary or preparatory school to one type or another of secondary school, and remain in the latter till sixteen'. This was accepted as official Labour Party policy, although when the party came to form a minority government in 1924 it found itself unable to implement the plan. In 1926 the Hadow Report endorsed the idea of 'primary' education followed at 11+ by secondary education for all, and proposed to establish secondary 'modern' schools for the less academic pupils. The school-leaving age, it was suggested, should be raised to 15 after five years. Some progress was made with new schools, but the 1931 financial crisis meant another application of the brakes. The leaving age was formally raised to 15 by the Education Act of 1936. To allow for the necessary provision of buildings and teachers, a three-year delay was built in, and 1 September 1939 was fixed as the starting-date. But on that day Hitler invaded Poland. The raising of the school-leaving age was again delayed.

Notes

1   Sir John Clapham, *An Economic History of Modern Britain*, vol. 3, Cambridge University Press, 1938, p. 519.
2   Quoted in John Terraine, *Impacts of War, 1914 and 1918*, Hutchinson, 1970, p. 48.
3   Harold Macmillan, *Winds of Change, 1914–1939*, Macmillan, 1966, p. 100.
4   F. W. S. Craig (ed.), *British General Election Manifestos, 1918–1966*, Political Reference Publications, 1970, pp. 3 and 7.
5   George Orwell, *Coming Up For Air*, 1939 (Penguin, 1962), pp. 125–6.
6   Quoted in B. Eichengreen, 'Unemployment in interwar Britain' in Anne Digby, Charles Feinstein and David Jenkins (eds), *New Directions in Economic and Social History*, vol. 2, Macmillan, 1992, p. 118.
7   Bentley R. Gilbert, *British Social Policy, 1914–1939*, Batsford, 1970, p. 61.
8   Quoted in Sidney Pollard (ed.), *The Gold Standard and Employment Policies between the Wars*, Methuen, 1970, p. 28.
9   Ibid., pp. 37–8.
10   Anthony Quiney, *House and Home. A History of the Small English House*, BBC, 1986, p. 144.
11   Quoted in John Stevenson, *Social Conditions in Britain Between the Wars*, Penguin, 1977, pp. 185–6.
12   George Orwell, *The Road to Wigan Pier*, 1937 (Penguin, 1966), p. 50.
13   Quoted in John Stevenson, op. cit., 1977, pp. 218–19.
14   John Burnett, *A Social History of Housing, 1815–1970*, Methuen, 1978, p. 230.
15   Alan Jackson, *Semi-Detached London*, Allen and Unwin, 1973, p. 210.
16   John Stevenson, op. cit., 1977, p. 43.
17   Melvyn Bragg, *Speak for England*, Knopf, 1977, p. 125.

Chapter thirteen

War and reconstruction, 1939–51

'Total war' describes the Second World War more aptly than it does the First, for civilians were involved every bit as much as members of the armed forces. The bomber could not distinguish between the two groups, and the last frail distinctions between combatants and non-combatants were blasted away. The factory worker making military equipment was in as much mortal danger as the infantryman using it. Indeed, until September 1941 the enemy succeeded in killing more civilians than servicemen. Altogether 74,172 tons of bombs (including the V-weapons) were dropped on Britain, compared with 1,350,000 tons dropped on Germany. Some 60,000 Britons were killed, and a further 237,000 injured. Arthur Marwick quotes a diary entry of 18 October 1940 which captures the mood of the time:

> We had got accustomed now to knowing we may be blown to bits at any moment. The casual scraps of news we get about results of raids bring this home better than statistics. Two girls go into a telephone box to send word they may be late home, as there is a raid on. Bombs fall close by. Both killed. A woman of ninety-four with six daughters in a large expensive house is hit. Two of the daughters die. What a picture! A family creeps out of its garden dug-out to get some supper. They sit down at table. Next minute they are all dead. We know this may happen to any of us. Yet we go about as usual. Life goes on.[1]

The great fear at the outbreak of the war was of the bomber; and newsreel footage in 1937 of the German bombing of Guernica, during the Spanish Civil War, and the Japanese bombing of Shanghai, did nothing to alleviate those fears. Basil Liddell Hart, an expert on strategy, wrote in 1939: 'Nearly a quarter of a million casualties ought to be anticipated . . . in the first week of a new war.' Mercifully, this turned out to be a wild exaggeration, for the total number of deaths in the United Kingdom from bombing was 51,509. On the other hand, material damage was greatly underestimated by the experts. Over 3.5 million homes were damaged or destroyed (two out of every seven); and for every civilian killed, 35 were rendered homeless. The House of Commons was destroyed, and Buckingham Palace was hit nine times. 'I'm glad we've been bombed,' said the queen, 'It makes me feel I can look the East End in the face.' The City and the East End of London, together with many provincial cities – including Liverpool, Coventry, Plymouth and Exeter – were devastated by bombing. Yet there was very little panic, and although nerves were stretched, there was actually a decrease in mental disorder, while figures for drunkenness were more than halved between 1939 and 1942. Production was damaged less seriously than might be imagined. Even in Coventry (much of which was flattened in a 10-hour raid on 14 November 1940) factories were back in full production within five days.

Unlike the early years of the First World War, there was none of the confusion of voluntary recruiting, for conscription began in June 1939, some three months before the war started. Men up to the age of 41 were called up in stages, while over a million men, too old or too young for the forces or in reserved occupations, had joined the Home Guard by the summer of 1940. The United Kingdom was the only country where the government took full powers to conscript and direct women. In 1941 provision was made for the conscription of women aged 20–30, and by 1943 the age range was extended to $18\frac{1}{2}$–50. Women were given the choice of the women's services, civil defence and certain essential war work. By the end of the war there were still fewer than a million women in the Auxiliary Territorial Service, the Women's Royal Naval Service and the Women's Auxiliary Air Force (although they made up 12 per cent of British military strength), but the number employed in munitions grew from 7,000 in 1939 to 260,000 by October 1944. The proportion of women employed in engineering and vehicle building rose from 9 per cent to 34 per cent; those in commerce from 33 per cent to a total of 62 per cent. Whether such an expansion marked a permanent change in women's roles is examined below.

Another device not systematically employed by other belligerent powers was the direction of labour, and by the summer of 1941 Great Britain had 49 per cent of its total occupied population employed upon government work of one kind or another. By a Statutory Order of 1940 the Minister of Labour had unrestricted powers to conscript labour, but with the major exception of mining (to which 22,000 'Bevin Boys' were compulsorily directed from 1943) individual conscription was rarely used. The government met its labour needs by persuasion rather than compulsion, and that this worked so smoothly was in large part due to the tact of Ernest Bevin, General Secretary of the Transport and General Workers' Union, who was made Minister of Labour from October 1940. The government more than ever needed the cooperation of the unions, membership of which rose by one-third (to 8 million) by the end of the war. This figure had never previously been reached. The TUC was able to influence decisions at the highest level; unions drew strength from the key positions in the government held by members of the Labour Party; and they came to be described by Churchill as a 'Fourth Estate'.

'The First World War,' says Alan Milward, 'had left massive files of invaluable administrative experience on the shelves of government, which in 1939 had often only to be reached for and dusted . . .' The administrative machinery necessary to conduct the war sprang speedily into existence, and there was a vast growth in government bureaucracy. By April 1940 the newly created Ministry of Food employed 3,500 people; by 1943 it employed 39,000. Economists, scientists and engineers were in demand, and many people felt that their expertise, however small, was used and valued for the first time. Many of the problems which had to be solved were the same as those posed by the First World War: the production of war equipment; increased production of food; and the equitable distribution of necessities to the civilian population. Many of the mistakes made were also the same, including over-recruitment from the mines, and an over-optimistic assessment of shipping needs and resources. While there had been much planning on paper before the war started, physical preparations had been few. The one exception to this was the creation of aircraft-building capacity since 1936, both by expanding existing aircraft firms, and by preparing 'shadow' aircraft factories set up by motor car and other manufacturers.

The weapons used by the forces were more complicated than those used between 1914 and 1918. At the start of the war, bomber engines had about 11,000 parts (by comparison the original Ford V 8 engine had 1,700), while the aeroplanes themselves had about 70,000. In 1939 some 7,940 aircraft were produced; by 1944 the number was 26,461. The production of wheeled vehicles increased three and a half times between the end of 1939 and the first quarter of 1943, that of high explosives five times, of guns seven and a half times, and of small arms, shells and bombs 10 times. Indeed, by 1942 the army had rifles for 10 years ahead, and troop-carrying vehicles for four.

Much of civilian industry was converted to the production of war *matériel*. More important than previous manufacturing experience in the engineering industry was sound management and strong organisational and entrepreneurial talent. Thus it was that a large chocolate manufacturing firm made rockets, and a football pools firm manufactured gun carriages. To make the weapons, machine tools were needed. There was therefore a great expansion in what had been one of the more backward sectors of the engineering industry, and the production of machine tools rose from 20,000 in 1935 to 35,000 in 1939 and 100,000 in 1942. There was a drive for new materials and new techniques. Aluminium was in great demand for aircraft production. There was an enormous (and permanent) increase in the output of this metal, aided initially by the collecting of kitchen pots and pans organised by Lord Beaverbrook, Minister of Aircraft Production. In 1940, for example, nearly as much aluminium 'scrap' was collected as had been manufactured in 1938. The American steel magnate Henry Kaiser pioneered the rapid construction of welded 'Liberty Ships', but the British Admiralty was not prepared to abandon the older technique of riveting until 1943, a change which involved delicate trade union negotiations as riveters saw their craft skills under threat.

The war is sometimes called 'the physicists' war', and there were indeed rapid advances in many branches of technology, especially electronics, optics, nuclear physics and chemical engineering. The production of radio valves increased from 12 million a year in 1940 to over 35 million in 1944, while the need to miniaturise equipment boosted research into solid state physics. There were advances in medicine (the development of antibiotics such as penicillin) and in surgery (for example, in the fields of skin-grafting and plastic surgery). Chemical advances included the development of insecticides, weapons in the war against insect-borne disease and a great boon to agriculture. Some developments were very slow, however. Sir Frank Whittle took out his patent for a gas turbine for jet propulsion in 1930, but it was not until July 1944 that Britain launched its first operative jet aircraft (the Gloster Meteor) into combat, having been beaten in that race by the Germans. Milward concludes:

> . . . the impression which pervades much literature on the subject, of lightning technological breakthroughs effected under the tremendous pressure of war, is a misleading one. There is no convincing evidence that the overall speed of technological advance was greater in wartime. The concentration of research on particular tasks greatly accelerated their achievement, but this was always at the expense of other lines of development.[2]

To this must be added the longer-term economic loss to Britain occasioned by its wartime need to share its knowledge with the United States, where it was exploited not only in the war but afterwards. For example, it was there that the British discovery, penicillin, was developed by the Oxford scientist, Howard Florey, while British nuclear efforts were also concentrated in the United States.

It was inevitable that British agriculture should be encouraged by the war. The total area of tilled land increased by 66 per cent between 1939 and 1944, and there was a shift from meat production to the growing of cereals for direct human consumption. In 1943 meat output had fallen to 69 per cent of its 1938 level while wheat production had risen to 200 per cent above that of 1940. Labour productivity increased, despite a decline of a little over 5 per cent in the regular male labour force. A great deal of food was grown in gardens and on odd plots of land, and the exhortation to 'Dig for Victory' struck a deep chord in a nation of gardeners. The transformation of food production was aided by the application of science and technology. There was a great increase in the amount of fertiliser used, while the number of tractors went up from 56,000 to 203,000 between 1939 and 1946.

Following the experience of the First World War, food was rationed, every basic item of daily diet being included except bread and potatoes. For essential foodstuffs fixed amounts were allocated which, by mid-1941, allowed for a weekly ration no larger than a comfortable pre-war household would have considered for a single helping: about half a pound (225 grams) of meat, one ounce (28 grams) of cheese, four ounces (112 grams) of bacon or ham, eight ounces (384 grams) of sugar, two ounces (56 grams) of tea, eight ounces (384 grams) of fats (including not more than two ounces (56 grams) of butter) and two ounces (56 grams) of jam or marmalade. For 'non-essential' items, such as sweets and canned goods, a 'points' scheme (which allowed a limited choice) was introduced, and this applied also to clothing and to household goods. The Board of Trade devised a 'Utility' scheme which guaranteed that clothing and many household items reached a reasonable standard of production. It has been estimated that personal consumption settled down at about the level enjoyed by the pre-war skilled artisan – which was, of course, an improvement for many. Health statistics showed a considerable improvement during the war. In 1944 infant mortality figures were the lowest on record, and there was a particularly impressive drop in Scotland. Expectant mothers and young children were given special treatment, including orange juice, cod liver oil, vitamins and cheap milk. School meals were provided for all schoolchildren.

How was the war to be paid for? Here again the politicians had learned from the experience of the First World War, and were wary of two things in particular: inflation and profiteering. This time 55 per cent of the cost of the war was paid for in taxes, a far higher proportion than before. In 1939 excess profits tax had stood at 60 per cent; it rose to 100 per cent in 1940. The standard rate of income tax was raised to 10s in the pound, and allowances were lowered, thus bringing the majority of industrial workers for the first time into the class of income-tax payers. In October 1938, for example (when the average adult male wage was £175 a year), a married man did not pay tax until he earned £225 a year, or £300 if he had one child. After 1944 (by which time the average adult male wage was £288) a man with one child paid tax at £161. To facilitate the collection of income tax, 'Pay As You Earn' was introduced in 1943. Indirect taxes were also exploited, both to raise revenue and to influence consumption in line with the needs of a war economy. Increased taxation did not relieve the government from the need to borrow, but its borrowing policy was now executed with far greater skill and sophistication than in the First World War. In the course of the war £14,800 million was raised in this way, of which only £770 million was produced by the printing press (that is, by raising the fiduciary banknote issue). Great discrimination was shown in appealing to different kinds of saver. The small saver was catered for by a National Savings movement (a legacy from 1914–18), while War Bonds and Savings Bonds were designed for the larger saver. 'Post-War Credits' – increased taxes set against a promise to repay part after the war – were also employed.

Much of the credit for the strong fiscal policies of the government must go to Keynes, who in 1940 published a pamphlet, 'How to pay for the war', and was brought in as a Treasury adviser (without pay!). Keynes revised the whole approach to budgetary policy, advocating a calculation of the national income as the basis upon which to determine the capacity to raise the resources for pursuing the war. The 1941 budget took this approach, an accompanying White Paper setting out the official estimate of national income and expenditure. Thus was introduced one of the key guides to modern economic policy-making.

Many of the goods which Britain needed for survival (especially aircraft and machine tools) were produced in the United States and there was, in consequence, a great drain on dollar reserves. To pay its way Britain sold many of its overseas capital assets. By the end of the war its net annual income from overseas investments was less than one-half the 1938 figure. Of its initial gold reserves of £450 million it had spent two-thirds on the war. Finally, it had by June 1945 increased its overseas debt by £3,000 million.

Until March 1941 all goods required from the United States had to be purchased, and by then Britain's dollar resources were virtually drained away. At this point the United States came forward with the idea of 'Lend-Lease', by which American goods could be provided without cash payment. Already in September 1940 President Roosevelt had traded 50 First World War destroyers in exchange for 99-year leases on naval and air bases. America, said Roosevelt, must become the 'Arsenal of Democracy', but the scheme was not without its opponents in Congress. Senator Robert Taft, opposing Lend-Lease, observed that, 'Lending war equipment is a good deal like lending chewing gum. You don't want it back'. In fact, Lend-Lease (authorised by Congress in an act 'to promote the defence of the United States') was a mixture of friendly generosity and hard-as-nails business dealing. There were strings attached. The Americans insisted that they were aiding Great Britain to fight Germany, and not to maintain its industrial power. No Lend-Lease goods could go into exports (which was, perhaps, reasonable) but even exports not made from Lend-Lease materials had to be reduced in order not to alarm American industrialists. Britain virtually ceased to be an exporting nation. By 1943 British exports were only 29 per cent of their 1938 level, although imports still ran at 77 per cent. Altogether Britain received something like $27,025 million in Lend-Lease goods. In its turn it supplied the United States with roughly $5,667 million (mainly in the form of military stores, services and petroleum). This reciprocal aid was without conditions; but although the British assumed a more or less permanent merger or 'special relationship' between the two countries the Americans accepted only a short-term combination, and that on a firm business footing. Five days after Japan surrendered in August 1945 President Truman announced that Lend-Lease had been completely stopped. Opposing further aid to Britain, one Congressman complained that it would promote 'too much damned socialism at home, and too much damned Imperialism abroad'.

The Second World War, like the First, had profound effects upon British society, but one new feature is worth considering, for some have argued that it acted as a great force for social change in the post-war world. This was evacuation. Plans were first laid early in the 1930s for evacuating civilians from cities in the event of air attacks, and by 1939 certain key priority classes had been identified. These were:

schoolchildren, to be evacuated in school units with their teachers; younger children accompanied by mothers or guardians; expectant mothers; and blind adults and the disabled who could be moved. The scheme was voluntary, but government propaganda exhorted parents to send their children to safety, while the closing of city schools left many working mothers with nowhere to send their children during the day if they were left behind. The first evacuees were moved out on Friday, 1 September 1939 and, by the evening of 3 September, a few hours after war had been declared, nearly 1.5 million people had been placed in reception areas. Not all the children went, and the average response in England was 47 per cent (38 per cent in Scotland). This was the period of the 'Phoney War', and by January 1940 over half of those evacuated had returned to their homes. When the blitz began in September 1940, a second wave of official evacuees, this time about 1.25 million in number, were moved to safe reception areas. It has been argued by some that the revelation to middle-class families in the reception areas of the appalling condition of children reared in the city slums encouraged class unity and fostered the desire for reform. Thus, A. J. P. Taylor has commented that 'The *Luftwaffe* was a powerful missionary for the welfare state'. There may have been a 'mixing' of social classes during the war (though more in spirit than in substance), but Arthur Marwick has pointed out that the effect of evacuation was that 'more often middle-class families were confirmed in their prejudices about the dirty fecklessness of the working class'. Rose Isserlin was a London school teacher at the time, and she wrote of the difficulties of evacuation to the small town of High Wycombe in Buckinghamshire:

> I had a boy of eleven in my class whose foster-mother complained that he was wetting the bed. Now children are very secretive, far more than most adults realize, and we couldn't get anything out of him at school: he didn't mean to wet the bed, but he did wet the bed. Finally one of our welfare workers went around to the house, and found that to get to the lavatory at night this boy had to go through his foster-parents' bedroom. And he had no chamberpot. As a result of the bedwetting he had become very stubborn, and he was a backward child to begin with. But after we persuaded them to let him have a chamberpot, everything was all right: he cheered up, his behaviour was better and his school work improved.
>
> Of course the faults were not all on one side . . . We had to keep the balance between children, landladies and parents. Whilst we did all in our power, as guests should do, to meet the wishes of our hosts, these were mostly so houseproud that life was very difficult.[3]

Strain is part of the common experience of war, but unlike the First World War there was now an absence of disillusionment, and the belief survived that the war was a just crusade against the evils of Nazism. This is not to say that people never grumbled, nor that they did not look forward to a better future.

Official endorsement of the idea of reconstruction formed an important part of government propaganda, and the Army Bureau of Current Affairs (somewhat to the alarm of Churchill and the War Office) became a centre of democratic and egalitarian views. Wartime conditions made many people dependent on state provision of services who before the war would have been fiercely independent. In 1938, for example, a government survey of all available hospital accommodation led to the establishment of an Emergency Hospital Service, which involved 80 per cent of all hospitals by March 1941. At first the scheme was devised for a very limited group of people, particularly air-raid casualties, but gradually it was extended (to 26 main categories of patient by 1944) with the consequence that many men and women experienced what was, in effect, an embryonic national hospital service. The Poor Law tradition of public hospitals could not long survive this onslaught. Another charity for the needy which became a general welfare provision was school meals. One in 30 children ate at school in 1940; by 1945, roughly one-third did so.

Universal provision of welfare services was a keynote of one of the most influential reports to come out of the war, the Beveridge Report of 1942. The early career of William Beveridge was noted earlier, and he stands as one of the great social reformers of the twentieth century. The Beveridge Report sold over 100,000 copies within a month of its publication, and a cheap edition was printed for circulation to the armed forces. Within a year sales had reached 256,000 for the full Report, and 369,000 for an abridged version. Its popular appeal was enormous, and in February 1943 the *Daily Mirror* commented on 'the depth of feeling in the country which has made the Beveridge Report, in itself of no paramount import-ance, into a symbol of the new Britain'. In fact, the Report *was* important, although, as the *Daily Mirror* correctly observed elsewhere, much of it consisted of the coordination of existing services. Beveridge argued that if the Allies could 'plan for a better peace even while waging war, they will win together two victories which in truth are indivisible'. Yet, strangely, the Beveridge Committee, which produced the Report, came about almost by accident – to survey the areas of workmen's compensation and social insurance. Beveridge dominated the com-mittee. He interpreted the terms of reference very widely, and what the Treasury representative imagined would be 'a sort of tidying up operation' ended up as a recommendation for fundamental changes in the welfare services. Beveridge was hailed as a new Bentham, and in its significance for social policy his Report was compared with the classic Poor Law Report of 1834. It had one distinct similarity with that Report – the principles were laid down before the evidence was taken! Representatives of 50 bodies gave evidence, but the sessions were often used by Beveridge as much to expound and publicise his own views as to extract information. 'Perhaps *I* am giving evidence on this,' he joked with a delegation from the TUC, after he had spent a morning trying to convert them to family allowances. Beveridge had many of the qualities of an evangelist, and some of his rhetoric had overtones of John Bunyan, as, for example, when he talked of the struggle against the 'five giants on the road of reconstruction' which he defined as Want, Ignorance, Squalor, Idleness and Disease.

The first principle that the Report laid down was that the whole system of social security should be financed by equal contributions from the worker, the employer and the state. Second, he argued that the different compartments of social insurance should be administratively unified. (Seven government departments dealt with cash benefits in 1941.) Third, he laid down that benefits and contributions should be paid at a flat rate and, with certain exceptions, should be standardised for different kinds of social need. The Report set out a series of proposals for a national health service, family allowances, full employment and a comprehensive system of social insurance designed to cover the whole community.

The degree of support which the Report secured confirms that Beveridge interpreted rather than created the spirit of the time. But it was too revolutionary for the Cabinet, and received a cautious official reception. A month after the Report had been published Churchill circulated a note to the Cabinet:

> A dangerous optimism is growing up about the conditions it will be possible to establish here after the war. Unemployment and low wages are to be abolished, education greatly improved and prolonged; great developments in housing and

health will be undertaken; agriculture is to be maintained at least at its new high level. At the same time the cost of living is not to be raised. The Beveridge plan of social insurance, or something like it, is to abolish want . . . The broad masses of the people face the hardships of life undaunted, but they are liable to get very angry if they feel they have been gulled or cheated . . . The question steals across the mind whether we are not committing our forty-five million people to tasks beyond their compass, and laying on them burdens beyond their capacity to bear. While not disheartening our people by dwelling on the dark side of things, Ministers should, in my view, be careful not to raise false hopes, as was done last time by speeches about 'homes for heroes', etc . . . It is because I do not wish to deceive the people by false hopes and airy visions of Utopia and Eldorado that I have refrained so far from making promises about the future.[4]

It has been the fault of many politicians to offer the British people more than they could fulfil. Churchill, whose overriding concern was to win the war, curiously offered less. Although his government initiated a great deal of social reform (the 1944 Education Act is a notable example) it was the Labour Party which was confirmed in the public mind as the party of the Beveridge Report. In February 1943, when the Coalition government half-heartedly endorsed the Report (but, at Churchill's insistence, left the necessary legislation to a post-war government) James Griffiths, a mining MP observed presciently, 'This makes the return of the Labour Party to power at the next election an absolute certainty'.

The years of austerity, 1945–51

On 7 May 1945 the Germans surrendered unconditionally, and five and a half years of total war in Europe came to an end. The war in the east continued, however, and there was the prospect that the final defeat of Japan might not be achieved for another 18 months. Some arrangement had to be made to legitimate the government, for the Parliament which now sat had been elected in 1935, 10 years before. Churchill resigned during the Whitsun recess in May 1945, and when Parliament reassembled he formed a caretaker government to take over until the results of a July general election were known. Polling day was fixed for 5 July but, in order that the votes of servicemen abroad might be counted (a mammoth task) the declaration of poll was arranged for 26 July. Success at the election would depend not just on electoral tactics, but on a whole electoral strategy – and here the Conservatives badly misjudged the mood of the nation. The task was not to gain a vote of confidence in the continuing war effort. It was, instead, a need to secure a mandate to win the peace, and so the interwar record of the parties was thrown into the balance. No one doubted Churchill's capacity as a war leader; as a leader of a reconstruction government his abilities were less clear. Churchill and Attlee had very different temperaments and very different political styles. 'A modest man with much to be modest about', and 'a sheep in sheep's clothing' is how Churchill described Attlee; but a more meaningful comparison between the two was made by a Cabinet colleague:

When Attlee takes the chair, Cabinet meetings are businesslike and efficient; we keep to the agenda, make decisions and get away in reasonable time. When Mr Churchill presides nothing is decided; we listen enthralled and go home, many hours late, feeling that we have been present at an historic occasion.[5]

13   Post-war austerity

The end of the war in 1945 did not lead to an end to shortages. Far from it. By 1948 rations had fallen well below the wartime average, and applied to some goods which had not been rationed during the war. Foremost among these was bread, which was rationed for two years from 1946.

Giles depicted a boy 'riding shotgun' on a baker's delivery cart (1). The *Daily Express* and *Punch* were aimed at different groups of readers. Many of the items which the smart middle-class couple look at with such longing (2) would have been beyond the means of *Daily Express* readers at any time.

1   Cartoon by Giles in the *Daily Express*, 4 July 1946. The caption reads: 'Now don't forget – any one hanging around with a wistful look in their eye – let 'em have it – bang, bang!'

2   'Memory market', *Punch*, June 1947

The Conservative election manifesto left much to be taken on trust, and stressed the traditional virtues of individualism and independence, rather than government planning for the future:

> We are dedicated to the purpose of helping to rebuild Britain on the sure foundations on which her greatness rests. In recent generations enormous material progress has been made. That progress must be extended and accelerated not by subordinating the individual to the authority of the State, but by providing the conditions in which no one shall be precluded by poverty, ignorance, insecurity, or the selfishness of others from making the best of the gifts with which Providence has endowed him.
>
> Our programme is not based upon unproved theories or fine phrases, but upon principles that have been tested anew in the fires of war and not found wanting. We commend it to the country not as offering an easy road to the nation's goal but because, while safeguarding our ancient liberties, it tackles practical problems in a practical way.

The Labour manifesto, *Let Us Face the Future*, although written in a somewhat bombastic style (the 'Czars of Big Business' were rounded upon) presented a much more coherent programme:

> The Labour Party makes no baseless promises. The future will not be easy. But this time the peace must be won. The Labour Party offers the nation a plan which will win the Peace for the People . . .
>
> The nation needs a tremendous overhaul, a great programme of modernisation and re-equipment of its homes, its factories and machinery, its schools, its social services.
>
> All parties say so – the Labour Party means it. For the Labour Party is prepared to achieve it by drastic policies of replanning and by keeping a firm constructive hand on our whole productive machinery; the Labour Party will put the community first and the sectional interests of private business after, Labour will plan from the ground up – giving an appropriate place to constructive enterprise and private endeavour in the national plan, but dealing decisively with those interests which would use high-sounding talk about economic freedom to cloak their determination to put themselves and their wishes above those of the whole nation.

It remained to be seen how the electors would vote. Churchill thought that the Conservatives would gain a majority of 30–80 seats, and even Attlee confessed in private that he thought his opponents would 'pull it off'. They were both wrong. The poll marked an electoral swing comparable to those of 1832 and 1906. A lady diner at the Savoy Hotel, with a logic only possible in Britain's class society, exclaimed: 'But this is terrible – *they've* elected a Labour Government, and *the country* will never stand for that.' Attlee's assessment was otherwise:

> I think, first of all, people wanted a positive new policy, and not an attempt to go back to the old. Secondly, there was by that time a good deal of feeling among many people against what was felt to be the one-man business Churchill was running. And there was a good deal of suspicion of the forces behind him – Beaverbrook in particular . . . And even those who would have liked Churchill weren't prepared to have him if it meant having the Tories too. They remembered Munich and they remembered pre-war unemployment. They didn't want the Tories again.[6]

'We are the masters now,' the Labour minister, Sir Hartley Shawcross, is generally quoted as saying (in fact he said, 'We are the masters at the moment', which is not quite the same thing). The Labour Party's success at the general election of July 1945 certainly supported this view. It had a very large majority – 393 members as against 213 Conservatives and a mere handful of Liberals. The political turning-point carried with it at least the potential of a social watershed, but opinions vary as to the degree of fundamental change which followed in Labour's 'peaceful revolution'. Within three months the Labour back-bencher, Woodrow Wyatt, put the question, 'What is the use of having an orderly revolution if it turns out not to be a revolution at all?' The left-wing journalist Anthony Howard later suggested that, 'Far from introducing a "social revolution" the overwhelming Labour victory of 1945 brought about the greatest restoration of traditional social values since 1660'.

Of the Labour MPs, 253 were new members who had not previously sat in the House. Many were young, in sharp contrast to the new Cabinet which, full of Labour veterans, had an average age of well over 60 – a seemingly unlikely bunch to inaugurate a new era. The change-over of government was overshadowed by world events. Ten days before Attlee took office the first atomic bomb was tested experimentally. Eleven days after he became Prime Minister the bomb was dropped on Hiroshima. Japan surrendered on 14 August. The war was over.

The new Labour government had a number of basic aims. The country's balance of payments had to be brought into equilibrium as quickly as possible, and the dollar gap had to be bridged. Second, the standard of living of the British people had to be maintained at a tolerable level. Third, it wished to play a leading part in world affairs and had therefore to maintain armed forces of an appropriate size. Finally, it had to remember its pledges of social and economic reform. On the first two of these aims there was very little room for manoeuvre.

The Labour Party could hardly have chosen a bleaker time at which to come to power. The war had wreaked havoc on the country and its economy. Enemy bombing had destroyed millions of houses, as well as factories and offices. Parts of the big cities had been razed to the ground, and many people had lost homes and possessions. The nation had suffered and had borne many hardships, and its wounds were not yet healed. Wartime controls had to be maintained, and some new ones were added. Sir John Anderson, Chancellor of the Exchequer in 1945, predicted that economic controls might have to be imposed for five more years if the balance between exports, reconstruction and consumption was to be maintained, and if the mistakes which had brought the damaging and short-lived boom after the First World War were to be avoided. Controls were applied at the pressure points of the economy, but there was no coordinated 'plan', if only because the supply position was changing too fast for one to be adhered to. Most people were prepared to accept controls as the price to be paid for the better world that was being built, but this acceptance was a wasting asset that would not endure for ever. Many rules were frustrating and irritating, like the examples quoted by J. Jewkes in *Ordeal by Planning* (1948):

> A market gardener requires a new shaft for a wheel-barrow, a piece of wood costing perhaps ninepence. A licence must be applied for from the surveyor of the district council on the appropriate form. The licence has to be registered and filed by the district surveyor and then presented to, registered and filed by the timber merchant. A local authority for roads wishes to improve visibility at a dangerous junction by substituting some twenty yards of iron fence for the

existing hedge. To obtain permission to do this five enormous forms and nine maps, some of them coloured, have to be prepared and submitted. The despatch of a small shipment of six drums of lubricating oil involves the filling in of forty-six forms, requiring forty-two signatures, not including the customer's invoice or delivery notes . . . Boxes containing fragments of wedding-cake sent to friends abroad are emptied and sent on empty because the export of confectionery is prohibited . . . A householder cannot obtain a replacement for a cracked wash-bowl without getting a licence from the local authority and having the bowl examined to prove it is unusable.[7]

The government's prinicipal economic concern was to raise output as fast as possible, especially of the export industries, but there were shortages of both capital and labour. It has been estimated that, at 1948 prices, the loss of capital during the war amounted to £9,000 million, or one-fifth of the 1939 stock. Direct damage accounted for £2,000 million of this; running down of capital and stocks amounted to £3,000 million; and overseas capital losses, £4,000 million. It was clear that much of this investment would have to be made by the government itself, for savings – which had been low in the 1930s – were reduced still further by high taxation. Taxation had to be kept high to control suppressed inflation, for wages had risen during the war and, without controls, there would be too much money chasing too few goods. Here the government faced a dilemma, for high taxation, while necessary to hold inflation in check and to pay for the promised welfare schemes, diminished savings and reduced incentives. Controls were therefore particularly persistent in the capital investment field, and there were tight building controls, and regulation of capital issues over £50,000. The running down of wartime requirements released some capital. About 6.9 million square metres of factory space was made available to peacetime industry, and machine tools worth £100 million from government factories were sold to private industry.

The economy suffered from a labour shortage. In spite of partial demobilisation there were still 5.2 million men and women serving in the armed forces, compared with 0.6 million in 1939. Four million more were still employed on munitions and other military production, compared with 1.4 million in 1939. Put another way, 42 per cent of the nation's workforce was either in the armed forces or was directly engaged in supplying them. Fewer than 8 per cent were supplying and maintaining the country's capital equipment, and only 2 per cent were producing goods for export. The net cost in foreign exchange of British forces overseas in 1946 alone was estimated at £225 million, or more than one-half of the balance of payments deficit of that year, and it was further reckoned that the nation was suffering from a labour shortage of about half a million people.

The government looked particularly in two directions to make up the numbers – to women, and to immigrants (either from Europe or the Commonwealth). The Ministry of Reconstruction had issued a draft report to Parliament on employment policy in 1944, in which economists advised that the war would not be followed by a slump, but by a period of shortages, and that 'the total manpower available will be insufficient to satisfy the total demand for goods'. Despite this, many women left employment at the end of the war, with the result that from 1947 the government had, once again, to embark upon a propaganda campaign to persuade them to return. One of the reasons why policy was not clearly thought through was because the nation was seen to be facing two opposing needs. Industry required workers; but, at the same time, there was the fear that the birth rate would return to the low levels of pre-war years. This anxiety was exacerbated by the dissemination of the studies of John Bowlby and other psychologists which purported to show the ill-effects of maternal deprivation in early childhood. On the one hand, therefore, were pressures to keep women at work, while on the other were forces pushing women back to their traditional roles as wives and mothers. The propaganda drive for women workers was consequently aimed largely at older women whose children were at school, and stress was laid on the country's temporary, rather than permanent need for women workers. One 1947 poster caption stated:

> Without the work of our women we could never have won the war. Now without it can we win the Peace? Many who are needed at home, and long to be there again, are staying on at their jobs until Britain is firmly on its feet again.[8]

That some women might 'long' for permanent employment seems to have been ignored. Although the number of women in work did increase, the post-war propaganda campaign to remobilize women was not a great success. In consequence, recruiting drives were launched overseas. The Commonwealth had responded promptly to the mother country's call for help during the war. Some 8,000 West Indians had joined the services, of whom 1,000 had become RAF flight crew; 900 Hondurans volunteered for forestry work in Scotland, and many Indians were brought to Britain for industrial training. After the war, the government positively encouraged immigration from the Commonwealth. The arrival in June 1948 of 492 persons, many of them ex-servicemen, on the *Empire Windrush*, was greeted with great enthusiasm, and many organisations (such as London Transport, British Rail and regional hospital boards) ran recruiting campaigns in the Caribbean. Displaced persons from Europe were also encouraged, and by 1950 more than 100,000 Lithuanians, Ukrainians, Poles, Latvians and Yugoslavs had been imported to swell the numbers of those who had been here since the war itself. Their labour was welcome, but by the mid 1950s upwards of half had moved on, either to the United States or to Commonwealth countries.

In the immediate post-war years there was great pressure on the balance of payments. Between 1936 and 1938 there had been an average debit balance of £43 million; for 1946 the estimate was about £750 million, and another £250 million in each of the two succeeding years. The abrupt end of Lend-Lease caused Britain to be presented with a rather curt bill for $650 million to cover war goods still in the pipeline, and this alone was enough to wipe out a third of the country's diminished gold and currency reserves. The capacity to export was not there. By 1944 exports had slumped to only 30 per cent of the 1938 level, and many markets – in Latin America and Asia, for example – had been voluntarily abandoned so that the factories which served them might be turned over to the production of munitions.

There was a great pressure to import, and consumer spending (which had been held down by the successful thrift campaigns and general scarcities of the war) could not for long be suppressed. The United States was the source of many desired goods, from petrol to nylons. Peter Wilsher writes that 'this was the great age when nylon stockings could be confidently relied on to purchase the affections of anything female from Nottingham to Novaya Zemlya, and the British Customs were kept busy during 1949's dollar crisis tracking down the illicit import of nylons, at 16s 6d a pair, as part of the highly organized traffic in "unsolicited US food parcels" '.

There was great pressure, too, on sterling. The Sterling Area came into official existence as a wartime exchange control measure in 1939. It included the Commonwealth countries (with the exception of Canada which was in the dollar area) and a number of other countries within Britain's commercial and political sphere which kept their currency reserves in London. The formal establishment of the Area meant that overseas members who had previously kept their reserves in London from habit or for convenience were now expected not only to keep them there, but to accept coordination of their use according to the needs of the Area as a whole. The pooling of reserves and the restrictions placed upon their use represented a reversal of the trend of the 1930s towards a reduction in United Kingdom direction of the monetary policies of the Sterling Area countries, but was one of those changes necessary to finance the war.

During the war and immediately thereafter, Britain made vast credit purchases from countries within the Sterling Area, which had the effect of building up massive sterling reserves in London for the countries concerned. By 1949 the total of £2,352 million was four and a half times the liabilities outstanding when the Area had been formally set up. Many of these countries (particularly India, which became independent in 1947) were able to make use of these paper reserves as an easy way to pay for goods and services which they imported from Britain without the need to produce a counterflow of exports. Although the weight of the liabilities frequently limited Britain's freedom of monetary manoeuvre, they also represented sacrifices on the part of their owners, for many belonged to countries which their populations had much lower living standards than people in Britain, even during the worst times of the war. Again, the countries of Latin America which sent supplies to Britain during the war were not recompensed by its exports to them, but trusted it with their sterling credits. As security they had British assets within their borders, and any attempt by Britain to default on the sterling balances would have led to confiscation. The pressures which the Sterling Area placed on the British economy have been the subject of much debate. Britain's obsession with the international status of sterling has been described as a hankering after past glories, but in the post-war years other agencies for international settlements were created and the Sterling Area lost some of its reason for existence.

Britain's post-war cash crisis could only be overcome by a massive injection of dollars, and the task of securing this from the United States was the last great task undertaken by Keynes. The initial hope was that the Americans would make a free grant-in-aid of $5,000 million in recognition of Britain's relatively bigger wartime sacrifice in defence of democracy. This request fell on deaf ears, as did the suggestion of an interest-free loan. Several times the British Cabinet came near to breaking off the talks, but the situation was desperate and, in the end, it had to settle for a loan of $3,750 million (30 per cent below expected requirements) to be repaid at 2 per cent over 50 years, starting in 1951. ($1.3 billion was still outstanding in 1993, when annual repayments, including interest, ran to about $137 million). Even this loan had damaging conditions tied to it, the most serious being a British guarantee that sterling would be made freely convertible into dollars as from 15 July 1947. However financially indebted to the Americans the British might be, there were those who argued patriotically, but not unrealistically, that it could still hold its head high. Thus *The Economist* wrote: 'Our present needs are the direct consequence of the fact that we fought earliest, that we fought longest, and that we fought hardest. In moral terms we are creditors.' The terms of the loan were humiliating to a proud nation, and were opposed by both right and left. Robert Boothby, a Conservative MP, likened the agreement to 'Munich', and accused the government of selling 'the British Empire for a pack of cigarettes'. From the left came cries that the Americans were using the loan to impede the pursuit of socialist policies in Britain. Many Americans clearly were afraid that the loan might prop up both British socialism and British imperialism, but the convertibility provision sprang from a desire to get away from the bilateral trading of the 1930s, and to open up multilateral trade where countries could buy and sell where they liked and settle up, in some universally acceptable currency, at the end of the day.

From the time of the granting of the loan early in 1946, pressure built up gradually. The severe winter of 1946–7 delayed the British export drive, possibly by nine months, and Hugh Dalton, the Chancellor of the Exchequer, anticipated that the American loan would be exhausted in the first half of 1948, a year earlier than expected. One factor in this depressing situation was the rising price of dollar goods. Nevertheless, the Americans insisted that Britain should keep to the terms of the agreement, and on 15 July 1947 – the appointed day – convertibility was introduced. There was immediately a much greater flight from sterling than had been anticipated. Until the convertibility clause was suspended with American agreement in mid-August, every holder of sterling tried to change it into dollars while the going was good for it was the United States which had the goods that they wanted. The net gold and dollar deficit of the Sterling Area jumped from £226 million in 1946 to £1,024 million in 1947, and by the time convertibility ended, only £77 million of the US loan remained. In September Stafford Cripps took over the Chancellorship, by which time, as Peter Wilsher says, 'the begging bowl was as good as empty'.

At this moment of economic chaos Marshall Aid made its appearance – a more magnanimous gesture by the United States, though still one tinged with self-interest. The first tentative elaboration of the scheme was made by the American Secretary of State, George Marshall, in a Harvard speech in June 1947. He called upon the European nations to help themselves by drafting a programme of mutual economic aid, to which the United States would make a substantial constribution. Instead of bringing separate shopping lists to America, as had been the case with Lend-Lease, the nations should get together and decide among themselves the best allocation of resources. Only then would the United States contribute. The plan was offered to eastern as well as western European countries, but the Russians refused to accept aid or to allow their satellites to do so. The Marshall Plan passed easily through Congress, and the first appropriations were made in April 1948. Previously, in March, the Organisation for European Economic Co-operation (OEEC) had been formed in Paris to act as the international coordinating body. Ultimately, more than $20,000 million was pumped into the international monetary system, Britain being allocated more funds than any other country. It received $3,189,800,000; France $2,713,600,000; West Germany $1,390,600,000. Marshall Aid was an immense boon. In 1948 the Board of Trade estimated that, had Marshall Aid not come to the rescue, rations of butter, sugar, cheese and bacon would have had to be cut by one-third, cotton goods would virtually have disappeared from the home market, timber shortages would have reduced the housing programme from about 200,000 new buildings a year to only 50,000, and shortages of other raw materials would have led to 1.5 million being unemployed.

In the early months of 1949 Britain's balance of payments position seemed healthier than at any time since the war, but the onset of recession in America drastically altered the situation. Britain had pinned its hopes of recovery on the USA as an ever-ready purchaser of its exports. By May the motor, cotton, wool textiles, engineering and whisky industries all suffered big drops in American exports. By the second quarter of 1949 all the progress in the balance of payments over the previous 18 months was wiped out. As confidence ebbed away there was a speculative rush against the pound, and in September it was devalued from $4.03 to $2.80. Devaluation probably came too late for it to have much effect, and produced no new flood of goods for export to dollar markets. Britain's exporters were already working flat out, and there was a shortage of workers. Nor could the higher prices of imports lead to a significant reduction, for government controls had already cut them to the barest minimum. British costs had in fact been kept down with remarkable success, thanks partly to a virtual wage freeze for the previous two years. Devaluation added to the cost of living (the price of bread went up by 25 per cent) and the country embarked on the wage-price leapfrog that was to be a feature of the next decades.

The 'new age' which the return of the Labour government inaugurated in 1945 had, for the most part, turned out to be drab and depressing. By 1948 rations had fallen well *below* the wartime average. The average man's allowance for one week was thirteen ounces (364 grams) of meat, one and a half ounces (42 grams) of cheese, six ounces (168 grams) of butter and margarine, one ounce (28 grams) of cooking fat, eight ounces (225 grams) of sugar, two pints (1.14 litres) of milk and one egg. During the war large quantities of dried egg had been imported from America. It gave a curious flavour to cakes, and might be cooked as a lurid leather pancake, in substitute for a real omlette. In February 1946 it vanished from the shops during the negotiations for the American loan. It was much missed. The *Daily Mirror* asked its readers to choose the dollar imports which they would most readily see reduced: cheese, dried egg, films, fruit, grain, meat, tinned and powdered milk, or tobacco. They voted overwhelmingly for a cut in films, with tobacco, fruit, and milk next on the list. But not the versatile egg. Eventually the government brought powdered egg back into the shops.

Bread (which, as Churchill pointed out, had not been restricted even in the darkest days of the submarine menace) was rationed in July 1946, in the face of a world wheat shortage. It remained rationed for the next two years. In 1950 flour, eggs and soap were derationed, but the last remnants of food rationing were not removed until 1954. Coal remained rationed until 1958.

In 1947 two new foodstuffs appeared on the market. The first was whalemeat, described by the shippers as 'rich and tasty – just like beaf steak'. Few people believed them. Later in the year 10 million tins of 'snoek', a South African fish, was brought in to replace the Portuguese sardine – its import was restricted because of exchange troubles. Few people liked this either, and by 1949 more than one-third of the snoek imported since 1947 remained unsold. Even the Minister of Food described it as 'one of the dullest fish I have ever eaten'.

While some were cooking the snoek, others were cocking the snook. These were the 'spivs' and 'barrow-boys' who thrived on the black market which always springs up in an economy beset with shortages. They were shady customers, many of whose wares had no doubt 'fallen off the back of a lorry', or were so-called 'export rejects', in the deliberate manufacture of which many made a living, such was the pent-up consumer demand at home. During five and a half years of war the people had consumed less than four years' normal supply of clothing, and less than three years' of household goods.

'Starve with Strachey and shiver with Shinwell', was a popular slogan. John Strachey was the Minister of Food; Emanuel Shinwell was Minister of Fuel and Power. The winter of 1946–7 was the worst since 1880 and proved to be an economic disaster of the first magnitude. That coal supplies might run out had been forecast in the previous autumn, but no action was taken to provide for the emergency until it arrived. The government then took extraordinary measures, including the shutting down of factories in order to build up stocks at the power stations. By the first week of February 2 million men were out of work, and it has been estimated that the crisis involved the loss of not far short of 20 per cent of exports. Coal supplies were vital, yet it proved impossible to regain the pre-war level of output, and even in 1950 – three years after the crisis – output had increased by less than 10 per cent. In the end it was oil which came to the rescue, supplying the whole of the expansion in demand for energy from the 1950s onwards, and displacing coal more and more in the 1960s and early 1970s.

Austerity seemed to be personified in Sir Stafford Cripps, Chancellor of the Exchequer from 1947 until his death in 1950. He was high-minded, puritanical, a vegetarian and a teetotaller. As President of the Board of Trade in 1946 he had taken a prominent part in mounting the exhibition 'Britain Can Make It', at the Victoria and Albert Museum in London. The aim was to display the range of British-designed and manufactured goods which were available for export, and the task of selecting exhibits and organising their display was given to the newly created Council for Industrial Design (now the Design Council). Not many of the exhibits were available for sale to the general public (who constituted a majority of the 1.5 million visitors) and the exhibition was nicknamed by some 'Britain Can't Have It'.

In the following years the success of the export drive proved outstanding, for even in real terms exports increased by 77 per cent between 1946 and 1950. Furthermore, they were regularly concentrated in the growth sectors of world trade, as figures for 1952–3 show. At that time, 65 per cent of exports comprised expanding commodities, as against a world average of 53.6 per cent. A notable success was the motor vehicle industry. The pre-war production peak of 526,000 cars, commercial vehicles and tractors was reached in 1947 and exceeded in 1948, when 626,000 vehicles were produced. By 1950 the figure was up to 903,000, excluding motor cycles. Western European recovery was much slower, with the result that 66 per cent of the European output of cars was produced by Britain in 1946–8, and it was still 52 per cent in 1949–50. As the general dollar shortage made American cars unattainable, export markets were wide open, and British industry took advantage. The advantage, however, was a temporary one, and Britain could only maintain it by producing vehicles competitive with those of the renascent European industry from the late 1950s. This it failed to do. As early as 1950 a Political and Economic Planning group report pointed to the faults of the industry: British manufacturers produced too many models; they built for domestic rather than foreign needs; and they neglected after-sales service and spares.

By 1950, however, economic prospects looked brighter than at any time since the war. But in June the Korean War broke out, and the government immediately embarked on a vast programme of rearmament. Within weeks a £3,400 million programme was mapped out (to be spent over three years), and this was soon increased to £4,700 million. This involved an immediate rise from £830 million in 1950–51 to £1,300 million in 1951–2. The war, combined with the effects of the 1949 devaluation, pushed up costs of living, and both prices and wages shot up. At the same time the diversion of productive capacity to defence work cut into the exports which devaluation might otherwise have boosted.

By the time the Korean War started, the decision had already been taken to allow the British people a symbolic pat on the back for their post-war achievements and sacrifices. Plans were laid for a Festival of Britain in 1951, which, in the words of its director-general, would prove a 'tonic to the nation'. The year 1951 was the centenary of the Great Exhibition, with which some interesting comparisons can be made. As before, the Festival had many detractors, in whose company Colonel Sibthorp would have felt at home. Sir Thomas Beecham described it as 'a monumental piece of imbecility', while the President of the Royal Academy argued that the site on London's South Bank would be a death trap because of overcrowding. Even the Festival office's switchboard girl is alleged to have answered the telephone with, 'Festering Britain here'! Securing a site presented a problem as it had done in 1851. An inter-departmental committee set up to consider the question recommended a 300-acre site at Osterley Park in London's outer western suburbs, but that scheme was abandoned when the government learnt that it would cost the taxpayer £70 million, and absorb a third of London's building labour for three years. There were also obvious points of dissimilarity between the two exhibitions, the major one being that the Great Exhibition of 1851 was international, whereas that of 1951 was definitely a Festival of *Britain*. For this reason it has been argued that the true precursor of the Festival was the 1924 British Empire Exhibition which had been held at Wembley. Both exhibitions were held six years after a great world war, and each served a basically similar purpose, although, as Dr Roy Strong writes:

> the Festival of Britain offered neither a mirror nor a window but rather an enchanted glass in which somehow the organizers, shorn of the magic of Empire, attempted to reconstitute a future based on a new secular mythology. The South Bank Exhibition set out to tell 'one continuous, interwoven story . . . of British contributions to world civilization in the arts of the people'. It was no longer written in terms of an apotheosis of the crown and its Empire-sustaining heroes, but of a 'people' whose past was 'like pages torn from a buried book' striving towards an insular self-sufficient Utopia. Worse even than 1924 it not only failed to look towards Europe, already well on the way to forming the European Economic Community, it even virtually eliminated the Commonwealth. Fiercely nationalistic, and anti-imperialist, it was, as Adrian Forty writes, a 'celebration of the achievements of the Labour Government'. For those wearied of war and its aftermath, the austerity, the shortages, the rationing, the never-ending queues, it made visible a brave New World . . . For that presiding genius of the Festival, Herbert Morrison, it made tangible to the masses the Utopia of the Welfare State, the salvation of society seen in terms of universal material provision, education and nationalisation. It was the world of the Education Act, the Town and Country Planning Act, the National Insurance Act, the New Towns and the National Health Sevice conjured into a momentary millenary vision.[9]

There is some point in Strong's idea of a 'momentary millenary vision', for the Festival perhaps marked the beginning of that particularly 1950s brand of political millenarianism that persuaded people, as Adrian Forty says, 'that happiness could be found through material possessions and plenty of shiny paint'. Charles Plouviez, who worked in the Festival office, makes a basically similar point:

> The Festival might almost be said to mark the beginning of our 'English disease' – the moment at which we stopped trying to lead the world as an industrial power, and started being the world's entertainers, coaxing tourists to laugh at our eccentricities, marvel at our traditions and wallow in our nostalgia. Labour's Festival of Britain begat, after a difficult gestation period, the Conservative Swinging Sixties.[10]

Welfare state and nationalisation

When the Labour Party came to power in 1945 it was with a great sense of euphoria. Hugh Dalton described in his memoirs how the new victors felt: 'There was exhilaration among us, joy and hope, determination and confidence. We felt exalted, dedicated, walking on air, walking with destiny.' Their destiny was to enter the Promised Land; but they soon found that it would not yet awhile flow with milk and honey – nor even with dried egg and canned fruit. Labour's manifesto promises had to be fulfilled in the cold climate of austerity, as fundamental economic problems were tackled. The vision was boundless: the complete transformation of society. It has to be admitted that this was never achieved, for the class foundations of British society, eroded a little at the edges, perhaps, remain to this day. Instead, the Labour government inaugurated the 'welfare state'. This was not a term favoured by Beveridge – who was in many ways the father of the concept – although it had first been used publicly by Archbishop William Temple in 1941. It entered the *Oxford English Dictionary* in 1955 as 'a policy so organised that every member of the community is assured of his due maintenance with the most advantageous conditions possible for all'. The term can be interpreted both narrowly and broadly. A rather narrow interpretation is offered by Professor Maurice Bruce in his book, *The Coming of the Welfare State*, where he states five objectives. These are: (1) to guarantee to everyone, in any circumstances, a decent standard of living, without this minimum income necessarily being earned through employment (i.e. thanks to insurance and assistance); (2) to protect everyone against the risks of daily life, such as illness and unemployment; (3) to help family life to develop and thrive (hence family allowances); (4) to treat health and education as public services; and (5) to develop and improve all public establishments that they may conduce to the betterment of personal life (housing, leisure activities, the environment, etc.). Such an interpretation can easily be regarded simply as an extension of the social services, and this is the definition of a welfare state given by the *Concise Oxford Dictionary of Current English* in 1964 – 'one having national health, insurance, and other social services'. Interpreted thus, the welfare state appears as the end product of a long evolution going back to the Liberal reforms of 1906 to 1914, the Victorian increase in state intervention, or even the Elizabethan Poor Law. However, the phrase can be understood in a wider sense – a society with a mixed economy and full employment, where individualism is tempered by state intervention, and where the working-class movement is both recognised and afforded its rightful place in the nation. This is more what the Labour Party planned to implement; although this revolution, too, had its evolutionary aspects, and its two masterminds were, in fact, both Liberals: William Beveridge and John Maynard Keynes. Labour admitted its debt to the past but, as its manifesto pointed out, it looked to the future. Unlike the period after the First World War there was little disillusionment – and even today most people would consider the war against Hitler to have been justified. Nor was there any hankering after 'the good old days'. Memories of the interwar period were that these were bad old days, and that the social policy of that and former periods was rigid, impersonal and paternalistic.

The key to the welfare state was that it would be universal, and thus free of discrimination, free of stigma. Such a worthy concept is not without its practical difficulties, as subsequent events have proved. Those in most need have not necessarily been those who have received most help, and some know better than others how to manipulate the universal provision to their own special advantage. Anthony Sampson wrote in 1971:

> The middle classes have learnt how to use the welfare state, and the service and grants that were originally meant to help the poor are quickly applied for by those who are already well off. State schools in middle-class areas become

middle-class schools; grants for extra bathrooms are taken up by owners of bijou houses; the middle-class lobbies concerned with the environment push up the values of middle-class districts, making them too expensive for others, and the cities become more segregated into rich and poor areas. The attempts to break out of this bourgeois enclosure prove abortive: *Which?*, the potential champion of the mass consumer, turns its attention to burglar alarms and making wills; the Arts Council prefers Covent Garden to fun palaces; the Open University recruits forty per cent of its students from the teaching profession.[11]

The issue was much discussed in the 1960s when, not for the first time, poverty was 'rediscovered'. The complacency of the 1950s that, through the welfare state, poverty was being steadily eroded, was dispelled by the studies of influential academics such as Peter Townsend, Richard Titmuss and Brian Abel-Smith, as well as by a number of official enquiries. A government survey in 1966, for example, concluded that 166,000 families, embracing 500,000 children, were living below the official subsistence level because of the low wages of the father. At the general election of that year the question of universal as against selective benefits was much discussed. The Conservative Party had always had reservations about the appropriateness of handing out benefits to all, whether or not they were in need, and in the 1960s the issue was debated with renewed vigour.

Universal provision of social services was one of the cornerstones of the 1942 Beveridge Report, some recommendations of which were implemented before the war was over. This was the case with family allowances, for example, for the Coalition government introduced the necessary legislation in February 1945, and the bill was seen through its last stages by the caretaker government in the following June.

The scheme for National Insurance was completed by two acts of 1946 and two of 1948. During the debate in the House of Commons on the second reading of the main bill on 6 February 1946 the question of costs was raised. Attlee replied in no uncertain terms, as *Hansard* reported:

The Question is asked – Can we afford it? Supposing the answer is 'No', what does that mean? It really means that the sum total of the goods produced and the services rendered by the people of this country is not sufficient to provide for all our people at all times, in sickness, in health, in youth and in age, the very modest standard of life that is represented by the sums of money set out in the Second Schedule to this Bill. I cannot believe that our national productivity is so slow, that our willingness to work is so feeble or that we can submit to the world that the masses of our people must be condemned to penury.

The question of whether Britain could or could not afford to introduce a welfare state in 1945 was hotly debated in the 1980s, when welfare provision became, once again, a matter of great political controversy. The economic difficulties which Britain faced in that decade led many people to seek the origins of the 'British disease', and a view was strongly put forward that Britain had thrown away a historic moment at the end of the Second World War by attempting to herald a New Jerusalem when the prime task should have been to concentrate on a fundamental reconstruction of the economy. This was the argument of the historian, Correlli Barnett, in an influential (but highly controversial) book, *The Audit of War*, published in 1986. Barnett argued that:

. . . it came to pass that a romantic vision a century and a half in the making had at last found incarnation in the committed programme of a British government with a crushing majority in Parliament. Yet the cost of realising this programme was to fall not on the richest country in the world, not on that Victorian and Edwardian Britain in which the vision first had gleamed and which had made the New Jerusalemers what they were, but on a country with a ruined export trade, heavily in debt to its bankers (the Sterling Area Commonwealth countries and the United States), and with huge and inescapable continuing burdens with regard to the war with Japan. Yet the wartime promoters of New Jerusalem had pursued their vision in the face of economic realities perfectly well known to them – on the best romantic principle that sense must bend to feeling, and facts to faith.[12]

Barnett argued that the British people's self-congratulation over their industrial record during the war was misplaced, and that the impressive total figures of war production hid the fact that Britain had been reliant on what he described as the 'American life-support machine'. The economy, he argued, had not been all that efficient during the war, and he subjected the aircraft industry, in particular, to a blistering attack. According to Barnett, British pride in the superiority of the beloved Spitfire to the Messerschmitt ME109 was misplaced, for it took two-thirds more man hours to build, and would have been priced out of any commercial market. Not only that, but the ME109 was built with German machine tools, while the British aircraft industry was heavily reliant on tools imported from the United States. The conclusion he drew was a clear one. Britain could in no way afford to embark on the expense of setting up the welfare state, and should have concentrated on the rebuilding and restructuring of its industrial base.

Such an interpretation of events found much sympathy with many Conservative politicians of the 1980s. 'I'm a Correlli Barnett supporter,' declared Lord Joseph in 1987, 'I believe that managements, helped by trade unions and helped by government, were not nearly effective enough.' At about the same time, Nigel Lawson, the Chancellor of the Exchequer, cited 'Correlli's book' as a major source of authority for his fiscal and social policies.

Barnett's thesis, however, has come in for considerable criticism from other historians. Jose Harris, for example, suggests that, 'Where Barnett goes astray . . . is in implying that all welfare policies have an identical and undifferentiated character, and in his curiously insular assumption that the welfare state stops at the English Channel'.[13] She points out that Britain's spending on welfare was not large in comparison to many of its competitors.

> Even in 1950, in a year in which much of Western Europe had only recently been rescued from economic collapse by the first instalments of the Marshall Plan, Britain's spending on social security as a percentage of gross domestic product was lower than that of West Germany, Austria and Belgium. By 1952 her social security expenditure was also lower than that of France and Denmark, in 1954 it was outstripped by that of Italy, in 1955 by Sweden, in 1957 by the Netherlands, and in 1970 by Norway and Finland. From that time onwards until the 1980s . . . Britain consistently devoted a lower proportion of national income to social security purposes than any other European country, with the sole exception of Switzerland.[14]

The cost of the programmes introduced after the war was not crippling. Expenditure on income maintenance after the war – pensions, workmen's compensation, poor relief, family allowances, etc. – made up a smaller percentage of the gross national product than did the welfare programmes of the 1930s, when unemployment was at a high level. The percentage spent on health was roughly equivalent to the pre-war figure, though after 1948 the Exchequer took over much expenditure that had previously been diffused among voluntary associations and individuals in the private sector. The total costs were manageable with sharply increased taxation. There was an inevitable expansion of the government bureaucracy. To the existing nucleus of about 5,500 dealing with insurance, another 34,000 were added as wartime pressures relaxed, and the new Ministry of National Insurance was located at Newcastle to provide regional employment.

The insured person paid a flat-rate contribution and received flat-rate benefits. Treating everyone the same was in the spirit of universalism, but it inevitably meant that contributions had to be fixed at an amount which the lowest-paid worker could afford, and hence benefits had to be pitched very near the level of subsistence. There were many who doubted that they reached even this level. As a safety net, the National Assistance Act of 1948 established a National Assistance Board as a remedial relief agency, empowered to assist those needy persons who passed a means test. Those assisted in this way comprised people whose insurance benefits failed to provide subsistence, and those who had exhausted the insurance entitlement or who had earned none.

The scope of health insurance had been considerably widened in 1942, when the income limit for participation was raised to £420, but it still covered only about half the population and included neither specialist nor hospital services, nor dental and optical treatment, nor hearing aids. Doctors were spread unevenly over the country, as were hospitals – of which there were more than 1,000 voluntary ones in England and Wales. A number of proposals for reforming the health service were put forward in the wake of the Beveridge Report, but the job of implementing Labour's scheme fell to Aneurin Bevan, the new Minister of Health. Bevan had seen poverty, ill-health and squalor in abundance. His father – a founder member of the Tredegar Working Men's Medical Society – had died in his arms of the dreaded miners' disease, pneumoconiosis. Bevan was ready for the battle that was about to be waged.

Three problems stood out: first, how to meet the cost of the service; second, how to sort out the administrative tangle; and third, how to incorporate into the public service the fiercely individualistic medical profession.

The cost of a National Health Service might be reduced by establishing an income limit for free services, but Bevan would have none of it, for this would lead to 'the creation of a two-standard health service, one below and one above the salt'. In his view, 'The essence of the satisfactory health service is that the rich and the poor are treated alike, that poverty is not a disability and wealth is not an advantage'. Individual freedom would remain, however, for those who could afford private treatment to seek it if they wished.

Administration posed a number of problems, for there were numerous vested interests to placate – local authorities, voluntary hospitals and teaching hospitals with their endowments and independent boards of governors and, most powerful of all perhaps, the medical profession itself. The result was that a rather cumbersome tripartite health service was established. Certain 'local health services' (many of a preventive nature) were allocated to the larger local authorities. These services included vaccination and immunisation, home nursing and health visiting, domiciliary midwifery and maternity and child welfare, and ambulances. The existing local authorities were not given hospital services, for which regional units were required. Bevan argued that to wait for the reform of local government which this would necessitate would involve unacceptable delay. Since this reform did not come about until the early 1970s, he was no doubt right. There was another reason why the hospitals were not transferred to the local authorities, however, and that was that the medical profession would not have it thus, fearing a loss of control. Instead, therefore, hospitals were allocated to Regional Hospital Groups, of which 13 were established in England, one in Wales, five in Scotland and one in Northern Ireland. The Regional Boards would appoint management committees for the 388 hospitals within the system, although the teaching hospitals retained a considerable degree of independence. The third strand of the system was the general practitioner service. In England and Wales 138 executive councils were set up (Scotland had 25) on which local professional interests were strongly represented.

The result of this administrative division was that a patient's relationship with the service was fragmented. An expectant mother, for example, would receive the aid of a midwife from the local authority, but the GP's services from the executive council. Should she need to see a consultant she would have to attend the hospital administered by the Regional Hospital Board (perhaps being conveyed there in a local authority ambulance). The original intention was that the three health services should be coordinated through local health centres, but few were built, partly because of the constraints of finance, but also because of unresolved conflict between the doctors and the local authorities as to their control.

The opposition of the medical profession to the National Health Service was the most serious that the Labour government encountered during the three years in which the major part of its programme was put into effect. The doctors' fears related first to the possibility that medicine would be completely nationalised and that doctors would become salaried servants of the state, thus losing their cherished professional status. Second, they were concerned about the remuneration they would receive within the National Health Service. The former question was one of power – the power of the state against the power of the doctors, as represented by the British Medical Association (BMA). The doctors could be very unsubtle in their arguments, as when Dr Charles Hill, the BBC 'Radio Doctor' and secretary of the BMA, observed that 'if the Bill comes into operation in anything like its present form it will represent something very much like that regime which is now coming to its sorry end at Nuremberg'. One feature of their professional practice upon which they tried to insist was the sale of medical practices, the goodwill of which was reckoned as a sort of retirement bonus for the outgoing practitioner. Bevan emphatically opposed this system, which failed to ensure that doctors set up practice where they were most needed. Instead he proposed two Medical Practices Committees, one for England and Wales and one for Scotland, whose approval would be required before a doctor could set up. Retiring doctors would receive a pension instead of selling their practice, which Bevan described as 'an evil in itself . . . tantamount to the sale and purchase of patients'.

The doctors kept up their opposition after the National Health Service Act was passed in November 1946 down to July 1948, when the service came into operation. Bevan made some concessions, and by the 'Appointed Day', 5 July a majority of general practitioners had applied to enter. By September more than 18,000 doctors in England and Wales out of 21,000 had decided to enter the service. Peter Jenkins describes the first year of the National Health Service thus:

> Within a year of its inception 41,200,000 people – ninety-five per cent of the eligible population – were covered by it. In the first year 8,500,000 dental patients were treated and 5,250,000 pairs of spectacles dispensed, illustrating the pent-up demand for the dental and ophthalmic services, which had never been a part of the old insurance system. Working people no longer had to test their own eyes at Woolworths. In the first year 187,000,000 prescriptions were

written out by more than 18,000 general practitioners . . . The National Health Service employed 34,000 people, and cost nearly £400,000,000 a year. In terms of money and manpower it became the second largest undertaking in the country – second to the armed forces. It was the largest single item in the civilian budget, and accounted for about $3\frac{1}{2}$ per cent of the national product.[15]

The National Health Service was not without its critics, and in 1953 the question of its cost was handed over to the Guillebaud Committee which reported three years later. The Committee ascribed 70 per cent of the increased costs to inflation, and found no evidence to support the widespread charge of extravagance. It therefore recommended no major change in the general administrative structure of the service. Against the rising costs must be set the achievements. In the first 10 years the number of in-patients treated in hospitals had increased by a million, or 30 per cent. Waiting lists had been reduced by about 90,000 from the peak year of 1950. Expenditure on new hospital building was rising, and there was a steady increase in the numbers of doctors and nurses. Whatever the shortcomings of the service, millions of people who had experienced the old system of medical care knew how much they had to be thankful for.

The nation's health was improved in other ways. During the war children and expectant mothers had been provided with free or heavily subsidised welfare foods and vitamins and the distribution of these was now expanded. Free milk was distributed in schools, and in 1948 about 98 per cent of the country's schoolchildren were drinking one-third of a pint daily. Food subsidies, which had been introduced on a modest scale in 1940, were also increased. An act of 1947 covered about three-quarters of farming produce, using guaranteed prices and deficiency payments to subsidise home-produced food and to offset the competition from foreign agriculture. These subsidies represented a heavy burden on the Exchequer, running at £485 million per annum in 1948. Farming productivity improved (by about 6 per cent a year) and a gradual reduction in the real costs of food subsidies became possible by the 1960s, without serious injury to farmers' confidence.

An attempt to provide for comprehensive regulation of the use of land was made by the Town and Country Planning Act of 1947. The old socialist dream of land nationalisation was abandoned as too complicated; instead, the state nationalised development rights. The act must be considered in relation to the National Parks and Access to the Countryside Act of 1949, and to the New Towns Act of 1946. The latter act empowered the Minister of Housing to construct new towns to take the overspill population of London and other big cities. The scheme was ambitious, and resulted in 29 'New Towns' (23 in England and Wales and 6 in Scotland). The first generation (1947–50) comprised a dozen towns, including Harlow, Hatfield and Basildon, most of which were situated around London. Beveridge became chairman of one Development Corporation: Newton Aycliffe, built on the site of a Royal Ordnance shell-filling factory in County Durham. A second generation of new towns, benefiting from the experience of the first, was completed between 1961 and 1971. Altogether, the new towns attracted 700,000 inhabitants between 1947 and 1970.

There was a pressing housing need at the end of the war. Aneurin Bevan was the responsible minister, and he inherited orders for 150,000 prefabricated houses, various powers to subsidise local authorities in slum clearance, and plans to restore the building industry's labour force which, at the end of the war, had shrunk to one-third of its former size. Building workers received A1 priority for demobilisation. There was no comprehensive building plan. Conservatives wanted private builders to be given their heads, but the Housing Acts of 1946 and 1949 continued and extended the policy of subsidised local authority housing. The act of 1949 had a certain historic significance, for it was the first to drop the phrase 'working class', further evidence of Labour's concern to make social provision universal. Shortage of raw materials was a major source of delays, and in 1946 some 20,000 people squatted in several hundred disused (and in some cases still used) army camps, having nowhere else to live. Powerless to evict such a large number, the government eventually passed 563 camps, together with their squatters, to local authority control. In 18 months from the end of the war, homes were provided, by new building or repair, for nearly 300,000 people; and 58,000 permanent, together with 92,000 temporary homes were completed. At the time of the 1951 census the number of occupied dwellings (13.3 million) was higher than in 1931, but households had grown even faster (to 14.4 million). The shortfall was therefore just about the same. Labour's housing achievement was somewhat limited, and the government was vulnerable to the Conservative promise at the 1951 general election that it would build 300,000 houses a year.

The most pressing educational need at the end of the war was to provide 70,000 new teachers and 600,000 new school places. Five thousand destroyed or damaged schools had to be replaced or repaired. Fifty-five country houses or military camps (they were often the same) were rapidly adapted as emergency training colleges, the first one to open being Wall Hall Training College in Hertfordshire, former home of J. P. Morgan Jr, the American banker. By 1951 the emergency colleges had produced 35,000 teachers by means of crash courses. No one suggested that the shortage of doctors should be met by the same method. The raising of the school-leaving age in 1947 required a further 168,000 new school places, and a Hut Operation for the Raising of the School Age (HORSA) was mounted. Just under 7,000 HORSA classrooms were provided, and these bleak huts house thousands of schoolchildren to this day. The act in fact contained a provision to raise the school-leaving age to 16, 'as soon as the minister is satisfied that it has become practicable'. It did not become practicable until 1972.

That a government intent on effecting a social revolution should have left the public schools unscathed is surprising. The schools had been investigated by the Fleming Committee in 1944, which, says Pat Thane, 'sufficiently confused the issue to make action avoidable'. Churchill – whose philosophy was 'Everything for the war, whether controversial or not, and nothing controversial that is not *bona fide* needed for the war' – persuaded R. A. Butler to leave the public schools out of his bill. The Prime Minister wrote: 'I think it would . . . be a great mistake to stir up the public schools question at the present time.' The schools were not without their critics, and the novelist, E. M. Forster, suggested that the young emerged from them with 'well-developed bodies, reasonably developed minds, and underdeveloped hearts'. It might be added that they also emerged with highly developed prospects. The Fleming Committee reported that out of 830 top civil servants, bishops, judges, members of the Indian civil service, dominion and colonial governors, directors of banks and railway companies, three-quarters had been to a public school (and half of them to the nine 'great' schools). Ten years later the situation had hardly changed, and if one takes Conservative and Labour MPs together one finds that in 1970, as in 1951, almost half had been to public schools.

If the 1944 act was silent on public schools, it was also silent on grammar schools, although secondary education was made free for all. After the war, secondary education tended to develop along tripartite lines, although J. Chuter Ede, Labour Parliamentary Secretary to the Board of Education in the Coalition government, said in April 1944: 'I do not know where people get the idea about three types of school, because I have gone through the Bill with a small toothcomb, and I can find only one school for senior pupils and that is a secondary school.' He should have known that people got the idea from the Norwood Report of 1943, chaired by a former headmaster of Harrow School. The Norwood Report, without a shred of psychological or sociological evidence, asserted that the educational system had 'thrown up' three 'rough groupings' of children with different 'types of mind'. These were, first, 'the pupil who is interested in learning for its own sake, who can grasp an argument or follow a piece of connected reasoning'; second, 'the pupil whose interests and abilities lie markedly in the field of applied science or applied art'; third, the pupil who 'deals more easily with concrete things than with ideas . . . abstractions mean little to him . . . his horizon is near and within a limited area his movement is generally slow'. For these three groups, three types of secondary school were needed – grammar, technical and 'secondary modern' schools.

Many objections were made to these assumptions. The historian of education, S. J. Curtis, was vehement in his judgement of the Report: 'Seldom has a more unscientific or more unscholarly attitude disgraced the report of a public committee.' The suggestion 'seems to be that the Almighty has benevolently created three types of child in just those proportions which would gratify educational administrators'.

In spite of the Norwood Report's poor reception the Labour Ministers of Education after 1945 chose to interpret the 1944 act in its light, and only a few education authorities experimented with 'multilateral' or comprehensive schools, among them the London County Council and Anglesey. Allocation of children to different types of secondary school necessitated selection at the age of 11+, and the rigidities thus imposed were passed down through the system so that junior schools were driven to stream children as early as 7 years of age, and streaming even penetrated the infant schools. Secondary modern schools for Norwood's third class of children were intended by the Ministry to have 'parity of esteem', but this could never be the case. Not only did grammar schools have more prestige, they had more resources – resulting in selection becoming a self-fulfilling prophecy.

The assumptions behind the tripartite system were challenged in the 1950s. First, the experience of the existing comprehensive schools was collated, notably by Robin Pedley. Second, doubts were raised about the part played by intelligence testing in the selection process. Third, sociologists began to enjoy a more prominent role in education thinking. The second and third phenomena were related. The margins of error in the 11+ examination were found to be wide enough to allow the wrong allocation of large numbers of children; and greater understanding was reached of the sociological and environmental factors influencing the performance of schoolchildren. Advocacy of comprehensive schools thus increased in the 1960s, but the grammar schools had their supporters too (technical schools for Norwood's second group of children had never really got off the ground). The question of comprehensive education thus became one of the major political controversies of that and the following decade.

Education reform under the Labour government failed to bring about a transformation of society. Likewise, nationalisation – so loudly heralded in the 1945 election manifesto – failed to bring about a transformation of the economy. Many of the centres of economic power were left untouched. Land was not nationalised, and landed power continued to be great. The City and the banking system survived unscathed. It is true that the Bank of England was nationalised. Indeed, the short act of five clauses and three schedules which effected the change takes pride of place as the first piece of post-war legislation on nationalisation. However, nationalisation of the Bank of England was in itself little more than a symbolic act, for the relationship between the Bank and the Treasury had long been intimate. Churchill recognised this when he gave the necessary legislation his blessing: 'The national ownership of the Bank of England does not in my opinion raise any matter of principle.'

By 1951, six nationalised industries produced a combined turnover of £2,235 million (equivalent to 17 per cent of gross domestic product) and employed a total of 10 per cent of the employed workforce (over 2.3 million people). Labour's declared aim with nationalisation was to take control of 'the commanding heights of the economy', but this proved illusory. Partly this has been because it was the export industries rather than those actually nationalised which really commanded the heights; and partly because there was an inherent ambiguity about the function the nationalised industries were to exercise. Sidney Pollard writes that 'the earlier Socialist hopes that the nationalised industries would usher in a regime of better industrial relations, a motivation of unselfishness and a social purpose in industry, were soon disappointed'. Instead, the nationalised industries found themselves caught between conflicting social and commercial objectives. If they made large profits they laid themselves open to the charge that they were abusing their monopoly position. If they made small profits (or, worse still, no profits at all) they were accused of being inefficient. At the same time as low railway freight rates and low coal prices were consciously used as a subsidy to private industry, the nationalised industries concerned were criticised for failing to make ends meet. Pollard's conclusion is that 'far from becoming the spearhead of a Socialist economy the nationalised industries remained anomalies in a private enterprise economy'.

From the worker's point of view, too, it is hard to see how nationalisation effected any great change. Labour came to power with an emotional attachment to nationalisation (which, as Clause IV, formed part of its constitution from 1918 until its eventual repeal in 1995) – but there were no *plans* as to how it should be implemented. Emanuel Shinwell sat for a mining constituency. He observed:

> I had listened to the Party speakers advocating State ownership and control of the coal mines, and I had myself spoken of it as a primary task once the Labour Party was in Power. I had believed, as other members had, that in the party archives a blue print was ready. Now, as Minister of Fuel and Power, I found that nothing practical and tangible existed.[16]

Nationalisation (which had first been proposed in legislation as far back as 1844, and was frequently debated in Parliament between 1918 and 1921) might have adopted a variety of forms. For example, the Labour Party could have chosen a syndicalist form involving control of the industry from below through a series of committees from shop floor to top management. Or one of the variants such as guild socialism or sovietism might have been adopted. These the party consistently refused to advocate, and the form actually taken was that of the public corporation. In order to prevent ministerial interference with the day-to-day running of the industries, boards were appointed under independent chairmen. The boards were to be responsible to the minister, who was in turn responsible to Parliament. Seen from the workers' viewpoint, 'the bosses' remained very much the same. Hopes that the corporation boards would include many workers were largely disappointed. Only the Central Electricity Authority achieved significant worker representation, and even there the average was under one-fifth. There were many reasons for this deficiency. The government was anxious that the boards should have ample management skills, while at the same time trade unions were often reluctant to put forward candidates. Attlee later recalled: 'They weren't always willing to cross over, nor were their men always willing for them to go in: a curious contradiction, because they talked of labour running the show and yet when you put a trade unionist in to help run a nationalised industry they tended to regard him as a bosses' man.' Management remained remote (and in some cases became even more remote) from the workers, and was often overcentralised and overbureaucratised.

The National Coal Board took over the mines on 1 January 1947. The Board faced a task of enormous proportions, and even with adequate management and resources, could not be expected to produce significant results until the 1950s. Shinwell, as Minister of Fuel and Power, was much criticised by some of his colleagues for the 1947 fuel crisis, which could not be entirely blamed on the severity of the winter. As well as facing problems on the supply side, throughout the 1950s the industry suffered from falling demand. The Clean Air Act of 1956 contributed to a decline in the demand of domestic consumers, while coal-using industries were increasing their fuel efficiency, and were turning to other sources of supply. Thus, while the home consumption of coal fell by 10 million tons in 1958, that of oil increased by the equivalent of 6.5 million tons.

Electricity and gas were nationalised in 1948, and in each case a strong argument could be put forward on the ground of increased efficiency. At one time there had been no fewer than 635 electricity undertakings throughout the country, and in London there were still 75 in 1947. Tariffs and voltages differed from one area to another, and the industry was regulated by over 240 acts of Parliament and Provisional and Special Orders. The British Electricity Authority took over this haphazard system, and local distribution was placed in the hands of 14 subordinate area boards. Gas supply was even more disorganised and inefficient, and control here was vested in a Gas Council and twelve Area Gas Boards.

Large sections of the transport industry were nationalised. The British Overseas Airways Corporation (BOAC) had been run as a public concern since 1940. In 1946 British European Airways (BEA) was formed as a public corporation. Independent airlines could operate charter flights and act as agents for the corporations. One problem which all airlines faced was the lack of a suitable British aircraft. The introduction of the De Haviland Comet in 1952 enabled BOAC to pay its way, but a series of disastrous crashes in 1953 and 1954 (proved to be due to metal fatigue) led to the plane's grounding, and the corporation was compelled to buy American aircraft. BEA experimented with the Vickers Viscount in 1950, and put the aeroplane on to regular scheduled service three years later. Yet, although it was highly successful, BEA also came to rely on American aircraft.

The Transport Act of 1947 established a British Transport Commission with the task of providing 'an efficient, adequate, economical and properly integrated system of public inland transport and port facilities'. The Commission's burdens were great, and as an undertaking it dwarfed even the giants of private industry. It was provided with five Executives – the Railway Executive, the Road Transport Executive, the Inland Waterways Executive, the London Transport Executive and the Hotels Executive – but these were not so much partners in an integrated whole as different organisations with individual problems.

The Conservatives pledged themselves to reorganise the Transport Commission, which they did after their return to power in 1951. An attempt to denationalise road haulage in 1953 ran into some difficulty. Many customers were satisfied with the regular, interconnected runs made by British Road Services. This, combined with the fact that there was no great rush by private enterprise to acquire road haulage assets when put on the market, led to a further act in 1956 which permitted the

Commission to retain that part of its haulage fleet not disposed of, amounting to some 8,000 lorries.

The major transformation of the railways had to wait until the publication of the Beeching Report in 1963. Despite some economies since 1945 it was estimated that half of the railway network was not meeting even the most obvious costs, and the report suggested the closure of a vast number of lines. At one time it looked as if no lines would be left north or west of Inverness, and Wales and the south-west of England were particularly affected. The report took a dispassionate and unsentimental look at railway economics, and studiously avoided social issues. In so doing, it highlighted one of the central dilemmas of the nationalised industries. Herbert Morrison, the leading exponent of the public corporation, wrote in 1953, that it 'must be no mere capitalist business, the be-all and end-all of which is profits and dividends. Its board and officers must regard themselves as the high custodians of the public interest'. Such a view left unresolved the question of pricing policies in what were monopolistic industries. A government White Paper issued by the Conservatives in 1961 put forward a different view. Although nationalised industries, it argued, have obligations of a national and non-commercial kind, they ought not to be regarded as social services absolved from economic and commercial justification.

With the possible exception of road transport, a strong economic case could be made out for nationalising each of the industries mentioned above, for all required massive injections of capital unlikely to be made by private enterprise. The major debate over nationalisation was reserved for iron and steel. The usual arguments for nationalisation could not be used. The industry was not particularly inefficient, it was not short of capital; and its prices were lower than in most other countries. Unlike the coal industry there was no long history of labour unrest, and no serious strike had affected it for 50 years. However, the industry was of great strategic importance to the economy and therefore raised great questions of principle and power. The Conservatives argued that the proposed nationalisation of iron and steel was a political and not an economic act. Churchill called on his powers of rhetoric: 'This is not a Bill, it is a plot, not a plan to increase production, but rather, in effect, at any rate, an operation in restraint of trade. It is not a plan to help our patient struggling people, but a burglar's jemmy to crack the capitalist crib.'

The industry came under government supervision in 1946. Morrison put forward a compromise scheme, but majority feeling in both the Cabinet and the party favoured full-scale nationalisation. A bill to this end was introduced in October 1948. It had a stormy passage through the House of Commons, and the fear that it would be blocked by the House of Lords was one of the factors which contributed to the introduction of the Parliament Bill. When passed in 1949, this effectively reduced the delaying power of the Lords to one year. The Iron and Steel Act, 1949, provided for the nationalisation of firms that had produced 50,000 tons of iron, or 20,000 tons of iron and steel, in 1946–7. For Labour it was a pyrrhic victory, for nationalisation of the industry was not an electoral asset and the industry became something of a political football. Steel was denationalised in 1954, renationalised in 1967, and denationalised, yet again, in 1988. This uncertainty did neither the industry nor the country any good. Taking the period from 1948 to 1960 there was a greater increase in production than in the previous 30 years, but Britain's progress compared unfavourably with other countries such as West Germany and Japan. The United Kingdom's crude steel production went up by 60 per cent between 1948 and 1960. In the same period world production more than doubled. The clash between government and industry, as well as technical conservatism, played a part in the final outcome.

The Iron and Steel Act was the last nationalisation measure to be brought before Parliament for 20 years. The early 1950s were something of doldrum years for the nationalised industries, and in the 1960s the arguments appeared to have died down. The Conservatives introduced fewer measures for denationalisation than was expected, partly because of the hesitation of some ministers, but also because fewer purchasers came forward for steel and road transport undertakings than had been anticipated. It was not until the 1980s that denationalisation again became an issue, when it formed part of the Conservative government's plans to 'privatise' the economy.

Notes

1 Arthur Marwick, *The Explosion of British Society*, Macmillan, 1971, p. 99.
2 Alan S. Milward, *War, Economy and Society, 1939–45*, Allen Lane, 1977, p. 180.
3 B. S. Johnson (ed.), *The Evacuees*, Gollancz, 1969, p. 145.
4 Winston S. Churchill, *The Second World War*, vol. IV, Cassell, 1951, p. 861.
5 Arthur Marwick, op. cit., p. 123.
6 D. N. Pritt, *The Labour Government, 1945–51*, Lawrence and Wishart, 1963, p. 29.
7 T. W. Hutchinson, *Economics and Economic Policy in Britain, 1946–1966*, Allen and Unwin, 1968, p. 56.
8 Quoted in Susan Carruthers, ' "Manning the factories": Propaganda and policy on the employment of women, 1939–1947', *History*, June 1990, p. 251.
9 Mary Banham and Bevis Hillier (eds), *A Tonic to the Nation*, Thames and Hudson, 1976, p. 8.
10 Ibid., p. 166.
11 Anthony Sampson, *The New Anatomy of Britain*, Hodder and Stoughton, 1971, p. 662.
12 Correlli Barnett, *The Audit of War*, Macmillan, 1986, p. 37.
13 Jose Harris, 'Enterprise and the welfare state: a comparative perspective' in Terry Gourvish and Alan O'Day (eds), *Britain Since 1945*, Macmillan, 1991, p. 55.
14 Ibid, pp. 43–4.
15 Michael Sisson and Philip French (eds), *The Age of Austerity*, Penguin, 1964, p. 242.
16 Quoted in Pauline Gregg, *The Welfare State*, Harrap, 1967, pp. 67–8.

Chapter fourteen

The long boom, 1951–73

The years of consensus

Despite the fact that Labour substantially increased its popular vote in 1951, the Conservatives, making even greater inroads into the Liberal vote (which fell from over 2.5 million in 1950 to less than 750,000 in 1951) were returned to power. They remained in office for the next 13 years. In 1945 the Conservatives had been supported by barely 30 per cent of the electorate while Labour enjoyed an actual majority of popular support, but after 1947 it began to pull up in the opinion polls. The defeat of 1945 had been traumatic, but the party subsequently put its house in order both by strengthening its electoral machine and by updating its ideas, under the impetus of men like R. A. Butler. The party slogan at the election of 1951 was 'Set the People Free', and the banner under which the Conservatives rode to victory was that of 'free enterprise'. This was given great prominence in the election manifesto:

> The attempt to impose a doctrinaire Socialism upon an Island which has grown great and famous by free enterprise has inflicted serious injury upon our strength and prosperity. Nationalisation has proved itself a failure which has resulted in heavy losses to the taxpayer or the consumer, or both. It has not given general satisfaction to the wage-earners in the nationalised industries. It has impaired the relations of the Trade Unions with their members. In more than one nationalised industry the wage-earners are ill-content with the change from the private employers, with whom they could negotiate on equal terms through the Trade Unions, to the all-powerful and remote officials in Whitehall.

All further nationalisation would be stopped, and the denationalisation of steel and road haulage was promised, but as it turned out, there was little turning back of the clock.

At first glance the achievements of the Conservatives during their 13 unbroken years in office appear impressive. There was uninterrupted full employment, and productivity increased faster than in any other period of comparable length since the beginning of the century. In 1964, total production was 40 per cent higher than in 1951. Housing was transformed. By 1964, one family in four was living in accommodation built while the Conservatives were in power, and half the population was living in owner-occupied housing as against a quarter in 1951. The number of teachers had risen by a third, and there was a threefold increase in the number of students following some course of further education or training. Pensions rose constantly, that of 1954 having 50 per cent more purchasing power than that of 1951. The number of hospital doctors rose by 30 per cent, GPs by 18 per cent and nurses by 40 per cent. This far exceeded the growth of population which stood at 7 per cent over the same period.

The strides in social welfare were accompanied by a sharp increase in private affluence. The Canadian economist J. K. Galbraith coined the phrase 'The Affluent Society' in 1958; and while his critique applied to America, it still seemed to have relevance to Britain at that time. In 1951 there were 2.5 million private cars in Britain, and 1 million television sets. By 1964 there were over 8 million cars and 13 million television sets. In 1956 only 8 per cent of households had a refrigerator; 33 per cent had one in 1962. In 1951, 1.5 million households had a private telephone; by 1966 the figure had risen to 4.2 million. About 5 million people went abroad for their holidays in 1964, a threefold increase since 1951. In 1951 the average weekly earnings of men over 21 stood at £8 6s. A decade later the figure had almost doubled to £15 7s. In 1966 it was £20 6s. Even allowing for inflation, the average standard of living had risen by over 30 per cent during the Conservatives' time in office – and there was no knowing where it would stop. R. A. Butler, Chancellor of the Exchequer in 1954, asked: 'Why should we not aim to double our standard of living in the next twenty-five years?'

However, writing in 1964 on the Conservative management of the economy in the previous 13 years, Samuel Brittan made the point that, 'Britain is at least as materialistic as any other Western country – but inefficient in its materialism'. He added that 'a better recipe for frustration would be difficult to find' than 'the combination of slow growth with a highly commercial and materialistic environment'. And growth *was* slow in comparison with other leading industrial nations. While the increase in total British production was 40 per cent, that of France doubled, West Germany's and Italy's went up two and a half times, and Japan's production quadrupled. Britain's position in the export league table was equally disappointing. Between 1951 and 1962 there was a 29 per cent increase in British exports, but those of France increased by 86 per cent, those of West Germany by 247 per cent, those of Italy by 259 per cent, and of Japan by 378 per cent. Production and exports failed to increase at a rate necessary to balance the growing consumption of domestic and imported goods, which accounts for the balance of payments crises threatening the economy almost every year from the mid-1950s onwards. When the Conservatives were defeated in 1964 they left the country with the most serious sterling crisis since the one that they had themselves inherited in 1951.

With the bulk of the electorate expecting an annual increment to their income and welfare, it was easy for governments in the 1950s to fall into the trap of seeking short-term gains rather than long-term growth, and the danger was increased by a political system in which comparatively small swings in the popular vote could have great repercussions on party strength at Westminster. It was therefore tempting for governments to direct economic policy towards party political ends. Two examples illustrate this: housing policy and the 'election budget'.

At the Conservative Party conference in 1950, the party adopted a target of 300,000 houses a year, and the promise to build them – written into the 1951 election manifesto – was undoubtedly a factor in the party's electoral victory. In 1951, the last year of the Labour government, the total number of houses built was 195,000. Once in power the Conservative minister responsible, Harold Macmillan, assisted by Ernest Marples, set to work with a will to meet the party's target. During 1952, 240,000 houses were completed, and in 1953 the magic figure of 300,000 was passed. In the following year a further 347,000 were built. However, making housing a top priority meant that other urgent programmes were delayed. The average rate of industrial building was lower in 1952–4 than it had been in 1951, and Britain's road-building programme lagged behind that of almost every other major industrial country. It was not until 1958 that the first $8\frac{1}{2}$-mile stretch of motorway was opened, and by 1965 Britain still had only 345 miles completed, compared with 2,000 miles in Germany and nearly 1,000 in Italy. Furthermore, valuable dollars were being spent on imported timber and construction materials, while labour and capital were diverted from other projects more vital to the reconstruction of the economy.

It might be argued that housing was a great social need; but while there is truth in this, it remains the case that the Conservative record on slum clearance was unremarkable. 'Few of the houses that appeared in their neat rows during the 1950s were earmarked for the inhabitants of Stepney or the Gorbals,' writes Michael Pinto-Duschinsky. The number of unfit dwellings was 847,000 in 1954. Eleven years later the figure had only fallen to 824,000. There were ideological grounds for the Conservatives acting as they did. Conservative leaders had great faith in 'a nationwide, property-owning democracy' (as Anthony Eden put it), and they felt that the extension of home ownership eroded socialist support and widened electoral support for themselves.

Similar factors underlay the budget of April 1955 which marked the successful operation of the economic power of the government in harmony with electoral considerations. There was, of course, nothing new about vote-catching measures, or seeking to take advantage at the polls from the state of the economy, but many people argue that 1955 saw the beginning of a trend to harmonise the electoral cycle with the business cycle, thus producing the 'electoral business cycle'.

Once the ideas of Keynes gained orthodoxy after the war, the budget became one of the principal means of exerting influence upon the economy. The idea was that when unemployment rose, or there were signs of unused industrial capacity, the Chancellor would reduce taxes or allow government spending to rise. More goods would be bought, and jobs would be created. But once a boom got out of hand the Chancellor would restrict business activity by raising taxes and taking a tougher line on government spending. The government thus sought to influence businessmen and consumers through their pockets, while leaving them to make their own decisions as to the way they should spend their money. Electoral advantage is to be won if a boom is coming along nicely in the crucial pre-election year, but in order that this should be so, recovery from the previous downturn in the economy might have to be held back. The brakes which the government had then applied might have to be kept on longer than was strictly necessary, or the boom might inconveniently come in the middle of the government's term of office. This puts the situation very crudely, for questions of timing are matters of judgement rather than objective fact, and it would be wrong to suggest a political conspiracy. As it happened, in 1955 the boom had come to a head 18 months before the next general election was ultimately due, and there was therefore the danger that, with the boom then collapsing, the government would be at an electoral disadvantage. However, the retirement of Winston Churchill on health grounds in April 1955 provided the opportunity for an election in May, around the very peak of the boom. The April budget, instead of applying the brakes as circumstances demanded, gave the accelerator a further push – by making cuts in purchase tax and reducing the rate of income tax by 6d. In the following month the Conservatives won the general election comfortably, and so the 'election budget' was added to the opinion poll as a weapon for electoral success. As Anthony Sampson puts it, the ruling party 'could both stoke up the fire, and measure the heat'.

The budget of April 1955 helped to push the country into that 'Stop-Go' economic management which was to bedevil the country into the next decade. The accelerator that was pushed in April led to a slamming on of the brakes in October, when an emergency budget had to be introduced because of the worsening economic situation. Purchase tax was raised again, higher postal charges were imposed, housing subsidies and government spending were cut. The crisis continued, and in February 1956 Bank Rate was raised to $5\frac{1}{2}$ per cent, and the restrictions were extended still further. A more severe budget in April 1955 would have eased the inflationary strain during that year, and would probably have made it possible to maintain the stability of prices and to continue the growth rates that had been achieved in 1953 and 1954. As it was, 'Stop-Go' gained momentum and the vicious circle made steady progress impossible.

In 1959, when the Conservatives won their third general election in a row, it began to look as though the two-party system had ceased to operate and that the Labour Party was doomed to perpetual opposition. One explanation that was offered was the so-called 'embourgeoisment thesis' which suggested that manual workers increasingly took on middle-class life-styles and values, which were reflected in more conservative and individualistic political views. A number of reasons were put forward to explain why this should be so, including the higher wages received by many workers; advances in technology which removed much physical exertion from work and made more people technicians controlling processes; and the movement of many workers from working-class communities to suburbs where there was less emphasis on social solidarity. However, several studies showed that the situation was more complicated than a simple expansion of the middle class at the expense of the working class. Most notable was a study of Luton car workers by J. H. Goldthorpe and a team of Cambridge sociologists, published in 1968 as *The Affluent Worker*. They showed that employees of all classes were becoming increasingly *instrumental* in their attitude to work, and that affluent workers were becoming more *privatized*. In other words, not only work, but also trade unions and politics were seen merely as means to an end (instrumentalism), as more and more workers sought the good life among their family and their friends (privatization). But workers did not become 'middle class', for the conditions of their lives were still significantly different from those of white-collar workers. As the sociologist A. H. Halsey puts it: 'The worker on the shop floor has little sense of being an expert; of commitment to a calling; of autonomy on the job; of obligation to produce high quality work, and he has little or no sense of identification with the organisation in which he works.' This view accords well with that of a worker at a Ford motor factory who commented:

It's got no really good points. It's just convenient. It's got no interest. You couldn't take the job home. There's nothing to take. You just forget it. I don't want promotion at all. I've not got that approach to the job. I'm like a lot of people here. They're all working here but they're just really hanging around, waiting for something to turn up . . . It's different for them in the office. They're part of Ford's. We're not, we're just working here, we're numbers.[1]

Ironically, while work provided the means to the good life, the worker could only earn those means by expending greater amounts of energy in a traditionally working-class way.

There were several consequences of the alienation of many workers from their jobs. The absence of job satisfaction and the low levels of trust and discretion which their working conditions afforded had serious implications for the long-term health of British industry, while the instrumental attitude of many workers meant that their political vote was more likely to go to the party which appeared to come up with the goods. What was occurring in the 1950s and 1960s, therefore, was not a permanent shift towards the Conservative-minded middle class, but the creation of an unstable middle ground for which the two main parties could compete (and, later, in their own countries, the Welsh and Scottish Nationalists). The party struggle was so close that at any election between 1950 and 1964 a net swing of 3 per cent from the Conservatives would have given victory to the Labour Party.

Together with the evenly matched electoral strength there was a striking measure of agreement on policy. This lead *The Economist*, in February 1954, to coin the term 'Butskellism', a conflation of the names of the Conservative and Labour Chancellors of the Exchequer, R. A. Butler and Hugh Gaitskell. From 1951 onwards there was no major issue which produced a fundamental cleavage between the official policy of the Conservatives and that of the Labour Party. Disagreement was much stronger *within* the Labour Party – over such questions as Clause IV of the party's constitution, which related to nationalisation – than it was between the leaders of the Labour Party and their political opponents. To achieve electoral success the parties had to secure the support of the 'floating' voters, who showed repeatedly that they were unable to distinguish between lasting prosperity and the ephemeral kind that was temporarily created for political purposes. Thus, the politics of consensus has been said to go hand in hand with the politics of bribery. To quote Pinto-Duschinsky again:

> The generation which came to maturity in the 1950s had been born in the Great War, schooled during the slump, conscripted in the Second World War and rationed for years afterwards. It had no inclination to forgo the security and comforts now within its grasp in the hope of long-term economic growth. The nation demanded the priority to consumption which the politicians willingly offered. Even during the final defection from the Conservatives, the electorate did not reject the pursuit of short-run materialist objectives, but only the Government's inability to achieve them to the extent it demanded.[2]

To satisfy the consumer meant that the government was nearly always prepared to expand demand more rapidly than was desirable, until brakes had to be applied as the country ran into balance of payments difficulties. This alternation of expansion and restriction ('Stop-Go'), while representing an attempt to manage the economy, was a negation of long-term economic planning. It involved a 'fine tuning' of demand which proved impossible in practice, in spite of (or because of) the increasing mass of economic data at the government's disposal. B. W. E. Alford makes the point that

> political argument, policy-making and economic analysis were suffused with an increasing flow of statistical data which in range and scale was quite unlike anything which had been experienced before: to such a degree that by [the early 1970s] the rate at which data were being generated exceeded, probably by a wide margin, the capacity to apply them in practical economic action. . . . But almost certainly the biggest problem is reliability. Close examination of even the main data series which form the canon of economic management soon reveals that they are subject to significant margins of error. In theoretical terms there are acutely difficult (and often insoluble) index number problems. In practical terms there is the age-old problem of accurate recording.[3]

Two sets of instruments for economic management were available to the government – fiscal and monetary. However, in the period down to 1970 the former were paramount. Anti-cyclical policy relied mainly on indirect taxation, the principal direct tax used being company taxation. By varying the allowances which might be set against liability for company taxation, the government could, in theory, stimulate or damp down re-equipment, and thus influence the total level of productive investment. According to the state of the business cycle, company taxation was varied six times between 1950 and 1960. It became clear, however, that this policy had two drawbacks. Repeated changes in tax relief introduced an undesirable element of uncertainty into business decisions, and many entrepreneurs no doubt felt too insecure, in such circumstances, to execute those plans for modernisation and technical adaptation that were so necessary. With this in mind, in 1961 the government announced that it would no longer use company taxation for purely anti-cyclical purposes. Such a tool was less effective than it might have been because it takes time to change investment plans, and so alterations to company taxation did not have that immediate bite which successful management of the business cycle makes essential. The same is true of changes in indirect taxation such as purchase tax and excise duties, which were altered nine times between 1951 and 1961. Because such changes could effectively be made only in the annual budget (or in an extraordinary autumn budget) the Chancellor had to estimate the appropriate levels well in advance, and these estimates frequently exceeded what was necessary to make the desired adjustment to spending and investment. Far from exercising a stabilising influence, therefore, fiscal policy could itself become an instrument of instability. This was the same with variations in public expenditure. As this spending (including that of the nationalised industries and local authorities) constituted 40 per cent of the total investment expenditure of the country, it provided a powerful lever. But again, there were delays involved which militated against changes in the level of public expenditure as a means of stabilising demand.

Not until 1961 did the government seek powers to change indirect taxation between budgets by regulation rather than by the usual processes of legislation. In that year the Chancellor acquired the power to vary indirect taxes on a range of consumer goods by 10 per cent between budgets. A second 'regulator' was the power to vary National Insurance contributions, but this was not used down to 1970.

Monetary measures, such as the control of interest rates and restrictions on credit, were an ancillary instrument of anti-cyclical policy, although they received renewed interest after 1951, when the Bank Rate was raised to $2\frac{1}{2}$ per cent from the 2 per cent at which it had remained since 1932. There was something appealing to a Conservative government in monetary policies, for they seemed to accord more with the ideals of the free market economy than did fiscal measures of direct controls. However, the Report of the Radcliffe Committee on the Working of the Monetary System showed in 1959 that the effect of credit restrictions on the actual level of demand, in either the field of investment or consumption, was uncertain. The Committee observed that the restriction of bank credit fell 'not on projects already in train, but on capital projects in their earliest planning stages, implying an effect on spending not immediate but many months later'.

One instrument of credit control which was found to be effective was the regulation of hire-purchase conditions so as to influence the volume of household expenditure. Between 1952 and 1960, hire-purchase regulations were changed 11 times, either in the minimum initial deposit required or by limiting the maximum period of repayment, or both. This method found favour with successive Chancellors as it could be applied quickly and was quick acting. However, because the amount of goods affected was small in comparison with total consumer buying, fluctuations in the demand for hire-purchase goods had to be made large, and this caused serious dislocation to the industries involved. Furthermore, people do not always behave as economic theory might infer, as Anthony Sampson suggests:

The techniques for controlling the spending of money are still, and must always be, a matter of perpetual controversy. The economy is often regarded by chancellors and bankers in homely, mechanical terms, in the language of accelerators and brakes, a touch of the tiller, stop and go, stoking up booms and damping them down, overheating or going off the boil. But the consumers and companies do not react in such straightforward ways; and the bankers' calculations are often defeated by the refusal of housewives and managing directors to react as they are expected to – to stop when they are told to go, or to have an orgy of spending (as happened in the consumers' revolt of 1968) when they are supposed to be tightening their belts or pulling in the reins.[4]

By 1961 the Conservatives had begun to shift their attention to economic planning on a broader scale. The economic crisis of July of that year led to the introduction of a 'pay pause' and to the setting up of the National Economic Development Corporation ('Neddy'). The pay pause, like Stafford Cripp's wage restraint in 1948–50, showed that the movement of money incomes could be held up for short periods. However, the injustice and inefficiency of inflation may actually be increased, for those in under-unionised occupations who tend to lag behind in the wages race are also the most vulnerable to income restraints and 'guidelines'. The pay pause of 1961 won no support from the TUC, which complained of a lack of consultation, and it foundered before the end of the year in a pay award in the electrical supply industry. The next attempt to introduce an incomes policy was not made until 1965 when Harold Wilson tried to secure one.

The National Economic Development Council (NEDC) had two tasks. The first was to provide a forum where businessmen, union leaders and the government could meet to discuss problems of modernisation and growth. The second was to provide a centre outside the Treasury – and modelled on French experience – to work out medium-term projections and to give advice on growth problems. During 1962 the NEDC came out strongly for a 4 per cent growth rate, based on over-optimistic estimates and projections. This growth rate took on the nature of a target and was formally approved as such by the NEDC in February 1963, almost half-way through the period to which it referred! The Conservatives were voted out of office before the failure of this 'planning' experiment became apparent, but the NEDC remained, and was supplemented by the Labour Government with a number of 'Little Neddies' – Economic Development Commissions for individual industries. By the end of 1964 there were nine of them, covering just over one-quarter of the working population. They produced some interesting reports on their industries and may well have had some beneficial effect on firms' policies.

Harold Wilson, Prime Minister in the Labour government returned in 1964, projected the image of the 'professional' in economic affairs, and had indeed started his career as a lecturer in Economics at the University of Oxford. His opposite number in the Conservative Party, Sir Alec Douglas-Home, appeared an amateur by comparison. Wilson declared: 'We are redefining and we are restating our socialism in terms of the scientific revolution . . . the Britain that is going to be forged in the white heat of this revolution will be no place for restrictive practices or outdated methods on either side of industry.' The 'white-hot' revolution in fact turned out to be rather tepid. Nevertheless, the Labour government did take speedy action. In 1964 a new Ministry of Technology was set up, together with a Department of Economic Affairs headed by George Brown. At first, he seemed to have some success, for he secured the consent of the unions to voluntary wage restraint, and he announced the first National Plan, a thick volume of some 500 pages, which was published in September 1965. The target of the National Plan was a 25 per cent increase in total national output between 1964 and 1970, involving an average annual increase of 3.8 per cent. However, the basic figures were 'political' rather than economic, in the sense that they represented what the government hoped would happen, and its desire that, through projections of this kind, firms would be inspired to take appropriate action. In fact, earlier deflationary moves by the government made the plan obsolete even before it was published, and it was soon abandoned and forgotten. There was meant to be 'creative tension' between the Department of Economic Affairs and the Treasury but, as Martin Ceadel puts it, the relationship was 'more tense than creative'. The Department of Economic Affairs was finally disbanded in 1969 and reabsorbed into the Treasury.

In February 1965 a Prices and Incomes Board was set up, but it lacked teeth and produced disappointing results. The setting up of the Industrial Reorganisation Corporation in January 1966 marked a further change of direction. The prevailing philosophy in the first 20 years after the war was hostile to monopoly in any shape other than nationalisation. A Monopolies Commission was set up in 1948, and the abuses which it publicised led to the Restrictive Practices Act of 1956 which provided for the registration of all restrictive agreements and their scrutiny by a new Restrictive Practices Court which could, if it so judged, declare any of them to be contrary to the public interest. By 1963, 2,430 restrictive agreements were voluntarily registered, and about 100 more came to light in various ways. The Registrar laid about 100 agreements before the Court, with the result that many of them were abandoned before their hearing was completed, while only a few which were judicially reviewed were found to be acceptable. As a result of these early unfavourable judgments over 1,500 agreements were abandoned or altered, while an unknown number were given up by the parties concerned in preference to registration. For two reasons, however, the legislation was less effective than at first it might appear. First, unwritten agreements often proved as effective as formal ones; and second, the government acted inconsistently, for while it hounded out some monopolies it encouraged others.

With the creation of the Industrial Reorganisation Corporation, the government set out to promote amalgamations intended to improve industrial efficiency. The change of policy brought about a large-scale amalgamation movement, and for a number of years industrial concentration increased rapidly, and was evident in many fields. In retail trading, multiple stores increased their share of trade from 22 per cent in 1950 to 35 per cent in 1966, while those very large concerns with more than 100 establishments (excluding cooperatives) increased theirs from 12.9 per cent in 1950 to 19.2 per cent in 1961. There were important mergers among insurance companies and in banking, and numerous amalgamations between manufacturing giants, for example the takeover of AEI by GEC in the electrical engineering field. It was calculated that by 1970 the 100 largest firms held around 40 per cent of the assets of British industry compared with under 20 per cent before the First World War. The government was therefore urged to acquire ownership of some of these large firms and to induce others to enter into planning agreements. At the same time the government found itself running several large firms (such as British Leyland) because of the financial difficulties they encountered. This was not unlike the situation in the 1930s when the Bank of England almost by accident had acquired a large stake in the British steel industry. It was, however, a trend which the Conservatives opposed; and the Industrial Reorganisation Commission was abolished soon after they returned to power in 1970.

The Conservatives opposed another Labour innovation – the selective employment tax, which was imposed in 1965. The tax was seen by the Labour government as a valuable source of revenue, but its main aim was to squeeze labour out of the services sector and into manufacturing industry. It is questionable whether much labour was shifted in this way and, in retrospect, the continuing poor performance of British manufacturing industry suggests that labour shortage was not the main impediment to greater growth and improved export performance.

Eyes frequently turned to Europe where many countries enjoyed faster growth rates than did Britain, and from 1957 – when the European Economic Community (EEC; now the European Union) was established – Britain's relationship with it was an issue which could not be ignored. The liberalisation of trade in the 1950s and the establishment of the EEC involved a progressive opening up of the markets of the member countries to one another, which brought about an enormous expansion in trade, particularly of manufactures. This, in turn, provided greater opportunities for specialisation within particular industries and corresponding gains in productivity. Britain was meanwhile supplying markets outside Europe – largely in the Commonwealth and Sterling Area – that were less dynamic and less inclined than before the war to offer preferential advantages to British suppliers. These markets were less buoyant than those of the EEC, and British exporters supplied a diminishing share of them. Exporters were therefore obliged to establish themselves in European markets which they had previously neglected. The result was that western Europe, which bought only half as much from Britain as the countries of the Sterling Area in the early 1950s, was buying as much by 1965, and a good deal more by 1970.

However, entry into the EEC entailed political arguments as well as finely balanced economic judgements which, combined with an ambivalent attitude towards its 'European-ness' which stretches back centuries, meant that more than 15 years passed before Britain finally became a member. Britain's attitude to Europe at the end of the Second World War was haughty, and reflected feelings that were themselves a compound of sentimental attachment to the Commonwealth and a desire to foster the 'special relationship' which it was thought existed with the United States. The Labour government was also determined to rid Britain of unemployment and poverty, and feared that any sacrifice of British sovereignty might damage that objective.

In March 1948 Britain, France and the Benelux countries signed the Brussels Treaty which united them for purposes of 'collaboration in economic, social and cultural matters, and for collective self defence', but Britain opposed French plans to create an all-European assembly and to set up a customs and economic union. A Council of Europe was formed by 10 countries in May 1949, but the British saw to it that it had no real powers. They were also able to ensure that the Organisation for European Economic Co-operation was set up in April 1948 in accordance with their own wishes and to the frustration of French supranational plans. By 1950 some of the Continental enthusiasts for European cooperation were becoming wary of the obstructive tactics of the offshore islanders and were ready to go it alone. In April 1951, therefore, France, West Germany, Italy, Belgium, the Netherlands and Luxembourg ('the Six') set up the European Coal and Steel Community. From such beginnings sprang the European Economic Community, created by the Treaty of Rome in March 1957. Under the terms of the treaty, the Six were to be transformed into a 'Common Market' over a period of 12–15 years. Some countries – including Britain, which hovered on the sidelines – wished the EEC to move faster towards free trade. The French, particularly under de Gaulle, tended to regard the period as too short, and in November 1958 they brought the free-trade area talks to an end. Britain's next step was to go ahead with the formation of the European Free Trade Association (EFTA), without the supranational political overtones of the EEC. In this it was joined by Austria, Denmark, Norway, Portugal, Sweden and Switzerland to make up 'the Seven', and EFTA came into being between December 1958 and January 1960. Europe was now truly at sixes and sevens. Britain received only minimal advantages from EFTA, for few tariff barriers in fact existed between it and its new partners. It intended it to be a bargaining counter in its negotiations with the EEC; but this plan misfired, for it merely seemed to confirm French suspicions than Britain's interests in Europe were narrowly commercial.

For reasons chiefly related to its agriculture and to its relationship with the Commonwealth, Britain made no further approaches to the EEC until July 1961, when the idea of entry was taken up by Harold Macmillan. He believed that the EEC had been a powerful stimulus to European economic growth since the war, and that Britain's entry would give its economy a much needed fillip. Sir Frank Lee, Permanent Secretary to the Treasury, was insistent on this point, arguing that British industrialists had for too long been feather-bedded by Commonwealth and Sterling Area markets. Entry into the EEC would give Britain entry into a rapidly developing market of 170 million people, although in order to take advantage of it, the country would have to make a great effort in the fields of new technology.

The Labour Party was split. Its leader, Hugh Gaitskell, argued that the economic arguments were nicely balanced, but that the terms of entry which Britain was likely to get would probably not be good enough to warrant joining. Within the Labour Party strong support for entry was given by George Brown and Roy Jenkins, the latter holding the view that the Commonwealth would, in the long run, benefit from Britain's entry:

> If by 1970 we are still a sluggish, crisis-ridden nation unable to provide substantial resources for development capital to the Commonwealth, whatever sentimental arguments the Commonwealth may produce during the months of negotiations, they will turn their backs on us far more than if they find that by being in Europe we are economically prosperous and dynamic and able to offer them the economic leadership which to some extent they need.[5]

Similar arguments were put forward by Macmillan and some of his colleagues with regard to relations with the United States. Only within the EEC would Britain be likely to maintain its influence on Washington, while the Americans might feel that with Britain a member, the EEC would become more outward-looking.

The Liberals approved of the EEC in general principle but, like the Labour Party, were concerned that the terms should not be to the country's disadvantage. The TUC sat on the fence. The National Farmers' Union was implacably opposed to entry. Most other influential groups were in favour and, if opinion polls are to be relied upon, by September 1962 those in favour of entry outnumbered opponents by some 50 per cent (although 'don't knows' constituted nearly a quarter of the respondents).

Britain's negotiator in Brussels, Edward Heath, was meanwhile having a difficult time. The feeling grew in Britain that, whatever the merits of the case, the Six were insisting on very hard terms. The feeling among the Six – prompted largely by de Gaulle – was that the many reservations which the British held on behalf of their agriculture and of the Commonwealth showed that it was insufficiently European. In January 1963 de Gaulle persuaded the Six to break off negotiations. There were many in Britain who breathed a sigh of relief. The issues were complex and the majority of people wavered between feelings of menace and vague feelings of hope which the EEC stirred up. The issue was not a major one in either the 1964 or the 1966 elections.

A levelling off of British exports to the EEC in the mid-1960s strengthened the case for entry, for the European market was still growing rapidly while Britain was not sharing proportionately in the expansion. This was partly because of deficiencies in its industries, but also partly due to its non-membership of the Community. Entry to the EEC would not of itself cure Britain's economic ills, but without entry the problems of revitalisation would prove as great if not greater. As the efficiency of the industries of EEC countries increased, they were more and more able to compete against British industry elsewhere. Studies of the economic consequences of entry continued, leading to the assertion that food prices in Britain would rise 10–14 per cent. The Common Agricultural Policy of the EEC was designed to benefit food exporting countries such as France. Britain, if admitted, might find itself shouldered with an extra balance of payments burden of some £200 million. Fears of higher food prices and uneasy feelings about 'rule by foreigners' made public opinion waver. However, the House of Commons gave the government overwhelming support for a fresh application in May 1967.

The Benelux states and Italy were strongly in favour of British entry; West Germany was equivocal; but still France proved unsympathetic. De Gaulle continued to profess that Britain was an Atlantic power rather than a European one, and he made discouraging remarks about Britain's need to achieve a 'profound economic and political transformation'. Entry was clearly going to be difficult for Britain in 1967. As it happened, de Gaulle interposed a second veto on 27 November.

Subsequent events moved in Britain's favour. De Gaulle was weakened by the French strikes and riots of 1968, and the increased vulnerability of the franc. Defeated in a referendum in April 1969, he resigned. In September, Willy Brandt became Chancellor of West Germany. He was sympathetic to Britain, and had the self-confidence (and national confidence) to stand up to the French. Britain's general election of 1970 resulted in a Conservative victory, and Edward Heath, an ardent Europeanist, became Prime Minister. By 1971 terms for Britain's entry had been hammered out; the formal treaty of accession was signed in January 1972; and a year later Britain entered the EEC. Any hopes that this alone would solve its economic problems were soon dispelled, and Britain's membership continued to be politically controversial, as will be seen in Chapter 15.

The permissive society

The affluent society was a consumers' society, and 1957 saw the birth of the Consumers' Association and its magazine, *Which?*. Within six months it had acquired 50,000 members, all dedicated to getting the best value from their steadily depreciating money. The Consumers' Association highlights the political power of those who sought material ends. It also highlights their intention not to be bamboozled by advertisers. Vast sums were beginning to be spent on advertising, for which a new medium became available with the introduction of commercial television in 1954 (in effect, a form of denationalisation, in that it broke the monopoly of the BBC). The 1960s marked the 'great detergent war' between Omo and Daz, the products respectively of the giant corporations Unilever and Procter & Gamble; by the middle of the decade detergent manufacturers were spending £18 million a year on advertising and promotion. Consumers had to get used to a new

The mini-skirt was launched by the French couturier, Courrèges, and made popular in Britain by such designers as Mary Quant. To many moral watchdogs it became a symbol of 1960s permissiveness. As skirts and dresses became shorter, the exciseman was faced with a problem. Previously length alone had determined the difference between women's clothing (liable to a 10 per cent purchase tax) and girls' clothing (which was tax-free). To solve the dilemma, from November 1965 bust size was included in the definition – anything from 32" being classed as women's clothing, and liable to tax.

vocabulary in which 'Giant' meant large and 'Large' meant medium, 'De Luxe' meant standard, and 'Standard' often meant basic beyond belief.

New devices were developed to hide from the consumer the impact of price rises, of which the principal one was trading stamps. Given in proportion to the amount of money spent, they were generally to the value of 6d in the pound, and could be exchanged for goods provided by the stamp company. Many people were attracted by the something-for-nothing principle which the stamps seemed to embody; many others preferred the price-cutting of stores which offered 'value for money'. In 1964 the Trading Stamps Act was passed, with the intention of regulating their use – laying down, for example, that stamps should be printed with a value expressed in coin of the realm and that they should, if desired by the receiver, be redeemable in cash. Stamps then found their own level, many shops discontinued them, and eventually they faded from the retail scene. It was also in 1964 that legislation brought resale price maintenance in line with other restrictive practices, thus further encouraging competition among retailers.

The 1950s saw the emergence of a newly identified group of consumers – the young. Teenagers became an identifiable group for the first time, and acquired a high status in society, judging from the attempts to appeal to them. A character in Colin MacInnes's novel, *Absolute Beginners* (1959), says of his elder brother, Vernon: 'He's one of the generations that grew up before teenagers existed . . . in poor Vernon's era . . . there just weren't any: can you believe it? . . . In those days, it seems, you were just an overgrown boy, or an undergrown man, life didn't seem to cater for anything else in between.' A number of factors accounted for the change. With the expansion of welfare services and with better housing and better feeding, children matured sexually at an earlier age (perhaps four to five years earlier than a century previously). However, a number of other trends – such as the raising of the school-leaving age and the greater proportion of children staying on at school – meant that more and more of these physically adult young people were remaining dependent on their parents, and were legally and politically under age. Not until 1970 was the age of majority reduced from 21 to 18. A second trend was demographic, namely a 20 per cent increase in the number of unmarried people aged 15–24, the legacy of the post-war baby boom. The third factor was the increasing spending power of the young, which marked them out as an identifiable market. By 1957 working boys under 21 were averaging £5 11s 0d a week and girls £4 3s 11d, and as the cash was largely free of tax and subject only to the often nominal contribution to household expenses, it was available for spending. The hourly pay-rates for juveniles, starting from a base in 1947, had outpaced adult women by 13 points and adult men by a clear 20 points, thus establishing that trend towards shrinking age-differentials that has continued to this day.

In 1959 teenagers had £830 million to spend, of which the largest proportion went on records. Their spending controlled over 40 per cent of the record market which began to undergo great changes. Whereas the old-style popular music spread over all ages and all strata of society, the new music had a special appeal for teenagers who developed a taste of their own. Old-style pop music projected an image of affluent sophistication – what has been described as 'the great white myth of style', where 'men in white dinner jackets sang to ladies in evening gowns on romantically lit terraces or the first-class decks of ocean liners'. New-style pop music was very different. In 1956 Bill Haley's film, *Rock Around the Clock*, hit Britain. Many towns banned it, and clergymen thundered from the pulpit that rock'n'roll was the devil's music (much as their predecessors in the 1920s raged against jazz). In such ways the 'generation gap' was born. Part of the attraction of rock'n'roll to young people, and of the antipathy to it of their elders, was its 'Americanness.' Aspects of American culture had been imported since the minstrel shows of the nineteenth century, but the post-war invasion seemed to many defenders of British (or, more precisely, 'English') culture, to be more insidious. To the young, however, the United States spoke of the exciting and the new. Blue jeans (made of the denim material that had long provided the working clothes of the American farmer and the English worker) now became an essential part of anti-establishment uniform.

There was a home-grown sartorial rebellion. Public alarm had already been raised by the appearance of the 'Teddy Boys' who arrived on the scene round about 1953 (the name first appeared in print in March 1954). The Edwardian style of clothing which was affected in exaggerated form had been worn for a short period after the war by many of the more dashing members of the middle and upper classes. When it spread to the working class, and they made their own additions (thick crepe-soled shoes and bootlace ties), the middle class were obliged to give it up. As one guards officer was heard to moan over a champagne cocktail: 'It means that absolutely the whole of one's wardrobe *immediately* becomes *unwearable*.' The Teddy Boys were among the first of the identifiable youth factions, to be followed in the 1960s by the 'Mods', whose taste ran to all things Italian. The Mods and 'Rockers' (successors of the Teddy Boys) were involved in a number of disturbances in seaside towns in 1964, which caused further alarm to the middle-aged and elderly.

The phenomenon of the Teddy Boys was a form of social protest, albeit a confused and imprecise one. Another more articulate protest was raised by the 'Angry Young Men'. John Osborne's play, *Look Back in Anger* (1956), was described by the *Annual Register* as 'the first play since the war to put the point of view of the younger generation at odds with its world'. That generation – young men of 25–30 – included also Kingsley Amis (*Lucky Jim*), John Wain (*Hurry on Down*) and John Braine (*Room at the Top*). They were mostly left-wingers, disappointed by the dullness and smugness engendered by the marriage of the affluent society and the welfare state. As the critic, Kenneth Tynan (himself an 'Angry Young Man') wrote, they were people whose childhood and adolescence had been scarred by economic crisis and war, who had grown up under a socialist government only to find that the class system remained intact. Although the movement started before Suez, that crisis confirmed for some the fallibility of British leadership and the limitations of British power in the world, fuelling their sense of frustration.

A third protest movement, which not only contained within its ranks teenagers and angry young men and women, but also the middle-aged and the middle class, was the Campaign for Nuclear Disarmament (CND), which flourished between 1958 and 1962. Unlike the movements mentioned above, CND was deliberate, organised and politically orientated, having as its object the unilateral renunciation by Britain of nuclear arms (it began testing the H Bomb after 1955). The 1960 demonstration was the largest to be held in Trafalgar Square since VE night, and at the London finale of the Aldermaston March in the following year 100,000 people were present. Opinion polls showed that CND had the support of between one-quarter and one-third of the British people. A. J. P. Taylor said at the time that CND appeared to be a 'movement of eggheads for eggheads', but in fact it appealed to many ordinary people, including housewives. The participation which it invited presaged much of the middle-class activism of the 1960s, when the apathy of British political life was shattered by many groups taking a firm and personal stand on such issues as motorway schemes, the siting of new airports and the invasion of suburban and village streets by heavy goods vehicles. That political activism continued through the 1970s and welled up again, with greater strength, in the 1980s and early 1990s.

The Campaign for Nuclear Disarmament was a great moral crusade in the tradition of nineteenth-century radicalism, and it sprang up at a time when moral codes were in a great state of flux, and the Victorian moral certainties were being weakened. There was a noticeable increase in crime. Between 1958 and 1962 the total number of indictable offences recorded by the police in England and Wales increased by 43 per cent, and in both 1963 and 1964 there was a 9 per cent increase over the previous year. In 1964 well over 1 million indictable offences were recorded by the police in England and Wales; and in Scotland, where the trend was similar, the number was 352,000. While an increase in criminality was a feature of the population as a whole, it was most apparent in the 17–21, 14–17 and even the 8–14 age groups. The increasing use of firearms in the committing of crimes led to stiffer penalties being imposed by the Firearms Act of 1965, while the general election of the following year was the first in which 'law and order' was a major campaign issue. As early as 1960 the Committee on Children and Young Persons had concluded that the upsurge in crime, which had at first been popularly attributed to the Second World War, was related to the whole course of material change and cultural evolution in the twentieth century. It observed:

> During the past fifty years there has been a tremendous material, social and moral revolution in addition to the upheaval of two wars. While life has in many ways become easier and more secure, the whole future of mankind may seem frighteningly uncertain. Everyday life may be less of a struggle, boredom and lack of challenge more of a danger, but the fundamental insecurity remains with little that the individual can do about it. The material revolution is plain to see. At one and the same time it has provided more desirable objects, greater opportunity for acquiring them illegally, and considerable chances of immunity from the undesirable consequences of so doing. It is not always so clearly recognised what a complete change there has been in social and personal relationships (between classes, between the sexes and between individuals) and also in the basic assumptions which regulate behaviour.[6]

The affluent society bred acquisitiveness. One of the principal credit cards was advertised with the slogan that it 'Takes the Waiting out of Wanting'. The same could be said of breaking and entering and larceny which were the most widespread crimes.

Moral codes became more personal, a fact which was recognised in the 1960s when many laws affecting personal behaviour were amended or abolished. One of the first public signs of a relaxation in the Victorian moral code was the acquittal of Penguin Books in 1959 in an obscenity trial arising from the publication of D. H. Lawrence's sexually explicit novel, *Lady Chatterley's Lover*; although the fact that there was a trial at all is an indication of the tenaciousness of older standards of morality. The struggle between rival moral codes was further exemplified by such phenomena as the Festival of Light, and Mary Whitehouse's National Viewers' and Listeners' Association, which attempted to 'clean up TV'.

The introduction in the 1960s of oral contraception ('the Pill') undoubtedly affected sexual relations, and in 1967 the Family Planning Act empowered local authorities for the first time to provide contraceptive services. Two other important pieces of legislation were passed in that year. The Abortion Act made it easier to secure a legal abortion; and the Sexual Offences Act (which applied to England and Wales) made a homosexual act between two consenting adults in private no longer a criminal offence.

In 1968 theatre censorship ended, and although it remained for the cinema, there was a relaxation of acceptable standards, as there was also with newspapers. In 1969 the Divorce Act abolished the concept of 'the matrimonial offence', and laid down instead that 'the sole ground on which a petition for divorce may be presented to the court by either party to a marriage shall be that the marriage has broken down irretrievably'.

It is easy to exaggerate the extent of permissiveness in the 1960s. There was no concerted programme of legislation, and each reform had to be argued on its merits by pressure groups which had to secure a parliamentary majority for reform without alienating their moderate supporters. In consequence, much legislation (in comparison with other countries, for example) was limited. Gay men, for example, could only engage in sex if they were over 21, and that was not changed when the age of majority was subsequently reduced to 18. Homosexuality was also banned in the armed services. In one direction the law swung the opposite way from permissiveness, and this was in the case of drug abuse which, like crime, was on the increase. In 1964 the Drugs (Prevention of Misuse) Act was passed, outlawing the possession of certain drugs, use of which had hitherto been legal, without a prescription.

The historian, Alan Sked, calls into question the depiction of Britain as a particularly permissive society;

> After all, in comparison with other countries, she seemed more reserved than many about the sexual revolution of the 'swinging sixties'. London may have invented the mini-skirt and striptease may have been imported as a cabaret act from Paris, yet live sex shows have never been allowed as happened in France or Scandinavia; homosexual bath-houses have never been established on the model of New York, San Francisco, Paris or Amsterdam; 'singles bars' of the American type have never been introduced; and the incidence of AIDS has been noticeably lower than in the USA, France or Germany. *No Sex Please, We're British* is, after all, still very much a box-office hit in London's West End.[7]

It is also possible to exaggerate the decline in influence of the Church. By the 1960s, the proportion of the population who were communicant members of churches was almost exactly the same as it had been at the end of the eighteenth century, namely, about 15 per cent; and the evidence of opinion polls suggested that some 90 per cent of the population still claimed a religious affiliation, even though church attendance had fallen since its nineteenth-century heights.

A disturbing feature of the 1950s and 1960s was an increase in racial tension. In 1931 the black population of Great Britain had been 100,000. By 1951 the number was 200,000. In 1958 there were race riots in Nottingham and in the Notting Hill district of London, and the government moved towards control. In anticipation of legislation, there was a dramatic rise in immigration in 1961, when 113,000 arrived from the West Indies and the Indian sub-continent. In 1962 the Commonwealth Immigration Act became law, and introduced a quota system for ordinary immigrants, with vouchers for those with special skills or actual jobs. Although polls showed that the measure had strong popular support there was bitter fighting in the House of Commons over the bill, Hugh Gaitskell being one of the most fierce opponents. However, when Labour returned to power, it abandoned its principled stand against restriction, the shock defeat of Patrick Gordon-Walker at Smethwick in the 1964 general election having shown the strength of public opinion on the immigration issue. 'Ever since the Smethwick election it has been quite clear that immigration can be the greatest political vote loser for the Labour Party if one seems to be permitting a flood of immigrants in and blight the central areas of our cities,' confided the Labour politician, Richard Crossman, in his *Diaries*, and on the same day he described immigration as 'the hottest potato in politics'.[8]

In February 1965 the Wilson government tightened the restrictions against un-skilled workers, but an attempt was made to balance the restraints with more positive moves against discrimination, and a rather weak Race Relations Bill was published in April. It set out to prohibit racial discrimination in public places, and introduced penalties against incitement to racial hatred. In 1966 a Race Relations Board was set up, but the tensions continued. Part of the trouble was the high concentration of immigrants in particular areas. In 1961 one-third were concentrated in London, with high proportions in Lambeth, Paddington and Kensington. A further 7 per cent were in Birmingham. Racial hatred was whipped up by the National Front, formed in 1966. Although it remained a minority party it was very strong in some constituencies. In April 1968, while a stronger Race Relations Bill was going through Parliament, Enoch Powell, a Conservative shadow minister, delivered the notorious speech in which he said that, 'Like the Romans I seem to see the River Tiber flowing with much blood'. A Gallup Poll showed 75 per cent of the population broadly sympathetic to Powell's views on restriction and repatriation, but he was instantly dismissed by Edward Heath from the Shadow Cabinet. The Race Relations Act was passed, and discrimination in employment and housing was banned. Much prejudice remained, however, and immigration was further restricted when the legislation was codified in the 1971 Immigration Act. It was apparent that Britain was making only slow progress towards becoming a multi-cultural society.

Economic growth

'The English disease,' Correlli Barnett argued in 1975, 'is not the novelty of the past ten or even twenty years . . . but a phenomenon dating back more than a century.' The problem, symptomised by a poor economic performance in comparison with its competitors, was clearly rooted deep in the nation's past, and had social and psychological causes as well as economic ones. The retardation of the British economy at the end of the nineteenth century was examined in Chapter 11, where it was pointed out that it was relative performance which was then the cause of concern, for the economy continued to grow in absolute terms. The same is true of the period after the Second World War. Over the 25 years from 1948 to 1973, growth was faster than at any previous period of equal length in British history. The gross domestic product doubled in real terms, and the average annual rate of increase was 2.8 per cent. This compares with a growth rate of 2 per cent in the 40 years before the First World War and a slightly higher rate between 1923 and 1937. However, while the British growth rate hovered around 2.5 to 3 per cent, that of the EEC countries was generally between 5 and 6 per cent, i.e. about twice as high. The significance of this difference has to be emphasised. A margin of, let us say, 0.5 per cent per annum takes some time to add up to a significant difference; but when there is a margin of 3 per cent per annum between two countries which have a level start, the fast-growing country will have twice the output of the slower within 25 years. Such differences may or may not represent differences in efficiency. If faster growth merely reflects a more rapidly rising working population and a cor-respondingly higher input of resources, this does not represent greater efficiency, nor will the growth be translated into higher living standards. However, the facts are that employment in Britain rose at roughly the same rate as in the EEC, so that the differences remain even if comparison is made in terms of output per head. The lag in production represented a lag in productivity, and was reflected in standards of living. In 1950 the standard of living had been higher in the United Kingdom than in any EEC country with the exception of Belgium. It was twice as high as in Italy and 50 per cent higher than in West Germany. By the early 1970s it had become lower than all EEC countries except Italy – with which, according to one calculation, it was roughly equal. Output per head in some major branches of manufacturing was 50 per cent higher on the Continent than in Britain. The manufacturing sector of the British economy was shrinking, and the poor performance of British industry has to be set alongside the relatively good performance of the services sector. The British purchased more foreign cars, refrigerators and transistor radios; foreigners came to Britain to insure their ships, learn how to farm, or to buy clothes at Marks and Spencer. In the 10 years after 1965 employment in manufacturing fell by 12 per cent.

Britain's low productivity was reflected in a failure to maintain its share of the world's export markets, despite the great efforts which were made in the early post-war period. From 21.3 per cent in 1937, Britain's share of the world's manufactured exports rose to 25.4 per cent in 1950, but then fell to 16.2 per cent in 1961 and 12.9 per cent in 1966. Britain's advantageous position in 1950 resulted from the temporary advantage which it enjoyed, being better placed for recovery from the effects of war than the ravaged economies of Europe and Japan. There were dangers in that position, however. There was a pressing demand from abroad for basic goods and equipment, while domestic consumers were desperate for anything that they could lay their hands on. The existence of these captive markets meant that emphasis was placed on short-term production, with little stress being laid on design, delivery or after-sales service. 'Unhappily,' says B. W. E. Alford, 'habits which may have had some virtue in times of relative scarcity became vices in times of relative abundance.'

It was the failure of exports to hold up which led to balance of payments crises, which the government attempted to solve by an application of the brakes. A vicious circle was set in being as Sidney Pollard describes: 'Failure in productivity led to losses in exports; these led to balance-of-payments difficulties, and these, in turn, led to Government short-term measures which were certain, in long term, to make the productivity failures worse and start the circle up again, in less favourable conditions, as soon as the restrictions were taken off.' On the other hand, competitors like West Germany (where the volume of manufactured imports rose by 233 per cent between 1953 and 1964, compared with 48 per cent in the United Kingdom) got caught up in what has been described as a 'virtuous circle'. There may have been several reasons why West Germany obtained a competitive start in the buoyant export markets of the 1950s. It did not bear the strains of rearmament which the Korean War imposed on Britain, and it may have had less of a labour problem. Whatever the cause, high export demand led to a rapid general rate of growth, which in turn led to high investment – in machinery, research, new products and overseas sales promotion. In such an atmosphere productivity grew quickly and export prices remained competitive.

Investment constituted a lower proportion of the domestic gross product in the United Kingdom than in any other country of western Europe. From 17 per cent in the early 1950s it rose to 22 per cent in the mid-1960s, and was still at that level in the early 1970s. In France and Germany investment averaged 24 per cent and 26 per cent of gross domestic product respectively in the 1960s, and it was as high as 34 per cent in Japan. If we take manufacturing investment alone, this appears to have absorbed less than 4 per cent of the gross national product of the United Kingdom in the 1960s, compared with above 5 per cent in Germany, over 6 per cent in France and about 9 per cent in Japan. Even Britain's low investment was not fully matched by improvement in output, for capital investment in manufacturing in fact grew faster than manufacturing output over the period after 1955 for which figures are available.

The low rate of investment meant that much British capital equipment became seriously outdated. It was estimated that by the end of 1961, for example, 60 per cent of the buildings and 38 per cent of plant and machinery in manufacturing and construction dated from before 1948. The outdatedness was much more serious in some industries than others. In the metal-using industries 50 per cent of all plant and machinery was built in 1947 or earlier, as was 43 per cent in paper and printing, and 39 per cent in textiles. Fourteen years may not seem long, but with the speed of twentieth-century technical progress it is an age. New investment was low for a variety of reasons, not least the repeated 'stops' decreed by the government as deflationary measures designed to correct an adverse balance of payments. High interest rates, credit restrictions and cuts in investment allowances all had an adverse effect upon investment, while the nationalised industries repeatedly had their investment programmes cut back or postponed. 'Stop-Go' inevitably affected the optimism and enterprise of businessmen, who found it difficult to plan ahead investment for a high rate of growth.

It is through investment that other factors operate upon growth, of which a principal one is technical change. Technical change has clearly dominated economic growth over the last two centuries; but how far does it explain the divergence of British and foreign rates of growth since the Second World War? The question is a difficult one to answer. The National Institute of Economic and Social Research has studied some of the major innovations of the post-war period, from float glass to jet engines, and suggests that the British record was *above* average in comparison with other countries. Britain has certainly continued to be in the forefront of scientific advance, as is evidenced by its share of Nobel prizewinners; but it could be argued that its concern has been excessively with pure science and with prestige technology, to the detriment of less conspicuous advances in technique which nevertheless form the mainstream of technological advance. Britain's high standing in pure science has clearly not been fully reflected in its post-war economic performance, and both Japan and Italy have demonstrated how much growth can be achieved despite a heavy dependence upon foreign knowledge. In 1973 Dr (later Sir) Ieuan Maddock, Chief Scientist to the Department of Technology and Industry, spoke of Japan's remarkable industrial success: 'This has been achieved by great attention to the very things we tend to overlook – detail design, quality control, technological marketing and a willingness to adapt to the customer's needs.' He thought that British engineers put too much emphasis on originality, and paid too little attention to overall costs, probable practical difficulties and commercial considerations.

The British aircraft industry is symptomatic of these attitudes. Bright ideas abounded. The first turbo-jets to go into civilian operation in the late 1940s were British, as was the first pure jet – the de Havilland Comet – which went into scheduled service in May 1952. The hovercraft, too, was a British invention. However, this undoubted aeronautical flair was not always sufficiently related to the more mundane problems of producing a finished aircraft at the right time, at the right price, and with the appropriate capabilities to attract foreign as well as British buyers. In 1957 Sir Roy Fedden, a distinguished aeronautical engineer, complained that British policy suffered from 'delusions of grandeur'. This tendency is illustrated by the experience of Rolls-Royce:

At Rolls-Royce, ever since the First World War, commercial values had not been allowed to intrude upon dedication to technical perfection. Its chairman replied to Anthony Sampson's question about profits in 1969: 'If you said we're here to make profits, we'd never be making aero engines: we'd have gone into property years ago.' In this special 'pure engineering' ethos, the disdain of the gentleman for the descent into the market place was reproduced, and obsession with production legitimized. The price was eventual bankruptcy in 1971.[9]

The Anglo–French Concorde project is another example of industry working at the frontiers of technical knowledge and ending up with a commercial failure – the aircraft having been described as 'the fastest white elephant of modern times'.

Foreign commentators frequently draw a contrast between working conditions in Britain and other countries such as Germany, Scandinavia or Japan, and they comment on class differences in British industry which, in their view, cause disharmony between employers and employed. The classic satire on this state of affairs was the 1959 Boulting Brothers' film, *I'm all right, Jack*, which depicted a pig-headed, work-shy working class and a snobbish, arrogant and corrupt upper class. Behind the caricature and the stereotypes there remained a disturbing element of truth. Britain had been only moderately strike-prone in the 1950s, but there was less room for complacency in the next decade. In 1965 the Labour government set up the Donovan Commission on Trade Unions and Employers. Its Report in 1969 stressed the growing frequency with which formal machinery was being bypassed in industrial negotiations, the loss of control by large unions over their rank and file, and the prevalence of unofficial strikes.

The greater multiplicity of unions than on the Continent gave greater scope for demarcation disputes which diverted the attention of management from more pressing matters of growth. Union rivalries remained strong, despite some important new alliances such as the Amalgamated Society of Boilermakers, Shipwrights, Blacksmiths and Structural Workers, the Engineers and Foundry Workers, and Electricians and Plumbers. The experience of countries such as Sweden (with a smaller workforce and a much shorter and simpler history of industrial relations than Britain) showed that the reorganisation of labour relations would inevitably be a lengthy process. In 1963 the economist Michael Shanks touched upon the basic insecurity of British workers:

> The chaos and defensive-mindedness which dominate British industrial relations reflect not union strength, but weakness. From this I draw two conclusions:
> 1 If we are to have a more dynamic society we must first have a more *equal* society – not in the sense of equality of income or wealth, but in the sense of an absence of class-barriers, a greater equality of educational opportunity, of status, of power: in a word, social equality.
> 2 To get this more equal society we need a stronger and more effective trade union movement, one which will give the worker confidence that his interests can be properly safeguarded in a world of change. Only in this way, I believe, can we finally lay to rest the ghost of the 'thirties. It is a remarkable and depressing fact that the experience of the mass depression of the pre-war years should have bitten so much more deeply into the working-class mind here than anywhere else. Other countries suffered more than we from the slump, but in no other major country is it so widely felt among the industrial workers that those days are bound sooner or later to return. Nowhere else are union attitudes so conditioned by the paramount need to prevent people from ever, at any time, losing their jobs – and nowhere else do they take a form more guaranteed, in the long run, to achieve just that dreaded end![10]

There is ample evidence that British industry has failed to attract top management talent as effectively as many of its competitors. Among the élite, business careers have enjoyed a very low status. A young graduate told an interviewer in the late 1950s that with regard to a job: 'My first choice was the Foreign Office, my second UNESCO, my third the BBC, my fourth *The Times*; then there was nothing left but teaching or business, and as I can't bear little boys, it had to be business.' There is nothing new in this. Michael Wiener, in *English Culture and the Decline of the Industrial Spirit, 1850–1980* cites the case of Frederick Lugard, the great colonial administrator. While at public school in 1875 he had to decide between the offer of a job in the business of his half-sister's husband, or the chance to sit for the Indian civil service examination. Lugard wrote:

> If I go in for this [the business job] I have to throw overboard the ICS which if I passed it would be an infinitely better thing besides being a thoroughly gentlemanly occupation, and look at it how I may, I can't bring myself to think that an Assistant in a Sugar Factory is such. Of course 'a gentleman is a gentleman wherever he is', but still the Lugards have been in the Army and in the Church, good servants of God or the Queen, but few if any have ever been tradesmen.

He decided to try for the Indian Civil Service, failed the examination, and went into the army instead. The different status of a civil service and a business career today is much greater than in France, for example. There, the governing élite share a similar educational background, and the French move freely between public administration and industry in a way which is quite alien to British practice.

For those who enter British management, certain backgrounds are likely to lead to speedier promotion than others. Thus, training in the law or accountancy (more gentlemanly activities) is likely to have an advantage for career advancement greater than expertise in engineering. In Britain, provision for technical education outran demand; in Japan, entrance into engineering programmes has been highly competitive, more so than for any other area except medicine. There are very few engineers and scientists in the administrative class of the British civil service, where government policy is formed. For example, of 280 recruits to that class between 1957 and 1962, only nine had a scientific background and four a mathematical one – 95 per cent of the intake, in other words, was non-scientific. In 1963 the Treasury had one scientist at its disposal, while the office of the Minister for Science also boasted only one! In industry, too, scientists and engineers were largely absent from top management. In 1959 the White Paper on Scientific and Engineering Manpower showed that in the machine-tool industry only 1.3 per cent of its employees were qualified scientists or engineers, and in shipbuilding and marine engineering the figure was as low as 0.6 per cent.

Management training lagged behind that of many overseas countries. The University of Pennsylvania introduced management as an academic study in 1881, but the establishment of university business schools in Britain had to wait until the late 1960s. In 1963 the NEDC recommended a management school in the interests of productivity, and the matter was taken up in the Robbins Report on higher education. Eventually, two postgraduate schools were established at the Universities of Manchester and London. That at London was sited in a magnificent Nash terrace house in Regent's Park. (The Administrative Staff College is at Henley – of Regatta fame – and many individual company schools are situated in country houses.)

To what extent can failure to maintain satisfactory levels of growth be blamed on government policies, or the lack of them? It has to be remembered that economic growth was only one of many ends which post-war governments had to pursue, for there was also the need to maintain full employment, to keep prices and exchange rates stable, to maintain a healthy balance of payments, and to promote the economic well-being of the regions. It was inevitable that at times these ends would clash, and Harold Macmillan (writing of his years as Prime Minister) likened economic management to the most delicate of balancing acts. Of course, politicians are reluctant to admit publicly that their policies involve the sacrifice of any significant objectives, and this may lead to evasiveness. As Sir Isaiah Berlin commented: 'The natural tendency of all but a very few thinkers [is] to believe that all the things they hold good must be intimately connected or at least compatible with one another.'

As well as having social and economic ambitions, politicians (and others) have diplomatic ones. Britain might have solved its economic problems more easily had it accepted sooner the fact that it had emerged from the war a greatly diminished power, no longer in the same rank as the Soviet Union or the United States. Its leadership of the Commonwealth did not prove an adequate counterweight. In 1962 the former US Secretary of State, Dean Acheson, declared: 'Britain has lost an empire, she has not yet found a role.' That role might have been the leadership of a new Europe, but Britain awoke late to the idea of a European Community, and did not become a member until 1973. Politicians found it hard to explain to the public Britain's economic, strategic and global position. Not only did they promise more than they could perform; the public demanded more than it was prepared to pay for.

Management of the economy since the war has been confronted with the twin devils of unemployment and inflation, and as soon as one is apparently held in check the other rears its ugly head. Immediately after the war unemployment seemed the more diabolic of the two. Attitudes were scarred by memories of the 1930s, and there was the expectation that the full employment of the war years would prove impossible to maintain. Mass Observation (a pioneer in Britain of the opinion poll) reported in 1942 that many people expected the war to be followed by a return to mass unemployment. Sir Oliver Franks, at that time Provost of Queen's College, Oxford, described in 1947 the forebodings of that time:

> The citizens and governments of most nation states fear the occurrence of large-scale unemployment more than any other disaster that can happen in peace. No government of the future can hope to stay for long in power if it lets large-scale unemployment destroy the physical and spiritual conditions of life among the people. The great depression of 1929–35 made in many ways a deeper and more permanent mark on this country than the war of 1939–45. It is noticeable in the present generation of undergraduates at my university . . . almost all of whom are deeply worried about securing employment . . . The world to which they look forward seems insecure, impoverished and uncertain. Their frame of mind looks back beyond the forties to the thirties. What they fear is large-scale unemployment.[11]

But if the maintenance of full employment was such an important goal, how was full employment to be defined? At any time *some* people will be out of work, either because of personal inabilities, or because they are changing jobs, or because their work is seasonal. Full employment is not the same as 100 per cent employment, but rather represents that band within which unemployment is tolerable. Beveridge thought that it could be held at 3 per cent. In a letter to him, Keynes observed that there was 'no harm in aiming at 3 per cent unemployment, but I shall be surprised if we succeed'. He thought around 6 per cent to be a more realistic figure. Bevin, in

April 1943, had held that emergency action would only be required if unemployment rose above 8 per cent. In fact, it proved possible to keep unemployment lower than even Beveridge's estimate, and only in the late 1970s did the rate begin to rise from 2.5 per cent or less to 5 per cent and upwards.

If there was disagreement about the level to which unemployment could be held down, there was a high measure of agreement on the inflationary dangers of 'over-full' employment. The distinguished economist A. C. Pigou argued that maintaining a very high level of unemployment might well require that 'a spiralling movement of inflation is allowed to develop, so that the money demand for labour is not stabilized upwards, but perpetually moves higher and higher ahead of the pursuing wage rate'. In *Full Employment in a Free Society* (1944), Beveridge himself warned:

> There is a real danger that sectional wage bargaining, pursued without regard to its effect on prices, may lead to a vicious spiral of inflation, with money wages chasing prices and without any gain in real wages for the working class as a whole . . . The fact remains there is no inherent mechanism in our present system which can with certainty prevent competitive sectional bargaining for wages from setting up a vicious spiral of rising prices under full employment.

The tension between those with their eyes on the unemployment figures and those with their eyes on inflation and exchange rates was described by Samuel Brittan in 1964 in *The Treasury Under the Tories*:

> In the 1950s and early 1960s the Treasury behaved like a simple Pavlovian dog responding to two stimuli: One is 'a run on the reserves' and the other is '500,000 unemployed'. On the whole (although not invariably), it was officials who panicked on the first stimulus, and ministers on the second. Each side usually managed to communicate its alarm to the others. Officials instinctively regard a rapid fall in the reserves as 'money running out of the kitty'. Politicians feel alarmed by unemployment figures, which they never adjust for seasonal factors (not that the Ministry of Labour does either in public), and which as a consequence always come to them as a nasty surprise.[12]

He argued that Treasury officials, together with many other senior civil servants, were particularly sensitive to inflation, for many came from an upper middle-class background and their families 'would tend to have small private incomes invested in government stock or other fixed interest securities, and would be thus ultra-sensitive to any threat of inflation or currency debasement'.

Protecting the value of the pound was a major concern of Chancellors after the war, as it had been in the interwar period. Such matters then, as between the wars, were tied up with international prestige – a longing to maintain Britain as the financial centre of the world. The interests of the 'City', where financial interest was only indirectly tied up with that of industry, were protected by a powerful lobby, while the all-powerful Treasury (which itself lacked adequate access either to economic science or to industry) too often followed the City's appraisal of any situation. To the problem of inadequate productivity, the financier's response was too often not 'produce more' but 'consume and invest less'. Of course, as Brittan puts it, there is 'the psychological point that "the pound" is easier to worship as an abstract symbol, however little it is understood, than a technocratic concept like growth or expansion, which needs a great deal of explanation and is even then not a good slogan with which to lead troops into battle'. If the pound had been allowed to weaken, exports might have been stronger, and industrial productivity in the long run might have been healthier.

454   The long boom, 1951–73

In the 1960s there was a greater enthusiasm for planning for economic growth, and both the NEDC and the Department of Economic Affairs were designed as forums, free from the constraints inevitably imposed by the Treasury, for making medium-term projections and planning growth. But while 'targets' might be set, there was no clear agreement on how they could be reached; and as the 1970s developed, any lingering consensus began to crumble.

1   Arthur Marwick, *Class: Image and Reality*, Collins, 1981, p. 327.
2   Vernon Bogdanor and Robert Skidelsky (eds), *The Age of Affluence*, Macmillan, 1970, p. 77.
3   B. W. E. Alford, *British Economic Performance 1945–1975*, Macmillan, 1988, pp. 13–14.
4   Anthony Sampson, *The New Anatomy of Britain*, Hodder and Stoughton, 1971, p. 546.
5   C. J. Bartlett, *A History of Postwar Britain*, Longman, 1977, p. 189.
6   Arthur Marwick, *British Society Since 1945*, Penguin, 1982, p. 149.
7   Alan Sked, *Britain's Decline: Problems and Perspectives*, Blackwell, 1987, p. 41.
8   Quoted in Colin Holmes, 'Immigration' in Terry Gourvish and Alan O'Day (eds), *Britain Since 1945*, Macmillan, 1991, p. 219.
9   Michael J Wiener, *English Culture and the Decline of the Industrial Spirit 1850–1980*, Cambridge University Press, 1981, p. 141.
10 Arthur Koestler (ed.), *Suicide of a Nation?*, Hutchinson, 1963, p. 66.
11 T. W. Hutchinson, *Economics and Economic Policy in Britain, 1946–1966*, Allen and Unwin, 1968, p. 25.
12 Samuel Brittan, *The Treasury Under the Tories*, Penguin, 1964, pp. 288–9.

Chapter fifteen

Britain transformed? 1973–90

Thatcherism

Margaret Thatcher was Prime Minister from May 1979 until November 1990. She led the Conservative Party to victory in three general elections; and she held office for longer than any other twentieth-century premier – and for an uninterrupted period longer than any other Prime Minister since Lord Liverpool (1812–27). It does not detract from that achievement that the degree of popular support for her policies varied greatly over time, and that opinion polls in 1981 showed her to be the most unpopular Prime Minister since the Second World War.

Margaret Thatcher was the first woman to become Prime Minister, just as she had been first woman to lead a major British political party when she took over from Edward Heath as leader of the Conservatives in 1975. When she became Prime Minister, the only ministerial office she had held was Education, traditionally seen as 'women's work' in the Cabinet, and not usually a stepping stone to high office. She notched up other firsts. Not even Winston Churchill (whom she greatly admired) had given birth to a personal 'ism', and it had taken *two* Chancellors of the Exchequer, Butler and Gaitskell, to father 'Butskellism', but she succeeded in conceiving an 'ism' all on her own when 'Thatcherism' entered the political vocabulary.

Thatcherism contained a number of distinct elements. In the first place, it harked back to many of those traditional middle-class values that would have been evident in the Grantham grocer's shop of the 1920s where Margaret Thatcher (née Roberts) grew up. The virtues which it extolled were those of the market: competition, individual initiative and an opposition to state intervention and bureaucracy. Second, it represented a backlash against trade union militancy in the workplace and permissiveness in the home, setting against them a belief in authority, law and order, the family, and individual freedom and responsibility. Thatcherism did not come out of the blue. If it struck a chord with many people, it was because the strings were already there. Many of them had been there for a decade or more, and we have to look back into the 1960s and early 1970s in order to trace the origins of the ideas which Margaret Thatcher took up, and to which she gave a name.

To the historian, there are dangers with a concept such as 'Thatcherism'. By taking the name of a single politician it suggests a radical change with the past, or a sudden discontinuity. But while such radical breaks with the past can be identified, they are fewer than we might think, and are likely to be caused by factors other than the arrival on the scene of a particular individual, however forceful that individual may be. Policies that we associate with the Thatcher governments, for example, had their counterparts in countries as far apart as France, Australia and the United States (where 'Reaganomics' was a contemporary theme). Margaret Thatcher cannot be praised or blamed for all of this. Because it makes periodisation easier, it is as tempting to talk of 'the Thatcher years' as it is of 'the Victorian age', without pausing to ask if the period is really as discrete as the title implies, or whether the homogeneity which is implicit is an accurate depiction of reality. We might question both assumptions. Certainly, there was Thatcherism before Margaret Thatcher as well as after her, while the Thatcher years are not all of a piece. It was sound political rhetoric to suggest that they were, of course. Andrew Gamble makes the point that although 'the 1987 manifesto presented the evolution of policy as a smooth and coherent progression, the reality was very different. Like all governments there was considerable improvisation and opportunism'.[1] The doctrines of Thatcherism became more coherent as the 1980s evolved, and much of the alleged coherence is a product of hindsight more than anything else. It has been argued that Thatcherism was more of an approach to leadership than an ideology. That approach is often depicted as confrontational rather than consensual. Her supporters defend this as 'conviction politics'. Her detractors recognise the quality, but value it differently. Denis Healey wrote in his autobiography:

> She saw consensus as a dirty word, because it meant a compromise between different interests or points of view. 'To me,' she said, 'consensus seems to be the process of abandoning all beliefs, principles, values and policies. So it is something in which no one believes and to which no one objects.' She told the diplomatist Tony Parsons while she was still in opposition that she regarded people who believed in consensus as 'quiclings and traitors'. But, though she insisted again and again that she stood for conviction against consensus, it has never been clear whether by conviction she means anything more than her current state of mind; the content of her conviction is simply the opinion she happens to hold on a particular issue at any particular time.[2]

The consensual politics represented by Butskellism continued after the men who had given their names to the idea had left the scene. Third parties, such as the Liberals, tried to make political capital out of the supposed similarities between the aims of the two major parties. Echoing a shampoo advertisement popular in the 1950s and 1960s, a Liberal Party poster, showing the faces of Harold Wilson and Edward Heath, asked the question, 'Which twin is the Tory?'. The consensus was based on a belief in economic growth; a mixed economy containing both state and private enterprises; economic planning; expanding welfare services; and 'corporatism', or a tripartite arrangement whereby the government came together with the representatives of labour and capital (mainly through the TUC and the Confederation of British Industry) to hammer out the problems of the economy. This consensus collapsed in the middle of the 1970s with the onset of recession. Demand for welfare provision grew at the very time that an insufficient rate of economic growth put constraints upon the ability to pay for them.

Within the Conservative Party, considerable ground was made by the New Right, an early focus for this opinion being Enoch Powell. As early as the 1950s he articulated the principles of liberal political economy, and was regarded as old-fashioned for doing so, for Keynesianism remained the economic orthodoxy. In the following decade he denounced inflationary economic policies, and opposed government high spending and intervention in the economy. To this he added a strain of political nationalism with attacks upon the EEC and outbursts against the permanent settlement of black immigrants in the United Kingdom. After his 'River of Blood' speech in 1968 he was expelled from the Conservative Shadow Cabinet, but he remained a focus for New Right thinking, having demonstrated the popularity of a political programme that was hostile to state intervention, and which articulated many popular frustrations and grievances.

In the mid-1970s the mantle passed to Sir Keith Joseph who was the founder of the Centre for Policy Studies, one of a number of 'think tanks' that sought to develop new strategies for the particular political parties which they supported. It was through the Centre for Policy Studies that he promulgated the doctrine of monetarism, derived from the Chicago economist, Milton Friedman. Edward Heath, then leader of the opposition, remained unconvinced, but Joseph found a staunch ally in Margaret Thatcher and in Sir Geoffrey Howe.

It should not be thought that the onslaught of the New Right was the only factor which led to the ending of consensus, for the Labour party was also obliged to rethink the management of the economy. Why this was so will be clearer once we have examined the extreme pressures which bore down on the economy from the early 1970s. In so doing we will be better able to appreciate the continuities between Thatcherism and that which proceeded it.

The management of the economy from the early 1970s

The long and worldwide post-war boom came to an end in the early 1970s, the result of a number of strains and seismic shocks, the epicentres of which ranged from the United States to the Middle East. Inflation in the industrial world rose from 5.3 per cent in 1972 to 11.9 per cent in 1974, and Britain's economic difficulties became such that in 1976 it suffered the humiliation (for an advanced industrial nation) of having to apply, cap-in-hand, to the International Monetary Fund for a loan.

The coordination necessary to avert a world recession could only come from the United States, but it was from that quarter that some of the problems themselves emerged. The Vietnam war, into which the United States had been sucked during the 1960s, proved to be hugely expensive. Between 1965 and 1973 more than three times as many bombs were dropped by American airmen as had been dropped by all United States aircraft in the Second World War. There was considerable social upheaval at home, especially among the poor of decaying inner-city areas, but warfare cut deeply into the funds that might have been applied to welfare. Indeed, one estimate suggested that each B52 bomber raid cost the equivalent of 27 elementary schools or 4,050 housing units. In these circumstances it proved politically imposs-ible to finance the war by taxation; instead, the government ran up massive deficits on its budget, as well as increasing the money supply. As its own industry switched towards war production, the United States increased its imports in order to maintain its consumption levels, with the result that the balance of payments also ran into deficit. This combination of budget deficits and balance of payments deficits pumped into the world's financial system a volume of dollars in excess of the US gold reserves. The time came, in August 1971, when European dollar holders began to switch out of the currency. The American response was to impose a 10 per cent import surcharge and to end the dollar's convertibility into gold. This brought to an end the system of stable exchange rates, based on dollars, that had been agreed at the Bretton Woods conference of 1944. Fixed exchange rates had helped to constrain inflationary pressures, for no country could allow inflation to get out of line with other economies without bringing about a balance of payments crisis. Now, inflation would simply result in a depreciation of the exchange rate.

The so-called long boom of the post-war years had, of course embraced the inevitable fluctuations in economic activity associated with the trade cycles of individual countries; but in the 1950s and 1960s these had tended not to be synchronised. Consequently, a high demand for raw materials from one country was offset by a lower demand from others, and this tended to keep down the price of primary products. However, growing integration of trade tended to bring the cycles closer together, with the result that a concerted boom (such as occurred from 1971 onwards) had the effect of sharply driving up the price of raw materials, such as metals, sugar, rubber and cotton. Political events could have a similar effect. Attempts to tune the economy so that a trade-cycle boom occurs in an election year have already been referred to in Chapter 14. British governments were not alone in devising 'election budgets'; but if elections in a number of major industrial countries should bunch together this, too, could have the effect of driving up world commodity prices. Just such a bunching occurred between May 1972 and March 1973 when elections took place in six of the Big Seven economies, together responsible for 78 per cent of the output of the developed world.

Of all the commodities which had price rises at this time the most important, by far, was oil. On 6 October 1973 – Yom Kippur, the holiest day in the Jewish calendar – Egyptian and Syrian troops launched an attack on Israel. In return, Israel occupied Arab territory. In an attempt to force western Europe and the United States to choose between their oil supplies and support for Israel, the Arab oil-producing countries imposed an oil embargo, cutting their supplies to western countries, including Britain, by 25 per cent. So inelastic is the demand for oil that between 1973 and 1975 a cut of 12.5 per cent in the production by members of the Organisation of Petroleum Exporting Countries (OPEC) led to a trebling of their total revenues. If the oil exporters had spent their surpluses, by increasing their imports from the industrialised world, the shock (even though severe) would only have been a temporary one. But not only did most of them have small populations but the governments of the Arab countries generally shielded their people from the temptations of western consumerism. As a consequence, the money piled up in bank accounts in Europe and the United States.

The effect on Britain was immediate and dramatic. The first significant discovery of oil in the United Kingdom Continental Shelf was made in 1969, but supplies were not brought ashore until 1975 (and then only at enormous expense). North Sea oil therefore offered no solution to the energy crisis engineered by Arab oil producers. The situation was one from which the miners, the power engineers and the train drivers took immediate advantage as they launched into industrial action in support of pay claims. The Chancellor of the Exchequer introduced an emergency budget in December, axeing £1,200 million from public spending, placing tight restrictions on credit, and announcing plans to move industry to a three-day week in the New Year, as coal supplies to the power stations dwindled. Early in February 1974 the National Union of Mineworkers announced a full-scale strike.The Prime Minister, Edward Heath, panicked and called a general election for the end of the month. The campaign was the bitterest that had been fought since the war. Both the major parties lost support and neither gained an overall majority in Parliament. After an unsuccessful attempt by Heath to form an alliance with the Liberals, he stepped down and Harold Wilson was appointed as Prime Minister. Wilson called a fresh election in October which strengthened his position, but an overall majority of only three, however skilfully managed, acted as a major restraint upon his freedom of action over the next four years.

After the election of October 1974, the government began immediately to rein back expenditure, but for a brief period inflation ran out of control. In 1974, prices rose by 19 per cent, and wage rates by 29 per cent, as groups of workers, who had got used to annually rising real incomes, fought to maintain their position. In the third quarter of 1975 inflation peaked at 26.5 per cent. More troubling even than this was that a situation had developed which orthodox Keynesian economic theory had seemed to hold impossible – high levels of inflation were accompanied by high levels of unemployment. 'Stagflation', as it came to be called, presented the government with problems that Keynesianism seemed unable to solve, for any moves to curb inflation were likely to exacerbate the unemployment situation, while attempts to reduce unemployment stoked the fires of inflation. The economy thus floundered along at a low rate of growth while the high rate of inflation continued to make British exports uncompetitive.

Following the collapse of the international system of fixed exchange rates, the pound had been allowed to float since 1972. By 1976 it had sunk. With the pound at its lowest level ever against the dollar, British currency reserves were exhausted, and the government suffered the indignity of having to apply to the International Monetary Fund (IMF) for international credits. Only days before, James Callahgan (who had succeeded Wilson as Prime Minister in April, after the latter's surprise resignation) had made an uncompromising speech at the Labour Party Conference on the country's economic problems:

> We used to think that you could spend your way out of a recession and increase employment by cutting taxes and boosting government spending. I tell you in all candour that that option no longer exists, and that insofar as it ever did exist, it only worked by injecting a bigger dose of inflation into the economy, followed by higher unemployment as the next step. Higher inflation followed by higher unemployment. We have just escaped from the highest rate of inflation this country has ever known; we have not escaped from the consequences: high unemployment. That is the history of the last twenty years.[3]

Even before Britain made its application for an IMF loan, the Chancellor of the Exchequer, Denis Healey, had embarked on policies that would later be defined as 'monetarist'. Cuts in public expenditure were announced in July, and the Chancellor announced that monetary growth should be held at about 12 per cent in 1976–7. The hope was that a clear signal of the amount of money that would be available to finance wages and prices would act as a restraining influence on trade unionists and businessmen. The rate of inflation did indeed fall and, for the first time since 1973, was below 10 per cent in 1978. However, Healey's financial disciplines were never fully accepted by the Labour Party as a whole, nor by the trade union movement. When the government failed to secure parliamentary approval for sanctions against the Ford Motor Company for conceding pay increases in excess of the published norm of 5 per cent, many unionists saw this as the end of pay restraint and rushed to put in pay claims. Some of the lowest paid jobs were those of unskilled workers in the public sector. The government's rejection of their large pay claims led to widespread strikes and other protests which developed into what became known as the 'Winter of Discontent' of 1978–9.

The disruptions of that winter aroused strong public resentment, as television and newspapers showed scenes of patients being turned away from hospitals and hearses being turned back from cemeteries. Water supplies became contaminated, and vermin-infested rubbish piled into mountains in the streets. It was the violent nature of much of the picketing that caused concern, as did the tactic of 'secondary picketing' against employers not directly involved in the dispute. It became increasingly clear to many that the trade union leadership had difficulty in influencing its members, the realisation of which resulted in the government's 'Concordat' with the TUC, reached in February 1979, being treated with some scepticism. The 'Winter of Discontent' did much to lose Labour the General Election of May 1979, although that was precipitated, not by the pay disputes, but by the removal of Scottish Nationalist Party support after a referendum on devolution which, while gaining a narrow majority of votes, failed to secure the 40 per cent support of the electorate required by the legislation.

In his *General Theory of Employment, Interest and Money*, Keynes had written:

> The ideas of economists and political philosophers, both when they are right and when they are wrong, are more powerful than is commonly understood. Indeed, the world is ruled by little else. Practical men, who believe themselves to be quite exempt from any intellectual influences, are usually the slaves of some defunct economist.

For 40 years Keynesian economic theory was the orthodoxy of most professional economists, to whom the *General Theory* became almost a biblical text. Yet it was not without its difficulties, The economist, Keith Smith, suggests:

> In some ways the General Theory is in the great tradition of pathbreaking scientific texts, meaning that it combines analytical innovations of great power, scope and complexity with passages that are confused, internally contradictory, generally tricky to decipher or just plain wrong.[4]

Scientists are able to fine-tune a rocket so that it can land on the Moon, or orbit Mars, but, however scientific they may claim to be, economists find it impossible to fine-tune an economy. An economy is not a machine, the performance of which can be monitored and forecast once it is set in motion. Forecasts of the performance of the economy are always hedged around with the qualification of *ceteris paribus* ('other things being equal'). But, in real life (if not on the pages of a textbook) the one certainty we may have is that other things never are equal Not only that, but economics is based on the assumption of the 'economic man' who always behaves rationally, and is motivated only by self-interest and the maximisation of profit. But real men (and women) differ from this amoral creature, which makes them both more difficult to predict and nicer to live with. To add to these regulatory problems, the situation by the mid-1970s was one which Keynes had not foreseen – high inflation and high unemployment running in tandem. For most of the post-war period governments were in agreement about the four principal objectives of economic policy: full employment; price stability; economic growth; and a balance of payments equilibrium. By the mid-1970s there was mounting scepticism that these four objectives were compatible. The change took place before Margaret Thatcher entered Downing Street, having been evident in the policies of Denis Healey; but when she became Prime Minister the tide ran fast against Keynesianism.

The new government declared that it would mount a three-pronged attack on Britain's economic problems. First, it would reduce public expenditure and curb the economic actions of the state through money-supply controls. Second, it aimed to stimulate private enterprise through incentives, especially a taxation policy designed to enable a greater retention of earnings, Third, it would restrict the actions of trade unions, not only in wage negotiations, but also in their capacity to resist changes in working practices. These three approaches aimed to tackle some of the long-standing problems of the economy as well as deal with immediate problems. The first priority was given to squeezing inflation out of the system, and the goal of full employment was pushed right down the agenda, where it was to remain for the next decade.

The economic policies of the new government were based not on Keynesianism but on monetarism, the belief that the money supply is the most important factor in determining the level of prices and expenditure. Although rooted in classical economics, modern monetarism owes much to the writings of the American economist, Milton Friedman. Friedman's argument was that inflation is only caused by increasing the money supply, and that as only governments can (lawfully) print money, only governments can cause inflation. And what only they can cause, only they can cure – by keeping the money supply under tight control. One problem with this, of course, is that money can be defined in various ways. Only governments may print banknotes or mint coins, but banks 'create' money through the creation of bank deposits, while in a modern economy there are a whole host of assets that may be considered 'near-money'. Which of all these definitions is the one that governments are supposed to follow? United States policy-makers recognise 40 different definitions of money. More modestly, their British counterparts generally settle for three; and of these the Thatcher government originally settled for M3, which consists of notes and coin in circulation, plus bank deposits. Strict control of this, it was believed, would bring down inflation with only temporary loss of output and jobs

Monetarism has certain attractions. A repeated refrain of Friedman was that monetary rules were crucial, and that political discretion should be eliminated since this had led to all the inflationary stagnation of the 1970s. In a sense, monetarism is seen by its advocates to work in a similar way to the gold standard; it took the management of the economy out of the hands of politicians. As Christopher Huhne puts it: 'Politicians were not to be trusted: monetary rules would serve to lash them to the helm so that they could avoid the sweet calls of the Sirens luring them on to the rocks.'[5]

Monetarism also possesses certain advantages when it comes to the *presentation* of economic policy, for this is not just a matter of theory, but is concerned with the government's credibility and ability to inspire public confidence. Indeed, a policy which can do this has attractions that transcend any theoretical merits it may possess. Business confidence is a fragile thing, and can be diminished if the public expect a policy not to be carried through, but to be reversed in the future. This was one of the factors inherent in 'Stop-Go', when the government's announcement of 'Full steam ahead' could be expected to be followed shortly by the equally strident command, 'Full steam astern'. Part of the problem is that economic management is like navigating in a fog, where the problem of steering the economy into the future is compounded by uncertainty as to where it actually is at the present. Not only can the government barely see where it is going, but the public has little means of telling whether the economic ship of state, with the government at the helm, is truly on course. If the government were steering (preferably with an auto-pilot that brooked no deviation) towards some clear marker buoy intermediate to its chosen destination, it would be in a better position to persuade the public that progress was truly being made. Such marker buoys presented themselves in the form of annual monetary targets.

Edward Heath had started with some of the same objectives as Margaret Thatcher, but had turned aside when the human consequences of his policies were apparent, in the form of recession and rising unemployment. She made determination a public virtue in its own right. 'There is no alternative' was a frequent rallying cry (shortened by journalists to 'Tina'). Mrs Thatcher deplored 'U-turns'. She punned: 'You turn if you want to. This lady's not for turning.' This was in October 1980, when it was already clear that the first of the monetary buoys had been overshot.

When the incoming Chancellor, Sir Geoffrey Howe, presented his first budget in June 1979, the prospects for economic recovery in that year were already diminishing. Following the Iranian revolution in January, oil prices were once again soaring, and they doubled in the course of the year. The British national income was not directly affected *in total* because, by now, the country was virtually self-sufficient in oil. But the price rise affected the distribution of income. The benefits to Britain of North Sea oil production went mainly to the government in the form of oil taxation. Some would argue, indeed, that this revenue helped to keep the government afloat by providing the revenue from which could be made those social security payments which tend to rise at times of recession. But British firms had to pay the increased world price. This, with increasing costs of other materials, pushed up the costs of manufacturing industry by 15 per cent. On top of this, firms were faced with higher interest rates when the Chancellor decided to raise the Minimum Lending Rate from 12 per cent to 14 per cent as a means of reaching his monetary targets. In November the rate was raised to the record level of 17 per cent. High interest rates worked their way through to exchange rates, as foreigners transferred their funds to sterling. As the pound rose in the foreign exchanges, Britain's exports became more expensive, while domestic producers had to face the competition of cheaper imports.

By the autumn of 1979 firms that found themselves in financial difficulties were trying to reduce their deficits by cutting back on employment, investment and stocks. But one firm's stock reduction leads to another firm's loss of orders. As that pattern continued, the country slid into the worst recession experienced by any industrial country since the 1930s. In 1978, 5,000 firms had gone into liquidation; in 1980, 27,000 were to do so. Between 1979 and 1981, manufacturing output fell by 15 per cent; the national income fell by just over 3 per cent; unemployment rose by 250 per cent; and inflation increased from under 10 per cent to over 20 per cent by the middle of 1980. This was a severe blow to a government which had placed the fight against inflation at the top of its agenda.

To what extent was this simply an unfortunate reflection of world recession, and to what extent the result of the government's own economic policies? Two factors point to the latter. In the first place, there are the simple facts of chronology, in that Britain entered its recession before the world recession really got going, which was not until 1982. Second, all countries faced much the same international problems, yet Britain's major industrial partners did not suffer recession on anything like the same scale

The March 1980 budget introduced the Medium Term Financial Strategy (MTFS), which set out to commit the government to a tightly defined course of action for four years, at the very least. The growth of the money supply was to be halved by 1983–4, and there was to be a progressive reduction in public spending. What was new was the understanding that the targets would not be adjusted. Instead, there was a commitment to aim at an arbitrary target, whatever the consequences. Everything was staked on success in bringing down the inflationary expectations of businesses and trade unionists. If this could be achieved, there were theoretical grounds for supposing that while unemployment would rise, it need not rise substantially. But there was a divergence of opinion as to the actual magnitude of output and job losses that could be expected. As it happened, increases in unemployment – running at 100,000 a month by the end of the year – were greater than the government had anticipated.

It was soon apparent that both monetary targets and targets for the reduction of public spending would be over-shot. The gap between government revenue and government spending – the Public Sector Borrowing Requirement (PSBR) –

widened as a result of the recession, as tax revenues diminished while social security expenditure on the unemployed increased. The Chancellor was determined to cut borrowing and, failing to persuade ministers to accept further spending cuts in their departments, had no other option but to raise taxes. This he did in the 1981 budget, sparking off a wave of protest, including a statement published in the *Guardian* and signed by 364 economists who predicted that government policies would deepen the depression.

The MTFS ('Mrs Thatcher's Final Solution' as Denis Healey irreverently dubbed it) remained part of government policy, but from 1982 the targets – which in any case were larger than those set in the 1980 budget – assumed, once more, their discretionary nature. In his 1982 budget statement the Chancellor said: 'The new target represents a realistic restatement of our intention to maintain a responsible monetary policy.' Responsible but no longer automatic; the auto-pilot had been switched off. Thereafter, strict monetarism was no longer followed, and the government placed more emphasis on the other elements of its economic strategy.

As if to mark the trough of the recession which was reached in 1981, the country was rocked by a series of urban riots starting in Brixton in April, and spreading to a number of cities across England in July. The causes were complex, but they point to some of the realities that lie behind statistical *averages*. Adult unemployment averaged around 10 per cent for the country as a whole, but it was higher for young people, the national average for those under 18 being over 30 per cent. For black people it was generally higher still. There were also considerable regional differences, as we shall see in the next section. When these elements coincided, as they did for young black people in the deprived parts of a city such as Liverpool, the mixture could be explosive. In October 1981 *The Times* described Mrs Thatcher as the most unpopular Prime Minister since records began.

In the spring of 1982, however, the standing of the Conservative government, and Mrs Thatcher's personal popularity in particular, were to soar. The cause was the short, but hard-fought war between Britain and Argentina over the sovereignty of the Falkland Islands. Whether war might have been avoided must be left for later generations to judge; but there can be no doubt that once the decision had been taken to oust the Argentinian invaders, swift and effective action was taken. Within three days of the Argentinian invasion a massive naval task force, the ships crammed with aircraft and troops, had embarked on the 8,000-mile journey to the South Atlantic. The action was also costly: in lives (225 British troops died, and nearly 600 Argentinians, equivalent to about half the population of the Falklands); and in money (the immediate cost to the British taxpayer was in the region of £900 million). As a result of the Falklands crisis, planned cuts in naval strength were whittled down, and the cost of garrisoning the islands helped to push up defence expenditure by 21 per cent in real terms between 1979 and 1985. There were immediate electoral gains for the Conservatives, who, in the general election of June 1983, won a landslide victory and, depite polling fewer votes than in 1979, secured the largest parliamentary majority since Labour's victory in 1945.

Although the 'Falklands Factor', in boosting national pride, contributed to the Conservative resurgence, there were other factors, too. In the 15 months since the 1982 budget the government had been able to lay claim not only to a military victory overseas, but to a number of economic victories at home. There were signs that trade union power was weakening, and that wage claims were moderating. Productivity was growing rapidly, as was output, and the inflation rate was falling, partly because of an easing of the growth in prices of imported commodities as a result of the world recession, and also because of lower mortgage rates following the easing of monetary policy. In his budget of March 1983 the Chancellor was able to announce substantial tax cuts.

There were a number of forces driving the recovery. As interest rates began to fall the industrial situation stabilised, and output increased as the destocking of 1979–81 came to an end. More important than this, however, was the growth in consumer demand which, between 1981 and 1987 grew at an annual average rate of 14 per cent. Disposable income, on the other hand, grew at an annual average of only 2.3 per cent, as the rise in earnings of those in work was offset by the fall in income suffered by the increasing number of unemployed. The increase in consumer expenditure, therefore, was only made possible because people began to save less and to borrow more. Between 1980 and 1988, annual borrowing from banks rose by over 100 per cent, and from building societies by over 230 per cent. It was not greater efficiency, therefore, nor an improved export performance which brought about the recovery, but the decision of the British people to consume more, and to go into debt (using credit cards, for example) in order to do so.

There were two sources from which the additional goods which British consumers purchased could come: domestic production and imports. The reality is that they came principally from the latter. The value of imported manufactures (1980 prices, £ million) rose from £23,470 in 1978 to £29,432 in 1980, and £49,736 in 1986. In 1976 Britain had a surplus in manufacturing trade of £5.5 billion. The figure was the same 10 years later – only by then it was a deficit. The 1980s therefore witnessed a major restructuring of the British economy. Despite the expansion of that decade (the longest continuous expansion in the post-war period) it was not until 1988 that United Kingdom manufacturing eventually regained its 1979 level, an experience markedly in contrast with comparable advanced economies. The oil industry expanded by over 50 per cent between 1980 and 1986, but most major categories of manufacturing had falling output at that time. It was elsewhere that expansion was to be found: in service industries such as distribution and retailing; and in banking and financial services which grew in response to the demand for credit. Whether or not the decline of Britain's manufacturing base presents a serious problem, or whether it simply represents a case of an economy wisely specialising in those areas where it has a comparative advantage, is a major question, and is discussed in a subsequent section.

The second half of the decade witnessed a great shake-up of financial markets, including the deregulation of the Stock Exchange (the 'Big Bang') in 1986, and the passage of the Financial Services Act in the same year. A more aggressive marketing of credit by financial institutions added fuel to the consumer boom. Personal credit expanded from £90.5 billion at the end of 1980 to more than £325 billion by 1988. By that year individuals' liabilities (such as their mortgages, personal bank loans and credit card debts) were averaging around 88 per cent of pre-tax incomes. A second stimulus was the rise in property values, which increased the wealth of house-owners to such an extent that they felt less need for saving and increased their consumption. For many people, their houses were earning as much or more than they earned at work. In London, for example, a person who bought a house in 1964, even with a 100 per cent mortgage, was sitting on around £60,000 in tax-free capital gains by 1989. Those gains could not be spent unless you 'traded down', which many elderly people did, taking some of the equity out of their homes for their retirement. Or you could borrow, as many people did by taking out second mortgages and spending the money on cars, or stereos, or holidays. By 1987 the Bank of England had given up any pretence that mortgages were intended for homes or home improvements.

By 1988–9 there were indications that the economy was once again over-heating, and interest rates were increased in 11 stages from 9 per cent to 15 per cent during the second half of 1988 and in 1989. Higher interest rates do not just affect consumer demand, for investment demand is also affected, and by the autumn of 1990 the United Kingdom economy was again showing signs of entering a period of recession.

Britain and the world

The degree of control which an individual government can exercise over its national economy has diminished in recent decades, partly as a result of a worldwide tele-communications revolution. There has been a surge in global capital flows that goes way beyond that which would be necessary to finance a booming world trade. A global communications system means that the world's financial markets work as one, 24 hours a day, right round the clock; for as one major exchange closes for the day, another is starting to trade. Each day around US$1 trillion are traded on the foreign exchanges of which, by the end of the 1980s, more than 90 per cent was speculative and unrelated to trade or capital investment. In such a borderless world, and with currency flows on such a scale, governments must needs surrender some of their control over their own currencies and fiscal policies. As Paul Kennedy puts it: 'Simply the awareness of the market's disapproval of certain measures (like raising taxes) can deter so-called sovereign governments from implementing them.'[6]

The globalisation of financial markets has been paralleled by the growth of multinational corporations, such as General Motors or Shell, which operate on a worldwide basis. Although we might think of General Motors as an American company and Shell as British (or, more accurately, Anglo–Dutch) multinational corporations such as these plan their actions on a global scale, serving their own interests rather than the interests of their country of origin. The 'home' country of multinational corporations is as likely as not to be somewhere such as the Cayman Islands or Liechtenstein or wherever tax and company law make it more profitable to register. The United Nations estimated that in 1980 350 multinationals accounted for 28 per cent of the total domestic product of the entire capitalist world. Such huge corporations have the power to alter the geography of world trade and industry. Separate operations in the production process can be located in the most profitable places for the multinational corporation itself. Research and development is likely to be located where there is an existing knowledge base and a highly skilled technical workplace exists. Advanced manufacturing processes may be located elsewhere, where high levels of skill allow the latest machinery to be used; while assembly and routine work will be centred on regions or countries where there is an abundance of cheap, low-waged labour. Finally, marketing is likely to be based in a major international centre such as New York, London or Paris, where financial, advertising and media services of a high order are available.

Against such corporate power (and the wealth of multinational corporations exceeds the wealth of many individual countries in which they operate) the power of individual governments is strictly limited. If pollution controls are too tight, then dirty processes will be relocated somewhere where there is limited environmental legislation or none at all. Tax liability will be reduced by shifting financial assets from country to country, while keeping them internal to the corporation. The decision to locate plant in one country rather than another can have a major impact on employment, and governments are often willing to offer concessions and inducements to encourage such investment. The British government offered more than £100 million in grants to the Japanese car company, Nissan, to encourage it to set up an assembly plant near Washington in Sunderland in the mid-1980s. Another factor, however, was the existence of a pool of relatively cheap, skilled labour. The British market for cars was important to Nissan, but more important still was the possibility of entry into the rest of the European Economic Community (EEC; European Community from 1987–93; now the European Union).

Britain's attitude to the EC can only be understood in the context of party politics, and the need of party leaders to keep together the coalitions of often competing interests and factions that represent political parties today. With only the minor parties of the centre (the Liberals and the Social Democrats) giving unequivocal support to the EEC, it is not surprising that public opinion on the issue of membership should waver. When Harold Wilson returned to Downing Street for a third term of office in March 1974, he was committed to renegotiating the terms of Britain's entry to the EEC, and these were put to the British people in a referendum in June 1975. On a two-thirds turnout, 67.2 per cent of the voters favoured continued membership. Of 68 counties, only the Shetland Islands and the Western Isles came out against. At other times, support was much less. Through to the middle of the 1980s, opinion polls showed only between a quarter and a third of the electorate in favour of membership of the EEC, after which there was a steady rise, with 55 per cent evaluating membership as 'a good thing' in a Gallup poll of May 1989. The timing of Britain's entry inevitably had some effect on public perceptions of the EEC. Britain's membership coincided with the onset of economic recession, whereas the original members had come to associate the Community with the rapid economic growth of the 1960s.

The 1975 referendum was opportune for Wilson, for the Heath government's confrontation with the unions had led to a deeply divided country. Renegotiation of Britain's entry to the EEC provided a welcome diversion, for it was an issue that did not divide people closely on lines of social class. However, in order to show that he and his Foreign Secretary James Callaghan were fighting as champions of the British people, Wilson was obliged to adopt a confrontational line during the negotiations. The changes to the terms of entry might have been achieved through normal diplomatic means, but the confrontational approach served domestic political purposes. The truth of this was not lost on Margaret Thatcher after 1979.

In 1979 Britain (with the third lowest gross domestic product per head in the EEC) would become the second largest net contributor to the Community's budget. Between 1979 and 1984 the Thatcher government was faced with the problem of correcting this imbalance, a task which the Prime Minister pursued in a characteristically determined manner, linking with it the reform of the Common Agricultural Policy.

In September 1990, *The Economist* described the Common Agricultural Policy as 'the single most idiotic system of economic mismanagement that the rich western countries have ever devised', while a writer in the *Financial Times* described it as a system where 12 diners all order the most expensive items on the menu because each of them knows that the bill is going to be split equally. At that time, over 70 per cent of EC spending was on agriculture and fisheries, the cost to a typical European family of four being of the order of £300 a year through higher food prices and £250 a year through taxation. The Common Agricultural Policy established a common tariff to give Community farmers protection against lower-cost non-EC producers. It also fixed minimum support prices for key foodstuffs, and guaranteed to purchase farm produce if prices fell below those levels, leading to the notorious 'butter mountains' and 'wine lakes'. Export subsidies also turned the EC into a major food exporter, taking third markets from other food-exporting countries, and straining relations with countries such as the United States, Canada and Australia.

The British government's insistence on reform of the Common Agricultural Policy reflected two things. First, Britain received comparatively little from the agricultural funds, and second it had to balance global interests against the more narrowly regional interests of the EC. The tensions between Britain's global interests and its European interests came into focus again with negotiations over the creation of a single European market by 1992. The launching of such a plan by the European Commission in 1985 reflected the degree to which the original ideals of the Treaty of Rome had yet to be met. By 1977 internal tariffs within the EEC had largely been eliminated, but there still remained formidable barriers to trade between the Community's members. Frontier delays and administrative paperwork imposed burdens on goods in transit. Differences in recognised qualifications prevented professional people from working outside their own country. Restrictions on competition for public-sector contracts favoured domestic suppliers. It was these barriers, and others like them, that the single European market was intended to wipe away; and two innovations meant that progress towards this end was likely to be more rapid than it had hitherto been. The first was the abandonment by the European Commission of attempts to impose common standards on the whole Community, in favour of laws which ensured mutual recognition of national standards within the EC. The second was the decision that voting within the European Council should be by qualified majority, preventing a single country from blocking liberalising legislation.

The removal of non-tariff barriers within the EC was fully consistent with Thatcherite attachment to free-market economics, but the Prime Minister perceived a danger that the EC might become excessively inwardlooking, and even protectionist against the rest of the world – 'Fortress Europe' as some called it. There were elements of the plan for a single European market that the British government did not find congenial: one was the proposal for monetary union; another was the so-called 'social dimension'. A 'Social Charter' would give workers a degree of protection over such issues as wages, social security benefits, and health and safety, not available outside the EC; but this would have the effect of putting up labour costs. The risk that this would make EC products uncompetitive might then lead to calls for excluding the free entry of goods from non-member states into the EC. Certainly, in the late 1980s, there was a determined effort on the part of multinational corporations to gain a foothold in the EC.

In September 1988 Margaret Thatcher made a speech in Bruges which attacked a number of aspects of the single European market. The press focused on those parts of the speech which stressed British nationalism, but the principle thrust of the Prime Minister's words were internationalist in tone, one of her guiding principles being that 'Europe should not be isolationist'. She was not prepared to accept a European superstate: 'We have not successfully rolled back the frontiers of the state in Britain, only to see them reimposed at a European level, with a European superstate exercising a new dominance from Brussels.'[7] Such pronouncements cheered anti-European factions at home, but encouraged Labour to look on the EC more sympathetically. Jacques Delors, the President of the Commission, received a standing ovation at the Trades Union Congress which he addressed in 1988, for many trade unionists came to believe that, with no hope of influencing the Thatcher government, the best chance of reaching some of their social objectives was through the EC.

Employment and changing patterns of work

The 1980s witnessed a major restructuring of the domestic economy, involving a drastic decline in the relative strength of the manufacturing sector, together with a rise in the contribution of service industries. The changes were to have a profound impact on the regional distribution of work, while the nature of work was itself changing under the influence of economic and technological pressures. By the end of the decade, people were beginning to ask whether the idea of 'the job' was being altered, in ways which might prove as dramatic in their transforming power as anything that had happened during the industrial revolution. Indeed, there were those who asked whether the signs showed that Britain, having been the first country to undergo industrialisation, might again be leading the world – but this time into 'deindustrialisation'. Whether this was a blessing or a curse became a matter of great debate. In the 1970s, many sociologists argued that the move towards a post-industrial society would generally improve the quality of life and work in the Western world. They were optimistic that dirty and unpleasant routine jobs in factories would die off, and that a greater proportion of people would be doing more rewarding jobs, in better surroundings, providing a variety of services to customers. This optimism was based on the faith that there would continue to be full, or near-full employment, and that it would be of a more pleasant and desirable type. It was soon apparent, however, that high levels of unemployment were likely to be the norm for a long time to come; while much work in service industries could be as unrewarding as work in manufacturing.

Britain's reliance on manufacturing has been steadily shrinking since its post-war peak in the early 1950s, when 36 per cent of the national income came from that source. Between 1966 and 1979 the gross domestic product increased by 29 per cent but manufacturing output grew by only 11 per cent. Between 1979 and 1981 production fell by 17 per cent, and the average annual growth rate of manufacturing was less than 1 per cent during the 1980s, a figure much lower than that of the 1960s. The place previously occupied by manufacturing was taken up by North Sea oil production and by the growth of services. Does this matter? Is 'manufacturing' more important than providing 'services'? Barry Supple has put the question this way: 'Why is the manufacture of ping-pong balls more worthy than the sale of educational services? Is the production of cigarettes and tanks inherently more useful than the supply of nurses or violinists?'[8] As Keith Smith points out: 'There is no law of economic life which says that Britain must export manufactures; there are other possible exports, notably services of various kinds. There are many who argue that Britain can and should develop its service exports as part of the solution to our economic problems.'[9]

It has always to be remembered that a *growing* economy is a changing economy, for growth does not consist simply of doing more of the same things. New ways of producing existing products have to be taken up in order to remain competitive; products themselves have to change as the pattern of demand alters; or new ways of earning a living have to be devised as comparative advantage shifts between one country and another in the world economy. Maybe there is no harm in relying on imported manufactures, provided that a country can continue to pay for them. But there's the rub. To what extent, and for how much longer, will North Sea oil continue to make a contribution to Britain's balance of payments? The only certainty is that this is a finite resource, but the extent to which new discoveries of oil will continue to be made, or new technology allow it to be extracted more efficiently, is uncertain. When the oil runs out, what then? Will services be able to fill the gap, bearing in mind that most are not traded internationally. According to IMF figures, only 18 per cent of world trade was in services in 1983, whereas 82 per cent was in goods, and half of all trade was in manufactures. Can a decline in manufacturing industry be reversed? A report of the House of Lords Select Committee on Overseas Trade, published in 1985, expressed concern on this point. It was argued that there was no guarantee that there could be a spontaneous rebirth of manufacturing at some point in the future, for once overseas markets had been lost and and an integrated manufacturing base had been destroyed, the costs of re-entry might be prohibitive.

A leader in the *Independent on Sunday* in November 1992 put the situation vividly, at the same time making comparisons with the nineteenth century:

> Baroness (then Mrs) Thatcher used to like Samuel Smiles and took some of her preaching from him. Self-help, the Smilesian gospel, was never far from her lips. But her reading of the Victorian moralist and biographer was highly selective. What gave Smiles his biggest kick was busy-ness, the sight of people and machines making things as bees might. The Thatcher era promised a different national salvation. We were to be busy, certainly, but not in the making of things: that was written-off in the fashionable shorthand of that time as 'old smoke-stack industry' and industrial romanticism. The future lay in 'services', in restaurants, banks, accountants, lawyers and PR men, as though the national exemplar was a cross between Disneyland and an issue of *Exchange & Mart*.
>
> We can now see this is folly. This year, in the middle of one of the worst recessions this century, Britain is heading for a deficit in its trade, imports over exports, of £13 bn. When and if consumer spending picks up, the consequences are awful to contemplate. More goods sucked in from abroad, an even larger deficit, an even weaker economy, an even weaker currency. In a world of free-money flows this deficit can certainly be financed, but in the long run the only signal of a healthy economy is a roughly equal balance of trade. This means that the gathering crisis of British manufacturing industry – what remains of it – is or should be the most important issue faced by the Government, because only a big manufacturing base can balance the books. Only 20 per cent of services are tradeable, and even those that are, such as tourism, do not have a large impact. In 1986 Sir John Harvey-Jones, then chairman of ICI, calculated that it would take an extra six million tourists, a 40 per cent rise, to replace ICI's contribution to the balance of payments.[10]

How is the weakness of Britain's manufacturing base to be explained? Any explanation must address itself to at least three problems: low productivity; a lack of suitably trained personnel; and an inadequate approach to research and development.

Labour productivity in manufacturing rose by 30 per cent between 1981 and 1986, compared with a mere 4 per cent between 1973 and 1979. The picture is not, however, as rosy as it might seem, in the first place, because some (but not all) of the productivity growth between 1981 and 1986 is to be explained by the mid-1980s economic upturn itself; for at such times manufacturing processes are more likely to be working at their optimum levels. Plant closures during the recession of the early 1980s might also explain some of the productivity growth, for if the least productive plants were shut down, then the average level of productivity would rise simply as an arithmetical consequence. Intuitively, this is an attractive explanation, but factories and plants close down for all sorts of reasons, and the few empirical studies that have taken place are sceptical that it is always the least efficient that close. Part of the explanation is undoubtedly a reformation in industrial relations with fear of redundancy and diminution of trade union power reducing resistance to new technology. Not that it should be thought that only the attitudes of workers changed, for the fear of plant closures or of take-overs act as a powerful incentive to efficiency on the part of managers although, as with all attitudinal changes, this is difficult to quantify.

The miraculous growth rates in productivity through the 1980s should not blind us to *absolute differences* in productivity between Britain and its competitors. A detailed study of Britain's eight top performing industries at the end of the 1970s showed them to be on average 40 per cent below the American level of productivity, while the eight lowest performing industries were 75 per cent below the American level. Such a large gap cannot have been closed in the 1980s. Indeed, a Treasury report relating to 1986 found that American output per hour exceeded British output by 32 per cent throughout the whole economy, once price differences between the two economies were allowed for. French output per hour was 17 per cent higher, and German output 5 per cent higher.

Productivity growth is partly dependent on the existence of a suitably trained workforce, able to take advantage of state-of-the-art production technology. Strange as it may seem, it is symptomatic of the problem that British managers, even at the height of the 1987–8 boom, reported relatively few skill shortages. That they failed to do so reflects the fact that their workers possessed adequate skills to cope with the basic production techniques, relatively simple machinery, and fairly unsophisticated products that were typical of much of industry. The problem is that the relatively unskilled nature of Britain's labour force militates against the development of a higher technology; but one of the first problems is to increase the demand for those skills by industrialists, many of whom are themselves unqualified. In fact, in 1985 the official Labour Force Survey indicated that one-fifth of those who described themselves as managers had no qualifications *of any description*.

The problem is a long-standing one, and was much debated towards the end of the nineteenth century when Britain's relative industrial decline was becoming apparent. There has been a persistent shortage of skilled craftsmen since the war. Michael Dintenfass observes that, 'They were scarce in the 1950s and 1960s when unemployment was low (there were 20,000 vacancies for engineering craftsmen in 1961) *and* in the 1970s and 1980s when unemployment was high'.[11] The gap at this level inhibits the introduction of sophisticated technology which could either not be operated at all, or could only be operated at an unintensive pace that would render the investment uneconomic. It means that production lines stop more frequently because machinery is badly used or not adequately maintained. It means also that highly qualified staff, such as graduate engineers, have to step in to sort out relatively simple problems simply because the intermediate technical skill is not there. An independent study in the mid-1980s showed that Britain was still bottom of the international league table of the five major industrial countries at *every* level of engineering and technological qualification except doctorates and technicians. There was a need to invest more in training. In 1980 investment in training by British industry measured a mere 0.15 per cent of revenues, as against 2 per cent in Germany and 3 per cent in Japan. It seems unlikely that business people will solve the problem all by themselves. While employers may gain from training their staff, there is always the danger that the employee, once trained, will leave to work for someone else. The temptation, therefore, is to poach trained personnel from rivals, rather than train people who may benefit someone else. The result is that all end up with an unsatisfactory level of skill.

The Industrial Training Act of 1964 created training boards that were to be financed by levies on firms with a supplement from the state. The boards consisted of representatives of employers, trade unions and the government. The levies, which were returned only to those firms which incurred training costs, were unpopular, for employers argued that investment in training was only worthwhile if the skills acquired were specific to their particular business, rather than transferable ones that might lead to trained employees being poached. The unenthusiastic attitude of many employers meant that the problem of untrained workers persisted, and in 1973 a semi-autonomous Manpower Services Commission (MSC) was established. Rather than attempt to force its own strategy upon employers and unions, the MSC operated a corporatist strategy and tried to work along consensual lines. The Thatcher government inherited this system in 1979, but corporatism was anathema to the Prime Minister, who was intent on 'returning management to the managers', and in the early 1980s many of the industrial training boards were abolished as being inconsistent with the government's free-market policies. Training continued to be a preoccupation of the government, although the politically pressing problem became what to do with the growing army of unemployed.

The poor performance of manufacturing has also resulted from Britain's attitude to research and development (R & D). In 1955 total R & D expenditure in the United Kingdom amounted to £187 million, which was the highest figure for any country in western Europe. However, 67 per cent of this was spent on defence, which included the development of nuclear power. British scientists and engineers were capable of highly imaginative and often path-breaking work, but R & D was poorly matched to the commercial needs of the economy. Britain tended to invest in prestigious defence and aeronautical projects rather than in fields such as vehicles, machinery and chemicals which featured more strongly in world trade. Britain's R & D was in precisely those areas where the United States was strongest, but the vast internal market of that country, together with the economies of scale that were possible there, meant that Britain was inevitably at a commercial disadvantage. In 1981 Sir Arthur Knight, a former chairman of the National Enterprise Board wrote:

> It seems that much of our massive programme of investment in defence-related high technology products was directed towards products which the Americans were bound to be able to manufacture more competitively . . . but these new activities were interesting and exciting and so they attracted a high proportion of our best young technologists; whereas in Germany the best young people were attracted into building up export-oriented, more down-to-earth mechanical engineering activities.[12]

As a percentage of net output, privately funded R & D actually declined between 1967 and 1975, a phenomenon that occurred in no other OECD (Organisation for Economic Cooperation and Development) country. Although this decline was subsequently halted, the British commitment to spending on R & D remained decidedly weaker than abroad, and by the early 1980s Britain had fallen to sixth place in the international league table. This decline showed in the number of patents filed. In 1963, British patents issued in the United States were equivalent in number to 57 per cent of the combined total from France and Germany. By 1985 it had fallen to 28 per cent. There were, of course, some outstanding successes in industries where R & D was taken seriously. In pharmaceuticals, for example, Glaxo developed the anti-ulcer drug, Zantac, which overtook its American competitor and went on to be the world's bestseller.

The declining contribution of manufacturing to the economy has inevitably been reflected in the occupational structure. Employment in manufacturing reached its peak in 1966, when the number of workers was 8.7 million. By 1992 that number had fallen to 4.4 million, with about half of that decline having taken place since 1979. At the same time there was a great expansion in service jobs. By the mid-1980s over 14 million people worked in service occupations, and they constituted by far the largest occupational grouping in the total labour force of 21.4 million in 1988. This shift has resulted in a decline in the number of manual workers, of whom there were 15.6 million in 1951, but only 13.3 million in 1981. Between the same years the proportion of employees doing manual work also fell, from 70 per cent to about 50 per cent.

The shift from manufacturing employment to tertiary employment has not been the only change in the nature of work that has taken place in Britain during the last generation or so. In the first place, growth in services has been accomplished by drawing upon new sources of labour rather than by redeploying the workers shed from manufacturing. The most important source of new labour has been women. They are still less likely than men to be in employment, although the gap has been steadily closing since the Second World War. Between 1984 and 1992, for example, the number of women in employment increased by 10 per cent, whereas the increase for men was less than 1 per cent. By the latter date women constituted 43 per cent of all persons in employment in the United Kingdom, compared with an average of 38 per cent within the EC as a whole. If we exclude the self-employed from the figures (where women constitute only 24 per cent of the total) the proportion of women in the workforce rises to 48 per cent. There are a number of reasons for this change. Much of the increase in employment has been in areas such as retailing, where women's presence had long been strong. In 1951 women constituted 51.6 per cent of sales employees; in 1971 the percentage was 59.4; but by 1981 it had risen to 77.8 per cent. Women continue to earn less than men; their average weekly earnings in 1992 being only 71 per cent of men's. They are also more likely to work part time, or to be employed on a casual basis.

The growth of part-time and casual work has been a feature of recent years. The difficult economic climate since the mid-1970s has encouraged firms to develop new working practices, with the aim of achieving greater flexibility. This may be with respect to changes in the level of economic activity (numerical flexibility) or to the nature of the activity itself (functional flexibility). There have been a number of elements in this transformation. In the first place, developments in technology permit a greater flexibility of production than ever before. Computer-aided design (CAD) and computer-aided manufacture (CAM), together with the use of robots, allow production lines to be altered more speedily, with the result that small-batch production becomes less costly. This makes it possible to produce small quantities to fill particular market niches and to respond more rapidly to changes in consumer tastes. However, in order to achieve this functional flexibility a more versatile workforce is required, for the new processes work more effectively when workers program and maintain the machines themselves, and are able to turn their hand to a variety of tasks. This type of working is most prevalent in Japan (which possessed 65–70 per cent of the world's industrial robots in 1990), although it is spreading to the more technically advanced companies in Britain. Responsiveness to changing levels of business activity, or numerical flexibility, is achieved by minimising the number of workers employed on a full-time basis. This leaves the firm free to take on temporary, part-time or casual workers when extra capacity is required; or certain activities may be contracted out. This last possibility raises an interesting point when it comes to the interpretation of statistical evidence. If a car manufacturer (for example) employs its own caterers, they will be classified as workers in the vehicle industry; if it decides to contract out that service, or even to set up a separate catering firm with responsibility for the work, then those jobs, even if done by the same people, will be classified under services. Part, but by no means all of the shift towards the service sector of the economy is to be accounted for in this way.

These changes in working practices have affected the service industries as well as manufacturing. Indeed, in the 1980s roughly 90 per cent of all part-time workers were employed in that sector. The result has been similar, however; namely a growing distinction between a 'core' of better-paid, largely male workers; and a 'periphery' of lower-paid workers, with less job security, who are often women.

There is another interpretation that can be put upon these changes, and that is that they are less the result of developments in technology and new products than they are of a change in the balance of power between employers and trade unions, with a swing significantly in favour of the former. When Margaret Thatcher assumed power in 1979 she declared her intention of clipping the wings of the trade unions, and she proceeded with the task in a steady and relentless manner. There can be no doubt that the 'Winter of Discontent' played a significant part in the defeat of Labour in the 1979 general election, and that there was much public unease about the apparent strength of trade unions within the state. The Conservative governments from 1979 set out to diminish the national political influence of the trade unions, as part of a three-pronged attack which also included the introduction of legislation to reduce the effectiveness of unions in workplace disputes, and the exertion of tighter discipline over the state's own employees.

In the 1960s and 1970s the trade union movement had played an important and direct role in national politics, and unions were represented on such corporatist bodies as the National Economic Development Council (NEDC). The TUC was widely and routinely consulted on matters of economic and social policy and, in return for being taken into the government's confidence, for a time accepted a responsibility for ensuring wage restraint. Margaret Thatcher set out to put an end to this political role. Bodies such as the NEDC were marginalised and, in a dismissive reference to consultation meetings at Downing Street between the government and trade union leaders, she expressed her resolve to end the period of 'beer and sandwiches'. She backed away from corporatism in other ways, too, such as reducing direct state involvement in wage bargaining, and refusing to intervene in plant closures and similar issues.

The second prong of the attack was reform of trade union legislation. This was carried through with considerable political acumen. For example, the government did not introduce an all-embracing piece of legislation that might have drawn the trade union movement into a pitched battle. Instead, it whittled away at union powers and immunities by a series of acts that spanned the decade. More subtly still, they were framed in such a way that each included an extension of members' rights while, at the same time, reducing the unions' institutional independence. Thus, the legislation could be presented as libertarian while its actual intention was authoritarian. Not that everything went the government's way. For example, the Trade Union Act of 1984 required all unions with political funds to seek new approval from members by a secret postal or workplace ballot. The aim was to weaken the links between the unions and the Labour Party, but by some highly skilful campaigning *all* the existing political funds were confirmed by large majorities, and there were even some additional gains made.

The third line of attack on union power was dependent on the fact that the state is itself a major employer, with nearly 30 per cent of all employed persons being in the public sector in 1980. The privatisation of some nationalised industries; the closure of parts of others (such as the coal mines, over which the miners fought a bitter year-long battle in 1984–5) and the restructuring of welfare services such as the National Health Service all impacted on the unions. So, too, did the withdrawal of collective bargaining rights from some groups of employees, including teachers and nurses, and the banning of trade unions from the Government Communications Headquarters (GCHQ) in 1984.

Trade union membership reached its height in 1974 when, for the first time in the history of the labour movement, union membership covered half the working population. Numbers fell markedly between 1979 and 1988, by which date more than 2 million members had been lost. Nevertheless, two out of five employees continued to be a member of a trade union. There can be no doubt that the policies of the Conservative governments bore heavily on trade unions, but it is equally clear that the high level of unemployment and changes to the structure of employment also had a key role in reducing membership.

Whether, as the government hoped, the reduction of trade union power will make British industry more efficient remains to be seen. The number of days lost through strikes has fallen, and was on average 0.2 days per worker in 1989. But, despite many people's perception, most workers have never been on strike in any case, and even in 1979, the year in which most days were lost through strikes since the Second World War, the figure was only 1.2 days per worker. This does not compare unfavourably with many of Britain's competitors, and is far less than the number of days lost through illness. By the end of the 1980s it was certainly less easy to use the trade unions as a scape-goat for the failings of industry for, as the labour relations director of Ford was reported as saying in 1985: 'If the trade unions have been significantly weakened by economic pressures or by industrial legislation, it has whipped away the crutch which managers have been using for the past 30 years.'[13]

Unemployment and the 'two nations'

Speaking in the House of Lords in November 1984, the Earl of Stockton (formerly Harold Macmillan) was moved to speculate: 'I foresee that in ten or fifteen years' time we shall never use the word "unemployment". We shall refer to the proper use of leisure and how to deploy it.' Implicit in this statement is the assumption that, whatever term we use to describe it, unemployment was likely to be around for some time to come; and in that he was proved right. But he was wide of the mark when he suggested that the unemployed would come to regard it as a 'proper use of leisure'. In the previous July, a Gallup poll had asked the question, 'What would you say is the most urgent problem facing the country at the present time?', to which 60 per cent had responded, 'unemployment' (it had been 80 per cent in July 1983, and was back up again to 79 per cent in 1985). Yet the political response was negligible.

For 30 years after the Second World War it was widely believed that no government could survive if unemployment rates went much above 3 per cent because neither the unemployed, nor the electorate at large, would tolerate it. Yet, in the spring of 1984, according to the International Labour Office definition of unemployment, there were 3.09 million out of work in Great Britain. It is important to state the definition being used when examining unemployment statistics. Linda McDowell has made the point that, 'Official statistics on unemployment serve a variety of purposes. Finding out how many people are unemployed is only one of them, and over the past decade it would seem to be the least important'.[14] There is nothing inherently cynical in such a statement, although the fact that the method of computing United Kingdom unemployment statistics was altered 17 times between

15   The 'wilderness picture'

On 15 September 1987 the Prime Minister Mrs Thatcher flew to Teesside to launch a new quango, the Teesside Development Corporation. Security was so tight that the press photographers had difficulty in taking satisfactory pictures. Eventually they asked her to walk towards them across a piece of waste land. John Voos, photographer for the *Independent*, snatched a picture of her as she walked away in order to get into position. The photograph which he took joined that select number of news photographs that have achieved the status almost of icons. The visual impact of the Prime Minister walking into what looks like post-industrial dereliction is somehow enhanced by the rays of the setting sun which seem to cast a halo around her head, the two elements creating great visual tension. In the distance are shadowy human forms which only add to the feeling of unease. The photograph became one of the all-time bestsellers of the *Independent's* syndication department, and appeared in many foreign newspapers. The picture is not entirely fair, partly because of the circumstances in which it was taken, and also because the site was quickly redeveloped as Teesdale, a commercial and industrial development which, with others sponsored by the Development Corporation, created 7,000 jobs. Can we ever expect a political photograph to be 'fair'? And how might different captions elicit different responses?

1980 and 1989 (almost invariably with the effect of lowering the figure) must surely raise eyebrows a little. Defining who is out of work does, of course, present definitional problems, just as does the definition of those who are 'in work'. Unpaid housework, for example, is not looked upon as employment, but by no stretch of the imagination could it *not* be regarded as work. A sample of housewives with pre-school children interviewed in 1974, did an *average* of 77 hours of domestic work a week.

By any kind of definition, and in comparison with its overseas competitors, unemployment in Britain was very high until 1986 (in the single month of December 1980, for example, the equivalent of Bradford's entire workforce was added to the dole queue). How, then, was political unrest contained? Fatalism is one factor. The government accepted unemployment as the price to be paid for bringing down inflation, which it made the over-riding aim of its economic policy; and opinion polls suggested that many members of the public, while remaining deeply anxious about the problem, came to accept the view that there was nothing that the government could do about it. Second, a period of unemployment, while experienced by increasing numbers of people, was not experienced by them in the same way, making it more difficult for 'the unemployed' to view themselves as a coherent group and to organise for the purposes of political protest. Unemployment, especially *long-term* unemployment, affected some groups more than others. Risk varied with age, gender, race, the degree of skill possessed, and the region where one lived. Those most likely to be unemployed were younger and older workers, with older workers more likely to suffer long periods of unemployment. Older people more easily become discouraged, and settle for early retirement or define themselves as ill rather than see themselves as long-term unemployed, and accept its inevitable loss of self-esteem. Young people drift in and out of casual and temporary jobs; those with family responsibilities have the greatest urgency in seeking fresh work; but, generally speaking, each distinct group has its own reason for not taking political action.

On the other hand, successive governments in the 1970s and 1980s introduced a number of employment and training programmes to deal with the problem of high unemployment. In 1983 the Youth Training Scheme (YTS) was set up to provide training and work-experience for school-leavers, and almost 1.2 million young people joined between April 1983 and March 1986. In 1986 YTS schemes were extended from one to two years, and the number of trainees increased by over 75,000 between December 1986 and December 1987. The scheme was not without its critics, one problem being that there was an inevitable tension between the twin aims of raising the general skill levels of new entrants to the workforce and reducing the number of young people who were unemployed. The status of different programmes within youth training varied, both for employers and for young people. Those which passed on skills that were in short supply in a local labour market proved attractive; but there were many others where on-the-job training was minimal and did little to enhance the employment prospects of the trainee, and where the aim of participating employers appeared to be no more than to exploit cheap labour. From 1988 people in the 16–18 age group were denied unemployment benefit, so that for those without a paid job youth training became the only source of income.

Programmes for adult and long-term unemployed have attracted similar criticism. In 1986 the Restart Programme was started to boost the morale and confidence of those who had been out of work for six months or more. Some job training was offered, and a Jobstart allowance of £20 a week for six months was payable if a full-time job was taken at a gross weekly wage of under £80. By the end of March 1988 only 2,900 people were in receipt of the allowance which critics, in any case, argued was a subsidy to employers who pay extremely low wages.

Whatever the merits of these schemes (and there were a number of others) they could not compensate for a lack of real jobs. That lack was felt more keenly in some parts of the country than in others; and this regional disparity in employment opportunities, together with a sharp contrast in the standard of living between those in work and those unemployed, once again led to the charge that Britain was made up of 'two nations'.

In 1988 Tony Champion of the University of Newcastle and Anne Green of Warwick University published the results of a survey which they had undertaken into the prosperity of 280 towns (excluding Northern Ireland). They used 10 measures of prosperity, which included such factors as unemployment (including the length of time people remained out of work), the proportion of people employed in certain service and high technology industries, and average house prices. The 10 most prosperous towns were (in rank order): Milton Keynes, Newbury, Didcot, Welwyn, Aldershot/Farnborough, Cambridge, Huntingdon, Hertford and Ware, Basingstoke and Woking/ Weybridge. The bottom 10 (with the lowest listed first) were: Holyhead, Mexborough, Barnsley, Pembroke, Cardigan, Stranraer, Doncaster, St Helens, Mansfield and Neath. The study found that there were wide variations *within* the regions, but that even the worst-performing towns in the south-east scored higher than a substantial proportion of those in places such as Yorkshire and Humberside. The detailed analysis which they undertook reinforced the idea of a North–South divide in Britain. They observed:

> The most striking result that emerges continually from these analyses is the great extent of the North–South divide. This conclusion would seem to be at variance with some recent studies and statements which have attempted to portray the situation of the North and its future prospects in a better light. In fact, the present study does not rule out the existence of brighter spots north of the Severn estuary-Lincolnshire line. It is just that the main weight of the evidence assembled here points to the North–South divide as the primary dimension in variations in economic health across Britain at the level of the Local Labour Market Area and indicates a widening of this gap in the 1980s.[15]

Official figures in 1988 showed that in terms of income per head the difference between the richest and the poorest region in Britain was at its widest for more than a decade. Income per head in the south-east (the richest region) was 44 per cent higher than in the poorest British region, which was Wales. It was also 53 per cent higher than in Northern Ireland. A decade before, the respective differences had been 29 per cent and 40 per cent. The contrast between the poorest regions and London was even greater. Average London incomes were 57 per cent higher than those in Wales and 67 per cent higher than those in Northern Ireland. However, these figures exaggerate the difference in standards of living between the regions for they assume that the prices of goods and services were equal. In many instances (such as the price paid for services, or house prices) this was not the case; but though the gap between the richest and poorest regions would be narrower, a noticeable gap yet remained.

There is another element in this comparison of incomes that we need to remember. Lower average incomes in the poor regions are a reflection of the fact that more people are out of work there. Regional disparities in unemployment are considerable. Between June 1979 and June 1986 there was a net loss of 745,000 jobs in Great Britain; but this figure is the result of 356,000 new jobs being created in the south-east, the south-west and East Anglia, while 1,107,000 jobs were lost in the rest of the country. This situation reflects the decline in manufacturing industry, where employment fell from 7.1 million in 1979 to less than 5 million in 1988. The loss of industrial jobs in specific areas could be devastating. In the summer of 1980 the steelworks which had dominated the town of Consett, in County Durham, closed down following the closure of the plateworks in the previous winter. Together, this meant the loss of 4,100 jobs. In the July of that year 1,400 young people in Consett left school; there were eight job vacancies in the town for them. New jobs were being created disproportionately in the South, with the growing service industries expanding most where population was also expanding, and with high-technology industries congregating around Cambridge and along the M4 corridor (Britain's 'Silicon Valley'). By the end of the 1980s, Hertfordshire had a higher proportion of industrial employees than either Greater Manchester or West Yorkshire.

Such regional inequalities as these spell economic and social tragedy for the poorest regions, but they have a very deleterious effect on the country as a whole, for two principal reasons. In the first place, a more even balance between North and South would allow the economy to run more efficiently, and at a higher level of growth. The events of 1987 and 1988 illustrate what happens at the moment. At that time, firms in the South began to experience shortages of labour and pressure on plant capacity. But while this 'overheating' was evident in the South, unemployment nationally was well over 2 million, with the North bearing the brunt. Despite this, inflation and balance of payments problems arose, and the Chancellor felt obliged to slow down the economy. Had economic activity been spread more evenly throughout the country the problems would have been reduced. Second, regional imbalances put pressure on the country's infrastructure. David Smith puts the problem clearly:

> Any shift in economic activity and population from North to South creates a major problem for public sector investment decisions. Schools, hospitals and roads are likely to be under-used in the North, but in short supply in the South. The difficulty is that if the government responds to such a shift by increasing infrastructural investment in the South at the expense of the North, then this has the effect of reinforcing the North–South divide, both in the direct employment opportunities it creates and in removing potential constraints on southern expansion.[16]

Since the 1930s, governments had developed regional policies in an effort to deal with the problems of regional decline, and these had been expanded in the 1960s. When the Conservatives came to power in 1979, however, such policies were placed on the back burner. Some claimed to see a political reason for this indifference, in that Conservative electoral support was strongest in the South and weakest in the North. However, a lack of enthusiasm for regional policies was consistent with the governments free-market approach, whereby businesspeople should be left to make their own decisions about where to invest. In the early 1980s, when jobs were needed *everywhere*, it could be argued that to wave the big stick in an attempt to get businesses to build new plant in places where they did not wish to go might result in potential jobs not being created at all. It was also the view of the Prime Minister that the unemployed should be prepared to move to other regions to find jobs, as she made clear in a speech to the Welsh Conservative Party Conference in July 1980. However, it was the speech of Norman Tebbit, then Secretary of State for Employment, which he gave to the Conservative Party conference in the following year that attracted more notice. He observed: 'I grew up in the thirties with an unemployed father. He did not riot – he got on his bike and looked for work until he found it.' Thus was born the phrase, 'On yer bike!', which, depending on your political viewpoint, summed up the virtues or the vices of Thatcherite self-help. There were many reasons why those out of work could not get on their bikes in order to find work. There were too many of them; and they were too far from where such jobs as existed were. They probably also lacked the skills that were necessary in the new industries, especially if they had been out of work for some time. Studies showed that the skilled were far more likely to migrate than the unskilled, and that when they did so they made it less attractive for employers to move to the more economically depressed areas. There was another factor which inhibited migration, however, and which reflected another aspect of regional inequality, and this was the great disparity in house prices between the North and the South. The Halifax Building Society reported in 1988: 'The gap between average house prices in London and the rest of the country is wider than it has been in living memory.' At the same time the boom in house prices was spreading out to the south-west and to East Anglia. The price gap made it hard for an owner-occupier to move south in search of work or better job opportunities. The owner of an averaged-priced house in, say Yorkshire or Humberside, could have sold it for £37,831 in 1988. But to purchase an equivalent house in Greater London would have cost £97,269; £88,706 in the rest of the south-east and £75,350 in East Anglia. The situation was no easier for council-house tenants. The demand for council accommodation almost invariably exceeds demand; and although the government implemented a National Mobility Scheme which required local authorities to let 1 per cent of vacant houses to newcomers from outside their area, only 24,000 moves were facilitated in the first five years of its existence.

Peter Riddell, political columnist and commentator for *The Times* observed in 1991:

> Overall, there has not been a split just into two groups, but into three, as John Rentoul has argued. 'There are now Three Nations, not Two, and the Thatcher Government has pampered not just the rich but even more that other, discreet Nation, the super-rich. The Three Nations are the haves, the have nots, and the have lots.' The haves are perhaps better described not as the rich but as the comfortably off majority – homeowners with jobs, including many skilled workers, with whom Mrs Thatcher has identified and who have sustained her parliamentary majority.[17]

Michael Ball sees the haves and the have-nots as 'privileged and powerful groups', and 'under-privileged and powerless groups':

> Successful groups include middle-aged, two-earner households in well-paid (typically private-sector) employment; those owning private property, especially home-owners; and people living in suburbs and rural areas, particularly in the South – what has been termed 'deep' or 'middle' England. Such groups are contrasted with the young and the old; single parents, the unemployed and the underemployed dependent on state benefits; those working in the public sector; people without private property, especially council house tenants; inner-city residents; and people in the North.[18]

Disparities in wealth increased during the 1980s. In the 11-year period from 1977 to 1988 the proportion of post-tax income taken by the richest fifth of the United Kingdom population rose from 37 per cent to 44 per cent, while the proportion taken by every other quintile fell, the share of the bottom fifth falling from 9 per cent to 7 per cent.

Poverty increased significantly throughout the 1980s. Between 1979 and 1983 the number of persons in families at or below the supplementary benefit level rose from just under 6 million to over 8 million. By 1987 the number had grown to around 9 million, a 50 per cent increase in less than a decade.

This trend towards greater inequality had several causes. The ending of pay controls meant that companies were able to pay substantial salary increases to directors and top executives, and six-figure salaries became commonplace. At the same time, successive tax changes greatly benefited the higher income earners. The government's view was that top managers and entrepreneurs needed financial incentives in order to encourage them to work harder. Margaret Thatcher put the view in 1985 that 'you are not doing anything against the poor by seeing that top people are paid well'. This attitude was consistent with those 'Victorian Values' which she extolled, and we return to them in a later section.

The welfare state, 40 years on

In 1983, after Margaet Thatcher's second electoral victory, Professor Ivor Crewe wrote that 'Keynes has been rejected, Beveridge has not'. If opinion polls are to be believed, the public's attachment to the welfare state actually strengthened in the 1980s. Gallup surveys, for example, regularly asked a question about the priority of cutting taxes as against extending government services such as health, education and welfare. In 1979 there was an even split, with 37 per cent of those polled favouring one option or the other. By the time of the 1987 general election the split was 61 per cent in favour of increased services, as against 12 per cent favouring lower taxes.

Three months after the Conservatives' third successive election win, John Moore, the Social Services Secretary, said in a speech:

> For more than a quarter century after the last war public opinion in Britain, encouraged by politicians, travelled down the aberrant path towards even more dependence on an even more powerful state. Under the guise of compassion people were encouraged to see themselves as 'victims of circumstance'.[19]

With Conservative stress on individual responsibility, and their determination to 'roll back the state', it was inevitable that many people should have felt anxiety about the safety of the welfare state in their hands, however loud might be their protestations that they intended to preserve it. To preserve, of course, is not the same as to keep unchanged; and it has to be said that whichever party had been in power in the 1980s, changes to the welfare state would have been inevitable. Indeed, considerable changes had already taken place since Beveridge had set out his plans in the 1940s. In the 1960s, for example, the 'rediscovery of poverty' had led to the targeting, by way of means tests, of those in particular need; while there had been a swing away from the idea of a free health service with the re-introduction in 1968 of prescription charges, and imposition of dental charges amounting to half the cost of treatment.

Britain in the 1980s was very different from the austerity of 40 years previously, when the foundations of the welfare state had been laid. Whatever its current economic problems, the country was wealthier than it had been then, and the living standards of those who were in work were much higher. The population was not the same, however, especially in its age structure. Improved health care and nutritional standards were among the factors which contributed to people living longer.

The age-balance of the population was shifting from the young to the elderly, as Table 15.1 shows. Such a demographic trend, with a projected overall rise in the dependent population skewed towards the elderly, inevitably calls for a policy response, as did the great rise in the number of unemployed.

Table 15.1   Dependent population per 100 population of working age, UK, 1971–86

Year	0–15	60/65–74*	Dependants aged 75–84	85+	All ages
1971	43.8	19.9	6.6	1.5	71.8
1981	37.1	20.0	7.9	1.8	66.8
1986	33.5	19.0	8.5	2.0	63.1
Projection 2025	34.1	23.3	11.3	3.9	72.6

*60–74 for women; 65–74 for men
Source: Central Statistical Office, Social Trends 18 (1988).

However, there was also much opinion supportive of changes to the welfare state because of what had come to be seen as defects in its current working. In the first place, the welfare state had failed to eliminate many of the problems which it had been set up to tackle. The five giants of Want, Ignorance, Squalor, Idleness and Disease were still an obstacle to progress; and although they may have been cut down in size since the Second World War, they were not yet dwarfs. In 1980, for example, the risk of death before retirement was seven-and-a half times as great for unskilled manual workers and their wives than it was for professional people. The final report of the Health Education Council before its abolition in 1987 noted major regional differences in health:

> Death rates were highest in Scotland, followed by the north and north west regions of England, and were lowest in the south east of England and East Anglia, confirming the long established North-South gradient. What is becoming increasingly clear from fresh evidence, though, is the great inequalities which exist between communities living side by side in the same region. Numerous studies at the level of local authority wards have pinpointed pockets of very poor health corresponding to areas of social and material deprivation. Alongside them, areas with much better health profiles can be detected and these exhibit more affluent characteristics. Although such deprived areas can be found throughout the country, the North has a higher concentration of them than the south and south east.[20]

In the following year, researchers at the Royal Free Hospital in London published findings which showed that whereas at the end of the Second World War there was only a quarter-inch (approximately 6 millimetres) difference in the average height of blue- and white-collar workers, the average height of male non-manual workers born in 1960 was now 5 ft 10½ in (approximately 1.79 metres), a full inch (about 2.5 centimetres) taller than manual workers.

Second, if the poor did less well than they should have done from universal provision (and educational performance was another indicator that this was the case), the middle class did rather well. It enjoyed a high score on two counts; both as consumers and as providers of the welfare state. As consumers, they possess the knowledge and the confidence to use the services that are on offer and to claim the benefits that are available. Not all people possess the capacity or the willingness to claim their entitlement. Thus, in 1979, only 55 per cent of eligible people claimed rent allowances, and only 60 per cent claimed free school meals. In 1986 the Central Statistical Office produced figures showing that the top 20 per cent of income-earners received benefits in kind from the state worth £1,700 per head, while the poorest 20 per cent received on average £1,510 per head. One of the principal reasons for this disparity was that far more of the children of better-off families stayed on in the sixth form of their schools. The class composition of university students remained almost the same as it had been in the 1920s, and many graduates found jobs as professionals in the public sector. The welfare state provides a great many middle-class people with a livelihood and with a valuable vested interest to protect. It should not be surprising that, at a time of economic uncertainty, the 'wealth-creating' private-sector professionals should round on them, as Professor Harold Perkin has convincingly demonstrated.

Third, there has been dissatisfaction with the sometimes labyrinthine bureaucracy of the welfare state, such that Baroness Wootton once suggested that 'Giant Complexity' should be added to Beveridge's other five. By the late 1980s there were over 100 Department of Health and Social Security leaflets on social security provision (although, to be fair, one of these was a list of all the others!).

Fourth, there has been the suggestion that the welfare state imposes impossible burdens on the economy. There are two strands to this argument. One is that the welfare state saps initiative and enterprise, leading to a 'dependency culture' that is inimical to economic growth; the other is that government expenditure on the welfare state 'crowds out' more productive investment. There is much about the idea of a 'dependency culture' that is not new, but harks back to Victorian ideas about the 'deserving' and the 'undeserving poor', and the idea of a criminal under-class. In recent years the idea of a permanent 'underclass' returned to this country largely through the works of American sociologists and political scientists such as Charles Murray of the Manhattan Institute for Policy Research. Their argument is that too extensive a benefit system removes from people their incentive to work. Instead they become dependent on government hand-outs, and refuse to integrate with mainstream society whose norms of behaviour they reject. Critics of the concept, which is by no means universally accepted, argue that it serves as a convenient means of finding scapegoats (be they social security 'scroungers' or unmarried mothers) for the problems of society.

The idea that public expenditure (which hovers around 40 per cent of the national income) 'crowds out' other, more productive investment in the private sector, was a constant refrain of Conservative governments in the 1980s, although why public economic activity should necessarily be any less 'productive' than private is not very clear. It is argued that high public expenditure, if financed by borrowing, pushes up interest rates and dissuades businesses from investment; but there is much empirical evidence to suggest that investment decisions are not determined by the cost of borrowing alone, but by businesses' expectations of demand and profitability.

Despite its declared intentions, the efforts of the government to reduce public spending were not very successful, and total expenditure remained remarkably stable (see Table 15.2). The composition, however, did change. Defence spending rose in the first half of the decade, consequent upon the Falklands War and Britain's continuing commitment to NATO. Spending on law and order increased throughout the decade, with crime remaining a major public anxiety. Spending on housing fell drastically. All of these changes were the result of policy decisions. Other changes

Table 15.2   Public expenditure on various services as a percentage of total government expenditure, 1979–1990

	1979–80	1981–2	1983–4	1985–6	1987–8	1989–90
Housing	7.3	4.1	3.7	3.0	2.7	2.9
Defence	11.9	12.2	12.6	12.9	12.2	11.7
Social security	25.9	28.5	29.9	31.3	31.5	29.7
Education and science	14.5	14.4	13.7	13.1	14.0	14.6
Health	12.1	13.1	12.7	12.7	13.4	13.8
Law and order	4.1	4.4	4.5	4.7	5.1	5.6

Source: Figures, based on HM Treasury *Public Expenditure Analyses*, derived from Nicholas Abercrombie, Alan Warde, *et al.*, *Contemporary British Society*, second edition, Polity Press, 1994, pp. 558–9.

were a side-effect of broader economic policies, especially the growth in spending on social security, which reflected persistent unemployment and its attendant problems.

With spending so high, New Right economists suggested that a more efficient way of providing welfare services would be through the competitive market rather than through the monopolistic state. The *social market* economy which they advocated would guarantee certain minimal standards, beyond which the freest possible scope would be given to private initiative. At the same time individual responsibility and free choice would be reasserted. There was nothing inherently new in this argument. Beveridge's philosophy had been that the state should make universal provision of welfare services such as national insurance, council housing, a national health service and state education, but that beyond those national minima people should be free to opt out into the private market. What was new was the movement towards reducing those minima (rather than enhancing or maintaining them), thus making the private, market option seem more attractive. Basic, state provision was to be regarded as a safety-net, beyond which people should be encouraged to make provision for themselves.

It was consistent with Margaret Thatcher's aim to 'roll back the state', that ministers argued that while the state would continue to provide the financing for the bulk of welfare state services, it was not necessary that the public sector should actually have to provide the services themselves. The contracting out of services to the private sector by competitive tendering was thus encouraged, as was the great nineteenth-century tradition of voluntary provision. The government might act through established voluntary organisations which, it was argued, were better placed than the state to distribute benefits. Thus, in 1987, for example, the Haemophiliac Society was given £10 million to pay out to haemophiliacs who had become infected by AIDS. Opponents of moves such as these argued that the government was forcing the recipients of aid to beg for charity, rather than to receive assistance as of right, and free of stigma.

The effects of introducing market principles into the welfare state can clearly been seen in the case of education and the National Health Service, although in neither case had policy changes been fully implemented by the time of Margaret Thatcher's fall from power in 1990.

Education

The 1960s and 1970s were decades of great change in education at every level, from the nursery to the university. In primary schools there was a marked trend towards the integration of learning and the breaking down of subject barriers within the curriculum. Such child-centred, 'progressive' methods were endorsed in 1967 by the report of the Central Advisory Council for Education, chaired by Lady Plowden. The thrust of that report was made clear by its opening words:

> At the heart of the educational process lies the child. No advances in policy, no acquisitions of new equipment have their desired effect unless they are in harmony with the nature of the child, unless they are fundamentally acceptable to him.

In secondary schooling the great move was away from selection at the age of 11, and the spread of comprehensive schools. In 1960, 4.7 per cent of the secondary school population of England and Wales was in such schools, a proportion which had risen to 31 per cent by 1970 (and 85 per cent by 1987). In higher education there was an expansion in the number of universities in the traditional mould, and the creation of new 'technological universities' and polytechnics. These changes were not implemented without a great deal of debate; and the comprehensive reorganisation of secondary education was a political football, kicked around by the Labour and Conservative Parties for more than a decade. Yet, having said this, it remains true that the period between 1944 and 1976 was one of relative consensus so far as education was concerned. There were three parties to this equilibrium. The central government provided the bulk of the finance for education and through its advisers at the Department of Education and Her Majesty's Inspectorate set out educational priorities and identified problems. In what was described as 'the great partnership', however, the solution to those problems was left largely to the initiative of local authorities, and there was in consequence a great diversity of educational provision, with certain authorities earning a reputation for their initiatives in particular fields. The local education authorities distributed the funds allocated by central government in accordance with political priorities that were defined *locally*. The third party to this educational triumvirate was the teachers, whose professional expertise was recognised by central and local government alike, and who possessed a considerable degree of discretion both in respect to what they taught and how they taught it.

In the mid-1970s there was much debate on the question of educational standards, both in respect of the child-centred education that had become the orthodoxy in most post-Plowden primary schools, and the non-selective and frequently unstreamed comprehensive schools. In 1976 a Department of Education and Science memorandum noted criticisms that schools 'have become too easy going and demand too little work, and inadequate standards of performance in formal subjects, from their pupils'; and drew attention to low pupil motivation and wide curriculum variation. The idea that the time had perhaps come for the establishment of some kind of 'core curriculum' was taken up by the Prime Minister, James Callaghan, in a keynote speech made at Ruskin College, Oxford, in October of that year. This speech inaugurated the so-called 'great debate' on education which culminated in the publication of a Green Paper, *Education in Schools*, in July 1977. This announced that the Secretaries of State (for Scotland and Wales and Northern Ireland had their own systems) were intending to initiate a 'review of curriculum arrangements', and to establish 'a broad agreement with their partners in the education service on a framework for the curriculum, and on whether part of the curriculum should be protected because there are aims common to all schools and pupils at certain stages'.

The idea of a national curriculum thus pre-dates the Conservative return to power in 1979, but the incoming government gave it a new emphasis. The role of 'their partners in the education service' was to be downplayed, for both local authorities and teachers came under increasing attack. In what was heralded as a process of decentralisation, local education authorities were to lose most of their powers to individual schools. Local management of schools (LMS) gave greater control of the school budget to headteachers and their governing bodies, and schools were strongly encouraged to 'opt out' of local authority control by becoming grant maintained, which entailed funds being allocated directly to them by the central government. However, on the basis that whomever pays the piper calls the tune, this in fact represented a massive swing towards centralisation, especially with the implementation of the National Curriculum after the passage of the Education Reform Act in 1988. Not only were local education authorities to lose their mediating influence, but teachers were to have their professional influence on education curtailed. Introducing his bill to the Conservative Party conference in 1986, the Secretary of State for Education Kenneth Baker remarked that 'Education can no longer be led by the producers – the academic theorists, the administrators, and even the teachers' unions . . . . Education must be shaped by the user – by what is good for the individual child and what hopes are held by the parent'.[21]

If education were to be taken away from the producers, the intention was to put it into the hands of the consumers. Ironically, the true consumers of education – children – were not consulted, and the tide was running fast against child-centred education. The consumers, in the government's eyes, were parents and business-people. Each were given increased representation on governing bodies, and it was hoped that businesspeople would not only inject sound business practice into the schools (the expertise of teachers, after all, being in teaching) but would be better placed to ensure that education met the needs of the economy. Parents were given the consumer's right to shop around for schools, for protected catchment areas were abolished and, since there were more school places than children to fill them, schools had to compete in the market place for pupils. The government showed less sympathy with parents when their wishes ran counter to its own intentions. A majority of London parents wished the Inner London Education Authority to continue, but for political reasons the government abolished it nonetheless.

There are, however, problems with applying market solutions to education. The 1988 Education Reform Act provided for compulsory testing of children at 7, 11, 14 and 16 (since modified), and required schools to publish the results, but the resulting league tables take no account of the particular social characteristics of the school and its catchment area. As Christopher Huhne wittily puts it: 'They are as if the camp cook of a polar expedition was pitted in competition with the chef of a three-star Parisian restaurant. Not surprisingly, the restaurant would win if the final result was the only measure, and no allowance was made for the difficulty of the cooking conditions or the availability of materials. In economic terms, exam results measure output rather than value added.'[22]

Some parts of the government's education programme moved more slowly than others. Although every encouragement was given to schools to 'opt out' of local authority control, the take-up was slower than the government had wished. Out of 26,000 secondary schools, only 70 had opted out by the spring of 1991, with a further 200 or so in the pipeline. The establishment of City Technology Colleges also moved forward slowly. The idea was to set up state-funded colleges, taking children of secondary school age, and giving them an education with a strong technological and business element – as the ill-fated technical schools had tried to do 40 or so years before. This time, however, industry and commerce were to sponsor such colleges in partnership with the central government (a case of calling on the 'pin-striped trousered philanthropists' as one commentator put it). The first of such colleges was opened in Solihull in 1988, and by September 1989 plans had been announced for a further 13.

Education is, perhaps, that welfare service of which the middle class take most advantage; and the Conservative reforms, while offering greater parental choice to all, are likely in practice to give more of it to middle-class parents than to others. One of the first policy changes instituted by the government, shortly after it came to power in 1979, was to allocate £60 million for an Assisted Places Scheme to help parents who wished to have their children educated privately, but could not afford the fees. By the middle of 1981, 5,500 children were participating in the scheme, of whom one in five had previously been receiving private education. Dr John Rae, Headmaster of Westminster School, described the scheme as 'like trying to deal with a famine by paying for a few children to have lunch at the Ritz', and other critics of the scheme suggested that it was the thin end of a wedge that was intended to lead to the general privatisation of education and the breaking up of the state system. Thinkers of the New Right also pushed the idea of a voucher system to bring free-market principles into education. Parents would be given vouchers to cover the cost of their children's education. They would be redeemed at state schools (which would have to fight for their share of the market) or they could be topped up out of the parents' pockets for use in private ones. The idea continued to be canvassed, but nothing had been done to implement it by the end of the decade.

The National Health Service

Ever since its introduction in 1948 the National Health Service (NHS) has been looked upon as the jewel in the crown of the British welfare state. It is the service with which most people have contact at some point in their lives. In the early 1980s an average of 100,000 people a day attended hospital accident and emergency departments. Each year about 9 million new patients attended out-patient clinics, and each member of the population made an average of three visits to the doctor. This high density of use, and the high regard that the public has for it (however much they may complain about its continuing defects) renders its reform a highly complex political issue. Not surprisingly, therefore, reform of the NHS was beset with difficulties and the government moved slowly. It was not until the very end of the 1980s that the government's fundamental proposals for change were set out in a White Paper, *Working for Patients*. Published in 1989, the White Paper set out plans for making the NHS more sensitive to patients' needs and to market forces.

The basic problem of health care is one of cost, but this is related to other issues including definitional ones. To what extent is 'health' merely the absence of 'illness'? How far is illness a personal matter, to be treated on an individual basis, and how far a social matter – determined by the kind of society in which we live? Some sociologists of health argue that since the advent of industrialisation, the determinants of death and illness in the West have gradually shifted from infectious diseases (spread by inadequate sanitation, overcrowding and malnutrition) to others, such as cancer and heart disease, and to problems such as mental illness and drug abuse. There is much evidence to support this view; but the question then arises as to how far these new problems arise from self-destructive behaviour (such as smoking or unhealthy diet) or from environmental factors such as industrial pollution. Either way, it is clear that health is not simply a medical matter. Many feminists have taken a similar line and, challenging the male-dominated professionalisation of medicine, have attempted to 'demedicalise' such natural female functions as menstruation and child-bearing. All of these questions pose fundamental questions for policy-makers. Should emphasis be placed upon removing from society, as far as is possible, those features which lead to illness and premature death (and these include such impalpable factors as stress); or should effort be concentrated on improving the rights and powers of people as consumers of medical services? In other words, is it *Patients First* (the title of a government consultative document issued in 1979) or is it first a healthy society? The importance of environmental issues was the clear message that came from the Black Report of 1980. A working group, under the chairmanship of Sir David Black, President of the Royal College of Physicians, was set up in 1977 by David Ennals, the Secretary of State for Social Service in the Labour government. Its task was to examine differences in health status between the social classes, and to consider the implications for policy. The group working party was not ready to report until after the general election of 1979, but its findings were so unwelcome to the Conservative government that it was, in effect, suppressed. Only 269 duplicated copies were originally made available, and it was not published by Her Majesty's Stationery Office as would normally be the case. In many respects this was an error of judgment on the part of the government, for, once the curiosity of the media was aroused, the report received much wider publicity than it might otherwise have done. The report was not welcome to the government because its main message was that differences in health between the social classes was more a function of standard of living than it was of the health system. The lower down the social scale you were the less healthy you were likely to be, and the higher the mortality of your children was likely to be also. Figures show that working-class parents are much less likely than those of the middle class to take their children to the doctor. Why this should be so is not altogether clear, but it seems unlikely that it is because they are less concerned about illness than that they perceive care to be both poor in quality and costly. In predominantly working-class areas it is indeed probable that health services are inferior or less accessible; but the difference also reflects the fact that, in general, working-class people are less efficient consumers of medical services than are members of the middle class. The latter are less likely to feel intimidated by doctors (who come largely from their own ranks) and they are more likely to possess the skills required to press for the care they need.

There are problems, then, in applying market solutions to health care, although they are political problems as much as economic ones. Advances in medical science and technology make new treatments available all the time. Most people do not choose to be consumers of such treatment, for they do not choose to be ill; but when they are ill, they naturally want the best treatment that is available. The political question, then, is to decide how much the nation can afford to spend on medical health care, and then to ensure that the money is spent efficiently and equitably.

An international comparison shows that the United Kingdom total health expenditure, at 5.8 per cent of the gross domestic product, was well below the OECD average and that, although it rose, it remained below that average throughout the 1980s (see Table 15.3). By the end of the decade there had been a move towards the private provision of health care, but the overwhelming

Table 15.3   International comparison of total and public health expenditure, 1980–90

	Total Expenditure (% GDP)			Public expenditure (% total expenditure)		
	1980	*1985*	*1990*	*1980*	*1985*	*1990*
UK	5.8	6.0	6.2	90	87	84
USA	9.2	10.5	12.1	42	41	42
OECD average	7.0	7.2	7.6	76	76	74

Source: Figures from OECD data in Nicholas Abercrombie, Alan Warde, *et al.*, *Contemporary British Society*, second edition, Polity Press, 1994, p. 392.

proportion was provided by the public sector. In contrast with this, spending in the United States was almost double the total spending of the United Kingdom, although around 60 per cent was provided privately. The figures suggest that Britain has not been profligate with national resources when it comes to health care, and comparisons with the more free-market United States show it to have been remarkably efficient. In 1980, for example, 20 per cent of spending in the United States went on administrative costs, compared with 3.8 per cent spent on the administration of the NHS.

It was nevertheless largely on the question of administration that the Thatcher administration concentrated. The publication of the Griffiths Report (*NHS Management Inquiry*) in 1983 led to the government requiring all health authorities to appoint chief executives with a view to achieving efficiency savings, a change that was in line with the government's over-riding aim of reducing public expenditure. In the winter of 1987–8 there was much public concern about the level of funding in the NHS, with considerable publicity being given to wards being closed and life-saving operations being postponed because of shortages of nurses. Although it had been intended that fundamental reform of the NHS would be left until a fourth term in office, the government brought forward its proposals which were incorporated in the National Health Service and Community Care Act 1990, the most far-reaching piece of legislation affecting health care to be passed since the NHS had been established. The act set out to establish within the NHS a surrogate market, but since patients do not possess the expertise to choose between one type of service or another, their GPs were to act as their agents, buying services from hospitals, depending on cost and availability. Groups of GPs were to become fundholders, receiving budgets out of the funding that would have gone to health authorities. At the outset the scheme was to apply only to the largest 9 per cent of practices covering a quarter of the population. However, there has been early evidence that the scheme is proving effective in improving standards of care as GPs shop around to get better services for their patients. The second change is to allow about 300 larger hospitals to set up as independent trusts within the NHS. They are free to compete with each other, and to expand those services at which they are particularly cost-effective, selling them both to health authorities on behalf of NHS patients, as well as to private patients.

It is too early yet to judge how successful these changes will be. While the notion of competition between different providers is gaining acceptance, critics still fear the re-introduction of a two-tier system, where the better-off turn increasingly to private health insurance while the rest are left with a National Health Service that is increasingly squeezed of funds.

Rolling back the state

The ideologies that win support at elections and the principles that guide the formulation of government policy need not necessarily be the same. For many years one of the main features of the Conservative Party's appeal to the electorate has been its antipathy to the state sector and to trade unions, and it won support from significant numbers of workers in the private sector and in non-unionised occupations. When in power between 1951 and 1964, however, the Conservative government found itself quite able to negotiate with the unions and to administer the public sector. It was in opposition, rather than in government, that the Conservatives professed to be the 'anti-state' party. After 1979 this changed. Ferdinand Mount, the head of Margaret Thatcher's Policy Unit in Downing Street from 1982 to 1984, argued that many of the reforms that came to be known as Thatcherism had been a twinkle in Tory eyes for decades. 'What is remarkable,' he argued, 'is not their originality but their implementation.'

Professor Harold Perkin, quoting a speech made by Margaret Thatcher at Newcastle in 1985, has suggested that:

> Margaret Thatcher and her allies made no secret of their dislike for state employees (with the notable exceptions of the police and the fire services and the armed forces) and of all those occupations dependent for their incomes on the taxpayer rather than the market. They believed them to be parasitic upon the creators of wealth and, undisciplined by market forces, almost by definition inefficient if not actually incompetent. Mrs Thatcher particularly disliked civil servants and academics (though she made good use of them), whom she bracketed with the clergy as representing the 'anti-industrial spirit' which she deplored: 'Nowhere is this attitude [suspicion of making money] more marked than in the cloister and the common room. What these critics apparently can't stomach is that wealth creators have a tendency to acquire wealth in the process of making it for others.' By contrast, the new entrepreneurs whom she admired 'didn't speak with Oxford accents. They hadn't got what people call the "right connections", they had just one thing in common. They were men of action.' There could be no clearer expression of the dichotomy in perception between the public- and the private-sector professionals.[23]

The idea of 'rolling back the state' was part of New Right philosophy which sought to diminish the role of the state in the economy and to restore the invisible hand of the market. This was to be achieved by deregulating industry (lowering or abolishing state controls over the private sector), and by privatisation (the returning to the private sector of industries and services which had been taken over by the state). Where the services of the state could not be transferred to the market, then the market would be brought to the state through such devices as competitive tendering, 'market-testing', and a stronger influence on the state apparatus of business people and business practice.

New Right rhetoric speaks of handing power back from the state to the people, but it could be argued that the trend of the 1980s was towards a massive transfer of power to the central government. This was evident, for example, in the onslaught which was made on local government, with local authorities losing a great many powers. There was a trend towards the setting up of extra-governmental organisations, better known as quangos (quasi-autonomous non-governmental organisations – a term first coined in jest in the late 1960s by Anthony Barker of the University of Essex). Quangos were appointed by ministers, and were subject to little, if any democratic control.

Professor Bernard Porter has argued: 'In one way or another, Britons were far more spied upon in the 1970s and 1980s than they had been for 200 years at the least, and possibly for the whole of their history.'[24] Reflection on the three-hundredth anniversary of the 'Glorious Revolution' of 1688 added to a debate on civil liberties; and the pressure group, Charter 88, was launched with the aim (among other things) of securing a Bill of Rights to enshrine civil liberties, and the introduction of an electoral system based on proportional representation. Even the *Spectator*, a conservative weekly paper, argued in 1989 that 'this government is far more interfering and bossy than any previous British administration this century. Whether you are a broadcaster, or a motorist, or a trade unionist, your liberties are markedly more restrained than they were ten years ago.'[25]

Nationalisation was originally seen as a way of making public utilities such as coal, power and the railways more efficient; and during the 1950s and 1960s the state-owned industries were held to have a good record of management, investment and productivity. In the late 1960s and 1970s the nationalised industries were added to, first with the *re*nationalisation of steel through the creation of the British Steel Corporation in 1967. The Post Office and the Royal Ordnance Factories, businesses which had previously been run directly as government departments, were converted into public corporations in 1969 and 1974 respectively. The trend towards state intervention in industry was reinforced by the willingness of successive governments to give financial support to private-sector industries that found themselves in difficulties (the so-called 'lame ducks'). Companies bailed out in this way included British Leyland (1975), and Rolls Royce (1971, 1978). As the 1970s progressed, the nationalised industries came increasingly to be criticised for inefficiency, and there was considerable discussion of the problem. Within the Conservative Party, Nicholas Ridley chaired a study group to consider denationalisation, but he saw the main scope to be for action in industries which had competitors, as he remained sceptical about disposing of the main utilities, which would entail the transfer of monopoly power from the public to the private sector.

When the Conservative Party was returned to power in 1979 it was the businesses operating in a competitive environment that were sold off first. Economic theory would suggest that there was some sense in this, although empirical evidence does not conclusively show that privately owned companies perform more efficiently than publicly owned ones. The position in the case of companies which operate in a monopolistic environment is different, for instead of increasing its profit by improving efficiency, it may simply raise the prices it charges to its customers. For this reason, moving such industries from the public sector to the 'free market' invariably leads to the ironic necessity of having to set up a regulator. An example is OFTEL, the Office of Telecommunications, set up under the Telecommunications Act of 1984 to regulate the privatised telecommunications industry. OFs abounded, others being OFGAS (the Office of Gas Supply set up under the Gas Act 1986), and OFFER (the Office of Electricity Regulation, established by the Electricity Act 1989).

Raising efficiency was not necessarily the only direct motivation for denationalisation. For example, it has been suggested that in the early days, before the movement to privatise gained a momentum of its own, denationalisation was seen as a means of breaking the power of the trade unions, which had always been strong in the public sector. Denationalisation could also contribute to a reduction in public sector borrowing, and release funds that could be used to finance tax cuts. This was because of the accounting convention that was employed. The government argued that since the purchase price appeared as public expenditure when assets were taken into public ownership, it was only logical that any funds raised by the sale of those

Table 15.4   Principal denationalisations, 1979–90

Year	Company or concern
1979, 1983, 1987	British Petroleum
1981, 1985	British Aerospace
1981, 1983, 1985	Cable and Wireless (telecommunications)
1982	Amersham International (radio and chemicals)
1982, 1985	Britoil
1983, 1985	Associated British Ports
1983	British Rail Hotels
1984	Enterprise Oil
1984	Jaguar (cars)
1984	Sealink (ferries and harbour)
1984	British Telecom
1986	British Gas
1987	British Airways
1987	Rolls Royce (aero-engines)
1987	British Airports Authority
1988	British Steel
1988	Rover Group (cars)
1989	Harland and Wolff (shipbuilders)
1989	Short Brothers (aviation)
1989	Regional water companies
1990	Regional electricity companies
1990	Electricity generation

assets back to the private sector should be regarded as *negative spending*. Thus, for any given borrowing target set by the government, asset sales allowed taxes to be lower and public spending to be higher. In this way the government raised £25,250 million between 1979 and 1989, around 90 per cent being realised after Nigel Lawson became Chancellor in 1983. In November 1985, in a vivid, but emotive phrase, Harold Macmillan described the process as 'selling the family silver'. Even some of those who would have disagreed with him felt that the selling off was arranged at too high a cost and at too low a price. The advertising campaign for the sale of British Telecom, for example, cost £12.4 million. Around 1 billion shares changed hands on the first day of trading, and within 24 hours the prices of shares went up by 90 per cent. Professor John Kay has argued:

> Whatever the wider economic consequences of privatization, it has proved a highly remunerative activity for three groups; the initial shareholders of privatized companies; the managers of the companies (whose salaries have risen sharply, in part to catch up with private sector levels); and the extensive group of professional advisers who have been involved in the privatization process.[26]

What have been the wider effects of privatisation? On the positive side, there is some evidence that the massive shake-up of the denationalisation programme implemented by the government has raised the performance level not only of the privatised companies themselves, but of those which still remained in state ownership. However, whether that shake-up could have been achieved by setting firmer financial targets without a change of ownership is another question. Customers were not always happy, however. British Telecom, for example, turned in record profits after privatisation, but MORI polls showed customer dissatisfaction with prices rising from 40 per cent in 1980 to 52 per cent in 1987. There was also a dissatisfaction with the quality of the service offered, although this improved markedly after much public rowing in 1987.

Other aspects of privatisation have included deregulation, and contracting out and competitive tendering of publicly financed services. An example of the former was the 1985 Transport Act which opened up bus transport to private competition. The previously dominant company in an area generally saw off much of the competition, but with loss-making routes closed (in rural areas, for example) and higher fares. Examples of services subjected to contracting out include catering, cleaning and laundry services in hospitals, and services such as refuse disposal and the supply of school dinners. The chief saving was usually on the wages bill, either by reducing staff or cutting wage rates; and it was often the already low-paid who suffered most.

Conservative rhetoric in the 1980s embraced the encouragement of a share-owning and a property-owning democracy. The campaign for the privatisation of the gas industry involved the slogan, 'Tell Sid'. The message was meant to be different from, say, 'Tell Jeremy', or 'Tell Samantha', and was intended to suggest that anybody, whatever his or her means, could acquire gas shares. By the time the offer closed, 4.5 million people had applied for shares (more than twice the number that had applied for shares in British Telecom). But in this, as in other flotations, many quickly sold their shares, and the proportion of individual shareholders continued its decline, as large financial institutions, such as pension funds and insurance companies, increased their holdings. Between 1963 and 1981 the proportion of individual shareholders fell from 54 per cent to 28 per cent, and was down to 25 per cent by 1987.

The idea of a property-owning democracy was not new, for the phrase had been coined by Anthony Eden as far back as 1948, and in the 1950s the Conservatives had embarked on a massive house-building programme which, it was thought, would not be without electoral advantage to themselves. Local authorities met a large share of the housing needs of the population, and at its peak at the end of the 1970s, about 32 per cent of all households in Britain were living in council houses. In the 1980s, however, the Conservatives set out systematically to dismantle this form of tenure. At first this was accomplished by the selling of council houses, and then, towards the end of the decade, it was through the transfer of whole estates to private landlords or housing associations. Although, as we have seen, general expenditure on the welfare state increased under the Thatcher administrations, housing was one of those services where there was a marked reduction of expenditure. At the beginning of the 1980s, central government subsidies to local authorities for current housing expenditure ran at £1.2 billion–£1.4 billion. By the end of the decade the figures were down to between £450 million and £500 million. Over a million dwellings were sold, for the proposition was very attractive to many tenants, to whom considerable discounts were offered on the 'market price' of their home, and ownership afforded greater scope for home-improvement. There were disadvantages however. Some found maintenance costs and mortgage repayments impossible to bear, and the least fortunate found their homes repossessed and themselves back on the housing list. The sales of council houses produced considerable capital receipts for local authorities but central government restrictions prevented them from using the money to build new houses or to repair the older ones. Increasingly, therefore, local authorities found themselves forced into a welfare role, housing families in what, in many instances, were little better than ghetto conditions.

The Thatcher administration had little sympathy for local government, and in the decade after 1979 some 50 acts of Parliament were passed which, in one way or another, aimed at reducing the independence of local authorities. The imperative for this was partly the perceived need to reduce public expenditure, but local authorities could also be seen as presenting a political challenge to Thatcherism. Such tensions between central and local government were not new of course, and the reorganisation of secondary education into comprehensive schools in the 1960s and 1970s provides a classic example of interplay between government at different levels when controlled by different political parties. During the early 1980s many Labour-controlled local authorities challenged the government both ideologically and in terms of practical politics. Across the river Thames from Westminster stands County Hall, originally the home of the London County Council and latterly of the Greater London Council (GLC), an authority with responsibilities for the whole of the metropolitan area. In the early 1980s the GLC challenged the government on many issues, and it was swept away in 1986, together with other metropolitan authorities, as part of government streamlining of local government. The attack on local government was made easier by the media attention which was focused on 'Loony Left' local authorities which, the government claimed, ignored ratepayers and pursued policies which helped destroy the local economy.

The Thatcher administration responded in several ways. One was to restrict the power of local authorities to raise local taxation, first by limiting rate increases (rate capping), and then (from March 1989 in Scotland, and from March 1990 in England and Wales) by a poll tax. This proved a political disaster of major proportions, and was quickly replaced by a property-based council tax, and a centrally determined business rate. Another way of limiting the power of local authorities was by removing services from their control, as in the case of further education (which was removed altogether) and the encouragement of schools to opt out. The trend, therefore, has been for local government to become squeezed between the increasing centralisation of the state and the spread of 'central government localism' or the appointment by the central government of non-elected bodies to administer services locally. Professor John Stewart of Birmingham University has spoken of 'the new magistracy' of government appointees who run colleges, opted-out schools and hospitals. He sees them as modern revivals of the early nineteenth-century magistrates who ran Britain before elected councillors were established. If it is a return to 'Victorian Values,' it is not one of those which Mrs Thatcher pressed most openly.

Values in a changing society

In January 1983, at the end of an interview by Brian Walden on the television programme, 'Weekend World', Mrs Thatcher extolled Victorian values:

I want to see one nation, as you go back to Victorian times, but I want everyone to have their own personal property stake . . . I want them to have their own savings which retain their value, so that they can pass things on to their children, so you get again a people, everyone strong and independent of government. Winston put it best. You want a ladder, upwards, so anyone, no matter what their background, can climb, but a fundamental safety-net below which no one can fall. That's the British character . . . Of course, we have basic social services, we will continue to have those, but equally compassion depends on what you and I, as individuals, are prepared to do. I remember my father telling me that at a very early age. Compassion doesn't depend upon whether you get up and make a speech in the market place about what governments should do. It depends upon how you're prepared to conduct your own life, and how much you're prepared to give of what you have to others . . . It's the sincere approach born of the conviction which I learned in a small town from a father who had a conviction approach.[27]

The theme of personal responsibility was one to which she returned again and again, and she continued to give fascinating insights into her thinking. In a *Woman's Own* magazine interview in October 1987, she remarked: 'There is no such thing as society. There are only individual men and women, and there are families.' This observation, and her reflection on 'Victorian values', should be taken together. Politicians of the right are not the only ones who raid history for inspiration. Politicians of all persuasions do it, although they bring back different trophies from their raids into the past. Left-wing politicians look back to the Victorian period, but see different values, or place a different interpretation on values. 'Self-help' is an example. In 1986 Sir Keith Joseph wrote an introduction to a new edition of Samuel Smiles's 1859 classic, giving it a Conservative slant; but 'self-help' in Victorian times meant different things to different people. To the middle class it was an individual virtue; to the working class it was a collective virtue, whereby people whose individual power was minimal joined together in order to help themselves. Neal Ascherson drew some of these points together in an article reflecting on yet another Thatcherite idea (this one emanating Douglas Hurd, Home Secretary from 1985–9), that of 'the active citizen':

Combinations, which in time became trade unions, were among the supreme expression of what used to be called, 'social love'. They rested on an idea of human dignity and responsibility which their members hoped to extend to all men. They believed that unity was strength, and that the nature of all men and women – not just those who gave surplus wealth to the poor – was in Goethe's words 'helpful and good'. They became a better example of Victorian 'responsibility' and 'social cohesion' (another phrase of Mr Hurd's) than the capitalists they fought. They remain still, with all their weaknesses, the standing army of active citizenship. But that's an army the Conservative Party would like to disband.[28]

Appeals to history as a justification for one's actions are likely to prove highly selective. (Appeals to the Bible may prove no less so, as in the case of Margaret Thatcher's version of the Good Samaritan, which laid most stress on his affluence.) The history books you choose to read will influence you, too. Three books in particular seem to have provided ammunition for the Thatcher administration. Martin J. Wiener's *English Culture and the Decline of the Industrial Spirit 1850–1980* stressed the failure of the educational system to inculcate the values that might have prevented Britain's economic decline. Harold Perkin's *The Rise of Professional Society: England Since 1880* stressed the triumph of the professional ideal, and the competition between public-sector and private-sector professionals. Correlli Barnett in *The Audit of War* blamed the creation of the welfare state for Britain's economic difficulties after the Second World War. Each of these books addressed the question of enterprise, and it was towards a re-awakening of an 'enterprise culture' that Conservative administrations made enormous efforts in the 1980s.

The task facing the government was a daunting one. A *New Society* survey in April 1977 on the attitudes of the British people to money and work revealed:

They are remarkably unambitious in a material sense. Very few sincerely want to be rich. Most people in Britain neither want nor expect a great deal more money. Even if they could get it, the vast majority do not seem prepared to work harder for it: most of our respondents thought we should work only as much as we need to live a pleasant life . . . It seems clear that the British people today prefer economic *stability* to rapid economic growth.

The distinguished sociologist Ralf Dahrendorf applauded these findings, saying that 'the desire to "live a pleasant life" rather than "work as much as one can for as much money as one can get", is a source of strength, not of weakness in Britain'. Others shared his optimism, and *The Times* had observed as far back as 1971 that 'The secret hope for Britain is indeed that the monetary obsession has penetrated our society less deeply than it has others. There are probably still more people in Britain who will give total effort for reasons of idealism than for reasons of gain'. But there were many who were pessimistic about the realities of a static economy. Edward Heath observed in 1973: 'The alternative to expansion is not, as some occasionally seem to suppose, an England of quiet market towns linked only by trains puffing slowly and peacefully through green meadows. The alternative is slums, dangerous roads, old factories, cramped schools, stunted lives.'[29]

The Thatcher governments' initiatives to encourage enterprise were far-ranging. They involved tax cuts, deregulation and the liberalisation of many controls, including the relaxation of restrictions on many professional groups to advertise. Much effort went into small business initiatives, including the setting up of local enterprise agencies to provide advice and stimulate the setting up of new businesses. Industrial aid was switched from subsidies to nationalised industries and blanket support of economically depressed regions, to projects which backed innovation, research and development, and the transfer of new technology. And so that the enterprise culture might be instilled at an early age, encouragement was given to links between industry and schools, while teachers (and those training to be teachers), as well as their pupils, were encouraged (and in the case of student-teachers, required) to engage in work-experience.

It is difficult to assess the effectiveness of these initiatives, partly because they were so broad. There was undoubtedly a rise in self-employment and the formation of new businesses. During the 1980s the number of self-employed people rose from around 1 million to more than 3 million by late 1988, over six times the increase of the previous 30 years. There is evidence, however, that there was a high turnover among the self-employed, a study of those in that category between the spring of 1986 and 1987, for example, showing that 440,000 entered self-employment while 250,000 left.

If the encouragement of enterprise represented an intention to turn the country back to 'Victorian' economic values, Conservative politicians in the 1980s showed a similar regard for their own version of 'Victorian' social values. In this retrospective quest for standards of behaviour, one period in particular was anathematised and that was the 1960s, the decade which was claimed to have heralded the 'permissive society'. Norman Tebbit was made chairman of the Conservative Party in 1985, in which year he published *Britain's Future: a Conservative Vision*. In it he extolled the virtues of individualism as opposed to collectivism, but he observed:

It would be wrong to blame all our ills upon collectivist policies. The effects of those policies have been dramatically worsened by the onset of the politics of the permissive society. Far from encouraging the greater self-discipline and responsibility, for which no doubt Mr Roy Jenkins hoped when he upheld the view that the permissive society is the civilised society, permissiveness compounded by the economic failure and personal irresponsibility engendered by the socialist state leads inevitably to the violent society . . .

[C]riminal behaviour [has not] increased because of poverty or unemployment: the 1930s was a time of very high unemployment but not of crime on today's scale. California is richer and more criminal than Britain

No. the trigger of today's outburst of crime and violence was deeper. It lies in the era and attitudes of post-War funk which gave birth to the 'Permissive Society' which, in turn generated today's violent society.

The permissives scorned traditional standards. Bad art was as good as good art. Grammar and spelling were no longer important. To be clean was no better than to be filthy. Good manners were no better than bad. Family life was derided as an outdated bourgeois concept. Criminals deserved as much sympathy as their victims. Many homes and classrooms became disorderly – if there was neither right nor wrong there could be no basis for punishment or reward. Violence and soft pornography became accepted in the media. Thus was sown the wind; and we are now reaping the whirlwind.[30]

Yet, as has been remarked in Chapter 14, the 1960s were not all that permissive, and even if Conservatives 20 years later professed to dislike the liberalising legislation of that decade, they did very little to alter it; a notable exception (as interesting for the light it sheds on Conservative attitudes to local government as to anything else) being Clause 28 of the 1988 Local Government Act which outlawed the 'promotion' of homosexual material by local authorities.

High on the political agenda was the fight against crime, for opinion polls showed that the fear of crime was rising faster than crime itself, and was becoming a problem in its own right. In 1981 the government instituted the first of a series of British Crime Surveys which showed that the average citizen would suffer a robbery once every five centuries; burglary once every 50 years; and assault resulting in injury (however slight) once every century. In the early 1980s a Briton's chances of being murdered were 25 per cent lower than they had been in the 1860s. So much for Victorian values! On the other hand, such 'average' figures concealed the fact that for some people, living in certain areas (particularly in inner-city areas and on bleak housing estates), the risks were such as to make fear of crime perfectly rational.

Public spending on law and order grew in real terms by 57.1 per cent between 1978–9 and 1987–8. The number of full-time police officers rose by 10,000, and the police were given sweeping new powers by the Police and Criminal Evidence Act 1984. The prison population rose from 49,700 in 1979 to 54,200 in 1986 (a higher proportion of the population than in any other country in western Europe), and a major prison-building programme was embarked upon, with eight being opened between 1985 and 1989. At the same time, thoughts were being turned to the privatisation of the prison service, which commenced on an experimental basis in the next decade.

The family, the school and the Church were seen by the government and its supporters as the nurseries of moral values, and blame for the perceived decline in behaviour was placed firmly at their door. Attention was frequently drawn to the number of single-parent families, estimated to number about 1 million in 1982, and containing about 1.6 million children. The proportion of children living with a single parent rose from 8 per cent in 1972 to 13 per cent in 1985. The proportion of single families in the 1970s had been about the same as that 100 years before, although the causation was different; in the 1870s death of a parent was the major cause, whereas in the 1980s it was more likely to be separation, divorce or non-marriage. Divorce was undoubtedly rising. In 1931, 0.5 persons per 1,000 people in England and Wales divorced. In 1961 the figure had risen to 2; by 1981 it was almost 12 per 1,000. Cohabitation was also on the increase. Only 5 per cent of women married in the 1950s reported having previously cohabited with their husbands. By the late 1980s, half of all couples marrying for the first time, and three-quarters of those marrying for the second time, had previously lived together.

The influence of organised religion is hard to estimate. The proportion of the adult population claiming membership of a Christian church fell from 20.7 per cent in 1970 to 15 per cent in 1987; but if one in seven of the adult population claimed church membership at the latter date, no more than one in ten went to church at all regularly. It would be quite difficult to claim that Britain in the 1980s was a Christian country, although not quite so difficult to claim that it was a religious country when members of other religions are included in what is, after all, a multi-faith society. That aspect of British society continued to make religious education in schools a highly controversial subject, just as it had been in Victorian times, although for different reasons. Many of those who supported Christian teaching in schools supported the Church only from the outside. They might have agreed with Lord Melbourne, Prime Minister when Queen Victoria came to the throne, who is attributed with saying, 'While I cannot be regarded as a pillar, I must be regarded as a buttress of the Church, because I support it from the outside'.

In the nineteenth century the Church of England was often looked upon as the buttress of the government, and the idea that it was 'the Tory Party at prayer' was not completely wide of the mark. In the 1980s, however, the Church was one of the sternest critics of the Thatcher administration, and little love was shown on the other side. The Archbishop of Canterbury and the Prime Minister differed over the service of thanksgiving at the end of the Falklands War; and the relationship between Church and government came to one of its lowest ebbs in 1985 with the publication of a Church of England report, 'Faith in the City', which focused on inner-city problems (and which a government spokesman described as 'Marxist').

Britain transformed?

It was unusual for a Conservative government to be so frequently criticised by the Church of England, but Margaret Thatcher had many brushes with the establishment, including the BBC and the civil service. Nothing could have made her strained relations with the establishment more vivid than the fact that (not once, but twice) members of Oxford University, her *alma mater*, refused her an honorary degree. She courted confrontation, and was frequently offered it.

In assessing the Thatcher years, it is important to distinguish the rhetoric from the reality, and the style from the substance. Peter Riddell comments:

> Mrs Thatcher's premiership . . . posed questions about the role of the state. As she decried the power of government over economic decisions, she centralized power over local government and other bodies which stood between Whitehall and the individual. She strengthened the power of the state to an extent not seen before. Some of her alleged centralism – the way she ran her Cabinet and Whitehall – disappeared with her and was only a memory within months of her resignation. But other aspects – the gradual erosion of the role of local authorities and the accretion of power in Whitehall – remained.[31]

Any assessment of 'conviction politics' has to start with the convictions themselves. Did the governments of the 1980s succeed in what they set out to do? The Thatcher administrations placed the cutting of inflation at the very top of their political agenda, but at the time of Margaret Thatcher's resignation retail-price inflation was running at 10.9 per cent, fractionally higher than when she came to power (although it fell back to single figures in the first half of 1991). The government planned to cut public expenditure and, as a proportion of gross domestic product, it did, although in real terms public spending rose by 16 per cent. The number of shareowners increased, as had been intended. From 7 per cent of the population, the number of shareholders rose to 21 per cent (roughly 11 million people), but the proportion of shares owned by individuals continued to decline. Home-ownership was up, from around 52 per cent to 66 per cent. However, families accepted by local authorities as homeless nearly doubled, and reached 146,000 in 1988. The Conservatives set out to reduce the power of the trade unions, and they succeeded. From a peak of 13.3 million in 1979, trade union membership fell to 10.5 in 1987; but although this was lower than for any year of the 1970s, it was about the same level as that which prevailed in the 1960s. The country had not become strike-free, and a wave of strikes in the summer of 1989 led journalists to talk of a 'Summer of Discontent', although officially recorded strikes were at a 55-year low in 1990. The Conservatives campaigned against crime: but notifiable crime recorded by the police went up 60 per cent in the 1980s. They did not set out to increase equality, and equality was not increased. Between 1979 and 1987 the living standards of the poorest fifth of the population increased by 1 per cent, while the wealthiest fifth gained 30 per cent. The aim of securing a 'classless society' was left to Margaret Thatcher's successor, John Major, to propound.

What of the future? Is there a case for arguing that the government's policies have finally brought to an end Britain's economic decline and have started to turn the economy around? Their supporters could point to the more rapid growth rates than other countries at the end of the 1980s, combined with higher profitability, and inward foreign investment (from such countries as Japan). There is some evidence, however, that Britain performs relatively well at those times when the world is performing relatively badly, as was noticeable in the 1930s. When the world's economic hare is tired, the British economic tortoise seems to perform well, but it falls behind when the world forces the pace a little. (The tortoise gets there in the end, it is true, but the course may be a long one.)

A noticeable trend of the 1980s was a deterioration in the balance of trade in manufactures, masked by an improvement in the oil balance, the contribution of which to gross domestic product rose from 1.7 per cent in 1978 to 6.5 per cent in 1984. Manufacturing industry continued to decline, but whether it was 'leaner and fitter', as the government proclaimed, or simply leaner, is debateable. For the greater part of the 1980s business investment stagnated, and when it began to rise sharply at the end of the decade, a high proportion of the increase went into the financial and commercial sector. In evidence to the House of Lords Committee on Overseas Trade in 1985, Lord Weinstock, the chairman of GEC, asked:

> What will the service industries be servicing when there is no hardware, when no wealth is actually being produced? We will be servicing, presumably, the production of wealth by others. We will supply the Changing of the Guard. We will supply the Beefeaters around the Tower of London. We will become a curiosity. I do not think that is what Britain is about. [32]

The House of Lords Select Committee on Technology and Science took a bleak view in 1991. There was, the committee reported, 'virtually no investment in manufacturing industry during the 1980s. If market forces alone are to determine the course of events it is conceivable that we will end up with no significant British owned manufacturing sector in the UK'. It remains to be seen if this is what comes about, and what the consequences might be if it does. All that can be predicted with any certainty is that the new millenium will involve many changes for Britain.

Thatcherism did not end with the resignation of Margaret Thatcher in November 1990, and the attempted transformation of the British economy and society which she hoped to achieve continued with her successor. When historians have the advantage of a longer perspective they may well argue that the real influences on Britain's development and upon its place in the world came from other quarters. The year 1990 witnessed the continuing break-up of the Soviet empire. It was the year in which Nelson Mandela was freed from prison, setting South Africa on the path back to the community of nations. In May a declaration was signed by Britain and 33 other countries at a United Nations Environmental Conference in Bergen, committing them to 'anticipate, prevent and attack the causes of environmental degradation', including ozone depletion and global warming. In July the World Health Organisation reported that AIDS was now the main cause of death for women aged 20–40. In the month prior to Margaret Thatcher's resignation, Germany once again became united. In the month after her departure, British and French engineers stood face to face beneath the Channel, as Britain's 8,000 years as an island came to an end.

Notes

1   Andrew Gamble, *Britain in Decline: Economic Policy, Political Strategy and the British state*, third edition, Macmillan, 1990, p. 191.
2   Denis Healey, *The Time of My Life*, Penguin, 1990, p. 489.
3   Quoted in Nick Gardner, *Decade of Discontent: The Changing British Economy Since 1973*, Blackwell, 1987, p. 100.
4   Keith Smith, *The British Economic Crisis*, revised edition, Penguin, 1989, p. 155.
5   Christopher Huhne, *Real World Economics*, Penguin, 1991, p. 146.
6   Paul Kennedy, *Preparing for the Twenty-first Century*, HarperCollins, 1993, p. 129.
7   Quoted in Stephen George, *Britain and European Integration since 1945*, Blackwell, 1991, p. 61.
8   Barry Supple, 'Fear of failing: economic history and the decline of Britain', *Economic History Review*, August 1994, p. 452.
9   Keith Smith, op. cit., 1989, p. 107.
10 'A last chance to honour our makers', *Independent on Sunday*, 1 November 1992.
11 Michael Dintenfass, *The Decline of Industrial Britain 1870–1980*, Routledge, 1992, p. 38.
12 Quoted in Keith Smith, op. cit., 1989, p. 92.
13 Quoted in Chris Wrigley, 'Trade unions, the government and the economy' in Terry Gourvish and Alan O'Day (eds), *Britain Since 1945*, Macmillan, 1991, p. 74.
14 Michael Ball, Fred Gray and Linda McDowell, *The Transformation of Britain: Contemporary Social and Economic Change*, Fontana, 1989, p. 196.
15 Quoted in David Smith, *North and South*, Penguin, 1989, p. 116.
16 Ibid. p. 120.
17 Peter Riddell, *The Thatcher Era and its Legacy*, Blackwell, 1991, p. 154.
18 Michael Ball, Fred Gray and Linda McDowell, op. cit., 1989, p. 448.
19 Quoted in Peter Riddell, op. cit, 1991, page 127.
20 Quoted in David Smith, op. cit, 1989, p. 33.

21   Quoted in Richard Johnson, 'Thatcherism and English education: breaking the mould, or confirming the pattern', *History of Education*, vol. 18, 1989, p. 114.

22   Christopher Huhne, op. cit, 1991, p. 91.

23   Harold Perkin, *The Rise of Professional Society*, Routledge, 1990, pp. 486–7.

24   Bernard Porter, *Plots and Paranoia: a History of Political Espionage in Britain, 1790 1988*, Routledge, 1992, p. 208.

25   Philip Marsden-Smedley (ed.), *Britain in the Eighties: The Spectator's View of the Thatcher Decade*, Paladin, 1991, p. 176.

26   Quoted in Peter Riddell, op. cit, 1991, p. 108.

27   Ibid., p. 3.

28   *Observer*, 16 October 1988.

29   Quoted in Martin J.Wiener, *English Culture and the Decline of the Industrial Spirit 1850–1980*, Penguin, 1985, p. 162.

30   Quoted in Robert Eccleshall, *English Conservatism Since the Restoration*, Unwin Hyman, 1990, p. 247.

31   Peter Riddell, op. cit., 1991, p. 245.

32   Quoted in Barry Supple, op. cit, 1994, p. 451.

Further reading

These suggestions are confined to books, but it will be appreciated that much of the most recent scholarship is to be found in articles. Annual bibliographies and reviews of current literature appear in a number of journals, including *The Economic History Review*, *Social History*, *Agricultural History Review*, *Journal of Transport History*, and *Victorian Studies*.

General economic history

A number of books cover the whole period or large parts of it, including Peter Mathias, *The First Industrial Nation* (Methuen, second edition, 1983); E. J. Hobsbawm, *Industry and Empire* (Penguin, 1969); Phyllis Deane and W. A. Cole, *British Economic Growth, 1688–1959* (Cambridge University Press, second edition, 1969); John Rule, *The Vital Century, England's Developing Economy 1714–1815* (Longman, 1992); Francois Crouzet, *The Victorian Economy* (Methuen, 1982); W. Ashworth, *The Economic History of England, 1870–1939* (Methuen, 1960); and Sidney Pollard, *The Development of the British Economy, 1914–1967* (Edward Arnold, second edition, 1969). Much recent research is made accessible in Anne Digby, Charles Feinstein and David Jenkins (eds), *New Directions in Economic and Social History*, vol. 2 (Macmillan, 1992). Many of the revisions of the New Economic Historians are included in Roderick Floud and Donald McCloskey (eds), *The Economic History of Britain Since 1700*, vols 1 and 2 (Cambridge University Press, 1981). Those particularly interested in econometric history are referred to D. N. McCloskey, *Econometric History* (Macmillan, 1987) and Roderick Floud, *An Introduction to Quantitative Methods for Historians* (Methuen, second edition, 1979).

The regional balance can be maintained with B. Lenman, *An Economic History of Modern Scotland, 1660–1976* (Batsford, 1977); S. O. Checkland, *Industry and Ethos: Scotland, 1832–1914* (Edward Arnold, 1984); G. E. Jones, *Modern Wales: A Concise History* (Cambridge University Press, 1984); A. H. John, *The Industrial Development of South Wales, 1750–1850* (University of Wales Press, 1951); and L. M. Cullen, *An Economic History of Ireland Since 1660* (Batsford, 1987).

Britain's economic development is set in a wider context in a number of books. Technological change in western Europe from 1750 to the present is the subject of David Landes, *The Unbound Prometheus* (Cambridge University Press, 1969). Sidney Pollard, *Peaceful Conquest: the Industrialization of Europe, 1760–1970* (Cambridge University Press, 1981) and Carlo Cipolla (ed.), *The Fontana Economic History of Europe* vols 3–5 (Fontana, 1973–6) set Britain's economic growth in a European context. Trans-Atlantic comparisons are made by Philip Bagwell and G. E. Mingay, *Britain and America: A Study of Economic Change, 1850–1939* (Routledge and Kegan Paul, revised edition, 1987).

Industrial change is the theme of A. E. Musson, *The Growth of British Industry* (Batsford, 1978). For transport history see Philip Bagwell, *The Transport Revolution from 1770* (Batsford, 1974), and H. J. Dyos and D. H. Aldcroft, *British Transport* (Leicester University Press, 1969). The most convenient history of technology is T. K. Derry and Trevor Williams, *A Short History of Technology* (Oxford University Press, 1960). Those who want a long history should study Charles Singer et al., *A History of Technology*, vols 4 and 5 (Oxford University Press, 1958).

Much economic history can be studied on the ground, two of many useful guides to industrial archaeology being R. A. Buchanan, *Industrial Archaeology in Britain* (Penguin, 1972) and John Butt and Ian Donnachie, *Industrial Archaeology in the British Isles* (Elek, 1979). A book which deals specifically with surviving relics of transportation is P. J. G. Ransom, *The Archaeology of the Transport Revolution, 1750–1850* (Guild Publishing, 1984). Artefacts are considered by Asa Briggs in *Victorian Things* (Batsford, 1988).

B. W. Clapp, *Documents in English Economic History: England Since 1760* (Bell, 1976), offers a good selection of primary sources.

General social history

The most comprehensive general history is F. M. L. Thompson (ed.), *The Cambridge Social History of Britain, 1750–1950*, vols 1–3 (Cambridge Univerity Press, 1990). J. F. C. Harrison, *The Common People* (Flamingo, 1984) covers a longer time span but has the great merit of quoting extensively from primary sources. Documents alone tell their story in Theo Barker (ed.), *The Long March of Everyman 1750–1960* (Deutsch/BBC, 1975), while a collection of sources covering a shorter period is J. T. Ward, *The Age of Change: 1770–1870* (Black, 1975).

Three series are of special interest. Hutchinson's *Social History of England* includes R. W. Malcolmson, *Life and Labour in England, 1700–1780* (1981); James Walvin, *English Urban Life, 1776–1851* (1984); and Pamela Horn, *The Rural World, 1780–1850* (1980). In the *Pelican Social History of Britain*, Roy Porter, *English Society in the Eighteenth Century* (1982); Jose Harris, *Britain, 1870–1914* (1994); John Stevenson, *British Society 1914–45* (1984); and Arthur Marwick, *British Society Since 1945* (1982) have so far appeared. The Longman series *Foundations of Modern Britain* takes in economic and political themes as well as social, and includes Geoffrey Holmes and Daniel Szechi, *The Age of Oligarchy: Pre-Industrial Britain 1722–1783* (1993); Eric J. Evans, *The Forging of the Modern State: Early Industrial Britain, 1783–1870* (1983); and Keith Robbins, *The Eclipse of a Great Power: Modern Britain, 1870–1975* (1983). These books contain useful compendia of information. The Longman series *A Social and Economic History of England* includes John Rule, *Albion's People: English Society, 1714–1815* (1992), and S. G. Checkland, *The Rise of Industrial Society in England, 1714–1815* (1964).

Dorothy Marshall, *Industrial England, 1776–1851* (Routledge and Kegan Paul, 1973) is good for the early period, as is Harold Perkin, *The Origins of Modern English Society, 1780–1880* (Routledge and Kegan Paul, 1971). Perkin followed up this book with *The Rise of Professional Society: England Since 1880* (Routledge, 1989).

The Victorian era is admirably covered by F. M. L. Thompson, *The Rise of Respectable Society: A Social History of Victorian Britain 1830–1900* (Fontana, 1988); J. F. C. Harrison, *Early Victorian Britain, 1832–51* (Fontana, 1979); and Geoffrey Best, *Mid-Victorian Britain, 1851–70* (Fontana, 1979). For the period from the mid-nineteenth century, see François Bedarida, *A Social History of England, 1851–1975* (Methuen, 1979); Judith Ryder and Harold Silver, *Modern English Society, 1850–1970* (Methuen, 1970);

and Janet Roebuck, *The Making of Modern English Society from 1850* (Routledge and Kegan Paul, 1973).

Two books by Arthur Marwick cover the twentieth century: *The Explosion of British Society, 1914–1970* (Macmillan, second edition, 1971) and *Britain in the Century of Total War* (Pelican, 1970). For this period, see also G. C. Peden, *British Economic and Social Policy, Lloyd George to Margaret Thatcher* (Philip Allan, second edition, 1991).

A number of social themes are examined in books which take a broad chronological sweep. Education is covered in Michael Hyndman, *Schools and Schooling in England and Wales: A Documentary History* (Harper and Row, 1978); John Lawson and Harold Silver, *A Social History of Education in England* (Methuen, 1973); James Murphy, *Church, State and Schools in Britain, 1800–1970* (Routledge and Kegan Paul, 1971); and David Wardle, *English Popular Education, 1780–1970* (Cambridge University Press, 1970). For housing, see John Burnett, *A Social History of Housing, 1815–1970* (Methuen, 1980), and Anthony Quiney, *House and Home: A History of the Small English House* (BBC, 1986). For leisure, see James Walvin, *Leisure and Society, 1830–1950* (Longman, 1978) in the series *Themes in British Social History*. The fields of 'Green History' are tilled by B. W. Clapp in *An Environmental History of Britain* (Longman, 1994).

Much social history can be illuminated by folk song. For this, see two books by Roy Palmer, *A Touch on the Times* (Penguin, 1974) and *The Sound of History: Songs and Social Comment* (Oxford University Press, 1988).

Chapter 1: Britain and the industrial revolution

A considerable number of early works on industrialisation have been made available in reprint, and often in facsimile. A particularly good series is the *Library of Industrial Classics*, published by Frank Cass. Included are (for example) Andrew Ure, *The Philosophy of Manufactures* (1835, reprinted 1967); William Dodd, *The Factory System Illustrated* (1842, reprinted 1968); P. Gaskell, *Artisans and Machinery (1836, reprinted 1968)*; and John Fielden, *The Curse of the Factory System* (1836, reprinted 1969). W. O. Henderson, *Industrial Society Under the Regency, 1814–18* (Cass, 1968) gives an insight into the industrial revolution through the eyes of European observers, whose accounts are transcribed. Selections of short extracts from documents will be found in E. Royston Pike, *Human Documents of Adam Smith's Time* (Allen and Unwin, 1974), and the same editor's *Human Documents of the Industrial Revolution in Britain* (Allen and Unwin, 1966).

A collection of essays which debate some of the larger issues is Joel Mokyr (ed.), *The British Industrial Revolution: An Economic Perspective* (Westview Press, 1993). N. F. R. Crafts, *English Economic Growth During the Industrial Revolution* (Clarendon Press, 1985) brings together much fresh quantitative analysis. For Britain on the eve of industrialisation see Peter Laslett, *The World We Have Lost* (Methuen, 1965) and three books by Leslie Clarkson: *Proto–Industrialisation: The First Phase of Industrialisation?* (Macmillan, 1985); *Death, Disease and Famine in Pre-Industrial England* (Gill and Macmillan, 1975) and *Pre–Industrial Economy in England* (Batsford, 1971). D. C. Coleman, *The Economy of England, 1450–1750* (Oxford University Press, 1977) also covers the centuries before industrial take-off.

The causes of the industrial revolution are analysed in Maxine Berg, *The Age of Manufactures* (Fontana, 1985); Alan Thompson, *Dynamics of the Industrial Revolution* (Arnold, 1973); R. M. Hartwell, *The Causes of the Industrial Revolution in England* (Methuen, 1970); and M. W. Flinn, *The Origins of the Industrial Revolution* (Longman,

1966). See also Peter Mathias, *The Transformation of England* (Methuen, 1979), and Neil McKendrick *et al.*, *The Birth of a Consumer Society* (Europa, 1982).

The agricultural revolution is examined by J. V. Beckett, *The Agricultural Revolution* (Blackwell, 1990); Michael Turner, *Enclosures in Britain 1750–1830* (Macmillan, 1984); E. L. Jones, *Agriculture and the Industrial Revolution* (Blackwell, 1974); E. L. Jones, *Agriculture and Economic Growth in England, 1650–1815* (Methuen, 1967); and John Addy, *The Agrarian Revolution* (Longman, 1972), a book which also contains documentary extracts. For the debate on the effect of enclosure upon the small landholder see G. E. Mingay, *Enclosure and the Small Farmer in the Age of the Industrial Revolution* (Macmillan, 1968).

Population growth is the subject of E. A. Wrigley and R. A. Schofield, *The Population History of England, 1541–1871: a Reconstruction* (Cambridge University Press, 1989); Neil Tranter, *Population Since the Industrial Revolution* (Croom Helm, 1973); Thomas McKeown, *The Modern Rise of Population* (Arnold, 1976); and H. J. Habakkuk, *Population Growth and Economic Development Since 1750* (Leicester University Press, 1972).

Overseas trade is covered by W. E. Minchinton (ed.), *The Growth of English Overseas Trade in the Seventeenth and Eighteenth Centuries* (Methuen, 1969); Ralph Davis, *The Rise of the English Shipping Industry in the Seventeenth and Eighteenth Centuries* (Macmillan, 1962); and Judith Blow Williams, *British Commercial Policy and Trade Expansion, 1750–1850* (Oxford University Press, 1972).

For internal transportation, see Charles Hadfield, *British Canals* (David and Charles, second edition, 1966); E. Pawson, *Transport and Economy: the Turnpike Roads of Eighteenth-Century Britain* (Academic Press, 1977); and Anthony Bird, *Roads and Vehicles* (Longman, 1969).

For invention, see A. Dutton, *The Patent System and Inventive Activity During the Industrial Revolution* (Manchester University Press, 1984). François Crouzet, *The First Industrialists: the Problem of Origins* (Cambridge University Press, 1985), and Stanley Chapman, *The Early Factory Masters* (David and Charles, 1967) look at the men behind the factory system, documents on which will be found in J. T. Ward, *The Factory System,* vol. 1, *Birth and Growth* (David and Charles, 1970). On capital formation, see C. H. Feinstein and S. Pollard (eds), *Studies in Capital Formation in the United Kingdom* (Oxford University Press, 1988). John Addy, *The Textile Revolution* (Longman, 1976) contains documentary sources, but for a fuller discussion see S. D. Chapman, *The Cotton Industry in the Industrial Revolution* (Macmillan, 1972). Other important industries are examined in M. W. Flinn, *The History of the British Coal Industry,* vol. 2, *1700–1830: The Industrial Revolution* (Clarendon Press, 1984); T. S. Ashton and J. Sykes, *The Coal Industry in the Eighteenth Century* (Manchester University Press, second edition, 1964); J. R. Harris, *The British Iron Industry 1700–1850* (Macmillan, 1988); and T. S. Ashton, *Iron and Steel in the Industrial Revolution* (Manchester University Press, second edition, 1951). The contribution of steam power is considered in E. Robinson and A. E. Musson, *James Watt and the Steam Revolution* (Adams and Dart, 1969). To capture the visual impact of the industrial revolution, see F. D. Klingender, *Art and the Industrial Revolution* (Paladin, 1972), and Asa Briggs, *Iron Bridge to Crystal Palace: Impact and Images of the Industrial Revolution* (Thames and Hudson, 1979).

Chapter 2: The social impact of industrialisation before 1850

The best collection of documents is Patricia Hollis (ed.), *Class and Conflict in Nineteenth-century England, 1815–1850* (Routledge and Kegan Paul, 1973). There are good sources on changing attitudes to industrialisation and urbanisation in Alasdair Clayre, *Nature and Industrialization* (Oxford University Press, 1977), and on responses to the coming of the machine in Humphrey Jennings, *Pandæmonium 1660–1886* (Deutsch,1985). W. H. Chaloner (ed.) *The Autobiography of Samuel Bamford* (Frank Cass, new edition, 1967) presents the life of a radical handloom-weaver who was present at Peterloo. Robert Owen's critique of society undergoing change will be found in his *Report to the County of Lanark* and *A New View of Society* (new edition with an introduction by V. A. C. Gatrell, Penguin, 1970).

For a critical discussion of Owen, see J. F. C. Harrison, *Robert Owen and the Owenites in Britain and America* (Routledge and Kegan Paul, 1969), and John Butt (ed.), *Robert Owen, Prince of Cotton Spinners* (David and Charles, 1971).

The best introduction to the development of class and class consciousness is R. J. Morris, *Class and Class Consciousness in the Industrial Revolution, 1780–1850* (Macmillan, 1979). See also E. P. Thompson, *The Making of the English Working Class* (Penguin, 1972); R. S. Neale, *Class and Ideology in the Nineteenth Century* (Routledge and Kegan Paul, 1972); John Foster, *Class Struggle and the Industrial Revolution* (Weidenfeld, 1974); R. S. Neale, *History and Class* (Basil Blackwell, 1983); and Robert Glen, *Urban Workers in the Early Industrial Revolution* (Croom Helm, 1984). For changes in class structure in the later nineteenth century, see Alastair J. Reid, *Social Classes and Social Relations in Britain, 1850 1911* (Macmillan, 1992).

Malcolm Thomis, *The Town Labourer and the Industrial Revolution* (Batsford, 1974) is an excellent survey, and also forms a valuable commentary on the classic work, *The Town Labourer, 1760–1832*, written by J. L. and Barbara Hammond (Longman, new edition, 1966). Duncan Bythell, *The Handloom Weavers* (Cambridge University Press, 1969) is the best book on the subject, while the same author's *The Sweated Trades* (Batsford, 1978) covers the whole phenomenon of outwork throughout the nineteenth century. For Luddism, see Malcolm Thomis, *The Luddites* (David and Charles, 1970). Social protest is more generally discussed in Malcolm Thomis and Peter Holt, *Threats of Revolution in Britain, 1789–1848* (Macmillan, 1977); John Stevenson, *Popular Disturbances in England, 1700–1870* (Longman, 1979); and D. G. Wright, *Popular Radicalism: The Working-Class Experience,1780–1880* (Longman, 1988). For the government response to popular protest, see Bernard Porter, *Plots and Paranoia: A History of Political Espionage in Britain,1790–1988* (Routledge, new edition, 1992).

On the standard of living controversy, see A. J. Taylor, *The Standard of Living in Britain in the Industrial Revolution* (Methuen, 1975). John Burnett discusses changes in diet in *Plenty and Want* (Routledge, third edition, 1989). Changing attitudes to work and leisure are the subject of Alasdair Clayre, *Work and Play* (Weidenfeld, 1974).

A collection of essays covering many aspects of the social impact of the industrial revolution is Patrick O'Brien and Roland Quinault (eds), *The Industrial Revolution and British Society* (Cambridge University Press, 1993).

Chapter 3: Landed society in the nineteenth century

Two valuable nineteenth-century works are available in facsimile: John Bateman, *The Great Landowners of Great Britain and Ireland* (1883; new edition with an introduction by David Spring, Leicester University Press, 1971); G. C. Brodrick, *English Land and English Landlords* (1881; new edition, David and Charles, 1968). The essays of Richard Jefferies give a good insight into rural society towards the end of the nineteenth century, an especially good collection being *Hodge and his Masters* (1880; new edition, MacGibbon and Kee, 1966). For changes at the turn of the century, see George Bourne (Sturt), *Change in the Village*, (1912, reprinted George Duckworth, 1966).

An excellent overview is provided by G. E. Mingay (ed.), *The Victorian Countryside* (Routledge and Kegan Paul, 1981) and the collection of essays by Mingay in *A Social History of the English Countryside* (Routledge, 1990). A general study of the early part of the period is E. W. Bovill, *English Country Life, 1780–1830* (Oxford University Press, 1962). For the later nineteenth century see G. E. Mingay, *Rural Life in Victorian England* (Heinemann, 1976).

For the landed gentry, see J. T. Ward and R. G. Wilson (eds), *Land and Industry: The Landed Estate in the Industrial Revolution* (David and Charles, 1971), and F. M. L. Thompson, *English Landed Society in the Nineteenth Century* (Routledge and Kegan Paul, 1963). The changing fortunes of the aristocracy are analysed in David Cannadine, *The Decline and Fall of the British Aristocracy* (Picador, 1992). Social mobility between the middle and upper classes is the subject of Leonore Davidoff, *The Best Circles* (Croom Helm, 1973).

There are many books on the public schools and the education of a gentleman, but three particularly good accounts are T. W. Bamford, *The Rise of the Public Schools* (Nelson, 1967); Brian Simon and Ian Bradley (eds), *The Victorian Public School* (Gill and Macmillan, 1975); and J. R. de S. Honey, *Tom Brown's Universe* (Millington, 1977).

For the Church in the countryside, see Owen Chadwick, *The Victorian Church*, part one (Black, 1966), together with Nigel Yates, *The Oxford Movement and Anglican Ritualism* (Historical Association, 1983); and B. I. Coleman, *The Church of England in the mid-Nineteenth Century* (Historical Association, 1980).

Pamela Horn, *Labouring Life in the Victorian Countryside* (Gill and Macmillan, 1976) is a good introduction to the humblest members of the landed interest. Rural discontent is the theme of A. J. Peacock, *Bread or Blood* (Gollancz, 1965); E. J. Hobsbawm and George Rudé, *Captain Swing* (Lawrence and Wishart, 1969); and J. P. D. Dunbabin, *Rural Discontent in Nineteenth Century Britain* (Faber and Faber, 1974). The growth of trade unionism among farm workers can be traced in Pamela Horn, *Joseph Arch* (Roundwood Press, 1971), while Arch's autobiography of 1898 was reprinted by MacGibbon and Kee in 1966.

Chapter 4: The course of agriculture to 1914

A good primary source for the early nineteenth century is the report of the Board of Agriculture on *The Agricultural State of the Kingdom* (1816; new edition, with introduction by G. E. Mingay, Adams and Dart, 1970). Several of the county reports of the Board of Agriculture have been reprinted in facsimile, for example, Charles Vancouver, *General Report of the Agriculture of the County of Devon* (1808; David and Charles, 1969). For the Anti-Corn Law League, see Norman Longmate, *The Breadstealers: The Fight Against the Corn Laws, 1838–1846* (Temple Smith, 1984), while a good source is the work of one of its executive committee members, Archibald Prentice, *History of the Anti-Corn Law League* (1853; new edition with introduction by W. H. Chaloner, Frank Cass, 1968). There are also relevant documents in Norman Gash, *The Age of Peel* (Edward Arnold, 1968). The classic of high farming is

James Caird, *English Agriculture in 1850–51* (1852; reprinted, Frank Cass, 1968).

There are several good general histories of agriculture, including J. D. Chambers and G. E. Mingay, *The Agricultural Revolution, 1750–1880* (Batsford, 1966); E. L. Jones, *The Development of English Agriculture, 1815–73* (Macmillan, 1978); and Christabel Orwin and E. H. Whetham, *History of British Agriculture, 1846–1914* (David and Charles, 1971). A valuable collection of essays will be found in W. E. Minchinton (ed.), *Essays in Agricultural History*, vol. 2 (David and Charles, 1968). Kenneth Hudson, *Patriotism with Profit* (Hugh Evelyn, 1972) deals with the spread of good agricultural practice. The development of agricultural machinery can be traced in G. E. Fussell, *The Farmer's Tools* (Andrew Melrose, 1952). For the agricultural depression, see P. J. Perry, *British Farming in the Great Depression, 1870–1914* (David and Charles, 1974).

Chapter 5: Social problems in the age of laissez–faire

A good, broad collection of documents is E. J. Evans (ed.), *Social Policy, 1830–1914* (Routledge and Kegan Paul, 1978). B. I. Coleman (ed.), *The Idea of the City in Nineteenth Century Britain* (Routledge and Kegan Paul, 1973) contains sources on evolving attitudes to urbanisation. E. J. Midwinter, *Victorian Social Reform* (Longman, 1968) combines documents with discussion. Other primary sources are included below in relation to the specific topics which they cover.

There are two useful accounts of social problems and their solution: Ursula Henriques, *Before the Welfare State* (Longman, 1979), and John Roach, *Social Reform in England, 1780–1880* (Batsford, 1978). The essays in A. P. Donajgrodzki (ed.), *Social Control in Nineteenth Century Britain* (Croom Helm, 1977) touch upon various aspects of that concept. On the problems of nineteenth-century cities see R. J. Morris and Richard Rodger (eds), *The Victorian City: A Reader in British Urban History 1820–1914* (Longman, 1993); Asa Briggs, *Victorian Cities* (Penguin, 1968); H. J. Dyos (ed.), *The Study of Urban History* (Edward Arnold, 1968), and the magnificent two volumes of H. J. Dyos and Michael Wolff, *The Victorian City* (Routledge and Kegan Paul, 1973).

For voluntarism, see F. Prochaska, *The Voluntary Impulse: Philanthropy in Modern Britain* (Faber, 1988).The transformation from individualism to collectivism in social policy is examined in A. J. Taylor, *Laissez-faire and State Intervention in Nineteenth Century Britain* (Macmillan, 1972); S. E. Finer, 'The transmission of Benthamite ideas, 1820–50' in Gillian Sutherland (ed.), *Studies in the Growth of Nineteenth Century Government* (Routledge and Kegan Paul, 1972); Derek Fraser, *The Evolution of the British Welfare State* (Macmillan, 1973); Peter Stansky, *The Victorian Revolution* (New Viewpoints, 1973); and Oliver MacDonagh, *Early Victorian Government* (Weidenfeld, 1977).

For the causes of poverty, see James Treble, *Urban Poverty in Britain, 1830–1914* (Batsford, 1979), and for a general, cultural overview see Gertrude Himmerlfarb, *The Idea of Poverty: England in the Early Industrial Age* (Faber, 1984). Anne Digby, *The Poor Law in Nineteenth Century England and Wales* (Historical Association, 1982) is a good short introduction to the Poor Law, and the same author's *Pauper Palaces* (Routledge and Kegan Paul, 1978) is an excellent case study based on Norfolk. Other useful books on the Poor Law are Paul Slack, *The English Poor Law 1531–1782* (Macmillan, 1990); Geoffrey Taylor, *The Problem of Poverty, 1660–1834* (Longman, 1969), a book which contains documents; Anthony Brundage, *The Making of the New Poor Law, 1832–9* (Hutchinson, 1978); Derek Fraser, *The New*

Poor Law in the Nineteenth Century (Macmillan, 1976); Brian Inglis, *Poverty and the Industrial Revolution* (Hodder and Stoughton, 1971); and two books by Michael Rose, *The English Poor Law* (David and Charles, 1971), which contains primary sources, and *The Relief of Poverty, 1834–1914* (Macmillan, second edition, 1986).

For public health, see F. B. Smith, *The People's Health, 1830–1910* (Croom Helm, 1979); Anthony Wohl, *Endangered Lives* (Methuen, 1984); Norman Longmate, *King Cholera* (Hamish Hamilton, 1966); and R. Woods and J. Woodward (eds), *Urban Disease and Mortality in Nineteenth Century England* (Batsford, 1984).

Housing is covered by S. D. Chapman (ed.), *The History of Working Class Housing* (David and Charles, 1971); Enid Gauldie, *Cruel Habitations* (Allen and Unwin, 1974); Anthony Wohl, *The Eternal Slum* (Arnold, 1971); and J. N. Tarn, *Working Class Housing in Nineteenth Century Britain* (Lund Humphries, 1971).

A good starting point for a study of crime is Clive Emsley, *Crime and Society in England, 1750–1900* (Longman, 1987). V. A. C. Gattrell and T. B. Hadden, 'Criminal statistics and their interpretation' in E. A. Wrigley (ed.), *Nineteenth Century Society* (Cambridge University Press, 1972) is a good source on crime rates, and the debate on crime and policing can be followed in J. J. Tobias, *Nineteenth Century Crime: Prevention and Punishment* (David and Charles, 1972) which contains documents; David Philips, *Crime and Authority in Victorian England* (Croom Helm, 1977); David Jones (ed.), *Crime, Protest, Community and Police in Nineteenth Century Britain* (Routledge and Kegan Paul, 1982); and Victor Bailey (ed.), *Policing and Punishment in Nineteenth Century Britain* (Croom Helm, 1981). Henry Mayhew and John Binny, *The Criminal Prisons of London* (1862, reprinted Frank Cass, 1968) is a good nineteenth-century source and Clarence Rook, *The Hooligan Nights* (1899, reprinted with an introduction by Benny Green, Oxford University Press, 1979) is good on teenage gangland in the 1890s.

Among books on religion, see especially D. Hempton, *Methodism, Politics and British Society, 1750–1850* (Hutchinson, 1984); W. R. Ward, *Religion and Society in England, 1790–1850* (Batsford, 1972); A. D. Gilbert, *Religion and Society in Industrial England* (Longman, 1976); Stuart Andrews, *Methodism and Society* (Longman, 1970) which includes documents; and Hugh McCleod, *Class and Religion in the Late Victorian City* (Croom Helm, 1974).

James Walvin, *A Child's World* (Penguin, 1982) is an excellent account of the experience of children 1800–1914, and includes education. Other useful books on elementary education are Michael Sanderson, *Education, Economic Change and Society in England, 1780–1870* (Macmillan, 1983); John Hurt, *Education in Evolution* (Rupert Hart-Davis, 1971); Alec Ellis, *Educating our Masters: Influences on the Growth of Literacy in Victorian Working-Class Children* (Gower, 1985); P. Gardner, *The Lost Elementary Schools of Victorian England* (Croom Helm, 1984); and Thomas Laqueur's book on the Sunday Schools, *Religion and Respectability* (Yale University Press, 1976).

Chapter 6: The great Victorian boom

R. A. Church, *The Great Victorian Boom* (Macmillan, 1975) is a good introduction, and there is a good collection of essays edited by the same author in *The Dynamics of Victorian Business* (Allen and Unwin, 1980). J. D. Chambers, *The Workshop of the World* (Oxford University Press, 1968) is a useful general economic history covering the years 1820–80. The arguments on technological change can be followed in H. J. Habakkuk, *American and British Technology in the Nineteenth Century* (Cambridge University Press, 1962), and S. B. Saul (ed.), *Technological Change: The United States and Britain in the Nineteenth Century* (Methuen, 1970).

Patrick Beaver, *The Crystal Palace* (Hugh Evelyn, 1970) covers both its construction and its contents, while the *Illustrated Catalogue of the Great Exhibition*, originally published by the *Art Journal*, is available in facsimile (Dover, 1970).

A general history of transportation in this period is Michael J. Freeman and Derek H. Aldcroft (eds), *Transport in Victorian Britain* (Manchester University Press, 1988). Jack Simmons, *The Victorian Railway* (Thames and Hudson, 1991) is specifically on this period. Whole libraries of books have been written on the railways. Among the general histories, the following can be recommended: Harold Perkin, *The Age of the Railway* (Panther, 1970); Michael Robbins, *The Railway Age* (Penguin, 1965); Jack Simmons, *The Railways of Britain* (Macmillan, second edition, 1968), and the same author's *The Railway in England and Wales, 1830–1914* (Leicester University Press, 1978). Books which deal with specific issues include Geoffrey Alderman, *The Railway Interest* (Leicester University Press, 1973); P. S. Bagwell, *The Railway Clearing House in the British Economy, 1842–1922* (Allen and Unwin, 1968); Terry Coleman, *The Railway Navvies* (Penguin, 1968); John R. Kellett, *The Impact of Railways on Victorian Cities* (Routledge and Kegan Paul, 1969); and Henry Parris, *Government and the Railways in Nineteenth Century Britain* (Routledge and Kegan Paul, 1965). For the impact of railways on the economy, see especially, T. R. Gourvish, *British Railways and the British Economy, 1830–1914* (Macmillan, 1980); G. R. Hawke, *Railways and Economic Growth in England and Wales, 1840–70* (Oxford University Press, 1970); P. O'Brien, *The New Economic History of the Railways* (Croom Helm, 1977); and Michael Reed (ed.), *Railways in the Victorian Economy* (David and Charles, 1969). Many nineteenth-century railway books are available in facsimile, a particularly interesting one being F. S. Williams, *Our Iron Roads* (third edition, 1883; reprinted by Gresham Books, 1981).

For shipbuilding, see J. Guthrie, *A History of Marine Engineering* (Hutchinson, 1971) and M. S. Moss and J. R. Hume, *Workshop of the British Empire: Engineering and Shipbuilding in the West of Scotland* (Heinemann, 1977).

The coal industry is covered by B. R. Mitchell, *Economic Development of the British Coal Industry, 1800–1914* (Cambridge University Press, 1984), and Brian Lewis, *Coal Mining in the Eighteenth and Nineteenth Centuries* (Longman, 1971) which contains documents.

For iron and steel, see T. S. Ashton, *Iron and Steel in the Industrial Revolution* (Manchester University Press, third edition, 1963); A. Birch, *The Economic History of the British Iron and Steel Industry, 1784–1879* (Frank Cass, 1967); and W. K. V. Gale, *The British Iron and Steel Industry: A Technical History* (David and Charles, 1967).

Engineering is dealt with in R. C. Floud, *The British Machine-Tool Industry, 1850–1914* (Cambridge University Press, 1976); L. T. C. Rolt, *Tools for the Job* (Batsford, 1965), and the same author's *Victorian Engineering* (Penguin, 1974). Rolt's life of *Isambard Kingdom Brunel* (Penguin, 1970) chronicles one of the greatest of the Victorian engineers. For the rise of the professional engineer, see R. A. Buchanan, *The Engineers: A History of the Engineering Profession in Britain, 1750–1914* (Jessica Kingsley Publishers, 1989); and for a lavish insight into the work of Victorian (and later) draughtsmen, see Ken Baynes and Francis Pugh, *The Art of the Engineer* (Lutterworth, 1981).

The development of banking can be traced in L. S. Pressnell, *Country Banking in the Industrial Revolution* (Oxford University Press, 1956); S. G. Checkland, *Scottish Banking: A History, 1695–1973* (Collins, 1975); Richard Roberts and David Kynaston, *The Bank of England: Money, Power and Influence, 1694–1994* (Oxford University Press, 1995) and J. H. Clapham, *The Bank of England: A History, 1694–1914* (Cambridge University Press, 1944). For the rise of the business corporation, see

P. L. Payne, *British Entrepreneurship in the Nineteenth Century* (Macmillan, 1974), and E. V. Morgan and W. A. Thomas, *The Stock Exchange: Its History and Functions* (Elek, second edition, 1969). For 'the City' in general, see David Kynaston, *The City of London*, vol. 1, *A World of its Own, 1815–1890* (Chatto and Windus, 1994).

Chapter 7: Britain and the world

General studies include C. J. Bartlett (ed.), *Britain Pre-eminent* (Macmillan, 1969); P. J. Cain, *Economic Foundations of British Overseas Expansion, 1815–1914* (Macmillan, 1980); and part three of Donald McCloskey, *Enterprise and Trade in Victorian Britain* (Allen and Unwin, 1981).

For overseas trade, see D. A. Firnie, *The English Cotton Industry and the World Market, 1815–96* (Clarendon Press, 1979); S. B. Saul, *Studies in British Overseas Trade, 1870–1914* (Liverpool University Press, 1960); and W. Schlöte, *British Overseas Trade from 1700 to the 1930s* (Oxford University Press, 1952).

The freeing of trade is discussed in Barry Gordon, *Economic Doctrine and Tory Liberalism* (Macmillan, 1979); Norman McCord, *Free Trade* (David and Charles, 1970); Barry Turner, *Free Trade and Protection* (Longman, 1971); and J. B. Williams, *British Commercial Policy and Trade Expansion, 1750–1850* (Oxford University Press, 1973). For the export of capital, see P. L. Cottrell, *British Overseas Investment in the Nineteenth Century* (Macmillan, 1975); A. R. Hall (ed.), *The Export of Capital from Britain, 1870–1914* (Methuen, 1968); and L. H. Jenks, *The Migration of British Capital to 1875* (Nelson, 1971).

A splendid collection of facsimile documents recounting the day-to-day realities of emigration is Paul Rees (ed.), *The Leaving of Liverpool: The Story of Nineteenth Century Emigration* (Merseyside Maritime Museum, 1986). Among useful books on emigration are Terry Coleman, *Passage to America* (Penguin, 1974); Charlotte Erickson, *Invisible Immigrants* (Weidenfeld, 1972); A. J. Hammerton, *Emigrant Gentlewomen* (Croom Helm, 1979); S. C. Johnson, *Emigration from the United Kingdom to North America* (Frank Cass, 1966); and Brinley Thomas, *Migration and Economic Growth* (Cambridge University Press, 1954). Eric Richards, *A History of the Highland Clearances*, vols 1 and 2 (Croom Helm, 1982, 1985) describes the forces which impelled so many Scottish men and women overseas.

Chapter 8: The middle class

For the values of the Victorian middle class, see James Walvin, *Victorian Values* (Deutsch, 1987), and Gordon Marsden (ed.), *Victorian Values* (Longman, 1990). Many of these values are extolled in Samuel Smiles, *Self Help*, first published in 1859 and regularly reprinted since then. As with other aspects of social history, some of the most vivid insights come through works of literature and biography. It would be tedious to catalogue even the major works which touch upon the Victorian middle class, but two extremes may be mentioned. George and Weedon Grossmith, *The Diary of a Nobody* (1892; re-issued Penguin, 1965) purports to be the journal of a City clerk, and is full of humour and bathos. Edmund Gosse, *Father and Son* (1907; Penguin, 1983) gives a vivid account of childhood in a family dominated by stern religious beliefs.

For the middle class in the early nineteenth century, see Leonore Davidoff and Catherine Hall, *Family Fortunes: Men and Women of the English Middle Class, 1780–1850* (Hutchinson, 1987). There are good sections on the middle class in the general social histories by Bedarida, Best and Harrison mentioned above, and to these should be added G. Kitson Clark, *The Making of Victorian England* (Methuen, 1965). Geoffrey Crossick (ed.), *The Lower Middle Class in Britain* (Croom Helm, 1977) is the best introduction to the lower echelons of the middle class, and may be read in conjunction with Gregory Anderson, *Victorian Clerks* (Manchester University Press, 1976), and Wilfred B. Whitaker, *Victorian and Edwardian Shopworkers* (David and Charles, 1973). For the rapidly growing professions, see W. J. Reader, *Professional Men* (Weidenfeld, 1966), as well as Harold Perkin, *The Rise of Professional Society*, listed above.

Middle-class lifestyles are firmly set against a background of rising aspirations in J. A. Banks, *Prosperity and Parenthood* (Routledge, 1954). Middle-class tastes in furnishing and home-making are well illustrated in John Gloag, *Victorian Comfort* (David and Charles, 1973), and in Jenni Calder, *The Victorian Home* (Batsford, 1977). For the moral and religious revival which affected the middle class particularly, see F. K. Brown, *Fathers of the Victorians* (Cambridge University Press, 1961); Muriel Jaeger, *Before Victoria* (Penguin, 1967); and Ian Bradley, *The Call to Seriousness* (Jonathan Cape, 1976). There are a number of essays on education in Peter Searby (ed.), *Educating the Victorian Middle Class* (History of Education Society, 1982).

Chapter 9: The labour movement in the nineteenth century

John Burnett, *Useful Toil* (Allen Lane, 1974) is a fascinating collection of working-class autobiographies spanning the period from the 1820s to the 1920s, and includes the experiences of women as well as men. A critical study of such autobiographies which quotes freely from 142 works dating from 1790 to 1850 is David Vincent, *Bread, Freedom and Knowledge* (Methuen, 1982).

General studies of the working class include: Asa Briggs and J. Saville (eds), *Essays in Labour History* (Macmillan, 1960); Alan Ereira, *The People's England* (Routledge and Kegan Paul, 1981); E. J. Hobsbawm, *Labouring Men* (Weidenfeld, 1968); Eric Hopkins, *A Social History of the English Working Classes* (Edward Arnold, 1979); David Kynaston, *King Labour: The British Working Class, 1850–1914* (Allen and Unwin, 1976); and John Benson, *The Working Class in Britain, 1850–1939* (Longman, 1989).

Peter Stearns, *Lives of Labour* (Croom Helm, 1975) compares changing experiences of work in Britain, Belgium, France and Germany. For stratification within the working class, see the short study by Robert Q. Gray, *The Aristocracy of Labour in Nineteenth Century Britain* (Macmillan, 1981), together with Geoffrey Crossick, *An Artisan Elite in Victorian Society* (Croom Helm, 1978), and Charles More, *Skill and the English Working Class, 1870–1914* (Croom Helm, 1980).

P. H. J. H. Gosden is the author of two books which deal with friendly societies and other forms of working-class self-help: *The Friendly Societies in England, 1815–75* (Manchester University Press, 1960), and *Self Help* (Batsford, 1973). A. Aspinall, *The Early Trade Unions* (Batchworth, 1949) contains a fascinating collection of documents on the early period, while Harry Bourne, *The Rise of British Trade Unions, 1825–1914* (Longman, 1979) combines documents with discussion. R. and E. Frow and Michael Katanka, *Strikes: a Documentary History* (Charles Knight, 1971) contains useful source material on that topic.

For trade unionism in general, see John Rule, *British Trade Unionism 1700–1850: The Formative Years* (Longman, 1988). Henry Pelling, *A History of British Trade Unionism* (Penguin, second edition, 1971), and H. A. Clegg, Alan Fox and A. F. Thompson, *A History of British Trade Unions since 1889*, vol. 1 (Oxford University Press, 1964). See also John Lovell and B. C. Roberts, *A Short History of the TUC* (Macmillan,

1968). Women and unionism is the subject of N. C. Solden, *Women in British Trade Unions, 1874–1976* (Gill and Macmillan, 1978).

For leisure see P. Bailey, *Leisure and Class in Victorian Britain* (Routledge and Kegan Paul, new edition. 1987); H. Cunningham, *Leisure in the Industrial Revolution* (Croom Helm, 1980); and James Walvin, *Leisure and Society, 1830–1950* (Longman, 1978).

Chapter 10: Women in the nineteenth century

A good collection of documents is in Patricia Hollis (ed.), *Women in Public* (Allen and Unwin, 1979), while contemporary sources are freely quoted in Carol Adams, *Ordinary Lives, a Hundred Years Ago* (Virago, 1982). Margaret Llewelyn Davies, *Life as We Have Known It* (Virago, new edition with introduction by Anna Davin, 1977) consists of the recollections, first published in 1931, of working women from the 1850s to the early decades of the twentieth century. Personal memory is the source behind E. Roberts, *A Woman's Place: An Oral History of Working Class Women, 1890–1910* (Blackwell, new edition, 1995). Dale Spender (ed.), *The Education Papers: Women's Quest for Equality in Britain 1850–1912* (Routledge and Kegan Paul, 1987) is a collection of documents on that subject.

A good general study is Sara Delamont and Lorna Duffin (eds), *The Nineteenth Century Woman* (Croom Helm, 1978), to which may be added two collections of essays edited by Martha Vicinus: *Suffer and Be Still* (Methuen, 1972) and *Widening Spheres* (Methuen, 1977). Carol Dyhouse, *Girls Growing Up in Late Victorian and Edwardian England* (Routledge and Kegan Paul, 1981) examines the way in which girls learnt their social roles, as do Joan Burstyn, *Victorian Education and the Ideal of Womanhood* (Croom Helm, 1980), and D. Gorham, *The Victorian Girl and the Feminine Ideal* (Croom Helm, 1982). On women's education, see Mary Cathcart Borer, *Willingly to School* (Lutterworth, 1976), and Josephine Kamm, *Hope Deferred* (Methuen, 1975).

Mary Wollstonecraft, *A Vindication of the Rights of Women* (1792; Penguin, 1982) is a classic text, and Emmeline Pankhurst, *My Own Story*, first published in 1914, is a good source on women's suffrage (Virago, new edition, 1979). Books which describe the long road to the vote include Andrew Rosen, *Rise Up Women*; Martin Pugh, *Women's Suffrage in Britain, 1867–1928* (Historical Association, 1980); and Jill Liddington and Jill Norris, *One Hand Tied Behind Us* (Virago, 1978).

The key role played by women in charitable work is the subject of F. K. Prochaska, *Women and Philanthropy in Nineteenth Century England* (Oxford University Press, 1980). The pioneering work of women in local government is the subject of Patricia Hollis, *Ladies Elect: Women in English Local Government 1865–1914* (Clarendon, 1987).

There is a good selection of documents on working women in E. Royston Pike, *Human Documents of the Victorian Golden Age* (Allen and Unwin, 1967), while Michael Hiley, *Victorian Working Women: Portraits from Life* (Gordon Fraser, 1979) contains much pictorial evidence. Other books on working women include E. Roberts, *Women's Work 1840–1940* (Macmillan, 1988); Wanda Neff, *Victorian Working Women* (Frank Cass, 1966); Ivy Pinchbeck, *Women Workers and the Industrial Revolution, 1750–1850* (Virago edition, 1981); Angela V. John, *By the Sweat of their Brow: Women Workers at Victorian Coal Mines* (Croom Helm, 1980); and Lee Holcombe, *Victorian Ladies at Work* (David and Charles, 1973) which concentrates on the middle class. Caroline Davidson, *A Woman's Work is Never Done* (Chatto and Windus, 1982) describes four centuries of housework.

For the impact of the First World War on women, see especially Arthur Marwick, *Women at War, 1914–18* (Fontana, 1977).

Chapter 11: A new era dawns, 1870–1914

W. H. B. Court, *British Economic History, 1870–1914* (Cambridge University Press, 1965) contains the best collection of documents on the economy, but to set Britain's performance against its European competitors three useful books are Tom Kemp, *Industrialisation in Nineteenth Century Europe* (Longman, 1969); Sidney Pollard and Colin Holmes, *Industrial Power and National Rivalry, 1870–1914* (Edward Arnold, 1972); and Sidney Pollard, *Peaceful Conquest: The Industrialisation of Europe, 1760–1970* (Oxford University Press, 1981). E. E. Williams, *Made in Germany* (new edition with introduction by Austin Albu, Harvester, 1973) is a splendid piece of polemical journalism, first published in 1896 with the intention of stirring British businessmen to greater efforts.

On the economy generally, see S. B. Saul, *The Myth of the Great Depression, 1873–96* (Macmillan, 1969) and D. H. Aldcroft and H. W. Richardson, *The British Economy, 1870–1939* (Macmillan, 1969). The debate on economic performance can be traced in the following works: D. H. Aldcroft (ed.), *The Development of British Industry and Foreign Competition, 1875–1914* (Allen and Unwin, 1968), and Donald McCloskey, *Enterprise and Trade in Victorian Britain*, especially part two (Allen and Unwin, 1981). On technical and scientific education, see Michael Argles, *South Kensington to Robbins* (Longman, 1964) and for a provocative condemnation of the attitudes of Britain's elite, see Martin J. Wiener, *English Culture and the Decline of the Industrial Spirit, 1850–1980* (Cambridge University Press, 1981).

On the newer industries the following are useful: I. C. R. Byatt, *The British Electrical Industry, 1875–1914* (Clarendon Press, 1979); Peter Mathias, *Retailing Revolution* (Longman, 1967); Frederick Alderson, *Bicycling: A History* (David and Charles, 1972); Roy Church, *The Rise and Decline of the British Motor Industry* (Macmillan, 1994); and William Plowden, *The Motor Car and Politics, 1896–1970* (Bodley Head, 1971). Two useful industrial biographies also deal with the motor car industry: Roy Church, *Herbert Austin* (Europa, 1979), and R. J. Overy, *William Morris* (Europa, 1976).

For general social histories of the period, see Jose Harris, *Private Lives, Public Spirit. A Social History of Britain, 1870–1914* (Oxford University Press, 1993) and Donald Read, *The Age of Urban Democracy: England, 1868–1914* (Longman, new edition, 1994). The best sources for suburban growth are H. J. Dyos, *Victorian Suburb* (Leicester University Press, 1966), and F. M. L. Thompson (ed.), *The Rise of Suburbia* (Leicester University Press, 1982). The other side of the coin – slums – can be approached through the extracts from social investigations contained in Peter Keating (ed.), *Into Unknown England* (Fontana, 1976). Other sources on social conditions are E. Royston Pike, *Human Documents of the Lloyd George Era* (Allen and Unwin, 1972), and Donald Read, *Documents from Edwardian England, 1901–15* (Harrap, 1973).

Three books on the origins of the welfare state which contain primary sources are Derek Fraser, *The Evolution of the British Welfare State* (Macmillan, 1973); J. R. Hay, *The Development of the British State, 1880–1975* (Edward Arnold, 1978); and Pat Thane, *The Foundations of the Welfare State, 1875–1945* (Longman, 1982).

For further discussion of the Liberal reforms, see J. R. Hay, *The Origins of the Liberal Welfare Reforms, 1906–14* (Macmillan, 1983); Jose Harris, *Unemployment and Politics* (Oxford University Press, 1972); Bentley B. Gilbert, *The Evolution of National Insurance in Great Britain* (Michael Joseph, 1966); and Henry Pelling, *Popular Politics and Society in Late Victorian England* (Macmillan, second edition, 1979).

Chapter 12: Britain between the wars

Alan Milward, *The Economic Effects of the World Wars on Britain* (Macmillan, 1970) compares the impact of both the First and Second World Wars on Britain, and may be read in conjunction with Arthur Marwick, *The Deluge: British Society and the First World War* (Penguin, 1967), and Gail Braybon, *Women Workers in the First World War* (Croom Helm, 1981). John Stevenson, *Social Conditions in Britain Between the Wars* (Penguin, 1971) has the merit of extensive quotations from contemporary sources. Other general studies of the interwar years include Stephen Constantine, *Social Conditions in Britain, 1918–1939* (Methuen, 1983); Ronald Blythe, *The Age of Illusion* (Penguin, 1964); Noreen Branson and Margot Heinemann, *Britain in the Nineteen Thirties* (Panther, 1973); and Sean Glynn and John Oxborrow, *Inter-war Britain: A Social and Economic History* (Allen and Unwin, 1976).

For the economy, see B. W. E. Alford, *Depression and Recovery? British Economic Growth, 1918–39* (Macmillan, 1975); Derek Aldcroft, *The Inter-war Economy; Britain, 1919–39* (Batsford, 1970); and Neil K. Buxton and D. H. Aldcroft (eds), *British Industry Between the Wars* (Scolar Press, 1979). The significance of Keynes is discussed in Robert Lekachman, *The Age of Keynes* (Allen Lane, 1967); D. E. Moggridge, *Keynes* (Fontana, 1976); and Michael Stewart, *Keynes and After* (Penguin, 1967). Keynes's *The Economic Consequences of the Peace* (1919) is available in a modern edition (Macmillan, 1971), and his essay, 'The Economic Consequences of Mr Churchill', is reprinted in Sidney Pollard (ed.), *The Gold Standard and Employment Policies Between the Wars* (Methuen, 1970). The economic policies of the various political parties can be discovered from F. W. S. Craig (ed.), *British General Election Manifestos, 1918–66* (Political Reference Publications, 1970), and the important 1928 report of the Liberal Industrial Inquiry, *Britain's Industrial Future* is available in reprint (Ernest Benn, 1977).

Stephen Constantine, *Unemployment in Britain Between the Wars* (Longman, 1980) includes a documentary section, and Margery Spring Rice, *Working Class Wives,* first published in 1939 (Virago, 1981), is an excellent source on the condition of the poorest in the 1930s. On social and economic policy, see M. A. Crowther, *British Social Policy, 1914–1939* (Macmillan, 1988); W. R. Garside, *British Unemployment, 1919–39: A Study in Public Policy* (Cambridge University Press, 1986); Bentley B. Gilbert, *British Social Policy, 1914–39* (Batsford, 1970); and Jim Tomlinson, *Problems of British Economic Policy, 1870–1945* (Methuen, 1981).

For 'moments of decision', see Julian Symons, *The General Strike* (Cresset, 1957), and for the problems of the coal industry, see Barry Supple, *The History of the British Coal Industry,* vol. 4, *1913–1946: The Political Economy of Decline* (Clarendon Press, 1987). See also Peter Fearon, *The Origins and Nature of the Great Slump, 1929–32* (Macmillan, 1979), and Charles P. Kindleberger, *The World in Depression, 1929–39* (Allen Lane, 1973). Colin Bell (ed.), *The Times Reports: National Government, 1931* (Times Books, 1975) is a good source for the crisis of that year.

Housing policy is discussed in Mark Swenarton, *The Politics and Architecture of Early State Housing in Britain* (Heinemann, 1981), and the interwar growth of suburbia is examined in Alan A. Jackson, *Semi-Detached London* (Allen and Unwin, 1973). Mark Pegg, *Broadcasting and Society, 1918–39* (Croom Helm, 1983) is a good source on the impact of the radio, as is Asa Briggs, *The History of Broadcasting in the United Kingdom,* vols 1 and 2 (Oxford University Press, 1961–5). For education, see Gerald Bernbaum, *Social Change and the Schools, 1918–44* (Routledge and Kegan Paul, 1967).

Andrew Thorpe, *Longman Companion to Britain in the Era of the Two World Wars* (Longman, 1994) is a valuable reference work.

Chapter 13: War and reconstruction, 1939–51

Norman Longmate, *The Home Front* (Chatto and Windus, 1981) is an 'anthology of personal experience', and draws heavily on letters, diaries and memoirs. Also good on the home front is Angus Calder, *The People's War* (Jonathan Cape, 1969). C. Jackson, *Who Will Take Our Children?* (Methuen, 1985) deals with evacuation. The growth of a wartime concern to reconstruct British society is traced in Paul Addison, *The Road to 1945: British Politics and the Second World War* (Jonathan Cape, 1975), while P. H. J. H. Gosden, *Education in the Second World War* (Methuen, 1976) describes the background to the major 1944 Education Act. Alan Milward, *War Economy and Society, 1939–45* (Allen Lane, 1977) deals comparatively with the major powers. Correlli Barnett, *The Audit of War: The Illusion and Reality of Britain as a Great Nation* (Macmillan, 1986) is a highly controversial interpretation of Britain's wartime economic record, very antipathetic to Labour's post-war plans for a welfare state. The book was of great significance to the development of New Right thinking.

For the post-war period in general, see B. W. E. Alford, *British Economic Performance, 1945–1975* (Macmillan, 1988); Terry Gourvish and Alan O'Day (eds), *Britain Since 1945* (Macmillan, 1991); N. F. R. Crafts and Nicholas Woodward (eds), *The British Economy Since 1945* (Clarendon Press, 1991); K. O. Morgan, *The People's Peace: British History, 1945–1990* (Oxford University Press, 1990); C. J. Bartlett, *A History of Postwar Britain 1945–74* (Longman, 1977); Arthur Marwick, *British Society Since 1945* (Penguin, 1982); Pauline Gregg, *The Welfare State* (Harrap, 1967); A. H. Halsey, *Change in British Society* (Oxford University Press, 1978); Michael Sissons and Philip French (eds), *The Age of Austerity, 1945–51* (Penguin, 1964); and V. Bogdanor and R. Skidelsky, (eds), *The Age of Affluence, 1951–64* (Macmillan, 1970).

Vivid snapshots of Britain at various points of time are provided in the works of Anthony Sampson (all published by Hodder and Stoughton): *Anatomy of Britain* (1962); *Anatomy of Britain Today* (1965), *New Anatomy of Britain* (1971) and *The Essential Anatomy of Britain* (1992).

A. Cairncross, *Years of Recovery: British Economic Policy, 1945–51* (Methuen, 1985), and K. O. Morgan, *Labour in Power, 1945–51* (Clarendon Press, 1984) are good on the post-war Labour governments. R. C. Birch, *The Shaping of the Welfare State* (Longman, 1974) has a section of documents. This may be used with Maurice Bruce, *The Coming of the Welfare State* (Batsford, fourth edition, 1968), which is also valuable for earlier periods. Jose Harris, *William Beveridge* (Oxford University Press, 1977) is the biography of a key figure in the history of the welfare state.

Nationalisation is discussed in W. Ashworth, *History of the British Coal Industry*, vol. 5, *The Nationalized Industry, 1946–1982* (Clarendon Press, 1986); David Heal, *The Steel Industry in Post-War Britain* (David and Charles, 1974); and R. Kelf-Cohen, *Twenty Years of Nationalisation: The British Experience* (Macmillan, 1969), written by a former government minister.

Chapter 14: The long boom, 1951–73

Many of the general surveys of post-war Britain give a good coverage of this period. Economic planning is analysed in a number of books including Samuel Brittan, *The Treasury Under the Tories, 1951–64* (Penguin, 1964); J. and A-M. Hackett, *The British Economy: Problems and Prospects* (Allen and Unwin, 1967); T. W. Hutchison, *Economics and Economic Policy in Britain, 1946–66* (Allen and Unwin, 1968); W. A. P. Manser, *Britain in Balance* (Longman, 1971); C. T. Sandford, *National Economic*

Planning (Heinemann, 1972); and Andrew Schonfield, *British Economic Policy Since the War* (Penguin, 1959).

On the so-called permissive society, see Alan Sked, *Britain's Decline: Problems and Perspectives* (Basil Blackwell, 1987). Stanley Cohen, *Folk Devils and Moral Panics: The Creation of the Mods and Rockers* (Basil Blackwell, new edition, 1987) is a useful study of youth culture.

For Britain's troubled relationship with the European Economic Community, see Stephen George, *Britain and European Integration Since 1945* (Blackwell, 1991). James Walvin, *Passage to Britain: Immigration in British History and Politics* (Penguin, 1984) is a good introduction to that topic

Chapter 15: Britain transformed? 1973–90

There is no shortage of books analysing Britain's relative economic decline, including Alan Sked, *Britain's Decline: Problems and Perspectives* (Allen and Unwin, 1987); Andrew Gamble, *Britain in Decline* (Macmillan, third edition, 1990); Keith Smith, *The British Economic Crisis: Its Past and Future* (Penguin, new edition, 1989); Michael Dintenfass, *The Decline of Industrial Britain, 1870–1980* (Routledge, 1992). For a discussion of the Wiener and Barnett theses see the essays in Bruce Collins and Keith Robbins (eds), *British Culture and Economic Decline* (Weidenfeld and Nicholson, 1990).

Peter Donaldson and John Farquar, *Understanding the British Economy* (Penguin, 1988); Christopher Huhne, *Real World Economics* (Penguin, 1990); Nick Gardner, *Decade of Discontent: The Changing British Economy since 1973* (Blackwell, 1987); and Peter Curwen (ed.), *Understanding the UK Economy* (Macmillan, second edition, 1992) cover economic developments during the period, and will help historians to come to grips with difficult economic concepts. David Smith, *The Rise and Fall of Monetarism* (Penguin, 1987) and the same author's *North and South: Britain's Economic, Social and Political Divide* (Penguin, second edition, 1994) cover those particular topics in greater depth.

On social changes during this period, see Nicholas Abercrombie, Alan Wade, Keith Soothill, John Urry and Sylvia Walby, *Contemporary British Society* (Polity Press, second edition, 1994), and Stephen Edgell and Vic Duke, *A Measure of Thatcherism: A Sociology of Britain* (HarperCollins, 1991).

There are many books on Thatcherism, and they are frequently polemical in tone. The student might refer, however, to Peter Riddell, *The Thatcher Era and its Legacy* (Blackwell, 1991), and Michael Ball, Fred Gray and Linda McDowell, *The Transformation of Britain: Contemporary Social and Economic Change* (Fontana, 1989). Philip Brown and Richard Sparks, *Beyond Thatcherism: Social Policy, Politics and Society* (Open University, 1989) is good on the development of New Right ideology and social policy.

For changes to the welfare state, see Rodney Lowe, *The Welfare State in Britain Since 1945* (Macmillan, 1993); Norman Johnson, *Reconstructing the Welfare State: A Decade of Change, 1980–1990* (Harvester Wheatsheaf, 1990); J. Brown, *The British Welfare State: A Critical History* (Blackwell, 1995); and Robert E. Goodwin and Julian Le Grand, *Not Only the Poor: The Middle Classes and the Welfare State* (Allen and Unwin, 1987).

Index

PEARSON EDUCATION LIMITED
Edinburgh Gate, Harlow, Essex CM20 2JE, England
and Associated Companies throughout the world.

First published 1987
Second edition 1996
Fourth impression 2000

Set in 10/11 pt Bembo (Linotron)

A catalogue record for this book is available from the British Library

ISBN 0 582 25721 2

Printed in Singapore (KIIL)

The publisher's policy is to use paper manufactured from sustainable forests.

For Jennifer, Ashley and Susannah

Acknowledgements

We are grateful to the following for permission to reproduce copyright material: Newspaper Publishing PLC for an extract from an editorial 'A last chance to honour our makers' in *Independent on Sunday* 1/11/92; Reed Consumer Books for extracts from English Journey by J. B. Priestley (pubd Heinemann 1934/Penguin 1977); Routledge for extracts from *The Rise of Professional Society* by Harold Perkin (1989); George T. Sassoon for the poem 'They' by Siegfried Sassoon.

We are grateful to the following for permission to reproduce photographs: Amalgamated Engineering and Electrical Union, page 253; Barnados, page 335; Birmingham Museum & Art Gallery, page 220; Bodleian Library, Oxford, page 328 above; British Library, page 5 below; By permission of the Syndics of Cambridge University Library, page 74; Derbyshire Record Office, by permission of the Derbyshire Archaeological Society (photo: Mike Williams) page 4; Express Newspapers plc, page 408; John Frost Newspaper Library, page 353 below left; John Gorman, page 256; Hulton Deutsch Collection, page 5 above, 115 below, 169, 170, 171, 172 above, 327 below; Illustrated London News Picture Library, page 7 above; Imperial War Museum, London, pages 351, 352, 353 above left, 353 below right, 354; The Independent/John Voos, page 475; Manchester Central Library, Local Studies Unit, pages 114, 115 above; Manchester City Art Galleries, page 7 below, 221; Mansell Collection, page 142 above; Courtesy Museum in Docklands, page 172 below; Punch, pages 75, 353 above right, 409; Collection at the Royal Holloway College & Bedford College, page 141 below; Shipley Art Gallery, Gateshead (Tyne & Wear Museums), page 287 above; UC Library, London, page 254, Tate Gallery, London, page 286; Topham Picturepoint, page 442; Tower Hamlets Local History Library and Archives, page 142 below; Victoria & Albert Museum, London, page 287 below; Central Library, Watford, page 141 above; Wellcome Institute Library, London, page 326.

We are unable to trace the copyright holders of the following material and would be grateful of any information that would enable us to do so, pages 6, 93, 139, 140, 233, 255, 325, 327 above, 328 below.

Cover: Popularity by Lambert, Museum of London